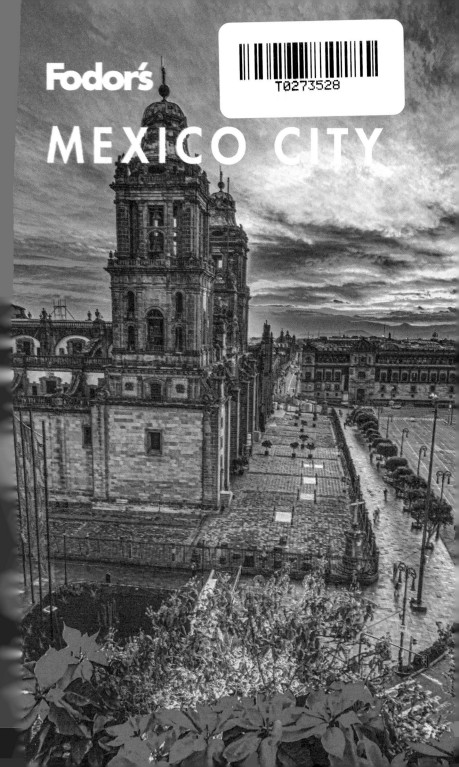

Fodor's

MEXICO CITY

T0273528

Welcome to Mexico City

First-time visitors to Mexico City are often surprised by the manageable pace and pleasing scale that defines many of its neighborhoods, from ritzy Polanco and San Ángel to historic Coyoacán and Condesa. As a wonderfully vibrant, culturally blessed metropolis that can keep museum-hoppers, discerning gourmands, history buffs, and design-minded shoppers entertained for days, it's little wonder that its cachet as a sophisticated, world-class travel destination continues to soar. As you plan your upcoming travels to Mexico City, please confirm that places are still open and let us know when we need to make updates by writing to us at editors@fodors.com.

TOP REASONS TO GO

★ **Food:** Savor everything from authentic street food to inventive globally inspired contemporary cuisine.

★ **Museums:** Fascinating collections of art and artifacts covering a vast range of eras and subjects fill Mexico City's more than 170 museums.

★ **Nightlife:** Sip Mexican-made mezcal, craft beer, fine wine, and pulque in the city's historic cantinas and hip lounges.

★ **Archaeological treasures:** Visit the legendary pyramids at Teotihuacán and view amazing pre-Columbian collections at several museums.

Contents

MAPS

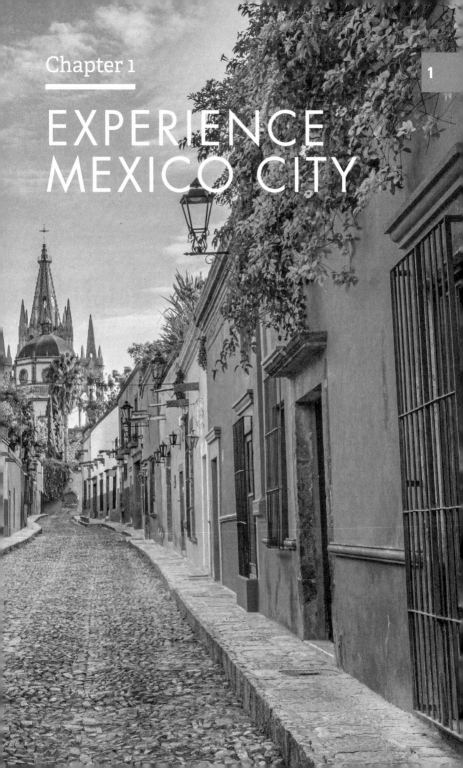

Chapter 1

EXPERIENCE MEXICO CITY

20 ULTIMATE EXPERIENCES

Mexico City offers terrific experiences that should be on every traveler's list. Here are Fodor's top picks for a memorable trip.

1 Palacio de Bellas Artes

Attend a symphony performance, view spectacular murals, check out the superb bookstore, or just admire the ravishing architectural elements of this iconic cultural space. *(Ch. 4)*

2 Día de Muertos

This joyful early November celebration of dead loved ones turns CDMX into a display of beautiful, often whimsical *ofrendas* for the entire month of October. *(Ch. 2)*

3 Xochimilco Canals

Enjoy a festive boat ride in a brightly painted *trajinera*— music and micheladas included—as you tour this network of ancient canals in the far south of the city. *(Ch. 13)*

4 UNAM's Cultural Attractions

A UNESCO World Heritage Site, the 2,500-acres of Mexico's most prestigious university is packed with superb museums, performances, and public art. *(Ch. 13)*

5 Museo Nacional de Antropología

Allow at least three hours to fully immerse yourself in this beautiful mid-century building filled with an unrivaled trove of pre-Hispanic archaeological treasures. *(Ch. 7)*

6 Fine Dining

Here you can dine on food prepared by some of the world's most hallowed chefs, including Enrique Olvera (Pujol), Jorge Vallego (Quintonil), Elena Reygadas (Rosetta), and countless others. *(Ch. 7, 8)*

7 Catedral Metropolitana

A tour of Latin America's largest cathedral is truly a walk through more than 300 years of history. Dominating the Zócalo, the building abounds with impressive religious art. *(Ch. 3)*

8 Zócalo

Flanking this stately, photogenic urban square, one of the world's largest, are some of Centro Histórico's most rewarding attractions. *(Ch. 3)*

9 Street Food

For some of the most flavorful (and inexpensive) meals in CDMX, order tamales, tortas, sopes, tacos, and more from any street vendor that's packed with diners. *(Ch. 3–14)*

10 Mezcal and Pulque

Both produced from agave, pulque uses the plant's fermented milky and slightly tart sap while artisanal mezcal has become the backbone of standout craft cocktail programs throughout the city. *(Ch. 3–14)*

11 Bosque de Chapultepec

A walk among the gardens and lakes of the city's most beloved green space is a delight. Outstanding museums abound here— don't miss Castillo de Chapultepec, with its sweeping vistas. *(Ch. 7)*

12 El Bazar Sábado

With its high-quality crafts and household goods, the Saturday market in San Ángel is reason enough to shop in this enchanting neighborhood. *(Ch. 12)*

13 Architecture in Condesa and Roma

Stroll the tree-shaded lanes of these charming neighborhoods rife with stately early 20th-century buildings. *(Ch. 8, 9)*

14 Museo Frida Kahlo

The lovely Casa Azul, where the iconic artist once resided, is today a fascinating museum and also a focal point of the charming and historic Coyoacán district. *(Ch. 11)*

15 Mercados

These colorful, typically historic halls packed with stalls selling fruit, seafood, flowers, crafts, candies, and street food are the lifeblood of most CDMX neighborhoods. *(Ch. 3–13)*

16 Torre Latinoamericana

Sip drinks, dine in one of the cafés, or head right to the 44th-floor observation deck of this mid-century tower to take in unparalleled views of the cityscape and surrounding mountains. *(Ch. 3)*

17 Juárez Nightlife

This trendy neighborhood buzzes with hip, arty bars set in chic restored mansions as well as the bustling dance clubs and LGBTQ+ hangouts of Zona Rosa. *(Ch. 5)*

18 Football Match at Estadio Azteca

Perhaps nowhere else in the country is Mexico's fervent embrace of fútbol more palpable than at a Club América game in this massive stadium. *(Ch. 13)*

19 Teotihuacán

If you have time for just one day trip, make it to these incredible 2,200-year-old ruins that include the world's third-tallest pyramid. *(Ch. 14)*

20 Diego Riviera Murals

The dynamic large-scale works of Rivera and fellow muralistas Orozco and Siqueiros can be viewed in museums and civic buildings throughout CDMX. *(Ch. 3, 4, 13)*

16

WHAT'S WHERE

1 Centro Histórico.
The city's historic core
is where you'll find
Latin America's largest
Zócalo and a slew of
essential museums and
historic sites.

2 Alameda Central.
Named for the charm-
ing park—the oldest in
the Western
Hemisphere—that
anchors it, Alameda
Central is rife with
cultural attractions.

**3 Juárez and Anzures
with La Zona Rosa.**
Bisected by Paseo de la
Reforma, here you'll
find the colonias of
Juárez, Cuauhtémoc,
and Anzures, including
the LGBTQ+ and night-
life-driven Zona Rosa.

**4 San Rafael and
Santa María la Ribera.**
These two historic
neighborhoods have
become the more
affordable and free-
spirited bastions of
edgy art and entrepre-
neurialism in the city.

**5 Polanco and Bosque
de Chapultepec.** The
1,695-acre Bosque de
Chapultepec contains
an enchanting array of
historic and newer
attractions. Immedi-
ately north, sprawling
and wealthy Polanco is
sometimes called
Mexico's Beverly Hills.

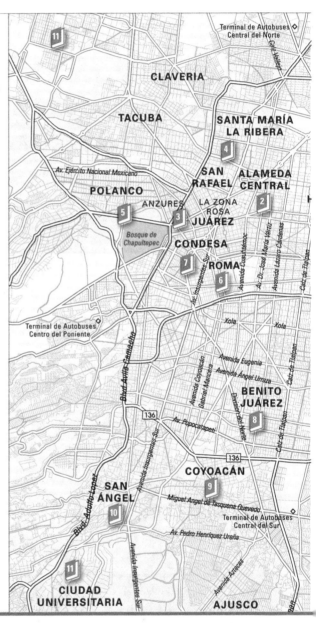

6 Roma. One of the trendiest neighborhoods in North America, Roma has few formal attractions but a seemingly endless supply of pleasing hangouts.

7 Condesa. A grand neighborhood of winding streets and Porfirian mansions, Condesa has transitioned from faded but elegant to hip and upwardly mobile.

8 Benito Juárez. A sweeping delegación made up of several unassuming, mostly middle-class colonias, Benito Juárez contains a number of lesser-known gems.

9 Coyoacán. Closely identified with the former home (now a museum) of its most famous resident, Frida Kahlo, the historic core of Coyoacán is one of the most appealing colonial neighborhoods in the Americas.

10 San Ángel. Like its easterly neighbor Coyoacán, this lively colonia that Diego Rivera called home is richly historic (and just plain old rich).

11 Greater Mexico City. Some of the city's top attractions—La Villa de Guadalupe, the canals of Xochimilco, the cultural institutions of UNAM (Universidad Nacional Autónoma de México)— lie outside the city center.

Mexico City Today

DEMOGRAPHICS

The population of Mexico City proper has increased by nearly 8% since 2010, to around 9.4 million, while the metro region, known as El Valle de México, has also grown at a similar rate, now clocking in around 22.4 million. The vast majority of the region's residents are Mexican nationals, most of them with a mix of Indigenous and European heritage (with about 20% self-identifying solely as Indigenous). But Mexico City has an enormous community of both permanent and semi-permanent expats (many living here from one six-month tourist visa to the next), and these numbers spiked significantly during the COVID-19 pandemic. It's estimated that nearly 12% of the city population is now foreign-born, the majority of them (upward of 700,000 residents) from the United States.

It's not clear how many of those expats who settled here during the pandemic have left, but anecdotally, the proliferation of trendy cafés, shops, and coworking spaces, along with the increased use of English, French, and other non-Spanish languages suggest the influx of foreigners continues to grow. As is always the case with gentrification, especially when spurred by outsiders, there are challenges. While some local business owners, landlords, and entrepreneurs benefit from these changes, many other locals have been impacted negatively; many are no longer able to afford skyrocketing rents and restaurant prices, and in some neighborhoods, they are outnumbered by foreigners who don't speak Spanish and earn their income in currencies that go much farther than the peso.

THE ECONOMY

Greater Mexico City is the country's economic powerhouse, generating about a quarter of the nation's GDP. The city's significant recent growth matches the rest of the country's, with CDMX serving as a huge banking, service, and construction sector as well as a leader in manufacturing industries metals, automotive parts, textiles, furniture, and cement. Tourism continues to grow as a significant economic contributor as well. The peso's value plummeted during the pandemic but has begun to rebound dramatically since 2023 and is currently trading at about 17.5 against the U.S. dollar, the strongest it's been since 2015. For many foreign visitors, while Mexico still represents an excellent value, costs have risen by about 40% to 50% since the start of the pandemic.

POLITICS

The mayor of Mexico City is considered the second most powerful elected official in the country after the president, and the role can also be a springboard to the presidency. Current president Andrés Manuel López Obrador, aka AMLO, previously served as Mexico City's mayor, as did Claudia Sheinbaum until 2023, when she resigned to run for president in 2024. Heavily favored to win, she's running against Xóchitl Gálvez; whoever wins, history will be made with the election of Mexico's first woman president. In 2024, voters will also decide on a new mayor of CDMX, with Clara Brugada—a member of the same Morena party as Sheinbaum and AMLO—considered to be the frontrunner. The success of Morena candidates in Mexico City reflects the city's leftward lean, particularly on social issues. There's a general cynicism in Mexico toward the government, however, and residents tend to invest more in their immediate communities and social networks than they do in elected officials.

SOCIAL ISSUES

Mexico City's progressive attitudes have made it a national trendsetter on issues like LGBTQ+ and reproductive rights, which advanced in the city before they did on a federal level. Chilangos also long supported legalizing recreational weed, which passed federally in 2021, and Mexico City continues to make big advances on environmental issues. After being named by the UN as the world's most polluted city in 1992, CDMX implemented a number of measures that have led to great improvements, and the city's annual air quality index is now 33rd in the world. Public transit continues to expand, the city has the largest bike-share network in Latin America, nearly 4,000 acres of city green space have been restored since 2018, buses and many factories now run on natural gas, and single-use plastic bags, food containers, and utensils in shops and restaurants were banned in 2021. One of the city's most pressing challenges is its dwindling water supply, the result of rapid growth and modernization paired with shrinking aquifers, an old and leaky infrastructure, and less reliable rainfall related to climate change. Low rainfall during the normally prolific summer monsoon season in 2023 led the city to enact drastic water-use restrictions. However, Herculean long-term efforts are underway to combat this crisis, including an overhaul of the city's water pipes, the implementation of rainwater catchment systems, and increased use of treated wastewater for landscaping.

EARTHQUAKES

Mexico City lies along the rim of the "Ring of Fire," a highly active earthquake and volcanic zone that extends along the Pacific Coast from Baja California all the way to the Guatemala border. About a half-dozen large (greater than a 7.0 magnitude on the Richter scale) quakes, or *terremotos*, have struck the country since 2017, two of them on September 19th in separate years (one—which caused tremendous damage and resulted in 370

deaths—in 2017 and the other in 2022). If that's not strange enough, September 19 is the anniversary of the devastating Mexico City earthquake of 1985, when at least 10,000 people lost their lives. Appropriately, each year on September 19, the city holds an earthquake-safety drill.

The epicenters of most quakes felt in the city are usually at least 100 miles outside Mexico City itself, but because the vast metropolis has been constructed on top of a former lake bed, much of the valley is susceptible to damage from even distant tremors. The city has, fortunately, made major advances in retrofitting older buildings and constructing new ones so that they can withstand damage from these often powerful seismic events.

It's important to be prepared for potential earthquakes when in Mexico City or the surrounding region. Always check or ask about evacuation routes and exit doors when you first arrive at a hotel or Airbnb. The city is served by a seismic alert system that can provide up to 60 seconds advance warning that an earthquake is imminent. The alarm speakers emit a repetitive whirring sound throughout the city—this is accompanied by a recorded (often rather garbled-sounding) announcement. When you hear this alert, if you're on the ground level or lower floor of a building, you should attempt to move outside and away from buildings as quickly as possible. If you're on a higher floor of a building or too far from exits to leave quickly, you should keep away from windows and exterior walls, get close to an interior wall, drop to your hands and knees, and—if possible—crawl under a sturdy table or desk. Never use elevators during an earthquake, as the building you're in may lose power.

What to Eat and Drink in Mexico City

MEZCAL
Typically produced by small artisan distilleries in only a handful of Mexican states, this potent spirit with an often smoky quality has become ubiquitous in CDMX and can be sipped straight-up or in an array of complex cocktails.

STREET FOOD
Even in upscale neighborhoods, street vendors serve up Mexican delicacies—not just tacos, quesadillas, and tamales, but slow-roasted arbacoa, *tortas* (sandwiches) overflowing with grilled meats, *sopes* (fried-masa discs topped with a slew of ingredients), and more.

CHAPULINES AND ESCAMOLES
Devotees eat *chapulines* (crickets) fried with salt by the handful, mixed with gaucamole, or ground in sauces, while *escamoles* (ant larvae) are best enjoyed with butter and garlic or in omelets—they look and even taste a bit like pine nuts.

CHURROS
Served by street vendors and in cafés alike (the El Moro chain has been famous for them since 1935), these long, curving, crispy doughnuts are best enjoyed with chocolate or *cajeta* (a milky caramel sauce).

ELOTE AND ESQUITES

Don't pass up the chance to snack on charred street corn slathered in chile powder, lime, cotija cheese, and either mayo or sour cream; these delicacies are known as *elote* when served on the cob or *esquites,* with the kernels shaved and served in a cup.

MEXICAN BREAKFAST

The morning meal in Mexico City is one of the loveliest times to socialize or even just relax or read by yourself over a leisurely paced meal. Dishes like chilaquiles with salted cecina meat and huevos divorciados provide a hearty and delicious yet generally inexpensive first course of the day. Don't forget your coffee or espresso, fresh-squeezed juice, fresh fruit, and flaky Mexican pastries.

REGIONAL CUISINES

In terms of food, Mexico is hugely diverse, and CDMX offers cuisines from every region. Examples include tender *cochinita pibil,* the slow-roasted pork dish of the Yucatán, and moles, the intensely complex sauces of fruits, nuts, chiles, and spices most typically associated with Oaxaca.

TACOS

Perhaps no snack more deliciously defines Mexico City dining than tacos. Small, soft, round corn tortillas are topped with a tantalizing array of fillings, including shaved spit-grilled pork with pineapples (*al pastor*) and braised stews (*guisados*).

TAMALES AND ATOLE

Roving as well as stationary street vendors dispense hearty tamales (with chicken or poblano chiles) all over town, especially for breakfast or a late-evening snack. Enjoy them with atole, a sweet and warm drink made with corn masa.

What to Buy in Mexico City

DÍA DE MUERTOS FIGURINES

These colorfully painted skeleton ornaments can be made of papier mâché, clay, wood, wax, or other materials and are wonderful to display year-round but especially during Día de Muertos.

CHOCOLATE

A tradition in Mexico that dates back centuries to ancient Mayan culture, chocolate-making thrives today, and CDMX has many fine purveyors, including makers of exquisite artisan bonbons like Que Bo! and Tout Chocolat.

TALAVERA POTTERY

These intricately pattered tin-enameled ceramic tiles and other works originated in Spain but have been made in Mexico for centuries. They're sold at several shops in CDMX.

MINIATURE OFRENDAS

Displayed prominently during Día de Muertos, meticulously detailed ofrendas can depict altars and other festive scenes. You'll also find dioramas of street-food vendors, mercados, and entire homes.

ALEBRIJES

These wildly colorful and whimsical folk art sculptures depicting everything from cats to butterflies to mythical beasts were originated by 20th-century artist Pedro Linares but are now crafted by many artists in a range of sizes.

CLOTHES

Mexico City has a growing crop of talented fashion designers earning international acclaim, among them Sandra Weil, Carla Fernández, and Suzzan Atala of Tuza. In more traditional shops and markets, look for distinctive traditional Mexican textiles, like embroidered huipil blouses, intricately patterned rebozo scarves, and handwoven Zapotec rugs.

LUCHA LIBRE MASKS

Whether you find them silly, creepy, or downright handsome, these fanciful emblems of Mexico's uniquely spirited wrestling culture make memorable souvenirs.

Mexican candy

COFFEE
A number of excellent cafés—including Cafe Avellaneda, Quentin, Buna 42, and Camino a Comala—sell high-quality, artisan-roasted coffee beans from the country's three prime coffee-producing states: Oaxaca, Chiapas, and Veracruz.

MEXICAN CANDY
Mexican candies are worth seeking out, especially the old-fashioned treats sold at Dulceria de Celaya, which include marzipan, candied fruits, and *cocada* coconut candies.

BEER
Until recently, the country generally favored mass-produced, German-style lagers like Negra Modelo and Dos Equis Amber. Thankfully, Mexico City's thirst for innovative craft brews—both domestic and imported—has skyrocketed since the mid-2010s, and *cervezas artesanales*, such as Cru Cru, Fauna, Hércules, and Insurgente, appear on many menus.

SALSAS
The city's traditional mercados are excellent sources for local spices, salsas, and mole and smoked chile pastes and powders. And if you're keen on making your own spice blend or guacamole at home, pick up a *molcajete*, a traditional bowl made of volcanic basalt.

Best Museums in Mexico City

CASTILLO DE CHAPULTEPEC

On a lofty hilltop in Bosque de Chapultepec this 18th-century castle once served as the presidential residence and is now an engaging history museum with grand city views.

MUSEO DE ARTE POPULAR

Vibrant, often brightly colored folk art—from textiles to ornately carved and painted figurines—collected from throughout Mexico fill this wonderful building with an exceptional museum shop.

MUSEO UNIVERSITARIO ARTE CONTEMPORÁNEO (MUAC)

The top reason for a trip to the impressive campus of UNAM is to tour this sleek art museum that presents world-class contemporary art exhibits.

MUSEO FRIDA KAHLO

The rambling colonial bright-blue house where Frida Kahlo was born and died is furnished much as she left it and provides an intimate look at her inspired, challenging life. Exploring the house allows you to get a sense of the personal style that influenced her iconic artwork, from the giant papier-mâché skeletons outside to the small religious tin paintings spread throughout the interior. You can also admire many of her early sketches, diary entries, and outfits.

MUSEO DEL CARMEN

Take a break from the throngs of weekend shoppers in San Ángel to tour this impressive early 17th-century religious building with a creepy but intriguing collection of mummies in its basement crypt. Established by Carmelite friars, it was never actually a convent, but it is still an active church.

MUSEO JUMEX

Not only is this one of the foremost contemporary art museums in Latin America, with works from the likes of Andy Warhol, Jeff Koons, and Damien Hirst, Jumex also has a terrace with great views of Carlos Slim's stunning Museo Soumaya.

Museo del Templo Mayor

MUSEO TAMAYO ARTE CONTEMPORÁNEO

Both a repository of works by renowned modernist Mexican painter Rufino Tamayo and a showcase of excellent changing exhibits, this handsome museum has something for everyone.

MUSEO DEL TEMPLO MAYOR

A beautifully designed archaeological museum interprets this 3-acre Aztec ruin adjacent to the Zócalo and discovered by accident in 1978. It also highlights thousands of pieces unearthed from the site and others across central Mexico. Don't miss the museum's centerpiece: the 8-ton disc depicting the moon goddess Coyolxauhqui.

PALACIO DE BELLAS ARTES

There may not be a more photographed or breathtaking building in the city than this domed opera house containing fabulous murals and terrific rotating art exhibits.

MUSEO NACIONAL DE ANTROPOLOGÍA

The cultural jewel of Bosque de Chapultepec ranks among the world's best archaeological museums and showcases an incredible trove of pre-Hispanic artifacts.

Mexico City Under the Radar

CINETECA NACIONAL
One of the world's largest, and least expensive, art-house cinemaplexes, this stunning contemporary film center on the Benito Juárez–Coyoacán border is a delight.

LUCHA LIBRE
To fully appreciate this no-holds-barred wrestling form that's been a tradition in Mexico since the 1860s, attend one of these spectacles held at two of the city's venues, Arena México in Alameda Central and the smaller Arena Coliseo in Centro Histórico.

BIBLIOTECA VASCONCELOS
One of the city's most striking works of contemporary architecture, the nation's largest library is great fun to explore inside and out in the surrounding gardens.

TROTSKY MUSEUM
Drawing just a fraction of the visitors of the neighboring Museo Frida Kahlo, the home where the tragic Russian dissident was assassinated contains fascinating exhibits and memorabilia, including bullet holes from his first assassination attempt and the study where he was murdered with a pickax.

TLALPAN CENTRO HISTÓRICO
With the historic charm of Coyoacán but far fewer visitors, this lively 17th-century neighborhood in the southern end of the city has friendly cafés and shops, plus beautiful architecture. The colorful historic houses and charming tree-lined plazas make you feel like you're very far away from the city.

MUSEO NACIONAL DE LAS INTERVENCIONES
This off-the-beaten-path museum set in a huge 17th-century former monastery contains remarkably well-designed exhibits on Mexico's surprisingly extensive war history, including the 1810-1821 War of Mexican Independence and the Mexican Revolution of the early 20th century.

Trotsky Museum

KIOSKO MORISCO
The centerpiece of charming Santa Maria la Ribera, this ornate 1880s Moorish pavilion is a wonderful spot for sipping coffee and people-watching. It was built to serve as the Mexico Pavilion at the 1884 World's Fair in New Orleans, but was relocated to its current location in 1910.

BIKING ON PASEO DE LA REFORMA
On Sunday morning, from 8 am to 2 pm, the main boulevard connecting Jardín de Chapultepec with Centro Histórico closes to car traffic and morphs into a festive bikeway beloved by locals and visitors alike.

ANTIGUO COLEGIO DE SAN ILDEFONSO
See an incomparable collection of works by muralists Rivera, Sisquieros, Leal, and Orozco on the interior walls of this somewhat overlooked Centro Histórico art museum. A former college, it's also where Frida Kahlo once studied.

PARQUE NACIONAL DESIERTO DE LOS LEONES
Escape from the crowds and spend an afternoon strolling through this gorgeous tract of greenery on the city's mountainous western edge.

A Brief History of Mexico City

Continuously inhabited since the 1300s (and sporadically inhabited for many centuries prior), Mexico City has seen its fortunes wax and wane over the millennia. Here are some of the key events that have shaped the city's, and the country's, development.

15,000–12,000 BC: Earliest nomadic tribes inhabit the lakes of Valle de México, the site of present-day Mexico City.

1400 BC–150 CE: Believed to be the oldest city in the Valle de México, Cuicuilco is inhabited, initially as a series of smaller communities and then becoming more concentrated from 800 to 600 BC, when the settlement's great pyramid was constructed.

600–200 BC: Small villages take root in the Teotihuacán Valley.

100 BC–700 CE: Teotihuacán thrives and then collapses over this 800-year period, with construction on the Pyramid of the Moon and Pyramid of the Sun having likely begun around AD 200. The ancient city's population is estimated to have reached its peak of about 200,000 around the 4th and 5th centuries.

245–315 CE: Xitle, an ash cone volcano, erupts, destroying what's left of Cuicuilco and creating the vast lava fields that still underlie a good bit of the southern half of the city.

900–1150 CE: The region is dominated by Toltec culture, which gives way to the Mexica (Aztecs) after the fall of the Toltec Empire in 1122.

1325–1521: The Aztecs establish the city-state of Tenochtitlan—the exact site of Mexico City's present day city center—on a series of islands in the middle of Lake Texcoco in 1325. The Aztec Empire and Tenochtitlan thrive over the next two centuries, with the city-state attaining a top population estimated to be anywhere between 300,000 and 700,000 inhabitants.

1519: The Spanish, led by Hernán Cortés, arrive in Tenochtitlan, having traveled from their landing point in Veracruz, and are initially received warmly by the city's Aztec ruler, Moctezuma II.

1521: Following more than a year of tensions and sometimes violent skirmishes, during which the Spanish fled the city for the community of Coyoacán, Cortés and his troops return and overrun Tenochtitlan, forcing the city's new king, Cuauhtémoc, to surrender. Although they keep much of Tenochtitlan's layout, the Spanish virtually destroy the Aztec city, building the city of Mexico—now the capital of New Spain—on top of it.

1521–1821: Over the next three centuries, as the kingdom of New Spain grows to include additional territories throughout Latin America, Mexico City grows rapidly in population and both economic and cultural clout, a period during which the valley's lakes are drained as settlement expands outwardly.

1810–1821: During a decade of insurgency and war, Mexico secures its complete independence from Spain on September 27, 1821, with Mexico City continuing its role as capital of the new nation.

1847–1848: U.S. troops occupy Mexico City during the Mexican-American War, an engagement that followed the U.S. annexation of Texas in 1845 and the ambitious expansionist designs of American President James K. Polk. The war ends with Mexico's defeat and the signing of the Treaty of Guadalupe Hidalgo in 1848. As a result, Mexico cedes present-day California and most of the current southwestern states to the United States.

1861–1867: The second and larger of two 19th-century wars between Mexico and France results in French occupation of Mexico City from 1863 through 1867, when Mexico prevails and the republic is restored.

1877–1911: A heroic general of the French-Mexican War, Porfirio Díaz assumes the presidency of Mexico by coup in 1877 and remains in this role, except for one term from 1880 to 1884, for seven more terms, until 1911. The full 36-year epoch is referred to as the *Porfiriato*.

1900: Greater Mexico City's population stands at about 500,000 (compared with 3.5 million in New York City and 5 million in London at the time).

1910–1920: The onset of the Mexican Revolution brings an abrupt end to the Porfirio Díaz regime and dramatically transforms the nation's, and Mexico City's, culture and government. The revolution ends in 1920, with Álvaro Obregón—a former commander of revolutionary forces—elected president.

1921: Secretary of Education José Vasconcelos launches the Mexican Muralist movement as a way to promote the ideals of the Mexican Revolution. Its heyday lasts into the 1970s and brings worldwide acclaim to numerous painters, particularly Diego Rivera, José Clemente Orozco, and David Alfaro Siqueiros.

1930: Greater Mexico City's population reaches 1 million.

1952: Construction begins on the massive and architecturally significant 2,500-acre main campus of National Autonomous University of Mexico (UNAM), which is named a UNESCO World Heritage Site in 2007.

1956: Torre Latinoamericana becomes Mexico City's first skyscraper and remains the country's tallest building, at 545 feet tall, until the 1982 construction of Torre Ejecutiva Pemex.

1958: Four years after Frida Kahlo's death, her former husband Diego Rivera donates her iconic blue Coyoacán house, Casa Azul, and its contents for it to become a museum.

1960: Greater Mexico City's population stands at 5.5 million.

1968: In October, Mexico City hosts the Summer Olympics. Just 10 days before the Opening Ceremonies, government forces murder 300 to 400 protesters gathered in Plaza de las Tres Culturas in Tlatelolco.

1971: Around 120 protesters, most of them students, are killed by government-trained forces in June's *Halconazo*, or Corpus Christi Massacre.

1985: More than 5,000 people are killed and 3,500 buildings are severely damaged or destroyed in an 8.1 magnitude earthquake.

1990: The population of greater Mexico City reaches 15 million.

1992: Mexico signs the North American Free Trade Agreement (NAFTA) with the United States and Canada (it's renegotiated as USMCA in 2019).

1994: The home and studio that Mexico's most influential modern architect Luis Barragán designed and lived in until his death in 1988 is turned into a museum.

2000: Vicente Fox is elected president on the PAN (Partido Acción Nacional) ticket, becoming the first non-PRI (Partido Revolucionario Institucional) in 71 years.

2016: At 807 feet tall, Torre Reforma becomes the city's tallest building.

2017: Exactly 32 years to the day after the 1985 quake, a 7.1 magnitude earthquake causes widespread damage and at least 370 deaths.

2018: Alfonso Cuarón's Mexico City–centered *Roma* becomes the first Mexican film to win Best Foreign Film at the Academy Awards (it also wins Best Cinematography and Best Director).

2018: The former mayor of Mexico City, Andrés Manuel López Obrado, better known as AMLO, is elected President of Mexico under the banner of the Morena party, which he founded in 2011.

2022: Torre Mítikah—a mixed-use complex set atop a swanky shopping mall—opens in the Benito Juárez delegación, on the border with Coyoacán. At 876 feet tall, it becomes the city's tallest building.

2023: Quintonil is named the second best restaurant in North America and the ninth best in the world by the U.K.'s prestigious *Restaurant* magazine. Pujol clocks in at 13, Rosetta at 49th, and Sud 777 at 70th.

2024: The population of greater Mexico City stands at about 22.4 million, although growth has slowed from a high of 63% during the 1950s to around 7.6% over the past decade.

What to Watch and Read

It's perhaps not surprising that many of the most memorable films and books about Mexico City explore themes of death, violence, and economic inequality, but often with a darkly or absurdly comedic bent. This massive, vibrant metropolis with a history that's at once inspiring and heartbreaking is an apt setting for tales that capture the full spectrum of the human condition. Here are some key works that shine a bold light on one of the world's most complex cities.

AMORES PERROS

This darkly funny, gritty anthology film from 2000 helped launch director Alejandro González Iñárritu into the current realm of Mexican cinematic royalty. Said to be influenced by Buñuel's *Los Olvidados,* the movie was shot in some of the capital's roughest neighborhoods.

DOWN AND DELIRIOUS IN MEXICO CITY BY DANIEL HERNANDEZ

Young California-born-and-bred journalist Daniel Hernandez chronicles his efforts to get in touch with his Mexican roots by partaking in a series of adventures in CDMX. The result is a colorful portrait of the capital and its subcultures in the 21st century.

FRIDA

Salma Hayek's portrayal of Frida Kahlo in this vivid 2002 biopic helped turn the artist into one of Mexico's most recognized and canonized figures, and her former home, Casa Azul—which appears in the film—into one of the city's most hallowed attractions.

HORIZONTAL VERTIGO BY JUAN VILLORO

This fascinating and often funny 2021 chronicle showcases the striking contradictions and singular quirks of life in the pulsing megalopolis that is Mexico City.

I'LL SELL YOU A DOG BY JUAN PABLO VILLALOBOS

The novelist Juan Pablo Villalobos set his comically absurd third novel in a Mexico City retirement-apartment complex filled with memorably odd and endearing characters.

THE INTERIOR CIRCUIT: A MEXICO CITY CHRONICLE BY FRACISCO GOLDMAN

Francisco Goldman followed up the raw, shattering memoir about his wife's death in a freak accident, *Say Her Name,* with this deeply personal account of learning to drive in his home city of CDMX, and subsequently exploring both its beauty and its social challenges.

THE LABYRINTH OF SOLITUDE BY OCTAVIO PAZ

The lionized Mexico City poet and Nobel Laureate Octavio Paz wrote this richly lyrical series of essays in 1950. They explore the country's complex identity, from its revolutions to its embrace of mortality by way of its Día de Muertos celebration.

LA CASA DE LAS FLORES

One of several Netflix original shows filmed in Mexico, this over-the-top and morosely funny paean to Mexican telenovelas recounts the desperate travails of a dysfunctional, wealthy Mexico City family.

LOS OLVIDADOS

The iconic Spanish auteur filmmaker and sometime Mexico City resident Luis Buñuel made this despairing, realist 1950 portrait of impoverished urchins trying to scrape by in a grim city slum. It was shot largely in the Romita section of Roma.

MADE IN MEXICO

Check out this often rollicking, at other times lyrical, documentary that showcases—and interviews—many of Mexico's most revered contemporary musicians and bands, including Lila Downs, Natalia Lafourcade, Kinky, Carla Morrison, Gloria Trevi, Adan Jodorowsky, Julieta Venegas, Molotov, and the amazing Chavela Vargas, who passed away in 2012, the year the film was released. A number of other cultural notables are also interviewed, from actors Diego Luna and Daniel Giménez Cacho to wrestler Blue Demon.

MASSACRE IN MEXICO BY ELENA PONIATOWSKA

In one of her most critically acclaimed works, celebrated French-Mexican journalist Elena Poniatowska provides a harrowing, carefully researched, and witness-corroborated account of the 1968 student massacre at Tlatelolco, shortly before the Summer Olympics.

MUSEUM

Alonso Ruizpalacios's largely fictionalized, stylistically filmed 2018 depiction of the strange but true 1985 heist of dozens of priceless treasures from the Museo Nacional de Antropología is a lot of fun. Gael García Bernal delights as one of two dim-witted slacker-students frustrated in their efforts to profit from their larceny. Ruizpalacios is also the force behind 2014's critically beloved indie flick *Güeros*, which was also filmed throughout Mexico City.

ROMA

Alfonso Cuarón's mesmerizing semi-auto-biographical tour de force masterfully and affectionately re-creates the Mexico City of his early 1970s childhood. The 2018 film is filtered through the unvarnished yet nevertheless poignantly sentimental lens of his family's maid, nanny, and confidant.

ROTTING IN THE SUN

Sebastián Silva's wildly off-color 2023 dark comedy filmed in and around an apartment beside Roma's Plaza Rio de Janeiro skewers the differences in privilege between classes and backgrounds in Mexico City.

THIS IS NOT BERLIN

This briskly paced, often quite funny film is based on director Hari Sama's wild coming-of-age in mid-1980s Mexico City and its queer and iconoclastic punk, art, and club scenes.

Y TU MAMÁ TAMBIÉN

One of the most beloved films of modern Mexican cinema, Alfonso Cuarón's 2001 road-trip dramedy starring then largely unknown actors Gael García Bernal and Diego Luna begins and ends in Mexico City.

Chapter 2

TRAVEL SMART

2

Updated by
Andrew Collins

★ **CAPITAL:**
Mexico City

♔ **POPULATION:**
9.21 million (city proper),
22.28 million (metro region)

💬 **LANGUAGE:**
Spanish

$ **CURRENCY:**
Mexican Peso

☎ **COUNTRY CODE:**
52

⚠ **EMERGENCIES:**
911

🚗 **DRIVING:**
On the right side of the road

⚡ **ELECTRICITY:**
127 v/60 cycles; plugs have
two or three rectangular
prongs

🕐 **TIME:**
1 hour behind New York (2
hours behind during daylight
savings time, which Mexico
no longer observes)

🌐 **WEB RESOURCES:**
www.mexicocity.cdmx.
gob.mx
www.visitmexico.com

✈ **AIRPORTS:**
MEX, NLU

UNITED STATES

Gulf of Mexico

CUBA

Cabo San Lucas ○

MEXICO

○ Cancún

Pacific Ocean

Puerto Vallarta ○

○ Querétaro

Tepotzotlán ○ ○ Teotihuacán
MEXICO CITY ✪
Cuernavaca ○ ○ Puebla
○ Taxco

Acapulco ○

BELIZE

GUATEMALA
HONDURAS

Know Before You Go

For a fast-paced, densely populated metropolis that's among the world's largest, Mexico City is surprisingly user-friendly. Still, to make the most of your time here, it's helpful to keep a few tips and customs in mind as you prepare for your visit.

EXCHANGING MONEY
As more and more businesses accept credit cards in Mexico City, even including some smaller vendors and stalls in mercados that have long been cash-only, it's becoming possible to travel with less cash on hand. Still, it's a good idea to carry roughly 1,000 to 1,500 pesos with you when you're out and about, as you'll inevitably encounter cash-only situations here and there. A good strategy is to make one large withdrawal (6,000 pesos or so) when you arrive in Mexico rather than making lots of smaller withdrawals, as the fees at ATMs (*cajero automáticos*) can add up fast. ATMs are easy to find in most neighborhoods, and you'll usually get a better exchange rate at an ATM that's part of a major bank than one in a restaurant or convenience store.

RIDE-SHARE APPS
Whatever your feelings are about Uber as a corporation, the ubiquitous ride-share app really is the most secure, cost-effective, and efficient way to navigate the city. Right from the moment you land at the airport, it's a more convenient option than the taxi stands, and it's almost always easier to call an Uber than to hail a taxi on the street. Uber rates in Mexico have risen considerably in recent years, especially during busy periods, but they're still usually far lower than what you'd pay in the United States or Europe. There are some other rideshare apps serving Mexico City, Didi being the most popular alternative, but it doesn't always allow users to register non-Mexican credit cards (in which case you'll have to pay in cash), and wait times for drivers are usually longer.

FASHION NORMS
One of the easiest ways to stand out as a tourist in Mexico City is to dress in shorts, sandals, and logo T-shirts. Unless they're going to and from the gym or running a quick errand, locals in Mexico City rarely dress so casually (this is starting to change slightly and gradually with younger generations). It's certainly not a faux pas to dress in whatever attire you feel comfortable in, but if you prefer blending in a bit more, consider wearing jeans or other pants or longer skirts and dresses as well as closed-toe shoes. The biggest reason for favoring these outfits that cover more of your body is that temperatures range greatly from morning to afternoon to evening in Mexico City.

LANGUAGE
Although English is widely spoken in areas popular with tourists, including Polanco, Roma, Condesa, and Juárez, it's still a good idea to learn a handful of basic Spanish phrases, especially terms you're apt to use in restaurants and shops. The effort is always appreciated, and if you're actually hoping to practice and improve your Spanish, you'll find that locals are consistently patient, friendly, and willing to engage with even your limited efforts to converse in Spanish. Outside the city center, even in Coyoacán and Santa María la Ribera, English is less widely spoken. It's always helpful to have a translation app like Google Translate or SpanishDict handy on your smartphone.

COSTS
There's certainly truth in the perception that for travelers from the United States, Canada, Europe, and many other parts of the world, Mexico is an extremely affordable destination. Food, services (anything from spa treatments to guided tours to Uber rides), museum admission, and Mexico-made products like clothing and crafts tend to be reasonably

priced here. But CDMX is one of the country's most expensive cities, and the recent strength of the peso may cut into your savings. Wine and spirits are typically priced closer to what you'd pay at home and can greatly increase your restaurant bill. And some luxury items, like electronics, jewelry, and rooms in upscale international hotels, can be quite expensive.

OPENING HOURS
For the most part, business hours in Mexico City are pretty similar to other big cities in North America. Some smaller shops close or have limited hours on Sunday, and museums tend to be closed on Monday or occasionally Sunday or Tuesday. Meal times at traditional restaurants tend to be from around 1:30 until 4:30 for lunch and 8:30 until 10 or even 11 for dinner, and dinner at such places often isn't served on Sunday. But many modern or international eateries serve food throughout the day. Bars usually close between midnight and 2 am, and very few businesses in Mexico City are open all night.

SAFETY
Despite the country's reputation for (mostly narco-related) violence, Mexico City is relatively safe for a giant metropolis, and crime rates are comparable to large U.S. cities like Dallas and Chicago. Take the same commonsense precautions you would when visiting any large city: don't carry or display valuables or large amounts of cash, don't leave your belongings unattended, and stick to populated and, at night, well-lit areas. But there's no need to take special precautions in order to have a safe and relaxing visit.

FOOD SAFETY
Most visitors eat and drink their way through this incredible food city without encountering any major health challenges. But mild stomach issues aren't uncommon, especially if you eat a lot of spicy salsas and rich street food, so it's wise to pack antidiarrheal and antacid medication. Avoid drinking tap water, but rest assured that restaurants use safe, filtered water to rinse produce and make ice. If you're feeling uneasy or have a sensitive stomach, stick with well-established restaurants with plenty of positive online reviews.

ALTITUDE
One of the world's highest major metropolises, Mexico City sits at 7,400 feet above sea level. If you're coming from lower altitudes, take it easy your first two or three days in town, giving your body time to acclimate. Shortness of breath, fatigue, and dizziness are common symptoms of altitude sickness. Get lots of rest and keep very hydrated (Mexico City also has a very dry climate). And limit your intake of alcohol, which affects the body much more quickly at high altitude.

ADDRESSES
As you make your way around the city, and especially when typing addresses into navigation or ride-share apps, always check that you're using not only the correct street address but also the correct neighborhood and postal code. Many street names in Mexico City appear in several different neighborhoods or in multiple iterations. Mixing up two similar-looking addresses can result in a long and costly Uber ride to an entirely different part of the city than you intended.

DRIVING IN MEXICO
Driving in Mexico is on the right side of the road, and traffic laws are quite similar to those in the United States and Canada. Note that when a traffic signal flashes green, it's indicating that the light is about to turn yellow. In Mexico, right turns are not permitted at a red light unless otherwise signposted. Perhaps the most important thing to keep in mind when driving in Mexico City is that many drivers do not follow the rules of the road. Drivers routinely run red lights, drive the wrong direction down one-way streets, fail to use turn signals, park illegally, and ignore signs and other regulations. Always keep alert about your surroundings and when in doubt, yield to other drivers, even if they're breaking the law.

Getting Here and Around

Air

Approximate flight times to Mexico City are 3 hours from Dallas, 4½ hours from Chicago and Los Angeles, 5 hours from Toronto and New York City, and 10 to 11 hours from London and Madrid.

AIRPORTS

The vast majority of the country's visitors arrive through massive Benito Juárez International Airport (MEX, officially Aeropuerto Internacional Benito Juárez), which is the city's main facility. This huge airport—the busiest in Latin America—is on the city's east side, just 7 km (4 miles) from Centro Histórico and 15 km (9 miles) from both Polanco and Coyoacán. It's a sprawling, rather dated airport consisting of two terminals, and although improvements continue to speed up the immigration and customs processes on arrival and security process on departure, Benito Juárez is at best an unmemorable gateway to Mexico City and at worst a chaotic, unwieldly facility that makes a poor first impression on visitors to a city that's so enjoyable in so many other ways.

Plans were well underway to construct a stunning, state-of-the-art, and much-needed new airport just east of the current one when Andrés Manuel López Obrador took office as Mexico's President in 2018 and promptly cancelled the plan (it has been one of his most prominent and controversial campaign promises). In order to reduce the growing flight congestion that had been plaguing Benito Juárez International Airport, which is the world's busiest airport with only two runways, AMLO converted a former air force base 35 km (22 miles) north of the city into a second commercial facility called Felipe Ángeles International Airport (NLU, officially Aeropuerto Internacional Felipe Ángeles and usually referred to

as AIFA). Opened in 2022, AIFA mostly handles cargo and domestic flights on smaller airlines like Viva Aerobus, the country's state-run Mexicana, and Aeroméxico's regional subsidiary, Aeroméxico Connect, which is currently the only airline offering international flights from this airport (to Dallas, Houston, and McAllen, Texas). There are quite a few flights, and the number is growing, to other cities throughout Mexico, however, and fares are often cheaper than from Benito Juárez International Airport. The catch is AIFA's location well north of the city. Especially if you're traveling here from a southern neighborhood like Coyoacan, your Uber or taxi ride increases from roughly 20 minutes to 60 or even 90 minutes depending on traffic, and the increased Uber or taxi fare may partly or entirely cancel out the lower airfare. If you're staying on the north side of the city, AIFA isn't quite so inconvenient—the drive there from Polanco or San Rafael is sometimes only 15 or 20 minutes longer than it is to Benito Juárez.

Although it currently has no direct international flights, one other airport that some visitors to Mexico City might consider—especially if they're headed to the Santa Fe neighborhood on the west side of the city—is Toluca International Airport (TLC, officially Aeropuerto Internacional Licenciado Adolfo López Mateos). It's served by Viva Aerobus and Volaris with flights to several Mexican airports that connect to the United States and elsewhere, such as Cancún, Guadalajara, and Monterrey. Like AIFA, however, what you might save in airfare you may surrender in Uber or taxi fare. From Centro Histórico, the drive to Toluca's airport is about 90 minutes; from Santa Fe business-oriented hotels and office towers, it's about 45 minutes (which is only slightly longer than the drive from Santa Fe to Benito Juárez).

GROUND TRANSPORTATION

By far the easiest and most efficient way to get between Benito Juárez International Airport and your accommodations in the city is by Uber or taxi, and of these, Uber is usually cheaper and often quicker. You can use your phone to order an Uber from the passenger pickup areas outside the arrivals areas in both terminals (cell service is usually reliable, but if you're unable to connect, the airport has free Wi-Fi); the fare to most locations in the center of the city as well as in southern neighborhoods like Coyoacán and San Ángel will typically run anywhere from MP120 to MP200. If you'd rather use a taxi, go to the official taxi stands outside the arrivals areas in either terminal; fares will generally run MP150 to MP250. Never flag an unlicensed taxi; if want to take a taxi to the airport from your hotel or Airbnb, ask the front desk or your host to arrange this for you in advance.

Given the ease and reasonable cost of using Uber and taxis to get to and from the airport, using public transportation isn't a popular option, especially for first-time and non-Spanish-speaking visitors. However, if you're looking to save money and feel comfortable using public transit, there are a couple of options with direct airport access. The city's Metrobús Line 4 has stops right outside Terminal 1 and 2; you'll have to buy a reusable Mexico City Metro Card (officially called an integrated mobility card, or *tarjeta de movilidad integrada*) from the ticket machine, and the fare is just MP6 per trip. Line 4 runs directly through Centro Histórico and along Reforma, and from it you can connect with other lines as well as with the Metro subway system. Speaking of which, the city's Metro Aérea Station, on (yellow) Line 5, is just a few steps from Terminal 1; you can buy a ticket from the machine or ticket window (or use

the aforementioned Mexico City Metro Card), and the fare is just MP5. Metro Line 5, however, curves around the north side of the city and so you'll need to change trains at least once to get to any of the more central neighborhoods.

🚲 Bicycle

Since the launch of EcoBici in 2010, this increasingly popular bike-share program has become one of the largest and most popular such systems in the world. Stations are located throughout the city's central neighborhoods, from as far north as Santa María la Ribera and Polanco and as far south as Coyoacán and San Ángel. It's easy for visitors to sign up: just download the EcoBici app, register on the website, or use your Mexico City Metro Card at any of the newer 4G stations (they're continuing to add more and more of these). You can use the app or Mexico City Metro Card to use bikes for an unlimited number of 45-minute rides; just pick up your bike and return it to the station nearest to your destination. If you exceed 45 minutes, your credit card will be charged a small fee, but you can avoid the fee by returning the bike within 45 minutes, waiting two minutes, and then taking it out again (at which time a new 45-minute session will start). There are four EcoBici plan options: MP118 for one day, MP234 for three days, MP391 for seven days, and MP521 for an annual plan.

Even in this vast metropolis with its infamous car traffic, biking isn't terribly difficult or dangerous; the city has created a growing network of bike lanes, and sticking with quieter side streets is another good way to ensure a safe journey. That said, always look carefully before crossing intersections, and if you plan on biking extensively, consider bringing your own bike helmet.

Getting Here and Around

Bus

The city's modern rapid transit bus system, the Metrobús, provides a cheap way to travel through many central neighborhoods, although for most visitors, it's not the most practical way to navigate the city. With the exception of Metrobús Line 1, which runs along Avenida de los Insurgentes and connects Avenida Reforma and the neighborhood of Condesa with San Ángel and UNAM/Ciudad Universitaria, the five Metrobús lines mostly travel to neighborhoods that are also easily reached by metro (subway) or to residential areas that aren't of much interest to tourists.

Also, in order to ride the Metrobús, you must purchase a reusable Mexico City Metro Card —these cost 15 pesos (cash only, although plans are underway to upgrade machines to allow payment by credit card and even smartphones) and are sold from the automated machines located at Metrobús stations and from metro stations and light rail ticket windows. You can then load up the card with up to 120 pesos in credit that you can also use for the city's metro, light rail, and EcoBici bikeshare system. Metrobus rides cost MP6 per trip. The fleet's red buses travel along fixed routes in their own dedicated lanes and pick up passengers at designated stations, just like the metro. Also like the metro, the Metrobus reserves the forward-most carriages for women and children. Note that the Metrobús is the only one of the city's handful of other bus systems that really make sense for short-term visitors exploring the city.

Car

With legendary intense traffic, a vastly sprawling road system that doesn't always adhere to a grid, hard-to-find parking, lots of one-way streets, a lack of traffic signs and signals, and countless obstacles (speed bumps, potholes, double-parked cars, cyclists, pedestrians), driving in Mexico City is not for the faint of heart. In most scenarios, it's unnecessary and potentially even a hindrance to rent a car. In terms of exploring the city, it's far more relaxing, efficient, and usually even cost-effective to let others— Uber drivers specifically—do the driving for you. Furthermore, you can get around the city's most popular neighborhoods on foot or via the fast-growing EcoBici bike-share network.

That being said, there are a few scenarios where renting a car *might* make sense. If you're staying in a quieter, less central neighborhood and your accommodation offers secure, off-street parking, it might be worth renting a car for at least part of your stay, especially if you're planning to cover a lot of ground and you actually feel pretty comfortable driving in big cities. A more compelling reason to rent a car is to make side trips to other destinations in the region. But even if you're headed out of town, given that Mexico has an excellent network of privately run bus companies that serve all of the major towns and cities you'd likely want to visit, a car isn't a necessity for exploring farther afield.

CAR RENTALS

Most major international car rental agencies have counters at the airports in Mexico City as well as satellite offices located in central neighborhoods. Rates from major companies can vary greatly but typically run about MP1,000 to MP1,300 daily or MP5,000 to MP8,000 per week, and—always read the fine print to be sure of this—that usually includes the basic liability coverage that's legally required of all drivers in Mexico. Assuming you're paying with a credit card that covers the CDW (collision damage waiver)—always check first—you should decline this additional coverage. If not, it's a good idea to purchase this; otherwise, you'll be responsible for any damage to the car, regardless of fault. It's also a pretty good idea to purchase additional liability insurance, which credit cards and U.S. and Canadian insurance policies do not cover, just to make sure you're adequately covered in the event of an accident that causes damage or injury to other parties. Extra insurance can add significantly to the cost of your rental, but for many visiting drivers with limited experience driving in Mexico, the peace of mind is worth the price. It's also best to ask for the price of your car rental to be quoted in Mexican pesos to avoid currency conversions that always favor the rental car company.

Beyond that, renting a car in Mexico is pretty similar to doing so elsewhere in North America—you need a valid driver's license and passport, you must be at least 21, you should return the car with a full tank (or at whatever gas level you received it), and you should carefully check your vehicle for any damage or defective equipment before heading out.

If you're only going to be using your rental car to make side trips outside the city, it's best to rent at the airport. This way you avoid having to drive much in the city itself. From the airport, generally well-marked roads access the main highways leading outside the city.

DRIVING

For the most part, in terms of rules and customs, driving in Mexico is similar to driving in the United States and Canada. There are a few things to watch for in and around Mexico City. Roads throughout the country, including the entire city, have speed bumps—known locally as *topes*—that do greatly help to reduce speeding and reckless driving. However, because they're sometimes unmarked and unpainted, it's fairly easy to make contact with a tope at too high a speed, causing the upheaval of your vehicle's occupants and contents, and maybe even damage to your car. The majority of streets in Mexico City lack traffic signals or signs; if you come to an unmarked intersection, the norm is for drivers to take turns, one car at a time, but your actual results may vary. Drivers here aren't necessarily any more aggressive than in other big cities; the best approach is to drive defensively, and pay close attention to your surroundings.

GASOLINE

Gas stations are widespread throughout Mexico City and in most larger towns outside the city, as well as along major highways. All gas stations are full-service; drivers may not pump their own gas, and it's customary to tip gas station attendants 5 or 10 pesos. Prices are in liters (a gallon contains just under four liters), with the cost of gas averaging about 20% higher than in the United States.

Getting Here and Around

PARKING

In Mexico City's most central neighborhoods, street parking can be hard to come by; on some streets it's metered (meters accept credit cards), and on others it's free. In less congested areas like Coyoacán, Santa María la Ribera, and even Roma Sur, you can sometimes find a spot on the street, and in these neighborhoods parking is usually free. You'll find quite a few parking garages and lots throughout the city, however, and these are invariably the safest places to park, especially overnight (it's never a great idea to park on the street after dark).

RULES OF THE ROAD

Driving in Mexico is on the right side of the road, and traffic laws are quite similar to those in the United States and Canada. Note that when a traffic signal flashes green, it's indicating that the light is about to turn yellow. In Mexico, right turns are not permitted at a red light unless otherwise signposted. Perhaps the most important thing to keep in mind when driving in Mexico City is that many drivers do not follow the rules of the road. Drivers routinely run red lights, drive the wrong direction down one-way streets, fail to use turn signals, park illegally, and ignore signs and other regulations. Always keep alert about your surroundings and when in doubt, yield to other drivers, even if they're breaking the law.

Ⓜ Metro

Mexico City's subway system is a wonder to behold. Its 12 color-coded lines ferry millions of visitors and commuters to most parts of the city quickly and efficiently, often much faster than traveling overland in the city's notorious traffic; rides cost MP5. You can buy single-ride tickets and reusable Mexico City Metro Cards (officially called integrated mobility cards) for MP15 at ticket windows in each station. If you're planning to use the Metro regularly, it makes sense to buy the Mexico City Metro Card and load it up with credit, which allows you to use the card in the metro as well as on the Metrobús, light rail, and EcoBici bikeshare systems. Metro stations are marked with graphical icons—a grasshopper, a fountain—as well as written names. The metro can be uncomfortably hot and sardine-packed during rush hour; women traveling solo may want to take advantage of the women-and-children-only cars, located at the front of each train. The metro is relatively safe, but it's always wise to keep a close eye on your belongings at all times, and to avoid using it late at night. The metro runs daily from 5 am until midnight.

 Ride-Sharing

Uber isn't just the most popular and widely used ride-sharing app in Mexico City; it's by far the most popular and widely used way for visitors to explore the city. Upon launching here in 2013, Uber effectively changed the navigation landscape. It's much cheaper here than in Europe and the rest of North America. A 30-minute ride between even neighborhoods a good distance from one another—say Coyoacán and San Rafael, which are 15 km (10 miles) apart—costs about MP150 to MP200 under normal conditions. Quick hops of 2 km or 3 km (a mile or two) can cost as little as MP40. Drivers are consistently reliable, and because you can easily call an Uber from your phone to virtually any address in the city at any hour of the day, and you never have to exchange physical money or credit cards, it's hard to overstate how profoundly the arrival of this company affected the city, and especially its popularity with visitors from other places. Many visitors, and even quite a few residents who've moved here from other countries, navigate the city entirely via Uber.

There are potential pitfalls, of course. The service's popularity has led to increased demand, which in turn has resulted in more frequent periods of surge-pricing, which can double or in rare instances triple the fare. During these busy periods, wait times for a driver can easily exceed 10 or even 15 minutes. With that in mind, even if you're able to count on using Uber for the vast majority of your trips around town, it's good to have a backup plan—such as having some familiarity with taking the metro or Metrobús, knowing how to get a taxi, or having a backup ride-share app. The second-most popular ride-share app in the city is Didi, but it tends not to allow riders to pay with credit cards from other countries. You can pay for your Didi ride with cash and fares are sometimes cheaper than with Uber, but it's also common for waits to be longer with Didi.

🚕 Taxi

Long saddled with a reputation for crime or at the very least unscrupulous drivers, taxis have improved considerably in Mexico City over the years, in part because competition from Uber and other ride-share apps has forced them to shape up a bit. Still, it's best to avoid hailing cabs from the street in Mexico City. Instead, either hire a taxi through a *sitio* booth—these are located on some busy streets and plazas, and also at airports, in bus terminals, and elsewhere. Another option is to have the staff at a hotel, restaurant, or bar call a radio taxi for you. And lastly, the city's government-run app (App

CDMX) comes with its own Mi Taxi service, which allows you to call a registered taxi from your phone the same way you would from a ride-share app. Using this app is also the one way that you can safely hail a cab from the street; when a cab stops for you, just enter its license plate number into Mi Taxi. The app will then list the driver's name and the make and model of the car (if it doesn't match, don't get in). The app also allows you to track your ride (and share this tracking information with a friend). Even though taxis have improved in Mexico City, fares still tend to be higher than riding with Uber, and the process is more cumbersome.

Train

Both within Mexico City and regionally, train travel in Mexico is far less prevalent than bus travel. However, Mexico City's Xochimilco Light Rail (or Tren Ligero) can be a useful option if you're planning to visit the canals in Xochilmilco, which are located in the southeastern corner of the city, a 45-minute to 75-minute drive from the city center. Uber rides this far can be spendy and cost MP200 or more. By light rail, it's about a 40-minute ride from the first station (Tasqueña) to the last (Xochimilco), and the fare is just MP5. However, Tasqueña station is at the end of the Metro Line 2, a 20- to 25-minute ride from the city center, so while you'll save a lot of money taking a combination of metro and light trail to Xochimilco, you won't necessarily save much or any time.

Essentials

🏃 Activities

Mexico City supports its professional sports teams with vigor. The city has professional baseball, basketball, and even American football teams, but the sport that Mexicans follow with intense passion is fútbol (or soccer, to Americans). The city is home to three of the country's top professional soccer teams: Club América, Cruz Azul, and the UNAM's Pumas. You can watch the first two teams in action at massive Estadio Azteca, which is one of the world's largest stadiums—attending games here, and even taking a tour of the stadium, is great fun for visitors. The Pumas play at Estadio Olímpico Universitario. Both venues are in the south of the city. Occasionally, major league baseball, football, and basketball teams play a game or two in Mexico City—it's best to search online to see when these are next scheduled (dates are usually announced months in advance).

The other spectator activity you might want to check out during your visit is Mexico's uniquely entertaining—some might even say bombastic—brand of wrestling, lucha libre. Matches take place primarily at two venues in the city, Arena México, which is the larger and more impressive of the two, located in Doctores near the border with Alameda and Roma Norte, and the smaller and somewhat shaggier Arena Coliseo, located in Centro Histórico.

🍽 Dining

As Mexico City's culinary reputation has continued to grow and thrive throughout the 21st century, increasing numbers of food lovers now plan their visits entirely around where they'll dine each day. And buzzy neighborhoods like Condesa,

Roma, and Juárez now rank among the city's most popular for exploring, despite having few museums and other formal attractions—for visitors, these charming quadrants are largely about eating, snacking, and sipping espresso drinks, craft beer, Mexican wine, and creative cocktails.

The dining scene in the national capital isn't defined by any one specific cooking style so much as it is a place to sample regional cuisines from throughout Mexico's 31 states. You'll find plenty of great sources of authentic fare from Oaxaca, Puebla, Sinaloa, Baja California, the Yucatan, and other regions known for their rich and varied dining. And great food in CDMX bridges every budget, from inexpensive street-food stands dispensing tacos, tortas, and tamales to high-end dining rooms helmed by chefs who present oft-changing menus based on what's fresh and in season.

Although many of the city's top dining destinations do focus their efforts chiefly on Mexican fare, many others offer a fusion of flavors influenced heavily by other parts of the world, particularly the Mediterranean and both southern and eastern Asia. Restaurants specializing in casual international fare—pizza, pasta, ramen, burgers, Thai curries, French pastries—also continue to make waves here. Dining purists sometimes eschew anything but purely Mexican cuisine when visiting CDMX, reasoning that it's silly to order a dish here that you can just as easily enjoy back home. Fair enough, but some of the city's most talented chefs specialize in international cuisine, often infusing their creations with Mexican ingredients and accents. It would be a shame to miss out on these places simply because they don't purport to specialize exclusively in traditional Mexican cuisine.

One final piece of advice: although Mexico City is several hours' drive from the sea and has relatively little agricultural within its city limits, it's the country's shipping and commercial crossroads. Fresh fish, produce, and other ingredients are delivered to the city's markets around the clock, and you can find both casual and upscale restaurants in CDMX that serve fresh seafood, salads, juices, and farm-to-table fare on par with any other region in the country.

PAYING

The vast majority of Mexico City's restaurants take credit cards, but a handful of smaller places do not. Food stalls in markets and on the street typically take only cash, although even this is changing gradually as some vendors now use smartphone apps that process credit card payments. Some of these smaller businesses charge a small fee if you pay with a credit card. It's always a good idea to have some cash on hand when dining in smaller establishments or in markets. It's customary to tip between 10% and 15% at restaurants; most foreign visitors, especially when dining at more upscale establishments, tip 15%. Note that when paying with a credit card, in most cases, your server will bring a portable credit card terminal to your table and ask you if you'd like to charge your tip (*propina*) to your credit card, let the server know *before* they run your card. To add 15%, you can just say, "con quince por ciento."

RESERVATIONS AND DRESS

At any of the city's internationally acclaimed restaurants—places like Pujol, Quintonil, and Rosetta—scoring a table can be challenging, or even impossible, without a reservation. Most of these establishments make it easy to book reservations online through their website or popular third-party apps like OpenTable or Resy, but if you really have your heart set on dining somewhere in particular, it's best to book well ahead—even a week or two in advance. Even at less-vaunted but still trendy spots around town, of which there are hundreds, if you can make a reservation, it's a good idea to do so, even the day you plan to go, just to avoid the disappointment of traveling some distance only to be turned away. Quite a few popular and upscale restaurants don't accept reservations, so be prepared for a possible wait at these places.

Although even the fanciest restaurants in Mexico City don't enforce strict dress codes, you're going to look quite out of place if you show up in shorts, a T-shirt, and sandals, and dressing too casually can also greatly diminish your chances of securing a table at a restaurant where you don't have a reservation. Jeans and a button-down shirt are fine, and really the norm, at even nicer restaurants, especially in the evening or during *la comida* on Sunday, which is the one daytime meal in Mexico City that locals tend to dress up a bit for.

MEALS AND MEALTIMES

Traditionally in Mexico the most substantial meal of the day is *la comida,* and it happens roughly between 1:30 and 4:30 pm. Breakfast is usually served in restaurants starting around 8 am, while Mexicans tend to prefer eating light at night, often enjoying a simple dinner (*la cena*) between 8:30 and 9:30 or even 10.

These customs sometimes confound visitors used to lunching around noon and saving their largest meal for dinnertime. But in diverse and cosmopolitan Mexico City, you'll find plenty of restaurants that serve meals at times that suit both visitors and locals, not to mention countless cafés, taquerías, and street vendors doling out quick bites throughout the day. The hipper and often more international restaurants that thrive throughout trendy

Essentials

dining districts like Roma, Condesa, and Juárez are especially likely to have meal times more in line with those in the United States or Europe. Just keep in mind that some establishments—especially more traditional ones—may not open for lunch until 1 pm, and if you show up for dinner before 8, you may encounter a fairly empty dining room. Also note that on Sunday, even many trendy international restaurants close by 6 or 7 pm.

Although not many restaurants in Mexico City specifically offer "brunch" menus, you'll find plenty of places that offer late-morning and early afternoon dining that's very typical of what might be called brunch in other parts of the world. Think expansive menus featuring a mix of breakfast and lunch dishes, along with free-flowing cocktails and a charming setting—there may even be live music. Especially in affluent neighborhoods like Polanco and San Ángel, wonderfully inviting brunchlike experiences abound on weekends and even at some restaurants during the week.

Finally, if you're a fan of the morning meal, take comfort in knowing that breakfast (*el desayuno*) is highly popular in Mexico City, and typically a great value. Many restaurants offer package deals (*paquetes*) that include your main dish, coffee, fresh fruit or fresh-squeezed juice, and—best of all—a decadently delicious pastry of your choosing.

SMOKING

In 2023, Mexico passed one of the world's strictest and most comprehensive anti-tobacco laws. Smoking had already been prohibited in all indoor public spaces, including restaurants and bars, since 2008. The ban now includes public outdoor spaces, such as restaurant patios, as well as public plazas and parks, and it applies to conventional cigarettes as well as e-cigarettes and vapes.

Prices in the reviews are the average cost of a main course at dinner or, if dinner is not served, at lunch.

What It Costs in Mexican Pesos			
$	$$	$$$	$$$$
AT DINNER			
under 150 MP	150 MP–300 MP	301 MP–450 MP	over 450 MP

⊕ Health and Safety

Despite its size and that it's the capital of a country that does have one of the Western Hemisphere's higher crime rates, Mexico City is quite safe for travelers. "Safe," of course, is a relative term, and crime statistics are notoriously thorny to compare from one place to another, because of different methodologies and variations in how accurately crimes are reported. Nevertheless, according to the most recent and widely reported statistics, Mexico City has fewer homicides per capita than Dallas, Denver, and Portland. Most of the violent crime in Mexico in recent years is related to narco-related organizations and has not been perpetrated against individuals who aren't involved in criminal activities. Random violence against visitors to Mexico is extremely rare—when it happens, it virtually always makes international headlines. With this in mind, assuming you steer clear of any criminal activity and you spend your time in Mexico City's most visitor-oriented neighborhoods—the ones covered in this guidebook—there's no more reason to worry about your safety here than you should be when visiting any major U.S. city.

This isn't to say that you shouldn't exercise commonsense precautions as you explore the city. Nonviolent crimes—pickpocketing, theft, scams—do happen here. Just as you would in any new place you're visiting, pay attention to your surroundings, avoid desolate or dark streets and parks, leave your valuables and large amounts of cash in your hotel room (and in your hotel safe, if there is one), and in general, just play it cautiously. The vast majority of locals you encounter in Mexico City will be kind and helpful—this is an exceedingly friendly city. More often than not, if you accidentally drop something on the street while you're walking—even cash—someone nearby will pick it up and return it to you. Trying to fit in and not stand out as a tourist is another way to avoid being targeted by anyone looking to take advantage of you. This is one more reason to consider avoiding the standard tourist "uniform" of shorts, flip-flops, and T-shirts, which will instantly mark you as an outsider. But again, Mexico City is by and large a safe and secure city, and even tourists who stand out are very unlikely to be a victim of even a petty crime.

The other safety issues to consider when visiting CDMX relate to eating and acclimating to the city's high (7,400 feet) elevation. In terms of food safety, there can be a greater risk of encountering stomach issues here than back home, in part because you're going to be trying new ingredients (and may be served some potentially spicy salsas, especially at taquerias and street-food stalls) and potentially eating more than you normally would at home. Understandably, given all the amazing food, people sometimes overindulge a bit here. But if you're dining in established restaurants that have

plenty of positive reviews on Google and other websites, there's no reason to worry about drinking the water and ice or eating fruit and other produce. These establishments are inspected by the health department and depend on both local and foreign patrons to succeed; they serve only filtered water for drinking and to wash produce and vegetables. Yes, food poisoning can happen at a nice restaurants in Mexico City, but it's no more likely to happen here than in New York City or London.

Street food is another matter. There's simply no way around the fact that food served from vendors on the street is potentially riskier than what's served in sit-down restaurants. Most visitors to CDMX experience the city's delicious and extremely affordable street food without having any major issues, but minor bouts of diarrhea or rumbling stomachs are probably more likely to happen the more you eat street food, and especially spicy street food. You can greatly reduce your odds of eating something disagreeable by ordering food only from very popular food vendors, by washing your hands before and after you eat (it's a good idea to bring some liquid hand gel with you), and by going easy on how much and how often you eat street food, especially the first couple of days of your trip.

The tap water that comes out of the faucet in Mexico City or really anywhere in Mexico is best avoided. This isn't to say that bodily chaos will ensue if you ingest a few drops of shower water or even if you use tap water from your hotel or Airbnb to brush you teeth. But the city's water pipes are notoriously old and creaky, and even most locals drink only filtered or bottled water.

Essentials

Whatever precautions you take, there's always a chance you'll have an upset stomach. Always travel with some anti-diarrheal medication and antacid tablets, and for that matter, whatever other medications you regularly take. Pharmacies are widespread and generally affordable throughout Mexico City, but some medications sold over the counter in the United States aren't available here (and vice versa). It's best to bring with you an ample supply of any medication you need. Mexico City also has a first-rate health-care infrastructure. If you need medical care, hotel staff and Airbnb hosts can help you find the nearest hospital, as can the staff at pharmacies.

Unless you're coming to CDMX from another high-altitude destination, altitude sickness is more likely to affect you here than stomach problems. Fortunately, most people experience only minor symptoms, and these tend to disappear after a few days of getting acclimated. The most likely discomforts are fatigue, shortness of breath, and dizziness, and if you take things slowly your first two or three days in the city, drink lots of water (Mexico City is very low in humidity, especially fall through spring), and get plenty of rest, you'll likely have no problems. Also go easy on alcohol consumption—the effects of alcohol are both faster and more intense at this altitude.

Immunizations

There are no immunization requirements for visitors traveling to Mexico for tourism. The CDC and WHO generally recommend the same vaccinations you'd likely want for traveling anywhere else in North America, including the latest flu shot and COVID-19 vaccination, but these are not required for entry.

Lodging

Mexico City has a mix of major international and domestic (Camino Real, Fiesta Inn and Fiesta America, Grupo Habita, and some others) brands that you'd expect of a major metropolis. Most of the larger properties are located in central neighborhoods popular with both leisure and business travelers—Centro Histórico, Alameda Central, Juárez, and Polanco—along with the almost exclusively business-driven Santa Fe district, on the western outskirts of the city (not an ideal place to stay unless you're doing business in that area). You'll also find a smattering of boutique inns, B&Bs, and Airbnbs in these areas, but the city's smaller properties tend to be located more in residential—and often historic—neighborhoods, such as Condesa, Roma, Santa María la Ribera, Benito Juárez, and Coyoacán. Overall, hotel rates in Mexico City are quite reasonable, but there are a handful of luxury properties that charge rates roughly comparable to those you'd pay in many U.S. and European cities. Airbnb is extremely popular in Mexico City, and also typically an excellent value.

FACILITIES

You can assume that all rooms have private baths and TVs unless otherwise indicated; in larger hotels and chain properties, rooms also almost always have phones and air-conditioning. In smaller B&Bs and Airbnbs, even upscale ones, rooms often lack phones and air-conditioning, which is a relatively uncommon feature (as is heating) in homes in this city with its relatively mild climate. If you're staying at a smaller property and these amenities are important to you, always ask ahead. Breakfast is noted when it is included in the rate—many larger and most smaller Mexico City hotels do offer this. Most of the city's larger hotels do have pools and gyms, and many have restaurants and bars; a few even have impressive spas. These sorts of amenities do vary a bit, however, and the reviews in this book call attention to properties with noteworthy dining, spas, and other perks.

PARKING

Renting a car in Mexico City is, for the most part, not recommended. Should you be using a car, keep in mind that many larger hotels do have garages and either valet or self-parking, and rates tend not to be exorbitant (typically under MP200 per night). Always check ahead if this feature is important to you. If you're staying at an Airbnb or a smaller property, check with your host about parking options, as this can vary considerably depending on the property and the neighborhood.

PRICES

Hotel rates in Mexico City tend not to vary a great deal seasonally. You might encounter slightly higher rates, and lower occupancy, during holiday periods and in summer, which is actually the rainy season—a fairly cool and wet time to visit—but also when families are more likely to spend time here.

RESERVATIONS

Always make a reservation when visiting Mexico City. Hotels often fill up, and rooms can be harder to come by from mid-October through early November (during Día de Muertos and the days leading up to it). But any time of year, popular hotels—especially smaller properties with a limited number of rooms—may book up days or weeks in advance.

Prices are the average cost of a double room during high season, not including especially expensive holiday or special-event rates.

What It Costs in Mexican Pesos				2
$	$$	$$$	$$$$	
FOR TWO PEOPLE				
under 2,000 MP	2,000 MP–4,000 MP	4,001 MP–6,000 MP	over 6,000 MP	

Travel Smart ESSENTIALS

ⓨ Nightlife

Mexico City has a remarkably vibrant and varied bar and club scene. Nightlife in the capital is perhaps a misnomer, given that you'll find plenty of locals and visitors sipping beer and cocktails for hours well before sunset, at least on weekends. Many bars here have appealing outdoor spaces, from cozy sidewalk tables and back gardens to spacious roof decks. And as is the case in many cosmopolitan cities, there's often a fine line between restaurant and bar, as many of the former have outstanding beverage programs and lively lounges, and many of the latter serve superb food, from light bar snacks to sophisticated tapas. If you're wanting a classic Mexico City experience, seek out one of the city's old-world, unpretentious cantinas or maybe a casual beer or pulque bar with TV screens airing fútbol games. You'll find these locals-oriented hangouts just about everywhere, from workaday residential areas to upscale neighborhoods. For a trendier and more current night on the town, seek out some of the hip mixology-driven cocktails bars, lively mezcalerías, craft-beer gardens, and swanky natural-wine bars that continue to open around town, especially in the adjacent neighborhoods of Roma, Condesa, and Juárez. Late-night clubbers will definitely want to check out the Zona Rosa section of Juárez, which has dozens of both mainstream and LGBTQ+ establishments. You'll find dance clubs

Where Should I Stay?

	NEIGHBORHOOD VIBE	PROS	CONS
Centro Histórico	A historic and central neighborhood, it's home to many of the city's top attractions.	Fairly safe; steps from many important museums; distinctive, often historic, hotels.	Heavy foot- and car traffic often lead to noise even at night; lacking in quaintness.
Juárez	Offers a mix of upscale and popular hotels along Paseo de la Reforma along with charming and historic residential blocks.	Quite safe; great selection of both larger and boutique-y hotels; short walk to Roma Norte and Alameda Central.	Modern Reforma lacks charm and dining options; can be noisy with car traffic and, in the historic sections, late-night bars.
Polanco	Wealthy neighborhood bordered by Bosque de Chapultepec, with a number of high-end hotels as well as fine shops and restaurants.	Very safe area; an easy and pleasant walk to the many attractions of Bosque de Chapultepec; several swanky hotels with top-notch amenities.	A little far from other popular neighborhoods, such as Centro Histórico and Roma; ritzy vibe isn't for everyone; lodging options tend to be expensive.
Roma	Trendy and sophisticated neighborhood filled with hip bars and restaurants.	Extremely safe; home to some of the city's most alluring, design-driven boutique hotels;; outstanding food scene.	A bit spendy, and the small hotels and Airbnbs here can book up well in advance; ultrahip vibe and huge numbers of non-Spanish-speaking expats can be off-putting for some.
Condesa	Leafy and historic district with beautiful architecture and charming restaurants and boutiques.	Extremely safe; close to Roma and Bosque de Chapultepec; a number of smartly designed boutique inns and Airbnbs; fantastic dining scene.	The few larger hotels are on the expensive side; streets can get crowded with pedestrians; the presence of so many expats and non-Spanish speakers can be off-putting.
Coyoacán	Endearingly historic and friendly neighborhood that's home to Museo Frida Kahlo.	Extremely safe; laid-back and quiet with a thriving café culture and some notable attractions; several appealing small inns and plenty of well-priced Airbnbs.	A 20- to 40-minute Uber ride from the city center; limited selection of hotels; might be a little too quiet for some.

catering to diverse crowds in other neighborhoods as well, from Polanco to Centro Histórico. There are also a number of bars and clubs that offer live music. You may encounter cover charges at these spots as well as in dance clubs. Most bars and lounges stay open until somewhere between midnight and 2 am while a handful of the city's top clubbing venues keep the beat alive until well after sunrise.

⊕ Passports and Visas

All visitors to Mexico require a valid passport that is valid for the duration of your stay. If you're entering as a tourist, you don't need a visa, but your stay will be limited to up to six months.

⊕ Performing Arts

CDMX is the country's arts capital, the home of such renowned performing arts groups as Ballet Folklórico de México, Orquesta Sinfónica Nacional, Ópera de Bellas Artes, and dozens of outstanding theater groups. There's also an extensive network of concert halls and arenas that draw many of the world's top touring music acts. By far the most renowned performance space in the city is the grand Palacio de Bellas Artes in Alameda Central. Most of the other key venues are in the city center, although some major concerts take place in the city's major sports stadiums, such as Estadio Azteca on the south side of the city and Palacio de los Deportes near the airport. One other major arts venue of note is Centro Cultural Universitario de la UNAM, the sprawling cultural complex of theaters and concert halls on the beautiful campus of Universidad Nacional Autónoma de México, on the south side

of the city. You can typically purchase tickets to top performing arts events in Mexico City through Ticketmaster.

CDMX is also a city of film lovers. Two major chains—Cinemex and Cinépolis—dominate the scene and have often fancy multiplex theaters throughout the city. These chains mostly show the same movies that you'll find back at home, but usually at a fraction of the price. For a more memorable movie-going experience, head to Cineteca Nacional, a gorgeously designed complex of cinemas, cafés, and film-related shops located at the southern end of Benito Juárez, near the border with Coyoacán.

⊕ Shopping

In most of the city's neighborhoods that are popular with visitors, shopping is a favorite pastime. This activity can mean anything from browsing the colorful stalls of local foods and crafts inside the numerous neighborhood mercados (markets) to strolling through fashionable neighborhoods like Roma, Condesa, Juárez, and Polanco and popping inside boutiques specializing in clothing, crafts, housewares, and art created in Mexico—not just CDMX but all around the country. The city also has a number of exceptional museum gift shops: notably those at Museo de Arte Popular, Museo Universitario Arte Contemporáneo (MUAC), Museo Tamayo, and Palacio de Bellas Artes. Other strengths in Mexico City when it comes to retail are bookstores, candy and chocolate shops, and stores specializing in mezcal, tequila, and Mexican wines. As you make your way around the city, and especially through upscale neighborhoods like Polanco and Santa Fe, you may notice that CDMX has a pretty enthusiastic appreciation for giant, sprawling shopping malls. These

Essentials

places cater mostly to the city's affluent residents, of which there are many, but they're not too exciting for visitors. As with malls in most of the world, most of the retailers are internationally known brands, and prices for goods imported to Mexico tend not to be any less expensive than they are in the United States or Europe.

💲 Tipping

Tipping is as commonplace and expected in Mexico as it is in the United States, but the amounts and percentages are a bit lower. It's always a good idea to keep some change on hand, although at restaurants and bars that accept credit cards, you can ask to add the tip (*propina*) to the bill before they run your card.

🏳 U.S. Embassy

Mexico City is home to about 85 embassies and consulates, and most offer consular services in the embassy building. The U.S. Embassy is located at Avenida Paseo de la Reforma 305 in the Cuauhtémoc/Juárez neighborhood.

📍 Visitor Information

The Mexico City Tourism Office has a very good tourism website (in both English and Spanish), at ⊕ *mexicocity.cdmx. gob.mx.* They also produce a handy app, App CDMX, which contains most of the information on the website. You can also visit the office (Secretaría de Turismo de la CDMX) in Condesa at Avenida Nuevo León 56, to ask questions and pick up brochures in person. The office is open weekdays 9–6.

Tipping Guides for Mexico City

Bartender	MP10–MP20 per drink or 10% to 15% of the total bill
Bellhop	MP10–MP30 per bag, depending on the level of the hotel
Coat Check	MP10–MP20 per coat
Hotel Concierge	MP50–MP100, depending on the service
Hotel Doorstaff	MP10–MP50 for help with bags or hailing a cab
Hotel Housekeeping	MP20–MP50 a day (in cash, preferably daily since cleaning staff may be different each day you stay)
Hotel Room Service	MP20–MP40 per delivery, even if a service charge has been added
Porter at Airport or Bus Station	MP10 per bag
Restroom Attendants	MP5 or small change
Skycap at Airport	MP10–MP20 per bag checked
Spa Personnel	15%–20% of the cost of your service
Taxi or Uber Driver	10%–15%
Tour Guide	10%–20% of the cost of the tour, per person
Valet Parking Attendant	MP40–MP100, each time your car is brought to you
Waiter	10%–15%, with 15% being the norm; many visitors do tip closer to 20% at higher-end restaurants

When to Go

There's really no bad time to visit this dynamic city with a temperate and generally pleasant climate year-round. However, each season has its charms as well as potential tradeoffs.

Winter: This is the city's coolest month, with average highs around 70° and nighttime lows in the low- to mid-40s. But as with most of the rest of the year, you can expect plenty of sunshine. Although this time of year may sound downright balmy to anyone visiting from upper North America or northern Europe, you still want to pack jackets and plenty of layers for those chilly evenings, especially if you're staying at an Airbnb that doesn't have heat (which is quite common in Mexico City). The city is very festive and warmly decorated during the Christmas season (note that in Mexico, the biggest day of celebration is December 24 rather than December 25), making December and early January a fun time to visit. As temperatures start to warm up a bit in February and March, the city's stunningly famous jacaranda trees show off their lavender blooms (their season lasts until around mid-April). Many people consider March to be the loveliest time of year in Mexico City, between the jacarandas and the mild, sunny temperatures.

Spring: This is the warmest time to visit Mexico City, as daytime highs climb into the low 80s in late April and into May. It's rarely uncomfortably hot except maybe in the very middle of the day, and only if you're outside in the sun. By late spring, several months of low rainfall have taken their toll on the city's flora—gardens can look a bit bare at this time, at least relatively (Mexico City is also fairly green).

There's often a slight surge in visitation, especially with families on spring break, between mid-March and mid-April.

Summer: If it's hot and humid back home during the summer months and you're craving cooler climes, summer in CDMX may be just what you need. This is the city's rainy season, a time when mornings tend to be warm and sunny, but afternoons consistently give way to overcast skies and sometimes torrential downpours. It rains an average of more than 5 inches per month from mid-June to mid-September (compared with less than a half-inch of rain per month from November through April). You will absolutely want to bring your umbrella. But visitors from hotter places often appreciate how green everything is in summer, and happily embrace the mild temperatures, with daytime highs in the mid-70s and nighttime lows in the upper 50s. Crowds, especially families off from school, tend to be a little higher in summer, but not dramatically so.

Fall: Like late winter and spring, the autumn months in Mexico City are sunny and warm but rarely too hot, making this an extremely popular and enjoyable season to visit. Daytime highs hover around the low- to mid-70s, with lows dipping down to the low 50s. The city celebrates Mexico's independence with great fanfare on September 16, and it begins preparing altars and ofrendas for Día de Muertos, which takes place officially November 1 and 2, as early late September. Other than the fact that you may encounter pretty sizable crowds during these aforementioned holidays, there are few downsides to visiting Mexico City in the fall.

Best Tours in Mexico City

In Mexico City, you'll find dozens of companies offering guided tours, in both English and Spanish, many of them fairly standard group excursions around the most prominent neighborhoods or out to Teotihuacán (which, because of its immensity as well as its distance from the city center, can be easiest to explore on an organized trip). Look beyond the usual fare, however, and you'll find several excellent outfitters that can provide an inside look at some of the city's most fascinating aspects, from mezcal and street food to LGBTQ+ history and street art.

Bikes and Munchies. Offering a fun and active spin on Mexico City food tours, this company with a young and friendly team of guides offers culinary excursions by bike. Options include street-food pedals through Condesa and Santa María la Ribera as well as popular food-and-history rambles through Centro Histórico. ☎ 55/4164–8518 ⊕ www.bikesandmunchies.com ✉ From MP900.

Club Tengo Hambre. This well-established, culinary-focused tour company is best known for its street-food hops around either Centro Histórico or Condesa, which include five or six diverse stops in a little under four hours. Other notable options include an inside stroll through famous Mercado Merced, an after-dark taco tour, and a mezcal tasting at one of the city's most exclusive small-batch distilleries. ☎ ⊕ www.clubtengohambre.com/mexicocity ✉ From MP1300.

Eat Like a Local Mexico City. With a focus on responsible tourism, this women-owned tour company stands out for its commitment to working only with restaurants and vendors who provide their workers with good pay and a positive work environment. These thoughtful, in-depth experiences include a street-food-focused introduction to Mexican cooking, a flower market brunch and mezcal tasting in Condesa, and a "Badass Mexican Women" food adventure. ☎ ⊕ www.eatlikealocal.com.mx ✉ From MP1900.

Ecotura. Mexico City is surrounded by incredible natural scenery, including some of North America's tallest and most rugged mountains. Book a full-day hiking tour to Iztaccíhuatl Volcano, Nevado de Toluca, or—in summer—a trip to a firefly sanctuary. Personalized custom trips to a number of additional natural wonders are also available. Rates include round-trip transportation from Mexico City, trekking poles, boxed lunches, and park admissions. ☎ 55/5555–9382 ⊕ www.ecotura.mx ✉ From MP1200.

Intrepid Urban Adventures. This internationally acclaimed company offers pretty standard Teotihuacán excursions, but it stands out for some more unusual tours, such as a night of experiencing mariachi, licha libre, and old-school cantinas as well as a quest for street food in some of the city's best mercados. ✉ Mexico City ☎ 506/4113–9300 ⊕ www.urbanadventures.com/en/mexico-city ✉ From MP850.

Mexico a Pie Walking Tours. This highly reputable outfitter whose name translates literally to "Mexico on Foot" offers an extensive menu of guided strolls at a wide range of price points. Experiences include tours of specific attractions like Museo Nacional de Antropología and Templo Mayor as well as trips through the famous flower market Mercado Jamaica or attending a lucha libre match followed by a mezcal tasting. ☎ 55/6014–2996 ⊕ www.mexicoapie.com ✉ From MP340.

Mexunitours. This company's enthusiastic, local guides offer regularly scheduled tours with a rich variety of themes, including Jewish history, LGBTQ+ heritage (covering three different areas), food, shopping, the Zócalo, and Coyoacán. They also offer side-trip adventures that include a Cuernavaca history excursion and trips to Teotihuacán. ✉ Mexico City ☎ 55/1355–2122 ⊕ www.mexunitours.com ✉ From MP1500.

Sabores México Food Tours. Although several outfitters have a culinary excursion in their tour line-ups, Sabores specializes exclusively in the city's most intriguing culinary offerings. Options include eating your way through Centro Histórico and Roma's top eateries as well as a particularly stimulating beer, mezcal, and taqueria adventure. ✉ Mexico City ☎ 55/5350–9565 ⊕ www.saboresmexico-foodtours.com ✉ From MP1600.

Street Art Chilango. Married couple and highly knowledgeable art experts Abril and Chris give wonderfully enlightening tours of Roma's incredible trove of street art. Contact them through their website to find out about upcoming tour dates or to arrange a private art tour. ✉ Av. Álvaro Obregón 112, Roma Norte ☎ 55/1364–0818 ⊕ www.streetartchilango.com ✉ From MP500 Ⓜ Insurgentes.

On the Calendar

Some of the best times of the year to visit Mexico City revolve around cultural celebrations, some that have been taking place for 500 years and others that are still relatively new. In addition to these high-spirited gatherings, keep in mind that Mexico City also observes a number of public holidays, during which normal business hours may be affected; a few to watch for, beyond Christmas and New Year's, include Dia de la Constitucion on Feburary 5, Benito Juárez's birthday on March 21, Easter week, Labor Day on May 1, and Dia de la Revolución on November 20.

February

Zona MACO. Held over five days in early February and growing in size and prestige every year, this remarkable contemporary art festival draws both national and international talents to feature their work at dozens of noteworthy galleries and art museums around the city. Additionally, a massive art and design expo takes place at Centro Citibanamex convention center northwest of Polanco, featuring art, furniture, jewelry, antiques, photography, and more. ⊕ www.zonamaco.com

March

Spring Equinox at Teotihuacán. During this day on which indigenous tribes throughout the Americas once ushered in the new growing season and gave praise to the sun's energy, tens of thousands of visitors—many dressed in the traditional attire of all white with one red garment, such as a ribbon or scarf—descend on the 2,200-year-old complex of pyramids north of the city.

Vive Latino. This two-day pan-Latin outdoor music festival takes place at Foro Sol, near the airport, and draws an impressive roster of internationally renowned talents in a variety of genres. In more recent years, non-Latin bands like Bad Religion, the Cardigans, and Portugal the Man have also been included in the lineup. ⊕ www.vivelatino.com.mx

June

Marcha del Orgullo LGBTTTIQAP+. Typically held the last weekend in June, the nation's largest and wildest Pride celebration is centered around the cluster of queer bars in Zona Rosa and features a hugely popular parade that commences at El Ángel de la Independencia and proceeds along Avenida Paseo de la Reforma to the Zócalo. A growing number of bars, hotels, restaurants, and even cultural attractions now hold related parties and events throughout the preceding week. ⊕ www.marchalgbtcdmx.org

September

Día de la Independencia. Here in Mexico, the beer-sodden Cinco de Mayo celebration that's so popularly hailed in the United States is barely even acknowledged (it's a celebration of Mexico's 1862 victory over the French during the Battle of Puebla). But Mexico's true Independence Day, which marks the start of Catholic priest Miguel Hidalgo's brave uprising in 1810, is hugely important. Throngs gather at the Zócalo outside Palacio Nacional on September 15 to loudly commemorate with fireworks and great fanfare Hidalgo's "el grito de Dolores," or "cry of Dolores" (Dolores, now Dolores Hidalgo, being the small town in Guanajuato where he initiated the rebellion). A huge parade is held the following day.

October

Feria Nacional del Mole. Head to the small colonia of San Pedro Atocpan in late October to celebrate—and sample myriad versions of—this complex, rich, and diverse dish claimed by both Oaxaca and Puebla. Although within Mexico City limits, this traditional community lies about an hour's drive from the city center (it's best to take an Uber or rent a car to get here). ⊕ *www.ferianacionaldelmole.com.mx*

November

Corona Capital. Held over a weekend at the Autódromo Hermanos Rodríguez racetrack near the airport, this Coachella-inspired music festival features performances by around 60 top rock, alternative, and pop talents. Headliners in recent years have featured Arcade Fire, Pulp, Alanis Morissette, Miley Cyrus, and My Chemical Romance. ⊕ *www.coronacapital.com.mx*

Día de Muertos. The Day of the Dead has become increasingly popular throughout the city in recent years (and, just before it, Halloween for that matter). Mexicans joyfully honor their dead by creating lavish and both joyful and poignant *ofrendas*—altars with *papel picado*, photos, images of saints, favorite foods, *pan de muerto* (Day of the Dead bread), candles, incense, and *cempasúchiles* (marigolds). It's celebrated with particular color and fervor in the historic plazas in Coyoacán, Xochimilco, Bosque de Chapultepec, and the small, off-the-beaten-path colonia of San Andrés Mixquic; there's a Day of the Dead Parade on Paseo de la Reforma too. Many attendees dress in skeleton costumes and wear skull makeup, and countless museums and other businesses set up impressive ofrenda exhibits during the weeks before or after.

December

Día de la Virgen de Guadalupe. On this day in 1531, an indigenous man claimed to have encountered the ghost of the Virgin Mary. Ever since, millions of Mexicans have made the pilgrimage to the site, which is now encased within the Basilica of Our Lady of Guadalupe on the city's north side. A good many of those pilgrims trek here—many on foot—on December 11 and 12, and throughout the city and country, midnight mass is held at churches and even local makeshift altars.

Great Itineraries

In this vast city that's absolutely packed with fascinating museums and attractions and must-experience restaurants and bars, you can easily find enough to keep you engaged and delighted for a week or even a month. Conversely, as anyone who's ever attempted to "do" Mexico City during a weekend layover en route to or from one of the country's beach resorts, there's simply too much to experience here to get much of a sense of CDMX in just 48 hours. In five days, however, you can enjoy a pretty satisfying first visit, getting acquainted with the city's most celebrated attractions and charming neighborhoods, and even venturing out to farther-flung attractions like the pyramids of Teotihuacán and the canals of Xochimilco.

Mexico City in Five Days

DAY 1: CENTRO HISTÓRICO AND ALAMEDA CENTRAL

Begin your day in the heart of the city at the **Zócalo,** admiring the ornate exterior and interior of stately **Catedral Metropolitana,** visiting the carefully restored ruins of **Templo Mayor,** and seeing the murals at either **Palacio Nacional** or **Antiguo Colegio de San Ildefonso.**

Walk west along pedestrianized **Calle Francisco I. Madero,** with its colorful people-watching, to the edge of the neighborhood, where you can take an elevator to the 44th-floor observation deck of **Torre Latino** for a sweeping view of the city and surrounding mountains. Back on the ground, cross the street and take a photo of the stately **Palacio de Bellas Artes** before venturing inside to see the incredible mural displays. Afterward, go for a stroll amid the gallery

of surrounding **Alameda Central** park. You may have time for a quick look inside the underrated **Museo Franz Meyer,** but your top priority should be viewing the colorful and often whimsical exhibits of **Museo de Arte Popular.** For dinner, you'll find some great options in these parts, but you're also relatively close to a pair of up-and-coming neighborhoods with great food scenes: **San Rafael** and **Santa María la Ribera.**

DAY 2: BOSQUE DE CHAPULTEPEC, CONDESA, AND ROMA

Kick things off with breakfast at one of the many charming cafes on or near lovely **Avenida Amsterdam** in **Condesa.** Give yourself all morning and maybe even the early part of the afternoon to stroll around the tree-lined paths and lush gardens of the city's most beloved green space, **Bosque de Chapultepec.** You won't have time to explore all of this park's impressive attractions, but definitely set aside time for the incomparable **Museo Nacional de Antropología** and the gracious **Castillo de Chapultepec,** with its impressive city views. The impressive **Museo Tamayo Arte Contemporáneo** is an excellent choice if you have time for one more.

Now that you've burned off some calories walking through Bosque de Chapultepec, use the rest of the day to make your own food-driven walking tour of arguably the city's leading culinary neighborhood, **Roma.** Try making it a leisurely by having a small bite to eat and a drink at three or four restaurants, saving room for churros or ice cream at the end. You could easily add expand this delicious adventure by hopping over to adjacent **Juárez** or backtracking through Condesa.

DAY 3: COYOACÁN AND SAN ÁNGEL

Get up early and take an Uber to the historic **Coyoacán** district, on the southern side of the city. Have breakfast at one of the neighborhood's charming cafes before touring iconic **Museo Frida Kahlo** (you will have needed to have purchased tickets well in advance). Follow this with a quick tour around the corner of the excellent **Museo Casa de Leon Trotsky,** and then venture inside the colorful **Mercado de Coyoacán** for a quick lunch.

In the afternoon, walk amid the happy crowds of the neighborhood's two adjacent public squares, **Jardín Centenario** and **Plaza Hidalgo.** Then continue your strolling west along narrow, cobblestone **Avenida Francisco Sosa,** one of the prettiest streets in the city. Give yourself a full hour to get to the heart of **San Ángel,** with its bounty of crafts shops and galleries (if it's Saturday, do not miss the vendors at **Bazaar Sábado**). If you're a serious art fan, it's well worth ending the day with a quick tour of **Museo Casa Estudio Diego Rivera y Frida Kahlo.**

DAY 4: TEOTIHUACÁN AND POLANCO

Located 31 miles north of the city center, **Teotihuacán** is one of the Western Hemisphere's most extensive and exceptional archaeological sites. It's a large complex that takes at least four hours to explore, and depending on traffic, it can take up to an hour each way to get there. If you're a devotee of exploring ancient ruins, make Teotihuacán a top priority—even if you're visiting Mexico City for only two or three days. If this kind of attraction is of only mild interest, you might consider skipping it, especially if it's your first time in CDMX, in favor of exploring more of the museums and neighborhoods in the city center.

Either way, save the final couple of hours of your day for a walk through swanky **Polanco,** a neighborhood that's somewhat on your way back to the city if you're returning from Teotihuacán. Anyone with an interest in contemporary art and architecture should take at least a quick tour of the free and quite striking **Museo Soumaya Plaza Carso** as well as **Museo Jumex** across the street, which often presents outstanding art exhibits.

DAY 5: XOCHIMILCO, TLALPAN, AND UNAM

As with visiting Teotihuacán, booking a ride in a gondola-like *trajinera* to explore the centuries-old canals of **Xochimilco** is on plenty of Mexico City must-do lists. And also like Teotihuacán, it takes about an hour each way to get to Xochilmilco. Given the investment of time, that these boat rides are most enjoyable for larger groups of friends, and that some visitors find this experience a bit overrated, you might want to think carefully about whether you'd rather pass on this and instead spend your time eating at amazing restaurants or touring outstanding museums in the city center. On the other hand, Xochimilco is a UNESCO World Heritage Site, and it is relatively easy to combine a visit here with some other worthwhile areas in the south of the city.

If you do go to Xochmilco, arrive later in the afternoon—it's actually more fun to take a ride around sunset. Earlier in the day, you could start your explorations by checking out the wealth of attractions on the campus of **UNAM (Universidad Nacional Autónoma de México),** which is also a UNESCO World Heritage Site, and also have lunch and go for a stroll through the charming and historic neighborhood of **Tlalpan,** which is relatively close to Xochimilco.

Helpful Phrases in Spanish

BASICS

Hello	Hola	**oh**-lah
Yes/no	Sí/no	see/no
Please	Por favor	pore fah-**vore**
May I?	¿Puedo?	**Pweh**-doh
Thank you	Gracias	**Grah**-see-as
You're welcome	De nada	day **nah**-dah
I'm sorry	Lo siento	lo see-**en**-toh
Good morning!	¡Buenos días!	**bway**-nohs **dee**-ahs
Good evening!	¡Buenas tardes! (after 2pm)	**bway**-nahs-**tar**-dess
	¡Buenas noches! (after 8pm)	**bway**-nahs **no**-chess
Good-bye!	¡Adiós!/¡Hasta luego!	ah-dee-**ohss/ah**-stah **lwe**-go
Mr./Mrs.	Señor/Señora	sen-**yor**/sen-**yohr**-ah
Miss	Señorita	sen-yo-**ree**-tah
Pleased to meet you	Mucho gusto	**moo**-cho **goose**-toh
How are you?	¿Cómo estás?	**koh**-moh ehs-**tahs**

NUMBERS

one	un, uno	oon, **oo**-no
two	dos	dos
three	tres	tress
four	cuatro	**kwah**-tro
five	cinco	**sink**-oh
six	seis	saice
seven	siete	see-**et**-eh
eight	ocho	**o**-cho
nine	nueve	new-**eh**-vey
ten	diez	dee-**es**
eleven	once	**ohn**-seh
twelve	doce	**doh**-seh
thirteen	trece	**treh**-seh
fourteen	catorce	ka-**tohr**-seh
fifteen	quince	**keen**-seh
sixteen	dieciséis	dee-**es**-ee-**saice**
seventeen	diecisiete	dee-**es**-ee-see-**et**-eh
eighteen	dieciocho	dee-**es**-ee-**o**-cho
nineteen	diecinueve	dee-**es**-ee-new-**ev**-eh
twenty	veinte	**vain**-teh
twenty-one	veintiuno	**vain**-te-oo-noh
thirty	treinta	**train**-tah
forty	cuarenta	kwah-**ren**-tah
fifty	cincuenta	seen-**kwen**-tah
sixty	sesenta	sess-**en**-tah
seventy	setenta	set-**en**-tah
eighty	ochenta	oh-**chen**-tah
ninety	noventa	no-**ven**-tah
one hundred	cien	see-**en**
one thousand	mil	meel
one million	un millón	oon meel-**yohn**

COLORS

black	negro	**neh**-groh
blue	azul	ah-**sool**
brown	café	kah-**fehg**
green	verde	**ver**-deh
orange	naranja	na-**rahn**-hah
red	rojo	**roh**-hoh
white	blanco	**blahn**-koh
yellow	amarillo	ah-mah-**ree**-yoh

DAYS OF THE WEEK

Sunday	domingo	doe-**meen**-goh
Monday	lunes	**loo**-ness
Tuesday	martes	**mahr**-tess
Wednesday	miércoles	me-**air**-koh-less
Thursday	jueves	hoo-**ev**-ess
Friday	viernes	vee-**air**-ness
Saturday	sábado	**sah**-bah-doh

MONTHS

January	enero	eh-**neh**-roh
February	febrero	feh-**breh**-roh
March	marzo	**mahr**-soh
April	abril	ah-**breel**
May	mayo	**my**-oh
June	junio	**hoo**-nee-oh
July	julio	**hoo**-lee-yoh
August	agosto	ah-**ghost**-toh
September	septiembre	sep-tee-**em**-breh
October	octubre	oak-**too**-breh
November	noviembre	no-vee-**em**-breh
December	diciembre	dee-see-**em**-breh

USEFUL WORDS AND PHRASES

Do you speak English?	¿Habla Inglés?	ah-blah in-**glehs**
I don't speak Spanish.	No hablo español	no **ah**-bloh es-pahn-**yol**
I don't understand.	No entiendo	no en-tee-**en**-doh
I understand.	Entiendo	en-tee-**en**-doh
I don't know.	No sé	no **seh**
I'm American.	Soy americano (americana)	soy ah-meh-ree-**kah**-no (ah-meh-ree-**kah**-nah)
What's your name?	¿Cómo se llama ?	koh-mo seh **yah**-mah
My name is . . .	Me llamo . . .	may **yah**-moh
What time is it?	¿Qué hora es?	keh **o**-rah es
How?	¿Cómo?	**koh**-mo
When?	¿Cuándo?	**kwahn**-doh
Yesterday	Ayer	ah-**yehr**
Today	hoy	oy
Tomorrow	mañana	mahn-**yah**-nah
Tonight	Esta noche	es-tah **no**-cheh
What?	¿Qué?	keh

What is it?	¿Qué es esto?	keh es **es**-toh
Why?	¿Por qué?	pore **keh**
Who?	¿Quién?	kee-**yen**
Where is . . .	¿Dónde está . . .	**dohn**-deh es-**tah**
. . . the bus station?	la central de autobuses?	lah sehn-**trahl** deh ow-toh-**boo**-sehs
. . . the subway station?	estación de metro	la es-ta-see-**on** del **meh**-tro
. . . the bus stop?	la parada del autobus?	la pah-**rah**-dah del ow-toh-**boos**
. . . the terminal? (airport)	el aeropuerto	el air-oh-**pwar**-toh
. . . the post office?	la oficina de correos?	la oh-fee-**see**- nah deh koh-**rreh**-os
. . . the bank?	el banco?	el **bahn**-koh
. . . the hotel?	el hotel?	el oh-**tel**
. . . the museum?	el museo?	el moo-**seh**-oh
. . . the hospital?	el hospital?	el ohss-pee-**tal**
. . . the elevator?	el elevador?	ehl eh-leh-bah-**dohr**
Where are the restrooms?	el baño?	el **bahn**-yoh
Here/there	Aquí/allí	ah-**key**/ah-**yee**
Open/closed	Abierto/cerrado	ah-bee-**er**-toh/ ser-**ah**-doh
Left/right	Izquierda/derecha	iss-key-**eh**-dah/ dare-**eh**-chah
Is it near?	¿Está cerca?	es-**tah sehr**-kah
Is it far?	¿Está lejos?	es-**tah leh**-hoss
I'd like . . .	Quisiera . . .	kee-see-**ehr**-ah
. . . a room	un cuarto/una habitación	oon **kwahr**-toh/**oo**-nah ah-bee-tah-see-**on**
. . . the key	la llave	lah **yah**-veh
. . . a newspaper	un periódico	oon pehr-ee-**oh**- dee-koh
. . . a stamp	un sello de correo	oon **seh**-yo deh korr-**eh**-oh
I'd like to buy . . .	Quisiera comprar . . .	kee-see-**ehr**-ah kohm-**prahr**
. . . soap	jabón	hah-**bohn**
. . . suntan lotion	bronceador	brohn-seh-ah-**dohr**
. . . envelopes	sobres	**so**-brehs
. . . writing paper	papel	pah-**pel**
. . . a postcard	una postal	**oo**-nah pohs-**tahl**
. . . a ticket	un billete (travel)	oon bee-**yee**-teh
	una entrada (concert etc.)	**oo**na en-**trah**-dah
How much is it?	¿Cuánto cuesta?	**kwahn**-toh kwes-tah
It's expensive/ cheap	Es caro/barato	es **kah**-roh/ bah-**rah**-toh
A little/a lot	Un poquito/mucho	oon poh-**kee**-toh/ **moo**-choh
More/less	Más/menos	mahss/**men**-ohss
Enough/too (much)	Suficiente/	soo-fee-see-**en**-teh/
I am ill/sick	Estoy enfermo(a)	es-**toy** en-**fehr**-moh(mah)

Call a doctor	Llame a un medico	**ya**-meh ah oon **med**-ee-koh
Help!	Ayuda	ah-**yoo**-dah
Stop!	Pare	**pah**-reh

DINING OUT

I'd like to reserve a table . . .	Quisiera reservar una mesa . . .	kee-**syeh**-rah rreh-sehr-**bahr** oo-nah **meh**-sah . . .
. . . for two people.	para dos personas.	**pah**-rah dohs pehr-**soh**-nahs
. . . for this evening.	para esta noche.	**pah**-rah **ehs**-tah **noh**-cheh
. . . for 8 PM	para las ocho de la noche.	**pah**-rah lahs **oh**-choh deh lah **noh**-cheh
A bottle of . . .	Una botella de . . .	oo-nah bo-**teh**-yah deh
A cup of . . .	Una taza de . . .	oo-nah **tah**-sah deh
A glass of . . .	Un vaso (water, soda, etc.) de...	oon **vah**-so deh
	Una copa (wine, spirits, etc.) de...	oona **coh**-pah deh
Bill/check	La cuenta	lah **kwen**-tah
Bread	Pan	pahn
Breakfast	El desayuno	el deh-sah-**yoon**-oh
Butter	mantequilla	man-teh-**kee**-yah
Coffee	Café	kah-**feh**
Dinner	La cena	lah **seh**-nah
Fork	tenedor	ten-eh-**dor**
I don't eat meat	No como carne	noh koh-moh **kahr**-neh
I cannot eat . . .	No puedo comer . . .	noh **pweh**-doh koh-**mehr**
I'd like to order . . .	Quiero pedir . . .	**kee**-yehr-oh peh-**deer**
I'd like . . .	Me gustaría . . .	Meh goo-stah-**ee**-ah
I'm hungry/thirsty	Tengo hambre/sed	**Tehn**-goh **hahm**-breh/seth
Is service/the tip included?	¿Está incluida la propina?	es-**tah** in-cloo-**ee**-dah lah pro-**pee**-nah
Knife	cuchillo	koo-**chee**-yo
Lunch	La comida	lah koh-**mee**-dah
Menu	La carta, el menú	lah **cart**-ah, el meh-**noo**
Napkin	servilleta	sehr-vee-**yet**-ah
Pepper	pimienta	pee-mee-**en**-tah
Plate	plato	
Please give me . . .	Me da por favor . . .	meh dah pohr fah-**bohr**
Salt	sal	sahl
Spoon	cuchara	koo-**chah**-rah
Sugar	ázucar	ah-**su**-kar
Tea	té	teh
Water	agua	**ah**-gwah
Wine	vino	**vee**-noh

Contacts

Air

AIRPORTS Benito Juárez International Airport. ✉ *Av. Capitán Carlos León S/N, Peñón de los Baños, Greater Mexico City* ☎ *55/2482–2400* ⊕ *www. aicm.com.mx* Ⓜ *Terminal Aérea.* **Felipe Ángeles International Airport.** ✉ *Circuito Exterior Mexiquense, Km 33, Santa Lucia, Zumpango de Ocampo, Edomex, Greater Mexico City* ☎ *55/5798–9800* ⊕ *www.aifa.aero.* **Toluca International Airport.** ✉ *San Pedro Totoltepec, Toluca de Lerdo, Edomex* ☎ *722/279–2800* ⊕ *www. aeropuertodetoluca.com. mx.*

🚌 Bus

BUS Metrobús Mexico City. ☎ *55/5578–2140* ⊕ *www. metrobus.cdmx.gob.mx.*

🚲 Bicycle

BICYCLE EcoBici. ☎ *55/5005–2424, 800/326–2421* ⊕ *www. ecobici.cdmx.gob.mx.*

🇺🇸 Embassy

U.S. Embassy Mexico City ✉ *Av. Paseo de la Reforma 305, Cuauhtémoc* ☎ *55/5080–2000* ⊕ *mx. usembassy.gov/es* Ⓜ *Chapultepec.*

Ⓜ Public Transit

METRO Metro Mexico City. ⊕ *www.mexicocity.cdmx. gob.mx/e/getting-around/ using-the-metro.*

🚆 Train

TRAIN Xochimilco Light Rail. ☎ *55/5539–2800* ⊕ *www.ste.cdmx.gob.mx/ tren-ligero.*

📍 Visitor Information

VISITOR INFORMATION Mexico City Tourism Office. ✉ *Av. Nuevo León 56, La Condesa* ☎ *55/5286–7097* ⊕ *www.mexicocity.cdmx. gob.mx* Ⓜ *Chilpancingo.*

Chapter 3

CENTRO HISTÓRICO

3

Updated by
Roshida Dowe

◉ Sights	🍽 Restaurants	🛏 Hotels	💼 Shopping	🍸 Nightlife
★★★★★	★★★★★	★★★★☆	★★☆☆☆	★★★☆☆

NEIGHBORHOOD SNAPSHOT

TOP EXPERIENCES

■ **The Zócalo.** Plaza de la Constitución, also called the Zócalo, is the largest square in Latin America and the central place to start your adventure in Centro Histórico.

■ **Templo Mayor.** All lovers of archaeology or history should check out Templo Mayor, a popular museum on the site of Mexica ruins.

■ **Catedral Metropolitana.** Built over a span of 250 years, Catedral Metropolitana showcases multiple architectural styles and is both a UNESCO World Heritage Site and the seat of the Mexican Catholic Archdiocese.

■ **Palacio Nacional.** This stunning building houses the office of the President of Mexico, a museum, and one of the largest Diego Rivera murals in the world.

GETTING HERE

As its name suggests, Centro Histórico is, historically, the city's geographic heart. Well-served by public transit, Centro is best reached by Metro Lines 1 (Isabel la Católica or Pino Suárez stops), Line 2 (Zócalo stop), or Line 8 (San Juan de Letrán stop). If coming or going early in the morning or late at night, ride-sharing is a good option, but the heavily congested streets can make entering in a private vehicle during the day complicated. Parking is hard to find here so don't plan to drive yourself into Centro.

PLANNING YOUR TIME

Centro Histórico is a must-see in the city, but that means you'll find lots of crowds here. The Zócalo, also known as the Plaza de Constitucion, is the central gathering point for the city. It hosts concerts, fairs, parades, and, most importantly, government events and protests. An online search for events in the area will tell you what events might be happening here on any given day; if it's a major one and your goal is to avoid crowds as much as possible, you might want to find another day to visit.

VIEWFINDER

■ When first designed, Torre Latinoamericana was the tallest skyscraper in Latin America. Standing at 44 floors, it no longer holds that title, but it still has a lot to offer. The *mirador* on the top floor provides expansive views of the city, beautiful by both day or night.

OFF THE BEATEN PATH

■ The Mercado Sonora, better known as the witchcraft market, lies just southeast of Centro and is the place where some in the city go for a cleansing with a witch doctor, to buy candles dedicated to Catholic saints, or to stock up on stacks of earthenware plates and cups for a just few cents each. Crowded and chaotic, Mercado Sonora is best visited on a tour with a local guide.

Centro Histórico is not only the heart of Mexico City, but it is where the modern history of the Americas began. Since its time as the center of the great Mexica city of Tenochtitlan, founded in 1325 on an island in the shallows of Lake Texcoco, the modern-day historic center has been the axis around which Mexico revolves.

This is where the Mexica kings performed their sacred rites (the pediments of their great stone pyramid are still visible just below street level at the Museum of the Templo Mayor), where the Spanish invaders established their colonial capital, and where modern Mexico has consummated its many revolutions. Centered on a grand ceremonial square, called the Zócalo, the neighborhood is both a living museum crowded with historic monuments, and also the most democratic space in a highly stratified city of more than 20 million people. On any given day, people from across the city and country flock here to shop for toys, school uniforms, or fabrics by the yard, to protest under the Zócalo's arcades, or simply to marvel at the nation's magnificent heritage as they wander down crowded pedestrian streets like Madero and Regina. Dotted with street stalls, cantinas, and precarious-looking churches—their foundations tilted from centuries of earthquakes—Centro is still the chaotic, graceful soul of the Western Hemisphere's greatest metropolis.

Centro Histórico North

Sights

Antiguo Colegio de San Ildefonso
SPECIALTY MUSEUM | Located in a colonial building with lovely patios, this former college started out in the 18th century as a Jesuit school for the sons of wealthy Mexicans. Frida Kahlo also famously studied here as an adolescent. It's now a splendid museum that showcases outstanding regional exhibitions, but the best reason to visit is the interior murals by Diego Rivera, José Clemente Orozco, and Fernando Leal. ⊠ *Calle Justo Sierra 16, Centro Histórico* ☎ *55/3602–0000* ⊕ *www.sanildefonso.org.mx* ✉ *MP50; free Sun.* ☾ *Closed Mon.* Ⓜ *Zócalo.*

Arena Coliseo
SPORTS VENUE | **FAMILY** | The smaller and less polished of the city's two lucha libre arenas, the Coliseo is (as its name suggests) round and (belying its grandiose namesake) has seen better days. But the space allows proximity to the crowd, which means the fighters ramp up spectators to compensate for the lack of bright lights and spectacle in their other

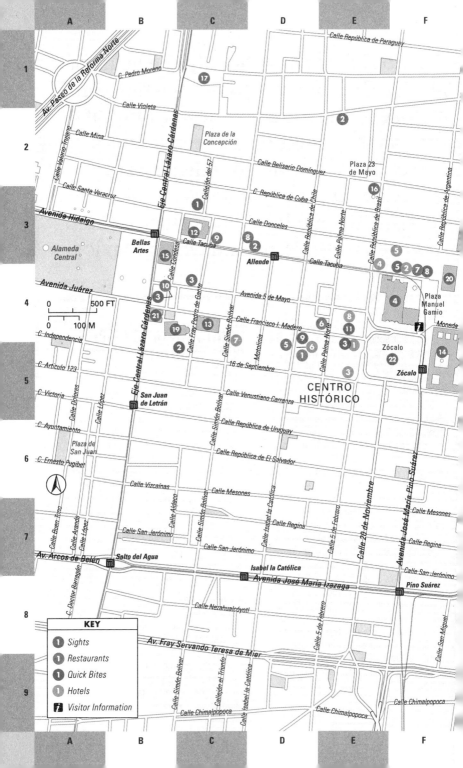

Centro Histórico North

Sights ▼

1 Antiguo Colegio de San Ildefonso **G3**
2 Arena Coliseo **E2**
3 Casa de los Azulejos ... **B4**
4 Catedral Metropolitana **F4**
5 Centro Cultural de España **F4**
6 Ex-Teresa Arte Actual **G4**
7 Mercado Abelardo L. Rodriguez **H3**
8 Museo Archivo de la Fotografía **F4**
9 Museo del Estanquillo **D4**
10 Museo José Luis Cuevas **G4**
11 Museo Mexicano del Diseño **E4**
12 Museo Nacional De Arte (MUNAL) **C3**
13 Museo Palacio Cultural Banamex **C4**
14 Palacio Nacional **F5**
15 Palacio Postal (Dirección General de Correos) **B3**
16 Plaza de Santo Domingo **E3**
17 Plaza Garibaldi **C1**
18 Sinagoga Justo Sierra **H4**
19 Templo de San Francisco **B4**
20 Templo Mayor **F4**
21 Torre Latinoamericana **B4**
22 Zócalo **F5**

Restaurants ▼

1 Azul Histórico **D5**
2 Café de Tacuba **D3**
3 Café La Pagoda **C4**
4 Casa Nela **H5**
5 Casino Español de Mexico **D5**
6 El Cardenal **E4**
7 La Casa de las Sirenas **F4**
8 Limosneros **C3**
9 Los Girasoles **C3**
10 Sanborns **B4**

Quick Bites ▼

1 El Callejón Café **C3**
2 Pastelería Ideal **C5**
3 Tacos de Canasta Los Especiales **E5**

Hotels ▼

1 Best Western Majestic Hotel **E5**
2 Círculo Mexicano **F4**
3 Gran Hotel Ciudad de México **E5**
4 Hostel Mundo Joven Catedral **E4**
5 Hotel Catedral **F3**
6 Hotel Downtown México **D5**
7 Hotel Histórico Central **C4**
8 Zócalo Central **E4**

3

Centro Histórico

CENTRO HISTÓRICO NORTH

home, Arena México. The fights start on Saturday at 7:30 pm; tickets are available at the box office or through Ticketmaster. ✉ *República de Perú 77, Centro Histórico* ☎ *55/5588–0266* ⊕ *www.cmll.com* 💷 *MP60* ⊘ *Closed Sun.–Fri.* Ⓜ *Garibaldi.*

Casa de los Azulejos (*House of Tiles*)
HISTORIC HOME | Originally built as a home in the 16th century, the "House of Tiles" only acquired the celebrated facade that lends it its name a century later when the material was likely introduced from the workshop of the Dominican friars in the nearby city of Puebla. The dazzling designs, along with the facade's iron balconies and bronze handrails, the latter imported from China, make it one of the most singular baroque structures in the city. The interior is also worth seeing for its Moorish patio, monumental stair-case, and mural by Orozco. The building is currently occupied by Sanborns, a chain store and restaurant; if you have plenty of time (service is slow), this is a good place to stop for a meal—espe-cially breakfast, when older men gather to read their newspapers around the snaking bar. There's also a store with a pharmacy, bakery, candy counter, and an ATM. ✉ *Calle Madero 4, at Callejón de la Condesa, Centro Histórico* ⊕ *www.san-borns.com.mx* Ⓜ *Bellas Artes, Allende.*

★ **Catedral Metropolitana**
CHURCH | The majestic cathedral that forms the northern side of the Zócalo is nothing less than the heart of Mexico City, its most famous building, and the backdrop to many of the country's most important historical events. Construction on the largest and one of the oldest Latin American cathedrals began in the late 16th century and continued intermittently throughout the next 300 years. The result is a medley of baroque and neoclassical touches. There are 5 altars and 14 chap-els, mostly in the ornate churrigueresque style, named for Spanish architect José Benito Churriguera (1665–1725). Like most Mexican churches, the cathedral

is all but overwhelmed by innumerable paintings, altarpieces, and statues—in graphic color—of Christ and the saints. Over the centuries, this cathedral began to sink into the spongy subsoil, but a major engineering project to stabilize it was declared successful in 2000. The older-looking church attached to the cathedral is the 18th-century Sagrario chapel. ✉ *Zócalo, Centro Histórico* ☎ *55/4165–4013* ⊕ *www.catedralmetro-politana.mx* 💷 *Free* Ⓜ *Zócalo.*

Centro Cultural de España
ART MUSEUM | The Cultural Center of Spain is an art space, restaurant, and bar in the heart of the neighborhood, just steps away from the Cathedral and the Templo Mayor and with beautiful views of both from its open-air rooftop. It was built in an area that Hernán Cortés himself assigned to his butler, Diego de Soto, though the land changed hands many times and the current building was constructed in the 18th century, well after the years of Cortés. Temporary exhibits housed in the seven exhibition rooms often highlight young artists and showcase current artistic trends. While the exhibitions are worth a look, there are also conferences and workshops held on a nearly daily basis for anyone inter-ested in art and culture. The rooftop bar, which hosts frequent live music events, is one of the neighborhood's better-kept secrets, with a balcony opening directly onto the Cathedral's magnificent dome and buttresses: easily one of the area's best views. Check out the center's web-site for listings. ✉ *Guatemala 18, Centro Histórico* ☎ *55/5521–1925* ⊕ *ccemx.org* 💷 *Free* ⊘ *Closed Mon.* Ⓜ *Zócalo.*

Ex-Teresa Arte Actual
ART MUSEUM | One of the more disori-enting buildings in Centro, the Ex-Te-resa was first established in 1616 as a Carmelite convent and now runs as a contemporary art space. The convent was shut down after 250 years, but the space reopened in its current iteration

in 1993. The two primary chapels lean precariously against one another, unsettled by centuries of seismic activity and resulting in a gravity-warping physical experience when you step inside. The space transforms dramatically with each new installation, but its vertigo-inducing power is constant. ⊠ *Licenciado Verdad 8, Centro Histórico* ✛ *Off Calle Moneda* ☎ *55/4122–8020* ⊕ *www.exteresa.bellasartes.gob.mx* ▨ *Free* ⊘ *Closed Mon.* Ⓜ *Zócalo.*

Mercado Abelardo L. Rodriguez

MARKET | Built in 1934 as a cultural complex and prototype for modern marketplaces around Mexico, the Mercado Abelardo L. Rodriguez is largely an ordinary neighborhood mercado today, with butchers, vegetable vendors, and juice stalls. The market's real claim to fame is its murals, painted by disciples of the greats in the arched entrances. ⊠ *Callejón Girón, Centro Histórico* ⊕ *www.facebook.com/MercadoAbelardoLRodriguez* ▨ *Free* Ⓜ *Zócalo.*

Museo Archivo de la Fotografía (*Museum of the Photography Archive*)

ART MUSEUM | The building that now houses the Museum of the Photography Archive is one of the oldest on the Zócalo, first built in the late 16th century as part of the property of the Nava Chávez family, founded by the canon priest Pedro Nava Chávez and passed down through his niece, Catalina de Nava. Decorated in a neo-Moorish style popular in Mexico's colonial period, the house became famous in 2006 when archaeologists uncovered a monolithic statue of the goddess Tlaltecuhtli under its floors. That same year, the building opened its doors for regular photography exhibitions, often focused on the work of Mexico's finest photojournalists. ⊠ *República de Guatemala 34, Centro Histórico* ☎ *55/2616–7057* ⊕ *www.cultura.cdmx.gob.mx/recintos/maf* ▨ *Free* ⊘ *Closed Mon.* Ⓜ *Zócalo.*

Museo del Estanquillo

SPECIALTY MUSEUM | First built as a jewelry store in 1892, the belle epoque–style Esmeralda Building has had various uses over the years, including as a government office, a bank, a disco called La Opulencia, and, since 2006, as the Museo de Estanquillo, housing the eclectic collection of the great 20th-century journalist, Carlos Monsiváis. The museum takes its name from the term used through the 19th and early 20th centuries for small neighborhood convenience shops, which stocked virtually everything a person could need. It's an appropriate name for a museum dedicated to rotating exhibitions drawn from a total collection of 20,000 individual pieces. Shows might range from cartoons, stamps, and etchings to photos, lithographs, drawings, and paintings from some of the greatest names in Mexican art; the collection is as diverse and democratic as Monsiváis was in his writing. The rooftop café and bookstore offer a stunning view over the domes of San Felipe Neri la Profesa and the hubbub of Madero below. ⊠ *Isabel la Católica 26, at Av. Madero, Centro Histórico* ☎ *55/5521–3052* ⊕ *museodelestanquillo.cdmx.gob.mx* ▨ *Free* ⊘ *Closed Tues., Fri., and Sat.* Ⓜ *Zócalo or Allende.*

Museo José Luis Cuevas

ART MUSEUM | Found within the refurbished Santa Inés convent, this inviting museum displays international modern art as well as work by Mexico's *enfant terrible*, José Luis Cuevas, one of the country's best-known modern artists (1934–2017). The highlight is the sensational *La Giganta* (*The Giantess*), Cuevas's eight-ton bronze sculpture in the central patio. It represents male-female duality and pays homage to Charles Baudelaire's poem of the same name. Up-and-coming Latin American artists appear in temporary exhibitions throughout the year. ⊠ *Academia 13, at Calle Moneda, Centro Histórico* ☎ *55/5522–0156* ⊕ *www.museojoseluiscuevas.com.mx* ▨ *MP30; free Sun.* ⊘ *Closed Mon.* Ⓜ *Zócalo.*

Museo Mexicano del Diseño

ART MUSEUM | This museum with a big gift shop (or shop with a small museum) and café features small expositions of contemporary Mexican design. The goals of the museum are to provide a space for design, to assist local designers, and to offer a location in which designers can make money from their craft. Exhibitions, open only through guided tours in Spanish every half hour from 10 am to 8 pm, are shown in a back room made of brick, where you can see the old archways from Cortés's patio, which was built, in part, on top of Moctezuma's pyramid. The shop is open to the public. ☒ *Madero 74, Centro Histórico* ☎ *55/5510–8609* ⊕ *www.mumedi.mx* ☒ *MP60* Ⓜ *Zócalo.*

Museo Nacional de Arte (MUNAL) (*National Art Museum*)

ART MUSEUM | FAMILY | The collections of the National Art Museum occupy one of Centro's most impressive neoclassical buildings, designed by Italian architect Silvio Contri in the early 20th century. The works in the permanent collection, organized in galleries around a gracious open patio and grand central staircase, span nearly every school of Mexican art, with a concentration on work produced between 1810 and 1950. José María Velasco's *Vista del Valle de México desde el Cerro de Santa Isabel* (*View of the Valley of Mexico from the Hill of Santa Isabel*) is on display; the collection also includes artists such as Diego Rivera and Ramón Cano Manilla. Keep an eye out for temporary exhibitions of works by Mexican and international masters. ☒ *Calle Tacuba 8, Centro Histórico* ☎ *55/8647–5430* ⊕ *www.munal.mx* ☒ *MP85* ⊘ *Closed Mon.* Ⓜ *Bellas Artes or Allende.*

Museo Palacio Cultural Banamex

(*Palacio de Iturbide*)

CASTLE/PALACE | Built between 1779 and 1785, this baroque palace—note the imposing door and its carved-stone trimmings—was originally a residence for the Counts of Moncada and the Marquises of Jaral de Berrio, a title created only five years earlier. The palace takes its name from Agustín de Iturbide, who stayed here for a short time in 1822. One of the military heroes of the independence movement, the misguided Iturbide proclaimed himself emperor of Mexico once the country finally achieved freedom from Spain. He was staying in the palace when he became emperor, a position he held for less than a year before being driven into exile. In the two centuries since, the house has been a school, a café, and a hotel. In 1964, the Palacio Iturbide became the property of Banamex, which oversaw its restoration and eventually reopened the space in 2004 as a cultural center, showing major exhibitions in the grand central atrium. ☒ *Calle Madero 17, Centro Histórico* ☎ *55/1226–0124* ⊕ *www.fomentoculturalbanamex.org* ☒ *Free* Ⓜ *Bellas Artes, Zócalo.*

★ **Palacio Nacional**

GOVERNMENT BUILDING | The center of government in Mexico City since the time of the Mexica (aka Aztecs), Palacio Nacional's long, volcanic stone facade is both a symbol of political power and a staging ground for acts of resistance. Construction of the national palace was initiated by Cortés on the site of Moctezuma II's royal residence and remodeled by the viceroys. Its current form dates from 1693, although its third floor was added in 1926. If it's open to the public, the entire building is worth a look, even just for the novel experience of wandering freely through an influential nation's primary seat of government, but most visitors come for Diego Rivera's sweeping murals on the second floor of the main courtyard. For more than 20 years, starting in 1929, Rivera and his assistants mounted scaffolds day and night, perfecting techniques adapted from Renaissance Italy's frescoes. The result is nearly 1,200 square feet of vividly painted wall space, titled *Épica del Pueblo Mexicano en su Lucha por la Libertad y*

Mexico City's most famous cathedral, Catedral Metropolitana, is stunning both inside and out.

la Independencia (*Epic of the Mexican People in Their Struggle for Freedom and Independence*). The paintings represent two millennia of Mexican history, filtered through Rivera's imagination; only a few vignettes acknowledge the more violent elements of some pre-Hispanic societies. As you walk around, you'll pass images of the savagery of the conquest and the hypocrisy of the Spanish priests, the noble independence movement, and the bloody revolution. Marx appears amid scenes of class struggle, toiling workers, industrialization (which Rivera idealized), bourgeois decadence, and nuclear holocaust. These are among Rivera's finest works—as well as the most accessible and probably the most visited. The palace also houses a minor museum that focuses on 19th-century president Benito Juárez and the Mexican Congress. Other exhibition spaces house rotating, and sometimes quite extraordinary, exhibitions, typically advertised on a large billboard in the Zócalo.

The liberty bell rung by Padre Hidalgo to proclaim independence in 1810 hangs high on the central facade. It chimes every eve of September 16, while from the balcony the president repeats "*El Grito,*" the historic shout of independence, to throngs of citizens below.

The Palacio Nacional has historically been open to visitors, but the administration of Andrés Manuel López Obrado changed this and private tours are currently not allowed. This is likely to change with the next presidential election in June 2024. ⊠ *East side of the Zócalo, Centro Histórico* ⊕ *Entrance through side door on Moneda* ⊕ *www.gob.mx/palacionacional/articulos/patrimonio-edificado* Ⓜ *Zócalo.*

★ Palacio Postal
(Dirección General de Correos)
NOTABLE BUILDING | Mexico City's main post office building, designed by Italian architect Adamo Boari and Mexican engineer Gonzalo Garita, is a fine example of Renaissance Revival architecture. Constructed of cream-color sandstone

Back in the Day

At the northeastern corner of Centro Histórico, past the notoriously dodgy market district of Tepito, the Archivo General de la Nación occupies the fortresslike structure once known as Lecumberri, Mexico City's most infamous penitentiary. Opened in 1900 by the dictator Porfirio Díaz, Lecumberri is a classic panopticon (a type of institutional building designed around a system of control) and the prison helped solidify Díaz's reputation as a modernizer abroad (elsewhere in the country, he maintained antiquated prison camps). By the time it was shut down in 1976, Lecumberri had become a byword for misery, torture, and government-ordained disappearances.

from Teayo, Puebla, and Carrara, Italy, it epitomizes the grand Eurocentric architecture common in Mexico during the Porfiriato—the long dictatorship of Porfirio Díaz (1876–1911). For many, it's one of Mexico's most splendid buildings. Tours in Spanish are available and can be booked on their website. ⊠ *Calle Tacuba 1, at Eje Central Lázaro Cárdenas, Centro Histórico* ☎ *55/5510–2999 museum, 55/4130–4000* ⊕ *www.gob.mx/correos-demexico* 🎫 *Free* Ⓜ *Bellas Artes.*

Plaza Garibaldi

PLAZA/SQUARE | Known as the birthplace of mariachi music in Mexico City, you'll likely see multiple mariachi bands performing in this plaza. The area around it isn't always safe after dark, so make your visit there during the daytime, and don't stray too far from the main roads. ⊠ *Eje Central Lázaro Cárdenas 43, Centro Histórico* Ⓜ *Garibaldi/Lagunilla.*

★ Plaza de Santo Domingo

PLAZA/SQUARE | Of all the plazas and public spaces in Mexico City, there is none more beautiful or harmonious than the Plaza Santo Domingo. The Mexica emperor Cuauhtémoc built a palace here, where heretics were later burned at the stake during the Spanish Inquisition. The plaza was the intellectual hub of the city during the colonial era and it remains one of the only places in the city to have maintained nearly all of its original

18th-century buildings. Today Santo Domingo's most iconic feature is the Portal de los Evangelistas, a sagging arcade casting shade over scribes working at typewriters and stands printing business cards and other stationery on old-fashioned ink presses. On the northern side of the plaza, the baroque Santo Domingo Church is all that remains of the first Dominican convent in New Spain. The convent building was demolished in 1861 under the Reform laws that forced clerics to turn over all religious buildings not used for worship to the government. ⊠ *Bounded by República de Cuba, República de Brasil, República de Venezuela, and Palma, Centro Histórico* ⊕ *mexicocity.cdmx.gob.mx/venues/plaza-de-santo-domingo* Ⓜ *Zócalo.*

Sinagoga Justo Sierra

SYNAGOGUE | FAMILY | This was the first center for the Ashkenazi Jewish community that arrived in Mexico after fleeing eastern Europe in the first decades of the 20th century; the synagogue fell out of regular use just two decades after its founding in 1941, when the community starting moving out to more prosperous districts of the city. Restored in 2010, it's now once again a community center, open daily to the general public and hosting frequent cultural activities, from seminars to musical performances to lending studio space to local artists. Guided tours of the synagogue are available on

The Palacio Nacional is the official residence of Mexico's president.

the third Sunday of each month at 11:30 am (MP100) and tours of the surrounding neighborhood, where many Jewish migrants once lived, are offered the second Sunday of each month at 10 am (MP200). For guided tours outside those dates contact the synagogue directly by email (✉ sinagogajustosierra@gmail. com). ✉ Justo Sierra 71, Centro Histórico ☎ 55/5522–4828 ⊕ www.sinagoga-justosierra.com 🖾 Free; tours MP100 ⊘ Closed Sat. Ⓜ Zócalo.

Templo de San Francisco

CHURCH | On the site of Mexico's first convent (1524), this church has served as a barracks, a hotel, a circus, a theater, and a Methodist temple. The main sanctuary's elaborate baroque facade is set past an iron gate and down a pretty flight of steps from street level. Inside, the Templo is one of the best places in Centro to get a sense of the seismic shifts that continue to unsettle Mexico City. Stand at the back of the nave and note the chandeliers, which appear frozen mid-swing: an effect of gravity combined with the incline of the aisle, which has sunken unevenly over the centuries. The church next door, in a French neo-Gothic style, was added later. ✉ Madero 7, Centro Histórico ☎ 55/5521–7331 ⊕ mexicocity. cdmx.gob.mx/venues/iglesia-de-san-fran-cisco-de-asis 🖾 Free Ⓜ Bellas Artes or Allende.

★ Templo Mayor

HISTORY MUSEUM | The ruins of the sacred shrine of the Mexica (also commonly known as the Aztec) empire, built here in the 14th century, were unearthed accidentally in 1978 by telephone repairmen and the vast, 3-acre archaeological site has since become the old city's most compelling museum. At this temple, whose two twin shrines were dedicated to the sun god Huitzilopochtli and the rain god Tláloc, captives from the empire's near-constant wars of conquest were sacrificed in rituals commemorated in carvings of skulls visible deep in the temple compound. The adjacent Museo del Templo Mayor contains thousands of pieces unearthed from the site and

In the middle of Mexico City, you'll find the 3-acre archaeological site known as Templo Mayor.

others across central Mexico, including ceramic warriors, stone carvings and knives, skulls of sacrificial victims, models and scale reproductions, and a room on the Spaniards' destruction of Tenochtitlán. The centerpiece is an 8-ton disk unearthed at the Templo Mayor depicting the dismembered moon goddess Coyolxauhqui. The proximity between Templo Mayor and Catedral Metropolitana is no coincidence. When the Spanish conquistadors defeated the Mexica empire, they intentionally destroyed their places of worship, and used the stones from the temples to build churches. ⊠ *Seminario 8, Centro Histórico* ☎ *55/4040–5600* ⊕ *www.templomayor.inah.gob.mx* ✉ *MP90* ⊙ *Closed Mon.* Ⓜ *Zócalo.*

★ Torre Latinoamericana

NOTABLE BUILDING | FAMILY | At the time of its completion in 1956, after eight long years of construction, the 44-story Torre Latina was Latin America's tallest building, a marvel of local engineering that proclaimed Mexico City as the most important metropolis in the Spanish-speaking world. Some of the best views of the city can be seen from the museums, restaurants, and cafés on floors 37 to 41 while the observation deck is on floor 44. Stop off at floor 38 to visit a museum that focuses on the history of the tower and the city or on the 40th floor for a drink at Bar Nivel 40, which gives you basically the same view for just the cost of a drink. In addition, the Bicentennial Museum on the 36th floor has documents from the early independence era. ⊠ *Eje Central Lázaro Cárdenas 2, at Calle Madero, Centro Histórico* ⊕ *www.torrelatinoamericana. com.mx* ✉ *MP220* Ⓜ *Bellas Artes.*

★ Zócalo

PLAZA/SQUARE | One of the world's largest urban squares, Mexico City's Zócalo is the clearest expression of the city's immense importance as the capital of New Spain: a showpiece of colonial power and wealth and, after independence, a symbol for every element of Mexico's complex political identity.

Zócalo literally means "pedestal" or "base"; in the mid-19th century, an independence monument was planned for the square, but only the base was built. The term stuck, however, and now the word "zócalo" is applied to the main plazas in many Mexican cities. Mexico City's Zócalo (because it's the original, it's always capitalized) is used for government rallies, protests, sit-ins, and festive events. It's the focal point for Independence Day celebrations on the eve of September 16 and is a maze of lights, tinsel, and traders during the Christmas season. Flag-raising and-lowering ceremonies take place here in the early morning and late afternoon.

Formally called the Plaza de la Constitución, the enormous paved square, the largest in the Western Hemisphere, occupies the site of the ceremonial center of Tenochtitlán, the capital of the Mexica empire, which once comprised 78 buildings. From the early 18th century until the mid-1900s, the plaza housed a market known as El Parián, specializing in luxury goods imported from Asia on the Manila Galleons, Spanish trading ships that crossed the Pacific from the Philippines to Acapulco. And while the Zócalo has seen the rise and fall of governments and movements for seven centuries, many of the rust-red facades that ring the plaza today—save for the first two floors of the emblematic Palacio Nacional and the Cathedral—were only added in the early 20th century, built in the neo-colonial style in fashion following the Revolution.

The Zócalo is the heart of Centro Histórico, and many of the neighborhood's sights are on the plaza's borders or just a few short blocks away. Even as the Mexican economy has gradually begun to centralize in recent years, the Zócalo remains the indisputable center of the nation. ⊠ *Bounded 16 de Septiembre, Av. 5 de Mayo, Pino Suárez, and Monte de Piedad, Centro Histórico* Ⓜ *Zócalo*.

 Restaurants

★ Azul Histórico

$$$$ | MEXICAN | An oasis in the middle of the chaos of Centro Histórico, you'll find excellent service and elegant versions of traditional Mexican dishes here. A variety of dishes from around the country are expertly prepared under the watchful eye of renowned chef Ricardo Muñoz Zurita. **Known for:** freshly made tortillas; upscale atmosphere; multiple varieties of mole. Ⓢ *Average main: MP500* ⊠ *Isabel la Católica 30, Centro Histórico* ☎ *55/5510–1316* ⊕ *www.azul.rest* Ⓜ *Zócalo, Allende.*

★ Café de Tacuba

$$$ | MEXICAN | An essential, if touristy, breakfast, lunch, dinner, or snack stop downtown, this Mexican classic opened in 1912 in a section of an old convent. At the entrance to the main dining room are huge 18th-century oil paintings depicting the invention of mole poblano, a complex sauce featuring a variety of chiles and chocolate that was created by the nuns in the Santa Rosa Convent in Puebla. **Known for:** live music by students dressed in medieval attire; classic tamales; old-school atmosphere. Ⓢ *Average main: MP400* ⊠ *Calle Tacuba 28, at Allende, Centro Histórico* ☎ *55/5521–2048* ⊕ *www.cafedetacuba.com.mx* Ⓜ *Allende.*

Café La Pagoda

$ | MEXICAN | FAMILY | Think of this as Mexico City's equivalent of your favorite all-day diner: open from 7 am to 4 am every day of the year, La Pagoda is the best of several (admittedly very similar) old school cafés lined up along the northern side of Avenida 5 de Mayo. The food is far from extraordinary, but the atmosphere is beyond charming, with its long bar and bright lights, service that borders on the maternal (expect to be called *mi amor* or *mi vida* at least once), solid breakfast dishes served all day, and a perfect café con leche to snap you out of a late-night or early-morning stupor. **Known for:** chilaquiles con cecina; all-day dining; late-night pozole, a traditional Mexican stew. $ *Average main: MP130* ⊠ *Av. 5 de Mayo 10, Centro Histórico* ☎ *No phone* ⊕ *www.cafelapagoda.com. mx* Ⓜ *Bellas Artes, Allende.*

★ Casa Nela

$ | MEXICAN | For more than 60 years, the shop Aquí es Oaxaca has anchored this block of Calle Santísima that serves as Centro's unofficial Little Oaxaca, selling tamales as well as the mole pastes and cured meats known in the region. When visitors started asking for full meals, Casa Nela was born, and so up a distressingly narrow flight of spiral stairs you'll find Oaxacan classics served in surprisingly peaceful surroundings. **Known for:** traditional mole negro; tlayudas, a typical Oaxcan dish; nice view over Calle Santísima. $ *Average main: MP100* ⊠ *Soledad 42, Centro Histórico* ⊹ *Entrance on Santísima* ☎ *55/5542–3754* ⊕ *casanela.com. mx* ⊟ *No credit cards* ⊗ *Closed Sun.* Ⓜ *Zócalo.*

Casino Español de Mexico

$$ | SPANISH | FAMILY | Housed on the mezzanine floor of the magnificent Casino Español, this restaurant is as classic as it gets: white tablecloths, coffered ceilings, formal service, and food straight out of the Iberian Peninsula, with a particular focus on dishes from the northern regions of Galicia, Asturias, and País Basco. The Casino was founded in 1863 as a club for Spanish immigrants to independent Mexico and relocated to its current, opulent home in 1905. **Known for:** amazing architecture; great carajillos (Mexico's beloved after-lunch coffee cocktail); early closing at 6 pm. $ *Average main: MP200* ⊠ *Isabel la Católica 29, Centro Histórico* ☎ *55/5521–8894* ⊕ *www.cassatt.mx* ⊗ *No dinner* Ⓜ *Allende, Zócalo, Isabel la Católica.*

El Cardenal

$$ | MEXICAN | FAMILY | An institution known for its classic Mexican cooking, today El Cardenal has locations all over the city, but the branch to try is on Calle Palma, in a three-story building in the florid style of the late 19th century. Inside, the atmosphere (think beige walls and white tablecloths) and food are old school; the best time to come is breakfast, when trays of pan dulces make for a pleasant prelude to eggs or chilaquiles. **Known for:** perfect Mexican breakfast; Oaxacan-style moles; family favorite for special-occasion dining. $ *Average main: MP250* ⊠ *Calle Palma 23, Centro Histórico* ☎ *55/5521–8815* ⊕ *www. restauranteelcardenal.com* ⊗ *No dinner* Ⓜ *Allende, Zócalo.*

La Casa de las Sirenas

$$$ | MEXICAN | The oldest portions of this 16th-century mansion were built using stones torn down from the Templo Mayor, which lies just feet away. At lunchtime, you may want to reserve a table on the atmospheric second-floor terrace overlooking the Zócalo, cathedral, and national palace, or simply stop at the ground floor patio for a drink in the shade of the towering cathedral across the street. **Known for:** nice craft beer and mezcal selection; mix of international and Mexican cuisine; outdoor seating. $ *Average main: MP400* ⊠ *República de Guatemala 32, Centro Histórico* ☎ *55/5704–3273* ⊕ *www.lacasadelassirenas.com.mx* ⊗ *No dinner Sun.*

★ Limosneros

$$$ | MODERN MEXICAN | With its dramatic volcanic-stone walls and sisal-rope ceiling, this upscale restaurant offers adventurously modern reinterpretations of pre-Hispanic Mexican cuisine. Start your meal with made-to-order tableside salsa (it's best with chapulines) and a sampling of several smaller dishes—like rabbit carnitas and beef tongue tamales—before graduating to a bigger plate of crawfish with a Yucatán relleno negro stew or octopus grilled with black onions, peas, and cherry tomatoes. **Known for:** interesting cocktails using Mexican spirits; emphasis on authentically indigenous Mexican ingredients; creative taco menu

The 44-story Torre Latinoamericana building looms large over Centro Histórico.

de dégustation. $ *Average main: MP420* ✉ *Ignacio Allende 3, Centro Histórico* ☎ *55/5521–5576* ⊕ *www.limosneros. com.mx* ⊗ *No dinner Sun.*

Los Girasoles

$$ | **MEXICAN** | When Los Girasoles ("the sunflowers") opened more than 30 years ago in Centro, it became the first in a wave of modern Mexican restaurants to take on a neighborhood dominated by century-old classics. Now it remains a good place to sip a cold beer and enjoy pre-Hispanic delicacies like *escamoles* (ant eggs), *gusanos de maguey* (agave worms), and *chapulines* (fried grasshoppers). **Known for:** outdoor dining; great views of one of the city's most gorgeous plazas; sunny decor. $ *Average main: MP240* ✉ *Plaza Manuel Tolsá, Xicotencatl 1, Centro Histórico* ☎ *55/5510–0630* ⊕ *losgirasolesmexico.com* Ⓜ *Allende, Bellas Artes.*

Sanborns

$ | **MEXICAN** | **FAMILY** | In 1917, the Sanborn brothers took over the iconic Casa de los Azulejos building to expand their drugstore business and now the popular stores-cum-restaurants, owned by billionaire Carlos Slim, populate every major town in Mexico. The menu plays it safe with decent Mexican standards and international options like burgers, soups, and club sandwiches, but the long, winding counter is one of the best places around for a solo coffee and breakfast, while happy hour deals at the endearingly old-fashioned upstairs bar are hard to beat. **Known for:** quality enchiladas; spectacular colonial setting; old-school atmosphere. $ *Average main: MP135* ✉ *Calle Madero 4, at Cinco de Mayo, Centro Histórico* ☎ *55/5518–3525* ⊕ *www.sanborns.com.mx.*

Coffee and Quick Bites

El Callejón Café
$$ | **CAFÉ** | Specializing in coffee and desserts, El Callejón Café should be your stop for a quick bite on the north side of Centro Histórico. Grab a pizza in the afternoon and enjoy the scenery. **Known for:** beautifully designed interiors; excellent coffees; casual but filling breakfasts. [$] *Average main: MP200* ✉ *Callejón Heroes del 57 #4, Centro Histórico* ☎ *55/1106–9692* 🌐 *www.facebook.com/elcallejoncafemx* 🕒 *Closed Sun. No dinner* [M] *Bellas Artes, Allende.*

★ **Pastelería Ideal**
$ | **BAKERY** | Since 1927, this venerable bakery has been supplying Chilangos with traditional European and Mexican pastries as well as savory rustic breads. Give yourself a little time to wander the aisles and make your way up to the second level to see the cake decorating area. **Known for:** dizzyingly enormous selection of desserts; Christmas cookies and roscas de reyes (king cakes); ornately decorated cakes. [$] *Average main: MP50* ✉ *República de Uruguay 74, Centro Histórico* ☎ *55/5512–2522* 🌐 *www.pasteleriaideal.com.mx* [M] *Zócalo.*

Tacos de Canasta Los Especiales
$ | **MEXICAN** | **FAMILY** | According to some food historians, *tacos de canasta* (literally "basket tacos") are the original taco and a street food par excellence as closely associated with the capital's unique culinary culture as tacos al pastor. Mostly made in the neighboring state of Tlaxcala and carried into the city in baskets (hence the name), tacos de canasta are cheap and tasty, slicked with fat and moisture from their journey, and stuffed with simple fillings like beans, potatoes, or chicken in adobo. **Known for:** quick and cheap dining; local classic; famed spot for tacos de canasta. [$] *Average main: MP60* ✉ *Madero 71, Centro Histórico* ✥ *West of the Zócalo* 💳 *No credit cards* [M] *Zócalo.*

Hotels

Best Western Majestic Hotel
$ | **HOTEL** | If your main interest for your trip is exploring the city's historic downtown, the atmospheric, colonial-style Majestic will give you a perfect location. **Pros:** perfect location for activities in Centro Histórico; great views of the Zócalo; restaurant serves all kinds of well-prepared international food. **Cons:** front units can be noisy with car traffic until about 11 pm; dated rooms; hard beds. [$] *Rooms from: MP2000* ✉ *Av. Madero 73, Centro Histórico* ☎ *55/5521–8600* 🌐 *www.majestichotel.com.mx* 🛏 *85 rooms* 🍴 *No Meals* [M] *Zócalo/Tenochtitlan.*

Círculo Mexicano
$$$ | **HOTEL** | With an obvious attention to detail and exceptional service, the Círculo Mexicano stands out in Centro Histórico. **Pros:** rooftop bar with amazing views; lovely steam room; small rooftop pool. **Cons:** many rooms have no exterior windows; noise from both the rooftop bar and the streets can reach rooms; no gym. [$] *Rooms from: MP4500* ✉ *Republica de Guatemala 20, Centro Histórico* ☎ *55/9689–0543* 🌐 *www.circulomexicano.com* 🛏 *25 rooms* 🍴 *Free Breakfast* [M] *Zócalo, Allende.*

Gran Hotel Ciudad de México
$$ | **HOTEL** | The rooms in this 1895 art nouveau beauty face either the iconic and bustling Zócalo or a less dramatic garden. **Pros:** great views from the fifth-floor restaurant; prime location during events in the Zócalo; the unique lobby, complete with chirping canaries and top-hatted staff. **Cons:** hotel often holds parties in lobby; area can be crowded and noisy; staff can be unhelpful. [$] *Rooms from: MP3750* ✉ *Av. 16 de Septiembre 82, at 5 de Febrero, Centro Histórico* ☎ *55/1083–7700* 🌐 *granhoteldelaciudaddemexico.com.mx* 🛏 *60 rooms* 🍴 *Free Breakfast* [M] *Zócalo/Tenochtitlan.*

Hostel Mundo Joven Catedral

$ | **HOTEL** | In the heart of downtown Mexico City, just behind the Catedral Metropolitana, this large hostel provides clean rooms at rock-bottom prices. **Pros:** excellent value for location; one of the best balconies in the area; co-working space in lobby. **Cons:** very few room amenities; noise from outside and inside the hostel permeates the rooms; shared bathrooms are often in the hallways. [$] *Rooms from: MP665* ✉ *República de Guatemala 4, Centro Histórico* ☎ *55/5518–1726* 🌐 *mundojovenhostels.com/en/hostel* 🛏 *19 private rooms, 23 dormitories with 134 beds* 🍴 *Free Breakfast* [M] *Zócalo/Tenochtitlan.*

Hotel Catedral

$ | **HOTEL** | This refurbished older hotel on a busy street in the heart of downtown is a bargain, with many of the amenities of the more upscale hotels at less than half the price. **Pros:** a good value in a super-central location; tasty daily buffet in hotel restaurant; 24-hour room service. **Cons:** the Catedral's bells chime every 15 minutes late into the night; noticeably old building; service levels are inconsistent. [$] *Rooms from: MP960* ✉ *Donceles 95, Centro Histórico* ☎ *55/5518–5232* 🌐 *www.hotelcatedral.com* 🛏 *117 rooms* 🍴 *No Meals* [M] *Zócalo/Tenochtitlan.*

Hotel Downtown México

$$ | **HOTEL** | Enjoy close proximity to the Zócalo and Alameda Central from your boho-minimalist hideaway in this exquisitely restored 17th-century building. **Pros:** stellar modern design; good location; low lighting creates a romantic ambience. **Cons:** some areas are a bit too dark; ground floor of the hotel feels like a continuation of the sometimes overwhelming neighborhood; rooms can be noisy. [$] *Rooms from: MP4000* ✉ *Isabel la Católica 30, Centro Histórico* ☎ *55/5130–6830* 🌐 *www.downtownmexico.com* 🛏 *17 rooms* 🍴 *No Meals* [M] *Zócalo/Tenochtitlan.*

★ Hotel Histórico Central

$$ | **HOTEL** | A superb choice in Centro Histórico, Histórico Central is the perfect location for those looking to explore Centro while feeling pampered. **Pros:** good on-site restaurant; free daily walking tours; café in the lobby provides free food to all guests 24 hours a day. **Cons:** surrounding area is noisy; outside area can get very crowded, especially during events; some rooms have no views. [$] *Rooms from: MP2600* ✉ *Símon Bolívar 28, Centro Histórico* ☎ *55/5521–2121* 🌐 *www.centralhoteles.com* 🛏 *85 rooms* 🍴 *Free Breakfast* [M] *Allende.*

Zócalo Central

$$ | **HOTEL** | This hotel couldn't have a better location—it's right on the Zócalo and close to a gaggle of museums, restaurants, and historic buildings. **Pros:** phenomenal location; breakfast and all day snacks included in room rate; free daily walking tours. **Cons:** busy location means that at times the areas outside the hotel are chaotic; rooms (and gym) are small; beds are a bit firm. [$] *Rooms from: MP3000* ✉ *Av. 5 de Mayo 61, at Zócalo, Centro Histórico* ☎ *55/5130–5138* 🌐 *www.centralhoteles.com* 🛏 *105 rooms* 🍴 *Free Breakfast* [M] *Zócalo/Tenochtitlan.*

🍸 Nightlife

Cabaret La Perla

BARS | The tiny, gritty Cabaret La Perla dates from 1946 and is now one of several popular gay bars lining the western end of Calle República de Cuba. Weekend drag shows are some of the city's best, with performances focusing on Mexican pop divas. ✉ *República de Cuba 44, Centro Histórico* ☎ *55/1997–9001* 🌐 *www.instagram.com/la_perla_bar_cabaret* [M] *Allende.*

La Botica

BARS | A small *mezcalería* located in the Hotel Downtown, La Botica is easily the best place in Centro Histórico for a mezcal. Though mezcalerías have proliferated

The Zócalo is the heart of Mexico City and frequently hosts events, protests, and political demonstrations.

in the area in the hopes of luring in tourists, few serve as respectable a selection in such a pleasant spot, with a list of 35 distillates from across the county and balcony views over the street below. ✉ *Hotel Downtown, Isabel la Católica 30, 2nd fl., Centro Histórico* ☎ *55/5497–3613* Ⓜ *Zócalo.*

La Ópera

BARS | One of the city's classic watering holes has attracted top personalities since it opened in 1870. Don't forget to have your waiter point out the bullet hole in the ceiling allegedly left by Mexican revolutionary hero Pancho Villa. Come at night for live mariachi and good tequila. ✉ *5 de Mayo 10, at Filomeno Mata, Centro Histórico* ☎ *55/5512–8959* ⊕ *www.barlaopera.com* Ⓜ *Allende.*

Marrakech Salón

DANCE CLUB | Over a decade after opening its doors on the gay-friendly end of Calle República de Cuba, El Marra (as this chaotic little slip of a place is affectionately known) remains as wild, crowded, and joyful as ever. Open to everyone, the crowd here skews young, queer, and ready to dance. ✉ *República de Cuba 18, Centro Histórico* ☎ *55/4843–4814* ⊕ *www.instagram.com/marrakech_salon-mx* Ⓜ *Bellas Artes, Allende.*

Pasagüero

LIVE MUSIC | In the early 2000s, this became one of the first bars to draw hip crowds from other parts of town to Centro. Since then, things have calmed down, but the bar remains a pleasant spot for an afternoon beer and a lively spot for live music, which might range from salsa to hip-hop to cumbia, on weekend nights after 9 pm. For a complete listing of upcoming events, visit their Facebook page. ✉ *Motolinía 33, Centro Histórico* ☎ ⊕ *www.facebook.com/Pasaguero* Ⓜ *Allende.*

Salón Corona

BARS | The famed *cervecería* opened this flagship cantina in 1928, three years after Corona beer was launched. Still a popular hangout for people who live or work in the neighborhood, it is one of the friendliest joints in town, and now boasts three other locations in Centro (all inexplicably within a two-block radius) and another in the Zona Rosa. Try a torta of *pulpo* (octopus) or *pierna* (roast pork leg) with your giant mug of beer. Photos on the wall show the clientele reacting to the 1986 World Cup at the heartbreaking moment defeat was snatched from the jaws of victory by the national team. ⊠ *Calle Bolívar 24, Centro Histórico* ☎ *55/5512–5725* ⊕ *www.saloncorona. com.mx* Ⓜ *Allende.*

Salón Tenampa

LIVE MUSIC | Juan Hernández opened Salón Tenampa in 1925, and was the first to introduce mariachi, originally a folk music of his home state of Jalisco, to Plaza Garibaldi. Now Plaza Garibaldi is *the* place to hear (and hire) not only mariachis, but also groups playing regional music styles from around Mexico. Spend the night under Salón Tenampa's historic brick arches sipping on tequila and hiring the mariachis by the song (prepare, if you can, to sing along). ⊠ *Plaza Garibaldi 12, Centro Histórico* ☎ *55/5526–6176* ⊕ *www.salontenampa.com* Ⓜ *Garibaldi.*

Zinco Jazz Club

LIVE MUSIC | A moody subterranean jazz bar tucked into the basement of an art deco building straight out of Gotham, Zinco is as chic a place to pass a night as Centro has to offer. Keep an eye on their website for up-to-date performances of some of the city's best musicians. ⊠ *Motolinía 20, Centro Histórico* ☎ *55/1131–7760 reservations* ⊕ *www.zincojazz.com* Ⓜ *Allende.*

Shopping

Dulcería de Celaya

CANDY | **FAMILY** | A haven for anyone with a sweet tooth since 1874, Dulcería Celaya specializes in candied pineapple, guava, and other exotic fruits; almond paste; candied walnut rolls; and *cajeta,* a thick caramelized milk similar to Argentine dulce de leche. There's another branch

in La Roma, but you have to come to Centro for the atmosphere. ⊠ *5 de Mayo 39, Centro Histórico* ☎ *55/5521–1787* Ⓜ *Zócalo.*

Oaxaca en Mexico

FOOD | **FAMILY** | Opened six decades ago, this family-run shop in the shadow of the Parroquia de la Sanísima Trinidad sells fresh products imported weekly from Oaxaca. Expect to find cheeses, herbs, chiles, and chocolate along with simple green-glazed pottery. ⊠ *Calle Santísima 16, Centro Histórico* ☎ *55/4036–2316* ⊕ *www.facebook.com/oaxacainmexico* Ⓜ *Zócalo, Merced.*

★ Portales de Mercaderes

JEWELRY & WATCHES | This arcade on the Zócalo has attracted merchants since 1524. It's lined with jewelry shops selling gold (often by the gram) and authentic Taxco silver at prices lower than those in Taxco, where the overhead is higher. The best shop is Sombreros Tardán, which specializes in fashionable hats of every shape and style; it's more or less in the middle of the arcade. ⊠ *Extending length of west side of Zócalo between Calles Madero and 16 de Septiembre, Centro Histórico* Ⓜ *Zócalo.*

Shops at the Downtown Hotel

SHOPPING CENTER | In the early 2010s, the 17th-century palace of the Miravalle family was turned into Centro's coolest hotel, which brought with it a collection of worthwhile shops arranged around its interior patios. The stores range from clothing stores like Casilda Mut, a tea shop, and a number of jewelry stores. ⊠ *Isabel la Católica 30, Centro Histórico* ⊕ *www.theshops.mx* Ⓜ *Zócalo, Isabel la Católica, Allende.*

★ Tianguis La Lagunilla

MARKET | Enormous La Lagunilla has been the site of trade and bartering for more than five centuries. It's open every Sunday, when vendors set up along Confort Street and along the alley connecting to Paseo de la Reforma, selling everything from antique paintings and furniture to old magazines and plastic toys. Dress down, and watch out for pickpockets. ⊠ *Comonfort 32, Centro Histórico* Ⓜ *Garibaldi, Lagunilla.*

Centro Histórico South

Sights

★ Museo de la Ciudad de México
HISTORY MUSEUM | One of Centro's most beautiful colonial palaces, built on land originally owned by Hernán Cortés's son Juan Gutiérrez de Altamirano, the Museo is both an excellent example of Mexico City's baronial 18th-century architecture and an interesting place for rotating exhibitions covering a wide range of subjects and interests. The original building was lost, with the current structure dating from 1778 when it was rebuilt as a palatial home for the counts of Santiago y Calimaya. By the early 20th century, the expansive structure had been broken into small, modest apartments, including one where the painter Joaquín Clausell (1866–1935) lived after arriving in Mexico City to study law. Claussel never finished his degree, instead going into exile due to his vocal opposition to the dictatorship of Porfirio Díaz. While in Europe, he learned to paint and ended up becoming one of the most important Impressionist painters in Mexican history. The museum displays historical objects from Mexico City, including antique maps. Clausell's studio is also open to the public, and its walls are covered with his work. Keep an eye out for the stone serpent's head, likely pilfered from the nearby Templo Mayor, embedded in the building's foundations on the corner of Pino Suárez and El Salvador. ⊠ *Pino Suárez 30, Centro Histórico* ☎ *55/5522–9936* ⊕ *www.cultura.cdmx. gob.mx* ☒ *MP40* 🕙 *Closed Mon.* Ⓜ *Pino Suárez.*

 Restaurants

Al Andalus
$$ | MIDDLE EASTERN | Housed in a magnificent 17th-century building, Al Andaluz makes some of the best Lebanese food in the capital and is a landmark for the Lebanese immigrant community that has been present here since the late 19th century. Its proximity to La Merced means that the numerous menu options—from classic spreads like hummus and baba ghanoush to delicate plates of raw kibbeh nayeh—are made with the freshest ingredients. **Known for:** outdoor dining; Arabic coffee; perfect baklava. Ⓢ *Average main: MP180* ⊠ *Mesones 171, at Las Cruces, Centro Histórico* ☎ *55/5522–2528* 🕙 *No dinner.*

Coox Hanal
$ | MEXICAN | FAMILY | Located up two flights of stairs, this neighborhood institution has turned out solid fare from the Yucatán since 1953 in a big, sunny spot filled with families and, on most afternoons, live music. If you turn up on a weekend lunch hour (usually from around 2 to 4 pm), expect to find a line winding down the staircase. **Known for:** cochinita pibíl, a popular slow-roasted pork dish from the Yucatán; family-friendly atmosphere and weekend crowds; sunny back patio. Ⓢ *Average main: MP90* ⊠ *Isabel la Católica 83, 3rd fl., Centro Histórico* ☎ *55/5709–3613* ⊕ *www.cooxhanal.com* 🚫 *No credit cards* 🕙 *No dinner* Ⓜ *Isabel la Católica.*

Danubio
$$$ | SPANISH | Prior to opening as a Basque-style seafood restaurant in the mid-1930s, Danubio was, as its name suggests, a German bar. Today, the place veritably reeks of old-world charm, with its formal service, pressed table linens, and a bar of whole fish for diners to choose from. **Known for:** long history of traditional fine dining; seafood power lunches; business friendly clientele. Ⓢ *Average main: MP350* ⊠ *Uruguay*

3, Centro Histórico ☎ *55/5512–0912* 🌐 *www.danubio.com* [M] *San Juan Letrán.*

Helu's

$ | **LEBANESE** | **FAMILY** | After 70 years in a tiny alley of a shop deep in Centro's fabric district on Calle El Salvador, Lebanese grocer and baker Helu's moved to bigger, shinier digs on Mesones, where they serve tasty shawarma on homemade *pan arabe* and empanadas *libanesas* stuffed with spinach, cheese, or meat. There are also Lebanese groceries like labneh and tahini for sale, popular with members of the community coming through the neighborhood for work. **Known for:** traditional baklava; homemade ingredients; community atmosphere. [$] *Average main: MP100* ✉ *Mesones 90, Centro Histórico* ☎ *55/5522–5130* 🌐 *helusproductosarabes.com* 🕒 *Closed Sun. and Mon. No dinner* [M] *Pino Suarez.*

La Corte

$ | **MEXICAN** | **FAMILY** | Open since 1932, La Corte is a sunny, cheerful spot for breakfast or a particularly ambitious rendition of what's known in Mexico as *comida corrida*: three-course meals at a set cost designed to eat quickly during a work lunch break. **Known for:** classic and substantial comida corrida; tasty enchiladas; great horchata. [$] *Average main: MP110* ✉ *República de Uruguay 115, Centro Histórico* ☎ *55/5542–7358* 🕒 *Closed Sun.* [M] *Pino Suárez.*

Roldán 37

$$ | **MEXICAN** | Just a handful of blocks from the entrance to La Merced, Roldán 37 may well be Centro's most surprising restaurant. Set over two floors in a 200-year-old house, the restaurant, run by chef Rómulo Mendoza, is an elegant oasis of high ceilings, French doors, and lovingly prepared family recipes, some drawn from Mendoza's grandmother's handwritten cookbook, which he keeps out of sight but on the premises. **Known for:** dishes made from long-standing family recipes; peace and quiet in an often busy neighborhood; early closing at 7 pm. [$] *Average main: MP250* ✉ *Roldán 37, Centro Histórico* ☎ *55/5542–1951* 🌐 *www.facebook.com/roldan37* [M] *Merced.*

Zéfiro

$$ | **MEXICAN** | The restaurant attached to the culinary school at the Claustro Sor Juana is one of Centro's best-kept secrets and one of its few options for fine dining. The cooking here leans toward the traditional with well-executed moles and classic antojitos like corundas and gorditas, but the space, tucked inside the school's quiet campus, is old-world elegant and the service is impeccable. **Known for:** regularly changing fixed-price menus; educating aspiring cooks; affordable fine dining. [$] *Average main: MP250* ✉ *San Jerónimo 24, Centro Histórico* ☎ *55/5130–3385* 🌐 *www.ucsj.edu.mx/zefiro* 🕒 *Closed Sun. and Mon. No dinner* [M] *Isabel la Católica.*

☕ Coffee and Quick Bites

Antojitos Mexicanos Las Escaleras

$ | **MEXICAN** | **FAMILY** | So named for its location blocking access to a narrow staircase, this tiny stall is known for its deep-fried quesadillas, a notch above others in the neighborhood. Be prepared for a line any time you visit. **Known for:** almost literal hole-in-the-wall location; takes orders by phone; delicious quesadillas de requesón. [$] *Average main: MP50* ✉ *5 de Febrero 52, Centro Histórico* ✥ *Look for a cluster of people gathered around an open doorway* ☎ *55/5709–1554* 💳 *No credit cards* 🕒 *Closed Sun.* [M] *Pino Suárez, Isabel la Católica.*

Baltazar

$ | **MEXICAN** | **FAMILY** | Before Mexico City had *al pastor* tacos, Puebla had tacos *arabes*, a kind of schwarma brought here by Lebanese immigrants in the early 20th century and adapted to the flavors and ingredients of the New World. Baltazar serves arguably the best rendition of the

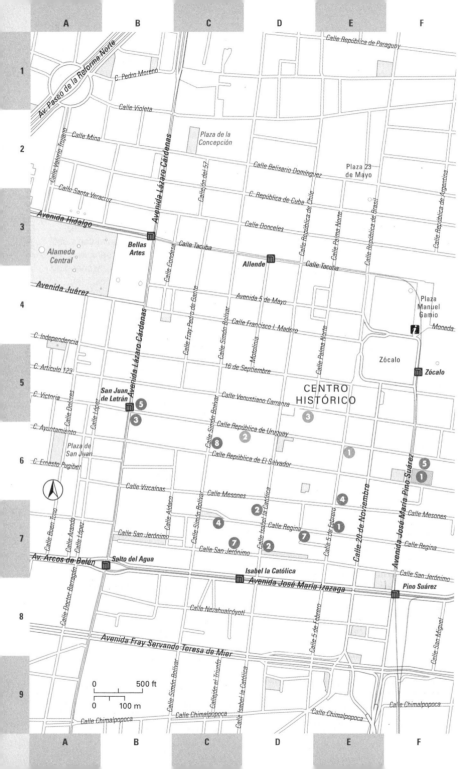

Centro Histórico South

Sights ▼

1 Museo de la
  Ciudad de México F6

Restaurants ▼
1 Al Andalus G7
2 Coox Hanal D7
3 Danubio B5
4 Helu's E7
5 La Corte F6
6 Roldán 37 .... H6
7 Zéfiro C7

Quick Bites ▼
1 Antojitos Mexicanos
  Las Escaleras E7
2 Baltazar D7
3 Café Equis H6
4 Café Jekemir C7
5 El Moro B5
6 El Nuevo Café Bagdad H7
7 Los Arcos de Regina D7
8 Los Cocuyos C6
9 Taquería Los Paisas H7

Hotels ▼
1 Hampton Inn & Suites
  Mexico City
  Centro Histórico E6
2 Hotel Punto Mx D6
3 Umbral, Curio Collection by
  Hilton D5

3

Centro Histórico CENTRO HISTÓRICO SOUTH

KEY

- ● Sights
- ● Restaurants
- ● Quick Bites
- ● Hotels
- 🛈 Visitor Information

dish in town along with some light, crisp falafel for vegetarians. **Known for:** retro diner-meets-taco stall aesthetic; good vegetarian options; delivery available. [$] *Average main: MP100* ✉ *Isabel La Católica 96, Centro Histórico* ☎ *55/5709–7967* 💳 *No credit cards* [M] *Isabel la Católica, Salto de Agua.*

★ **Café Equis**

$ | **COFFEE** | Open since 1930, this coffee spot on one of Centro's most hectic streets is one of liveliest places in town to sip a *cortado* (espresso mixed with warm milk). Café Equis is by no means a third-wave coffee joint—the beans here, entirely from Mexico, are a touch over-roasted and you won't find any plant milks on offer—but with its painted walls and lively air, it's a bona fide institution. **Known for:** beautiful paintings; great break spot near La Merced; long history in the Mexico City coffee world. [$] *Average main: MP20* ✉ *Roldán 16, Centro Histórico* ☎ *55/5522–4263* 💳 *No credit cards* 🕒 *Closed Sun. No dinner* [M] *Merced.*

Café Jekemir

$ | **LEBANESE** | **FAMILY** | The main location of a small local chain founded in 1938 by a family of Lebanese immigrants, Jekemir recently moved to one of Centro's prettiest plazas, at the end of the pedestrianized Calle Regina. One of precious few places in Centro to sit outside, Jekemir is still a family-owned operation. **Known for:** rare sidewalk seating; peaceful atmosphere; decent pastries. [$] *Average main: MP60* ✉ *Regina 7, Centro Histórico* ☎ *55/5709–7086* 🌐 *www.cafejekemir.com* 🕒 *Closed Sun.* [M] *Isabel la Católica.*

El Moro

$ | **MEXICAN** | **FAMILY** | In the past few years, this classic *churrería* (churro shop) has exploded across the city, opening branches decked out in chic blue-and-white. But the original location, open since 1935 on the Eje Central (previously Avenida San Juan Letrán), is a cozy, two-story maze of wooden beams, ceramic tiles, and stained glass. **Known for:** some of the city's best churros; delicious hot chocolate; historic location. [$] *Average main: MP50* ✉ *Eje Central Lázaro Cárdenas 42, Centro Histórico* ☎ *55/5512–0896* 🌐 *www.elmoro.mx* [M] *San Juan Letrán, Salto de Agua.*

El Nuevo Café Bagdad

$ | **MEXICAN** | **FAMILY** | Open since 1955, Café Bagdad occupies a long narrow room in an 18th-century house on the Plaza de la Aguilita, one of several plazas in Centro's rundown and hectic but charming eastern side. Coffee beans are toasted and ground on-site and simple but hearty *comida corrida* (all-inclusive meals that include soup of the day, rice, beans, tortillas, and fruit juice) comes at an affordable MP80. **Known for:** great breakfasts; outdoor seating; pretty setting in an often-ignored corner of town. [$] *Average main: MP80* ✉ *Plaza de la Aguilita, Plaza de San Juan José Baz 4, Centro Histórico* ☎ *55/5542–3802* 💳 *No credit cards* [M] *Merced.*

Los Arcos de Regina

$ | **MEXICAN** | **FAMILY** | On weekend mornings there's hardly a corner in Mexico City without a stall selling *barbacoa*, a traditional dish made by slow-cooking meat in an underground pit. This cozy spot on Calle Regina is a notch above the usual: warm, friendly, and family-run, with good tacos, *consomé* (soup made from the drippings of the meat), and a superior selection of salsas. **Known for:** friendly atmosphere; outdoor seating; good option for brunch. [$] *Average main: MP50* ✉ *Regina 45, Centro Histórico* 🕒 *No dinner Sun.–Tues.* [M] *Isabel la Católica.*

★ **Los Cocuyos**

$ | **MEXICAN** | Centro's most famous tacos are available all day from this hole-in-the-wall *puesto* (stall), but are best experienced in the early hours of the morning after several rounds of beer. The tacos here are all beef and are small, so plan on trying at least three. **Known for:**

late-night dining; tacos de campechano (tacos with multiple layers of longaniza and suadero); unique beef tongue tacos. *[$] Average main: MP30 ✉ Bolívar 59, Centro Histórico ☎ 55/5518–4231 💳 No credit cards [M] Salto de Agua, San Juan Letrán, Isabel la Católica.*

★ Taquería Los Paisas

$ | **MEXICAN** | **FAMILY** | You'll know this all-day taco spot (open 8 am to midnight, seven days a week) from the crowds that take over the corner outside. The main draw here are tacos de bistec—thin cuts of beef cooked on a flat top—and a staggering array of toppings from mashed potatoes to boiled beans to pico de gallo that could make a solid meal on their own. **Known for:** tacos with impressive showmanship; tortillas straight off the press; cheerful, family-friendly atmosphere. *[$] Average main: MP100 ✉ Jesus María 131–C, Centro Histórico 💳 No credit cards [M] Pino Suárez, Merced.*

Hotels

Hampton Inn & Suites Mexico City Centro Histórico

$$ | **HOTEL** | **FAMILY** | Located only a few short blocks from the main attractions in Centro Histórico, this hotel is a great choice for travelers who want a comfortable place to stay at a reasonable price. **Pros:** free breakfast included; great location; attentive staff. **Cons:** small gym; can be quite loud in rooms; traffic can make reaching the hotel difficult. *[$] Rooms from: MP2200 ✉ Calle 5 de Febrero 24, Centro Histórico ☎ 55/8000–5000 🌐 www.hilton.com 🛏 160 rooms 🍴 Free Breakfast [M] Zócalo.*

Hotel Punto Mx

$$ | **HOTEL** | **FAMILY** | A basic hotel in a great location, Hotel Punto Mx provides more value than style. **Pros:** great location; very affordable; some rooms have private terraces. **Cons:** hard beds; inconsistent service; thin walls mean guests can hear neighboring rooms. *[$] Rooms from: MP2200 ✉ República de Uruguay 47, Centro Histórico ☎ 55/5512–7064 🌐 www.hotelespuntomx.com 🛏 60 rooms 🍴 Free Breakfast [M] San Juan de Letrán.*

Umbral, Curio Collection by Hilton

$$$ | **HOTEL** | Built in 1924 and beautifully designed and furnished, this is a great choice for those looking for comfort and style in the area. **Pros:** nice fitness Center; some rooms have Juliet balconies; rooftop pool and restaurant. **Cons:** busy location; some rooms are sparsely decorated; a few rooms have no natural light. *[$] Rooms from: MP4200 ✉ Calle de Venustiano Carranza 69, Centro Histórico ☎ 55/1203–2600 🌐 www.hotelumbral.com 🛏 59 rooms 🍴 No Meals [M] Zócalo.*

Nightlife

Bar Mancera

BARS | Dim and elegant with a long wooden bar, stained glass, and high-backed chairs, Bar Mancera is perhaps the best preserved of all Centro's early 20th-century watering holes. Founded in 1912, just two years after the beginning of the Mexican Revolution, this is the perfect place to sit back with a tequila or a beer and imagine yourself living in the optimistic days after the fighting had ended and a new political order had emerged. *✉ Venustiano Carranza 49, Centro Histórico ☎ 55/5521–9755 🌐 www.facebook.com/barmancera [M] Isabel la Católica, Zócalo.*

El Depósito

BARS | Centro's branch of one of the city's best craft beer bars has a handful of outdoor tables on a pretty pedestrian street and serves up to 150 beers, roughly 80% of them made in Mexico. Look out for beer brands like Colimita, Wendlandt, and Insurgentes. *✉ Isabel la Católica 96, Centro Histórico ☎ 55/5709–2404 🌐 www.eldeposito.com.mx [M] Isabel la Católica.*

Hostería La Bota

BARS | Open since 2005 as part of a larger project to revitalize Centro Histórico, La Bota has since become a neighborhood institution. Set in a long, convivial room, its walls plastered with pictures and objects, the space participates in cultural and literary projects for the neighborhood while providing one of the warmest, coziest places around for a beer and Spanish-inflected snacks like *pan de tomate* and cheese and meat boards. ⊠ *San Jerónimo 40, Centro Histórico* ✛ *Corner of Isabel la Católica* ☎ *55/5709–9016* Ⓜ *Isabel la Católica.*

La Faena

BARS | With its endearingly faded elegance and beguiling collection of vintage bullfighting artwork, costumes, and memorabilia, this cavernous cantina from the 1950s feels decidedly from another era. Along with its wonderful neighbor, Bar Mancera, it occupies the 1535 Palacio del Marqués de Selva Nevada. Although international hipsters have gained a foothold, La Faena still entices a steady flow of old-timers and often features mariachis, live Latin jazz, and dancing. ⊠ *Calle de Venustiano Carranza 49, Centro Histórico* ☎ *55/5510–4417.*

★ La Mascota

BARS | One of Centro's most atmospheric cantinas, La Mascota seems perpetually packed, even when in reality only a few tables are full. Cheerful, bright, and frenetic, it's also among the relatively few remaining cantinas to offer free *botanas* (snacks), listed on a short rotating menu, with every drink. ⊠ *Mesones 20, Centro Histórico* ☎ *55/5709–3414* Ⓜ *Isabel la Católica.*

Shopping

Cerería de Jesús

SPECIALTY STORE | It's easy to miss this century-old candle shop in the thrum of pedestrian traffic along the eastern stretch of Venustiano Carranza Street, but step inside and you'll find marvelous creations in technicolor wax, from graceful taper candles in every shade of white, bone, and cream to elaborate towers of flowers dyed jade, ocher, and violet. ⊠ *Venustiano Carranza 122–C, Centro Histórico* ☎ *55/5542–1651* ⊕ *www.cereriadejesus.com* Ⓜ *Zócalo.*

El Palacio de Hierro

DEPARTMENT STORE | Upscale department store El Palacio de Hierro is noted for items by well-known designers and its seductive advertising campaigns. There are freestanding branches throughout the city, as well as anchor stores in malls such as Centro Santa Fe, Mexico's largest mall. If you're in need of any practical purchases, there's a good chance you'll find them here, but otherwise, it's not much different from any other department store. ⊠ *Av. 20 de Noviembre 3, Centro Histórico* ☎ *55/5728–9905* ⊕ *www.elpalaciodehierro.com* Ⓜ *Zócalo.*

Chapter 4

ALAMEDA
CENTRAL

4

Updated by
Roshida Dowe

☉ Sights · ★★★☆☆ · 🍴 Restaurants · ★★★★☆ · 🛏 Hotels · ★★★☆☆ · 🛍 Shopping · ★★★★☆ · 🍸 Nightlife · ★★☆☆☆

NEIGHBORHOOD SNAPSHOT

TOP EXPERIENCES

■ **Monumento a la Revolución.** As its name implies, this is one of the city's most famous monuments, an ode to the Mexican Revolution with amazing city views at the top.

■ **Palacio de Bellas Artes.** A museum and a performing arts venue, Bellas Artes also houses art-related municipal departments.

■ **Embracing local life in Alameda Central.** While historically a place to see and be seen, Alameda Central is now a place for the more mundane parts of everyday life in CDMX: locals shopping at markets, friends spending time together, and dog walkers managing their packs.

■ **Chinatown.** This neighborhood includes Mexico City's tiny Chinatown, which was once a refuge for Chinese immigrants from around the country.

GETTING HERE

Separated from Centro Histórico by Eje Central in the east and Colonia Juárez by Avenida Bucareli in the west, Alameda Central is easy to reach by car and connected to virtually every corner of the city by public transit. Metro lines 1, 2, 3, and 8 all stop here at the major hubs Balderas, Salto de Agua, Bellas Artes, and Hidalgo. Four lines of the Metrobus stop in or near the neighborhood, with lines 3, 4, and 7 all making stops at Hidalgo (3 runs south to La Roma, 4 loops around Centro, and 7 follows Reforma east and west). Metrobus line 1, which follows Insurgentes, the city's longest avenue, from north to south, stops just west of the Revolution Monument in neighboring Tabacalera.

PLANNING YOUR TIME

This area tends to be very congested so plan on getting around by walking instead of driving. Getting a taxi off the street isn't the best choice, so when leaving the neighborhood, taking an Uber is recommended. When using a ride sharing app, try to get away from the extremely busy areas as the traffic will dissuade many drivers from accepting a fare.

VIEWFINDER

■ Near the corner of Avenida Juárez and the Eje Central, pop into the local branch of the Sears American department store, take the elevator to the top floor, and grab a seat for an overpriced coffee at Gran Café de la Ciudad. You'll get a perfect view of the Palacio Bellas Artes.

First built in the 16th century as a patch of public green space at the western edge of the capital, the Alameda has long been a place where the city and its residents could show off. First it was wealthy residents in the late 18th century who came here to perform their elaborately choreographed courtships, then the dictator Porfirio Díaz chose this as the site for his grand belle epoque monument to the arts, the Palacio Bellas Artes. Later, it was gay men in the 1960s who came for late-night rendezvous under cover of the decaying historic center's anonymous darkness.

Long overshadowed by the Torre Latina and the Palacio Bellas Artes, two of Mexico City's most iconic landmarks, the Alameda was renovated in 2012 and has once again become a lively center of public life in the city, as well as a flash point for conflicts over gentrification in the city's historic *barrios populares*.

Immediately surrounding the plaza you'll find a discordant mix of restaurant chains and local institutions hanging on to their foothold in the neighborhood with impressive ferocity even as real estate developers attempt to push them out (be sure to patronize the latter and skip the former). South of the Alameda, the fancy facades along Avenida Juárez give way to fluorescent-light minimalls filled with lighting stores, some of the city's best food and craft markets, and a small Chinatown. To the north, the Colonia Guerrero remains somewhat dicey at night, but it's nevertheless one of the city's more interesting central neighborhoods with a few sights worth checking out.

Sights

★ Alameda Central
CITY PARK | FAMILY | The manicured gardens of the Alameda Central at the western edge of Centro Histórico have been the heart of Mexico City life since the height of the city's pre-Hispanic glory, when informal markets were held here. Strolling around the park today remains a

Within Alameda Central, you'll find the Benito Juárez Hemicycle, a monument commemorating the 26th president of Mexico.

great way to break up sightseeing in the neighborhood. During the week it's quite lively, but you'll be able to find a shaded bench for a few moments of rest before heading off to more museums. Food vendors throughout the park sell all kinds of snacks, from ice cream to grilled corn on the cob. In the early days of the vice-royalty, the Inquisition burned its victims at the stake here. Later, national leaders, from 18th-century viceroys to Emperor Maximilian and the dictator Porfirio Díaz, envisioned the park as a symbol of civic pride and prosperity. *Life in Mexico,* one of the quintessential texts on daily life in the colonial period, written by the British countess Frances Calderón de la Barca, describes how women donned their finest jewels to walk around the park even after independence. Over the centuries it has been fitted out with fountains and ash, willow, and poplar trees; through the middle of the 20th century, it became a popular gay cruising ground. Today, the Alameda is one of the best places in town to see people from all walks of life, mingling in the shadow of some of the city's most iconic buildings. ⊠ *Bordered by Av. Juárez, Eje Central Lázaro Cárdenas, and Av. Hidalgo, Alameda Central* Ⓜ *Bellas Artes, Hidalgo.*

Arena México

SPORTS VENUE | FAMILY | In operation for more than 80 years, this is Mexico's biggest venue for lucha libre. Pyrotechnic matches, complete with big screens and grand entrances, are held every week on Tuesday at 7:30 pm, Friday at 8:30 pm, and Sunday at 5 pm. Tickets range from MP60 to MP600 depending on quality of seats and the day of the week, with the more expensive matches typically held on Friday and Sunday. Tickets are available through Ticketmaster or at the venue. ⊠ *Dr. Lavista, between Dr. Carmona and Dr. Lucio, Alameda Central* ☏ *55/5588–0508* ⊕ *www.cmll.com* 🖃 *MP60* ⊙ *Closed Mon., Wed., Thurs., and Sat.*

Biblioteca de México

LIBRARY | The building that now houses one of several national libraries scattered around the city was first designed as a cigarette factory at the end of the 18th century. A grid of nine square modules, including open courtyards lined with neoclassical columns, construction on the building lasted from 1793 through 1807. Within a year, the building had taken on other uses, including as a prison. By the middle of the struggle for Mexican independence, which lasted from 1810 to 1821, the building had become an armory. After decades of multiple uses, a substantial part of the building was dedicated as part of the new national library system and eventually inaugurated as such in 1946. Today, the library houses the collections of several of Mexico's most celebrated writers. It's also a beautiful place to sit with a book of your own. Guided tours through the library's elegantly staid courtyards are available by request from Tuesday through Saturday. For more information, visit the library's website. ⊠ *De La Ciudadela 4, Alameda Central* ☏ *55/4155–0830* ⊕ *www.bibliotecademexico.gob.mx* Ⓜ *Buenavista.*

Casa Rivas Mercado

HISTORIC HOME | Built by the renowned architect Antonio Rivas Mercado between 1893 and 1898, the recently restored Rivas Mercado House is among the finest freestanding homes in the city's central neighborhoods and one of the remaining reminders of the *colonia* Guerrero's heyday as one of the city's more fashionable districts. The house was also the childhood home of writer and intellectual Antonieta Rivas Mercado, a great cultural gatekeeper of early 20th-century Mexico. A contributor to the avant-garde Teatro Ulises and the now-legendary literary magazine *Los Contemporáneos*, Rivas Mercado died tragically in 1931 at age 30 by shooting herself on the altar at Notre Dame. The house is open for guided tours at 10 am and noon on weekends, which must be reserved via email. ⊠ *Heroes 45, Alameda Central* ☏ *55/2591–6666* ⊕ *www.casarivasmercado.com* ☒ *MP450* ⊘ *Closed weekdays* Ⓜ *Hidalgo.*

Centro Cultural Universitario Tlatelolco

HISTORY MUSEUM | If you fly into Mexico City at night, there's a good chance you'll spot the tower of this museum; located on the south side of the Plaza de las Tres Culturas, its stoic modernist facade is clad in Moorish starbursts of red and purple neon. The museum hosts regularly rotating exhibitions of contemporary art, often experimental in nature, and a moving permanent memorial to the 1968 massacre that occurred on the plaza, installed in honor of that event's 50th anniversary. ⊠ *Av. Ricardo Flores Magón 1, Alameda Central* ☏ *55/5117–2818* ⊕ *tlatelolco.unam.mx* ☒ *MP40* ⊘ *Closed Mon.* Ⓜ *Garibaldi-Lagunilla.*

★ Centro de la Imagen

ARTS CENTER | FAMILY | One of the city's most interesting museums, Centro de la Imagen shares the old Ciudadela building with the Biblioteca de México. Remodeled just a few years back, the extensive gallery spaces work cleverly to transect and interact with the historic structure and are devoted to reflections on photographs as both historical documents and art. The library near the entrance has a significant collection of photobooks. Guided tours in English can be arranged for free via the website with several weeks' notice. ⊠ *Plaza de la Ciudadela 2, Alameda Central* ☏ *55/4155–0850* ⊕ *centrodelaimagen.cultura.gob.mx* ☒ *Free* ⊘ *Closed Mon. and Tues.* Ⓜ *Balderas.*

Colonia Doctores

NEIGHBORHOOD | Named for the fact that many of its main thoroughfares are named for noted medical doctors, the neighborhood was established in the late 1890s, right before Roma and Condesa. Home to the 42-acre campus of prestigious Hospital General de México, the famous lucha libre venue Arena México, and a number of

4

Alameda Central

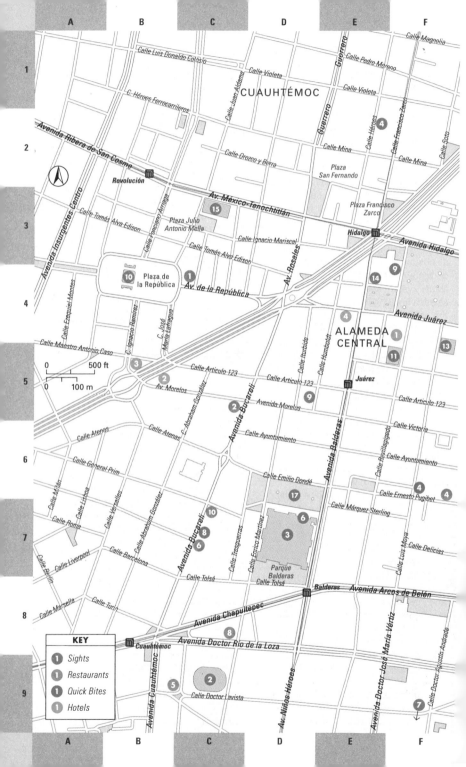

Alameda Central

Sights ▼

1 Alameda Central.................. **G4**
2 Arena México..................... **C9**
3 Biblioteca de México **D7**
4 Casa Rivas Mercado.............. **E2**
5 Centro Cultural
  Universitario Tlatelolco **G1**
6 Centro de la Imagen.............. **D7**
7 Colonia Doctores **F9**
8 Karen Huber Gallery.............. **C7**
9 Laboratorio Arte Alameda........ **F4**
10 Monumento a la Revolución **B4**
11 Museo de Arte Popular **F5**
12 Museo Franz Mayer.............. **G3**
13 Museo Memoria y Tolerancia **F5**
14 Museo Mural Diego Rivera....... **E4**
15 Museo Nacional de San Carlos...**C3**
16 Palacio de Bellas Artes.......... **H4**
17 Plaza de la Ciudadela **D6**
18 Plaza de las Tres Culturas **G1**

Restaurants ▼

1 Arango **C4**
2 Café La Habana................... **C5**
3 Cocina Mi Fonda................. **G7**
4 El Puerto de Alvarado............ **F6**
5 El Rancho Birrieria **B9**
6 Farmacia Internacional **C7**
7 Fonda Mi Lupita.................. **G7**
8 Fritz............................. **C8**
9 Mesón Del Cid **D5**
10 Tirasavia **C7**

Quick Bites ▼

1 Café El Cordobés **G6**
2 El Huequito **G6**
3 Finca Don Porfirio **H5**
4 Panque de Nata Queretanas..... **F6**
5 Ricos Tacos Toluca............... **G7**
6 Taco de Oro XEW................ **G7**

Hotels ▼

1 Hilton Mexico City Reforma **F4**
2 Hotel Imperial Reforma **B5**
3 Le Méridien Mexico City......... **B5**
4 One Ciudad de
  México Alameda.................. **E4**

prominent governmental buildings as well as some impressive old mansions, Doctores abounds with cantinas, bars, nightclubs, and pulquerías—some a bit dodgy, but others with increasing cachet among in-the-know locals. Doctores does have a reputation for crime, especially as you venture farther east and south; the issues are more commonly robbery and car theft than violent crime, but do exercise common sense when walking around this neighborhood, and go with friends or by Uber after dark. ⊠ *Bound by Av. Cuauhtémoc, Eje 3 Sur/Dr. Ignacio Morones Prieto, Eje Central/Lázaro Cárdenas, and Av. Chapultepec/Av. Arcos de Belén, Alameda Central* Ⓜ *Balderas.*

Karen Huber Gallery

ART GALLERY | Open since 2014, this white-box gallery up a flight of stairs on Avenida Bucareli focuses primarily on contemporary painting. It is one among a crop of art- and design-focused spaces to have opened recently near the Alameda, and has launched the careers of several artists currently on the rise in the international art scene. ⊠ *Av. Bucareli 120, 2nd fl., Alameda Central* ☎ *55/5086–6210* ⊕ *www.karen-huber.com* 🖾 *Free* ⊗ *Closed Sun. and Mon.* Ⓜ *Balderas.*

Laboratorio Arte Alameda

ART MUSEUM | The facade of this refurbished building from the 1950s has a colonial air, but inside is one of the most contemporary art museums in town, with a mission to explore how art intersects with science and technology. There is a space for contemporary and often experimental art, a display area for video and photographs, and a room where artists whose works are not displayed in other museums and galleries can exhibit. These are not necessarily young artists, but those who have yet to become truly established. ⊠ *Dr. Mora 7, Alameda Central* ☎ *55/8647–5660* ⊕ *inba.gob.mx/recinto/32* 🖾 *MP45; free Sun.* ⊗ *Closed Mon.* Ⓜ *Hidalgo.*

★ Monumento a la Revolución

MONUMENT | The bronze art deco dome of the monument commemorating Mexico's bloody, decade-long revolution, which began in 1910, gleams like a beacon at the end of Avenida Juárez, one of the Alameda's busiest thoroughfares. Take an elevator to the observation deck up top, which offers 360-degree views of the city, or admire the Oliverio Martinez sculptures that adorn the four corners of the monument from below. There's also a small café and museum devoted to the history of the Revolution accessible at an additional cost. Lit up nightly at 10 pm, the monument is a moving sight. At the base of the pillars lie the remains of important figures from 20th-century Mexican history, including those of Pancho Villa. ⊠ *Plaza de la República, Alameda Central* ☎ *55/5592–2038* ⊕ *mexicocity.cdmx.gob.mx/venues/monument-to-the-revolution* 🖾 *From MP150* Ⓜ *Revolución.*

★ Museo de Arte Popular

ART MUSEUM | Set in an art deco former fire station (the building itself is reason enough for a visit), the Muso de Arte Popular maintains a gloriously diverse collection of folk art from all of Mexico's 32 states. Expect to find elaborately painted pottery from Guerrero, trees of life fashioned from clay in Mexico State, textiles woven in Oaxaca and Chiapas, and carved masks from Michoacán. Don't forget to stop at the on-site store on your way out for an exceptional collection of crafts sourced directly from communities around the country, by far the highest quality products you'll find in the city. ⊠ *Revillagigedo 11, Alameda Central* ⚓ *Entrance on Independencia* ☎ *55/5510–2201* ⊕ *www.map.cdmx.gob.mx* 🖾 *MP60; free Sun.* ⊗ *Closed Mon.* Ⓜ *Juárez or Hidalgo.*

Within the Museo Mural Diego Rivera, you'll find one of Rivera's most famous murals called "Dream of a Sunday Afternoon in Alameda Central Park."

Museo Franz Mayer

ART MUSEUM | FAMILY | Housed in the 16th-century Hospital de San Juan de Dios, this museum houses thousands of works collected by Franz Mayer, who emigrated from his native Germany to Mexico in 1905 and went on to become an important stockbroker. The permanent collection includes 16th- and 17th-century antiques, such as wooden chests inlaid with ivory, tortoiseshell, and ebony; tapestries, paintings, and lacquerware; rococo clocks, glassware, and architectural ornamentation; and an unusually large assortment of Talavera (blue-and-white) ceramics. The museum also has more than 700 editions of Cervantes's *Don Quixote*. The old hospital building is faithfully restored, with pieces of the original frescoes peeking through. You can also enjoy a great number of temporary exhibitions, often focused on modern applied arts. ⊠ *Av. Hidalgo 45, at Plaza Santa Veracruz, Alameda Central* ☎ *55/5518–2266* ⊕ *www.franzmayer.org. mx* ✉ *MP85* ⊗ *Closed Mon.* Ⓜ *Bellas Artes or Hidalgo.*

Museo Memoria y Tolerancia

SPECIALTY MUSEUM | FAMILY | Located inside a gleaming building by Ricardo Legorreta and situated across the street from Alameda Central, this impressive museum presents a poignant, thoughtful, and appropriately disturbing examination of the Holocaust and other atrocities around the world, including the genocides in Armenia, Cambodia, Guatemala, Rawanda, the former Yugoslavia, and Darfur. Compelling rotating exhibits have shined a light on Gandhi, LGBTQ rights, migrants and refugees, and other issues related to human rights. ⊠ *Av. Juárez 8, Alameda Central* ☎ *55/5130–5555* ⊕ *www.myt.org.mx/myt* ✉ *MP130* ⊗ *Closed Mon.*

★ Museo Mural Diego Rivera

ART MUSEUM | Each one of Diego Rivera's Mexico City murals is equal parts aesthetic revelation and history lesson, offering large overviews of Mexican history, allegorical vignettes from daily life, or, in the case of the single mural on display at the Museo Mural Diego Rivera, a

The iconic Palacio de Bellas Artes is Mexico City's most important cultural center.

visual rolodex of important figures in the nation's history. That mural, *Sueño de una Tarde Dominical en el Parque Alameda* (*Sunday Afternoon Dream in the Alameda Park*), was originally painted on a lobby wall of the Hotel Del Prado in 1947–48 with the controversial inscription "God does not exist," which was later replaced with the bland "Conference of San Juan de Letrán" to placate Mexico's conservative Catholic elites. The 1985 earthquake destroyed the hotel but not the mural, and this small, laser-focused museum was built across the street to house it. Like most of Rivera's murals, this one serves a didactic purpose as well, providing a veritable who's who of Mexico's most important historical figures; their identities are helpfully outlined in English and Spanish on panels facing the painting. ⊠ *Balderas 202, Alameda Central* ⊹ *Entrance on Calle Colón* ☎ *55/1555–1900* ⊕ *www.museomuraldiegorivera.inba.gob.mx* ⊠ *MP45; free Sun.* ⊘ *Closed Mon.* Ⓜ *Hidalgo.*

Museo Nacional de San Carlos
HISTORY MUSEUM | FAMILY | The San Carlos collection occupies a handsome, 18th-century palace built by Manuel de Tolsá in the final years of Mexico's colonial period. Centered on an unusual oval courtyard, the neoclassical mansion became a cigarette factory in the mid-19th century, lending the *colonia* its current name of Tabacalera. In 1968, the building became a museum, housing a collection of some 2,000 works of European art, primarily paintings and prints, with a few examples of sculpture and decorative arts ranging in styles. ⊠ *Mexico-Tenochtitlan No. 50, Alameda Central* ☎ *55/8647–5800* ⊕ *mnsancarlos.inba. gob.mx* ⊠ *MP65; free Sun.* ⊘ *Closed Mon.* Ⓜ *Revolución or Hidalgo.*

★ Palacio de Bellas Artes
NOTABLE BUILDING | Of all the monumental structures in Mexico City's city center, there is probably none more iconic than the Palacio Bellas Artes, with its orange dome, its elaborate belle epoque facade, and its magnificent interior murals.

Construction on this colossal white-marble opera house began in 1904 under the direction of the Europhilic dictator Porfirio Díaz. The striking structure is the work of Italian architect Adamo Boari, who also designed the city's post office; pre-Hispanic motifs trim the facade, which leans toward the opulence of the belle epoque while also curiously hinting at the pared-down art deco style that would take hold in the Mexican capital in just a few years. The beginning of the Revolution in 1910 brought construction to a halt and threw the country into economic turmoil for a decade. By the time construction commenced again, the political, economic, and aesthetic world of Mexico had changed dramatically, resulting in an interior clad in red, black, and pink marble quarried in Mexico (the white exterior is from Carrara, Italy) and clear, straight lines that complement the murals by the great Mexican triumvirate of Siqueiros, Orozco, and Rivera, which you can visit for a fee. There are interesting temporary art exhibitions as well, plus an elegant cafeteria and a bookshop with a great selection of art books and magazines.

Palacio Bellas Artes is also home to the Museum of the Palace of Fine Arts, the National Architecture Museum, Ballet Folklorico, the National Opera Company, and many other cultural offerings. ⊠ *Eje Central Lázaro Cárdenas and Av. Juárez, Alameda Central* ☎ *55/8647–6500* ⊕ *www.palacio.inba.gob.mx* ⌦ *MP85; free Sun.* ☉ *Closed Mon.* Ⓜ *Bellas Artes.*

Plaza de la Ciudadela

PLAZA/SQUARE | FAMILY | Located between the craft market of the same name and the 18th-century building that today houses one of the city's most important libraries and a photography museum, the Plaza Ciudadela is one of the liveliest squares in town, particularly on weekends when older couples come to dance. After lingering (or stepping in for a dance lesson of your own), browse the book and record stalls that line Balderas, the major avenue that borders the plaza toward the east. ⊠ *Between Av. Balderas, Emilio Donde to north, José María Morelos to south, and Enrico Martínez to west, Alameda Central* Ⓜ *Balderas.*

★ Plaza de las Tres Culturas

PLAZA/SQUARE | A short distance north of Centro and Alameda, the neighborhood of Tlatelolco, with the Plaza de las Tres Culturas at its heart, is easily among the most historically significant corners of the city. Before the arrival of the Spanish, Tlatelolco was a breakaway city-state from the great Mexica city of Tenochtitlan. Memorialized in Rivera's murals at the Palacio Nacional, its market was the commercial heart of both cities. The ruins of Tlatelolco, no less impressive than those of the Templo Mayor but much less frequently visited, form the center of the Plaza de las Tres Culturas, surrounded by important buildings from different stages of the city's history. To the east, the 16th-century Colegio de Santa Cruz de Tlatelolco, the first European institution of higher learning in the Americas, stands in slender profile against the monolithic block of the Tlatelolco housing projects, a masterpiece of Mexican modernism built between 1960 and 1965 by the legendary architect Mario Pani. In 1968, this became the backdrop for the infamous Tlatelolco massacre, when the Mexican military opened fire, at the orders of the president, into a crowd of peaceful student protestors, arguably the city's most important political moment since the Revolution. Short of the Zócalo itself, there is no place in Mexico City more heavily imbued with history. ⊠ *Plaza de las Tres Culturas, Tlatelolco, Alameda Central* ⊹ *North across Reforma from Lagunilla antiques market* ⊕ *www.tlatelolco.inah.gob.mx* Ⓜ *Garibaldi-Lagunilla, Tlatelolco.*

 Restaurants

★ Arango

$$$ | **MODERN MEXICAN** | Exceptional modern French-Mexican cuisine, charming service, and—most of all—spectacular floor-to-ceiling views of Monumento de Revolución and the Reforma skyline create a memorable experience at this stylish restaurant perched dramatically atop an art deco office building in Tabacalera. Food highlights include esquites with braised oxtail, duck confit with fragrant and fruity mole sauce, and grilled octopus. **Known for:** dramatic skyline views; creative versions of French and Mexican dishes; well-crafted cocktails. $ *Average main: MP450* ⊠ *Av. de la República 157, 7th fl., Alameda Central* ☎ *55/5705–5034* ⊕ *www.arangorestaurante.com.*

★ Café La Habana

$$ | **CAFÉ** | In a city with as much depth and history as Mexico City, Café La Habana still manages to stand out. Opened in 1952, it has hosted famous writers (Gabriel García Márquez, Roberto Bolaño, and Octavio Paz, to name a few) and revolutionaries (Che Guevara and Fidel Castro planned the Cuban revolution over coffee here), and yet with all its fame, this unhurried and simple diner is a laid-back place to take a break from the world. **Known for:** incredible history; decent food that takes a backseat to the ambience; great coffee. $ *Average main: MP150* ⊠ *Av. Morelos 62, Juárez* ☎ *55/5535–2620* Ⓜ *Juárez.*

Cocina Mi Fonda

$ | **MEXICAN** | **FAMILY** | If you're looking for the platonic ideal of a Mexico City fonda (the small, home-style restaurants that feed much of the city's population each day), you need look no farther than this sunny mainstay between the Mercados San Juan and Arcos de Belén. The food here is simple, classic, and always served with love, from the famous paella to the daily, three-course comida corrida. **Known for:** time-warp 1950s decor; home-style cooking; prix-fixe lunches. $ *Average main: MP110* ⊠ *López 101, Alameda Central* ☎ *55/5521–0002* ⊟ *No credit cards* 🕐 *Closed Mon. No dinner* Ⓜ *Salto de Agua.*

El Puerto de Alvarado

$$ | **MEXICAN** | **FAMILY** | This seafood stand in the Mercado San Juan sells some of the market's freshest fish, which are also served up as ceviches and tostadas for diners who stop at the tables across the aisle. This is the place to try fresh *almejas chocolatas* ("chocolate" clams, named for the color of their giant shells), so fresh they'll move under a squirt of lime juice. **Known for:** raw seafood including excellent ceviche; incredibly fresh fish; traditional market atmosphere. $ *Average main: MP175* ⊠ *Mercado San Juan, Ernesto Pugibet 21, Alameda Central* ✛ *Enter market and head down 1st aisle inside door* ☎ *55/5512–6095* ⊟ *No credit cards* 🕐 *No dinner* Ⓜ *San Juan Letrán, Salto de Agua.*

El Rancho Birrieria

$$ | **MEXICAN** | When the last match ends at Arena Mexico, slip outside and down the block to this spot for a big bowl of *birria*, a hearty beef stew ideal for a chilly night. The vibe is all neon, metal chairs, and blaring banda music, a continuation of the zero-subtlety atmosphere at the arena, but the birria is tasty and the doors open late. **Known for:** live banda, salsa, or rock on Friday night; loud and raucous crowds; deals on beers. $ *Average main: MP150* ⊠ *Doctor Carmena y Valle 31, Alameda Central* ☎ *55/5588–2387* Ⓜ *Cuauhtemoc.*

Farmacia Internacional

$$ | **CAFÉ** | **FAMILY** | Located on Bucareli, a grand avenue lined with opulent turn-of-the-century apartment buildings, Farmacia Internacional is a perfect specimen of a café: all warm wood, pleasant light, good coffee, and the kind of light, simple cooking that can feel hard to come by in this neighborhood. Stop in for a freshly baked cookie in the morning, a

glass of wine in the evening, or a midday salad. **Known for:** fantastic egg dishes; nice, concise wine list; cozy atmosphere. $ *Average main: MP150* ✉ *Bucareli 128, Alameda Central* ☎ *55/5086–6220* ⊕ *www.facebook.com/internacional. farmacia* ⊘ *No dinner Sat. and Sun.* Ⓜ *Juárez, Balderas.*

★ Fonda Mi Lupita

$$ | **MEXICAN** | **FAMILY** | Some of the best mole to be found in central Mexico City comes out of a giant clay pot that, at first glance, looks bigger than the entire dining room of this modest, family-run fonda. Opened in 1957, Fonda Mi Lupita specializes in mole from the eastern side of Mexico state, where the dish leans toward the rich, savory flavors of *mu lato* chilies. **Known for:** authentic home cooking; traditional atmosphere; enchiladas en mole. $ *Average main: MP150* ✉ *Buen Tono 22, Local 4, Alameda Central* ⊹ *Entrance on Calle Delicias* ☎ *55/5521–1962* ⊕ *fondamilupita.wixsite.com/molenupcial* ⊘ *No dinner* Ⓜ *Salto de Agua.*

★ Fritz

$$ | **GERMAN** | Close to the border of the Juárez neighborhood sits this locals' favorite German restaurant, which has been in business since 1947. Serving authentic German food and a very extensive list of German beers, it has been paid a visit by many famous players in Mexican history, as proudly displayed on the walls near the bar. **Known for:** house-made pretzels and mustard; pork sauerbrauten in creamy gingersnap sauce; hard-to-find German beers. $ *Average main: MP250* ✉ *Av. Dr. Río de la Loza 221, Alameda Central* ☎ *55/5709–2305* ⊕ *www.elfritz.rest* ⊘ *Closed Mon.* Ⓜ *Cuauhtémoc, Balderas.*

Mesón Del Cid

$$$ | **SPANISH** | This alluring *mesón* (tavern) exudes Old Spain with stained-glass windows and a roaring fireplace. On weekdays, classic dishes such as paella, spring lamb, suckling pig, and Cornish hens with truffles keep customers happy,

4

Alameda Central

but on Saturday night this place comes into its own with a four-course medieval banquet (starting at 8:30 pm), including a procession of costumed waiters carrying huge trays of steaming hot viands. **Known for:** traditional Spanish cooking; unique menu featuring rabbit, goat, quail, and blood sausage; Saturday night medieval banquet complete with entertainment. $ *Average main: MP325* ✉ *Humboldt 61, Alameda Central* ☎ *55/5521–6998* ⊕ *www.mesondelcid.com.mx* ⊘ *No dinner Sun. and Mon.* Ⓜ *Juárez.*

Tirasavia

$$ | **MEXICAN** | A pretty café on the border of Centro and Juárez, with a focus on farm-to-table cuisine, Tirasavia is a sweet, sunny spot for a coffee, breakfast, or a cold beer or glass of wine in the afternoon. Set in the street-level corner of a spare, glass-and-concrete modernist building occupied by architecture firms, photo studios, and a design company, this place is the happy cousin to its moodier, bolder neighbors and as pleasant a place as any for a quick refuel. **Known for:** gorgeous design with onyx counters and sage-green

walls; pretty presentations of breakfast standards; outdoor tables. [$] *Average main: MP250* ✉ *Bucareli 108, Alameda Central* ☎ *55/4053–4602* 🌐 *tirasavia.com* 🕒 *Closed Sun.* [M] *Juárez, Balderas.*

Coffee and Quick Bites

Café El Cordobés

$ | **CAFÉ** | **FAMILY** | A corner coffee spot clad in dark wood with an impossibly narrow upstairs balcony, El Chavelete is a pleasant spot to stop for a pick-me-up in the vicinity of San Juan. You can also grab your coffee to-go from the window that opens to the sidewalk. **Known for:** faux-colonial aesthetic; repairs and sales of coffee equipment; fun vantage point over a bustling street. [$] *Average main: MP50* ✉ *Ayuntamiento 18, Alameda Central* ☎ *55/5512–5545* [M] *San Juan Letrán.*

El Huequito

$$ | **MEXICAN** | General consensus says that this miniscule taco stand on the border between the Plaza San Juan and Chinatown serves the best al pastor in Centro, and has been doing so since 1959. There are now three branches around the neighborhood, and several more scattered around town, but the original remains the best by far. **Known for:** crowded but quick meals; sidewalk dining; legendary tacos. [$] *Average main: MP150* ✉ *Ayuntamiento 21, Alameda Central* ☎ *55/5510–3746* 🌐 *www.elhuequito.mx* [M] *San Juan Letrán.*

Finca Don Porfirio

$$ | **CAFÉ** | At the top of the Sears building, you'll find an only okay coffee shop with one of the city's most famous and beautiful views of Bellas Artes. You will need to buy something to enter, so grab a drink or a pastry and enjoy the view below. **Known for:** mediocre drinks and food; long lines; most photographed view of Bellas Artes in town. [$] *Average main: MP200* ✉ *Sears, Av. Juárez 14, Alameda Central* ☎ *55/6650–4036* [M] *Bellas Artes.*

Panque de Nata Queretanas

$ | **BAKERY** | **FAMILY** | You'll know this tiny storefront by the cluster of people waiting patiently on the sidewalk for a full loaf or single serving of *panque de nata*, pound cake made in a style traditional to the nearby state of Queretaro. Pillowy, buttery, and sweet, a piece makes for a perfect snack while winding your way through the nearby Ciudadela and San Juan markets. **Known for:** hole-in-the-wall atmosphere; delicious homemade pastries; quick service. [$] *Average main: MP20* ✉ *Luis Moya 82, Alameda Central* 🌐 *www.instagram.com/panquedenata* 💳 *No credit cards* [M] *Balderas, Juárez.*

Ricos Tacos Toluca

$ | **MEXICAN** | You'll recognize this bustling corner stall near the Mercado San Juan by the tangling garlands of chorizo hanging over its flat top. And while the taqueros here serve perfectly good tacos of many varieties, the reason you're here is the fragrant, herbal chorizo *verde,* or green chorizo, from the nearby city of Toluca, stained emerald with herbs and green chiles. **Known for:** fast and buzzy stall open one day a week; sidewalk dining; city's best chorizo verde. [$] *Average main: MP60* ✉ *Lopez 103, Alameda Central* 🌐 *www.facebook.com/ricostacos-toluca* 💳 *No credit cards* 🕒 *Closed Sun.* [M] *San Juan Letrán, Salto de Agua.*

Taco de Oro XEW

$ | **MEXICAN** | **FAMILY** | Founded 65 years ago and moved to its current location three decades back, Taco de Oro specializes in *cochinita pibíl*, the beloved dish of slow-roasted pork from the Yucatán. This small restaurant doesn't have much seating inside, so be prepared to eat on a bench on the sidewalk or stand outside. **Known for:** bright and cheerful decor; quick service; family specializing in Yucatán stew. [$] *Average main: MP50* ✉ *Lopez 107, Alameda Central* 💳 *No credit cards* 🕒 *No dinner Sun.* [M] *Salto de Agua.*

Hotels

Hilton Mexico City Reforma
$$$ | **HOTEL** | The abstract red-and-blue mural in the lobby and cantilevered gray facade add a dramatic flourish to this hotel in the city's historic center. **Pros:** double junior suites with a kichenette and dining area are available for long-term stays; indoor and outdoor pool; walking distance to several sights. **Cons:** street noise can be heard in the rooms; can be crowded with convention attendees; additional charge for Wi-Fi. [$] *Rooms from: MP5900* ✉ *Av. Juárez 70, Alameda Central* ☎ *55/5130–5300* 🌐 *www.hilton.com* 🛏 *456 rooms* 🍴 *No Meals* [M] *Juárez.*

Hotel Imperial Reforma
$$ | **HOTEL** | Suiting its name, this hotel occupies a stately late 19th-century building with a corner cupola right on the Reforma alongside the Glorieta de las Mujeres que Luchan, a monument to women's struggles. **Pros:** good restaurant; great location for visiting Centro Histórico, Alameda Central, and Reforma; quiet elegance and personal service. **Cons:** rooms really need an update; dated furniture; small bathtubs. [$] *Rooms from: MP2400* ✉ *Paseo de la Reforma 64, Centro Histórico* ☎ *55/5705–4911* 🌐 *www.hotelimperial.mx* 🛏 *65 rooms* 🍴 *No Meals* [M] *Juárez.*

Le Méridien Mexico City
$ | **HOTEL** | This comfortable, all-suites hotel right in the middle of the Reforma Avenue action is perfectly located to get you just about anywhere in the city in no time. **Pros:** central location; charming library-like café-bar; spacious rooms. **Cons:** basement pool/fitness center area is nicely lit but a bit musty; area around the hotel can get dark; rooms need an update. [$] *Rooms from: MP1850* ✉ *Paseo de la Reforma 69, Alameda Central* ☎ *55/5061–3000* 🌐 *www.lemeridien.com* 🛏 *160 suites* 🍴 *No Meals* [M] *Juárez.*

One Ciudad de México Alameda
$ | **HOTEL** | A central location across from the Alameda Central is the main selling point for this property catering to business travelers on a budget. **Pros:** central downtown location; budget-friendly rates; nice breakfast included. **Cons:** few amenities; small rooms; atmosphere is a bit impersonal. [$] *Rooms from: MP1300* ✉ *Av. Juárez 88, Cuauhtémoc* ☎ *55/5130–0030* 🌐 *www.onehotels.com* 🛏 *117 rooms* 🍴 *Free Breakfast* [M] *Juárez.*

Nightlife

Bósforo Mezcaleria
BARS | There's only one thing in Mexico City about which there is neither controversy nor argument: Bosforo is the absolute best place in town for mezcal (as the weekend crowds can attest). The music is trippy, the vibe is sexy, and the selection of mezcals, many served from unmarked bottles by small producers, comes from across the country. No place in town—and few places in all of Mexico—offers such a rich variety of flavors and styles. Dark, steamy, and nearly always packed, this is a place to surrender and drink whatever comes your way. ✉ *Luis Moya 31, Alameda Central* ☎ *55/5512–1991* [M] *Juárez.*

Cantina Tío Pepe
BARS | One of a handful of cantinas competing for the title of oldest in Mexico (it was founded over a century ago), Tío Pepe is about as atmospheric as it gets. A Tiffany-style stained glass window, a heavy wooden bar running the length of the room, swinging wooden doors, and unflattering fluorescent lights add up to make this the paradigmatic Mexico City cantina. ✉ *Av. Independencia 26, Alameda Central* ☎ *55/8044–5884* 🌐 *www.cantinatiopepe.com* [M] *Bellas Artes, San Juan Letrán.*

Enigma AntroBar

CABARET | This nightclub is known for its drag contests, musical tributes, and overall exciting entertainment. Things get going on the later side and reservations are recommended. Drinks come tableside from attentive servers, with all seats in the house having a solid view of the stage. ⊠ *Calle General Prim 9, Alameda Central* ☎ *55/1321–2239* ⊕ *www.facebook.com/EnigmaAntroBar* Ⓜ *Balderas.*

5 Caudillos

LIVE MUSIC | A classic cantina in the colonia Tabacalera, 5 Caudillos serves up *botanas* (snacks) that rotate through weekly specials, with options like *chamorro* (roasted pork shank) and *solomillo* (pork loin) drawing crowds on Thursday. Musicians play daily after 4 pm. ⊠ *Av. Plaza de la República 127–B, Alameda Central* ☎ *55/5705–3003* Ⓜ *Hidalgo, Revolución.*

Jardín Juárez

BEER GARDENS | What was until recently an empty lot on one of the city's busiest avenues is now the closest thing Mexico City has to a beer garden: there's a small green lawn, picnic tables, potted plants hanging from a postindustrial steel grid, and big open windows in the concrete facade that open onto the traffic outside. The bar serves a wide range of craft beers, including several on tap that are made in-house. The food tends toward barbecue standards like burgers and hot dogs. You may occasionally stumble upon a band playing or a trivia night. For more details, check out their website. ⊠ *Av. Chapultepec 61, Alameda Central* ⊕ *www.facebook.com/jardinjuarezcdmx* Ⓜ *Balderas.*

La Azotea

BARS | One of the relatively few terrace bars in the city, La Azotea ("The Rooftop") occupies a small space in the restored art deco building known as Barrio Alameda. Technically a restaurant serving sandwiches and grilled meat, La Azotea is a beautiful place for an afternoon beer (they have a good list of craft brews) with gorgeous views over the trees of the Alameda and the spire of the Torre Latino. It closes early at 10:30 pm. ⊠ *Calle Dr. Mora 9, Alameda Central* ☎ *55/5518–5023* ⊕ *azoteadebarrio.com* Ⓜ *Hidalgo.*

Las Duelistas

BARS | One of the best, and certainly the most famous, of the city's remaining pulquerías, La Duelistas is most first-timers' bar of choice for sampling fermented agave sap. Always busy, Las Duelistas is a psychedelic trip of a place. Try a sampler of the day's *curados* (pulques flavored with pureed fruits and vegetables). Just keep in mind that it's cash-only. ⊠ *Aranda 28, Alameda Central* ☎ *55/1394–0958* ⊕ *www.facebook.com/PulqueriaLasDuelistas* Ⓜ *Salto de Agua.*

Pulquería La Hija de los Apaches

BARS | An emblematic pulquería of the colonia Doctores, Hija de los Apaches is a perfect place for a prefight drink before wandering a block over to Arena México. Serving up mugs of fermented agave, flavored in house with pureed fruits and vegetables, Hija de los Apaches turns into a salsa club most evenings of the week. There's no doubt it's a lively, down-to-earth, singularly Mexico City kind of place. ⊠ *Doctor Claudio Bernal 149, 2nd fl., Alameda Central* ☎ *55/4056–1648* Ⓜ *Cuauhtemoc.*

★ Salón Los Angeles

DANCE CLUB | The slogan of this classic dance halls says it all: "Whoever doesn't know Los Angeles doesn't know Mexico." A flashback to the hot pink splendor of Mexico's mid-century boom years (it opened in 1937), Salón Los Angeles is a fairly quiet place on most nights, where older couples from the surrounding neighborhood come to dance to live bands playing salsa, cumbia, and danzón. But when big acts come through town, the hall, large enough for 600 people, bursts to life. These are the nights to be here, so keep an eye on the line-up on their website. Just note that this is out of the way for most city visitors, so plan to take an Uber to get here. ⊠ *Lerdo 206, Alameda Central* ☎ *55/5597–8847* ⊕ *www.salonlosangeles.mx.*

Terraza Cha Cha Chá

BARS | This expansive rooftop bar at the edge of the Plaza de República combines elements of modernist chic, tiki bar greenery, and Mexican crafts in a way that, against all odds, works beautifully. Combine that with extraordinary views of the Monument of the Revolution and this makes for a great place to spend an afternoon or evening over beers (or something stronger). ⊠ *Av. de la República 157, 6th fl., Alameda Central* ☎ *55/5705–2272* ⊕ *www.terrazachacha-cha.com* Ⓜ *Revolución.*

Performing Arts

Ballet Folklórico de México

FOLK/TRADITIONAL DANCE | **FAMILY** | The world-renowned Ballet Folklórico de México is a visual feast of Mexican regional folk dances in whirling colors. Lavish and professional, it's one of the country's most popular shows. Though the offices and rehearsal space are in the colonia Guerrero, performances are held at the Palacio de Bellas Artes on Wednesday at 8:30 pm and Sunday at 9:30 am and 8:30 pm or 9 pm, with additional shows scheduled intermittently throughout the year (check the website for more information). Tickets range in price MP370–MP1,560 and can be purchased via Ticketmaster or directly at the Bellas Artes box office. Most hotels and travel agencies can also secure tickets. ⊠ *Av. Juárez and Eje Central Lazaro Cardenas, Alameda Central* ☎ *55/8647-6500 box office* ⊕ *www.balletfolkloricodemexico.com.mx* Ⓜ *Bellas Artes.*

Orquesta Sinfónica Nacional

MUSIC | **FAMILY** | Mexico's National Symphony Orchestra plays regularly throughout the season at the Palacio

Bellas Artes, along with visiting orchestras from around the globe. It's one of the best (and most affordable) excuses to enter the iconic building's spectacular main hall. Tickets range from MP1,000 to MP180. ⊠ *Av. Juárez and Ave Lazaro Cardenas, Alameda Central* ☎ *55/4122–8040* ⊕ *www.osn.inba.gob.mx* 🎫 *MP100* Ⓜ *Bellas Artes.*

Teatro Metropólitan

CONCERTS | **FAMILY** | Opened in the 1940s as a cinema, the Metropólitan closed down following the 1985 earthquake that devastated the city and did not reopen until more than a decade later when it reopened the doors to its neoclassical hall in the form of a top concert venue. Today, the Teatro Metropólitan plays host to major pop and rock acts from Mexico and around the world. ⊠ *Av. Independencia 90, Alameda Central* ☎ *55/5510–1045 box office* ⊕ *www.teatrometropolitan.mx* Ⓜ *Juárez.*

🛍 Shopping

Artículo 123

SPECIALTY STORE | A shop, restaurant, and gallery, Artículo 123 first opened in this area otherwise dominated by electricians and hardware stores back in 2012. The food leans toward southeast Asian while the shop up front sells pretty keepsakes and gifts sourced from around Mexico, from carved stone mezcal glasses to cotton napkins and woven hats. ⊠ *Artículo 123 123, Alameda Central* ☎ *55/5512–1772* ⊕ *www.articulo123.com* Ⓜ *Hidalgo.*

★ **Mercado de Artesanías la Ciudadela**

SOUVENIRS | **FAMILY** | This market is a one-stop shop for all the gifts, souvenirs, and keepsakes you might need. Loaded with stalls selling everything from hammocks to beaded Huichol jewelry to woven palm hats, Ciudadela is a mixed bag to say the least, both in terms of quality and prices. But with a little patience, you will almost certainly find something special to take home. ⊠ *Balderas and Plaza de la*

Ciudadela, Alameda Central ✛ *Entrances on plaza and Balderas* ☎ *55/5510–1828* ⊕ *www.laciudadela.com.mx* Ⓜ *Balderas.*

★ Mercado San Juan

FOOD | Over the years, this traditional neighborhood market has refashioned itself as the city's gourmet food market. Its stalls are crowded with edible flowers, wild mushrooms, fresh seafood flown in from the coast, and spots that specialize in insect snacks like *chicatanas* (a species of flying ants) and *gusano de maguey* (agave grubs). Notably pricey, this is not a place where most people come for their daily shopping, but it's atmospheric nonetheless, with its cheeses, cured meats, and a great espresso bar in the form of Triana Café Gourmet that serves good drinks with a smile over a bright orange counter. ✉ *Ernesto Pugibet 21, Alameda Central* ☎ *55/2248–6633* Ⓜ *Salto de Agua, San Juan Letrán.*

★ Tienda del MAP

CRAFTS | **FAMILY** | The shop at the entrance to the Museo de Artes Populares is easily the best place in town to buy high-quality crafts from around the country. Even if you don't have time to visit the museum's galleries, the museum store itself is a sort of minimuseum with its shelves and racks stocked with textiles and pottery from many of the region's major craft regions, each piece marked with the name of the artisan who made it. Prices are higher here than in other places around town, but so is the quality and the overall financial benefit to the artist. ✉ *Revillagigedo 11, Alameda Central* ✛ *Corner of Independencia* ☎ *55/5510–3133* ⊕ *www.tiendamap.com.mx* Ⓜ *Juárez or Hidalgo.*

Chapter 5

JUÁREZ AND ANZURES WITH LA ZONA ROSA

Updated by
Megan Frye

◉ Sights	🍴 Restaurants	🛏 Hotels	🛍 Shopping	🍸 Nightlife
★★★☆☆	★★★☆☆	★★★☆☆	★★★☆☆	★★★★★

NEIGHBORHOOD SNAPSHOT

TOP EXPERIENCES

■ **LGBTQ+ Pride.** La Zona Rosa is historically known as the city's most LGBTQ+-friendly neighborhood. June's Pride month celebrations are best experienced along Reforma Avenue, and are an unforgettable way to get to know CDMX.

■ **Monumento a la Independencia.** Arguably the most iconic statue in Mexico City is this one of the Greek goddess Nike, which stands 22 feet tall above a 118-foot column in the middle of Reforma Avenue; it honors the heroes of the Mexican Revolution.

■ **Drinks with a view.** Visit the 38th floor of the rooftop bar at Sofitel, known as Cityzen Bar, for the most expensive cocktails in the city with an unrivaled view.

■ **Nightlife in La Zona Rosa.** Go bar-hopping in La Zona Rosa and La Juárez on a Saturday night. The streets will be popping—just stay in well-lit areas and follow the crowds.

■ **Reforma Avenue.** This is the street with the most activity in the city, including protests and marches. If you encounter one, it's best to stay on the sidelines and observe, but it's still a great way to get a sense of Mexico City's energy and passion.

GETTING HERE

Bordering Centro Histórico, Roma Norte, Condesa, Polanco, and the Bosque de Chapultepec, these neighborhoods (including Colonia Cuauhtémoc) are extremely well situated for exploring the city. Uber fares from the airport and Centro Histórico range from MP70 to MP170, depending on traffic. The area, with the exception of Anzures, is well-served by public transport, with two subway lines (1 and 3) and the Metrobus (line 1).

PLANNING YOUR TIME

■ There's a lot to see in these neighborhoods, so traveling by foot is recommended when possible. Zona Rosa is often busy, and where it's busy in Mexico City, there are usually pickpocketers, but in general, these neighborhoods are considered safe both night and day. Exercise extra caution on lonely streets at night on the edge of La Juárez.

■ With the exception of residential Anzures, these neighborhoods have a drastically different vibe from day to night. Daytime is mostly local office workers taking a coffee or lunch break. At night, ample bars in La Zona Rosa and upscale restaurants in La Juárez attract revelers and diners in droves.

ART IN THE WILD

■ La Juárez is one of the best neighborhoods in the city to experience a variety of street art. There's not much you have to do, just wander around. The majority of the artwork you see is from Mexican artists, especially from the city itself. Themes include Mexican kitsch such as Day of the Dead "Catrinas," Mesoamerican mythology and legend, and famous cultural characters such as the now-ubiquitous Frida Kahlo.

Reforma Avenue is one of Mexico City's most celebrated and visited avenues. It cuts across the city, connecting its most important business and government districts. The neighborhoods surrounding it (Colonia Juárez, Cuauhtemoc, and Zona Rosa along with nearby Anzures) are bustling with activity, each offering unique ways of experiencing local life.

Adjacent to the city center, Colonia Juárez is essentially an extension of it and represents Mexico's eclectic "all things European" period of architecture that engulfed the city in the late 1800s and early 20th century. As politicians, bankers, and other high-society types moved away from the city's bustling center, La Juárez became a sort of suburb for downtown. Recently, it regained popularity with a flurry of new restaurants, bars, and shops. Just north of La Roma and Condesa, it's also receiving the inevitable overflow of those booming neighborhoods while still maintaining its less-frequented-by-tourists nature, making it still friendly to the artistic set, at least for now.

La Zona Rosa is part of La Juárez and makes its home in the southwest corner of the colonia, nestled between Reforma Avenue and Insurgentes. "The Pink Zone" has been known for decades as the city's main LGBTQ+ neighborhood. With its streets lined with kitschy sex shops, beauty salons, nail parlors, gay bars, karaoke clubs, Asian restaurants, and the occasional embassy, this is one neighborhood that truly never sleeps.

Separated from Juárez by Paseo de la Reforma Avenue, one of Mexico City's broadest and most connected thoroughfares, Colonia Cuauhtémoc is at once big business and residential. With many international banks and other companies, it is one of the main business sections of the city. But take a step away from busy Reforma and you'll find the neighborhood is also home to office workers and people who lived in the area before any of its tall buildings appeared. Colonia Cuauhtémoc also has a number of small restaurants that cater to its increasingly diverse inhabitants.

Just northwest of Juárez and bordering the northeast side of Bosque de Chapultepec (the city's main park), **Anzures** is a small colonia lined with leafy boulevards and two-story art deco homes, its skyline dotted only by a few tall apartment and office buildings. Quiet by nature, and even more so since the 2017 earthquake left some of its buildings uninhabitable, it functions as a suburb of neighboring Polanco and Cuauhtémoc while still effectively being right in the middle of all the action. The charm of this neighborhood is simply how peaceful it is.

Sights

★ Diana la Cazadora
FOUNTAIN | Constructed over the course of four years and completed in 1942 by Mexican sculptor Juan Fernando Olaguíbel Rosenzweig, this celebrated fountain of Diana the Huntress stands nine feet tall. The one-ton bronze homage to the Roman goddess was originally designed nude, then was covered for more than two decades due to public and political outcry until she was liberated into her natural form again in 1967. She had originally been unveiled at Bosque de Chapultepec and then moved to an obscure location, from which she was rescued and moved to the city's bustling Paseo de la Reforma in 1992. ⊠ *Paseo de la Reforma and Calle Sevilla, Cuauhtémoc* Ⓜ *Sevilla.*

El Museo del Chocolate
SPECIALTY MUSEUM | **FAMILY** | This museum tells the history of chocolate, referencing archaeological evidence of the magical substance from different locations across Mesoamerica. You will see what a fresh cacao pod looks like, and will be able to taste toasted seeds. Learn about the cultural significance that chocolate has played in Mexico over a millennia, as well as the role it plays in the world today. From a room dedicated to sculptures made of chocolate to utensils used to prepare chocolate to the insects that dominate its growing regions and cultivation, there is little you'll be lacking in chocolate knowledge once you spend an afternoon here. ⊠ *Calle Milán 45, Juárez* 🕿 *55/5514–1737* ⊕ *www.mucho.org.mx* 🎟 *MP80* Ⓜ *Cuauhtémoc, Balderas.*

Lodos Gallery
ART GALLERY | This art gallery has spent years mounting group and solo shows from a diverse range of artists, both local and international. ⊠ *Turin 38B, Alameda Central* 🕿 *55/2121–6765* ⊕ *www.lodosgallery.info* 🕓 *Closed Sun. and Mon.* Ⓜ *Juárez, Hidalgo.*

★ Monumento a la Independencia (*Ángel de la Independencia*)
MONUMENT | Known as El Angel, this Corinthian column topped by a gilt angel is the city's most uplifting monument, built to celebrate the 100 anniversary of Mexico's War of Independence. Beneath the pedestal lie the remains of the principal heroes of the independence movement; an eternal flame burns in their honor. As you pass by, you may see one or more couples dressed in their wedding apparel, posing for pictures on the steps of the monument. Many couples stop off here before or after they get married, as a tribute to their own personal independence from their parents. ⊠ *Traffic circle bounded by Calle Río Tiber, Paseo de la Reforma, and Calle Florencia, Juárez* Ⓜ *Insurgentes.*

★ Zona Rosa LGBTQ District
NEIGHBORHOOD | Mexico City is home to one of the world's largest and most visible LGBTQ+ communities. Although you'll find gay or very mixed hangouts all over town, the epicenter of queer nightlife and rainbow flags is the Zona Rosa district of Juárez. Within this always bustling quadrant, you'll find nearly 20 LGBTQ+ bars and clubs, a handful of sex boutiques, and dozens of other more mainstream lounges, fast-food restaurants, music clubs, and the like. On a weekend evening, Zona Rosa pulses with revelers from all walks of life, the majority under 35 or so; pedestrianized Calle Génova almost feels like the CDMX equivalent of Bourbon Street in New Orleans. The more gay-frequented spots, including venerable hangouts like Kinky and Boy Bar, are predominantly along

calles Amberes and Florencia south of Paseo de la Reforma, but there are a few notable exceptions—such as Baby and Rico—farther east on the Avenida Insurgentes side of the neighborhood. ✉ Bound by Av. Insurgentes Sur, Paseo de la Reforma, Av. Chapultepec, and Calle Florencia, La Zona Rosa Ⓜ Sevilla, Cuautémoc.

 Restaurants

★ Amaya
$$$$ | MODERN MEXICAN | At this elegant but unpretentious bistro, acclaimed chef Jaír Telléz presents a seasonally changing menu of internationally inflected contemporary Mexican dishes. Seafood figures prominently in the mix, both raw (in ceviche and aguachile) and cooked (fried soft-shell crab, grilled octopus), and there are always a couple of robustly flavored game options, perhaps braised rabbit stew or lamb ribs. **Known for:** ceviches and aguachiles; impressive and diverse natural wine and craft beer list; creative desserts with house-made ice creams. $ Average main: MP700 ✉ Calle Gral. Prim 95, Juárez ☎ 55/5592–5571 ⊕ www.amayamexico.com ☯ Closed Sun.

Bellinghausen
$$$ | MEXICAN | This cherished Zona Rosa spot (open daily from 1 pm to 7 pm) has been in service for more than 100 years and its partially covered hacienda-style courtyard at the back, set off by an ivy-laden wall and fountain, is still a mid-day magnet for executives and tourists alike. A veritable army of waiters scurries back and forth serving tried-and-true Mexican favorites. **Known for:** filete chemita (broiled steak with mashed potatoes); chamorro Bellinghausen (make-your-own tacos of minced lamb shank); high-end service without the price tag. $ Average main: MP400 ✉ Londres 95, at Niza, La Zona Rosa ☎ 55/5207–6749 ⊕ www. bellinghausen.mx Ⓜ Cuauhtémoc.

Bistrot Arlequin
$$ | FRENCH | Here you'll find everything you would expect from a petite bistro: an intimate environment open to the street, comforting food, good music that's not too loud, and excellent French wines. Start by ordering the house specialty, hailing from Lyon, France: fish quenelles with your choice of various sauces. **Known for:** traditional French bistro atmosphere; popular carne bourguignonne; clafoutis for dessert. $ Average main: MP180 ✉ Río Nilo 42, at Río Panuco, Cuauhtémoc ☎ 55/5207–5616 ⊕ www. facebook.com/BistrotArlequin ☯ No dinner Sun. Ⓜ Sevilla.

Comedor Lucerna
$$ | INTERNATIONAL | This buzzy spot and communal eatery adorned with street art on the outside and vibrant colors on the inside is always busy. With four different kitchens to choose from (pizzas, hot dogs, hamburgers, or seafood) and a full-stocked bar, the offerings here would suit most people's palates and is great for trying a variety of foods or for people who simply have different tastes than their dining companions. **Known for:** casual atmosphere and communal dining; funky decor by local artists; live music on Thursday. $ Average main: MP300 ✉ Calle Lucerna 51, Mexico City ☎ 55/5535–8665 ⊕ www.facebook.com/ ComedorLucernaOficial Ⓜ Cuauhtémoc.

El Dragón
$$ | CHINESE | The former ambassador to China was so impressed by El Dragón's lacquered Beijing duck that he left behind a note of recommendation (now proudly displayed on one of the restaurant's walls) praising it as the most authentic in Mexico. The duck is roasted over a fruitwood fire and later brought to your table, where the waiter cuts it into thin, tender slices, though it's served with flour tortillas instead of the traditional Chinese steamed pancakes. **Known for:** a good place to splurge on a meal; a mix of regional Chinese cuisine, with a focus

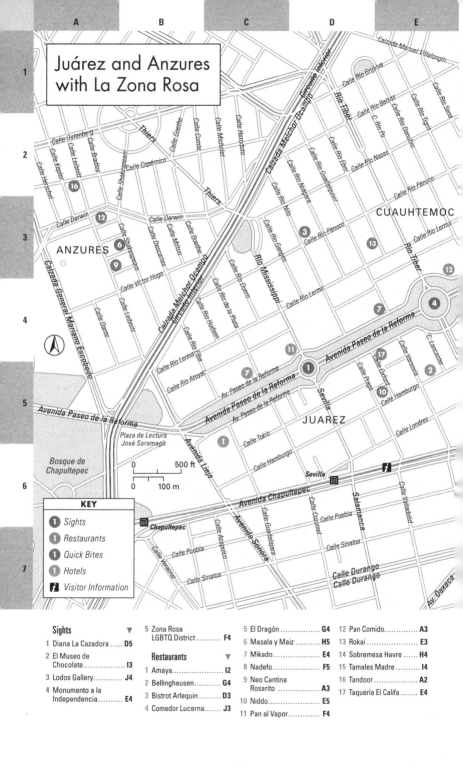

Juárez and Anzures with La Zona Rosa

ANZURES

CUAUHTEMOC

JUAREZ

Bosque de Chapultepec

Plaza de Lectura José Saramago

Avenida Paseo de la Reforma

Avenida Chapultepec

| 0 | 500 ft |
| 0 | 100 m |

KEY

- ① Sights
- ① Restaurants
- ① Quick Bites
- ① Hotels
- 🖬 Visitor Information

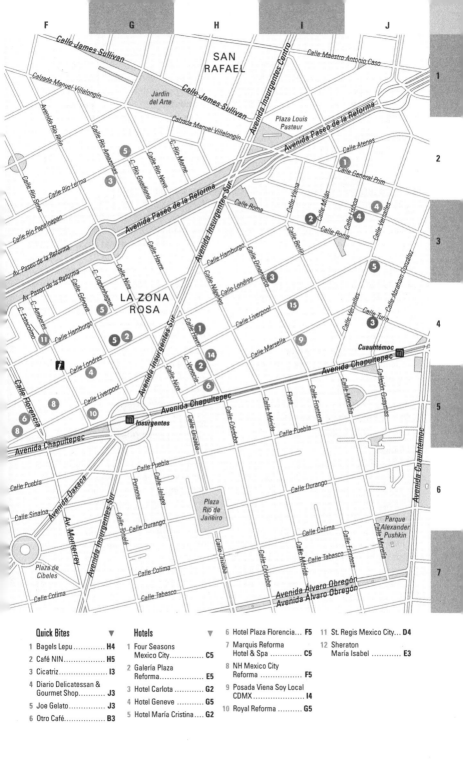

Quick Bites	▼
1 Bagels Lepu **H4**	
2 Café NIN **H5**	
3 Cicatriz **I3**	
4 Diario Delicatessan & Gourmet Shop........... **J3**	
5 Joe Gelato **J3**	
6 Otro Café **B3**	

Hotels	▼
1 Four Seasons Mexico City **C5**	
2 Galería Plaza Reforma **E5**	
3 Hotel Carlota **G2**	
4 Hotel Geneve **G5**	
5 Hotel María Cristina **G2**	

6 Hotel Plaza Florencia... **F5**
7 Marquis Reforma Hotel & Spa **C5**
8 NH Mexico City Reforma **F5**
9 Posada Viena Soy Local CDMX **I4**
10 Royal Reforma **G5**

11 St. Regis Mexico City... **D4**
12 Sheraton María Isabel **E3**

on Beijing; ideal location for a meal while out exploring. $ *Average main: MP260* ⊠ *Hamburgo 97, between Génova and Copenhague, La Zona Rosa* ☎ *55/5525–2466* Ⓜ *Cuauhtémoc.*

Masala y Maiz

$$$ | FUSION | Established by wife-and-husband chefs Norma Listman (born in Mexico) and Saqib Keval (born in the U.S. to Indian farmers from East Africa), this intimate bistro presents an intriguing fusion menu of dishes that reflect the owners' diverse heritage with a special focus on exploring social justice through the medium of food. In the morning, you might try heirloom beans in a tamarind adobo sauce with a fried egg and puffy bhatura bread, while lunch favorites include the signature masala fried chicken with Indian and Mexican spices, cardamom sweet potato puree, and herb chutney. **Known for:** flavorful India-meets-Mexico cuisine; an exciting (but spendy) list of natural wines; leisurely weekend brunches. $ *Average main: MP600* ⊠ *Calle Marsella 72, Juárez* ☎ *55/1313–8260* ⊕ *www.masalaymaiz.com* ⊘ *Closed Tues.*

Mikado

$ | JAPANESE | Strategically positioned a few blocks west of the U.S. embassy and close to the Japanese embassy, this spot is notable for its varied sushi and teppanyaki options. A fine Japanese chef and a cheerful mix of Japanese embassy workers and young Mexicans also make Mikado a real treat. **Known for:** hibachi grills in view of diners; plentiful vegetarian options; excellent yakimeshi, a fried-rice dish. $ *Average main: MP200* ⊠ *Paseo de la Reforma 369, at Río Guadalquivir, Cuauhtémoc* ☎ *55/5525–3096* Ⓜ *Sevilla.*

Nadefo

$$$ | KOREAN | Nestled close to busy Avenida Chapultepec, Nadefo is one of the many Korean restaurants in this part of southern Zona Rosa. Each table comes with a grill and the option to grill your meat right in front of you, and the dishes are varied, with popular Korean sides brought out as accompaniment. **Known for:** traditional Korean barbecue; gigantic ramen soup bowls; long waits if you come during peak hours. $ *Average main: MP300* ⊠ *Calle Liverpool 183, La Zona Rosa* ☎ *55/5525–0351* ⊕ *www.facebook.com/NadefoMX* Ⓜ *Sevilla.*

Neo Cantina Rosarito

$$$$ | MEXICAN | It's easy to visit Mexico and only dine at restaurants and bars that are made with foreign tastes and currencies in mind, but if that's not your style, check out Neo Cantina. It's not a classic cantina, as the name suggests, but a new take on the tradition, where classics like flautas, loaded molcajete, tacos, and sopes get a slightly gourmet update, and cocktails are varied and plentiful. **Known for:** perfectly cooked steaks; delicious tuna tartar; live music and karaoke. $ *Average main: MP500* ⊠ *Leibnitz 67, Anzures* ☎ *56/2614–0232* ⊕ *www.instagram.com/neocantinarosarito* ⊘ *Closed weekends* Ⓜ *Chapultepec.*

Niddo

$$$ | ECLECTIC | This bustling café open for breakfast and dinner, with a few sidewalk tables and an art deco aesthetic turns out tasty, globally influenced victuals throughout the day, including bagels and lox, eggs shakshuka, chilaquiles, and fluffy pancakes with a rotating array of toppings in the morning to a variety of creative sandwiches, pastas, and salads later in the day. There's also an impressive array of pastries, desserts, and espresso drinks as well as mimosas and other cocktails. **Known for:** first-rate espresso drinks; diverse breakfast and brunch fare; delicious brownies, cookies, and pastries. $ *Average main: MP400* ⊠ *Dresde 2, Juárez* ☎ *55/5525–0262* ⊕ *www.niddo.mx.*

Pan al Vapor

$$ | ASIAN | This small diner isn't anything special from the outside, but upon entering, your eyes will immediately be drawn

The fountain of Diana la Cazadora (Diana the Huntress) is one of the most recognized features of Paseo de la Reforma.

to the colorful steamed breads with animal faces that sit next to the cash register. Specializing in said bread, ramen lunch specials, and other Japanese and Korean delicacies, the food comes quick so it's a good stopping point for a bite to eat on a busy day of exploring. **Known for:** meal packages focusing on Japanese specialties; young and diverse crowd; cozy and welcoming atmosphere. $ *Average main: MP200* ✉ *Estocolmo 24, La Zona Rosa* ☎ *55/5207–4554* ⊕ *www. facebook.com/Omandupanalvapor* Ⓜ *Sevilla, Cuauhtémoc.*

Pan Comido

$$ | **VEGETARIAN** | This bright space along one of Anzures's busiest roads is usually bustling, but not often crowded. As one of the neighborhood's only fully vegetarian and vegan eateries, it specializes in healthy options including fresh-squeezed juice, coffee, and gluten-free dining options. **Known for:** breakfast and lunch specials; digital nomad hangout; popular meeting place for friends and co-workers. $ *Average main: MP200* ✉ *C.*

Darwin 118, Anzures ☎ *55/6386–0192* ⊕ *www.facebook.com/elpancomido* Ⓜ *Chapultepec.*

★ Rokai

$$ | **JAPANESE** | An immediate success since it opened on a quiet side street in Colonia Cuauhtémoc, tiny Rokai is perhaps the most authentic Japanese restaurant in a city where cream cheese, chipotle mayo, and bottled hot sauce adorn many a sushi roll. Japanese chefs Hiroshi Kawahito and Daisuke Maeda use immaculately fresh fish brought in daily from Mexico's various coasts, primarily Baja California and Oaxaca, and turn it into sushi and sashimi, as well as cooked dishes. There's also a ramen restaurant next door, bearing the same name and ownership. **Known for:** traditional omakase tasting menu that is a bargain for the quality; reservations typically needed; vegetarian ramen dishes. $ *Average main: MP300* ✉ *Río Ebro 87, Cuauhtémoc* ☎ *55/5207–7543* ⊕ *edokobayashi.com.*

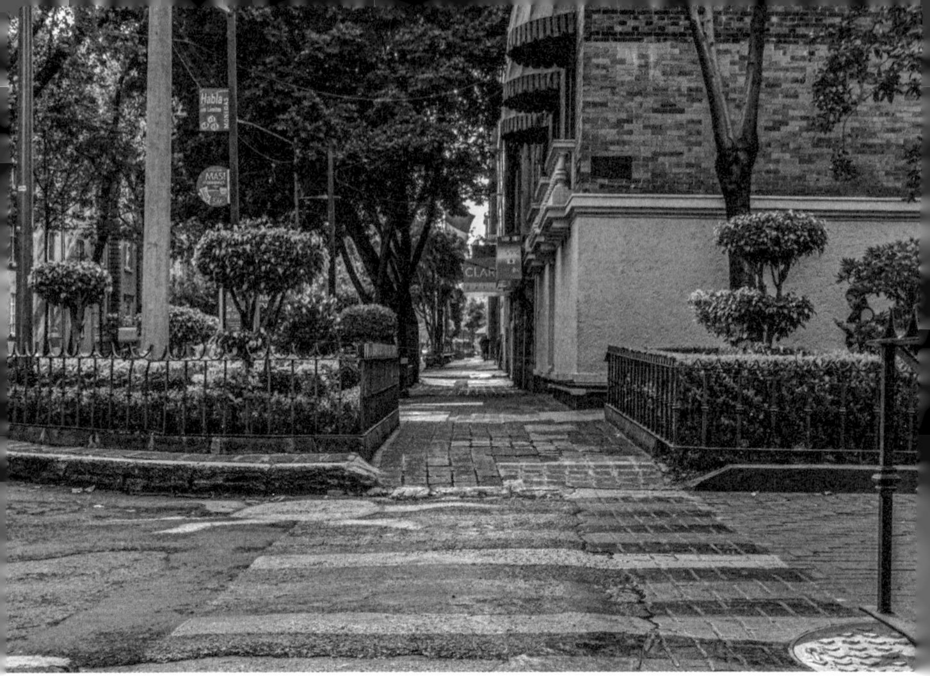

You'll find several rainbow crosswalks in La Zona Rosa, a nod to its role in the city's LGBTQ+ scene.

★ **Sobremesa Havre**

$$$$ | **MEXICAN** | A true culinary experience, Sobremesa offers group cooking courses throughout the week with chefs and house staff in a renovated early 20th-century building. No industrial utensils, blenders, ovens, or other kitchenware is used, with the idea being to replicate home-cooking styles and recipes; guests are treated to a meal of their own creation in the school's beautiful dining room at the end of each three-hour course. **Known for:** cooking classes in a bright kitchen space; Mexican-style home cooking, with some diverse cuisines thrown in; entertaining and interactive dining option. [$] *Average main: MP1400* ✉ *Havre 70, Juárez* ☎ *55/5941–4521* 🌐 *www.sobremesa.mx* [M] *Cuauhtémoc.*

★ **Tamales Madre**

$$ | **MEXICAN** | If its building's divine design doesn't call to you immediately from the street, you will be enchanted as you take a step down, literally, into the sunken communal dining area, which also doubles as the kitchen where outstanding tamales are prepared before your eyes. The service is personalized, and the high ceilings make way for shelves to show off a number of beautiful artifacts from around Mexico as well as books about Mexico's almighty corn. **Known for:** sweet and savory vegetarian and vegan tamales (and one organic chicken option); surprisingly gourmet tamales; tasty hibiscus and tamarind juice. [$] *Average main: MP200* ✉ *Calle Liverpool 44a, Juárez* ☎ *55/5705–3491* 🌐 *www.tamalesmadre.com* [M] *Cuauhtémoc.*

Tandoor

$$ | **INDIAN** | Indian and Pakistani cuisine are not easy to come by in Mexico City, much less of the high quality variety, but Tandoor is a welcome exception. The exquisitely decorated space, featuring items from India and Pakistan, is welcoming and intimate with plenty of space between tables. **Known for:** tandoor oven specialties; views overlooking a charming leafy street; natural mango

Dining with Food Allergies and Sensitivities

Mexican food has always been very meat heavy, but vegetarian and vegan options are becoming more widespread throughout Mexico City. While eating vegetarian here has long been pretty reasonable to do, even with street food, going vegan takes a little extra effort as most vegetarian dishes include dairy products and tortillas are sometimes prepared with small amounts of lard. But good news for those going gluten-free: the typical Mexican diet does not depend on a lot of bread.

One word to the wise, however: a lot of cooks use powdered chicken broth in their stews and soups (although not usually at vegetarian joints), so ask if they use *caldo de pollo en polvo* if you're trying to be a true vegetarian.

For people with Celiac disease, this is also a must as it often contains gluten, too. For those with gluten sensitivity, the amount of gluten in said broth is not usually enough to cause problems.

Some restaurants in areas more frequented by foreigners will offer allergy information on their menus and will often have someone who speaks English on staff. Otherwise, you'll have to rely on at least decent Spanish to let a restaurant know that you have a specific allergy. Restaurants are generally as accommodating as they can be, though beware that most mole dishes are prepared with some kind of nut. If in doubt, say *"soy alérgico(a) a los mariscos"* for fish/shellfish, *las nueces* for a nut allergy, and *los lacteos* for dairy.

lassis (without an excess of sugar). $ *Average main: MP300* ⊠ *Calle Copérnico 156, Anzures* ☎ *55/5545–6863* ⊕ *www. tandoor.com.mx* Ⓜ *Metro Polanco.*

Taquería El Califa

$$ | **MEXICAN** | When you're craving a light bite or even a substantial meal late at night, this big and lively eatery hits the spot with its vast menu that goes well beyond tacos, including *costras* (addictive "tacos" with crispy shells made of grilled cheese), chicken pastor, and Hidalgo-style arrachera barbacoa. Open nightly until 4 am and with several other CDMX locations, Califa has table service, a clean and light dining room, and menus with detailed food descriptions, making it one of the city's more appealing—if slightly pricier—taqueria experiences. **Known for:** several dishes with fried cheese; clean and attractive dining room; nice list of aguas frescas and craft beers. $ *Average main: MP200* ⊠ *Av. Paseo de la Reforma*

382, Juárez ☎ *55/5511–9424* ⊕ *www. elcalifa.com.mx.*

☕ Coffee and Quick Bites

★ Bagels Lepu

$$ | **BAKERY** | Bagels are not common in Mexico, but luckily Bagels Lepu single-handedly satisfies many a craving in the city. While it might just be the most expensive sandwich you'll find here, these homemade bagels are delicious, and the desserts and coffee are both delightful. **Known for:** soups of the day; pet-friendly outdoor seating; house-made cream cheese. $ *Average main: MP300* ⊠ *Havre 52, Juárez* ☎ *55/7350–9890* ⊕ *bagelslepu.com* ⊗ *Closed Mon.* Ⓜ *Cuauhtémoc.*

Café NIN

$$ | **INTERNATIONAL** | This exquisitely designed eatery feels like entering a mansion. A bit like a labyrinth, the service is quick and the menu extensive with

breakfast through dinner options specializing in fresh ingredients. **Known for:** excellent coffee and fresh juice blends; beautifully designed space; international vibe. [$] *Average main: MP300* ✉ *Havre 73, Juárez* ☎ *55/9155–4805* 🌐 *www.cafenin.com.mx* [M] *Cuauhtémoc.*

Cicatriz

$$$ | **CAFÉ** | Depending on when you visit, this hip hangout can serve as a cheerful breakfast nook for chia pudding and egg sandwiches, an afternoon coffee or teahouse with light salads and a delicious smoked-eggplant-harissa dip, or an evening lounge with craft cocktails and well-curated (though pricey) wines. Whatever the time of day, there's almost always a crowd that tends toward the fashionable, artsy side. **Known for:** creative, healthy salads, snacks, and baked goods; first-rate coffees and cocktails; trendy people-watching. [$] *Average main: MP300* ✉ *Calle Dinamarca 44, Juárez* ☎ *No phone* 🌐 *www.cicatrizcafe.com* [M] *Cuauhtémoc.*

★ Diario Delicatessen & Gourmet Shop

$$ | **SANDWICHES** | This small, design-focused deli and café has preserved its original wood ceiling, which sits high over the few two-person tables. The menu is small but high quality, with meat and cheese plates, sandwiches, bagels, and salads along with an impressive tea and coffee selection. **Known for:** Mexican coffee varieties; mezcal, wine, honey, and other goods for sale; some of the best charcuterie boards in the city. [$] *Average main: MP300* ✉ *Calle Lucerna 50b, Juárez* ☎ *55/5131–8009* 🌐 *www.diariodelicatessen.com* [M] *Cuauhtémoc.*

Joe Gelato

$ | **ITALIAN** | **FAMILY** | This gelato shop features flavors that are inventive, inspired by the Mexican palate. Friendly service from the owner himself gives it a homey vibe, where you can sit and enjoy your dessert or order coffee and tea. **Known for:** homemade quality gelato; unique flavors like beet and bergamot, avocado, and cacao and pistachio; quiet nook for relaxing. [$] *Average main: MP100* ✉ *Calle Versalles 78, Juárez* ☎ *55/6842–0904* 🌐 *www.facebook.com/JoeGelatoMx* ⏲ *Closed Mon.* [M] *Cuauhtémoc.*

Otro Café

$ | **CAFÉ** | On a hidden corner in Anzures, this chic café is pleasant for working and reading or just grabbing a cup of coffee to go. The selection of teas and infusions is impressive, and it's the only café with an underground, tucked-away vibe in the entire colonia. **Known for:** tranquil space in a tranquil neighborhood; one of the few cafés in Anzures; ideal for digital nomads and working from home days. [$] *Average main: MP80* ✉ *Shakespeare 78, Anzures* ☎ *55/2624–3464* 🌐 *www.otrocafe.mx* ⏲ *Closed Sun.* [M] *Metro Polanco, Chapultepec.*

Hotels

★ Four Seasons Mexico City

$$$$ | **HOTEL** | Among the most luxurious hotels in the capital, this eight-story oasis with a traditional inner courtyard was modeled after the 18th-century Iturbide Palace. **Pros:** outstanding level of service; great on-site dining; fabulous spa with pool and gym. **Cons:** hotel itself is very large and easy to get lost in; it's a franchise, so doesn't have much local flair; all amenities are (as expected) expensive. [$] *Rooms from: MP13,500* ✉ *Paseo de la Reforma 500, Mexico City* ☎ *55/5230–1818* 🌐 *www.fourseasons.com/mexico* 🛏 *240 rooms* 🍴 *No Meals* [M] *Chapultepec.*

Galería Plaza Reforma

$$ | **HOTEL** | Location gives this ultramodern hotel an edge; it's on a quiet street, but plenty of shops, restaurants, and nightspots are nearby. **Pros:** good quality-to-price ratio; rooftop pool with a good view of the city; all rooms are clean and bright, with small work areas. **Cons:** many conferences held here; small rooms; decor is a bit generic. [$] *Rooms from:*

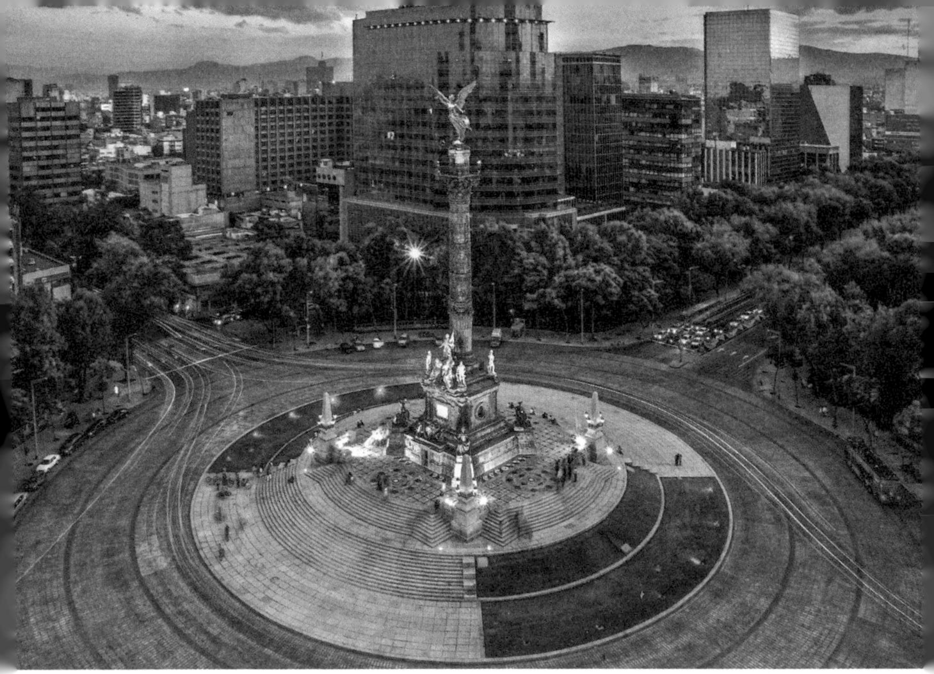

The Monumento a la Independencia was built to commemorate the 100th anniversary of Mexico's independence.

MP2000 ✉ *Hamburgo 195, at Varsovia, Juárez* ☎ *55/5230–1712* 🌐 *www.galeriaplazahotels.com.mx/en/reforma* 🛏 *436 rooms* 🍴 *No Meals* [M] *Sevilla.*

Hotel Carlota

$$ | HOTEL | Catering to a youthful, see-and-be-seen crowd of clubbers and fashionistas, this uber-cool design hotel also houses a hipster-approved lifestyle boutique and a buzzy mod-Mex restaurant. **Pros:** chic, updated design; great location and free bikes; outdoor bar and pool area. **Cons:** a little pricey; expensive minibar; outside noise can be high. [$] *Rooms from: MP2800* ✉ *Calle Rio Amazonas 73, Cuauhtémoc* ☎ *55/5511–6300* 🌐 *www.hotelcarlota.mx* 🛏 *36 rooms* 🍴 *No Meals* [M] *Cuauhtémoc.*

Hotel Geneve

$$ | HOTEL | This five-story 1907 hotel, referred to locally as El Génova, has a pleasant lobby whose atmosphere successfully combines elegance and whimsy. **Pros:** great price for what you get; historic, retro ambience; in the heart of the Zona Rosa. **Cons:** service is only so-so; needs some updating; some rooms have a high noise level. [$] *Rooms from: MP2370* ✉ *Londres 130, Juárez* ☎ *55/5080–0800* 🌐 *www.hotelgeneve.com.mx* 🛏 *229 rooms* 🍴 *No Meals* [M] *Cuauhtémoc.*

Hotel María Cristina

$ | HOTEL | Impeccably maintained since it was built in 1937, this Spanish colonial–style gem is a Mexico City classic. **Pros:** you get a lot for your money here; good food at on-site restaurant; classic colonial vibe. **Cons:** rooms aren't that exciting; spaces could use updating; hit-or-miss service. [$] *Rooms from: MP1775* ✉ *Río Lerma 31, Cuauhtémoc* ☎ *55/5566–9688* 🌐 *www.hotelmariacristina.com.mx* 🛏 *150 rooms* 🍴 *No Meals* [M] *Cuauhtémoc.*

Hotel Plaza Florencia

$ | HOTEL | The lobby of this hotel may be weighted with heavy furniture, but the rooms upstairs are bright, modern, and, most importantly, soundproofed against the traffic noise of the busy avenue below. **Pros:** excellent location; very clean; higher floors have views of the Angel Monument. **Cons:** decor is dated; generic style; some rooms are dark. [$] *Rooms from: MP1800* ✉ *Florencia 61, Juárez* ☎ *55/5242–4700* 🌐 *hotelespf.com.mx* 🛏 *142 rooms* 🍴 *No Meals* [M] *Sevilla.*

★ Marquis Reforma Hotel & Spa
$$ | **HOTEL** | This plush, privately owned member of the Leading Hotels of the World is within walking distance of the Zona Rosa. **Pros:** luxury at a fraction of the price of bigger chains; excellent spa; staff successfully blends white-glove service with personal warmth. **Cons:** the design sensibility in common areas can feel a bit dated; additional charges can add up; needs some minor updates. [$] *Rooms from: MP3700* ✉ *Paseo de la Reforma 465, La Zona Rosa* ☎ *55/5229–1200* 🌐 *www.marquisreforma.com* 🛏 *211 rooms* 🍴 *No Meals* [M] *Sevilla.*

NH Mexico City Reforma
$ | **HOTEL** | There's a stylish lobby cocktail lounge and a restaurant that serves excellent international cuisine in this 1960s-era business hotel. **Pros:** in the heart of Zona Rosa; decent on-site restaurant; excellent view of the neighborhood from the rooftop pool terrace. **Cons:** particularly business focused, so seems a little impersonal; generic style; lacks some comfort elements. [$] *Rooms from: MP2000* ✉ *Liverpool 155, Juárez* ☎ *55/5228–9928* 🌐 *www.nh-hotels.com* 🛏 *306 rooms* 🍴 *Free Breakfast* [M] *Sevilla.*

Posada Viena Soy Local CDMX
$ | **HOTEL** | Hidden away in a quiet spot three blocks from the hustle and bustle of the Zona Rosa, this hotel is convenient to restaurants, bars, and shops, but much more affordable than some of its more central counterparts. **Pros:** the staff couldn't be nicer; overall a great deal; good location. **Cons:** elevator and hallways are a little musty; could use some updates; price gouging for special events. [$] *Rooms from: MP1000* ✉ *Marsella 28, corner of Dinamarca, Juárez* ☎ *55/5592–7312* 🌐 *www.soylocal.co* 🛏 *88 rooms* 🍴 *No Meals* [M] *Cuauhtémoc.*

Royal Reforma
$ | **HOTEL** | The immaculate marble lobby of the modern Royal Hotel, beloved by international travelers, is filled with plants and the exuberant conversation of its guests. **Pros:** decent prices; excellent location; nice views if you're on one of the top floors. **Cons:** it's a Best Western property, which means that some things are more generic; needs some updates; Wi-Fi reportedly spotty. [$] *Rooms from: MP1660* ✉ *Amberes 78, Juárez* ☎ *55/9149–3000* 🌐 *hotelroyal-reforma.com* 🛏 *162 rooms* 🍴 *No Meals* [M] *Cuauhtémoc.*

Sheraton María Isabel
$ | **HOTEL** | The first international chain hotel in Mexico City still has an incomparable location and exemplary service. **Pros:** perfect location across from the Angel Monument and the Zona Rosa; good breakfast options; reliable brand. **Cons:** service is hit-or-miss; some spaces need updating; generic style. [$] *Rooms from: MP1860* ✉ *Paseo de la Reforma 325, Juárez* ☎ *55/5242–5555* 🌐 *www.marriott.com* 🛏 *827 rooms* 🍴 *No Meals* [M] *Sevilla.*

★ St. Regis Mexico City
$$$$ | **HOTEL** | The intimate layout and bespoke service here provide the ultimate sanctuary from urban chaos—despite being in one of the city's busiest sections and in one of the tallest towers. **Pros:** phenomenal service; peaceful ambience with good soundproofing in all rooms; world-class spa and fitness center, complete with yoga studio. **Cons:** expensive add-ons; not a good place to go if you don't like rich people; almost too quiet in public areas. [$] *Rooms from: MP10,500* ✉ *Paseo de la Reforma 439, Juárez* ☎ *55/5228–1818* 🌐 *www.marriott.com/en-us/hotels/mexxr-the-st-regis-mexico-city* 🛏 *224 rooms* 🍴 *No Meals* [M] *Sevilla.*

Airbnb in Mexico City

Since the foreign tourism to Mexico City boom began around 2015, several key neighborhoods in the city have changed dramatically, with new restaurants and bars popping up that cater to more upscale tastes and budgets. La Juárez is one of these zones, and it's also one of the city's colonias with the highest number of Airbnbs, the now famous online platform for short-term apartment stays.

Some former tenants say they have been forcefully and illegally evicted from their homes as entire apartment buildings are renovated for Airbnbs with higher per-night rates; in some cases, the one-night price for an apartment equates to an entire week's salary for the average Mexican. Rents have doubled or tripled in La Juárez and other neighborhoods over the past several years and the September 19, 2017, earthquake didn't help, as many buildings crumbled or were left uninhabitable, making for even fewer housing options in an already overwhelmed city. That same year, Mexico City's government ruled to enforce a 3% accommodation tax for anyone who seeks to stay in the city, instead of just for guests of the city's hotels. No other legal measures have been taken to regulate Airbnb or other similar platforms yet, much to the distress of many city residents.

🍸 Nightlife

Baby

DANCE CLUB | Drawing a pretty gender-diverse crowd of mostly under-thirty-somethings, this wildly popular LGBTQ club offers up a varied menu of dance genres—anything from reggaeton to electronic. If you need a break from the pulsing crowds and intensely pink lighting within, head to the pleasant side patio. It's in Zona Rosa, but a few blocks east of the Calle Amberes bar strip. ⊠ *Londres 71, Juárez* ☎ ⊕ *www.instagram.com/babyclubmexico.*

Bar Milán

BARS | The young and the hip favor this bar, a 10-minute walk northeast of Zona Rosa. Upon entering, you need to change pesos into *milagros* (miracles), which are notes necessary to buy drinks throughout the night. The trick is to remember to change them back before last call. ⊠ *Milán 18, at General Prim, Juárez* ☎ *55/5592–0031* ⊕ *www.barmilan.com.mx* Ⓜ *Balderas.*

★ Cabaretito Fusión

DANCE CLUB | This little cabaret offers entertainment six nights per week, ranging from drag shows and burlesque to exotic dancers and impersonators. There's nothing dull about a night at Cabaretito, and it's a welcoming space for all. Bottle service is available, and you'll find plenty of alcohol to lower your inhibitions and fit in with the rollicking crowd eager for a good time. ⊠ *Londres 77, Juárez* ⊕ *www.cabaretito.com.mx/* Ⓜ *Cuauhtémoc.*

Calle Genova

GATHERING PLACE | Closed off for pedestrians and lined with bars, this street is basically one long pub crawl, spanning several blocks and all kinds of different establishments. You'll be approached with menus by the hype people for various bars as you walk; feel free to take a quick look and move on to the next option if a place doesn't interest you (they're used to it). La Terraza and Bukowski's Bar are particularly good for people-watching and drinks, although you're better off looking elsewhere for dining. ⊠ *Calle Genova, between Paseo de la Reforma and Calle Liverpool, Juárez* Ⓜ *Cuauhtémoc.*

El Scary Witches Bar

BARS | A nod to international counter-culture, with a special appreciation for everything goth, this bar is purposely dark and always bumping out industrial, metal, and rock tunes into the street. It's tight quarters and slightly confined, but you'll feel like you're part of a special, all-black-wearing club when you enter. Find a spot to squeeze in and wait for your server to come by with a menu that includes wine, mezcal, an impressive variety of international and artisanal Mexican beers, and cocktails served in skull-shape mugs. ⊠ *Oslo 3, La Zona Rosa* ☎ *55/5207–8416* ⊕ *www.facebook. com/elscarywitches* Ⓜ *Cuauhtémoc.*

★ Hanky Panky Cocktail Bar

BARS | If you're looking for it, you'll eventually find it, but you won't find it if you aren't looking for it. With a strict, secret location, Hanky Panky is one of Mexico City's few Prohibition-era-style speakeasies. Award-winning mixologists come and go from here to highlight their specialties abroad, while always bringing something back with them. Reservations are required, and when you arrive, you'll have to ask around (as in up and down the block) in order to find the entrance—it's part of the charm. Inside is dark, with leather booths and a 10-seat bar. Many cocktails are based on Mexican mixology magic, though there's plenty of international flavors as well; you won't be disappointed with something spicy. ⊠ *Calle Turín, between Calle Versalles and Abraham González, Juárez* ☎ *55/9155–0958* ⊕ *www.hankypanky.mx* Ⓜ *Cuauhtémoc.*

Nicho Bears & Bar

BARS | Zona Rosa's prime hangout for bearish gay guys and their admirers actually draws a pretty varied crowd. It acts as a generally more mature alternative to the more raucous crowds you'll find in many of the bars around the corner on

Calle Amberes. It's open only Thursday through Saturday night. ⊠ *Londres 182, Juárez* 🚇 ⊕ *www.bearmex.com.*

★ Parker & Lenox

LIVE MUSIC | First you meet Parker, a classy diner with windowside black leather booths and an exquisite wooden bar serving up gourmet pub fare. Then, at night, you meet Lenox, a tucked away, acoustically ideal live music venue with green leather booths and not a bad seat in the house. With live music throughout the week, including international acts and local tributes (think Quentin Tarantino night featuring your favorite soundtracks), locals love Lenox for its speakeasy vibe and chilled-out jazz club ambience. ⊠ *Calle Milán 14, Juárez* ☎ *55/7893–3140* ⊕ *www.facebook.com/parkerandlenox* Ⓜ *Cuauhtémoc, Balderas.*

Tokyo Music Bar

LIVE MUSIC | Across the hallway from ultrahip restaurant Emilia, this bar has a speakeasy vibe, phenomenal music, and an inventive cocktail list, including nonalcoholic options. They keep things super chill with vinyl records lining green marble-faced walls, and a DJ spins everything from current to old-school R&B hits. ⊠ *Río Panuco 132, Cuauhtémoc* ☎ *55/8662–4064* ⊕ *www. facebook.com/tokyomusicbar* Ⓜ *Sevilla.*

🎭 Performing Arts

Hojas de Té

FOLK/TRADITIONAL DANCE | Perhaps the best place to see flamenco in the city, this space doubles as a performance studio and school. With live performances and occasional dinners, a bar with wine, beer and mezcal, and performances hosted by the school's students as well as international performers, it's an intimate space that transports you from the clubs of Zona Rosa to the hills of Andalucia. Check the website for a full schedule. ⊠ *Oslo 7, Juárez* ☎ *55/5207–8416* ⊕ *www.hojasdete.org* Ⓜ *Cuauhtémoc.*

Teatro Milán

THEATER | Intimate and affordable, Teatro Milán and its joint theater Foro Lucerna regularly present work by Mexican artists and feature local actors. From comedy to drama to ballet, the space changes nightly depending on the work it's showcasing. With 250 seats, everyone is entitled to a great view of the stage. Check the website for show dates and times. ⊠ *Calle Lucerna 64, Juárez* 🕾 *55/5535–4178* ⊕ *www.teatromilan.com* Ⓜ *Cuauhtémoc.*

Shopping

★ Bazar Fusion

SPECIALTY STORE | One of the best places in the city to go souvenir or gift shopping, Bazar Fusion specializes in Mexican-made clothing, beauty products, shoes, and goodies like mezcal and salsa. On weekends, it expands with vendors taking over the hallways selling different items, mostly based on local and organic themes (think bath products, jewelry, accessories, and cooking goods), as well as art. Spanning various aesthetics, artisan products from all across Mexico are featured; as big and diverse as the country is, Bazar Fusion does a good job at representing much of it with textiles and other artistry from across the Republic. ⊠ *Londres 37, Juárez* 🕾 *55/5511–6328* ⊕ *www.casafusion.com.mx* Ⓜ *Cuauhtémoc.*

★ Carla Fernández

CLOTHING | One of the country's most vaunted fashion labels, Carla Fernández displays and sells its gorgeously edgy women's garments—known for their geometric patterns and Mexican textiles—in this spacious boutique in Juárez. The original store is a few blocks away in Roma and there's a third outpost in Centro Histórico. ⊠ *Calle Marsella 72, Juárez* 🕾 *55/5511–0001* ⊕ *www.carlafernandez.com* Ⓜ *Insurgentes.*

Casa Caballería

CLOTHING | A store for the modern gentleman, Casa Caballería is designed to offer styles for men from different walks of life and varied interests. The space is well organized in what feels like a tailor's shop from more chivalrous times. From suits and colognes to jewelry and satchels, it has a boutique vibe with personalized service. The majority of goods here are from Mexican designers, though some Spanish and South American clothing can be found, too. ⊠ *Havre 64, Juárez* 🕾 *55/5207–3216* ⊕ *www.casacaballeria.com* Ⓜ *Cuauhtémoc.*

Cihuah

CLOTHING | French designer Vanessa Guckel moved to Mexico City in 2008 as an architect and five years later, she started her label Cihuah ("woman" in Nahuatl) to explore the intersections of architecture and clothing, the built environments closest to our bodies. At her studio and showroom Guckel displays clothing that uses experimental materials and geometric forms ranging from the indigenous Mexican *huipil* to elongated rectangles of cloth that zip into skirts and capes. ⊠ *Havre 68, Juárez* 🕾 *55/7427–5622* ⊕ *www.cihuah.com* Ⓜ *Juarez, Hidalgo.*

Fonart

CRAFTS | Located on the ground floor of the Secretariat of Welfare building on Paseo de la Reforma, the main retail outlet FONART (the National Fund for the Promotion of Handicrafts) is one of the country's best sources for authentic Mexican crafts: colorful embroidered textiles, ornate glassware, folk dolls, terra-cotta cookery, carved wood boxes, Day of the Dead figures, and more. You'll pay a bit more here than in many other markets and shops around the city, but FONART products are carefully selected directly from the best artisans in the country, who are in turn guaranteed a fair wage. There are a few other FONART locations around the city, including a very large branch in Benito Juárez on Avenida

Patriotismo. ⊠ *Paseo de la Reforma 116, Juárez* ☎ *55/5546–7163* ⊕ *www.gob.mx/ fonart* Ⓜ *Juárez.*

★ Jorge Cuesta Librería de Paso
BOOKS | With volumes in multiple languages, Jorge Cuesta Librería de Paso is a great spot to find academic writing on any number of subjects in Mexico, as well as out-of-print copies of international and Mexican literature. The bookstore, named after a Mexican poet and scientist, is packed to the gills with antiques, too (some of which are for sale), on which nary an inch is spared for all the books within its walls. ⊠ *Calle Liverpool 12, Juárez* ☎ *55/5546–1742* ⊕ *www. instagram.com/libreria_jorgecuesta* Ⓜ *Cuauhtémoc.*

Loose Blues
VINTAGE | Selling vintage clothing with a heavy emphasis on Japanese style, from shoes to denim to ceramics, the space is both well curated and slightly unexpected. Head upstairs for a privileged view of the hip Juárez neighborhood, where a restaurant serves Japanese fare including sushi, noodle dishes, and tea. ⊠ *Calle Dinamarca 44, Juárez* ☎ *55/5546–4359* ⊕ *www.facebook.com/LOOSEBLUES44* Ⓜ *Cuauhtémoc.*

Mercado Insurgentes de Artesanías y Platería
MARKET | Also referred to as either Mercado Zona Rosa or Mercado Londres, this is the neighborhood's largest crafts market, featuring artistry from across Mexico, including jewelry, ceramics, and clothing. Vendors here can be intense, calling you to their stalls with promises of low prices (which you may or may not find). The market is an entire block deep, with entrances on both Londres and Liverpool. Most of the stalls sell silver and pewter, or crafts like serapes and ponchos, baskets, pottery, fossils, jade, obsidian, amber, and onyx. Expect to pay slightly higher prices here than at the Mercado Artesanal de la Ciudadela. Opposite the market's Londres entrance is Plaza del Angel, a small, upscale shopping mall, the halls of which are crowded by antiques vendors on weekends. ⊠ *Londres 154, between Florencia and Amberes, Juárez* ⊕ *Tlatelolco, Garibaldi-Lagunilla.*

Plaza del Angel
ANTIQUES & COLLECTIBLES | Shopping in the maze of antiques stores of Plaza del Angel is at its liveliest on Saturday. Combine a trip here with one to the Mercado Insurgentes, the crafts market across the way, for a full day of shopping. ⊠ *Between Londres and Hamburgo, opposite Mercado Insurgentes, Juárez* Ⓜ *Centro Médico.*

Somos Voces
BOOKS | This inclusive store prides itself on being a bookshop, cultural space, and café geared toward LGBTQ+ customers. Colorful and stocked with magazines, games, gifts, and a variety of books on sexuality, it gives way to a quiet coffee shop with excellent pastries. The space is ideal for working or meeting in small groups. Open mike nights, book club meetings, and drag shows make up the regular event listings. ⊠ *Calle Niza 23, La Zona Rosa* ☎ *55/5533–7116* ⊕ *www. somosvoces.com.mx* Ⓜ *Cuauhtémoc.*

Tienda INAH
SOUVENIRS | Next to the city's offices of the National Institute of Anthropology and History is a gift shop similar to what you'd find at the National Museum of Anthropology down the road. With ancestral Mexican handicrafts such as ceramics, weavings, and jewelry as well as books, magazines, and other media about Mexico's pre-Columbian past, it's a great spot to peruse if you don't have time to make it to the museum. ⊠ *Hamburgo 135, La Zona Rosa* ☎ *55/4166–0770* Ⓜ *Sevilla, Cuauhtémoc.*

SAN RAFAEL AND SANTA MARÍA LA RIBERA

Updated by
Megan Frye

⊙ Sights   🍴 Restaurants   🛏 Hotels   ◉ Shopping   🍸 Nightlife

★★☆☆☆   ★★★☆☆   ★★☆☆☆   ★★☆☆☆   ★★★☆☆

NEIGHBORHOOD SNAPSHOT

TOP EXPERIENCES

■ **An underground art scene.** Art-forward experiences such as galleries and communal art spaces occur seemingly out of nowhere; there's always something going on and it's mostly new and up-and-coming artists.

■ **Biblioteca Vasconcelos.** This massive library is one of the largest in Latin America, but books are just one part of the appeal here. There are plenty of events to keep culture aficionados happy, from book launches to concerts and plays.

■ **The Moorish Kiosk.** A beautiful North African–inspired gazebo is the protagonist of the central park in Santa María la Ribera. Kids and dogs run around the perimeter, while elderly couples meet up for salsa dancing in front of it multiple times per week. It's a true centerpiece of life.

■ **Theaters in San Rafael.** In the 1950s, as the population of Mexico City began to soar and it became more and more well-known on the world's cultural stage, San Rafael became the theater neighborhood. There are still about a dozen theaters of small and medium, private and community, in the colonia.

GETTING HERE

Just 3 km (just under 2 miles) from the western edge of Centro Histórico and bordering La Juárez neighborhood, these residential neighborhoods are great for experiencing the city's real life and also being close to the action. Uber fares from the airport or city center run about MP90–MP200, depending on traffic. The neighborhoods are also served by three subway lines (2, 8, and B). As they both border Insurgentes, the main north–south artery of the city, they also are well connected to the Metrobus line 1.

OFF THE BEATEN PATH

■ **El Chopo Cultural Market.** Originally started outside the Museo del Chopo, El Chopo Cultural Market is a *tianguis* (a Nahuatl, or Aztec, word for regularly occurring outdoor marketplaces) that has served as a counterculture gathering space for decades. Now located just outside the Buenavista train station on Saturday mornings, it's a favorite for those looking to peruse vinyl records, T-shirts, zines, and other similar items. Find it at the corner of Calle Juan Aldama and Calle Luna, behind the Buenavista train station in Colonia Buenavista, the neighboring colonia from Santa María la Ribera.⊠ *C. Juan Aldama, Buenavista, Metro Buenavista.*

PLANNING YOUR TIME

■ One could cross both Santa María la Ribera and San Rafael by foot in less than an hour (roughly 3 km [1½ miles]), starting along Jaime Torres Bodet in Santa María la Ribera, which connects to Miguel E. Schulz in San Rafael. Street parking is available in most places. While generally considered safe, it's a good idea to exercise caution in both neighborhoods if on an empty street at night.

Two of Mexico City's first official neighborhoods outside of Centro Histórico, San Rafael and Santa María la Ribera have been considered well-located residential areas since the late 19th century. These neighboring colonias in the Cuauhtémoc borough have some similarities, but there's much that changes when you cross the Avenida Ribera de San Cosme.

First off, Santa María la Ribera is a lot busier than San Rafael. There are more restaurants, a coffee shop on seemingly every corner, and a number of beloved cantinas, and its activity is largely based around the late 19th-century Moorish Revival gazebo. The neighborhood has had its ups-and-downs over the years, but during the day, you'll see more parents picking up their children from school and elderly locals going about their daily business. Perhaps slightly rough around the edges for some, Santa María la Ribera feels like a small pueblo surrounded by a very large city.

Just south of Santa María la Ribera and north of Cuauhtémoc, San Rafael is mostly residential, with wide sidewalks, a few very good restaurants, long-running taquerías, classy cantinas and chill cafés, and its most famous offering: theaters. It's notably quieter than Santa María la Ribera, but equally as well situated to exploring the city. San Rafael could be said to hide its secrets well: it's not flashy and there aren't as many young people or foreigners around (although with its relatively low rents that

will likely change soon). But for now, it remains a storied neighborhood, with a history focused primarily on its number of theaters that have been in operation since the 1950s; some, like Cine Opera, have closed down but are in the process of renovation—an apt metaphor for San Rafael as a whole.

⊙ Sights

★ Biblioteca Vasconcelos

LIBRARY | With nearly 600,000 books, magazines, and international newspapers, this is the largest library in Mexico. It covers more than 410,000 square feet, with rows of catwalks leading up to its six-story ceiling. Opened officially in 2006, the space is regarded as having some of the most unique architecture of any public building in the city. An auditorium regularly hosts concerts, lectures, and other cultural events. Computers are available for public use, as is Wi-Fi. The massive building, which also houses the graffitied skeleton of a gray whale, is surrounded by gardens boasting palm trees and moonflowers. ⊠ *Eje 1, Santa*

Did You Know?

Originally created as the Mexico Pavilion for the 1896 World Fair, the Kiosko Morisco, or the Moorish Kiosk, is built of stunning panels that can be disassembled and moved if needed.

María la Ribera ✢ *North corner of Aldama* ☎ *55/9157–2800* ⊕ *www.bibliotecavas-concelos.gob.mx* Ⓜ *Buenavista.*

Casa de Cultura San Rafael

ART GALLERY | This cultural space and art gallery was created to give community members a way to interact with local artists, take workshops and classes ranging from yoga to ceramics, and generally participate in San Rafael's burgeoning arts culture. ✉ *C. Jose Rosas Moreno 110, San Rafael* ☎ *55/5705–2219* 🎫 *Free* ⊘ *Closed Sun.* Ⓜ *San Cosme.*

Jardín del Arte Sullivan

CITY PARK | This very centrally located park that divides Cuauhtémoc from San Rafael is best known for its all-day artisan market on Sundays. This is an excellent spot to people-watch, eat local snacks, and pick up souvenirs of all kinds, from traditional handicrafts to hip clothes. The artists are primarily Mexican, and representative of all corners of the country. ✉ *Calz. Manuel Villalongín 46, San Rafael* ⊕ *jardindelarte.mx* 🎫 *Free* Ⓜ *Revolucion.*

★ Kiosko Morisco (*The Moorish Kiosk*)

NOTABLE BUILDING | **FAMILY** | Built by Mexican architect José Ramón Ibarrola, the Moorish Kiosk was meant to serve as the Mexico Pavilion at the 1884 World's Fair in New Orleans. It was relocated to Mexico in 1910 and placed where it now stands, as a proud symbol of Santa María la Ribera. Designed in the Moorish Revival architectural style known as neo-Mudejar, which was popular at the time in Spain, it is made of wrought iron and wood painted in blue, red, and gold, and is topped with a glass cupola dome. It sits in the principal plaza of the colonia, and draws photographers and lovers (it's not uncommon to see a modeling shoot going on or a couple in a deep embrace) as well as families. Its sheer size is enough to accommodate even occasional dance classes and events. ✉ *Kiosko Morisco de Santa María la Ribera, Santa María la Ribera* ✢ *Central park area of Santa María la Ribera* Ⓜ *Buenavista.*

Mercado la Dalia

MARKET | **FAMILY** | A classic Mexican market with labyrinth-like aisles, you'll find everything you could possible want for sale, from fresh produce to clothing and kitchenwares. Vendors are set up outside in front of the market, too. It's a great place to stop for a quick *comida corrida*, an affordable three-course midday meal, at any one of the market's stalls in the prepared food sections. This market is a little less hectic than others around the city, so it's worth checking out if crowds are not exactly your thing. ✉ *Calle Sabino 225, Santa María la Ribera* 🚇Ⓜ *Buenavista.*

Museo Experimental El Eco

ART GALLERY | This contemporary gallery space encourages the appreciation of diverse artistic languages, including modern art that fits within the building's unique parameters. Operated in alliance with the National Autonomous University of Mexico, it features national and international artists as well as performances and gatherings from cabaret to pop-up dinners and tastings. ✉ *C. James Sullivan 43, San Rafael* ☎ *55/5535–4351* ⊕ *eleco.unam.mx* 🎫 *Free* ⊘ *Closed Mon.* Ⓜ *San Cosme.*

Museo de Geología

SPECIALTY MUSEUM | Operated by the National Autonomous University of Mexico, the city's geology museum features multiple mammoth skulls and an entire hadrosaurid dinosaur fossil. Gems and minerals from around the world, but mostly Mexico, adorn impeccably preserved antique glass and wooden showcases. The large and expertly polished pieces of selenite from northern Mexico are particularly impressive, as is the architecture of the building itself, built in 1906. The beautiful colonial building enjoys a privileged location overlooking Santa María la Ribera's central park. ✉ *Jaime Torres Bodet 176, Santa María la Ribera* ☎ *55/5547–3948* ⊕ *www.*

geologia.unam.mx/igl/museo 🎟 *MP30* 🕒 *Closed Mon.* [M] *Buenavista.*

★ Museo Universitario del Chopo
ARTS CENTER | This 603,000-square foot contemporary art space features several galleries of mostly Mexican visual and video artists, an auditorium for concerts, readings, and lectures, and a large rotating gallery space that features performance art. Operated by the National Autonomous University of Mexico, El Chopo is known for representing, honoring, and celebrating vast elements of contemporary culture and subcultures of Mexican society. ✉ *Calle Dr. Enrique Gonzalez Martinez 10, Santa María la Ribera* ☎ *55/5546–3471* 🌐 *www.chopo.unam.mx* 🎟 *MP40* 🕒 *Closed Mon. and Tues.* [M] *Revolucón.*

🍴 Restaurants

★ Cantina Salón París
$$ | **MEXICAN** | A large cantina with a sizeable lunch and dinner crowd, Salon París is an emblematic fixture of the neighborhood. A focused menu features Mexican bar food (think tortas, shrimp soup, and steaks) and varied liquor options (specifically Mexican beer, international rums, tequilas, and digestive liqueurs like Campari and Fernet). **Known for:** chamorro (braised pork shanks) on Thursday; tlacoyos (traditional corn masa stuffed with beans or cheese, cooked on a grill, topped with cheese and salsa); live music and soccer games on the television. [$] *Average main: MP200* ✉ *Jaime Torres Bodet 152, Santa María la Ribera* ☎ *55/5541–7319* 💳 *No credit cards* [M] *Buenavista.*

Chicago Bernie's Beef Bike
$$ | **BURGER** | **FAMILY** | This peculiar restaurant name (for this latitude) is thanks to the Midwestern owner who started making delicious burgers on a cart from the back of his bike. These gratuitous-in-every-way burgers quickly became well-recognized across the city and its San Rafael location has become one of the busiest restaurants in the neighborhood. **Known for:** gluttonous burgers; wide variety of beer; fast, friendly service. [$] *Average main: MP275* ✉ *Ignacio Manuel Altamirano 86, San Rafael* ☎ *55/7204–7184* 🌐 *www.instagram.com/chicagobernies* [M] *San Cosme.*

Cochinita Power
$$ | **MEXICAN** | It's not hyperbole to say that there are few interiors in the city as pink as the decor within this diner just near the San Cosme metro station. Cochinita Power specializes in Yucatecan food (read: pork and habanero salsas) with a set-up somewhere between a food cart and a restaurant, but without the hustle and bustle of standing and eating on the street. **Known for:** tasty and cheap pork-focused dishes from the Yucatan; guanabana juice; habanero pickled onions. [$] *Average main: MP150* ✉ *Ignacio Manuel Altamirano 19, San Rafael* ☎ *55/7589–6676* 🌐 *www.facebook.com/cochinitapowermx* 💳 *No credit cards* [M] *San Cosme.*

★ Coyota
$$ | **MEXICAN** | Working only with ancestral Mexican ingredients and with a focus on local products and traditional fermentation processes, the dishes at Coyota are some of the most accessible and exciting in the city. Everything served here is Mexican in origin, including beverages that run the gamut from the expected (mezcal and beer) to the less common including local ciders and kombucha. **Known for:** fun, relaxed environment; cool bar vibe; truly authentic dining experience with all Mexican ingredients. [$] *Average main: MP300* ✉ *Jardín Mascarones, Santa María la Ribera* ☎ *55/2524–0426* 🌐 *www.instagram.com/coyota_mx* 🕒 *Closed Mon.–Wed.* [M] *San Cosme.*

El Comedor de San Pascual Bailongo
$$ | **MEDITERRANEAN** | This intimate but elegant (for the neighborhood) diner has small tables in a quiet space with a reclaimed feel and appropriately

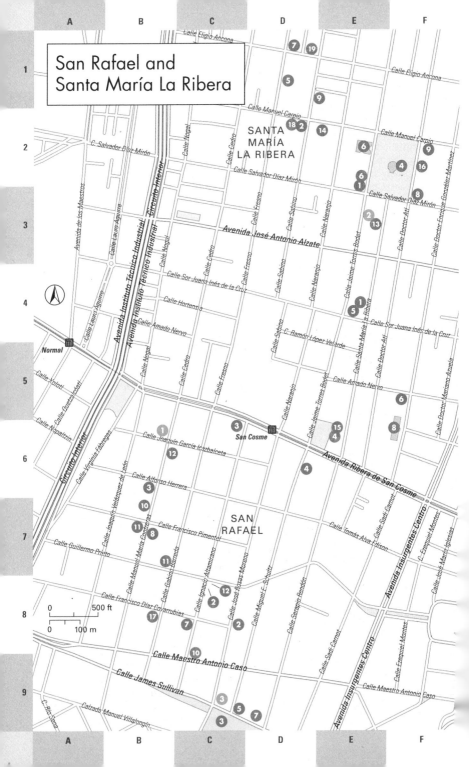

San Rafael and Santa María La Ribera

SANTA MARÍA LA RIBERA

SAN RAFAEL

Normal

San Cosme

Calle Eligio Ancona
Calle Eligio Ancona
Calle Manuel Carpio
Calle Manuel Carpio
C. Salvador Díaz Mirón
Calle Salvador Díaz Mirón
Calle Salvador Díaz Mirón
Avenida José Antonio Alzate
Calle Sor Juana Inés de la Cruz
Calle Sor Juana Inés de la Cruz
Calle Hortensia
Calle Amado Nervo
C. Ramón López Velarde
Calle Amado Nervo
Avenida Ribera de San Cosme
Calle Joaquín García Icazbalceta
Calle Alfonso Herrera
Calle Francisco Pimentel
Calle Tomás Alva Edison
Calle Guillermo Prieto
Calle Francisco Díaz Covarrubias
Calle Maestro Antonio Caso
Calle James Sullivan
Calzada Manuel Villalongín

Avenida de los Maestros
Avenida Instituto Técnico Industrial
Circuito Interior
Circuito Interior
Calle Lauro Aguirre
Calle Nogal
Calle Cedro
Calle Fresno
Calle Sabino
Calle Naranjo
Calle Jaime Torres Bodet
Calle Santa María La Ribera
Calle Doctor Atl
Calle Doctor Enrique González Martínez
Calle Doctor Mariano Azuela
Avenida Insurgentes Centro
Calle Sadi Carnot
C. Ezequiel Montes
C. José María Iglesias
Calle Miguel E. Schultz
Calle José Rosas Moreno
Calle Ignacio Altamirano
Calle Gabino Barreda
Calle Manuel María Contreras
Calle Joaquín Velázquez de León
Calle Virginia Fábregas
C. Río Sena
Calle Xólotl
Calle Chalchitl
Calle Nagalzotzin
Calle Serapio Rendón
Calle Ezequiel Montes
Calle Maestro Antonio Caso

0   500 ft
0   100 m

KEY

- 1 Sights
- 1 Restaurants
- 1 Quick Bites
- 1 Hotels
- ℹ Visitor Information

Sights ▼

1 Biblioteca
  Vasconcelos **H3**
2 Casa de Cultura
  San Rafael **C8**
3 Jardín de Arte
  Sullivan **C9**
4 Kiosko Morisco **F2**
5 Mercado la Dalia **D1**
6 Museo de
  Geología **E2**
7 Museo Experimental
  El Eco.................... **D9**
8 Museo Universitario del
  Chopo **F6**

Restaurants ▼

1 Cantina Salón París **E3**
2 Chicago Bernie's
  Beef Bike **C8**
3 Cochinita Power **C6**
4 Coyota..................... **E6**
5 El Comedor de
  San Pascual Bailongo... **E4**
6 El Corral del Chivo **E2**
7 El Guapo Grill............ **D1**
8 Kolobok **F3**
9 La Oveja Negra **D1**
10 La Periquita Tacos
   Arabes **C9**
11 La Santa **B7**
12 La Tía **B6**
13 María Ciento 38 .... **E3**
14 Mercado Morisco **E2**
15 Naan **E6**
16 OaxacAquí................ **F2**
17 Pakaa **B8**
18 Pollos Ray **D2**
19 Tencüi................... **D1**

Quick Bites ▼

1 Alebrije................... **E4**
2 Bello Café................ **D2**
3 Benigna.................. **B6**
4 Camino a Comala **D6**
5 Esquina Barragán **C9**
6 Estanquillo El 32......... **F5**
7 Finca Don Porfirio
  Cafetería II **C8**
8 La Vaca de
  Muchos Colores **B7**
9 MojiGato Café............ **F2**
10 Panadería 220........... **B7**
11 Tacos El Güero **B7**
12 Vendaval
   Cooperativa **C8**

Hotels ▼

1 El Patio 77 .... **B6**
2 Hotel Casa de Nina **E3**
3 Hotel Stella Maris **C9**

6

San Rafael and Santa María la Ribera

minimalist decor. With juicy burgers, salmon carpaccio, and crunchy thin-crust pizza, the menu caters to a wide audience. **Known for:** fried barbacoa tacos; house-made craft beer; great tapas, including an excellent eggplant Parmesan. [$] *Average main: MP300* ✉ *Calle Sor Juana Ines de la Cruz 67, Santa María la Ribera* ☎ *55/2630–2227* 💳 *No credit cards* 🕓 *Closed Mon.* [M] *Buenavista.*

El Corral del Chivo

$$ | **MEXICAN** | **FAMILY** | A beloved family spot with indoor and outdoor seating overlooking Santa María la Ribera's main park, you can smell the *birria* (goat meat) from a block away. The service is quick and the menu is not entirely varied, but its specialties have kept people coming for years. **Known for:** excellent birria tacos; grilled meats and vegetables; great pozole, traditional Mexican stew. [$] *Average main: MP200* ✉ *Jaime Torres Bodet 152, Santa María la Ribera* ☎ *55/5547–5609* 💳 *No credit cards* [M] *Buenavista.*

★ **El Guapo Grill**

$$ | **ARGENTINE** | Mexico City is arguably the capital of all Latin America, and for that reason you'll see plenty of restaurants from immigrants of the region, especially South America. El Guapo Grill is Argentine to the max, so expect lots of meat and red wine. **Known for:** slightly upscale Argentine steak house; delicious choripan (chorizo sandwich); authentic jugo de carne. [$] *Average main: MP300* ✉ *Calle Eligio Ancona 207, Santa María la Ribera* ☎ *55/6718–7771* 🌐 *www.facebook.com/Guapogrill* 🕓 *Closed Mon.* [M] *Buenavista.*

Kolobok

$$ | **RUSSIAN** | One of few Russian restaurants in the city, Kolobok showcases cuisine from Russian immigrants who came to Mexico after various Eastern European diasporas. A small space featuring just 10 wooden tables, the decor is homey with Russian music playing and murals depicting the Russian countryside, and the food is as authentic as it gets in Mexico. **Known for:** traditional Russian dishes like meat-stuffed cabbage rolls; a mean borscht; Baltika Russian beer. [$] *Average main: MP300* ✉ *Calle Salvador Díaz Mirón 87, Santa María la Ribera* ☎ *55/5541–7085* 🌐 *www.kolobok.com.mx* 💳 *No credit cards* [M] *Buenavista.*

★ **La Oveja Negra**

$$ | **MEXICAN** | **FAMILY** | Busy and stylish, this is a popular classic in the Santa María la Ribera neighborhood, located in an older building that has retained its original high ceilings and tile work. Known for having slightly higher prices than usual for the area, it's also recognized for excellent service, taste, and variety of traditional Mexican dishes, but the star is the barbacoa (slow-roasted sheep meat) and pulque. **Known for:** plato oveja (goat cheese, chorizo, and chicharrón); waits on weekends; traditional Mexican cocktails. [$] *Average main: MP250* ✉ *Calle Sabino 225, Santa María la Ribera* ☎ *55/5643–4781* 💳 *No credit cards* 🕓 *Closed Mon.–Thurs.* [M] *Buenavista.*

La Periquita Tacos Arabes

$ | **MEXICAN** | A popular lunch spot on a bustling corner of San Rafael, the *tacos arabes* (Arabic tacos) are always a delight here. With the pork cooked on a spit yelling distance from your table and pita bread replacing tortillas, it's a local and long-standing favorite of the neighborhood. **Known for:** late night eats; al pastor tacos; gigantic tortas. [$] *Average main: MP100* ✉ *Calle Maestro Antonio Caso 125, San Rafael* ☎ *55/5546–0456* [M] *San Cosme.*

La Santa

$ | **PIZZA** | **FAMILY** | This tiny pizzeria has more space on its sidewalk than its interior, which is mostly a kitchen that prepares thin-crust Argentine style pizzas, empanadas, and salads. The service is attentive and the prices are low. **Known for:** tasty empanadas; affordable gourmet pizzas; occasional wait for a table. [$] *Average main: MP200* ✉ *C. Gabino Barreda 83, San Rafael* ☎ *55/7098–5275* 🌐 *www.*

lasantapizza.com.mx/en-us ⊘ *Closed Mon.* Ⓜ *San Cosme.*

La Tía

$ | **MEXICAN** | **FAMILY** | In the residential neighborhood of San Rafael, La Tía is clearly a local favorite. Even with dozens of tables, it still doesn't match the demands of locals who crave the taste of homemade cooking and Mexican specialties such as *chile en nogada* (poblano chiles stuffed with picadillo) in August and September and less common cuisine for Mexico, such as mozzarella-and-spinach stuffed chicken breasts. **Known for:** always changing daily specials; quick service; weekday lunch crowds. Ⓢ *Average main: MP85* ⊠ *Manuel María Contreras 20, San Rafael* ☏ *55/5546–0157* ⊕ *www.facebook.com/LaTiaRestaurante* ⊟ *No credit cards* Ⓜ *San Cosme.*

★ María Ciento 38

$ | **SICILIAN** | Romantic and tucked away, María Ciento 38 is perhaps the most upscale eatery in the neighborhood. The authentic Sicilian cuisine is homemade and prepared fresh daily, which means the limited seats are in high demand and reservations are recommended. **Known for:** great weekend brunch; Sicilian-style pizzas; excellent wine selection. Ⓢ *Average main: MP150* ⊠ *Santa María La Ribera 138, Santa María la Ribera* ☏ *55/7159–2039* ⊕ *mariaciento38.com* Ⓜ *Buenavista.*

Mercado Morisco

$$ | **INTERNATIONAL** | This hip space is a communal eatery featuring six stalls with neon signs advertising everything from pulque (lightly alcoholic fermented agave nectar) to seafood tacos and Colombian arepas. Nestled among tortillerías, hardware stores, and apartments, it's easy to walk past it unless you happen to glance inward to spot the brightly decorated market and its picnic table–esque seating. **Known for:** wide variety of foods; pet-friendly location; hipster atmosphere. Ⓢ *Average main: MP150* ⊠ *Manuel Carpio 144, Santa María la Ribera*

☏ *55/8190–9600* ⊕ *www.facebook.com/morisco.mercado* Ⓜ *Buenavista.*

Naan

$ | **ASIAN FUSION** | One of the first purely vegan options in the area, this hidden spot serves more South Asian fusion rather than the traditional Indian fare that's advertised. Still, it's a great option for vegans, with very affordable prices, a lively color scheme featuring brightly painted peach and turquoise walls, and five white tables alongside the kitchen. **Known for:** vegan lassis; samosas with mango chutney; spinach croquets in tomato sauce. Ⓢ *Average main: MP120* ⊠ *Santa María La Ribera 12, Santa María la Ribera* ✛ *Enter through Jardín Mascarones Park* ☏ *55/6380–6168* ⊕ *www.naanmx.com* ⊟ *No credit cards* ⊘ *Closed Sun.* Ⓜ *San Cosme.*

OaxacAquí

$$ | **MEXICAN** | **FAMILY** | If you've been dreaming about Oaxacan cuisine, but don't have the time to travel there, this authentic restaurant that serves up breakfast, lunch, and early dinners is the next best thing. Service can be a bit chaotic but always friendly, and the quality of the food makes up for any wait. **Known for:** horchata with fresh melon and walnuts; red and black moles; great tlayuda, a traditional Oaxacan dish. Ⓢ *Average main: MP150* ⊠ *Dr. Atl 207, Santa María la Ribera* ☏ *55/4150–7187* ⊟ *No credit cards* ⊘ *No dinner* Ⓜ *Buenavista.*

Pakaa

$$ | **PORTUGUESE** | A charming little place perfect for lunch or early dinner, Pakaa specializes in Portuguese cuisine, though, of course, it's not uncommon to find a serrano pepper and some salsas on the table (this is Mexico after all). With a bright and welcoming atmosphere inside, it also has outdoor seating along a relaxed stretch of San Rafael. **Known for:** delicious octopus and mussel dishes; nice sangria and wine lists; Portuguese bitoque. Ⓢ *Average main: MP150* ⊠ *Calle de Francisco Díaz Covarrubias 36–B,*

San Rafael ☎ *55/3783–7755* ⊕ *pakaares-taurante.wixsite.com/jantaresreservas* ⊗ *Closed Sun.* Ⓜ *San Cosme.*

Pollos Ray

$$ | **MEXICAN** | **FAMILY** | One thing you can always count on in Mexico City, and Mexico for that matter, is excellent roasted chicken. While popular with locals, the dish is often overlooked by foreigners in favor of flashy tacos, but you should visit this small, sidewalk eatery and try its delicious marinated chicken; there are also grilled vegetables and salsas to make your own tacos. **Known for:** local favorite; affordable chicken dishes; variety of salsas. $ *Average main: MP150* ✉ *Manuel Carpio 158, Santa María la Ribera* ☎ *55/8681–6535* ⊕ *www.pollosray.com* Ⓜ *San Cosme.*

★ Tencüi

$$ | **MEXICAN** | One of the hottest restaurants in the city, this spot serves gourmet touches on Mexican classics with playful inventiveness and traditional ingredients. The base of all plates here, most of which are vegetarian, is mushrooms; even the drinks and the desserts have a fungi element to them. **Known for:** experimental Mexican vegetarian cuisine; fungi-lovers paradise; unique cocktails. $ *Average main: MP300* ✉ *Eligio Ancona 191, San Rafael* ☎ *55/1033–2167* ⊕ *www.instagram.com/tencui.mx* ⊗ *Closed Mon.* Ⓜ *San Cosme, Buenavista.*

☕ Coffee and Quick Bites

★ Alebrije

$$ | **INTERNATIONAL** | Located in a renovated garage, Alebrije is loaded with plants, couches, and tables, good for working or chatting during the day and an ideal date spot in the evening. String lights and antique fixtures provide warm-toned light, dancing off the exposed brick as you eat sandwiches and drink hot chocolate, wine, or beer. **Known for:** bagels (hard to find in Mexico City!); eggplant and goat cheese chapatas;

molletes (open-faced Mexican sandwiches). $ *Average main: MP150* ✉ *Santa María La Ribera 84, Santa María la Ribera* ☎ *55/2630–2972* ⊕ *www.facebook.com/AlebrijeArteYCultura* ⊗ *Closed Sun.* Ⓜ *Buenavista.*

Bello Café

$ | **CAFÉ** | Just around the corner from the famed Moorish Kiosk, this open-air coffee and tea spot also specializes in fresh pastries. Specializing in Mexican coffee, it's also a place to go and buy a bottle of mezcal, cacao, local honey, and even artisanal Mexican beers. **Known for:** bright, friendly atmosphere; 10 different ways to brew your coffee; cocktails with coffee, mezcal, and coffee-brewed beer. $ *Average main: MP50* ✉ *Manuel Carpio 158, Santa María la Ribera* ☎ *55/4757–6046* ⊕ *www.facebook.com/BelloCoffee* ⊟ *No credit cards* Ⓜ *Buenavista.*

Benigna

$$ | **SPANISH** | This open-air locale charms with its curated selection of wines and vermouths along with delicious mocktails and coffee drinks. With a small menu of tapas-inspired snacks, it is a nice place to hang out solo for a while or meet up with friends. **Known for:** unique wines; local artwork for sale; delicious tapas. $ *Average main: MP200* ✉ *Manuel María Contreras 35, San Rafael* ☎ *55/704–7245* ⊕ *www.facebook.com/Benigna.mx* ⊗ *No dinner Sun.* Ⓜ *San Cosme.*

★ Camino a Comala

$ | **CAFÉ** | Just a block from the busy Avenida Ribera de San Cosme, this quiet and elegantly designed hideaway offers respite from the crowds of nearby Metro San Cosme. Decorated with antiques and smelling of freshly roasted coffee, it's the kind of place where you can disappear for a quiet afternoon of reading or a nice meal alone or with a travel companion. **Known for:** house-made bread and pastries, baked fresh daily; plant-based breakfasts; hand-tossed pizzas. $ *Average main: MP50* ✉ *Miguel E. Schultz 7, San Rafael* ☎ *55/5592–0313* ⊕ *www.*

caminoacomala.com Ⓜ *San Cosme, Revolución.*

★ Esquina Barragán

$$ | **CAFÉ** | Black-and-white tiles give this bright space an impeccably clean and welcoming vibe. With its own house mezcal, wines, and beers, it can also be a place to gather for a drink or grab a light dinner. **Known for:** house-made pastries; excellent molletes and vegetarian chilaquiles; views of the Jardín de Arte. $ *Average main: MP150* ⊠ *Miguel Schultz 146, San Rafael* ☎ *55/7651–9605* ⊕ *www.instagram.com/esquina_barragan_bistro* ⊟ *No credit cards* ⊘ *Closed Mon.* Ⓜ *Revolución.*

★ Estanquillo El 32

$ | **MEXICAN FUSION** | This is a place where the neighborhood elders gather during the day to eat their tamales and drink their coffee, but where you'll find mostly young, artist types in the evenings. With a wide variety of Mexican artisanal beers and an impressive stock of unique mezcals as well as Mexican coffee, the space is open to the street, like a former garage, and has a couple very well-behaved house dogs keeping everything in check. **Known for:** paté de conejo (rabbit paté) with herbs and tomato on rye bread; tamal de huitlacoche (corn fungus, a delicacy); relaxed atmosphere with books and magazines to browse. $ *Average main: MP100* ⊠ *Calle Dr. Enrique Gonzalez Martinez 32, Santa María la Ribera* ☎ *55/5535–2310* ⊕ *www.facebook.com/EstanquilloEl32* ⊟ *No credit cards* ⊘ *Closed Sun.–Tues.* Ⓜ *Revolución.*

Finca Don Porfirio Cafetería II

$ | **MEXICAN** | **FAMILY** | This charming colonial-era café is open to the street, with regulars, families, and digital nomads regularly making appearances. It's bustling, maybe a bit too bustling for some folks to focus on work, but the price-to-quality ratio is impressive, as is its selection of Mexican-style hot chocolate, which range from spicy to sweet to bitter. **Known for:** variety of gourmet hot chocolates;

delicous pastries and Mexican breakfasts; setting on a beautiful tree-lined street. $ *Average main: MP50* ⊠ *Ignacio Manuel Altamirano 107, San Rafael* ☎ *55/5332–5962* Ⓜ *San Cosme.*

La Vaca de Muchos Colores

$ | **INTERNATIONAL** | This is a small and comfy spot to stop in and grab a bite to eat or enjoy a beer, wine, or coffee. It feels immediately like a good friend's (stylish) living room and is ideal for catching up with companions or coming in alone with a book. **Known for:** grasshopper and goat cheese chapatas; tasty frappuccinos; good Mexican beer menu. $ *Average main: MP100* ⊠ *Manuel María Contreras 52, San Rafael* ☎ *55/5535–0233* ⊟ *No credit cards* ⊘ *Closed Sun.* Ⓜ *San Cosme.*

MojiGato Café

$ | **CAFÉ** | A darling nook ideal for cat lovers, couches and cushions make for comfortable seating in a small, quiet space. You might have to duck your head to get in, but it serves as an espresso, tea, and coffee shop as well as a gift shop for all things cat-related. **Known for:** delicious, fresh croissants; adorable and affordable cat memorabilia; board games to play while you eat and drink (some of which are cat-theme). $ *Average main: MP35* ⊠ *Manuel Carpio 92, Santa María la Ribera* ☎ *55/5547–9993* ⊕ *www.facebook.com/MojiGatoCafe* ⊟ *No credit cards* Ⓜ *Buenavista.*

★ Panadería 220

$ | **BAKERY** | Designed as a walk-up and take-out café, this locale is adored for its divine pastries. Despite its small space, the number of delicious beverages and baked goods they prepare is as impressive as they are delicious. **Known for:** guava bread (a pastry stuffed with marmalade); very small space with limited seating; tasty espressos or Americanos to go. $ *Average main: MP50* ⊠ *Manuel María Contreras 45, San Rafael* ☎ *55/5161–8623* ⊕ *www.instagram.com/panaderia220* ⊘ *Closed Mon.* Ⓜ *San Cosme.*

A Tale of Two Neighborhoods

Two of the first "suburbs" of Mexico City's center, both Santa María la Ribera and San Rafael faced disrepair and neglect in the late 1980s, some argue as a result of the deadly 1985 earthquake, which damaged a lot of the central area of the city and left people looking for more stable ground in other parts of the capital. Crime took over, especially in Santa María la Ribera. But one stroll down the streets of these neighborhoods today and it's clear they have since cleaned up their acts: Santa María la Ribera in particular has become a bohemian gathering space for those looking to escape the rising rents and high activity zones of more gentrified parts of the city.

The richness of San Rafael and Santa María la Ribera can be seen in the diversity and excellence of their architecture. Although less popular with visitors today, the building of these neighborhoods was clearly no afterthought. At once reflecting the city's Porfiriato architecture phase (referring to the dictatorship of Porfirio Díaz during the late 19th and early 20th centuries in which anything considered "European" was encouraged) and the folklore present in many of Mexico's most enchanting villages, it is not uncommon to see Baroque, European Gothic, Renaissance, and art deco buildings here side-by-side. Walking the calm streets of these neighborhoods is the best way to take in their architectural treasures.

★ Tacos El Güero

$ | **MEXICAN** | Although its name is barely visible on the sun-faded awnings, this neighborhood taquería is busy on most nights. It's a true local's spot and its bright lights are visible from the street; you'll know it from the number of people mostly patiently waiting to place their orders (food is available to go as well). **Known for:** excellent al pastor tacos; busy crowds and long lines on weekends; other Mexican favorites like suadero tortas and gringas. [$] *Average main: MP40* ✉ *Manuel María Contreras 59, San Rafael* ☎ 💳 *No credit cards* [M] *San Cosme.*

★ Vendaval Cooperativa

$ | **BAKERY** | An anticapitalist communal space, bakery, and kitchen, this feminist cooperative has been serving handmade goods since 2017, in resistance to unhealthy working situations and overarching franchises without a soul. Their homemade breads use a unique fermentation process, and they also sell sweets, snacks, coffee, and tea. **Known for:** excellent sourdough bread; regularly hosting feminist workshops; welcoming gathering space. [$] *Average main: MP50* ✉ *Guillermo Prieto 46, San Rafael* ☎ *55/1154–2667* 🌐 *www.instagram.com/vendavalcooperativa* 🕒 *No dinner Sun.* [M] *San Cosme.*

Hotels

★ El Patio 77

$$ | **B&B/INN** | This boutique hotel is tucked into quiet, residential San Rafael, but is still well-located for exploring the city's central neighborhoods. **Pros:** impressive remodeled space; simultaneously cozy and hip; about as eco-friendly as a city hotel can get. **Cons:** introverts might be overwhelmed by socializing in common areas; some street noise since it's close to a main road; water pressure in this neighborhood is not the best. [$] *Rooms from: MP2300* ✉ *Joaquin Garcia Icazbalceta 77, San Rafael*

Operated by the National Autonomous University of Mexico, El Chopo is one of Mexico City's most treasured cultural centers.

☎ 55/5592–8452 🌐 www.elpatio77.com 🛏 8 rooms 🍴 Free Breakfast [M] San Cosme.

★ Hotel Casa de Nina

$ | B&B/INN | This boutique hotel takes sustainability seriously and makes guests feel at home on one of the quiet and quaint streets of Santa María la Ribera, not even a block from the colonia's central park. **Pros:** complimentary gym use and breakfast; perfect for exploring Santa María la Ribera; stunning, charming space with beautiful rooftop garden. **Cons:** no on-site parking; potential for street noise; some rooms have very little natural light. *[$] Rooms from: MP1650 ✉ Jaime Torres Bodet 139, Santa María la Ribera ☎ 55/4176–3924 🌐 www.hotelcasanina.com 🛏 8 rooms 🍴 Free Breakfast [M] San Cosme.*

Hotel Stella Maris

$ | HOTEL | FAMILY | This clean and comfortable hotel comes with all the expected amenities as well as a rooftop pool and terrace that offers an excellent view of the Reforma Avenue skyscraper district. **Pros:** great location for exploring; awesome rooftop pool; good on-site restaurant. **Cons:** along a loud and busy main road; not particularly unique or exciting in terms of design; frequent complaints about Wi-Fi. *[$] Rooms from: MP1400 ✉ C. James Sullivan 69, San Rafael ☎ 55/5566–6088 🌐 sites.google.com/view/hotel-stella-maris 🛏 114 rooms 🍴 No Meals [M] San Cosme.*

🍸 Nightlife

Don Fer's

LIVE MUSIC | More of a bar than a restaurant, it effectively functions as both. With live music on the weekends, it also has an open dance floor and a karaoke hall, depending on the night. The crowd is mostly locals and regulars, but it has a welcoming vibe to strangers as well. If you're hungry, try the flautas, beer specials, and *tacos de cochinita* (seasoned pork). *✉ Calle Sabino 245, Santa María la Ribera ☎ 55/6363–2507 [M] Buenavista.*

138

La Malquerida

BARS | Specializing in pulque, this is a traditional Mexico City type of pulquería. There's no bells or whistles here, just a nice variety of pulques (natural and flavored) to sample alongside other cocktails and beer. Its swinging doors open to a modest space, a clear locals' favorite. ✉ *Jaime Torres Bodet 117, Santa María la Ribera* ☎ *55/1270–4119* Ⓜ *Buenavista.*

★ La Polar

GATHERING PLACE | **FAMILY** | This lively cantina is known for its barriga and mariachi performances as well as roving Norteño and cumbia bands that perform in the massive, two-story space under blinding lights. Since opening in 1934, La Polar has earned its status as a tradition in the San Rafael area and as one of the most beloved gathering spaces in the whole city. ✉ *Calle Guillermo Prieto 129, San Rafael* ☎ *55/5546–5066* Ⓜ *San Cosme, Normal.*

★ Mad Chela

BREWPUBS | This craft beer bar represents Mexico's burgeoning artisanal brew culture in a relaxed and fun atmosphere. In the country that gave you Corona and Bohemia, a more sophisticated beer culture is growing slowly but surely, especially in recent years. Check out this tiny little spot where you can find beer from all over the world, including several from Mexico. ✉ *Santa María La Ribera 136 A, Santa María la Ribera* ☎ ⊕ *www.instagram.com/madchela* Ⓜ *Buenavista.*

 Performing Arts

Teatro San Rafael

THEATER | From cabarets and comedies to dramas and monologues, Teatro San Rafael (part of the greater Teatro Manolo Fabregas theater company) is one of the most beloved spots in the city to catch local talent onstage. An intimate theater space, it also offers acting classes and a variety of shows each weekend, and some during the week. ✉ *Virginia Fábregas No. 40, Santa María la Ribera* ☎ *55/5592–2142* ⊕ *carteleradeteatro.mx/teatro/centro/teatro-san-rafael* Ⓜ *San Cosme.*

Shopping

Tienda Orgánica

GENERAL STORE | Although its size and appearance is the same as most small corner stores in the city, Tienda Orgánica specializes in organic and local foods such as kombucha, coffee, dairy products, and even local tobacco rolled with medicinal flowers. It's a good spot to shop for delicious gifts to take home or, if you're staying a while, to do some quality grocery shopping. ✉ *José Antonio Alzate 46–B* ☎ *55/3983–3703* ⊕ *www.facebook.com/organica.stamarialaribera* Ⓜ *Buenavista.*

Chapter 7

POLANCO AND BOSQUE DE CHAPULTEPEC

Updated by
Roshida Dowe

● Sights   🍴 Restaurants   🛏 Hotels   ● Shopping   🍸 Nightlife

★★★★☆   ★★★★★   ★★★★☆   ★★★★☆   ★★★☆☆

NEIGHBORHOOD SNAPSHOT

TOP EXPERIENCES

■ **History lessons.** The most visited museum in the entire country, Museo Nacional de Antropología offers a deep dive into the entire history of Mexico.

■ **Upscale shopping.** Known as the Beverly Hills of Mexico, Avenida Presidente Masaryk is a trendy shopping location full of designer stores.

■ **Live music.** A staple for big shows, Auditorio Nacional is a great place to watch concerts.

■ **CDMX's biggest park.** With 1,600 acres, Bosque de Chapultepec is home to some stunning green spaces, several museums, and Castillo de Chapultepec, one of only two royal palaces in North America.

■ **Modern art.** One of several art museums in Bosque de Chapultepec, Museo de Arte Modern is a beautiful place to spend an afternoon exploring.

■ **Stunning architecture.** Grand colonial mansions grace many of Polanco's leafy side streets while Museo Soumaya Plaza Carso's silver cloudlike exterior is one of CMDX's most memorable buildings.

OFF THE BEATEN PATH

■ Bosque de Chapultepec is divided into three sections from east to west, with most of the park's attractions concentrated in the first, easternmost section. However, if you're looking for solitude or to enjoy some of the park's lesser-known wonders, consider stopping by the second section in the center of the park. This part is pet-friendly and home to the Papalote Museo del Niño, a great science, technology, and art museum for kids. At the Museo Jardín del Agua, a tribute to the city's water system, you can see murals and an impressive fountain created by Diego Rivera.

GETTING HERE

Polanco is notoriously hard to reach by public transport, with only one Metro stop serving the central section of the neighborhood (Auditorio Metro station and the Campo Marte Metrobus station also offer some coverage on its southern border). Ride-share apps like Uber and Didi will likely be an easier choice, although many attractions can be reached on foot from Metro Polanco. For shorter distances, there are Ecobici stations nearby. Bosque de Chapultepec is similarly tricky to navigate, with three Metro stations dotted around its border. Get off at Metro Chapultepec for the castle and the Museo de Arte Moderno and the Auditorio station for the Museo Nacional de Antropología and Museo Tamayo.

PLANNING YOUR TIME

■ From high-end shopping on Avenida Masaryk to the sprawling Bosque de Chapultepec just south of it, you're more likely to run out of time than to run out of things to do in Polanco. Sunday is the busiest day in the neighborhood, so avoid popular places that might have a long line. Many restaurants are closed on Monday, so work that into your plan as well.

A neighborhood known primarily for its high-rise business hotels and fine-dining restaurants, Polanco offers a central location in the city along with a few key sights like the stupendous main branch of the Museo Soumaya. The area developed as an escape from the crowded city center for Mexico City's upper-middle class in the mid-20th century, rapidly urbanizing in the aftermath of the 1985 earthquake. Today, real estate in Polanco is some of the most expensive in the city.

Polanco's main thoroughfare, Avenida Presidente Masaryk, is lined with upscale stores including Louis Vuitton, Gucci, and Tiffany & Co., as well as boutiques stocking local labels. In between Avenida Masaryk and Parque Lincoln, the Polanquito district is packed with restaurants and cafés. To the south, Polanco is bordered by Bosque de Chapultepec, named for the *chapulines* (grasshoppers) that populated it long ago. Chapultepec is the city's largest park, and home to a castle, a lake, and five world-renowned museums.

You can easily spend an hour at each Bosque de Chapultepec museum, with the exception of the Museo Nacional de Antropología, which is huge compared to its sister institutions. There you can have a quick go-through in two hours, but to appreciate the fine exhibits, a full day is more appropriate. Tuesday through Friday are good days to visit the museums and stroll around the park. On Sunday and Mexican holidays, they're often packed with families, and if you get to the Museo Nacional de Antropología after 10 am on a Sunday, you can expect to spend considerable time waiting to enter. If you have time to visit only one of Bosque de Chapultepec's museums, make it the Museo Nacional de Antropología.

Bosque de Chapultepec and Paseo de la Reforma

 Sights

★ **Bosque de Chapultepec**
CITY PARK | This 1,600-acre green space, literally translated as Chapultepec Forest, draws hordes of families on weekend

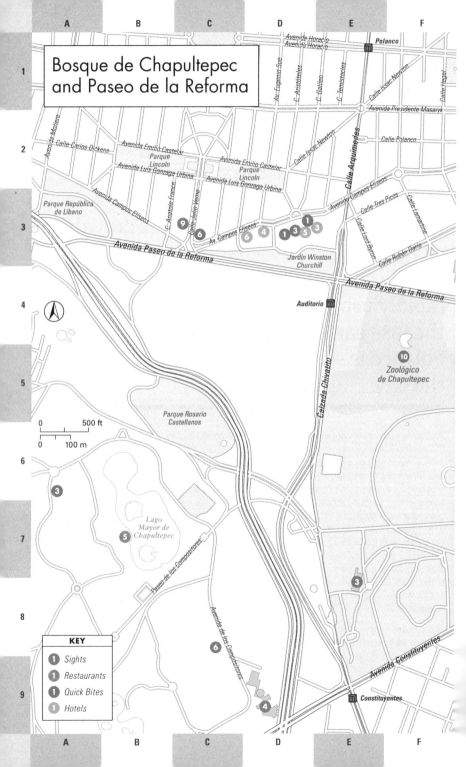

Bosque de Chapultepec and Paseo de la Reforma

KEY

- ① Sights
- ① Restaurants
- ① Quick Bites
- ① Hotels

Sights ▼

1 Bosque de Chapultepec **G6**
2 Castillo de Chapultepec............ **I6**
3 Complejo Cultural de los Pinos.... **E8**
4 El Papalote, Museo del Niño **D9**
5 Museo de Arte Moderno **J5**
6 Museo Jardín del Agua............ **C8**
7 Museo Nacional de
   Antropología **G4**
8 Museo Tamayo
   Arte Contemporáneo.............. **I4**
9 Oscar Román Gallery.............. **C3**
10 Zoológico de Chapultepec........ **F5**

Restaurants ▼

1 Au Pied de Cochon............... **D3**
2 Cantina El Bosque **J6**
3 Chapulín **D3**
4 El Mirador de Chapultepec **J6**
5 LagoAlgo........................... **B7**
6 Makoto.............................. **C3**

Quick Bites ▼

1 Amado **D3**
2 Churrería el Moro.................. **I1**
3 City Café **A6**

Hotels ▼

1 Camino Real Polanco **J3**
2 Grand Fiesta Americana
   Chapultepec........................ **J4**
3 Hyatt Regency Mexico City........ **E3**
4 J.W. Marriott Hotel
   Mexico City Polanco **D3**
5 Presidente InterContinental
   México............................. **D3**
6 W Mexico City **D3**

7

Polanco and Bosque de Chapultepec

BOSQUE DE CHAPULTEPEC AND PASEO DE LA REFORMA

outings, along with cyclists, joggers, and horseback riders into its three sections, which are divided from east to west by major roads. The first section is the oldest and the most frequented, as it is closest to the city center and home to many museums and other attractions. The second section is much quieter, with plenty of space for recreational activities, while the third section is largely undeveloped and generally functions as an ecological reserve.

At the park's principal entrance, the *Monumento a los Niños Héroes* (Monument to the Boy Heroes) commemorates the young cadets who, it is said, wrapped themselves in the Mexican flag and jumped to their deaths rather than surrender during the U.S. invasion of 1847. To Mexicans, that war is still a troubling symbol of their neighbor's aggression: it cost Mexico almost half its territory—the present states of Texas, California, Arizona, New Mexico, and Nevada.

Other sights in the first section of Bosque de Chapultepec include a castle, three small boating lakes, a botanical garden, and the Casa del Lago cultural center. You'll also find Los Pinos, the ex-residential palace of the president of Mexico, which is now open to the public for the first time thanks to Mexico's current president, Andrés Manuel López Obrador. ⊠ *Av. Reforma, Polanco* ⊕ *chapultepec. org.mx* ✉ *Free* ☉ *Section 1 closed Mon.* Ⓜ *Chapultepec, Auditorio, Constituyentes.*

★ Castillo de Chapultepec

CASTLE/PALACE | The castle on Cerro del Chapulín (Grasshopper Hill) within Bosque de Chapultepec has borne witness to all the turbulence and grandeur of Mexican history. In its earliest form it was an Aztec palace, where the Mexica made one of their last stands against the Spaniards. Later it was a Spanish hermitage, gunpowder plant, and military college. French emperor Maximilian used the castle, parts of which date from 1783, as his residence, and his example

was followed by various presidents from 1872 to 1940, when Lázaro Cárdenas decreed that it be turned into the Museo Nacional de Historia.

Displays on the museum's ground floor cover Mexican history from the conquest to the revolution. The bathroom, bedroom, tea salon, and gardens were used by Maximilian and his wife, Carlotta, in the 1860s. The ground floor also contains works by 20th-century muralists O'Gorman, Orozco, and Siqueiros, and the upper floor is devoted to temporary exhibitions, Porfirio Díaz's malachite vases, and religious art. From the garden and terrace, visitors can enjoy sweeping views of the city skyline. ⊠ *Bosque de Chapultepec, Section 1, Polanco* ☎ *55/5256–5464* ⊕ *mnh.inah.gob.mx* ✉ *MP90* ☉ *Closed Mon.* Ⓜ *Chapultepec.*

Complejo Cultural de los Pinos

HISTORIC HOME | Built in the early 20th century on land formerly owned by Emperor Maximillian, this site was home to Mexican presidents from 1934 until 2018. Since then, it has become a cultural space and museum open to the public. ⊠ *Calz de Rey, Polanco* ⊕ *Bosque de Chapultepec Section1, North of the Constituyentes Metro station* ☎ *55/4155–0200* ⊕ *www. lospinos.cultura.gob.mx* ✉ *Free* ☉ *Closed Mon.* Ⓜ *Constituyentes.*

El Papalote, Museo del Niño

CHILDREN'S MUSEUM | **FAMILY** | Six theme sections compose this excellent interactive children's discovery museum: My Body, Living Mexico, My Home and Family, My City, the Ideas Laboratory, and the Little Ones Zone, all together comprising more than 200 exhibits. There are also workshops, an IMAX theater (note that tickets are discounted if purchased with museum tickets), a store, and a restaurant. Although exhibits are in Spanish, there are some English-speaking staff on hand. ⊠ *Av. Constituyentes 268, Section 2, Polanco* ☎ *55/5237–1781* ⊕ *www. papalote.org.mx* ✉ *MP215* ☉ *Closed Mon.* Ⓜ *Constituyentes.*

Museo de Arte Moderno

ART MUSEUM | The Modern Art Museum's permanent collection has many important examples of 20th-century Mexican art, including works by Mexican school painters like Frida Kahlo—her *Las dos Fridas* is possibly the most famous work in the collection—Diego Rivera, José Clemente Orozco, David Alfaro Siqueiros, and Olga Costa. There are also pieces by surrealists Remedios Varo and Leonora Carrington. ⊠ *Bosque de Chapultepec, Paseo de la Reforma, Section 1, Polanco* ☎ *55/8647–5530* ⊕ *mam.inba.gob.mx* ▩ *MP85; free Sun.* ☾ *Closed Mon.* Ⓜ *Chapultepec.*

Museo Jardín del Agua

SPECIALTY MUSEUM | FAMILY | Located in Chapultepec's second section, this small museum includes a fountain created by Diego Rivera and the Cárcamo de Dolores, part of Mexico City's hydraulic system. The Cárcamo de Dolores was designed by architect Ricardo Rivas and built in 1951 to commemorate the completion of the Sistema Lerma, an integral part of Mexico City's water infrastructure. Inside, you'll find an impressive mural, also by Rivera, called *El Agua, Origen de la Vida* (Water, Origin of Life). The fountain is one of the park's most interesting public art works, depicting the formidable Tláloc, the Aztec god of rain, in mosaic. ⊠ *Bosque de Chapultepec, Av. Rodolfo Neri Vela, Polanco* ☎ *55/5515–0739* ⊕ *www.chapultepec.org.mx/actividad/jardin-del-agua-museum* ▩ *MP22* ☾ *Closed Mon.* Ⓜ *Constituyentes.*

★ Museo Nacional de Antropología

HISTORY MUSEUM | FAMILY | Architect Pedro Ramírez Vázquez's outstanding design provides the proper home for one of the finest archaeological collections in the world. Each salon on the museum's two floors displays artifacts from a particular geographic region or culture. The collection is so extensive that you could easily spend days here, and even that might be barely adequate.

The 12 ground-floor rooms treat pre-Hispanic cultures by region, in the Sala Teotihuacána, Sala Tolteca, Sala Oaxaca (Zapotec and Mixtec peoples), and so on. Objects both precious and pedestrian, including statuary, jewelry, weapons, figurines, and pottery, evoke the intriguing, complex, and frequently warring civilizations that peopled Mesoamerica for the 3,000 years preceding the Spanish invasion. Other highlights include a copy of the Aztec ruler Moctezuma's feathered headdress; a stela from Tula, near Mexico City; massive Olmec heads from Veracruz; and vivid reproductions of Mayan murals in a reconstructed temple. Be sure to see the magnificent reconstruction of the tomb of 7th-century Mayan ruler Pakal, which was discovered in the ruins of Palenque. The nine rooms on the upper floor contain faithful ethnographic displays of current indigenous peoples, using maps, photographs, household objects, folk art, clothing, and religious articles.

Explanatory labels have been updated throughout, some with English translations, and free tours are available at set times from Tuesday through Saturday. ⊠ *Bosque de Chapultepec, Paseo de la Reforma at Calle Gandhi, Polanco* ☎ *55/5553–6266* ⊕ *www.mna.inah.gob.mx* ▩ *MP90* ☾ *Closed Mon.* Ⓜ *Auditorio.*

★ Museo Tamayo Arte Contemporáneo

ART MUSEUM | Within its modernist shell, the sleek Rufino Tamayo Contemporary Art Museum contains paintings by noted Mexican artist Rufino Tamayo as well as temporary exhibitions of international contemporary art. The selections from Tamayo's personal collection, which he donated to the Mexican people, form the basis for the museum's permanent collection and demonstrate his unerring eye for great art; he owned works by Picasso, Joan Miró, René Magritte, Francis Bacon, and Henry Moore. ⊠ *Bosque de Chapultepec, Paseo de la Reforma at Calle Gandhi, Polanco* ☎ *55/4122–8200*

The Castillo de Chapultepec is the architectural highlight of Bosque de Chapultepec.

⊕ *www.museotamayo.org* ✉ *MP85; free Sun.* ⊗ *Closed Mon.* Ⓜ *Chapultepec.*

Oscar Román Gallery

ART GALLERY | Works—mostly paintings with a contemporary edge—by Mexican artists pack this large gallery. Downstairs, the main gallery exhibits a different artist each month while an upstairs gallery holds the permanent collection. ✉ *Julio Verne 14, Polanco* ☎ *55/5280–0436* ⊕ *www.galeriaoscarroman.mx* ⊗ *Closed Sun.* Ⓜ *Campo Marte.*

Zoológico de Chapultepec

ZOO | FAMILY | In the early 16th century, Mexico City's zoo in Chapultepec housed a small private collection of animals belonging to Moctezuma II; it became quasi-public when he allowed favored subjects to visit it. The current zoo opened in the 1920s, and has the usual suspects, as well as some superstar pandas. A gift from China, the original pair—Pepe and Ying Ying—produced the world's first panda cub born in captivity (much to competitive China's chagrin). Today, a descendent of those original pandas, Xin Xin, is one of only three pandas in the world not owned by China. Chapultepec is also home to a couple of California condors plus hippopotamus, giraffes, and kangaroos. The zoo includes the Moctezuma Aviary and is surrounded by a miniature train depot, botanical gardens, and two small lakes. You'll find the entrance on Paseo de la Reforma, across from the Museo Nacional de Antropología. ✉ *Bosque de Chapultepec, Calz. Chivatito, Polanco* ☎ *55/5553–6263* ⊕ *data.sedema.cdmx.gob.mx/zoo_chapultepec* ✉ *Free* ⊗ *Closed Mon.* Ⓜ *Auditorio.*

🍴 Restaurants

Au Pied de Cochon

$$$ | FRENCH | Open around the clock inside the Hotel Presidente InterContinental, this fashionable bistro continues to seduce well-heeled chilangos with high-end French classics. The oysters are flown in from France as well as Baja California; the roasted leg of pork with béarnaise sauce is the signature dish; green-apple sorbet with Calvados is a delicate finish. **Known for:** late-night atmosphere; extensive wine list; impressive breakfast menu. [S] *Average main: MP400* ⊠ *Campos Elíseos 218, Polanco* ☎ *55/5327–7756* ⊕ *www.aupieddeco-chon.rest* Ⓜ *Auditorio.*

Cantina El Bosque
$$$ | **MEXICAN** | An old-school cantina, come here for the vibes and the excellent service. You'll find classic Mexican meat and seafood dishes. **Known for:** indoor and outdoor seating; attentive service; vintage Mexican decor. [S] *Average main: MP400* ⊠ *Cl. 13 de Septiembre 29, Polanco* ☎ *55/5256–5370* ⊕ *www.ins-tagram.com/cantinaelbosque* ☉ *Closed Mon.* Ⓜ *Chapultepec.*

Chapulín
$$$$ | **MEXICAN** | Inside the Hotel Presidente InterContinental, you'll find elevated traditional Mexican ingredients like *huit-lacoche*, a type of fungus that grows on corn, and *chapulines*, or grasshoppers. If you visit for breakfast, order the blue corn chilaquiles for a nourishing start to the day. **Known for:** leafy terrace seating; artistic presentation; authentic recipes. [S] *Average main: MP800* ⊠ *Hotel Presidente InterContinental, Campos Elíseos 218, Polanco* ☎ *55/5327–7789* ⊕ *www.chapulin.rest* Ⓜ *Auditorio.*

★ El Mirador de Chapultepec
$$$ | **MEXICAN** | Set in a handsome old building on a sliver of city blocks wedged between Parque Chapultepec and the Circuito Bicentenario freeway (you may find it easier to Uber than walk here), El Mirador is a venerable old cantina that's been drawing a crowd of regulars since Porfirio Díaz was in office—1904 to be exact. In a dining room of paneled walls and white napery, well-dressed waiters whisk about with plates of pork tongue stewed in a rich chipotle-tomato sauce and tribilín, a flavorful dish of raw beef, fish, and shrimp marinated ceviche-style in olive oil, lime, onions, and roasted chiles. **Known for:** people-watching in the colorful side bar; slightly formal, clubby ambience; old-school traditional Mexican favorite. [S] *Average main: MP450* ⊠ *Av. Chapultepec 606, Polanco* ☎ *55/5286–2161* ⊕ *www.cantinaelmirador.com* Ⓜ *Chapultepec.*

LagoAlgo
$$$ | **MEXICAN FUSION** | Part art gallery and part restaurant, LagoAlgo is the best place to have a meal that's actually in Bosque de Chapultepec. The focus in the kitchen is on fresh, local cuisine with strong Mexican flavors. **Known for:** beautiful art; farm-to-table Mexican dishes; exceptional views. [S] *Average main: MP375* ⊠ *Bosque de Chapultepec, Polanco* ⊹ *On west side of Lago Mayor* ☎ *55/5515–9585* ⊕ *www.lago-algo.mx* ☉ *No dinner* Ⓜ *Constituyentes, Auditorio.*

Makoto
$$$$ | **JAPANESE** | Japanese chef Makoto Okuwa brings his energizing point of view to Mexico's rich culinary heritage. The dishes are beautifully presented; main dishes like the black cod miso and short rib maki offer a complex blend of flavors. **Known for:** edomae-style sushi; fresh local seafood; trendy interior. [S] *Average main: MP750* ⊠ *Campos Elíseos 295, Polanco* ☎ *55/5281–5686* ⊕ *www.makotopolanco.com* ☉ *No dinner Sun.* Ⓜ *Auditorio.*

☕ Coffee and Quick Bites

Amado
$$ | **BAKERY** | Inside the Hyatt Regency Mexico City, one of the city's best *pastelerías* will satisfy even the most discerning sweet tooth. Here European-style chocolate tarts sit alongside all classic *pan dulce* as well as a selection of sweets, salads, and sandwiches. **Known for:** intriguing pastries; experimental flavor combinations; magnificent cakes. [S] *Average main: MP250* ⊠ *Hyatt Regency, Campos Elíseos 204, Polanco* ☎ *55/5083–1234* ⊕ *www.instagram.com/pasteleriaamado* Ⓜ *Auditorio.*

The Museo Jardín del Agua celebrates how Mexico City uses water and gardens in many of its public works.

Churrería El Moro

$ | **BAKERY** | **FAMILY** | A branch of the historic churro restaurant in Centro Historico, this is a great place to stop and take a break on the eastern edge of Polanco. Delicious churros, hot chocolate, milk shakes, and coffee will satisfy your sweet tooth here. **Known for:** richly flavored churro dips; most popular churros in town; modern interior. $ *Average main: MP60 ⊠ Calz. Gral. Mariano Escobedo 501, Polanco ☎ ⊕ www.elmoro.mx* Ⓜ *Polanco.*

City Café

$$ | **CAFÉ** | **FAMILY** | A local chain, this location of City Café is the perfect place to grab breakfast, lunch, or a quick snack in Bosque de Chapultepec. It's located in Section 2 close to Lago Mayor and offers a menu filled with healthy choices. **Known for:** charming outdoor dining; good quick bite for parkgoers; healthy salads and sandwiches. $ *Average main: MP300 ⊠ Av. de los Corredores, Polanco ⊹ West of Lago Mayor ☎ 55/5272–1096* ⊕ *www.citycafe.mx* ☾ *Closed Mon. No dinner* Ⓜ *Constituyentes, Auditoro.*

Hotels

Camino Real Polanco

$$ | **HOTEL** | About the size of Teotihuacán's Pyramid of the Sun, this sleek, low-slung, 8-acre megalith was designed by Mexico's modern master, Ricardo Legorreta. **Pros:** great architecture and art; small but well-outfitted gym; terrific nightlife options. **Cons:** too large for some people's liking; draws many conferences; no spa. $ *Rooms from: MP3100 ⊠ Mariano Escobedo 700, Polanco ☎ 55/5263–8888* ⊕ *www.caminoreal.com ⇆ 677 rooms* ⍩ *No Meals* Ⓜ *Chapultepec.*

Grand Fiesta Americana Chapultepec

$$$ | **HOTEL** | Sleek and contemporary, this stylish hotel stands opposite the Bosque de Chapultepec, close to the city's main shopping area, and five minutes from the Auditorio Nacional. **Pros:** rooms are angled to maximize views; great location for visiting the most popular part of the

Fine Dining in Mexico City

Polanco has been the hub of Mexico City's fine-dining scene since at least the year 2000, when Enrique Olvera redefined Mexican food with the opening of his beloved restaurant Pujol. Quintonil, ranked at number nine on the 2023 World's 50 Best Restaurants list, is also found here, headed up by power couple Alejandra Flores and Jorge Vallejo. While tacos do occasionally feature on these upscale menus, Mexican haute cuisine is varied, modern, playful, and gorgeously plated.

Generally, Polanco's affluent residents tend to favor seafood, steak, and locally sourced greens, and the dress code at these places is often more relaxed than similar establishments in the United States. The neighborhood's fine-dining restaurants also buck the nationwide trend of closing in the early evening (after the day's most important meal, lunch), with most staying open until 11 pm or midnight. While Polanco may lack Condesa's youthful cool, its eateries deliver on taste, sophistication, and quality every time.

park; large rooms with comfortable beds. **Cons:** not all views are great; on-site restaurants could be better; many amenities cost extra. $ *Rooms from: MP4224* ✉ *Mariano Escobedo 756, Polanco* ☎ *443/310–8137* ⊕ *www.grandfiestamericana.com* ⬧ *203 rooms* ⦿ *No Meals* Ⓜ *Chapultepec.*

Hyatt Regency Mexico City
$$$ | HOTEL | Occupying a prime Polanco position adjacent to the Bosque de Chapultepec, this hotel is a seven-minute walk from the anthropology museum. **Pros:** comfortable beds; great location; considering that this is one of the most elegant places to stay in the city, discounted weekend rates are quite tempting. **Cons:** large property so it lacks some intimacy; the rooms are on the basic side; most of the lobby is a restaurant so there aren't many places to hang out besides the rooms. $ *Rooms from: MP5350* ✉ *Campos Elíseos 204, Polanco* ☎ *55/5083–1234* ⊕ *mexicocity.regency.hyatt.com* ⬧ *773 rooms* ⦿ *No Meals* Ⓜ *Auditorio.*

JW Marriott Hotel Mexico City Polanco
$$$$ | HOTEL | In keeping with its genteel neighborhood, this high-rise hotel has personalized service and cozy public areas; nothing overwhelms here. **Pros:** beautifully decorated; good on-site restaurants; exceptionally attentive service. **Cons:** some of the rooms are small; more expensive than other hotels in the area; noise from the street may disturb at night. $ *Rooms from: MP8750* ✉ *Andrés Bello 29, at Campos Elíseos, Polanco* ☎ *55/5999–0000* ⊕ *www.marriott.com* ⬧ *314 rooms* ⦿ *No Meals* Ⓜ *Auditorio.*

★ Presidente InterContinental México
$$$ | HOTEL | Regularly playing host to various heads of state (Barack Obama stayed here in 2009), the InterContinental's expansive atrium lobby has parquet floors, thick walls, oversize furniture, and Talavera pottery, which is also showcased throughout the property. **Pros:** beautiful lobby; excellent on-site restaurant options; gorgeous views from public areas and certain rooms. **Cons:** standard rooms are cramped; can be packed with conference attendees; large size means it lacks a certain warmth. $ *Rooms from: MP4800* ✉ *Campos Elíseos 218, Polanco* ☎ *55/5327–7700* ⊕ *www.intercontinental.com* ⬧ *700 rooms* ⦿ *No Meals* Ⓜ *Auditorio.*

★ **W Mexico City**

$$$ | **HOTEL** | The first W hotel in Latin America grooves with its bright colors, clever lighting, and a lobby that brings to mind a cool 1960s airport lounge. **Pros:** gorgeous decoration with thoughtful touches of Mexican culture; tech-friendly amenties; beautiful spa and fitness center. **Cons:** not a great choice for families with small children; no swimming pool; ultramodern design is not for everyone. [$] *Rooms from: MP5200* ✉ *Campos Eliseos 252, Polanco* ☎ *55/9138–1800* 🌐 *www.wmexicocity.com* 🛏 *237 rooms* 🍴 *No Meals* [M] *Auditorio.*

Nightlife

Blue Bar

BARS | The lounge in the Camino Real Hotel, southeast of Polanco, has a sophisticated crowd, mellow music, and good martinis—a relaxing stop if you're staying in the hotel or just passing through. Lighting and overall color schemes are, as you probably guessed, blue tinged. There are several seating areas; furnishings are eclectic but are heavy on mid-century modern pieces. One area has a translucent floor that's lighted from below and set over water—very cool, very blue. ✉ *Camino Real, Mariano Escobedo 700, Polanco* ☎ 🌐 *www.caminoreal.com* [M] *Chapultepec.*

Karisma

BARS | This welcoming cantina, established in 1976, is an old-school hold-out in the neighborhood, with a traditional Mexican food menu, outdoor seating, and wine, beer, and spirits on offer. The prices are reasonable, considering the location near some of Polanco's top hotels; English menus are available. ✉ *Campo Eliseos 219, Polanco* ☎ *55/7653–8289* 🌐 *www.facebook.com/karismacantina* [M] *Campo Marte.*

La No. 20

BARS | Part of a national chain, La No. 20 is an upscale cantina with slick decor and high-end mixology service. Mariachi bands roam the bar, while young professionals dine on satisfying (if pricey) old-school Mexican cuisine. Try to nab a table on the terrace for the full experience. ✉ *Andres Bello 10, Polanco* ☎ *55/5281–3524* 🌐 *www.cantina20.com* [M] *Auditorio.*

Living Room Bar

BARS | At the W Hotel, Living Room is a lounge-style bar packed with intriguing design touches and creative cocktails. Living Room has a more happening ambience than your average hotel bar, thanks to resident DJs that spin regularly in the evenings. ✉ *W Mexico City, Campos Elíseos 252, Polanco* ☎ *55/9138–1800* 🌐 *www.marriott.com/hotels/travel/mexwm-w-mexico-city* [M] *Auditorio.*

Performing Arts

Auditorio Nacional

PERFORMANCE VENUES | **FAMILY** | A popular concert venue, you can also watch a variety of performing arts here, including opera, ballet, and rock concerts by Mexican artists. The great part about this space is that there are really no bad seats. Tickets can be purchased at the box office or on Ticketmaster. If you buy at the box office, tickets are buy one, get one free on Thursday. ✉ *Av. Paseo de la Reforma 50, Bosque de Chapultepec* ☎ *55/9138–1350* 🌐 *www.auditorio.com.mx* [M] *Auditorio.*

Danza de los Voladores

FOLK/TRADITIONAL DANCE | The mind-blowing Mesoamerican dance, the Danza de los Voladores, is performed outside the Museo Nacional de Antropología and looks more like skydiving. Four men are tied by their feet to a long pole which they then jump off, weaving through the air to the beat played by the Caporal standing on top. Although this fertility ritual is performed by several ethnic groups, it is often associated with the city of Papantla in Veracruz. Make sure to

leave a donation if you enjoyed the show, which is performed almost continuously during museum hours every day except Monday. ⊠ *Grutas 770, Polanco* ⌖ *Outside Museo Nacional de Antropología* Ⓜ *Auditorio.*

Shopping

Librería Porrúa

BOOKS | This branch of the popular Mexican bookseller is conveniently located in Bosque de Chapultepec and includes an open-air café. Although the selection of English books is limited, the store is beautifully designed with a panorama of the surrounding greenery and the lake. ⊠ *Bosque de Chapultepec, Paseo de la Reforma, Bosque de Chapultepec* ⌖ *Across from Museo Nacional de Antropología* ☎ *55/5212–2242* ⊕ *www.porrua. mx* Ⓜ *Chapultepec.*

Polanco

Sights

Acuario Inbursa

AQUARIUM | **FAMILY** | This Mexico City attraction has been a hit since it opened, attracting long lines of people eager to see the largest aquarium in the country. A visit to the site starts four stories underground, at the "bottom of the ocean," and moves upward toward the surface. Thousands of species of fish, sharks, rays, eels, jellyfish, and more swim among the ruins of a sunken ship, vibrantly colored coral, and gracefully swaying kelp, all dramatically lit in huge tanks. The "rain forest" exhibit is home to reptiles and amphibians such as Mexico's endangered, curious-looking ajolote salamander. ⊠ *Av. Miguel de Cervantes Saavedra 386, Polanco* ☎ *55/5395–4586* ⊕ *www.acuarioinbursa.com.mx* 🚇 *MP280* Ⓜ *San Joaquín.*

Galería Alfredo Ginocchio

ART GALLERY | Founded in 1988 by Alfredo Ginocchio as Praxis Mexico, this now-eponymous gallery promotes distinguished work from Mexico and elsewhere in Latin America. Its relatively small but interesting collection features a different artist every couple of months, alongside a variety of sculptures and paintings by familiar names including Santiago Carbonell. ⊠ *Arquímedes 175, Polanco* ☎ *55/5255–5700* ⊕ *www. ginocchiogaleria.com* ⊘ *Closed Sun.* Ⓜ *Polanco.*

Museo Jumex

ART MUSEUM | Founded by an heir to the Jumex juice fortune, this contemporary art museum is located just across the way from the Museo Soumaya, and though the subdued travertine building that houses it is not as eye-popping as Carlos Slim's shiny silver cloud next door, the exhibition design of the Jumex is arguably superior. Shows draw from the museum's 2,700-strong collection, which includes boldfaced names like Jeff Koons, Damien Hirst, and Andy Warhol, as well as temporary exhibitions of work by international contemporary artists. There's also an on-site café and store. ⊠ *Blvd. Miguel de Cervantes Saavedra 303, Polanco* ☎ *55/5395–2615* ⊕ *www. fundacionjumex.org* 🚇 *Free* ⊘ *Closed Mon.* Ⓜ *San Joaquin or Polanco.*

★ Museo Soumaya Plaza Carso

ART MUSEUM | One of Mexico City's most well-known architectural icons, Museo Soumaya houses the valuable art collection of billionaire philanthropist Carlos Slim, as well as visiting exhibitions. The museum's Plaza Carso branch sits just beyond the edge of Polanco and contains sculptures by Rodin and Dalí and paintings from old masters to modernists and impressionists, including works from the likes of Leonardo da Vinci, El Greco, Tintoretto, Monet, and Picasso. But there are also many Mexican artists represented, including Diego Rivera.

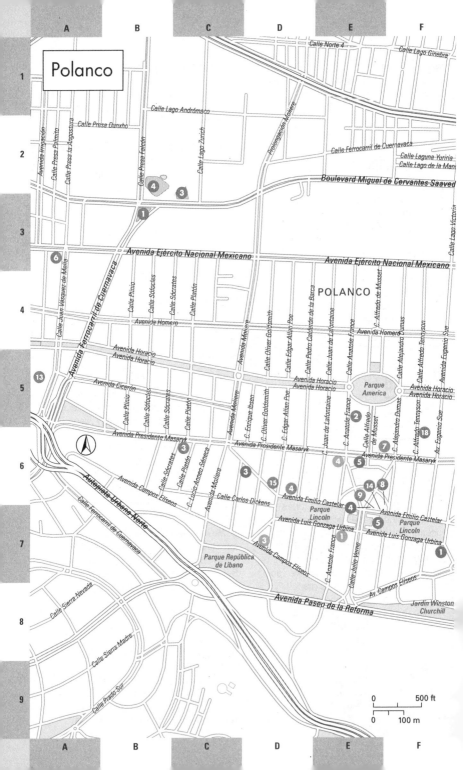

Sights ▼

1 Acuario Inbursa.................. **B3**
2 Galería Alfredo Ginocchio........ **H5**
3 Museo Jumex...................... **C3**
4 Museo Soumaya Plaza Carso.... **B2**
5 Parque Lincoln.................... **E7**

Restaurants ▼

1 Agua & Sal **G7**
2 Aúna............................... **E5**
3 Belfiore **C6**
4 Blanco Castelar................... **D6**
5 Cabanna **I6**
6 Caldos D'Leo **A3**
7 Cambalache....................... **F6**
8 Comedor Jacinta **F7**
9 Emilio.............................. **E7**
10 Entremar.......................... **I5**
11 Farina **G6**
12 Fougasse **G7**
13 Hacienda de los Morales......... **A5**
14 Ivoire.............................. **E7**
15 La Barra de Fran.................. **D6**
16 La Docena **J4**
17 Porfirio's **H6**
18 Pujol **F6**
19 Quintonil **G6**
20 Siembra Comedor **J4**

Quick Bites ▼

1 Caffe Biscottino................... **F7**
2 El Farolito Polanco............... **H5**
3 El Turix **D6**
4 Joselo............................. **E7**
5 Klein's **E6**
6 Maison Belen **G7**
7 Peltre Lonchería **I5**
8 Signora Mariola................... **H5**
9 Tortas Royalty **J5**

Hotels ▼

1 Casa Polanco **E7**
2 Habita Hotel **H6**
3 Hotel Polanco **D7**
4 Las Alcobas **E6**
5 Orchid House...................... **I7**

The reflective exterior of the Museo Soumaya is one of the city's most popular photo ops.

Each floor of the museum has a different layout, and you walk along curving ramps (not unlike those in the Guggenheim Museum in New York City) to get from one floor to another. Designed by the Mexican architect Fernando Romero, Slim's son-in-law, the $70 million building has a shape some have likened to a silver cloud, and is covered by thousands of hexagonal aluminum tiles. ✉ *Blvd. Miguel de Cervantes Saavedra 303, Polanco* ☎ *55/1103–9800* 🌐 *www.museosoumaya.org* 🎫 *Free* [M] *Polanco, San Joaquín.*

Parque Lincoln

CITY PARK | **FAMILY** | This park offers a welcome respite in the center of Polanco, surrounded by buzzing shops and restaurants. It is named for its statue of Abraham Lincoln (there's also one of Martin Luther King Jr.), but its clock tower is equally recognizable as the logo for the neighborhood's Metro station. There's a small lake, a children's playground, an aviary, and the Teatro Ángela Peralta, an open-air theater. On Saturday, Parque Lincoln hosts Polanco's weekly *tianguis*, or local market. ✉ *Emilio Castelar 163, Polanco* [M] *Polanco.*

🍴 Restaurants

★ Agua & Sal

$$$ | **SEAFOOD** | Specializing in fresh seafood, you'll find bright, crisp flavors and a fantastic variety of seafood options here. Start your meal with one of their ceviche varieties, and follow it with a plate or two to share—perhaps the esquites con camaron, a mayo-based corn dish loaded with shrimp. **Known for:** huge portions great for sharing; variety of fresh seafood; excellent ceviche. [$] *Average main: MP450* ✉ *Campo Eliseos 199-A, Polanco* ☎ *55/5282–2746* 🌐 *www.aguaysal.com.mx* 🕓 *No dinner Sun.* [M] *Auditorio.*

Aúna

$$$$ | **MEXICAN FUSION** | Both a café and a restaurant, Aúna turns locally sourced ingredients into fantastic meals with an international flair. It's an impressive collaboration between chef Fernando Torres and chef Jorge Vallejo from famed

Polanco restaurant Quintonil. **Known for:** open, airy atmosphere; simple yet delightful roasted organic chicken; natural wines and craft beers. $ *Average main: MP550* ✉ *Anatole France 139, Polanco* ☎ *55/9237–5157* ⊕ *www.instagram.com/auna.mx* Ⓜ *Polanco.*

Belfiore

$$$$ | **ITALIAN** | Quite a few CDMX restaurants do upscale Italian food well, but this romantic, warmly lighted trattoria stands out for serving some of the finest pizzas around. Each thin-crust pie is crisped to perfection in the wood-fired oven on view at the front of the dining room—the pie layered lavishly with burrata and prosciutto is worth the splurge. **Known for:** wood-fired pizzas with premium toppings; extensive Italian wine list; classic Italian desserts. $ *Average main: MP500* ✉ *Av. Pdte. Masaryk 514, Polanco* ☎ *55/5282–0413* ⊕ *www.instagram.com/belfioreristorante* Ⓜ *Auditorio.*

★ Blanco Castelar

$$$$ | **INTERNATIONAL** | The architecture here is just as impressive as the food, with the restaurant housed inside a Californian colonial-style mansion built in 1940. Diners can choose from an international menu with Mexican flourishes (like the tacos de lechon confit) or an impressive tasting menu. **Known for:** park views; dramatic dishes; trendy crowd. $ *Average main: MP600* ✉ *Emilio Castelar 163, Polanco* ☎ *55/5027–0321* ⊕ *www.blancocastelarmx.com* Ⓜ *Campo Marte.*

Cabanna

$$$ | **MEXICAN** | This laid-back seafood eatery brings the beach to Mexico City. Try the fresh taco Gobernador or tostada Punta Mita accompanied by a michelada. **Known for:** fast service; good for groups; Sinaloa-style seafood. $ *Average main: MP350* ✉ *Av. Presidente Masaryk 134, Polanco* ☎ *55/5545–2225* ⊕ *www.cabanna.com.mx* Ⓜ *Polanco.*

Caldos D'Leo

$$ | **MEXICAN** | A stalwart of northwestern Polanco since 1966, this traditional restaurant offers a taste of home-style Mexican fare. Choose from a menu of hot breakfasts, soups, moles, and enchiladas, then enjoy the efficient service and simple yet satisfying flavors. **Known for:** wholesome chicken soup; long lunches; great value Mexican classics. $ *Average main: MP250* ✉ *Av. Ejército Nacional 1014 B, Polanco* ☎ *55/5557–6760* ⊕ *www.grupoleos.com.mx* Ⓜ *Polanco.*

Cambalache

$$$$ | **ARGENTINE** | This beef-lover's dream is popular with everyone from businessmen to young families. Everything is grilled, from the Argentine beef and Australian lamb to the whitefish in a mild chile sauce. **Known for:** generous portions of classic Argentine cuisine; passionate staff; high-quality ingredients. $ *Average main: MP700* ✉ *Alejandro Dumas 122, Polanco* ☎ *55/5280–2080* ⊕ *www.cambalacherestaurantes.com* Ⓜ *Auditorio.*

★ Comedor Jacinta

$$ | **MEXICAN** | Inspired by his mother's cooking, chef Edgar Núñez (of Sud777 fame) opened the unpretentious Comedor Jacinta in 2016. Like most *comedores*, Jacinta offers a typical *comida corrida*, or set lunch menu, alongside a fully vegetarian option. **Known for:** regional seafood dishes; homey feel; convenient location. $ *Average main: MP300* ✉ *Virgilio 40, Polanco* ☎ *55/5086–6965* ⊕ *comedorjacinta.com* Ⓜ *Polanco.*

Emilio

$$$$ | **EUROPEAN** | Emilio is a popular all-day eatery in Polanquito, combining Italian, Mexican, and Spanish influences. The sidewalk seating is matched with a casual menu of imaginative shared plates and cocktails (try the tacos *de pato confitado*) while a classic European menu is served on the pleasant terrace upstairs. **Known for:** weekly specials; charming outdoor seating; park views. $ *Average main: MP600* ✉ *Emilio Castelar 107,*

Polanco ☎ *55/5281–7812* ⊕ *www.emilior-est.com* ☾ *No dinner Sun.* Ⓜ *Auditorio.*

★ Entremar

$$$ | SEAFOOD | Located in the shadows of Parque Uruguay, Entremar is the lesser-known sister restaurant of the popular Roma Norte seafood restaurant Contramar; both share the same menu as well as the same attentive service. Luckily, it's much easier to get a table at Entremar, but you'll still be enjoying the same high-quality dishes like the pescado contramar, a filet of fish seasoned on one side with red adobo rub and parsley on the other. **Known for:** delightful desserts; beautiful park views; fantastic seafood. Ⓢ *Average main: MP400* ⊠ *Hegel 307, Polanco* ☎ *55/5531–2031* ⊕ *www.entremar.com* Ⓜ *Polanco.*

Farina

$$$ | ITALIAN | With a focus on wood-fire pizzas and veggie-packed salads, Farina delivers uncomplicated Italian food. The outdoor terrace makes for a cozy and romantic meal, including a full bar. **Known for:** exquisite tiramisu; friendly vibes; good Italian wine list. Ⓢ *Average main: MP350* ⊠ *Av. Isaac Newton 53–1, Polanco* ☎ *55/7825–9921* ⊕ *www.farinarest.com/polanco* Ⓜ *Polanco.*

Fougasse

$$ | BAKERY | FAMILY | Part bakery, part restaurant, you won't be disappointed whether you stop here for a quicker bite or a full sit-down for dinner. The star of the show is the roulette, a round, flaky pastry reminiscent of a croissant and served plain or with savory or sweet toppings and fillings. **Known for:** excellent service; limited bar menu; freshly baked breads and pastries. Ⓢ *Average main: MP200* ⊠ *Emilio Castelar 34, Polanco* ☎ ⊕ *www.fougasse.com.mx* Ⓜ *Auditorio.*

Hacienda de los Morales

$$$$ | MEXICAN | Built in the 17th century on the site of a mulberry farm, this hacienda has been transformed into one of Mexico's most elegant dinner spots. The atmosphere outclasses even the food, which consists of both Mexican classics and more experimental dishes that incorporate Spanish and Mediterranean influences. **Known for:** gorgeous colonial architecture; creative flavor combinations; a variety of live music while you dine. Ⓢ *Average main: MP600* ⊠ *Juan Vázquez de Mella 525, Polanco* ☎ *55/5283–3055* ⊕ *www.haciendadelos-morales.com* ☾ *Closed Mon. No dinner Sun.* Ⓜ *Campo Marte.*

Ivoire

$$$$ | MODERN FRENCH | The epitome of Polanquito chic, Ivoire brings a touch of France to Mexico. The interior is reminiscent of a Parisian bistro, complete with cane chairs and indoor plants, and the menu features fondue, escargot, and artichokes. **Known for:** delicate French dishes; Instagram-friendly aesthetic; group-friendly terrace overlooking the park. Ⓢ *Average main: MP500* ⊠ *Emilio Castelar 95, Polanco* ☎ *55/5280–0477* ⊕ *www.instagram.com/ivoiremx* Ⓜ *Polanco.*

La Barra de Fran

$$$ | SPANISH | This contemporary Spanish tavern plates up Mexico City's top tapas, alongside paella and other delicacies. The *jamon serrano* is freshly carved and the red wine is full bodied; both are made to be shared. **Known for:** local crowds; imported meats and cheeses; small space so reservations are smart. Ⓢ *Average main: MP400* ⊠ *Av. Emilio Castelar 185, Polanco* ☎ *55/5280–6650* ⊕ *www.labarradefran.com* Ⓜ *Campo Marte.*

La Docena

$$$ | SEAFOOD | Known primarily for its succulent oysters, La Docena also offers an expansive menu of steaks, jamón ibérico, and burgers. Don't miss the octopus, the grilled oysters, and the cocktails either. **Known for:** quiet location away from the crowds; wide array of seafood options; lovely outdoor seating on the patio. Ⓢ *Average main: MP450*

✉ Homero 135, Polanco ☎ 55/5255–2066 🌐 www.ladocena.com.mx [M] Polanco.

Porfirio's

$$$$ | **MODERN MEXICAN** | Named after the Mexican dictator whose 31-year reign sparked the Mexican Revolution, Porfirio's does classic Mexican steak and seafood dishes very well. The service and atmosphere are quiet during the day, with DJs taking over after dark. **Known for:** extensive wine list; top-notch service; traditional chile relleno. [$] *Average main: MP500* ✉ *Av. Presidente Masaryk 214, Polanco* ☎ *55/5280–1494* 🌐 *www.porfirios.com.mx* [M] *Polanco.*

Pujol

$$$$ | **MEXICAN** | The internationally acclaimed chef at Pujol, Enrique Olvera, continuously reinvents traditional Mexican dishes and their presentation, and is largely responsible for the country's gastronomic revolution. The dining experience here can be described as educational and hedonistic, and the seven-course menus are designed to create a holistic flavor experience. **Known for:** exquisite local flavors; creative menu pairings; generally hard to get into. [$] *Average main: MP3500* ✉ *Tennyson 133, Polanco* ☎ *55/5545–4111* 🌐 *www.pujol.com.mx* 🕒 *Closed Sun.* ☞ *Children under 12 discouraged* [M] *Polanco.*

★ Quintonil

$$$$ | **MEXICAN** | Named after a wild green herb often found in *milpas*, a Mesoamerican crop-growing system, Quintonil was opened in 2012 by chef-owner Jorge Vallejo. Today, Vallejo eschews fussiness to let the local ingredients shine: smoked trout from nearby Zitácuaro or a salad of greens and herbs from the floating gardens of Xochimilco. **Known for:** accessible fine dining; thoughtful ingredient pairings; prix-fixe menu only. [$] *Average main: MP750* ✉ *Isaac Newton 55, Polanco* ☎ *55/5280–1660* 🌐 *www.quintonil.com* 🕒 *Closed Sun.* ☞ *Children under 12 discouraged* [M] *Polanco.*

★ Siembra Comedor

$$$$ | **MEXICAN** | At Siembra Comedor, the diverse dishes are elevated and delectable, with both the decor and the menu heavily centering around corn. Whether you choose tacos, octopus, or a rib eye, your meal won't disappoint. **Known for:** fresh homemade tortillas; beautiful decor; corn-focused dishes. [$] *Average main: MP500* ✉ *Newton 300, Polanco* ☎ *55/5244–5766* 🌐 *www.instagram.com/siembra.tortilleria* 🕒 *Closed Mon. No dinner Sun.* [M] *Polanco.*

☕ Coffee and Quick Bites

★ Caffe Biscottino

$$ | **CAFÉ** | This tiny café on the corner of Parque Lincoln pours the best espresso in the neighborhood, with a simple yet satisfying breakfast menu and homemade pastries (including vegan, gluten-free, and kosher options). The coffee is sourced from Chachaxtla in Veracruz, and always freshly roasted. **Known for:** excellent sourdough bread; specialized coffee; blue corn scones. [$] *Average main: MP150* ✉ *Luis G Urbina 4, Polanco* ☎ *55/5280–2155* 🌐 *www.instagram.com/caffebiscottino* 🕒 *Closed Sat.* [M] *Auditorio.*

★ El Farolito Polanco

$ | **MEXICAN** | **FAMILY** | In operation since 1962, you'll find an impressive array of tacos, tortas, agua frescas, and more here. Sit at the counter and watch the chefs whip up meals at an impressive speed. **Known for:** delicious chicharrón de queso (fried cheese); quick service; great tacos el pastor. [$] *Average main: MP70* ✉ *Av. Isaac Newton 130, Polanco* ☎ *55/5250–2322* 🌐 *www.elfarolito.com.mx* [M] *Polanco.*

★ El Turix

$ | **MEXICAN** | Polanco's most beloved taquería serves tacos, tortas, and *panuchos* of *cochinita pibíl*, the Yucatecan specialty of achiote-marinated pork. People from all walks of life, from hipsters to construction workers to businesswomen, line up throughout the day for a quick fix, topped with the habanero salsa and pickled red onion (and Montejo beer) typical of the Yucatán. **Known for:** authentic atmosphere; no-nonsense service; best cochinita pibíl in the neighborhood. [$] *Average main: MP100* ✉ *Emilio Castelar 212, Polanco* ☎ *55/5280–6449* [M] *Polanco, Campo Marte.*

Joselo

$ | **CAFÉ** | The coffee at Joselo is great, as is the location, in the center of stylish Polanquito. The sandwiches and sweets are tasty, but you'll be lucky if you snag an outdoor table during meal times, so you may prefer to get your caffeine fix to go and enjoy it across the road in Parque Lincoln. **Known for:** consistently delicious espresso; outdoor seating; late hours for a café. [$] *Average main: MP100* ✉ *Emilio Castelar 107, Polanco* ☎ *55/5281–0849* 🌐 *www.facebook.com/joselocafe* [M] *Auditorio.*

Klein's

$$ | **MEXICAN FUSION** | **FAMILY** | This popular deli has been serving up affordable Mexican-Jewish fusion in Polanco since 1962. You'll find hotcakes, waffles, and chili dogs on the menu alongside chilaquiles and enchiladas, all topped with a large range of house-made salsas. **Known for:** family atmosphere; diner classics; extensive menu. [$] *Average main: MP200* ✉ *Av. Presidente Masaryk 360B, Polanco* ☎ *55/5281–0862* 🌐 *www.kleins.mx* [M] *Polanco.*

Maison Belen

$$$ | **FRENCH FUSION** | A colorful French-Mexican fusion café, Maison Belen offers pastries and hearty breakfasts. The space itself is small, but the outdoor seating provides an excellent opportunity for people-watching over a pain au chocolate. **Known for:** glorious eggs Benedict; freshly baked bread; warm decor. [$] *Average main: MP320* ✉ *Emilio Castelar 31, Polanco* ☎ *55/5280–3715* 🌐 *www.maisonbelen.mx* [M] *Auditorio.*

Peltre Lonchería

$$ | **MEXICAN** | With several branches across the city, Peltre is an easy budget option in ritzy Polanco. Like traditional *loncherías*, this modern version has an extensive menu covering everything from chilaquiles negros to sopa Aguascalientes. **Known for:** best pan de muerto relleno (a type of pastry) in the city; contemporary design; great coffee and juices. [$] *Average main: MP150* ✉ *Francisco Petrarca 253, Polanco* ☎ *55/7824–2010* 🌐 *www.facebook.com/loncheriapeltre* [M] *Polanco.*

Signora Mariola

$$ | **MEXICAN** | The perfect spot for a quick coffee or pastry, Signora Mariola is a tiny place with very few tables placed on the sidewalk outside, so be prepared to take your meal to go as you stroll through Polanco. The croissants and bread are to die for, and the Mexican breakfasts are tasty and light. **Known for:** grab-and-go pastries; seasonal cakes; impressive pour-over coffee. [$] *Average main: MP150* ✉ *Av. Horacio 518, Polanco* ☎ *55/6273–8723* 🌐 *www.instagram.com/signoramariola* [M] *Polanco.*

★ Tortas Royalty

$ | **MEXICAN** | Chilangos (as Mexico City's residents are often known) are notorious for putting everything in a sandwich, even going as far as to create the carb-heavy *guajolota*, or *torta de tamal*. Convenient, filling, and cheap, tortas are the perfect fuel for a day of sightseeing and Royalty, Polanco's favorite sandwich shop, offers excellent versions of them. **Known for:** freshly baked bread; delicious consomé de pavo (turkey); fast service. [$] *Average main: MP55* ✉ *Horacio 227, Polanco* ☎ *55/5250–2118* [M] *Polanco.*

Hotels

Casa Polanco

$$$$ | **HOTEL** | This house-turned-hotel provides an intimate setting for travelers staying in the Polanquito area. **Pros:** very

intimate feeling atmosphere; beautifully renovated home originally built in the 1940s; complimentary minibar and snacks. **Cons:** not child-friendly; pricey; can be too quiet for travelers looking for nightlife. [$] *Rooms from: MP13,700* ✉ *Luis G. Urbina 84, Polanco* ☎ *55/5125–0800* 🌐 *www.casapolanco.com* 🛏 *19 rooms* 🍴 *Free Breakfast* [M] *Auditorio.*

Habita Hotel

$$$ | **HOTEL** | Its design strikes a harmonious balance between style statements and minimalism, but the location of this hotel, on one of the city's poshest avenues, is its main selling point. **Pros:** beautiful pool; great location; panoramic views from the bar. **Cons:** rooftop bar is noisy late into the night; small, basic rooms; gym is tiny. [$] *Rooms from: MP4500* ✉ *Av. Presidente Masaryk 201, Polanco* ☎ *55/5282–3100* 🌐 *www.hotel-habita.com* 🛏 *36 rooms* 🍴 *No Meals* [M] *Polanco.*

Hotel Polanco

$ | **HOTEL** | This small hotel right off Parque Lincoln and not far from Chapultepec park offers an exclusive Polanco zip code at a much better price than the larger hotels nearby. **Pros:** good value for the neighborhood; nice location; strong Wi-Fi. **Cons:** rooms are tiny and in need of renovation; no restaurant on-site; you get what you pay for in terms of service. [$] *Rooms from: MP1920* ✉ *Edgar Allan Poe 8, Polanco* ☎ *55/5280–8082* 🌐 *hotel-polanco.com* 🛏 *71 rooms* 🍴 *No Meals* [M] *Auditorio.*

★ Las Alcobas

$$$$ | **HOTEL** | A favorite of celebrities and dignitaries, this boutique member of Marriott's Luxury Collection is on Polanco's most exclusive shopping street, a block from charming Parque Lincoln Polanco. **Pros:** beds are soft and heavenly; 24-hour butler service; great location. **Cons:** hydromassage bathtubs are small, tend to malfunction, and cannot be used after 9 pm; no pool; small gym. [$] *Rooms from: MP8700* ✉ *Presidente Masaryk 390, Polanco* ☎ *55/3300–3900* 🌐 *www.lasalcobas.com* 🛏 *31 rooms* 🍴 *No Meals* [M] *Polanco.*

Orchid House

$$$ | **HOTEL** | A boutique hotel with only eighteen rooms, Orchid House provides an intimate experience for its guests. With an acclaimed in-house restaurant (get the pizza), it's a convenient place to stay in a beautiful part of Polanco. **Pros:** wonderful on-site restaurant; comfortable beds; excellent location. **Cons:** certain rooms on the smaller side; inconsistent service; some rooms have no natural light. [$] *Rooms from: MP4000* ✉ *Campo Elíseos 76, Polanco* ☎ *55/5183–2798* 🌐 *www.orchidhousehotels.com* 🛏 *18 rooms* 🍴 *Free Breakfast* [M] *Auditorio, Polanco.*

🍸 Nightlife

El Deposito

BARS | Domestic and international beers take the spotlight here. With a weekday happy hour and plenty of food options, this is a great choice for anyone who just wants a place to hang out without any of the pretentiousness that can frequently come with nightlife in this area. ✉ *Av. Ejército Nacional Mexicano 468, Polanco* ☎ *55/7045–0950* 🌐 *www.eldeposito.com.mx* [M] *Polanco.*

Gin Gin

COCKTAIL BARS | Dark and a little spooky, Gin Gin is a real scene, from the skull-lined, red-lit entryway to the hookah smoke-filled bar area. Enjoy a cocktail at the bar, and watch the night unfold. ✉ *Calderon de la Barca 72, Polanco* ☎ *55/5477–0123* 🌐 *www.gingin.mx* [M] *Polanco, Auditorio.*

★ Habita

BARS | The Habita Hotel rooftop showcases a magnificent view of the city from its hip open-air bar and terrace. The lounge area with its fireplace is a great place to chill out without catching a chill. Sipping a selection from the range of mezcals on offer will also do the trick. On some nights, you can watch vintage movies projected onto the building across the street. ✉ *Av. Presidente Masaryk 201, at Lamartine, Polanco* ☎ *55/5282–3100* ⊕ *www.hotelhabita.com* Ⓜ *Auditorio.*

Limantour

COCKTAIL BARS | Popular with tourists, this cocktail lounge is known for having friendly bartenders and tasty drinks. Food is available as well so it's a great place to spend an evening. ✉ *Oscar Wilde 9, Polanco* ☎ *55/5280–1299* ⊕ *www.limantour.tv* Ⓜ *Polanco.*

Scotch

BARS | A small bar with delicious cocktails, Scotch is a great place to stop after dinner in Polanco. Although ccasionally filled with smoke from cigarettes or sparklers, the music and the vibes make up for that. ✉ *Pasaje Polanco, Julio Verne 110, Polanco* Ⓜ *Auditorio, Polanco.*

Shopping

Antara Polanco

MALL | **FAMILY** | One of only a few outdoor malls in the city, Antara Polanco has a collection of upscale stores that includes Carolina Herrera, Zara, Hugo Boss, and Coach as well as branches of several luxury stores that are also found along the neighborhood's ritzy Avenida Presidente Masaryk; there are plenty of dining options, too. ✉ *Ejército Nacional 843, Polanco* ☎ *55/4593–8870* ⊕ *www.antara.com.mx* Ⓜ *San Joaquín.*

Bomboti

HOUSEWARES | A two-story home goods store on a quiet street, Bomboti is where you go to find unique decorative pieces. Head to the second floor for larger pieces. ✉ *Hegel 232, Polanco* ⊕ *www.bomboti.com* Ⓜ *Polanco.*

★ El Palacio de Hierro

DEPARTMENT STORE | This upscale department store is mostly filled with high-end designer collections. While it is a local chain, this location of El Palacio de Hierro stands out from the rest of the stores, thanks to its floor after floor of designer goods for men and women. You'll likely find something here you won't be able to get anywhere else. After making your way up to the top floor, stop at the La Terraza Palacio for a quick bite or a cocktail in the extensive food court. ✉ *Av. Moliere 222, Polanco* ☎ *55/5283–7200* ⊕ *www.elpalaciodehierro.com* Ⓜ *Polanco.*

Ikal

CLOTHING | A large, upmarket concept store on Masaryk Avenue, Ikal aims to celebrate local independent labels. From luxury fashion and footwear to hard-to-find homewares and jewelry, the store curates a contemporary feel while maintaining a distinctly Mexican perspective. ✉ *Av. Presidente Masaryk 340A, Polanco* ☎ *55/8954–3612* ⊕ *www.ikalstore.com* Ⓜ *Polanco.*

Lago

CLOTHING | This sophisticated Latin American design store offers a collection of pieces from Peru, Colombia, Ecuador, Argentina, Brazil, and Mexico. Here you'll find leather goods, ceramics, clothing, and accessories from emerging and established brands. The two-story space itself is similarly impressive, with six huge windows facing out onto the street and creative product displays inside. ✉ *Av. Presidente Masaryk 310, Polanco* ☎ *55/7261–9343* ⊕ *www.lagolatam.com* Ⓜ *Polanco.*

★ Onora

HOUSEWARES | In collaboration with artisans all over Mexico, Onora sells handmade homewares and textiles that you might recognize from the city's chicest boutique hotels. The store was founded in 2014, with a minimalist yet luxurious philosophy and a commitment to elevating fine Mexican design. If you're looking for Mexican handicrafts that are a step above what you might find in the local markets, Onora is the right place. ✉ *Lope de Vega 330, Polanco* ☎ *55/5203–0938* ⊕ *www.onoracasa.com* Ⓜ *Polanco.*

Pasaje Polanco

MALL | In the heart of Polanco, you'll find this open-air shopping center lined with mostly locally owned and operated stores. Opened in 1938 and bordered by Avenida Masaryk (the most famous shopping district in the city), the stores here might not be exceptional, but the location and the people-watching are. ⊠ *Av. Masaryk 360, Polanco* ☎ *56/1771–0404* ⊕ *www.instagram.com/pasajepolancocd-mx* Ⓜ *Polanco, Auditorio.*

Raquel Orozco

CLOTHING | Known for her feminine color palette and extravagant silhouettes, Raquel Orozco is part of the new guard of Mexican fashion designers. This Polanco boutique is her flagship store, stocked with a full range of clothing and accessories. Pieces can also be found at the Palacio de Hierro department stores in Polanco and Santa Fe and at a second boutique in Antara Fashion Hall. ⊠ *Emilio Castelar 227–B, Polanco* ☎ *55/5280–5081* ⊕ *www.raquelorozco.com* Ⓜ *Polanco, Campo Marte.*

★ Sandra Weil

CLOTHING | Peruvian designer Sandra Weil opened this shop, her first boutique in Mexico City, in 2012. Combining traditional craftsmanship with high-quality fabrics, including pima cotton, alpaca wool, and silk, her bold designs have become a go-to for the capital's trendsetters. Weil's dresses and separates can be found at stores throughout Mexico, as well as in Miami and Houston, but this one has the most extensive collection. ⊠ *Horacio 907, Polanco* ☎ *55/2292–4808* ⊕ *www.sandra-weil.com* Ⓜ *Polanco or Campo Marte.*

★ Tane

JEWELRY & WATCHES | This store is a mine of perhaps the best silverwork in Mexico—jewelry, flatware, candelabras, museum-quality reproductions of archaeological finds, and bold designs by young Mexican silversmiths. The Masaryk shop is one of several in the city, including locations in the Four Seasons and in the upscale Centro Santa Fe. Outside this Polanco branch, you'll find an Instagram-famous bright pink wall with a neon sign that sums up most visitors' sentiments: *Mexico mi amor.* ⊠ *Av. Presidente Masaryk 430, Polanco* ☎ *55/5282–6200* ⊕ *www.tane.com* Ⓜ *Polanco, Campo Marte.*

★ Uriarte Talavera

CERAMICS | With a workshop in operation since 1824, Uriarte Talavera has been making the Talavera pottery emblematic of the town of Puebla for two centuries. If you can't make it to Puebla to see the workshop yourself, this store is a nice substitute, where you can still purchase original handmade Talavera. ⊠ *Galileo 67–A, Polanco* ☎ *55/5280–4406* ⊕ *www.uriartetalavera.com.mx* Ⓜ *Polanco.*

Chapter 8

ROMA

8

Updated by
Andrew Collins

👁 Sights	🍴 Restaurants	🛏 Hotels	🛍 Shopping	🍸 Nightlife
★★☆☆☆	★★★★★	★★★★★	★★★★☆	★★★★★

NEIGHBORHOOD SNAPSHOT

TOP EXPERIENCES

■ **Avenida Álvaro Obregón.** This broad boulevard with a charming tree-lined median decked with public art is perfect for leisurely walks. It bisects Roma Norte and is lined with fashionable restaurants, bars, and boutiques.

■ **Plaza Río de Janeiro.** Arguably the most enchanting of the neighborhood's handful of public squares, this rectangular park with a bronze replica of Michelangelo's *David* in the center is a great spot for people-watching. Several fashionable restaurants with sidewalk seating line its perimeter.

■ **Craft cocktails.** Home to the world-renowned bar Licorería Limantour, Roma is the neighborhood to explore if you want to experience what North America's most talented mixologists are up to. Other lounges with destination-worthy beverage programs include Gin Gin, Maison Artemisia, and Rayo.

■ **Romita.** To get a sense of Roma's historic roots, go for a stroll through this refreshingly untrendy quadrant of narrow lanes, which is anchored by a 1530s church and was occupied by Mexica long before the Spaniards arrived.

PLANNING YOUR TIME

As with Condesa to its west, Roma is an incredibly popular neighborhood that lacks any major attractions. As the main draw is its wealth of extraordinary restaurants and bars, along with an intriguing mix of art galleries and shops, a good strategy is to allow for an hour or two before or after dining in Roma to walk its tree-shaded streets and admire its regal architecture. Another fun way to plan your visit here is to set aside a full day to eat and drink your way through the neighborhood, starting with breakfast at a hip café and culminating with late-nights drinks at a fashionable bar.

GETTING HERE

■ Roma is easily reached by Uber and Metro as well as being an easy walk from the hotels on or near Paseo de la Reforma. Roma consists of two halves: the quieter and more prosaic Roma Sur and the trendier and much larger Roma Norte, which has an east and a west side divided by one of the city's most prominent north–south thoroughfares, Avenida Insurgentes. This chapter is focused almost entirely on Roma Norte, but to make it a bit easier to navigate, we've divided our coverage between the areas north and south of the major east–west thoroughfare, Avenida Álvaro Obregón. Two other major streets, Avenida Cuauhtémoc and Avenida Chapultepec, form Roma's eastern and northern borders, respectively. This is generally a safe neighborhood for strolling, but take a little extra care when walking on quieter side streets after dark. Roma has several metro stations, all on its borders, including the Sevilla, Insurgentes, and Cuauhtémoc stops on the 1 line, the Hospital General stop on the 3 line, and Centro Médico stop on both the 3 and 9 lines.

Although it contains only a handful of small museums and cultural attractions, Roma has become one of Mexico City's essential destinations, especially since its lightning-fast gentrification in the 2010s. This is the neighborhood where you're most likely to hear the voices of foreigners as you amble about, experiencing the area's essential activities: shopping, gallery-hopping, dining, and drinking.

The neighborhood is divided into Roma Sur and Roma Norte, and most of the action is in the latter district, which is also the much larger of the two (Calle Coahuila is the dividing line). Exceedingly trendy, Roma's rapid rise has led to both newfound respectability and soaring rents, but its restaurants and shops still offer better values than comparable establishments in Polanco and other high-end districts in the city.

Like its western neighbor Condesa, Roma was developed in the early 1900s on a huge tract of land owned previously by two Spanish countesses; the area was turned into an aristocratic enclave of stately homes, quite a few of which still stand today. By the 1940s and 1950s, many of the city's wealthiest residents began moving to newer and fancier developments farther west and south. Roma—far more than even Condesa—became better known for its rough-and-tumble cantinas, pool halls, dance clubs, and nightspots of questionable repute. The neighborhood's nadir followed the

1985 earthquake, but the rock-bottom rents of the 1990s and early 2000s—along with an amazing stock of grand beaux-arts and art nouveau mansions—helped spur its transformation into a center of edgy fashion, avant-garde art, innovative dining, and clever theme bars catering to a mix of styles, ages, and orientations.

The lower portion of Roma borders Condesa along Avenida Insurgentes Sur. At Calle Guanajuato, however, Roma Norte leaps across Insurgentes and follows a rather meandering border with Condesa for several blocks to the west. In this area, even many locals don't know (and likely don't care) whether they're in Condesa or Roma Norte, and there's little discernible difference between the look and feel of either district. Busy and wide Avenida Chapultepec forms Roma's northern border with Juárez, and similarly busy Avenida Cuauhtémoc separates the neighborhood from Doctores, to the east.

Roma North of Av. Álvaro Obregón

Sights

Avenida Álvaro Obregón

STREET | Roma's main east–west boulevard is wide and tree-lined, with a central promenade that's studded with sculptures and fountains. With dozens of restaurants, bars, cafés, and shops lining either side, Álvaro Obregón is an ideal place to stroll and take in occasional cultural exhibitions and events like classic car shows and public art displays. ⊠ *Av. Álvaro Obregón, between Avs. Cuauhtémoc and Sonora, La Roma* Ⓜ *Insurgentes.*

Casa Lamm Cultural Center

ARTS CENTER | Inside this imposing early 20th-century mansion and its connected buildings, artists are nurtured and browsers are welcomed in the airy exhibition spaces, a library, a bookstore, a wide range of courses, a café, and a swanky restaurant called Nueve Nueve that serves upmarket contemporary Mexican and international cuisine. All of the spaces surround a beautiful courtyard, and the restaurant—set inside a modern glass-walled addition—offers particularly nice views. ⊠ *Av. Álvaro Obregón 99, La Roma* ☎ *55/5525–1332* ⊕ *www.casalamm.com.mx* ✄ *Free* Ⓜ *Insurgentes.*

Fuente de Cibeles

PLAZA/SQUARE | This striking fountain anchors the busy traffic circle in Roma Norte's northwestern quadrant, an exact copy of the neoclassical Plaza de Cibeles fountain found in Madrid (which depicts the Roman goddess of fertility, Cybele, in a carriage pulled by lions). The surrounding traffic circle is officially called Plaza Villa de Madrid, although most locals just called it Plaza Cibeles. Six streets intersect here, and there's a lively flea market, Mercado Cibeles, held on weekends on the narrow lane running southeast to Avenida Insurgentes (Calle El Oro). There are a number of prominent restaurants on or within a few steps of the circle, including the famously sceney seafood eatery, Contramar, and branches of the popular coffee-pizza eateries, Cancino and La Ventanita, which have large swaths of sidewalk tables curving around the northwestern arc of the circle. ⊠ *Plaza Villa de Madrid, at Av. Oaxaca and Calle de Durango, La Roma* Ⓜ *Insurgentes.*

★ Galería OMR

ART GALLERY | Set within a typical-looking Roma house with an early 20th-century stone facade, Galería OMR has been a leader in the city's contemporary arts scene since it opened in 1983. It contains dramatic, light-filled exhibit spaces on two levels as well as an art library, a bougainvillea-filled courtyard, and a roof-deck with grand views of the neighborhood. The gallery also has a strong presence in international art fairs and art magazines. ⊠ *Calle Córdoba 100, La Roma* ☎ *55/5511–1179* ⊕ *www.omr.art* ⓧ *Closed Sun. and Mon.* Ⓜ *Insurgentes.*

MAIA Contemporary Gallery

ART GALLERY | An essential stop on any gallery stroll through Roma, MAIA occupies part of one of the more striking mansions on elegant Calle Colima, the Porfirian-era Casa Basalta, with exhibition spaces connected by a long, columned veranda. The gallery represents a mix of up-and-coming and more established contemporary talents, and the shows here make great use of the dramatic architecture. Casa Basalta also houses a handful of other businesses, including a few small restaurants, an ice cream shop, and a couple of clothing boutiques. ⊠ *Calle Colima 159, La Roma* ☎ *55/8662–0085* ⊕ *www.maiacontemporary.com* ✄ *Free* ⓧ *Closed Mon.* Ⓜ *Insurgentes.*

★ MODO (Museo del Objeto de Objeto)

ART MUSEUM | Literally the Museum of the Object of the Object, MODO presents fascinating rotating exhibits from an immense collection of some 150,000 objects dating back to the early 19th century, all with some relationship to design. The building itself is a series of relatively compact gallery spaces inside a gracious Porfirian art nouveau mansion on one of Roma's prettiest streets. This trove of objects was donated by collector Bruno Newman, the museum's founder, and it's really intended to celebrate prosaic objects of everyday use that aren't often celebrated in museums: recent exhibitions have featured vintage sneakers, household appliances, political posters and propaganda, beer and liquor bottles, erotica, lucha libre memorabilia, and rock music. The little gift shop is terrific, too, filled with original, captivating items, large and small, practical and whimsical. ⊠ *Calle Colima 145, La Roma* 🕾 *55/5533–9637* ⊕ *www.elmodo.mx* ✉ *MP60* 🕑 *Closed Mon.–Thurs.* Ⓜ *Insurgentes.*

Museo Soumaya–Casa Guillermo Tovar de Teresa

HISTORIC HOME | Part of Carlos Slim's growing collection of cultural holdings that operate—always with free admission—under the aegis of Soumaya Museum, this classic late 19th-century Porfirian mansion was formerly owned by the late historian and art collector Guillermo Tovar de Teresa. The grand, if imposingly formal, home is filled with priceless antiques and artwork, including an important painting of Archangel San Rafael by noted religious painter Miguel Cabrera, fine porcelain and glassworks from both Europe and Spanish Colonial Mexico, and Tovar de Teresa's huge library of historic books. Walking amid the Oriental rugs, gilt-framed mirrors and paintings, and sweeping drapes give a nice sense of what it might have felt like to live in one of the city's grandest homes, but the real treat here is visiting the romantic, cloistered garden, with its huge ferns, flowering plants, and curving pathways—it's a peaceful little green treasure in the heart of a bustling

neighborhood. ⊠ *Calle Valladolid 52, La Roma* 🕾 *55/1103–9800* ⊕ *www.museosoumaya.org* ✉ *Free* Ⓜ *Sevilla.*

★ Plaza Río de Janeiro

PLAZA/SQUARE | Perhaps the most picturesque—and oft-photographed—of Roma's several public squares, this large rectangular plaza was laid out as part of the neighborhood's formal development into an upper-class residential district in 1903. Near the neighborhood's northern border and the more frenetic Gloria de los Insurgentes traffic circle, the Plaza attracts dog walkers, joggers, shoppers, and passersby of all stripes. The fountain, anchored by a bronze replica of Michelangelo's *David*, is the square's social focal point, and you'll find a handful of inviting cafés and restaurants on its different sides, including Pigeon, Marmota, Sartoria, and Buna. Ornately detailed early 20th-century mansions fringe the plaza, the most famous being the redbrick *Casa de las Brujas* (Gouse of the Witches), so named for its soaring conical turret's resemblance to a witch's hat. ⊠ *Calle Orizaba, at Calle de Durango, La Roma* Ⓜ *Insurgentes.*

★ Romita

NEIGHBORHOOD | Before real estate developers established most of Roma as a fashionable residential neighborhood in the early 1900s, this small quadrant of narrow lanes thrived as an off-the-beaten-path village for centuries. Originally occupying one of the many small, low islands of massive Lake Texcoco, the area was inhabited by Mexica (aka Aztecs) well before the arrival of Spaniards. As the city and then Roma and neighboring Juárez and Doctores districts grew up around it, Romita retained a distinct—and decidedly more working-class—personality and independence. You can get some sense of what it might have looked like in the mid-20th century by watching Luis Buñuel's heart-wrenching 1950 film, *Los Olvidados,* which was filmed here. Romita's name is said to derive from its

8

Roma ROMA NORTH OF AV. ÁLVARO OBREGÓN

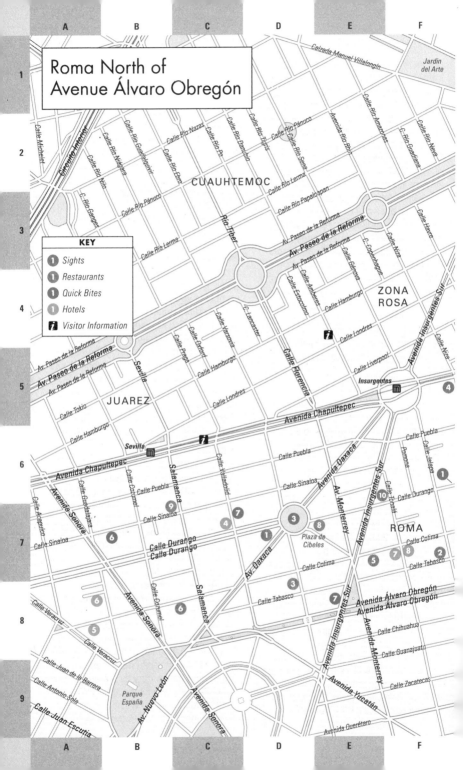

Roma North of
Avenue Álvaro Obregón

KEY

- 1 Sights
- 1 Restaurants
- 1 Quick Bites
- 1 Hotels
- *i* Visitor Information

Sights ▼

1 Avenida Álvaro Obregón................. G7
2 Casa Lamm Cultural Center.......... G7
3 Fuente de Cibeles....... D7
4 Galería OMR............. H7
5 MAIA Contemporary Gallery G7
6 MODO (Museo del Objeto de Objeto) G7
7 Museo Soumaya-Casa Guillermo Tovar de Teresa.......... C7
8 Plaza Río de Janeiro ... G6
9 Romita I5

Restaurants ▼

1 Contramar D7
2 Dooriban.................. F7
3 Fonda Fina............... D8
4 Fugaz...................... F5
5 Huset...................... E7
6 Kura Izakaya C8
7 La Docena I7
8 La Tecla E7
9 Lorea B7
10 Loup Bar E6
11 Marmota................. G6
12 Máximo Bistrot H7
13 Meroma.................. G7
14 Peltre Lonchería H8
15 Rosetta................... G7
16 Sartoria G6
17 Wabi Sushi G7

Quick Bites ▼

1 Cafe Trucha F6
2 Caravanserai............ G7
3 Gonzalitos I6
4 Helados Cometa G7
5 Panadería Rosetta...... G7
6 Raku Café................ B7
7 Taquería Orinoco E8

Hotels ▼

1 Brick Hotel............... G7
2 Casa Izeba............... G7
3 Colima 71 .... I6
4 Durango 219 .... C7
5 Hotel Villa Condesa..... A8
6 La Palomilla B&B A8
7 La Valise F7
8 Nima Local House Hotel F7
9 Stanza Hotel.............. I7

The Museo del Objeto de Objeto explores the use of diverse objects used in the name of artistic design.

resemblance during the mid-1700s to a neighborhood in Rome, Italy, that was similarly rife at the time with large trees. To get a feel for the neighborhood, walk along one of its narrow lanes to Plaza Romita, a tranquil tree-shaded courtyard with park benches and a central fountain that's flanked on its eastern side by the small, 1530s Rectoria San Francisco Javier Church. The neighborhood's liveliest street, Real de Romita, has a few shops and cafés, including La Perla de la Roma, Veganísimo Loncheria, and Vocablo Café y Poesía; down another lane you'll find the headquarters of the acclaimed craft bewery, Cru Cru. ✉ *Callejón de Romita 24, La Roma* [M] *Cuauhtémoc.*

🍴 Restaurants

★ Contramar

$$$ | SEAFOOD | Come before 1 pm or make an online reservation to avoid the long wait at this airy seafood haven, a power-lunch spot for the creative and celebrity sets since it opened in 1998 (there's often less of a wait for the casual outside tables). While the people-watching is prime, your attention will be on the food: start with the famed tuna tartare tostadas, then try some fish cooked al pastor or a bowl of clam chowder, minced soft-shell crab or octopus tacos, or the huge butterflied pescado Contramar with red chile. **Known for:** see-and-be-seen crowd; some of the freshest seafood in Mexico City; octopus aguachile. [$] *Average main: MP395* ✉ *Calle Durango 200, La Roma* ☎ *55/5514–3169* 🌐 *www.contramar.com.mx* [M] *Sevilla.*

Dooriban

$$ | KOREAN | This trendy, casual spot with a long wooden bar serves up some of the best Korean food in the city, including classics like beef bulgogi, kimchi-fried rice topped with a fried egg, bibimbap, and—arguably the star of the menu—crispy Korean fried chicken wings with *gochujang* (fermented chiles). There's also a nice selection of kefirs and kombuchas to sip, plus wine and craft beer. **Known for:** spicy braised tofu appetizer; soju spirits; chocolate mousse with yuja-fruit jelly. $ *Average main: MP210* ✉ *Calle Tabasco 189, La Roma* ☎ ⊕ *www.instagram.com/dooriban* ⊗ *Closed Mon. and Tues.* Ⓜ *Insurgentes.*

★ Fonda Fina

$$$ | **MODERN MEXICAN** | Partly founded by Quinonil's celebrity chef Jorge Vallejo, Fonda Fina serves modernly interpreted Mexican classics, such as raw tuna tostadas with citrus oil and a gaujillo-chile vinaigrette or a casserole of beef cheeks braised in a green mole sauce with smoked cauliflower. One popular way to choose your meal here is to mix and match your protein (rib-eye, octopus, and pork among them) with any of several vegetable garnishes and about 10 salsa options—the servers are happy to recommend tasty pairings. **Known for:** casually chic dining room; regional Mexican fare with a modern twist; creative cocktails. $ *Average main: MP320* ✉ *Calle Medellín 79, La Roma* ☎ *55/5208–3925* ⊕ *www.instagram.com/fondafinamx* ⊗ *No dinner Sun.* Ⓜ *Insurgentes.*

Fugaz

$$ | **SEAFOOD** | At this unpretentious, cozy spot on the north edge of Roma, the short menu of tapas-size plates changes according to what chef Giuseppe Lacorazza picks up that morning at the city's leading seafood market. The focus is always on sustainability and fresh produce—think bonito crudo with tamarind and tangerine, smoked-mackerel quesadillas, steamed clams with spring peas and basil, or Veracruz-style shellfish stew. **Known for:** artfully plated sustainable seafood; nice mezcal selection; ever-changing list of creative desserts. $ *Average main: MP240* ✉ *Calle Cerrada Orizaba 3–3B, La Roma* ☎ *55/3566–0298* ⊕ *www.instagram.com/fuuuugaz* ⊗ *Closed Mon.–Wed. No lunch* Ⓜ *Insurgentes.*

★ Huset

$$$ | **CONTEMPORARY** | You can opt for either of the two distinct experiences in this stylish Calle Colima restaurant: dining in the early 20th-century town house that overlooks the busy street below or sitting in the much more casual and social covered outdoor section with a green living wall. The menu changes seasonally but might feature crab tostadas with grapefruit, ginger, and arugula or fillet of beef with pureed potatoes and a soy-caramel emulsion. **Known for:** late night dining; sophisticated wood-fired cuisine; innovative cocktails. $ *Average main: MP365* ✉ *Calle Colima 256, La Roma* ☎ *55/5511–6767* ⊕ *www.instagram.com/husetroma* ⊗ *Closed Mon.* Ⓜ *Insurgentes.*

★ Kura Izakaya

$$$ | **JAPANESE** | Savor deftly crafted modern Japanese fare—yakitori skewers, oden and ramen bowls, tempura, udon noodle, raw shellfish, and sushi and sashimi—in this inviting, contemporary space with a variety of seating options, including private tatami rooms. The menu stand-outs are many, including a serrano-wagyu beef roll and shrimp mapo tofu. **Known for:** huge menu designed for sharing; attractive dining areas with ample natural light; diverse alcohol menu. $ *Average main: MP320* ✉ *Calle Colima 378, La Roma* ☎ *55/7989–3102* ⊕ *www.instagram.com/izakaya_kura* Ⓜ *Sevilla.*

La Docena

$$$ | **SEAFOOD** | This boisterous, upmarket seafood spot is an especially fun late-night option, but also popular for weekend brunch. The menu blends Mexican and American (especially New Orleans) seafood traditions and features several kinds of po'boys, aguachile and sashimi, grilled soft-shell crab, and a pretty good variety of steaks and meatier items. **Known for:** lively, chatter-filled dining room; oysters on the half shell and other raw-bar items; serving food until very late at night. $ *Average main: MP340* ✉ *Av. Álvaro Obregón 31, La Roma* ☎ *55/5208–0833* ⊕ *www.ladocena.com.mx* Ⓜ *Insurgentes.*

La Tecla

$$ | **MEXICAN** | This popular veteran of the city's modern Mexican culinary scene is still a mainstay for reasonably priced, consistently well-prepared dishes like huitlacoche risotto with corn and poblano chiles, and grilled prawns with a sweet-spicy tamarind-guajillo reduction. The space is refined, relaxed, and ideal for conversation, and there are a few tables on the sidewalk overlooking Plaza Villa de Madrid and Fuente de Cibeles. **Known for:** artfully plated contemporary fare; excellent selection of Mexican wines; soursop mousse with mango sauce. $ *Average main: MP290* ✉ *Calle de Durango 186A, La Roma* ☎ *55/5525–4920* ⊕ *www.latecla.mx* ⊗ *No dinner Sun.* Ⓜ *Insurgentes.*

Lorea

$$$$ | **MODERN MEXICAN** | Meals in this minimalist dining room are among the most refined and romantic culinary adventures in Roma. Local chef-owner Oswaldo Oliva spent years abroad honing his craft at some of Spain's most hallowed restaurants, and he shares his farm-to-table approach here in the form of exquisitely plated, ethereal bites that change seasonally, but you can expect a number of Mexico-centric ingredients, such as huitlacoche, tomatillos, and honeycomb. **Known for:** beautifully plated farm-to-table cuisine; tacos made on a comal with interesting fillings (octopus, huitlacoche); exceptional selection of wine, cocktails, and artisanal beers. $ *Average main: MP480* ✉ *Calle Sinaloa 141, La Roma* ☎ *55/9130–7786* ⊕ *www.lorea.mx* ⊗ *Closed Sun. and Mon.* Ⓜ *Sevilla.*

Loup Bar

$$ | **WINE BAR** | This cozy wine-cave-like space, located beneath the wildly popular cocktail-piano bar Artemisia, stands out from the city's growing clutch of vino bars for its devotion to natural bottles, from German orange wines to heady, bold Rhône blends (nearly all are priced over MP1,000—and many are much costlier—so budget accordingly). But there's also a quite reasonably priced menu of tasty French-inspired bar fare, including a savory Wagyu beef tartare with piquillo chiles, fried Brussels sprouts with a garlic-lemongrass dressing, and lamb couscous with olives and preserved lemon. **Known for:** impressive natural wine list; tasty French bar fare; hip and intimate setting. $ *Average main: MP260* ✉ *Calle Tonalá 23, La Roma* ☎ *55/5299–6931* ⊕ *www.loupbar.mx* ⊗ *Closed Sun.* Ⓜ *Insurgentes.*

★ **Marmota**

$$$ | **MODERN AMERICAN** | The creative cuisine served in this chic restaurant with sidewalk tables overlooking pretty Plaza Río de Janeiro is inspired by the time the chef-owners spent in the Pacific Northwest of the United States. Typical fare from the regularly changing menu includes wild boar sausage with pickled blackberries or clams steamed with white wine, panceta, spring peas, and parsley. **Known for:** outstanding wine list; classic grilled cheese sandwich with cheddar and bacon; lovely outdoor seating. $ *Average main: MP320* ✉ *Plaza Río de Janeiro 53, La Roma* ☎ *55/8870–4242* ⊕ *www.marmota.mx* ⊗ *Closed Sun.* Ⓜ *Insurgentes.*

★ **Máximo Bistrot**

$$$$ | **MODERN FRENCH** | One of the capital's most sought-after dining experiences has moved from its unassuming original digs to a much more spacious and rather swanky space. Chef Eduardo García crafts complex French-Mediterranean-Mexican dishes like sea scallops with a raspberry "aguachile," lobster risotto, and tagliatelle pasta with a wild boar ragout—nothing outlandish but always perfectly executed. **Known for:** stone crab, lobster, sea urchin, and other rarefied seafood; decadent desserts; exceptional wine list. $ *Average main: MP720* ✉ *Av. Álvaro Obregón 65 Bis, La Roma* ☎ *55/5264–4291* ⊕ *www.maximobistrot.com.mx* ⊗ *Closed Sun.* Ⓜ *Insurgentes.*

★ Meroma

$$$$ | **CONTEMPORARY** | The mid-century-modern design of this fashionable, trendy, and yet somehow still unpretentious restaurant feels distinct from its grandiose Porfirian neighbors, and so does the seasonally inspired small-plate-focused cuisine, which is heavy on fresh vegetables, hand-made pastas, and seafood. A foie gras terrine is served with a zesty apple-shiso-rhubarb-port sauce, while tender, slow-roasted lamb is served with crushed falafel, braised eggplant, labneh, fried pistachios, and a green zhug sauce. **Known for:** house-made pastas tossed with seasonal ingredients; distinctive mid-century-modern aesthetic; noteworthy cocktail, beer, and wine list. [$] *Average main: MP470* ✉ *Calle Colima 150, La Roma* ☎ *55/5920–2654* 🌐 *www.meroma.mx* 🕒 *Closed Sun. and Mon.* [M] *Insurgentes.*

Peltre Lonchería

$$ | **MEXICAN** | This stylish mid-century-modern lunchroom offers a contemporary take on classic Mexican and American comfort fare, like ham-turkey-gouda sandwiches with a fried egg on top, cochinita pibíl, and beef milanesa tortas with salsa verde. There's nothing fancy about this place, but it's great for a light in-between meal, late-night snack (it's open til 11 pm), or breakfast, which features a similarly extensive variety of favorites, from huevos rancheros to French toast slathered in berries and agave honey. **Known for:** hearty sandwiches and tortas; house-made jams, snacks, and peltre (pewter) kitchenware for sale; good coffee drinks (including cold brew with horchata). [$] *Average main: MP155* ✉ *Av. Álvaro Obregón 86, La Roma* ☎ 🌐 *www.instagram.com/peltre_loncheria* [M] *Insurgentes.*

★ Rosetta

$$$$ | **MODERN ITALIAN** | Regarded as one of the best female chefs in the world, Elena Reygadas worked for years at London's Michelin-starred Italian restaurant Locando Locatelli before moving back to her hometown to open Rosetta in a stunning early 1900s belle epoque mansion. Despite the perfect risottos and handmade pastas in varying shapes, what her cuisine primarily takes from Italy is reliance on local and seasonal ingredients (the olive oil is from Baja California, the burrata cheese made in the town of Atlixco)—but much of the food has a creative Mexican heart. **Known for:** superb modern Italian fare; drinks in the swanky upstairs cocktail bar, Salon Rosetta; rosemary–olive oil ice cream with fresh herbs for dessert. [$] *Average main: MP530* ✉ *Calle Colima 166, La Roma* ☎ *55/5533–7804* 🌐 *www.rosetta.com.mx* 🕒 *Closed Sun.* [M] *Insurgentes.*

Sartoria

$$$ | **MODERN ITALIAN** | This uberhip osteria with a cool arched dining room overlooking Plaza Río de Janeiro is justly famous for the fresh handmade pastas of internationally renowned chef Marco Carboni—think gnocchi with a 12-hour ragu of beek cheek, lamb, sausage, and pork leg, or tagliolini tossed with lobster, lemon, tarragon butter, and fish roe. Portions are a bit small, so consider ordering a side or two of the marvelous Creole tomatoes with burrata, pesto, and preserved lemon. **Known for:** handmade artisanal pastas; fine coffees in adjoining Buna café; gorgeous, chicly modern dining room. [$] *Average main: MP420* ✉ *Calle Cerrada Orizaba 42, La Roma* ☎ *55/7265–3616* 🌐 *www.sartoria.mx* 🕒 *No dinner Sun.* [M] *Insurgentes.*

Wabi Sushi

$$ | **SUSHI** | This cute hole-in-the-wall sushi and sake bar with several outdoor seats and a cozy interior turns out some of the best Japanese food in the city. There's a wide assortment of nigiri sushi, including bluefin tuna, spicy scallop, and sea urchin, plus creative maki rolls like kampachi with ume and asparagus, along with soft-shell crab tempura, yakimeshi with foie gras and eel sauce, rib-eye

Roma is one of the best neighborhoods to just stroll around on foot or bike.

tataki, and teriyaki salmon-mushroom bowls. **Known for:** outdoor tables looking toward Plaza Río de Janeiro; chef who trained under acclaimed Japanese sushi master; well-curated list of Japanese sakes and whiskies. [$] *Average main: MP285* ✉ *Calle Cerrada Orizaba 76, La Roma* ☎ *55/5941–4815* 🌐 *www.wabisushi.mx* [M] *Insurgentes.*

☕ Coffee and Quick Bites

★ Cafe Trucha

$$ | **MEDITERRANEAN** | This fashionably casual spot owned by the talented chefs at neighboring Marmota is a great option for anything from sipping espresso drinks while you work to noshing on creative Mediterranean-meets-Pacific Northwest bar snacks while you mingle with friends. Highlights from the kitchen include house-made potato chips with creme fraiche and caviar, one of the best Caesar salads in town, Portuguese tinned sardines, burrata with figs and tomatoes, and a selection of cheeses with figs and honey. **Known for:** fresh-baked goods and fine coffee in the morning; landscaped outdoor seating overlooking Plaza Río de Janeiro; craft cocktails. [$] *Average main: MP165* ✉ *Plaza Río de Janeiro 53, La Roma* 🌐 *www.instagram.com/cafetrucha* 🕒 *Closed Sun. No dinner Mon.–Thurs.* [M] *Insurgentes.*

Caravanserai

$ | **CAFÉ** | This Paris–meets–Silk Road–inspired teahouse on a lively street corner along Avenida Álvaro Obregón is a wonderful spot to sip interesting hot and iced teas (nearly 200 blends are available, from spicy chais to delicate white teas) while watching passersby from a sidewalk table or cozied up in one of the warmly furnished interior rooms. French-Asian desserts are offered, too, including green tea cakes and tarte tatin. **Known for:** intimate and inviting space; tea blends in a vast range of flavors; tarte tatin and other desserts. [$] *Average main: MP80* ✉ *Calle Cerrada Orizaba 101, La Roma* ☎ *55/7090–6157* 🌐 *www.caravanserai.com.mx* [M] *Insurgentes.*

★ Gonzalitos

$$ | **MEXICAN** | This itty-bitty taqueria on a less swanky block of famous Calle Colima has a big following for its hearty tacos prepared in the style of Monterrey. **Known for:** Norteño-style barbacoa tacos; casual sidewalk seating; spicy vampirito cocktails. [$] *Average main: MP150* ✉ *Calle Colima 71, La Roma* ☎ 🌐 *www.instagram.com/barbacoagonzalitos* ⏲ *Closed Mon.* [M] *Cuauhtémoc.*

Helados Cometa

$ | **ICE CREAM** | Pop inside this tiny café for first-rate ice cream and sorbets in interesting flavors like ginger-hibiscus, chocolate-mint, and raspberry-green tea. There are a few stools and two little tables, but the best plan is to take your purchase to enjoy by the fountain at Plaza Río de Janeiro. **Known for:** gourmet sorbets and ice creams; cute, cozy space; short walk to Plaza Río de Janeiro. [$] *Average main: MP75* ✉ *Calle Colima 162, La Condesa* ☎ 🌐 *www.heladoscometa.com* [M] *Insurgentes.*

★ Panadería Rosetta

$$ | **BAKERY** | Just a block away from the famous restaurant that inspired it, this wildly popular bakery is worth the often long wait for a table to savor a fantastic breakfast, lunch, or even a sweet treat to break up your day. The flaky pastries here are second to none—try the blueberry-lavender scones, guava rolls, or mamey-filled berliners. **Known for:** long lines, especially on weekends; heavenly French-style pastries and coffee; charming tree-shaded sidewalk seating along elegant Calle Colima. [$] *Average main: MP165* ✉ *Calle Colima 179, La Roma* ☎ *55/5207–2976* 🌐 *www.instagram.com/panaderiarosetta* [M] *Insurgentes.*

Raku Café

$ | **CAFÉ** | This diminutive, modern café turns out some of the finest Kyoto-sourced matcha green tea in the city as well as exceptional house-roasted coffee drinks, which are served in beautiful hand-thrown ceramic mugs. Have a seat on one of the little benches fashioned out of tree trunks or at one of the sidewalk tables ensconced within a landscaped wooden platform. **Known for:** matcha tea; tasty sandwiches and pastries; well-crafted espresso drinks and cold brew. [$] *Average main: MP65* ✉ *Calle Sinaloa 188, La Roma* ☎ *55/5553–0850* 🌐 *www.instagram.com/rakucafe_mx* [M] *Insurgentes.*

★ Taquería Orinoco

$ | **MEXICAN** | There are few more satisfying experiences after a night of dancing and drinking than devouring a plate of tacos at this taqueria with a spacious dining room on Avenida Álvaro Obregón. Fillings include *trompo* (al pastor), chicharrón with spicy house-made salsa, and beef; a side of the crunchy fried *papas orinoco* potatoes is a must. **Known for:** late-night tacos; great people-watching; guayaba popsicles. [$] *Average main: MP85* ✉ *Av. Álvaro Obregón 179, La Roma* ☎ *55/5514–6917* 🌐 *www.taqueriaorinoco.com* [M] *Insurgentes.*

Hotels

Brick Hotel

$$$$ | **HOTEL** | An opulent English manor-style mansion from the early 20th century has been transformed into arguably Roma's most exclusive lodging, an intimate urban resort with first-class amenities and rooms outfitted with sumptuous touches like premium sound systems, Mexico-made Persea Apothecary bath products, and in-room climate control. **Pros:** several bars and restaurants; luxurious full-service spa; steps from trendy dining and shopping. **Cons:** expensive; some rooms lack balconies; in a very busy part of Roma. [$] *Rooms from: MP6250* ✉ *Calle Cerrada Orizaba 95, La Roma* ☎ *55/9155–7610* 🌐 *www.itbrickhotel.com* 🛏 *17 rooms* 🍴 *No Meals* [M] *Insurgentes.*

★ Casa Izeba

$$$ | B&B/INN | This somewhat unassuming art deco–style town house beside famed Panadería Rosetta is considered one of the neighborhood's lodging gems, thanks to its chic yet unfussy modern design, abundance of peaceful common terraces (including a gorgeous roof deck), and desirable location. **Pros:** located on one of Roma's prettiest streets; morning pastries from Panadería Rosetta; one of the few small inns in Roma that welcomes kids of all ages. **Cons:** you'll have to climb some stairs to reach upper floors; always lots of pedestrians on this street; though delicious, the continental breakfast is on the light side. $ *Rooms from: MP5250 ⊠ Colima 183, La Roma ☎ 55/4873–3306 ⊕ www.casaizeba. mx ➷ 8 rooms ⧾ Free Breakfast* Ⓜ *Insurgentes.*

★ Colima 71

$$ | HOTEL | Designed by one of the country's leading architects, this pale-green contemporary boutique hotel with a mid-century-modern vibe features spacious rooms with fully equipped kitchens, large balconies with tables and comfy chairs, organic Yucateco bath products, and a stunning collection of contemporary art. **Pros:** thoughtful, efficient staff; several areas to work and socialize (including a hip coffee bar); full kitchens and spacious rooms make this great for longer stays. **Cons:** front rooms receive some street noise; not suitable for kids under 13; in a busy neighborhood. $ *Rooms from: MP3650 ⊠ Colima 71, La Roma ☎ 55/4166–7467 ⊕ www. colima71.com ➷ 16 rooms ⧾ Free Breakfast* Ⓜ *Cuauhtémoc.*

Durango 219

$$ | HOTEL | This six-story boutique hotel on the side of Roma Norte closer to Bosque de Chapultepec and Avenida Reforma offers uncluttered contemporary rooms with smart TVs, fast Wi-Fi, and stand-alone rain head showers, but instead of a conventional front desk, guests communicate with the highly efficient staff through text messages or phone calls. **Pros:** rooms have balconies with great neighborhood views; excellent location near Condesa and many restaurants; nice restaurants on roof and ground floor. **Cons:** lacks front desk, gym, and common spaces; rooms on lower floors receive some noise from street and ground-level restaurant; rooms are a bit on the compact side. $ *Rooms from: MP3000 ⊠ Calle de Durango 219, La Roma ☎ 55/3225–3142 ⊕ www.durango219.com ➷ 12 rooms ⧾ No Meals* Ⓜ *Sevilla.*

Hotel Villa Condesa

$$ | B&B/INN | With no sign out front and a location on a quiet street a block from Roma's border with Condesa, this inviting oasis anchored by a restored two-story Porfirian mansion stands out for its lovely staff, delicious food, and tasteful balance between old-world elegance and modern convenience. **Pros:** peaceful yet central setting close to parks and Avenida Amsterdam; very good guest-only on-site restaurant; beautifully decorated common rooms and landscaped terraces. **Cons:** bit of a walk from the heart of Roma; least expensive rooms can feel a little cramped; Internet can be a little slow. $ *Rooms from: MP3000 ⊠ Colima 428, La Roma ☎ 55/5211–4892 ⊕ www. villacondesa.com.mx ➷ 15 rooms ⧾ Free Breakfast* Ⓜ *Chapultepec.*

★ La Palomilla B&B

$$ | B&B/INN | This cozy, reasonably priced B&B located down a private alley has seven simple but inviting rooms with white color schemes that contrast with brightly colored Mexican-made pillows, crafts, and decorative accents, along with charming common spaces that include an indoor patio, a sunny terrace, and a dining area with a full kitchen. **Pros:** owners use eco-friendly products and practices; delicious full breakfasts; convenient base for both Roma and Condesa. **Cons:** some rooms have private baths accessed from the hall; smaller property lacking big-hotel amenities; not a good fit for young kids. [$] *Rooms from: MP2200* ✉ *Segunda Cerrada Guadalajara 10, La Roma* ☎ *55/7587–8995* 🌐 *www.lapalomillabnb.com* 🛏 *7 rooms* 🍴 *Free Breakfast* [M] *Sevilla.*

★ La Valise

$$$$ | B&B/INN | The Terrace Suite at La Valise is one of the most dramatic guest rooms in the city, with a plush king-size bed on tracks that allows it to slide right out onto the rooftop balcony, where you have the option of spending the night beneath a canopy of stars, but the other two rooms in this magical little B&B also exude character and luxury. **Pros:** the exceptional breakfasts are served in your suite; highly professional and thoughtful staff; enormous, gorgeously appointed rooms. **Cons:** often booked up well in advance; steep rates; in a very busy part of the neighborhood. [$] *Rooms from: MP7800* ✉ *Calle Tonalá 53, La Roma* ☎ *55/5965–2585* 🌐 *www.lavalisecdmx.com* 🛏 *3 suites* 🍴 *Free Breakfast* [M] *Insurgentes.*

★ Nima Local House Hotel

$$$$ | B&B/INN | For an ultraromantic urban getaway, it's hard to beat staying at this intimate Spanish Colonial mansion on one of the city's most enchanting streets—the knowledgeable and efficient staff pampers guests at every turn, with everything from nightly aromatherapy turn-down service to massage and reiki sessions in a serene spa cabin. **Pros:** sublime breakfasts; highly desirable location; variety of bespoke experiences and packages are available. **Cons:** not a good fit for kids; in a very busy neighborhood; highest rates of any hotel in Roma. [$] *Rooms from: MP11,000* ✉ *Colima 236, La Roma* ☎ *55/7591—7175* 🌐 *www.hotelnima.com* 🛏 *4 rooms* 🍴 *Free Breakfast* [M] *Insurgentes.*

Stanza Hotel

$ | HOTEL | An anomaly in fashionable Roma, this seven-story budget hotel built in the early 1970s won't win any prizes for its design, but with spacious if nondescript rooms, a friendly staff, and close proximity to the neighborhood's trendy restaurants and shops, it's a solid pick if you're looking to save money. **Pros:** excellent location near restaurants and overlooking Jardín Pushkin; the suites are enormous; affordable rates. **Cons:** feels a bit dated and faded; very small gym; tends to attract a lot of younger partying guests. [$] *Rooms from: MP1460* ✉ *Av. Álvaro Obregón 13, La Roma* ☎ *55/5208–0052* 🌐 *www.stanzahotel.com* 🛏 *130 rooms* 🍴 *No Meals* [M] *Cuauhtémoc.*

🍸 Nightlife

Bar Oriente

DANCE CLUB | Bright lighting and a bold color scheme create a striking vibe for singing karaoke, watching live bands, dancing, sipping craft cocktails, and nibbling on Japanese-Mexican-fusion bar snacks in this quirky late-night space that draws a mix of artists, club kids, and style-makers. Music tends toward the playful and accessible—think trash disco, alternative, reggae, and pretty much anything that gets the diverse crowd moving. Oriente's two private karaoke rooms are great for small parties (they hold up to 30 guests). ✉ *Calle de Durango 181, La Roma* ☎ *55/3239–9887* 🌐 *www.instagram.com/bar_oriente* [M] *Insurgentes.*

Blanco Colima

BARS | Ensconced within one of the most opulent Porfirian mansions in Roma, this urbane bar is a dramatic setting for well-crafted cocktails and tasty tapas. Located in the mansion's former courtyard, the bar is just one element of the building's rambling series of dining spaces (which also includes an oyster bar and a more formal high-end farm-to-table restaurant), but it's also arguably the most delightful of the venues to pass time in. ✉ *Calle Colima 168, La Roma* ☎ *55/5511–7527* 🌐 *www.blancocolimamx.com* [M] *Insurgentes.*

Strolling Around Old-World Romita

A ramble through the northeastern corner of Roma, centered on the prehistoric village of Romita, offers visitors a laid-back experience that is still relatively free of the gentrification that characterizes the rest of neighborhood. Start by visiting the narrow lanes that lead away from **Plaza Romita** and its nearly 500-year-old church, Rectoria San Francisco.

From there, meander a few blocks south to **Jardín Pushkin**, a pretty swath of greenery that's popular with dog walkers and contains one of the better playgrounds in Roma. On Sunday, it also hosts a bustling flea market. The stretch of Colima bordering Jardín Pushkin contains an interesting mix of shops—including a couple of popular vintage stores—that reflect Roma's eclecticism.

Diagonally from Jardín Pushkin to the northeast, across wide Avenida Cuauhtémoc and on the edge of the steadily gentrifying but still somewhat rough-around-the-edges Doctores neighborhood, another pleasant spot to go for a stroll is **Jardín Dr. Ignacio Chávez,** which was created following the destruction of several buildings in the 1985 earthquake. It's fringed by towering pine trees, and on weekends, it's the site of Tianguis de Antigüedades, a popular antiques market. If you're in the mood to haggle, the vendors here have a reputation for price flexibility, especially if you're willing to buy more than one item from the same seller.

Back at Plaza Romita, one last patch of benches and trees lies just a block north at **Plaza Morelia,** a small, semicircular pocket park with a lush canopy of greenery. There are no markets here, and the pace is sleepy, but it's still a nice spot for dog-walkers and families. From just a half-block south of here, you can follow Calle Puebla back into Roma's trendy heart.

★ **Casa Franca**

LIVE MUSIC | The glow of flickering candles welcomes visitors to this swish Parisian-style bar that presents live jazz and blues bands several days a week, along with a menu of designer pizzas, Mediterranean tapas, wine, and cocktails. It's a popular spot on weekends, and reservations are recommended if you want a table. Around the corner, sister restaurant Franca Bistro serves a more extensive food menu and has a similarly classy but laid-back air about it. ⊠ *Calle Mérida 109, La Roma* ☎ *55/5208–2265* ⊕ *www.instagram.com/casa.franca* Ⓜ *Insurgentes.*

★ **Covadonga**

BARS | This grand, cavernous 1940s-era cantina has a long antique bar to one side and a kitchen serving up tasty Asturian Spanish fare. It's filled nightly with the sounds of the *tercera edad* (a polite phrase for the elder generation) playing exuberant games of dominoes and millennials chatting about their adventures at Roma's latest gallery opening. ⊠ *Calle Puebla 121, La Roma* ☎ *55/5533–2701* ⊕ *www.instagram.com/cantinacovadonga* Ⓜ *Insurgentes.*

Cru Cru Brew

BREWPUBS | In a two-story redbrick brewery on a quiet alley in historic Romita, you can sample some of Mexico City's finest craft brews, from a crisp golden pale ale to a toasty and rich porter. There's a small selection of bar food, and occasionally musicians perform. ⊠ *Callejón de Romita 8, La Roma* ☎ ⊕ *www.casacerveceracrucru.com* Ⓜ *Cuauhtémoc.*

Gin Gin

BARS | You'll find some of the city's most esteemed mixologists slinging drinks in this swanky cocktail bar in a grand old house off Cibeles. The menu changes regularly, but you might try El Viejo Reyes with Ancho Reyes (a poblano and ancho-chile liqueur from Puebla), Siete Misterios Doba-Yej mezcal, Angostura bitters, and flaming orange oil, or Gin Gin's take on a mule with Bombay Sapphire, ginger, yerba buena, cane syrup, lime, and soda. There are tasty food options, too. There are additional locations in Condesa, on the eastern side of Roma Norte, and in Polanco, but this one has the most inviting ambience. ⊠ *Av. Oaxaca 87, La Roma* ☎ *55/5248–0911* ⊕ *www.gingin. mx* Ⓜ *Seviila.*

Jardín Chapultepec

BEER GARDENS | On Roma's northern border with Colonia Juárez, this long and narrow order-at-the-bar beer garden is populated by picnic tables and lushly landscaped, making it surprisingly easy to forget the traffic noise outside (especially if you snag a seat near the back). The beer selection is vast, and you'll find plenty of notable brews from Mexico's up-and-coming artisanal brewers. There's burgers, sandwiches, and other pub fare, too, along with a selection of cocktails. ⊠ *Av. Chapultepec 398, La Roma* ⊕ *www.instagram.com/jardinchapultepec* Ⓜ *Insurgentes.*

★ La Bodeguita del Medio

LIVE MUSIC | At this welcoming, lively Cuban joint set in a grand but faded mansion that wouldn't look the least out of place in Havana, every surface is splashed with graffiti. Inspired by the original Havana establishment where Hemingway once lapped up mojitos, La Bodeguita also serves inexpensive Cuban food and sells Cuban cigars. Much of the time, live salsa, timba, and rumba bands provide entertainment. ⊠ *Calle Cozumel 37, La Roma* ☎ *55/5553–0246* ⊕ *www. labodeguitadelmedio.com.mx* Ⓜ *Sevilla.*

★ Maison Artemisia

BARS | A small group of French and Mexican friends created this inviting, cosmopolitan bar with a top-flight mixology program that features local botanicals and bitters as well as a house-brand Absinthe distilled in Paris. The relatively short cocktail menu changes weekly but always features some novel creations. There's live jazz, blues, soul, and other music once or twice a week. Downstairs, you'll find sister establishment, Loup Bar, which specializes in natural wines. ⊠ *Calle Tonalá 23, La Roma* ☎ *55/6303–2471* ⊕ *www.maisonartemisia.com* Ⓜ *Insurgentes.*

Patrick Miller

DANCE CLUB | At this long-standing, high-energy, Friday-only "danceteria," DJs spin 1980s pop classics, disco, and techno while the flamboyant patrons, a fairly even mixture of gays and straights, compete in theatrical dance-offs. Prepare to sweat. ⊠ *Calle Mérida 17, La Roma* ☎ ⊕ *www.instagram.com/patrick_miller_oficial* Ⓜ *Insurgentes.*

★ Pulqueria Los Insurgentes

BARS | Behind the colorfully muraled facade of this wildly popular pulqueria, you'll find three floors to enjoy plain and flavored (blackberry, guayaba, mamey, apricot, mango) versions of the milky millennia-old beverage distilled from the fermented sap of the very agave plants that give us mezcal and tequila. The most popular seating area, especially on warm evenings, is the expansive roof-deck. Top DJs and occasional live bands provide a nice beat to the socializing. And if you're not much for pulque, fear not: there's a full selection of liquor and beer, plus nachos, tacos, burgers, and the like. ⊠ *Av. Insurgentes Sur 226, La Roma* ☎ *55/5207–0917* ⊕ *www.instagram.com/ pulqueriainsurgentes* Ⓜ *Insurgentes.*

★ Rayo

BARS | Reservations are a good idea, especially on weekends, at this beautiful bar perched on the rooftop of a dapper

Roma's streets are filled with colorful Art Nouveau buildings.

early 20th-century town house that houses the similarly trendy restaurant Fonico on the ground floor. You can sample the superb, inventive cocktails before deciding on which one you'd like to order. ✉ *Calle Salamanca 85, La Roma* ☎ *55/6385–2051* ⊕ *www.rayococktailbar. com* Ⓜ *Sevilla.*

Traspatio

BARS | This cool backyard-garden space with a retractable roof to protect from the elements is a great place to hang out with friends on a warm afternoon or evening. It's part of the Milagrito del Corazón mezcal group, and sure enough, there's a good variety of cocktails featuring the spirit. Plus, there's a decent selection of pub grub, including vegetarian options. There's a slightly quieter upper-level terrace if you prefer a bit more privacy. ✉ *Calle Córdoba 81, La Roma* ☎ *55/5207–4309* ⊕ *eltraspatio.mx* Ⓜ *Insurgentes.*

Performing Arts

Centro Cultural Teatro 1 y 2

THEATER | A diverse range of concerts, theatrical performances, and other entertainment are presented at these two big venues in the northeastern Romita section of the neighborhood. ✉ *Av. Cuauhtémoc 19, La Roma* ☎ *55/5514–1935* ⊕ *www.carteleradeteatro.mx* Ⓜ *Cuauhtémoc.*

🛍 Shopping

Concept Racer

CLOTHING | You don't actually have to ride a Harley to appreciate shopping in this small, beautifully designed shop that specializes in bespoke motorcycle gear and apparel. The sturdy but stylish belts, denim jackets, canvas weekend bags, and offbeat gifts appeal to anyone seeking high-quality, rugged goods and clothing. ✉ *Calle Colima 267, La Roma* ☎ ⊕ *www. conceptracer.com* Ⓜ *Insurgentes.*

The Roma of Alfonso Cuarón

The sights and sounds of Alfonso Cuarón's *Roma* can be a little hard to find in today's Mexico City, but the Oscar-winning 2018 film that the director based on his—and his family maid's—life in an upper middle-class household residing amid the fading glory of early 1970s Roma Sur was shot on location. Cuarón's actual childhood home is in Roma Sur at Calle Tepeji 21, but the house that appears in the film is across the street at Tepeji 22.

The elementary school where maid Cleo takes the youngest boy to school is Kinder Condesa, at Calle Tlaxcala 105, and the movie's famously gripping hospital scene was shot at Centro Médico Nacional Siglo XXI, at the corner of Avenida Cuauhtémoc and Eje 3 Sur. Many other scenes were shot in Centro Histórico, including a meal between Cleo and Adela at the restaurant La Casa del Pavo and the facade of Teatro Metropólitan concert hall.

Happening

CLOTHING | This buzzy boutique on a quiet side street carries a lot of interesting locally made clothing, shoes, and accessories as well as lotions, soaps, and whimsical household goods. The colorful ceramics and glassware make wonderful gifts or keepsakes. ☒ *Calle Tabasco 210, La Roma* ☎ *55/5919–1254* ⊕ *www.instagram.com/happeningstore* Ⓜ *Insurgentes.*

★ Librería Casa Bosques

BOOKS | Set in fashionable building with a small cluster of art- and design-related spaces, this small, beautiful bookstore specializes in titles related to art, architecture, fashion, and photography. You'll also find a selection of handmade stationary and paper goods as well as interesting locally made gifts, including artisan chocolates. Casa Bosques often hosts signings and readings as well. ☒ *Calle Córdoba 25, La Roma* ☎ *55/9627–9987* ⊕ *www.casabosques.net* Ⓜ *Insurgentes.*

180°

CLOTHING | This boutique carries modish fashion for the city or the beach, much of it by young, Latinix talents. You can browse slick sunglasses by Mexican-born Miami designer Sunny Patoche, Mónica Márquez chunky women's boots, stylish Paruno men's shoes, and the store's own print tote bags and playful T-shirts. There's an interesting selection of skateboards, too, as well as books and other whimsical gifts. ☒ *Calle Colima 180, La Roma* ☎ *55/5525–5626* ⊕ *www.180grados.mx* Ⓜ *Insurgentes.*

★ Originario

FURNITURE | On the ground floor of a handsome Porfirian town house, this striking showroom displays the colorful furniture and housewares of celebrated designer Andrés Gutiérrez. These often chunky, curvy pieces, from lamps and bookends to end chairs and dining tables, are cast in eye-catching colors and make bold design statements. His pieces often look as though they'd fit perfectly in one of Luis Barragán's homes. ☒ *Calle Colima 249, La Roma* ☎ *55/7179–4558* ⊕ *www.instagram.com/originario.originario* Ⓜ *Insurgentes.*

Sangre de mi Sangre

JEWELRY & WATCHES | Artist Mariana Villarreal creates one-of-a-kind jewelry in this small boutique on the ground floor of the stately beaux-arts Balmori Mansion near Casa Lamm Cultural Center. Stop in and browse her collections of silver and gold earrings, necklaces, and rings, often with inlaid precious stones. Naturalistic, neo-Gothic motifs—skulls, bumblebees, stars, leaves—figure prominently in

Roma, especially Romita, is known for its impressive street art.

her whimsical designs. ✉ *Calle Orizaba 101, La Roma* ☎ *55/5511–8599* ⊕ *www. sdemis.com* Ⓜ *Insurgentes.*

★ Vintage Hoe

CLOTHING | This playfully named shop opened by a Cuban-American stylist who relocated to CDMX has been a beacon in the city's fashion community since 2007. Look to the unabashedly over-the-top boutique for carefully curated men's, women's, and unisex threads from top international design houses as well as shoes, bags, and home accessories. ✉ *Calle Jalapa 27, La Roma* ☎ *55/6275–5424* ⊕ *www.instagram.com/vintagehoe-store* Ⓜ *Insurgentes.*

Viriathus

ANTIQUES & COLLECTIBLES | In this rambling, historic Roma Norte town house, two brothers and business partners with a passion for collecting one-of-a-kind historical memorabilia and antiques sell their treasures to the public. Just walking through each room is great fun—more so, really, than touring some of the city's somberly baroque house-museums.

You'll find expensive and rare items (a 1790s map of the Americas, a 1930s oak credenza) along with a number of smaller and more affordable pieces, including model ships, vintage valises, fine books, and framed artwork. ✉ *Calle Mérida 10, La Roma* ☎ *55/2624–3552* ⊕ *www. viriathus.com.mx* Ⓜ *Insurgentes.*

Roma South of Av. Álvaro Obregón

 Sights

Huerto Roma Verde

FARM/RANCH | This eco-minded organic urban farm is one of the more unusual spaces in the city center—it occupies an expansive corner lot beside Roma Sur's attractive, wooded Jardín Ramón López Velarde Park. Built largely from repurposed materials, the farm is easy to spot from the giant temple-like structure by its entrance, made up of hundreds of blue plastic water bottles with a palm tree growing through the center. The center offers workshops and classes open to the public on sustainability, recycling, organic and hydroponic gardening, yoga, temazcal, dance, jewelry-making, slow-food cooking, and much more. And there are regular eco-markets featuring a wide range of sustainable products. Visitors are welcome to saunter around the property, admiring the eclectic artwork, patting the many friendly and free-ranging cats (most of which are up for adoption through the farm), and spotting a bounty of potted plants and leafy gardens. ⊠ *Calle Jalapa 234, La Roma* 🕾 *55/5564–2210* ⊕ *www.huertoromaverde.org* 🖂 *Free* Ⓜ *Hospital General.*

★ Laguna México

ARTS CENTER | In Doctores just a block from Roma and Avenida Álvaro Obregón, this historic textile factory has been transformed into a collaborative art and design space that serves as both showcase and incubator. From the street you'd hardly know it was here—you need to knock on the door to gain entry. But the public is welcome to drop in, order a well-crafted latte from the cool café (which is also an inviting spot to work on your laptop), check out the bookstore specializing in titles about design, and explore the building's unique architecture. Many of the galleries and studios inside sell their works to the public, but Laguna also hosts a wide range of cultural activities, including dance classes, art workshops, design expos, and various lectures. Above all else it offers visitors a terrific opportunity to interact with the city's constantly evolving creative scene. ⊠ *Calle Dr. Lucio 181, Doctores* 🕾 ⊕ *www.lagunamexico.com* 🖂 *Free* Ⓢ *Closed Sun.* Ⓜ *Niños Héroes/ Poder Judicial.*

Plaza Luis Cabrera

PLAZA/SQUARE | Designed around the same time and in a somewhat similar style to Plaza Río de Janeiro, which is a few blocks due north, this stately plaza centered on an elliptical reflecting pool and fountain is one of the most enchanting spots in Roma to sit with a cup of coffee and soak up the streetscape. Art installations are regularly set up around the pool's tree-shaded perimeter, and the streets flanking the eastern and western sides of the plaza contain several imposing Porfirian mansions, some of which now house restaurants and cafés. If you'd rather frequent a more locally grown business than the ubiquitous, albeit attractive, Starbucks on the northwest corner, try Cafe Toscano, at the southwest end of the plaza, which makes a nice break for coffee and cake or a glass of wine and a sandwich. And across the street, Porco Rosso, the U.S.-style barbecue joint with several locations around the city, is a fun place to eat and socialize. ⊠ *Calle Orizaba, between Calles Guanajuato and Zacatecas, La Roma* Ⓜ *Insurgentes.*

★ Terreno Baldío Arte

ART GALLERY | This prestigious gallery represents acclaimed artists like Emilio Rangel, known for his playful and sometimes erotic depictions of pop cultural icons like Miss Piggy and Elvis; Javier Marín—whose massive sculptures, such as *Cabeza Vainilla* (Vanilla Head) have been installed in a number of prominent spaces around the world; and about a dozen other diverse talents. The gallery itself occupies an imposing mansion whose interior has been given a striking, light-filled contemporary redesign. It's recommended that guests get in touch to make an appointment before visiting. ⊠ *Calle Orizaba 177, La Roma* 🕾 *443/396–0722* ⊕ *www.terrenobaldio.com* 🖂 *Free* Ⓢ *Closed Sun.–Tues.* Ⓜ *Hospital General.*

🍴 Restaurants

★ Bar El Sella

$$$ | **SPANISH** | This old-time cantina a block from the eastern edge of Roma opened in 1950 and continues to attract crowds of both locals and

Did You Know?

One of the neighborhood's many leafy parks, Plaza Luis Cabrera was created as a counterpart to Plaza Río de Janeiro in Roma Norte.

tourists-in-the-know. There's nothing fancy about the brightly lit dining room, but the authentic Spanish food is up there with the best in the city and includes slow-cooked octopus, chorizo with cabrales cheese, Spanish omelets with asparagus, and *chamorro* (a fall-off-the-bone pork shank braised in a heady achiote sauce). **Known for:** no-frills old-fashioned cantina ambience; great people-watching; authentic Spanish fare. $ *Average main: MP320* ✉ *Calle Dr. Balmis 210, La Roma* ☎ *55/5578–2001* 🌐 *www.barelsella.mx* 🕒 *Closed Sun. No dinner* [M] *Hospital General.*

BOU

$$ | CAFÉ | Equal parts artisan bakery, leisurely hangout, and all-day café, this airy space on a picturesque Roma corner has two large and lushly landscaped dining areas and serves an array of enticing international treats. Start the day with blueberry pancakes or a hearty plate of chilaquiles verdes; later in the day, consider a classic bacon-gouda cheeseburger on a fluffy brioche bun or a slice of the flavorful vegetarian lasagna. **Known for:** decadent pastries and cakes; delicious all-day breakfast fare; espresso, tea, and cacao drinks. $ *Average main: MP210* ✉ *Calle Tonalá 110, La Roma* ☎ 🌐 *www.instagram.com/bou_mx_* 🕒 *Closed Mon.* [M] *Insurgentes.*

Broka Bistrot

$$$ | MODERN MEXICAN | You'll find one of Roma's prettiest dining rooms—with high brick walls and lush greenery set around a two-story interior courtyard with plenty of natural sunlight—in this moderately upscale and somewhat unassuming restaurant that turns out excellent globally influenced bistro fare. Consider the Vietnamese shrimp dumplings in a fragrant soy-shiitake sauce or tuna tartare tostadas to start, before choosing among the soft-shell-crab tacos, grilled Pacific snapper, or rabbit carnitas among the mains. **Known for:** soft-shell crab tacos; lovely light-filled courtyard dining room; good cocktails. $ *Average main: MP350* ✉ *Calle Zacatecas 126, La Roma* ☎ *55/4437–4285* 🌐 *www.brokabistrot.com* 🕒 *No dinner Sun.* [M] *Insurgentes.*

Cafebreria El Péndulo

$$ | ECLECTIC | The grand, three-story Roma location of this local chain of stunningly designed bookstore-cafés is a wonderful destination for brunch, cocktails, or late-night snacking, either on the breezy roof-deck or seated on one of the comfy lounge chairs inside. Try the pancakes with bananas and blueberries early in the day, or one of Roma's top burgers later in the day, and don't overlook the extensive dessert selection. **Known for:** weekend brunch; lots of veggie options; huge selection of books to browse before or after you eat. $ *Average main: MP200* ✉ *Av. Álvaro Obregón 86, La Roma* ☎ *55/5574–7034* 🌐 *www.pendulo.com* [M] *Insurgentes.*

★ Chico Julio

$$ | SEAFOOD | For all the buzzy seafood restaurants in Roma, not one serves a better aguachile than this casual, affordable spot decorated like an old fishing shanty, with mermaid wall sconces, mounted fish, and seaside bric-a-brac. Everything here—including fish-and-chips, smoked-marlin tostadas, octopus-chorizo tacos, and salmon burgers—is fresh and boldly flavored, and you can add even more spice by choosing a few salsas from the extensive condiment bar (some of these are *muy picantes,* so ask for advice if you're wary). **Known for:** aguachile and ceviche; variety of grilled-fish tacos; big selection of housemade salsas. $ *Average main: MP180* ✉ *Jalapa 126, La Roma* ☎ *55/2124–5276* 🌐 *www.instagram.com/chicojuliocdmx* [M] *Insurgentes.*

Comedor de los Milagros

$ | LATIN AMERICAN | Always packed with locals—including plenty of expats from other parts of the Americas—watching fútbol on TV or enjoying the live music, this welcoming two-story Roma Sur

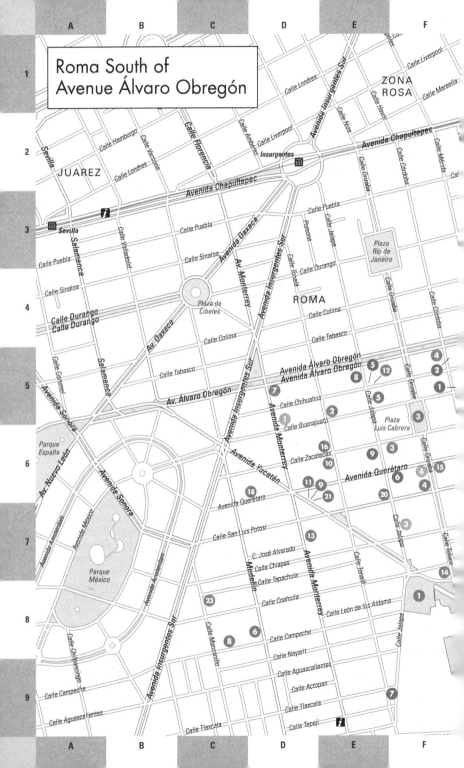

Roma South of Avenue Álvaro Obregón

Sights ▼

1 Huerto Roma Verde **F8**
2 Laguna México **I5**
3 Plaza Luis Cabrera....... **F5**
4 Terreno Baldío Arte...... **F6**

Restaurants ▼

1 Bar La Sella **H6**
2 BOU **E5**
3 Broka Bistrot............. **F6**
4 Cafebreria El Péndulo... **F5**
5 Chico Julio............... **E5**
6 Comedor de los
  Milagros **D8**
7 Delirio Mónica
  Patiño **D5**
8 El Hidalguense **C8**
9 El Parnita **D6**
10 Em **E6**
11 Expendio de Maíz
   Sin Nombre.............. **D6**
12 Farina **E5**
13 Galanga
   Thai Kitchen............. **D7**
14 Kiin Thai-Viet Eatery..... **F7**
15 La Pitahaya Vegana **F6**
16 Lalo! **E6**
17 Maíz de Cacao **G5**
18 Mercado Roma **D6**
19 Mog Bistro............... **H5**
20 Mux....................... **E6**
21 Páramo................... **D6**
22 Pargot................... **G7**
23 Taquería El Jarocho.....**C8**

Quick Bites ▼

1 Casa Cardinal **F5**
2 Casa Tassel.............. **F5**
3 Churrería El Moro....... **H4**
4 El Auténtico
  Pato Manila **H5**
5 Eno **E5**
6 Forte...................... **F6**
7 Tamales Doña Emi....... **F9**
8 Tres Galeones............ **E5**
9 Tsubomi.................. **E6**

Hotels ▼

1 Casa Goliana **D6**
2 Four Points by Sheraton
  Mexico City,
  Colonia Roma **G4**
3 Ignacia Guest House.... **F7**
4 NaNa Vida CDMX........ **F6**

8

Roma ROMA SOUTH OF AV. ÁLVARO OBREGÓN

mercado contains more than a dozen food stalls set around a central dining area with communal tables. Cuisines from mostly Central and South America are featured, including Brazilian feijoada, Peruvian ceviche, and Salvadoran arepes. **Known for:** wide variety of cuisines from throughout Latin America; festive, unpretentious vibe; live music. $ *Average main: MP140* ✉ *Calle Medellín 221, La Roma* ☎ *55/7158–0044* ⊕ *www. instagram.com/comedordelosmilagros* Ⓜ *Chilpancingo.*

Delirio Mónica Patiño

$$ | **MEDITERRANEAN** | This gourmet market, artisan bakery, and sidewalk café with a prime location on Álvaro Obregón is a top destination for any meal, but especially breakfast and brunch, when you might try French toast with whipped cream and fresh fruit or Greek-style baked eggs with jocoque, olives, tomato sauce, and grilled pita. The rest of the day, the eclectic but slightly Mediterranean-leaning menu features tortas and toasts (like the one with smoked trout, pickled beets, and capers) as well as lasagna, lamb moussaka, and other heartier dishes. **Known for:** savory and sweet baked goods; leisurely breakfasts and brunches; gourmet house-made jams, oils, and other goodies to take home. $ *Average main: MP220* ✉ *Av. Monterrey 116, La Roma* ☎ *55/5584–0870* ⊕ *www. delirio.mx* Ⓜ *Insurgentes.*

★ El Hidalguense

$$ | **MEXICAN** | This laid-back restaurant has been serving Hidalgo-style lamb *barbacoa* to grateful Mexico City residents since the 1990s. Friday through Monday afternoon only, fresh lamb from owner Moisés Rodríguez's Hidalgo farm is roasted for 12 hours over mesquite and oak in an underground pit, then served in charred agave leaves. **Known for:** excellent lamb barbacoa tacos; friendly, local crowd; variety of pulques. $ *Average main: MP185* ✉ *Calle Campeche 155,*

La Roma ☎ *55/5564–0538* ⊕ *www.instagram.com/elhidalguense_restaurante* ▭ *No credit cards* ⊙ *Closed Tues.–Thurs. No dinner* Ⓜ *Chilpancingo.*

El Parnita

$ | **MEXICAN** | The logo says "tradición desde 1970," but in fact El Parnita is a more recent addition to Roma's lunch scene: a hip, updated take on the simple family-owned fonda. The menu consists of *antojitos* (snacks like tacos, tostadas, and ceviches), from recipes culled from the family's travels throughout the country, such as *rellenito*, a chipotle chile stuffed with cheese and beans in a sauce of *piloncillo* (unrefined brown sugar) from Zacatecas; and tacos *viajeros*, homemade tortillas piled with pork loin and leg long cooked in citrus, from Michoacán. **Known for:** festive people-watching scene; affordable regional Mexican fare; great micheladas. $ *Average main: MP140* ✉ *Av. Yucatán 84, La Roma* ☎ *55/5264–7551* ⊕ *www.elparnita.com* ⊙ *Closed Mon. No dinner Sun.* Ⓜ *Insurgentes.*

★ Em

$$$$ | **CONTEMPORARY** | Occupying the intimate, refined space that was the original location of renowned Máximo Bistrot, this romantic farm-to-table restaurant is the brainchild of celebrated chef Lucho Martínez, an alum of both Máximo and Quintonil. Em's exciting menu varies according to the chef's inspiration and the season's bounty, but you might start with steak tartare with black truffles and a pain perdue brioche before graduating to braised short ribs with a rich peanut-based mole sauce or a fragrant, earthy porcini mushroom risotto. **Known for:** romantic, intimate dining room; knowledgeable waitstaff; sumptuous omakase menus with well-chosen wine pairings. $ *Average main: MP620* ✉ *Calle Tonalá 133, La Roma* ☎ *55/3543–3275* ⊕ *www.itsemilia.rest* ⊙ *Closed Tues. No lunch* Ⓜ *Insurgentes.*

★ Expendio de Maiz Sin Nombre

$ | MEXICAN | The owners of this tiny Roma kitchen with volcanic-rock floors and walls are devoted to preserving Mexico's ancient culinary traditions, including the *nixtamalización* process of grinding corn into tortilla dough, which is used to create exquisite yet simple breakfast and lunch fare that changes day to day, according to what's in season. You might enjoy anything from corn tacos filled with fresh cheese, *hoja santa* (a peppery Mexican herb), and squash blossom, to a blue-corn tortilla topped with avocado, ants, and salsa. **Known for:** corn tortillas produced following centuries-old Mesoamerican traditions; seasonally changing breakfast and lunch fare; covered sidewalk seating. $ *Average main: MP90* ✉ *Av. Yucatan 84, La Roma* ☎ *55/2498–9964* ⊕ *www.instagram.com/exp_maiz* ⊘ *Closed Mon. No dinner* Ⓜ *Insurgentes.*

Farina

$$$ | MODERN ITALIAN | In this intimate pizza place, you'll find a generous selection of excellent thin-crust pizzas and handmade pastas, plus a good variety of cocktails and wines. The pizzas come with red or white bases, with the truffle oil, gorgonzola, and wild-mushroom pie being a favorite among the latter, and the pie with Brie, mozzarella, pepperoni, and cherry tomatoes standing out among the "rosso" pies. **Known for:** creative thin-crust pizzas; good selection of wines by the glass; late-night hours. $ *Average main: MP380* ✉ *Calle Chihuahua 139, La Roma* ☎ *55/5160–1644* ⊕ *www.farinarest.com* Ⓜ *Insurgentes.*

★ Galanga Thai Kitchen

$$$ | THAI | Fans of Thai food who are frustrated by the lack of options in the capital can flock to this stellar restaurant set inside a dramatic, spacious 19th-century mansion. The artfully prepared dishes here can hold their own with any you'll find in North America—it's best to share a few dishes, such as duck in a red curry of pineapple, eggplant, and lychee; a southern-style pad Thai with soft-shell crab, tamarind sauce, and coconut milk; and the dessert of fried bananas with house-made chrysanthemum ice cream. **Known for:** inventive, boldly flavored Thai cuisine; excellent wine and cocktail list; rich desserts with homemade ice cream. $ *Average main: MP430* ✉ *Calle Monterrey 204, La Roma* ☎ *55/6550–4492* ⊕ *www.instagram.com/galangathaihouse* ⊘ *No dinner Sun.* Ⓜ *Insurgentes.*

★ Kiin Thai-Viet Eatery

$$ | THAI | This younger sibling to Galanga offers a more varied menu that includes both Thai and Vietnamese fare at slightly lower prices, but as with the original restaurant, the food is flavorful, expertly prepared, and delicious. The solarium-style space creates the feel of dining in an art nouveau birdcage, and there's outdoor seating on a side patio as well. **Known for:** beautiful, plant-filled dining room; creative desserts with house-made ice creams; teas, wines, and creative cocktails in adjacent Somsaa Wine & Tea Room. $ *Average main: MP285* ✉ *Calle Cerrada Orizaba 219, La Roma* ☎ *55/7095–7421* ⊕ *www.instagram.com/kiinthaivietmx* ⊘ *Closed Mon. No dinner Sun.* Ⓜ *Hospital General.*

Lalo!

$$ | CONTEMPORARY | The walls are decked with cartoon figures and bursts of color at this lively space that differs from its more sophisticated and spendier night-time sister restaurant, Máximo Bistrot. Come in the morning to feast on smoked-salmon bagels with poached eggs, acai bowls with seasonal fruit, and croque monsieur sandwiches, while afternoons are the time for gourmet pizzas, pastas, ceviche, roasted chicken, and other satisfying fare. **Known for:** pizzas with creative toppings; lushly landscaped sidewalk seating area; artisanal beer. $ *Average main: MP280* ✉ *Calle Zacatecas 173, La Roma* ☎ *55/5564–3388* ⊕ *www.eat-lalo.com* ⊘ *Closed Mon. No dinner* Ⓜ *Insurgentes.*

La Pitahaya Vegana

$$ | VEGETARIAN | Although the availability of vegan cuisine has come a long way in Mexico City in recent years, few restaurants are devoted exclusively to it, but this small café produces some of the tastiest and most beautifully plated plant-based fare in town. Tortillas at La Pitahaya are as bright pink as the walls (they're dyed with beet juice—the tortillas, that is), and they come with equally bright, fresh fillings like cauliflower with coconut cream and pineapple, and pastor-style oyster mushrooms. **Known for:** customizable vegan burgers with a variety of toppings; waffles and chilaquiles for breakfast; house-brewed kombucha. $ Average main: MP200 ⊠ Calle Querétaro 90, La Roma ☎ 55/7159–2918 ⊕ www.lapitahayavegana.mx Ⓜ Hospital General.

Maíz de Cacao

$ | MEXICAN | Part of the city's warm embrace and advocacy of Mesoamerican culinary traditions, this diminutive café with Mexican folk art on the walls specializes in dishes made with—as the name suggests—corn and chocolate. Tuck into a plate of blue-corn tamales with mildly spicy pork rib meat, eggs grilled with chiles in banana leaf, or cheese gorditas, washing everything down with corn atole or indigenous chocolate drinks (all of which are also available in the form of refreshing *paletas*, or popsicles). **Known for:** corn tortillas and tamales made with Mesoamerican nixtamalization practices; cute, cheerful dining space with an open kitchen; traditional indigenous corn and chocolate drinks (and popsicles). $ Average main: MP120 ⊠ Calle Córdoba 148, La Roma ☎ 55/9080–2963 ⊕ www.instagram.com/maizdecacao Ⓜ Hospital General.

Mercado Roma

$ | ECLECTIC | About 55 vendors offering everything from elevated short-order street food to refined farm-to-tables victuals operate out of this trendy food hall with a popular artisan beer bar, the Biergarten, on the third-floor rooftop space, which is also home to a whiskey bar. The first floor features stalls and a patio seating area, and a smaller mezzanine offers still more options. **Known for:** plenty of to-go options; different food choices for every taste; lively and fun rooftop beer garden. $ Average main: MP135 ⊠ Calle Querétaro 225, La Roma ☎ 55/5564–1396 ⊕ mr.mercadoroma.com Ⓜ Insurgentes.

★ **Mog Bistro**

$$ | ASIAN FUSION | This rambling, seemingly always-packed restaurant is one of the city's pioneers in genuinely sophisticated, authentic modern Asian (mostly Japanese) cuisine. The food, which is artfully presented in small plates, bowls, and bamboo steamers, spans Thailand, Japan, and China, with highlights being several varieties of ramen, shimp pad thai, hamachi sashimi, sushi rolls, and Chinese sausage. **Known for:** colorful tropical cocktails; late-night dining; about a dozen varieties of ramen. $ Average main: MP270 ⊠ Calle Frontera 168, La Roma ☎ 55/5264–1629 ⊕ www.instagram.com/mogbistro Ⓜ Hospital General.

Mux

$$ | MEXICAN | The menu of this sleek corner space with striking ceramics and statuary lining the walls celebrates the flavorful cuisine of the scenic mountain town of Malinalco, about 70 miles southwest of Mexico City. Some of the more interesting dishes include a starter of chilacayote squash with mint and citrus and a yellow-tomato pico de gallo salsa, and a main dish pork ribs served with a rich red mole sauce. **Known for:** creative interpretations of regional Mexican cuisine; beautiful art-filled dining room; plantain-cream tart for dessert. $ Average main: MP280 ⊠ Calle Jalapa 189, La Roma ☎ 55/9039–6990 ⊕ www.instagram.com/mux_mexico Ⓜ Hospital General.

Páramo

$$ | **MODERN MEXICAN** | Depending on the time of day and your mood, this buzzy warren of smartly designed nooks can be a fun options for drinks and a leisurely mid-afternoon lunch or for a late-night feast of ceviche and tacos with creative fillings like hibiscus flowers, seared tuna, and longaniza sausage. Keep in mind that it gets packed here on weekends, so scoring a table and receiving your order can be slow, but everything here—from the food to the drinks—is delicious. **Known for:** cool, trendy vibe; delicious, creatively prepared tacos; big crowds and relatedly iffy service on weekend nights. [$] *Average main: MP220* ✉ *Av. Yucatan 84, La Roma* ☎ *55/5941–5125* 🌐 *www.instagram.com/paramo_roma* [M] *Insurgentes.*

★ **Pargot**

$$ | **MODERN MEXICAN** | One of the tiniest yet most beautifully designed restaurants in Roma, this strangely wonderful bistro serves boldly flavored contemporary Mexican cuisine from a short, always-changing menu created by an alum of Pujol and El Bulli. Options might include a tostada topped with smoked leeks, (a charred Yucatecan chile paste) and avocado mousse, or an (a fried, puffed tortilla) filled with crabmeat and corn and topped with a puree of spring peas and mint. **Known for:** just a handful of tables inside and on the sidewalk (so smart to reserve ahead); sleek, minimalist design; orange and natural wines. [$] *Average main: MP300* ✉ *Calle de Chiapas 46, La Roma* ☎ *56/3470–4481* 🌐 *www.instagram.com/pargotrestaurant* 🕒 *Closed Mon.* [M] *Hospital General.*

Taquería El Jarocho

$ | **MEXICAN** | This old-time neighborhood institution has weathered Roma's booms and busts since 1947 and is today far more than a taqueria, although tacos de guisados (filled with rich, stewed ingredients) are still the restaurant's main draw. Try authentic fillings like *moronga* (ground blood sausage with onions and chiles), beef tongue in a olive-tomato Veracruz sauce, or traditional lamb barbacoa. **Known for:** famous tacos de guisados; big, inexpensive portions; refreshingly untrendy ambience. [$] *Average main: MP80* ✉ *Calle Tapachula 94, La Roma* ☎ *55/5574–5303* 🌐 *www.taqueriaeljarocho.com.mx* [M] *Chilpancingo.*

Coffee and Quick Bites

Casa Cardinal

$ | **CAFÉ** | A lovely, inviting spot for a light meal, Casa Cardinal employs a team of well-trained baristas devoted to producing some of the finest coffee drinks in the neighborhood, using the method of your choice (Aeropress, Japanese siphon, Chemex pour-over, and a few others—plus very good mochas). There's always cool music playing, and you can dine inside or out at one of the sidewalk tables. **Known for:** well-crafted coffee drinks; hip but unpretentious vibe; sandwiches and stroopwaffles. [$] *Average main: MP80* ✉ *Calle Córdoba 132, La Roma* ☎ *55/6721–8874* 🌐 *www.instagram.com/casacardinal* [M] *Insurgentes.*

★ **Casa Tassel**

$ | **CAFÉ** | When you're seeking a calm break from the bustle of the big city, have a seat in this dainty and diminutive tearoom with white painted walls, a brick ceiling, and shelves piled high with beautiful teacups, kettles, and bins of tea. You'll find an impressive array of tea blends as well as yerba mate, and a staff who prepares every drink with great care—in fact, the shop offers classes in tea tasting. **Known for:** tea cakes and baguette sandwiches; knowledgeable and friendly staff; extensive and quirky selection of teaware. [$] *Average main: MP80* ✉ *Calle Córdoba 110, La Roma* ☎ 🌐 *www.instagram.com/casatassel* [M] *Insurgentes.*

★ Churrería El Moro

$ | **CAFÉ** | This festive and always packed spot has been a mainstay for sweet tooths since 1935. The best plan is to share an order or two of long, crispy churros with at least two dipping sauces (condensed milk, chocolate, and—maybe the best—cajeta are your options), along with a churro ice-cream sandwich. **Known for:** churros with sweet dipping sauces; churro ice-cream sandwiches; Spanish and Mexican hot chocolate. $ *Average main: MP65* ⊠ *Calle Frontera 122, La Roma* ☏ *No phone* ⊕ *www.elmoro.mx* Ⓜ *Cuauhtémoc.*

★ El Auténtico Pato Manila

$ | **ASIAN FUSION** | Tucked inside the small El Mercado Amazónico on the east edge of Roma, this tiny offbeat Asian-Mexican-fusion taqueria features duck in every one of its handful of dishes, all of them addictively good. In addition to both Mexican- and Asian-style taco preparations (the Peking duck–inspired "Kim" version is especially tasty), you can enjoy ginger-duck-filled wontons and spring rolls as well as duck tortas. **Known for:** Asian Peking-duck tacos; interesting house-made Asian-Mexican salsas; slow-grilled duck baguettes. $ *Average main: MP110* ⊠ *Guanajuato 19, La Roma* ☏ *55/5138–9611* ⊕ *www.instagram.com/patomanila* Ⓜ *Insurgentes.*

Eno

$$ | **MODERN MEXICAN** | World-famous Pujol mastermind Enrique Olvera is the talent behind Eno, a smart-casual bakery and café on a lively Roma Norte street corner (there's another location in Polanco). The airy brick-ceilinged spot with a handful of sidewalk tables is great for a light meal, dessert, coffee, or atole (a warm Mesoamerican corn drink) from early morning until late at night, with breakfast especially popular. **Known for:** delicious egg and veggie breakfast dishes; fresh-baked cookies and pastries; Mesoamerican drinks, like atole and amaranto.

$ *Average main: MP265* ⊠ *Calle Chihuahua 139, La Roma* ☏ *55/7576–0919* ⊕ *www.eno.com.mx* Ⓜ *Insurgentes.*

Forte

$ | **CAFÉ** | Although this cozy, discrete café is in Roma Norte, it's at the southern end of the less frenetic neighborhood, making it a nice option for a relaxed coffee break or a light snack. The artisan house-baked goods here are superb, from sourdough pizzas to flaky croissants and other French pastries. **Known for:** stellar coffee drinks (and coffee-infused craft beer on tap); house-baked pastries; sourdough pizza nights on weekends. $ *Average main: MP70* ⊠ *Calle Querétaro 116, La Roma* ☏ ⊕ *www.instagram. com/fortebreadcoffee* ⊗ *No dinner Sun.* Ⓜ *Hospital General.*

Tamales Doña Emi

$ | **MEXICAN** | Try to arrive early to ensure that you get your choice of delicious tamales from this casual little shop with a handful of sidewalk tables—they sometimes sell out quickly, especially on weekends. Devotees of the hearty tubes of steamed corn masa come from all over the city, drawn by the extensive selection of fillings, including figs-and-cream cheese, chicken mole, pork with mushrooms in red sauce, and black beans with cheese and *chapulines* (grasshoppers). **Known for:** sweet and savory tamales with inventive fillings; coconut atole; quick counter service. $ *Average main: MP90* ⊠ *Corner of Calles Jalapa and Tlaxcala, La Roma* ☏ *55/4535–0103* ⊕ *www.instagram.com/tamalesdemi* ⊗ *Closed Mon. No dinner* Ⓜ *Centro Médico.*

Tres Galeones

$ | **SEAFOOD** | The lively, tiny Mexico City location of the popular seafood spot in Tulum has just a handful of tables inside and on the sidewalk. It's a perfect stop for a light snack—try the pibíl-style octopus or pastor-style fish tacos, a ceviche tostada, or a heartier garlic-shrimp burrito. **Known for:** seafood tacos and burritos; ceviche tostadas; ice-cream sandwiches. [$] *Average main: MP145* ✉ *Guanajuato 53, La Roma* ☎ *55/5419–3964* 🌐 *www.tresgaleones.mx* [M] *Insurgentes.*

Tsubomi

$ | **BAKERY** | This cozy bakery/café is a source of singularly delicious Japanese and European treats, both savory and sweet, as well as more substantial fare like grilled teriyaki chicken and curry and rice. Matcha cakes, orange pastries, and perfectly crafted baguettes and sandwiches are among the top options. **Known for:** baguette and rustic-bread sandwiches with Japanese and European fillings; good bet for a meal if in the southern end of Roma; colorfully frosted cakes and pastries. [$] *Average main: MP135* ✉ *Calle Tonalá 346, La Roma* ☎ *55/1334–4352* 🌐 *www.tsubomimexico.com* 🕓 *Closed Mon. No dinner* [M] *Insurgentes.*

🛏 Hotels

Casa Goliana

$$ | **B&B/INN** | Within this refined early 20th-century mansion, graciously appointed rooms with tastefully neutral color schemes, plush linens, and original architectural details appeal to a discerning crowd who wish to be close to Roma's fantastic restaurants but in a quieter section that's slightly removed from the neighborhood's sometimes frenetic nightlife. **Pros:** exceptional full breakfast included; luxurious bedding and bath products; great central location that's also close to Condesa. **Cons:** rooms facing street can hear some traffic noise; only a handful of moderately priced rooms; might feel a tad formal for some tastes. [$] *Rooms from: MP3500* ✉ *Guanajuato 199, La Roma* ☎ *55/6811–3948* 🌐 *www.casagoliana.com* 🛏 *8 rooms* 🍴 *Free Breakfast* [M] *Insurgentes.*

Four Points by Sheraton Mexico City, Colonia Roma

$$ | **HOTEL** | Although this seven-story property—it's one of the largest in the neighborhood—isn't particular trendy, it does have warmly appointed contemporary rooms with floor-to-ceiling windows, attractive white-tile showers, and ultra-comfy beds. **Pros:** one of Roma's few hotels that warmly welcomes pets; very nice fitness center; rooftop bar with great neighborhood views. **Cons:** cookie-cutter room design; no pool; some rooms have drab interior views. [$] *Rooms from: MP3600* ✉ *Av. Álvaro Obregón 38, La Roma* ☎ *55/1085–9500* 🌐 *www.marriott.com* 🛏 *90 rooms* 🍴 *No Meals* [M] *Cuauhtémoc.*

★ **Ignacia Guest House**

$$$ | **B&B/INN** | One of the most alluring of the several posh, intimate B&Bs that occupy stately Porfirian-era mansions in Roma, this 1913 house has been enlarged with a dramatic glass-and-metal contemporary addition that encircles a peaceful courtyard with a living wall, cactus garden, and fountain that functions as social focal point—and is also just a wonderfully relaxing place to read or relax. **Pros:** friendly, highly personalized service; calm Roma Sur location; exceptional breakfasts and happy hour cocktails included. **Cons:** not suitable for kids under 13; Roma Sur location is a slight walk from many of the neighborhood's top restaurants; a bit pricey. [$] *Rooms from: MP4400* ✉ *Calle Jalapa 208, La Roma* ☎ *55/2121–096* 🌐 *www.ignacia.mx* 🛏 *9 rooms* 🍴 *Free Breakfast* [M] *Hospital General.*

★ **NaNa Vida CDMX**

$$ | **B&B/INN** | This smartly designed boutique inn is filled with thoughtful touches and whimsical creative flourishes, including colorful contemporary paintings and murals by up-and-coming artists, co-working and yoga rooms, and complimentary coffee, Mexican candies, and

even mezcal shots. **Pros:** very reasonable rates for the neighborhood; exceptionally helpful and kind staff; lots of inviting indoor and outdoor common spaces. **Cons:** some rooms are a bit small; on a busy street (though close to many dining options); no elevator. $ *Rooms from: MP2900* ⊠ *Calle Cerrada Orizaba 161, La Roma* ☎ *55/5574–5789* ⊕ *www.nanavida. com* 🡒 *14 rooms* ❘◎❘ *No Meals* Ⓜ *Hospital General.*

Nightlife

Bar Félix

BARS | A favored fixture along the voguey nightlife row that is Avenida Álvaro Obregón, Félix is a popular, dimly lit cocktail bar at first glance. Head down the side hallway to the back, however, and you'll find a chatter-filled garden pizzeria that rakes in sizable crowds until late into the evening—the pies here are pretty tasty, too. ⊠ *Av. Álvaro Obregón 64, La Roma* ☎ *55/5160–1791* ⊕ *www.instagram.com/felixpizzabar* Ⓜ *Insurgentes.*

Departamento

BARS | Meant to evoke the inviting, laid-back trappings of a friend's (very large) *departamento*—or apartment—this often packed lounge has DJs spinning trancy tunes on turntables. It's a fun place to chill and mingle before going clubbing, or a place to enjoy while the night is winding down. Some nights there's live music. ⊠ *Av. Álvaro Obregón 154, La Roma* ☎ *55/4089–4652* ⊕ *www.instagram.com/departamento_studiobar* Ⓜ *Insurgentes.*

★ Jazzatlán Capital

LIVE MUSIC | The Mexico City branch of a famous Latin swing jazz club in the historic town of Cholula (just outside Puebla), this energetic spot has a few different areas, including the live music area where bands perform both traditional and contemporary tunes. On other levels, there's a tap room serving craft beers and a full restaurant with gastropub fare. ⊠ *Calle Guanajuato 239, La Roma* ☎ *55/1390–1631* ⊕ *www.jazzatlan.club* Ⓜ *Insurgentes.*

La Chicha

BARS | A low-key neighborhood hangout with kitschy decor, string lights, and reasonably priced craft beers, cocktails, and globally inspired tapas, La Chicha is a few blocks south of Roma Norte's flashier and more crowded Álvaro Obregón bar strip. It's a much more mellow place to meet locals and a generally easy spot to find a table. There's another location at Cineteca Nacional in Coyoacan. ⊠ *Calle Orizaba 171, La Roma* ☎ *55/1906–8115* ⊕ *en.lamaschicha.com* Ⓜ *Hospital General.*

★ La Roma Brewing

BREWPUBS | Below the popular restaurant Páramo, this lively spot with vaulted brick ceilings offers up one of Roma's most extensive selections of craft beers on tap and by the bottle. Order a flight to sample a few different kinds of ale, which range from aromatic sours to hoppy Pacific Northwest–style IPAs. There's a good selection of gastropub fare as well such as tacos, chili dogs, nachos, and chocolate brownies. ⊠ *Av. Yucatan 84, La Roma* ☎ ⊕ *www.laromabrewing.com* Ⓜ *Insurgentes.*

★ Licorería Limantour

BARS | Much-lauded and regularly named among the world's 10 best cocktail bars, Limantour looks nevertheless remarkably approachable—a narrow, neatly designed space with one of the city's first truly serious mixology programs (hence its phenomenal reputation). The surprisingly affordable drinks, like the herbal Green Park (with gin, celery bitters, basil, lime, and egg white) and the Machete (San Cosme mezcal with tangerine liqueur, grapefruit and lime extract, agave syrup, and spearmint), delight the senses and explain why ardent cocktail aficionados flock here. You'll find tasty bar snacks, too. ⊠ *Av. Álvaro Obregón 106, La Roma* ☎ *55/5264–4122* ⊕ *www. limantour.tv* Ⓜ *Insurgentes.*

Vinamore

WINE BAR | This charming, tiny spot with modern wooden tables and white brick walls has quickly become a go-to for its thoughtfully curated selection of wines. You can also build your own cheese-charcuterie board to accompany your sipping, and cannoli are available for a sweet ending. ⊠ *Calle Guanajuato 78, La Roma* ☎ *55/7651–5981* ⊕ *www.vinamoremx. com* Ⓜ *Insurgentes.*

 Performing Arts

★ Cine Tonalá

FILM | Three or four indie and foreign films show daily at this terrific little arthouse cinema in Roma Sur. The space also contains myriad places to hang out before or after your movie, including a roof terrace with occasional live music or stand-up comedy, a bookstore, and a café with good pizzas, burgers, and other casual pub fare. ⊠ *Calle Tonalá 261, La Roma* ☎ *55/2663–7293* ⊕ *www.cinetonala.mx* Ⓜ *Centro Médico.*

Shopping

Global Comics Noveno Arte

BOOKS | This flashy-looking space carries one of the best selections of comic books and graphic novels in the city, including a number of hard-to-find titles. ⊠ *Calle San Luis Potosí 109, La Roma* ☎ *55/5913–1318* ⊕ *www.globalcomics. com.mx* Ⓜ *Hospital General.*

Kameyama Shachuu

HOUSEWARES | Both serious and amateur chefs are drawn to this shop for its radiant Sakai Takayuki knives. Available in a wide range of designs and types of handles, they are hand-forged on-site using a style that's been carefully maintained in Osaka for 800 years. ⊠ *Av. Álvaro Obregón 230, La Roma* ☎ *55/1866–2362* ⊕ *www.instagram.com/kameyamashachuu* Ⓜ *Insurgentes.*

★ Mercado Medellín

MARKET | Inside this colorfully painted brick market building that's officially named Mercado Melchor Ocampo, you'll find rows and rows of stalls stocked with sausages, bacalao, nopales, candies, spices, nuts, mole pastes, and sauces of every kind, plus small restaurants selling tasty street-food bites like pozole, arrachera, chile rellenos, Cuban ice cream, and Colombian coffee. It's one of the better organized and less chaotic of the city's many traditional mercados, and it stands out for having vendors hawking goods from a number of other Latin American countries. It's an excellent place to shop for snacks as well as other kinds of gifts, from locally made crafts to household goods. There's also an enormous section devoted to flowers. ⊠ *Calle Campeche 101, La Roma* ☎ *55/5264–1467* ⊕ *www.facebook.com/ mercadomedellincdmx* Ⓜ *Chilpancingo.*

★ Proyecto Rufina

HOUSEWARES | The mission of this beautiful little boutique is to promote and pay consistent and fair wages to artisans and clothing designers from throughout Mexico. The major draw here is women's fashion, including stylishly casual blouses, jackets, pants, and sweaters in earthy hues and constructed with natural fabrics. But there's also an extensive collection of goods for the kitchen and home, including pillows, candles, bowls, and planters. There's a second location in Condesa. ⊠ *Calle Jalapa 151, La Roma* ☎ *55/3039–6072* ⊕ *www.proyectorufina. com* Ⓜ *Insurgentes.*

Retroactivo

MUSIC | One of a few shops around Roma where you can find vinyl LPs, this funky little shop has an especially impressive selection, including hard-to-find treasures from Latin America and Europe. And you can listen before you buy on a handful of turntables in the store. Prices are fair, and the cheerful staff is very helpful.

✉ *Calle Jalapa 125, La Roma* ☎ *55/7158–
5701* ⊕ *www.instagram.com/retroacti-
vo_records_oficial* Ⓜ *Insurgentes.*

Roma Vintage
SECOND-HAND | One of the better
vintage shops in town, this small but
well-stocked boutique is part of a small
collection of stores run by curator and
stylist Nata Paniagua. You'll find a range
of fashionable goods here: retro T-shirts,
leather jackets, designer labels, jewelry,
sunglasses, cowboy boots, and much
more. ✉ *Calle Guanajuato 31, La Roma*
☎ ⊕ *www.instagram.com/romavin-
tagemx* Ⓜ *Hospital General.*

Chapter 9

CONDESA

Updated by
Andrew Collins

● Sights	🍴 Restaurants	🛏 Hotels	🛍 Shopping	🍸 Nightlife
★★★☆☆	★★★★★	★★★★★	★★★★☆	★★★★☆

NEIGHBORHOOD SNAPSHOT

TOP EXPERIENCES

■ **Avenida Amsterdam.** One of the most enjoyable streets for strolling in the entire city, this elliptical circuit with a verdant, tree-shaded median is lined with fashionable cafés and restaurants.

■ **Cocktail-bar hopping.** Although sophisticated coffeehouses and restaurants abound in Condesa, the cocktail mixology scene is perhaps what jumps out the most. Hip lounges like Antolina, Baltra, Caimán, and the rooftop lounge at Hotel CondesaDF are all hot spots.

■ **Casa Luis Barragán and Casa Gilardi.** View the striking, vibrantly colored architecture of Mexico's arguably most renowned architect in these two homes, both of which are open by advance reservation only but a must for design fans.

■ **San Miguel Chapultepec art galleries.** This small but inviting mostly residential neighborhood that borders Condesa to the west abounds with prominent art spaces, including Galeria RGR, Kurimanzutto, and LABOR.

GETTING HERE

La Condesa is easy to reach and navigate by Uber, metro, or on foot. It's just south of prominent Avenida Paseo de la Reforma, and it's flanked by two other important roads, Aveninda Insurgentes and the Circuito Bicentenario freeway. One of the city's safest and most picturesque neighborhoods for strolling, it's within walking distance of Roma and Bosque de Chapultepec as well as the Sevilla, Chapultepec, and Juanacatlán Metro stops on the 1 line, and Chilpancingo and Patriotismo stops on the 9 line. To get from upper Condesa to the outer sections covered in this chapter, such as Escandón and San Miguel Chapultepec, it's a 30- to 45-minute walk—consider Uber or take the metro to the Tacubaya or Constituyentes stop.

PLANNING YOUR TIME

■ Although it's easy to get a feel for Condesa's charms with just an afternoon of sauntering along its tree-shaded streets, you could also walk through this enchanting neighborhood every day for a week and still continue to discover new and engaging spots—especially leisurely cafés and bars dispensing delicious food and drinks. Even when it's crowded with foodies and revelers (weekend evenings in particular), Condesa never feels overwhelming, and you can always pause in one of its leafy parks. It is not a neighborhood with many formal attractions, but if you're keen on exploring the architecture of Luis Barragán or you're a fan of art galleries, set aside at least an additional half day to visit the artsy neighboring colonia of San Miguel Chapultepec.

Filled with striking 1920s and 1930s architecture, tree-lined streets, and both classic and trendy bars and eateries, Condesa is usually mentioned in the same breath as its similarly cool neighbor, Roma. Many people treat the two areas as one large district, but Condesa retains its own distinct history and personality, and it generally feels more established and less hipsterized than Roma. It also has a supply of tiny parks and promenades, many on crescents and down hidden lanes, all with lush greenery, especially its two most famous parks, España and México.

Condesa is a trove of grand, artful architecture—much of it historic, but you'll also find a number of eye-catching modern buildings, few of them rising higher than five or six stories. As you walk around, be sure to look up, as grand balconies and sweeping roof-decks are part of the visual picnic. Angular art deco structures with expansive casement windows mingle beside ornate and slightly curvier art nouveau beauties, while many of the newer structures have sheer glassy facades and huge terraces decked with ferns, flowers, and shrubs. Condesa sustained heavy damage following the massive earthquake of 1985, and many of the neighborhood's newer buildings replaced those that collapsed or were condemned. Exactly (to the day) 32 years later, the 2017 earthquake caused further destruction; even today it's possible to detect cracks in building facades and extra structural supports. For the most part, however, Condesa looks and feels enchanting, with a carefree elegance and a decidedly bohemian vibe.

Condesa's grandeur dates back generations. It's named for Spanish contessa (or *condesa*) Miravalle, who owned the land (as well as Roma and much of Tacubaya) throughout the city's colonial era. In the early 1900s, the contessa's vast property had been sold and subdivided, and it quickly became a desirable place to live among wealthy supporters of Mexico's aristocratic Porfirio Díaz regime, which ended in 1911. The neighborhood's grand avenues, lush parks, and glorious art nouveau and art deco buildings were developed over the next three decades. Like Roma, Condesa experienced a downturn during the latter half of the 20th century that was greatly exacerbated by the '85 earthquake. Following this period and well into the 1990s, the neighborhood began to attract artists and counterculture types drawn to its gorgeous old buildings and newfound affordability.

Today the neighborhood vibe spans youthful, monied, LGBTQ+, touristy, hipster, entrepreneurial, digital nomad, and artsy, and this diverse blend results in some of the best people-watching in the city. Condesa also has one of Mexico City's most eclectic dining and drinking scenes, with an abundance of everything from cheap old-school taquerias and casual international restaurants to a growing number of voguish bistros and darkly lit craft-beer bars and mezcalerias. Much of the action is along the broad avenidas Tamaulipas, Michoacán, and Nuevo León as well as elliptical Avenida Amsterdam—all of these streets have gracious, landscaped medians down their centers. The neighborhood's dense green foliage is alluring any time of year, but in late winter (mid-February to mid-April), it's especially gorgeous as the neighborhood's many jacaranda trees bloom with lavender flowers.

Additionally, this section covers Escandón, a more middle-class neighborhood that extends south from Condesa's border of Avenida Benjamín Franklin to the Viaducto Alemán Highway. And it covers one of the city's somewhat hidden, although increasingly fashionable, urban gems, the small colonia of San Miguel Chapultepec. Quieter than Condesa but with similarly striking architecture of all styles and periods from the past century or so, this neighborhood adjacent to the south edge of Bosque de Chapultepec is crisscrossed with narrow, tree-shaded lanes and boasts a smattering of buzzy restaurants and cafés. For now at least, it remains mostly residential, but the top draw are two iconic house/museums designed by Luis Barragán (including the celebrated architect's own home) and a trove of contemporary art galleries that are among the most prestigious in the city. If you're looking to base yourself close to both Bosque de Chapultepec and Condesa and Roma, this is an excellent neighborhood to stay in (there are quite a number of Airbnbs, though few actual hotels).

Condesa

Sights

★ Avenida Amsterdam

STREET | An elliptical avenue that feels like it could be in Paris or Madrid minus the unusually lush semitropical foliage, Amsterdam was designed in the early 1900s as the outer perimeter of a racetrack that would eventually become Parque México. Today it's among the best streets in the city for a stroll. The two lanes of auto traffic are divided by a landscaped median with a paved sidewalk, old-fashioned street lamps, and a smattering of art nouveau tiled benches. There are three roundabouts connecting Amsterdam, each named for one of the city's cloud-scraping peaks: Popocatépetl, Iztaccihuatl, and Citlaltépetl. This is also one of the best streets for admiring the neighborhood's distinctive residential architectural, from ornate art deco and art nouveau beauties to strikingly contemporary mid-rise towers. Although predominantly residential, the ground floors of many of these buildings contain hip coffeehouses, ice-cream shops, bistros, and bars, along with a handful of noteworthy boutique shops. The avenue completely encircles Parque México, and at the northwestern side of the ellipse, you can walk from Parque México just two blocks along restaurant-lined Avendia Parras to reach Parque España. ✉ *Av. Amsterdam, La Condesa* [M] *Chilpancingo.*

Hydra + Fotografía

ART GALLERY | In this building painted in boldly colored abstract designs, shutterbugs and admirers of art photography can take classes and workshops, view contemporary gallery shows, and peruse the extensive selection of photography books. ✉ *Calle Tampico 33, La Condesa* ☎ *55/6819–9872* 🌐 *www.hydra.lat* 🎟 *Free* 🕒 *Closed Sun. and Mon.* [M] *Chapultepec.*

Parque España

CITY PARK | Like nearby Parque México, this slightly smaller but no less alluring 16½ acre urban oasis was laid out in the early 1920s by architect José Luis Cuevas, who was also responsible for planning much of the surrounding Hipódromo section of the Condesa neighborhood. It opened officially in September 1921, during the centennial celebrations of the Mexican War of Independence. A focal point of Parque España is the dramatic, modern sculpture and fountain installed in 1974 in honor of statesman and Mexican Revolutionary General Lázaro Cárdenas. It's a figurative depiction of the outstretched palm of then President Cárdenas, welcoming Republican refugees of the Spanish Civil to Mexico during the late 1930s. Both the statue and the park in general are popular places to sit with a book or watch locals strolling with their dogs. It's filled with flower beds, native shrubs, a small pond, and a playground. ✉ *Av. Nuevo León at Av. Sonora, La Condesa* [M] *Sevilla.*

★ Parque México

CITY PARK | **FAMILY** | Condesa's other green lung, the 22-acre Parque México lies just southeast of its slightly smaller and slightly older sister, Parque España. Among its many enchanting features, you'll find a gracious duck pond, a large children's playground, fountains, a strikingly ornate art deco iron clocktower, and dozens of footpaths passing by emerald gardens, topiary shrubs, and towering specimen trees. The park was constructed in 1927 on the site of a former racetrack, which explains the circular road, Avenida México, looping its perimeter and the name of the colonia in which its officially located, Hipódromo (hippodrome) Condesa. The park is lined with handsome buildings, including some of the best examples of art deco in the city. Dozens of cafés, taquerias, and bars are within a couple of blocks of the park, making it a great spot to enjoy a casual bite to eat. ✉ *Av. Michoacán at Av. México, La Condesa* [M] *Sevilla.*

🍴 Restaurants

★ Anónimo

$$ | **ITALIAN** | This tremendously popular corner bistro, the brainchild of acclaimed Mexican-German chef Klaus Mayr, is a stylish candlelit space to mingle with friends and dine on well-prepared thin-crust pizzas and house-made pastas. The classic Caesar salad makes a perfect opener before tucking into plates of lasagna Bolognese, duck-and-corn-filled agnoloti, and the white pizza topped with bacon, caramelized onions, and honey. **Known for:** outstanding cocktail list; lively music from a well-curated playlist; soft-serve ice cream topped with baklava or fruit compote. [$] *Average main: MP300* ✉ *C. Atlixco 105, La Condesa* ☎ *55/3709–9049* [M] *Patriotismo.*

★ Azul Condesa

$$$ | **MEXICAN** | When it comes to authentic Mexican food, chef and food historian Ricardo Muñoz Zurita literally wrote the book with his *Diccionario Enciclopédico de la Gastronomía Mexicana* (*Encyclopedia of Mexican Food*). Here in his art-filled, elegant Condesa restaurant, you can sample some of his superb regional Mexican dishes, such as beef drizzled in a smoky Oaxacan mole that takes three days to make, Veracruz-style fish, or ancient Mayan dishes from the Yucatán.

ROMA

Sights ▼

1 Avenida Amsterdam..... **F4**
2 Hydra + Fotografía...... **D2**
3 Parque España.......... **E4**
4 Parque México **F5**

Restaurants ▼

1 Anónimo **C6**
2 Azul Condesa............. **E5**
3 Botánico **D7**
4 Café Milou **D2**
5 Canton Mexicali **G3**
6 Chilpa **F7**
7 Deigo Ramen............. **F7**
8 La Guerrerense **E6**
9 La Vinería **D5**
10 Lardo **C3**
11 Le Bon Bistro............. **G6**
12 Maizajo **B4**
13 Malcriado Café **C6**
14 Mendl Delicatessen..... **E6**
15 Merkavá **F4**
16 Merotoro.................. **F6**
17 Ostería 8 .... **C2**
18 Pasillo de Humo.......... **E6**
19 Patagonia................ **D6**
20 Rojo Bistrot **F4**
21 Specia.................... **G6**

Quick Bites ▼

1 Cafe Escandon.......... **D9**
2 Chiquitito Café **D7**
3 El Farolito **D8**
4 El Tizoncito **C6**
5 Enhorabuena Café...... **D4**
6 Frëims..................... **F4**
7 La Buena Birria MX **G7**
8 Molino El Pujol **C7**
9 Nevería Roxy............. **C4**
10 Nieve de Olla **C6**
11 Ojo de Agua **E6**
12 Qüentin Café **F4**
13 Saint...................... **C7**
14 Tacos Hola................ **E5**
15 Taquería El Greco........ **E5**

Hotels ▼

1 Andaz Mexico City
   Condesa **F7**
2 Hotel CondesaDF **E3**
3 Hotel San Fernando
   La Condesa **F6**
4 Maria Condesa........... **C6**
5 Mondrian Mexico City
   Condesa **F7**
6 Octavia Casa **C6**
7 Red Tree House **E7**
8 Stella
   Bed & Breakfast......... **E6**
9 Tao Suítes **D6**

KEY

1 Sights
1 Restaurants
1 Quick Bites
1 Hotels
i Visitor Information

Known for: cochinita pibíl; authentic Mexican breakfasts; chocolate dessert tamales. $ *Average main: MP440* ⊠ *Av. Nuevo León 68, La Condesa* ☎ *55/5286–6380* ⊕ *www.azul.rest* Ⓜ *Sevilla.*

★ Botánico

$$$ | MODERN MEXICAN | With tables neatly arranged in one of Condesa's most romantic gardens, this trendy spot showcases the creative international cuisine of chef Alejandra Navarro, formerly of world-famous Quintonil. The menu changes regularly and reflects seasonal ingredients, but typical fare includes flame-roasted beets with a chimichurri sauce, mussels steamed in a coconut-lemongrass broth, and organic smoked and roasted chicken au jus with new potatoes and a robust green sauce. **Known for:** long and well-curated wine and cocktail list; spectacular setting amid towering cacti and succulents; exceptional service. $ *Average main: MP420* ⊠ *Alfonso Reyes 217, La Condesa* ☎ *55/5271–2152* ⊕ *www.facebook.com/botanicomx. mx* ☉ *Closed Mon.* Ⓜ *Chilpancingo.*

★ Café Milou

$$ | FRENCH | There's often a slight wait for one of the marble tables in this chic, intimate wine bar on the border with Roma Norte—it has a loyal following among the city's trendier residents. Enjoy a glass of Muscadet or Grenache-Carignan—or perhaps an espresso and pan au chocolate in the morning—while savoring deftly prepared modern French tapas, like pork rilletes; Niçoise salad with tuna confit, egg, anchovies; and North African tagine with couscous and almonds. **Known for:** eggs Benedict and scrambled eggs with gravlax for breakfast; late-night dining and drinking; well-curated French wine list. $ *Average main: MP240* ⊠ *Av. Veracruz 38, La Condesa* ☎ *55/7866–4575* ⊕ *www.cafemilou.com* ☉ *No dinner Sun.* Ⓜ *Chapultepec.*

Canton Mexicali

$$ | CHINESE FUSION | In a gray house with red trim and awnings that are lit up at night brighter than a Christmas tree, this extremely popular restaurant near the border with Roma specializes in the distinct brand of Chinese food that's popular in the Baja city of Mexicali. Start with the chiles rellenos stuffed with ground seasoned pork, garlic, and ginger before moving on to flavorful main dishes, such as Szechuan-style dan dan noodles, beef chop suey, and shrimp chipotle. **Known for:** house-distilled baijiu (a Chinese spirit); festive, conversation-filled dining room; five-spice chocolate cake with vanilla ice cream. $ *Average main: MP285* ⊠ *Av. Álvaro Obregón 264, La Condesa* ☎ *55/1701–1479* ⊕ *www.cantonmexicali.com* Ⓜ *Sevilla.*

Chilpa

$ | MEXICAN | Chilaquiles are by far the top draw at this friendly brunch spot a block from Avenida Amsterdam; it also offers up a nice selection of other all-day dishes, from fruit-yogurt bowls and avocado toast with eggs and goat cheese to molletes topped with butter, beans, Oaxacan and manchego cheeses, and pico de gallo. The chilaquiles are build-your-own: you choose your sauce (chipotle, habanero, and more), protein (eggs, chicken breast, cecina steak, vegan chorizo), and other ingredients (anything from asparagus to panela cheese)—with enough toppings, this can be a dish to last you the entire day. **Known for:** cheerful, open-air seating; generous portions; freshly squeezed juices and organic kombuchas. $ *Average main: MP165* ⊠ *Chilpancingo 35, La Condesa* ☎ *55/5264–4976* ⊕ *www.chilpa.mx* ☉ *No dinner* Ⓜ *Chilpancingo.*

★ Deigo Ramen

$$ | RAMEN | There's often a pretty sizable crowd waiting for a seat at the long, narrow bar inside this hip ramen parlor, a fast-casual version of one of the city's most beloved Japanese restaurants,

Diego & Kaito, in Del Valle. One of the only spots in town that serves food 24/7, Deigo has a fairly short but sweet menu of well-prepared dishes, with chashu (pork belly, egg, and wakame seaweed) and corn-butter-miso among the favorites. **Known for:** hearty meat and vegan ramens; takoyaki octopus balls; calpis, a noncarbonated Japanese soft drink. $ *Average main: MP290* ⊠ *Tlaxcala 165, La Condesa* ☎ ⊕ *qrco.de/bd7U7j* Ⓜ *Chilpancingo.*

La Guerrerense

$$ | SEAFOOD | Fans of Baja-style seafood flock to this bustling counter inside the Parián Condesa food hall for fresh, delicious crab tostadas, *caracol* (sea snail) ceviche, oysters and clams on the half shell, and shrimp and octopus cocktails. Enjoy your food at one of the casual tables, imagining you're at the beach in Ensenada, where the original La Guerrerense (which was much lauded by Anthony Bourdain) is located. **Known for:** raw shellfish, ceviches, and aguachiles; seafood tacos; variety of delicious house-made salsas. $ *Average main: MP300* ⊠ *Av. Nuevo León 107, La Condesa* ☎ *55/8376–5332* ⊕ *www.laguerrerense. com* ⊗ *No dinner Sun.* Ⓜ *Chilpancingo.*

★ Lardo

$$$ | MEDITERRANEAN | At this more casual and free-wheeling sibling to famed Rosetta restaurant and bakery, sit at one of the cozy café tables in the sun-filled, shabby-chic dining room and fill up on exceptional grilled, panfried, and oven-baked modern Mediterranean fare served on whimsical antique china. Highlights from the extensive menu include grilled rustic bread topped with tomato and anchovies, blistered-crust pizzas topped with eggplant and ricotta, and rabbit liver ravioli with a rabbit ragù. **Known for:** creative, contemporary Mediterranean cuisine; stunning desserts, some featuring homemade ice cream; baked goods and light fare available from the take-out window. $ *Average*

main: MP380 ⊠ *Calle Agustín Melgar 6, La Condesa* ☎ *55/5211–7731* ⊕ *www. facebook.com/lardomexico* ⊗ *No dinner Sun.* Ⓜ *Chapultepec.*

La Vinería

$ | MEDITERRANEAN | This cozy, well-established restaurant and wine bar is ideal for conversation and lingering over a light meal from the eclectic menu that shows Mexican, Spanish, and Italian influences. Try the wild mushrooms and goat cheese in pastry with brandy sauce, the steak tartare with curly french fries, and the cajeta crepes for dessert. **Known for:** low-key, quiet ambience; excellent Eurocentric wine list; interesting mix of new-world and old-world cuisine. $ *Average main: MP260* ⊠ *Av. Fernando Montes de Oca 52A, La Condesa* ☎ *55/5211–9020* ⊕ *www.lavineria.com.mx* ⊗ *No dinner Sun.* Ⓜ *Juanacatlán.*

Le Bon Bistro

$$$ | FRENCH | One of the newer and decidedly modern French restaurants that abound and, indeed, fit in perfectly amid Condesa's vaguely Parisian vibe, this dapper bistro is a charming option when you're seeking a slightly fancy but still unpretentious dinner out. You'll find all the classics here, well-prepared and artfully plated, including salade niçoise, filet mignon, duck leg confit, and beef bourguignonne. **Known for:** attractive sidewalk seating on Avenida Amsterdam; beautiful desserts (especially the chocolate mousse); attentive service. $ *Average main: MP360* ⊠ *Av. Amsterdam 225, La Condesa* ☎ *55/5087–2132* ⊕ *www.facebook.com/lebon.bistromx* ⊗ *No dinner Sun.* Ⓜ *Chilpancingo.*

Malcriado Café

$$ | ECLECTIC | Open from 8 in the morning until late every evening (it closes a little earlier on Sunday night), this unpretentiously stylish café with a covered sidewalk terrace fits the bill for a wide range of occasions. Early in the day, it's a favorite for well-crafted espresso drinks, shakshuka, and French toast, but as the day continues, patrons drop by for smoked-trout sandwiches, French onion soup, and to share a bottle of from the short but well-chosen wine list. **Known for:** relaxed, intimate vibe; coffee-based cocktails; sticky toffee pudding. $ *Average main: MP240 ⊠ Calle Atlixco 127, La Condesa* ☎ *55/6199–2805* ⊕ *www. malcriado.mx* Ⓜ *Patriotismo.*

★ Maizajo

$$$ | **MODERN MEXICAN** | Run by Santiago Muñoz, formerly of the famous regional Mexican restaurant Nico's, this casually stylish rooftop restaurant showcases the talented chef's devotion to traditional preparations and ingredients (including the centuries-old nixtamalization process of producing corn tortillas). Highlights from the creative menu include barbecue-duck tacos, *huaraches* (oval-shaped masa tortillas) topped with braised oxtail, and grilled striped bass with pasilla chiles and heirloom tomatoes. **Known for:** casual downstairs taco bar and shop; fresh fruit cocktails; strawberries with an atole (corn) cream and honey for dessert. $ *Average main: MP330 ⊠ Fernando Montes de Oca 113, La Condesa* ☎ *55/7959–8540* ⊕ *www. maizajo.com* ☾ *Closed Mon. No dinner Sun.* Ⓜ *Juanacatlán.*

★ Mendl Delicatessen

$$ | **JEWISH DELI** | Fans of authentic Jewish deli fare flock to this rather chic modern deli with sidewalk seating facing toward gracious Parque México. You'll find all the classics here, prepared with care, including potato latkes with apple compote, Reuben sandwiches, smoked whitefish salad, cured lox bagels, and slow-cooker brisket. **Known for:** inviting indoor and outdoor seating; soul-warming matzo ball soup; challah French toast. $ *Average main: $300 ⊠ Citlaltépetl 9, La Condesa* ☎ *55/9347–9944* ⊕ *www.mendl.mx* ☾ *No dinner* Ⓜ *Chilpancingo.*

★ Merkavá

$$$ | **ISRAELI** | In this sleek, narrow dining room, the best strategy for enjoying some of the city's best Israeli fare is to order the selection of 7 or 14 *salatim* (cold dishes), which include tomatoes with eggplants and honey, tamarind-cured beets, baba ghanoush, labneh with zaatar, and a host of other easily shared delectables. From the oven, you can't go wrong with the roasted cauliflower with mint yogurt, potato latkes with sour cream (and optional caviar), or grilled whole chicken with fried artichokes. **Known for:** halva for dessert in a variety of flavors; shrab al loz (an almond drink sweetened with rose water and pistachio); great creative cocktail list. $ *Average main: MP420 ⊠ Av. Amsterdam 53, La Condesa* ☎ *55/5086–8065* ⊕ *www.bullandtank.com* ☾ *Closed Mon. No dinner Sun.* Ⓜ *Sevilla.*

Merotoro

$$$ | **MODERN MEXICAN** | The esteemed team behind Roma's Contramar also operates this glitzy see-and-be-seen bistro specializing in a rarefied take on the contemporary cuisine of Baja California. The oft-changing menu veers toward rich and beautiful, with dishes like sea urchin–cream rice with crispy soft-shell crab, preserved beef tartare with serrano chile aioli and chapulines, and braised lamb with creamy potatoes, turnips, and bok choy. **Known for:** refined Baja California cuisine; sophisticated service; dessert cheese plate with caramelized fig. $ *Average main: MP430 ⊠ Av. Amsterdam 204, La Condesa* ☎ *55/5564–7799* ⊕ *www.merotoro.mx* Ⓜ *Chilpancingo.*

★ Pasillo de Humo

$$$ | **MODERN MEXICAN** | Located upstairs at the bustling Parián Condesa, an arcade mostly of food stalls, Pasillo de Humo and its gorgeous atrium-style space is at once sophisticated but easygoing. The kitchen produces flavorful, authentic Oaxacan fare, including tlayudas with grasshoppers, chorizo, strips of chile, and

other traditional toppings, plus octopus grilled with a *hauchimole* (guaje-seed mole) sauce and pork belly with fruit mole, plantains, sweet potato puree, and roasted pineapple. **Known for:** tlayudas with a variety of toppings; authentic Oaxacan fare; house-made ice creams with unusual flavors. [$] *Average main: MP355* ✉ *Av. Nuevo León 107, La Condesa* ☎ *55/5211–7263* 🌐 *www.facebook.com/pasillodehumo* 🕑 *No dinner Sun.* [M] *Chilpancingo.*

Patagonia

$$$ | **ARGENTINE** | Dine at one of the sidewalk tables here when you're craving first-rate Argentinean-style steaks and other expertly prepared grills, such as grilled veal osso buco, pork shoulder with caramelized sweet potatoes, and sous vide confit of octopus with roasted potatoes and aioli. There's an excellent Argentina-focused wine list, and the desserts (including a cardamom-lemon crème brûlée) are impressive. **Known for:** attractive sidewalk seating; perfectly prepared Argentinean-style steaks; late-night dining. [$] *Average main: MP340* ✉ *Campeche 345, La Condesa* ☎ *55/5211–8032* 🌐 *www.facebook.com/patagoniaparrilladecampo* [M] *Chilpancingo.*

Ostería 8

$$ | **MODERN ITALIAN** | A modern, warmly lit neighborhood spot, Ostería 8 uses mostly organic, regional ingredients in its handmade pastas and thin-crust pizzas. The pie topped with jamón Serrano, mascarpone, and fresh arugula is a favorite, while tagliatelle pasta with guanciale, wild mushrooms, garlic, and white wine shine among the pastas. **Known for:** personal-size focaccia pizzas; vanilla ice cream with nuts and an aged-balsamic drizzle; noteworthy Italian wine selection. [$] *Average main: MP240* ✉ *Calle Sinaloa 252, La Condesa* ☎ *55/5212–2008* 🌐 *www.facebook.com/osteria8* 🕑 *Closed Sun.* [M] *Chapultepec.*

Rojo Bistrot

$$$ | **FRENCH** | The bright-red vintage neon sign and mustard-hue facade of this corner bistro overlooking Avenida Amsterdam will have you feeling as though you've stumbled into Paris's Latin Quarter. The short chalkboard menu changes nightly but might feature grilled salmon with an orange-star anise sauce or beef fillet with olives, sundried tomatoes, and roasted potatoes. **Known for:** warm Parisian-style vibe; classic French bistro fare; views of charming Avenida Amsterdam. [$] *Average main: MP365* ✉ *Av. Amsterdam 71, La Condesa* ☎ *55/5211–3705* 🌐 *www.facebook.com/rojobistrot* 🕑 *No dinner Sun.* [M] *Sevilla.*

Specia

$$$ | **POLISH** | The famous roasted duck with an apple-based stuffing, mashed potatoes, and a baked apple bathed in blueberry sauce has made Specia a wildly popular destination, but the refined Polish restaurant with 1920s-inspired Jazz Age artwork serves a number of other tasty dishes, too. Consider the lamb goulash, seasoned with paprika and tomato, or the slow-grilled rabbit loin with cabbage and beets. **Known for:** apple-stuffed roasted duck; refined Polish food; elegant art-filled dining room. [$] *Average main: MP430* ✉ *Av. Amsterdam 241, La Condesa* ☎ *55/5564–1367* 🌐 *www.specia.mx* 🕑 *No dinner Sun.* [M] *Sevilla.*

☕ Coffee and Quick Bites

Cafe Escandon

$$ | **CAFÉ** | Part cute vintage store (with clothing, housewares, jewelry, and antique toys) and part café, this homey spot in Escandón is the sort of place you want to linger. The all-day breakfast menu features a number of hearty dishes, including the house dish: poached eggs over ham, bacon, and roast beef with hollandaise sauce; plus, there's a good selection of pastas, sandwiches, and other tasty fare available later in the day. **Known for:** quirky, living room–esque

Condesa's streets are intersected with lots of charming pocket parks.

vibe; hearty breakfasts served all day; antiques and crafts for sale. $ *Average main: MP180* ✉ *Calle Sindicalismo 53, Escandón, La Condesa* ☎ *55/2614–2376* ⊕ *www.facebook.com/cafescandon* ⊗ *No dinner Sun.* Ⓜ *Chilpancingo.*

Chiquitito Café
$ | CAFÉ | For a refreshing caffeine pick-me-up in the southern reaches of Condesa, pop into this cute and cozy third-wave espresso bar that serves delicious breakfasts and sandwiches, too. Students and freelancers work away on their laptops in the triangular white-brick interior space, while you're more likely to spy friends gabbing at the sidewalk tables. **Known for:** tasty baguette and bagel sandwiches; cakes and pastries; artisanal coffee drinks. $ *Average main: MP100* ✉ *Calle Alfonso Reyes 232, La Condesa* ☎ *55/5211–6123* ⊕ *www.chiquititocafe. com* ⊗ *No dinner Sun.* Ⓜ *Chilpancingo.*

El Farolito
$ | MEXICAN | A neighborhood favorite since 1962, this spacious taqueria with a striking black awning and red-and-white color scheme offers up hefty platters of delicious tacos and other classics. Try the *costras crujientes,* in which the meat is wrapped in fried cheese before being wrapped in a tortilla, or any of the *alambres al carbón* with bacon, onions, chile poblano, and any number of fillings. **Known for:** open hours well past midnight most evenings; horchata, jamaica, tamarindo, and other juices; churros with cajeta, chocolate, and condensed milk. $ *Average main: MP140* ✉ *Cerradas Altata 19, La Condesa* ☎ *55/5515–2380* ⊕ *www. elfarolito.com.mx* Ⓜ *Chilpancingo.*

El Tizoncito
$ | MEXICAN | You shouldn't leave this sprawling, casual place without trying one the tacos al pastor, which come in a variety of styles—long-running El Tizoncito claims to have invented the now iconic dish. This festive spot also serves excellent pozole, tacos *choriquesos* (grilled chorizo slathered in melted mozzarella), marinated *huesitos* (ribs) with guacamole, and plenty of other street-food-style options. **Known for:**

famous tacos al pastor; open hours until well after midnight; elote (corn) cake for dessert. $ *Average main: MP125* ✉ *Av. Tamaulipas 122, La Condesa* ☎ *55/5286–7321* ⊕ *www.eltizoncito. mx* Ⓜ *Patriotismo.*

Enhorabuena Café

$$ | CAFÉ | From morning through early evening, this casual, contemporary café that opens to a quiet, tree-lined street near Parque España welcomes a mix of regulars and tourists with bountiful plates of Mexican and international breakfast dishes, soups, salads, and sandwiches. The menu tends toward healthy and fresh, with mango-granola bowls, toasted ham-and-gruyere brioche sandwiches, green juices, and fine teas and lattes. **Known for:** chilaquiles verdes; house-made sodas, juices, and sipping chocolates; relaxing ambience with outdoor seating that's perfect for work or socializing. $ *Average main: MP170* ✉ *Calle Atlixco 13, La Condesa* ☎ *55/9155–6654* ⊕ *www.instagram.com/enhorabuenacafe* ⊗ *No dinner Sun.* Ⓜ *Chapultepec.*

Frëims

$$ | CAFÉ | Although there's a small indoor dining room, the big draw here is the expansive patio with a retractable glass roof, tall ivy-covered walls, and tables of varying sizes. It's a great place to relax or work on your laptop for a few hours, and there are enough tasty pressed-sandwich (try the Croque Madame), salad, and soup options to make a meal of it. **Known for:** late-night dining; waffles and waffle sandwiches; well-crafted coffee drinks. $ *Average main: MP175* ✉ *Amsterdam 62B, La Condesa* ☎ *55/9130–8449* ⊕ *www.freims.mx* ⊗ *No dinner Mon. and Tues.* Ⓜ *Sevilla.*

La Buena Birria MX

$ | MEXICAN | This unassuming spot beside a gas station near the border of Condesa and Roma has developed a loyal following for its hearty and affordable *birrias* (meat stews). The signature dish is the birriamen, basically

a Mexican-Japanese fusion of flavor packed with tender pork carnitas, onions, cilantro, and spices, but other delicious options include quesabirria tacos oozing with melted cheese, and the restaurant's spin on chilaquiles, birraquiles. **Known for:** casual outdoor seating area; fast and friendly service; famous birriamen. $ *Average main: MP140* ✉ *Campeche 218, La Condesa* ☎ *55/5264–4976* ⊕ *www. facebook.com/labuenabirriamx* ⊗ *Closed Mon. No dinner* Ⓜ *Chilpancingo.*

★ Molino El Pujol

$ | MODERN MEXICAN | Legendary chef and Enrique Olvera, a devoted practitioner of making tortillas according to tradition and with only the highest-quality ingredients, opened this hole-in-wall shop and café, in part to expand his world-famous Polanco restaurant to the masses. The short menu is basically an ode to maíz, featuring elote and esquites, *enmoladas* (chicken mole enchiladas), avocado-hoja santa tacos, chilaquiles con mole, huitlacoche tamales, and other perfectly prepared botanas (for breakfast and lunch). **Known for:** house-made tortillas, salsas, and mole to go; tamales with creative fillings; cheerful outdoor seating area. $ *Average main: MP125* ✉ *General Benjamín Hill 146, La Condesa* ☎ *55/5271–3515* ⊕ *www.pujol.com.mx* ⊗ *No dinner* Ⓜ *Patriotismo.*

Nieve de Olla

$ | ICE CREAM | All of the delicious homemade ice cream at this popular, eco-conscious dessert spot is served in waffle cones or bowls with edible spoons—no plastics or inorganic materials are used here. There are always about a dozen flavors on hand, including seasonal specials like (marigold) and pineapple-basil as well as regular favorites like lemon pie and marzipan. **Known for:** good people-watching from the sidewalk tables; unusual seasonal ice cream flavors; eco-friendly practices and materials. $ *Average main: MP80* ✉ *Alfonso*

Reyes 122, La Condesa ☎ *55/2748–0380* 🌐 *www.nievedeolla.com* [M] *Patriotismo.*

★ Ojo de Agua

$$ | **CAFÉ** | This fast-expanding Mexican chain of health food café-markets has one of its busiest but prettiest locations in Condesa, overlooking one of Avenida Amsterdam's most photographed fountains. Choose from an extensive array of combination juices and smoothies, plus excellent, if somewhat pricey, salads and sandwiches, like roasted turkey with manchego and ginger sauce. **Known for:** delicious smoothies in numerous flavors; fresh produce and healthy snacks to go; prime location with outdoor seating. [$] *Average main: MP285* ✉ *Citlaltépetl 23C, La Condesa* ☎ *55/2155–6466* 🌐 *www.grupoojodeagua.com.mx* [M] *Chilpancingo.*

Neveria Roxy

$ | **ICE CREAM** | **FAMILY** | Throughout the day, Condesa's traditional Mexican ice-cream parlor—and its several other locations around the city—packs in kids and hipsters alike with its *nieve* (sorbet) flavors like *maracuyá* (passionfruit) and *tuna* (prickly pear cactus fruit) and its *helado* (ice cream) flavors, including *rompope* (eggnog) and macadamia. Popular since it opened in 1946, it's distinctly old-school, with teal vinyl chairs, white tables, and bright fluorescent lights, but the quality is first-rate. **Known for:** old-school ambience; lots of regional Mexican fruit flavors; ice-cream sundaes. [$] *Average main: MP50* ✉ *Fernando Montes de Oca 89, La Condesa* ☎ *55/5286–1258* 🌐 *www.neveriaroxy.com.mx* [M] *Juanacatlán.*

★ Qūentin Café

$ | **CAFÉ** | With a more charming setting than the original location in Roma, this buzzy third-wave coffeehouse is set along leafy Avendia Amsterdam and offers comfy seating in its plant-filled interior and on the sidewalk. The baristas are knowledgeable and professional, whether crafting a *carajillo* (a refreshing cocktail with iced espresso and Licor 43, a fragrant herbal liqueur), a *cascara* (tea brewed with coffee cherries), or a single-origin pour-over. **Known for:** carefully sourced small-batch coffees from around the world; artisanal chocolates and pastries; coffee-based cocktails. [$] *Average main: MP80* ✉ *Av. Amsterdam 67A, La Condesa* ☎ *55/7312–6188* 🌐 *www.facebook.com/quentincafemx* [M] *Sevilla.*

Saint

$ | **BAKERY** | Extraordinarily delicious baked goods and savory breads are dispensed at this cute French-style bakery in the south end of Condesa. Highlights include rich pain au chocolate, doughnuts bursting with strawberry jam, creamy flan, and crunchy cinnamon palmiers. **Known for:** well-made espresso drinks; some of the best sourdough bread in the city; chewy chocolate chip cookies. [$] *Average main: $65* ✉ *General Benjamín Hill 146–1, La Condesa* ☎ *55/8848–1224* [M] *Patriotismo.*

★ Tacos Hola

$ | **MEXICAN** | This simple, tiny taqueria is a favorite standby for tacos *guisados,* a completely addictive style with stewed and richly seasoned braised meats like *higado* (beef liver topped with avocado), chicken mole, and a tuna-sardine blend. Hola stands out from the pack for its variety of vegetarian and vegan options, including squash, Swiss chard, nopales, and *quelites,* a distinctive Mexican herb that's commonly used in soups and stews. **Known for:** great location on Avenida Amsterdam; plenty of fresh vegetarian selections; fillings displayed in attractive stone bowls on the counter. [$] *Average main: MP100* ✉ *Av. Amsterdam 135, La Condesa* ☎ *55/8669–8455* 🌐 *www.facebook.com/tacos.hola68* 🕒 *No dinner Sun.* [M] *Chilpancingo.*

Taquería El Greco

$ | **MEXICAN** | At this no-frills, old-fashioned take-out taqueria, shaved meat rotates enticingly on a spit before an open flame, practically daring you not to try a plate of the Árabe-style (wrapped in grilled pita bread) tacos al pastor, plus tortas, grilled meats, and a long menu of other short-order snacks. It's a great, cheap Condesa option when you're hungry and on the run. **Known for:** handy location near both Parque México and Parque España; flan and key lime pie; tacos Árabes. $ *Average main: MP85* ⊠ *Av. Michoacán 54, La Condesa* ☎ *55/3934– 0040* ⊘ *Closed Sun* Ⓜ *Chilpancingo.*

Hotels

★ Andaz Mexico City Condesa

$$$ | HOTEL | This trendy outpost of Hyatt's stylishly upmarket Andaz brand, located inside an enormous restored art deco building, has spacious, tech-savvy rooms with large windows and plush bedding, as well as the greatest array of amenities in the neighborhood, including a full-service spa and multiple dining and drinking options. **Pros:** extremely convenient both to Condesa and Roma; fabulous infinity rooftop pool on the 17th floor; well-outfitted spa and gym. **Cons:** just off very busy Avenida de los Insurgentes; as the largest hotel complex in the neighborhood, it can feel a bit impersonal; the breakfast buffet, which costs extra, is pretty unmemorable. $ *Rooms from: MP5600* ⊠ *Aguascalientes 158, La Condesa* ☎ *55/5977–1234* ⊕ *www.hyatt.com/andaz* ⤢ *213 rooms* ⦿*No Meals* Ⓜ *Chilpancingo.*

★ Hotel CondesaDF

$$$ | HOTEL | It's all about the details at this hip hotel with a quiet, picturesque setting overlooking Parque España, from rooms outfitted with eye-catching custom-designed furniture and Malin & Goetz bath products to a library of coffee table books about Mexican history and culture. **Pros:** smartly designed contemporary rooms; steps from Condesa's notable restaurants and shops; rooftop terrace has great views of the leafy neighborhood. **Cons:** some rooms are a bit small; bars and restaurants are often crowded and noisy on weekends; service

Back in the Day

9

Condesa CONDESA

As you walk along two of the neighborhood's most picturesque streets, avenidas Amsterdam and México, you may wonder about their distinctive elliptical shapes. In fact, Avenida México sits atop a former racetrack—in which Parque México formed the center—where both horse and auto races took place in the 1910s; Avenida Amsterdam forms an outer perimeter "ring road" encircling it.

can be a little brusque at times. $ *Rooms from: MP6000* ⊠ *Av. Veracruz 102, La Condesa* ☎ *55/5241–2600* ⊕ *www.condesadf.com* ⤢ *40 rooms* ⦿*Free Breakfast* Ⓜ *Chapultepec.*

Hotel San Fernando La Condesa

$$ | HOTEL | Part of the hip Austin, Texas–based Bunkhouse Hotel group, this casually chic boutique hotel set inside a 1940s apartment building is just a few steps from both Parque México and Avenida Amsterdam, and offers light-filled rooms with Bluetooth speakers, mini-refrigerators stocked with premium snacks for purchase, and a handful of suites with terraces. **Pros:** well-thought-out rooms with original architectural details; great little lounge with good food and drink; amazing location in Condesa's prettiest section. **Cons:** some rooms lack much in the way of a view; least expensive rooms are pretty compact; street noise can be a problem, especially weekend evenings. $ *Rooms from: MP3600* ⊠ *Iztaccihuatl 54, La Condesa* ☎ *55/1334–4653* ⊕ *www.bunkhousehotels.com* ⤢ *19 rooms* ⦿*Free Breakfast* Ⓜ *Chilpancingo.*

Maria Condesa

$$ | **HOTEL** | This laid-back but sophisticated boutique hotel on a slightly busy street corner features 16 rooms that have been designed with locally crafted products. **Pros:** covered open-air roof terrace with neighborhood views; lots of terrific restaurants just steps away; bath products and some furnishings designed by Pineda Covalin boutique. **Cons:** linens and towels are a bit thin; not suitable for children; in a somewhat noisy part of the neighborhood. $ *Rooms from: MP3300* ✉ *Calle Atlixco 132, La Condesa* ☎ *55/5286–5828* ⊕ *www.mariacondesa. com.mx* ⟿ *16 rooms* ⅋⊘⅋ *Free Breakfast* Ⓜ *Patriotismo.*

Mondrian Mexico City Condesa

$$$ | **HOTEL** | Sharing a lobby and some amenities with the similarly upscale Andaz hotel, this contemporary art-themed hotel with dynamic murals in the guestrooms occupies part of a large mid-20th-century building designed by celebrated architect Jose Luis Benlliure and filled with see-and-be-seen lounges and restaurants, including Skybar Condesa, with its sweeping city and mountain views. **Pros:** fun, upbeat design and color scheme; several excellent dining options; full-service spa and fitness center. **Cons:** there can be a noisy, party vibe in the common areas; large property can feel a bit impersonal; guests must make reservations to use the rooftop pool belonging to the Andaz. $ *Rooms from: MP4200* ✉ *Aguascalientes 156, La Condesa* ☎ *55/8889–0356* ⊕ *book. ennismore.com/hotels/mondrian/mexico-city-condesa* ⟿ *183 rooms* ⅋⊘⅋ *No Meals* Ⓜ *Chilpancingo.*

★ **Octavia Casa**

$$$$ | **B&B/INN** | Established by the designer behind Mexico's acclaimed Octavia fashion line, this intimate, exquisitely designed modern boutique hotel has appeared in international design magazines with good reason—the minimalist-chic rooms convey a deep sense of serenity and harmony, with their geometric angles, earthy tones, soft lighting, and high ceilings. **Pros:** truly artful contemporary design; on a quiet street; helpful staff always anticipates the needs of guests. **Cons:** a few blocks from the heart of Condesa's restaurant and retail scene; not suitable for children; on the pricey side. $ *Rooms from: MP7100* ✉ *Av. Amatlan 126, La Condesa* ☎ *55/7338– 9520* ⊕ *www.octaviacasa.mx* ⟿ *7 rooms* ⅋⊘⅋ *Free Breakfast* Ⓜ *Chilpancingo.*

★ **Red Tree House**

$$ | **B&B/INN** | Set in a charmingly restored, art-filled 1930s compound just off delightful Avenida Amsterdam and steps from a slew of great bars and restaurants, this easygoing, quiet inn offers a range of accommodations, from simple, wallet-friendly garden units to fanciful suites and two-bedroom apartments with full kitchens and terraces. **Pros:** warm, personalized service; complimentary breakfast and afternoon wine; lush gardens and art-filled common spaces. **Cons:** the most economical rooms are a bit small; neighborhood can get a little busy and noisy on weekends; often books up weeks in advance. $ *Rooms from: MP2600* ✉ *Culiacan 6, La Condesa* ☎ *55/5584–3829* ⊕ *www. theredtreehouse.com* ⟿ *22 rooms* ⅋⊘⅋ *Free Breakfast* Ⓜ *Chilpancingo.*

★ **Stella Bed & Breakfast**

$ | **B&B/INN** | It's rare to find such an affordable and attractive guesthouse in such a popular neighborhood, much less directly on charming Avenida Amsterdam, but this clean and simply furnished inn built in the 1930s by prominent architect Francisco Serrano is a true gem, with its restored art deco architectural details, carefully chosen artwork, and airy common terrace. **Pros:** on one of the city's prettiest streets; kind and helpful owners; generous breakfast with rotating main dishes. **Cons:** surrounding neighborhood can get noisy and crowded; some rooms lack a view; furnishings are somewhat basic. [$] *Rooms from: MP1100* ✉ *Av. Amsterdam 141, La Condesa* ☎ *55/9264–7863* 🌐 *www.stellabb.com* 🛏 *7 rooms* 🍴 *Free Breakfast* [M] *Chilpancingo.*

Tao Suites

$ | **B&B/INN** | Located on a slightly busy street corner just a few blocks from charming Avenida Amsterdam, this early 20th-century inn has attractively priced, spacious rooms, some of which are interconnected with access to kitchens and can be rented together as two- or three-bedroom suites. **Pros:** lots of great restaurants nearby; thoughtful and helpful personal service; gorgeous art deco design details. **Cons:** street noise can be an issue for rooms in front; some rooms lack balconies; somewhat strict cancellation policy. [$] *Rooms from: MP1700* ✉ *Campeche 345, La Condesa* ☎ *55/4356–9472* 🌐 *www.taosuites.mx* 🛏 *6 rooms* 🍴 *Free Breakfast* [M] *Chilpancingo.*

Nightlife

★ Antolina

BARS | This stylish mezcaleria and gastropub has a smartly decorated tile-floor interior as well as plenty of sidewalk tables. In addition to artisanal mezcal and cocktails, there's a great wine and craft beer selection and well-prepared modern Mexican food to snack on. ✉ *Aguascalientes 232, La Condesa* ☎ *55/5211–6845* 🌐 *www.facebook.com/antolinacondesa* [M] *Chilpancingo.*

★ Baltra

COCKTAIL BARS | This snug and stylish hideout just off Avenida Amsterdam is decorated with framed butterflies and bird illustrations and offers up an enticing list of innovative cocktails—try the Old George Sour with Altos Plata tequila, cardamom, and cucumber, or any of the several fine mezcal elixirs. The tight space with just a handful of seats inside and a few more on the sidewalk can get busy on weekends, but if you can snag a table, it's a lovely place to chat with friends or mingle with new ones. It's owned by the same team behind the Roma's famous Licorería Limantour. ✉ *Iztaccihuatl 36D, La Condesa* ☎ *55/5264–1279* 🌐 *www.baltra.bar* [M] *Chilpancingo.*

★ Caimán

BARS | This sleek and rather spare cocktail and natural-wine bar on the ground floor of Casa Nuevo Leon hotel stands out for its long list of expertly prepared cocktails and its well-chosen selection of very interesting wines, including pét-nats and still wines from Baja's Valle de Guadalupe, along with selections from Georgia, Portugal, New Zealand, and other vino-centric parts of the world. There's also a tempting selection of seafood-focused bar bites, including anchovy toast, smoked-oyster pâté, and crab-salad sandwiches. ✉ *Av. Nuevo León 120, La Condesa* ☎ *55/1046–9814* 🌐 *www.casanuevoleon120.com* [M] *Chilpancingo.*

Drunkendog

BREWPUBS | With more than 35 beers on tap and more seating than nearby beer haven El Trappist, this is another of the city's best bets for sampling unusual beers from around the world (or purchasing cans and bottles to go). It's dog-friendly, too. There's a second location in the charming southern Mexico City neighborhood of Tlapan. ✉ *Av. Nuevo León 4A, La Condesa* ☎ *55/4945–4273* 🌐 *www.drunkendog.mx* [M] *Sevilla.*

El Centenario

PUB | This traditional 1940s cantina in the heart of Condesa serves up tasty Spanish- and Mexican-style tapas, inexpensive drinks, and loads of atmosphere. Tables go fast, so prepare to saddle up to the bar. ✉ *Av. Vicente Suárez 42, La Condesa* ☎ *55/5553–5451* [M] *Patriotismo.*

★ El Trappist

BREWPUBS | This diminutive bar along nightlife-rich Avenida Álvaro Obregón is further evidence of Mexico City's increasingly fervent embrace of craft beer. As the name suggests, it has a particular soft spot for Belgian beers, but you'll find a little bit of everything here, including some bottles from smaller, cult brewers around the world, as well as one of the most current selections of up-and-coming Mexican producers. The friendly bartenders really know their stuff, too. ✉ *Av. Álvaro Obregón 298, La Condesa* ☎ *55/5916–4260* ⊕ *www.facebook.com/eltrappistbarbieres* Ⓜ *Sevilla.*

Felina

BARS | There's no signage outside this darkly seductive bar with blue-and-gold velvet seats and an intentionally distressed exterior, but everyone from postgallery-goers to hipster cocktail enthusiasts make their way here, six nights a week (they're closed Monday). The atmosphere is low-key, and the kitchen turns out pretty good bar food. ✉ *Calle Ometusco 87, La Condesa* ☎ *55/5277–1917* Ⓜ *Patriotismo.*

★ Hotel CondesaDF

COCKTAIL BARS | One of the most fashionable cocktail venues in the neighborhood, this contemporary open-air rooftop bar is perched atop the chic Hotel CondesaDF. Hang with friends beneath a white umbrella on one of the wide arm chairs or snag a table overlooking the lush foliage of Parque España. In addition to well-crafted drinks, there's a menu of tasty sushi and other Japanese-fusion snacks. ✉ *Av. Veracruz 102, La Condesa* ☎ *55/5241–2600* ⊕ *www.condesadf.com* Ⓜ *Chapultepec.*

★ Hugo

WINE BAR | Mingle with the fashionable crowd that frequents this trendy wine bar on the border of Condesa and Roma Norte. The focus is mostly on natural wines, with many selections from Europe but also a good number from Mexico's own esteemed Valle de Guadalupe. A nice selection of share-worthy small plates—pastas, beef tartare, eggplant caponata—are available, too.

Hugo is a cousin of its hip neighbor, Cafe Milou. ✉ *Av. Veracruz 38, La Condesa* ☎ *55/9224–6882* ⊕ *www.hugoelwinebar.com* Ⓜ *Chapultepec.*

★ La Clandestina

COCKTAIL BARS | A womblike, intimate space with shelves adorned with countless bottles of mezcal, La Clandestina is one of four establishments in Roma and Condesa operated by Mezcales Milagrito, an artisanal distiller in Oaxaca (La Lavandería, El Palenquito, and Traspatio are the others). The fun here is in sampling some of the many different varieties, ideally straight up (take your time and sip slowly) so that you can taste the different complexities. There's also an extensive list of creative cocktails as well as tlayudas and other light bar snacks. ✉ *Av. Álvaro Obregón 298, La Condesa* ☎ *55/5212–1871* ⊕ *laclandestina.mx* Ⓜ *Sevilla.*

Salón Malafama

BARS | This long bustling bar ranks among the city's most popular pool halls. Since there's often a wait for the tables (it's two-for-one games before 4 pm), the bar area is an always buzzy gathering spot. There are often contemporary photography exhibits on the walls, and pretty good pub fare is served, too. ✉ *Av. Michoacán 78, La Condesa* ☎ *55/5553–5138* ⊕ *www.salonmalafama.com* Ⓜ *Patriotismo.*

Tom's Leather Bar

BARS | A dark back room and naked, muscular, bar-top dancers make for a cruise-y atmosphere at this long-popular Condesa gay bar. It doesn't attract as much leather gear anymore, but is a favorite of otters, bears, and guys who favor Scruff as their favorite hookup app. ✉ *Av. Insurgentes Sur 357, La Condesa* ☎ ⊕ *www.toms-mexico.com* Ⓜ *Chilpancingo.*

Xampañería

WINE BAR | A wall of windows allows the fashionable patrons of this posh champagne bar to enjoy views of lush Parque

España. Inside, beneath a coffered ceiling and vintage light fixtures, you can sip bubbly or any number of well-poured cocktails while noshing on upscale bar fare. There's also seating on the rooftop deck. ⊠ *Av. Nuevo León 66, La Condesa* ☏ *55/4432–4073* Ⓜ *Chilpancingo.*

 Performing Arts

★ Foro Shakespeare

THEATER | On a quiet street in the northwestern corner of the neighborhood, this highly regarded performing arts nonprofit presents dozens of plays and other kinds of shows—film, music, dance—throughout the year. Although the name may have you expecting classic Elizabethan fare, Foro Shakespeare is devoted to diversity and social impact, and often presents edgy and provocative material. The organization collaborates with a number of noteworthy partners, including La Compañía de Teatro Penitenciario, which aims to help inmates reintegrate through art and culture. The theater also has an inviting all-day restaurant, La Bambalina, and a great little bookstore, Libreria Paso de Gato. ⊠ *Calle Zamora 7, La Condesa* ☏ *55/5256–0014* ⊕ *www.foroshakespeare.com* Ⓜ *Chapultepec.*

Un Teatro

THEATER | Check the website of this small theater space with a cute Mexican restaurant (La Callejera Condesa) to see what's on. The options include a wide range of performances like modern dance, experimental theater, spoken word, and other generally incisive and often funny material. ⊠ *Av. Nuevo León 46, La Condesa* ☏ *55/2623–1333* ⊕ *www.unteatro.org* Ⓜ *Sevilla.*

Shopping

Buck House

SHOES | This tiny little shoe boutique stocks an impressively big selection of beautifully crafted leather sneakers, sandals, boots, Oxfords, and loafers. They've been making fine leather shoes in Mexico City since 1955. ⊠ *Av. Tamaulipas 38, La Condesa* ☏ *55/5162–7532* ⊕ *www.buckhouse.com.mx* Ⓜ *Chilpancingo.*

Carmen Rion

CLOTHING | Linen dresses by this Mexican designer are done in palettes and patterns that bring to mind (and sometimes incorporate) traditional Mexican textiles, embroidery, and lace. The draping and layering, however, are very contemporary. Skirts and wraps that flow elegantly—often in vertical lines—are juxtaposed with structured, sometimes architectural bodices and tops. Ties, fastenings, and jewelry are equally tantalizing, the latter often combining wood, silver, and seedpods. Rion has been recognized not only for her unique designs, but also for her ethical practices, which have included working with Mexican artisans to create her garments. ⊠ *Av. Michoacán 30–A, La Condesa* ☏ *55/5264–6179* ⊕ *www.carmenrion.com* Ⓜ *Chilpancingo.*

★ Karani-Art

CRAFTS | Visit this shop to check out the extensive collection of Mexican-made clothing and textiles in stunning, colorful patterns, from folk-art-print T-shirts, caps, and boots to beautiful handbags and ceramics. There's a nice mix of items for all ages, including young kids. There are a few additional locations around the city. ⊠ *Citlaltépetl 36A, La Condesa* ☏ *55/5264–0616* ⊕ *www.karaniart.com.mx* Ⓜ *Chilpancingo.*

La Increíble Librería

BOOKS | Small but with a well-chosen selection of books, this fun and free-spirited bookstore puts an emphasis on art and architectural titles. It also has benches where you can enjoy a cup of coffee while you peruse any books you're thinking about purchasing. There's a nice assortment of decorative gifts and knickknacks for sale, too. ⊠ *Av. Amsterdam 264, La Condesa* ☏ *55/9350–0125* ⊕ *www.instagram.com/laincreible_condesa* Ⓜ *Chilpancingo.*

★ **Librería del Fondo de Cultura Económica**
BOOKS | Located within the strikingly white Cultura Económica Rosario Castellanos cultural center and containing more than 250,000 books on exhibit, this outstanding bookstore with a dramatically illuminated black-and-white ceiling and plenty of comfy armchairs also contains a café and art gallery. One of Condesa's hubs of intellectualism, the center regularly presents films, lectures, readings, and other events. ⊠ *Av. Tamaulipas 202, La Condesa* ☏ *55/5276–7110* ⊕ *www.fondodeculturaeconomica.com* Ⓜ *Patriotismo.*

Sabrá Dios
WINE/SPIRITS | With a superb selection of small-batch mezcals, this tiny shop is a must if you're looking for a great sippable Mexican souvenir or gift. The staff is extremely knowledgeable and helpful, and you'll find (and can sample) some truly special, and spendy, bottles here, but others are more in the 400 to 600 pesos range. You'll also find a few other specialty food items, such as Oaxacan coffee and *sal de gusano*, salt with ground agave-fattened worms. ⊠ *Av. Veracruz 15, La Condesa* ☏ *55/5211–7623* ⊕ *www.facebook.com/sabradiosmezcal* Ⓜ *Chapultepec.*

★ **Tout Chocolat**
CHOCOLATE | Owner and chocolatier Luis Robledo, who trained with Daniel Boulud in New York and at the prestigious L'école de Grand Chocolat in Paris, was named best pastry chef in Latin America in a República del Cacao competition. In his light and cheerful boutique on Avendia Amsterdam, you can shop for exquisite bonbons in intriguing flavors (cardamom–chocolate ganache, calamansi, mezcal-sea salt, and pineapple-ginger), or have a seat and sip a lusciously rich hot chocolate or mocha. There's also a selection of cakes, cookies, and French macarons. ⊠ *Av. Amsterdam 154, La Condesa* ☏ *55/5211–9840* ⊕ *www.toutchocolat.mx* Ⓜ *Chilpancingo.*

San Miguel Chapultepec

 Sights

Casa Gilardi
HISTORIC HOME | Just a few blocks from Casa Estudio Luis Barragán, you'll find the famed architect's final design project. This narrow, deep house looks modest from the street, but its light-pink facade hints at something interesting within. Indeed, a tour of this house that Barragán constructed in 1976, well after he'd retired professionally, reveals many of the trademark features that characterize his design approach: boldly colored walls, geometrically shaped windows that allow light to filter in at interesting angles, and a stunning back patio anchored by a jacaranda tree. There's also an almost miragelike indoor swimming pool. A visit here is a must for devotees of Barragán, but anyone with an interest in design will enjoy a tour. Because the occupants of the house still reside here (their son gives the tours), visiting does require a little effort: advance reservations are required (you must call or email), and tours are offered only twice a day on weekdays and once on Saturday morning. ⊠ *Calle General Antonio León 82, San Miguel Chapultepec, San Miguel Chapultepec* ☏ *55/5271–3575* ⊕ *www.casagilardi.mx* ✉ *MP600* ⊘ *Closed Sun.* Ⓜ *Juanacatlán.*

★ **Casa Luis Barragán**
HISTORIC HOME | Bold colors, lines, and innovative designs are among the most ubiquitous features of Mexico City architecture, and this modernist approach can in large part be traced to Luis Barragán, who lived and worked in this home—now designated as a UNESCO World Heritage Site—from the year he built it (1947) until his death in 1988. The architect's singular aesthetic is apparent throughout the house: in the angular staircases, sharp angles, ample natural light, and bold colored accent

Luis Barragán and Mexico City Modernism 9

Arguably Mexico's most famous architect, Luis Barragán (1902–88) designed some of the most striking and recognizable structures in the city, although his output was greatly limited by how selectively he accepted work. He also greatly influenced illustrious architects like Tadao Ando and Frank Gehry, along with his most important Mexican protege, Ricardo Legoretta. Barragán espoused clean lines, bright colors, and geometric shapes and angles that infused his designs with ample light and interesting shadows. Like Frank Lloyd Wright, he also pioneered the integration of his building designs with their natural settings. In addition to visiting Barragán's home studio and neighboring Casa Gilardi, there are a number of places in greater Mexico City where you can view works he either created.

One must-visit is **Jardines del Pedregal**, a residential subdivision that Barragán developed in the late 1940s in the desolate, volcanic lava-strewn foothills south of San Ángel. Here you can see one of the first homes he ever built, **Casa Pedegral**, and its former stable, **Tetetlán**, which is now a restaurant, architectural library, yoga studio, and boutique shop. Tours of the pink rectilinear home, which was fully restored in 2016, can be arranged by appointment.

If you're a true fan, you might consider driving 16 km (10 miles) out to see the **Torres de Satélite**, which rise some 170 feet above the highway that leads into the white-collar, mid-century suburb for which they're named. Along with artists Jesús Reyes Ferreira and Mathias Goeritz, Barragán created the 1957 sculptural cluster of five narrow obelisks painted in primary blue, red, yellow, and white. It's another 19 km (12 miles) north to visit one of Barragán's most extensive intact designs, **Cuadra San Cristobal Los Clubes,** a sprawling equestrian hacienda the artist created in 1968 (tours of the stables, the Fuentes de los Amantes, and the landscaped gardens can be arranged by emailing cuadrasancristobal@gmail.com).

The works of his ardent and prolific disciple Legoretta are sometimes, especially the early ones, mistaken for Barragán's. Notable Legoretta structures in Mexico City include the striking hot-pink 1968 **Hotel Camino Real** near Polanco, the **Comisión de Derechos Humanos del Distrito Federal** in Coyoacán, the **Papalote Museo del Niño** and redesign of **Chapultepec Zoo** in Bosque Chapultepec, **Museo Memoria y Tolerancia** and surrounding Plaza Juárez, and **Torre BBVA México** on Avenida Reforma. His firm also designed much of **Centro Nacional de las Artes (CENART),** the huge arts center and educational campus east of Coyoacán that was built in 1994 in collaboration with seven other architects. With its bright colors and sharp angles, CENART looks almost to be a direct homage to Barragán's aesthetic and ideas.

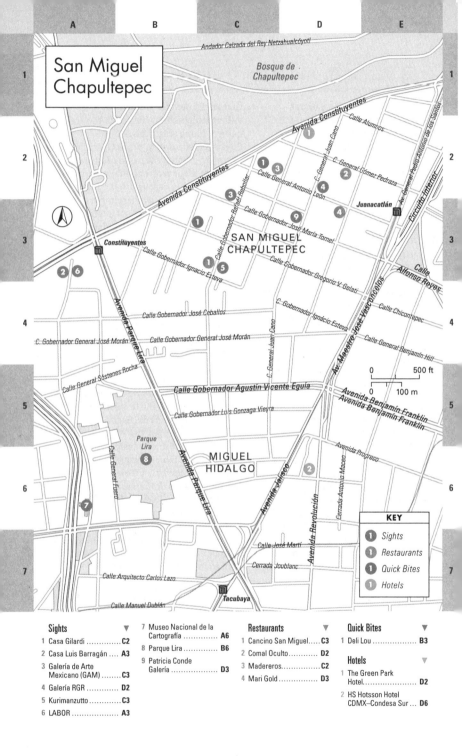

San Miguel Chapultepec

Luis Barragán was famous for his exterior architectural designs, but the inside of Casa Barragán is just as impressive as its outside.

walls. Visits are by self-guided or guided tours, both of which must be purchased by advance reservation. Book online, and keep in mind that tour slots open roughly a month in advance and sell out almost immediately, so plan accordingly. Tickets are also quite expensive, and it costs an extra 500 pesos for permission to take photos. Across the street from the house is a small, peaceful garden with chairs, a reflection pool, lush foliage, and restrooms—this serves as a waiting area before tours begin, although it's free and open to the public (as is the museum's excellent bookstore), and it's a pleasant spot to take a break. The easiest route to the house is via the pedestrian pathway and stairs that border the highway, leading from the Constituyentes Metro station. ⊠ *General Francisco Ramírez 12, San Miguel Chapultepec* ☎ *55/8104–0688* ⊕ *www.casaluisbarragan.org* ⊠ *MP450* ☉ *Closed Sun.* Ⓜ *Constituyentes.*

Galería de Arte Mexicano (GAM)

ART GALLERY | Founded in 1935 and set in a beautifully restored house from that period, the GAM was the first place in Mexico City dedicated full-time to the sale and promotion of art. It's played an important role in many Mexican art movements since then and continues to support the country's most important artists. GAM also publishes an impressive catalog of books, which are available at the gallery's bookstore. ⊠ *Gobernador Rafael Rebollar 43, San Miguel Chapultepec* ☎ *55/5272–5529* ⊕ *www.galeria-deartemexicano.com* ⊠ *Free* ☉ *Closed weekends* Ⓜ *Constituyentes.*

Galeria RGR

ART GALLERY | One of the most respected galleries in the neighborhood, RGR occupies a striking, angular concrete building with ample space for hosting the exhibitions of often large-scale works by contemporary Latin American artists. Begun in Venezuela in 2012, the gallery has become increasingly acclaimed—it's

been in its current home since 2018.
✉ *Calle General Antonio León 48, San Miguel Chapultepec* ☎ *55/8434–7760* ⊕ *www.rgrart.com* 🚇 *Free* ⊙ *Closed Sun.* Ⓜ *Juanacatlán.*

★ Kurimanzutto

ART GALLERY | Renowned architect Alberto Kalach (of Biblioteca Vasconcelos fame) converted this former lumber yard into an internationally acclaimed contemporary art gallery in San Miguel Chapultepec, using polished wood, cement floors, and a curving metal-plated spiral staircase to set a dramatic stage for the well-attended exhibits. Often ranked among Latin America's most influential art spaces, Kurimanzutto represents about three dozen established and emerging talents and has a second location on New York City's Upper East Side. The on-site bookstore has a small but carefully curated collection of titles. ✉ *Calle Gobernador Rafael Rebollar 94, San Miguel Chapultepec* ☎ *55/5256–2408* ⊕ *www.kurimanzutto. com* 🚇 *Free* ⊙ *Closed Sun. and Mon.* Ⓜ *Constituyentes.*

LABOR

ART GALLERY | About 20 esteemed contemporary artists show at this spacious, airy gallery across the street from both Casa Estudio Luis Barragán. Like its neighbor, the gallery is a prominent work of Mexican modernist design, having been built in 1948 by functionalist architect Enrique del Moral, who resided here for many years. Both solo and group shows usually run for a couple of months, and the openings always draw a cadre of big names in the art world. The adjoining gardens, with benches and tables, are a relaxing spot to take a break from art viewing. ✉ *General Francisco Ramírez 5, San Miguel Chapultepec* ☎ *55/6304–8755* ⊕ *www.labor.org.mx* 🚇 *Free* ⊙ *Closed Sun.* Ⓜ *Constituyentes.*

Museo Nacional de la Cartografía

HISTORY MUSEUM | Established in 1999 within the walls of a dramatic church that was part of a 17th-century monastery

(most of which is now occupied by a military installation across the street), this free and rather underrated museum tells the story of Mexico's history, its formation into a republic, and even aspects of its demographics and economics (there are hydrography and mining maps, for example) through a series of maps and even more ancient codices that date back to the early days of New Spain. These documents cover the walls of the entire domed structure, and in the transept there's also a display of map-making equipment, from antique sextants to clunky GPS devices from the early 2000s. Signage is in both Spanish and English. Ironically (or perhaps as some sort of cosmic joke), using the map on your phone to get to this museum on the western edge of Tacabuya—just a 15-minute walk from Condesa—can be a bit tricky. The museum sits in the middle of a fenced-in island of sorts, surrounded by busy two-lane roads on all sides; to get in, go to the intersection of Anillo Periférico and Avenida Observatorio and go through the unmarked pedestrian underpass, which leads to a small plaza in front of the museum. ✉ *Av. Observatorio 94, Tacubaya, La Condesa* ☎ *55/5272–6686* ⊕ *www.gob.mx/sedena/acciones-y-programas/museo-nacional-de-la-cartografia* 🚇 *Free* ⊙ *Closed Mon.* Ⓜ *Tacubaya.*

Parque Lira

CITY PARK | This hilly green space on the border of San Miguel Chapultepec and Tacubaya includes a maze of tree- and shrub-lined pathways as well as one of the largest children's playgrounds close to Condesa. The central fountain, beside a pergola with a massive bougainvillea tree looming over it, is a lovely place to sip coffee, read a book, or chat with friends. Adjacent to the park's southeast corner, you'll find Museo Casa de Bola (⊕ *www.museoshaghenbeck.mx/ museo-casa-de-la-bola*), which is open by appointment only or during special events (it's a popular wedding venue). The magnificent 16th-century villa belonged to San José de Tacubaya, and its 13 ornately decorated rooms are filled with fine European (predominantly French) tapestries, finery, decorative objects, and furniture that dates over the past few centuries. ✉ *Av. Parque Lira 136, San Miguel Chapultepec* ☎ *55/5412–0522* 🎫 *Free* [M] *Tacubaya.*

Patricia Conde Galería

ART GALLERY | The main draw of this gallery with spare, angular exhibit rooms is that it's one of the only art spaces in Mexico City with a primary focus on contemporary photography. About 30 artists show here regularly, and there are about six to eight temporary shows throughout the year. ✉ *Calle General Juan Cano 68, San Miguel, San Miguel Chapultepec* ☎ *55/5290–6345* 🌐 *www.patriciaconde.online* 🎫 *Free* 🕒 *Closed Sun.* [M] *Constituyentes.*

🍴 Restaurants

Cancino San Miguel

$$ | **PIZZA** | Near several art spaces in San Miguel Chapultepec (and across the street from famed Kurimanzutto), this upbeat, stylish Italian restaurant has a lovely brick patio that fills with creative types after gallery openings. The roasted potatoes with truffle oil and Parmesan is a worthy starter, and there are some nice pasta and salad options, but the star is the pizza, including a distinctly Mexican-style pie topped with huitlacoche, Oaxacan cheese, corn, and jalapeños. **Known for:** affordable thin-crust pizzas; sangria, clericot, and other wine-based cocktails; on-site coffeehouse and breakfast spot, La Ventanita. [$] *Average main: MP200* ✉ *Calle Gobernador Rafael Rebollar 95, San Miguel Chapultepec* ☎ *55/4333–0770* 🌐 *www.archipielagomx.com/cancino* [M] *Constituyentes.*

Comal Oculto

$ | **MEXICAN** | Tuck into plates of exquisitely prepared, traditional Mexican snacks like tlacoyos, sopes, flautas, and quesadillas with rich sauces and authentic, carefully curated ingredients. **Known for:** simple, beautifully designed space; interesting ingredients like braised lamb, wild mushrooms, and pork confit; fresh fruit aguas. [$] *Average main: MP130* ✉ *Calle General Gómez Pedraza 37, San Miguel Chapultepec* ☎ *55/8988–2557* 🌐 *www.facebook.com/comaloculto* 🕒 *Closed Sun. and Mon. No dinner* [M] *Juanacatlán.*

★ **Madereros**

$$$ | **MODERN MEXICAN** | The specialty of this trendy San Miguel de Chapultepec restaurant helmed by a veteran of famed eatery Pujol is food prepared with an open flame, such as grilled sirloin with an eggplant puree and roasted vegetables, but you'll also find a number of classic Mexican and Italian dishes, from shrimp aguachiles to house-made casarecce pasta with a hearty ragu sauce. Dining is inside one of the neighborhood's well-preserved 1930s homes, but there's also a pleasing sidewalk terrace bracketed by cacti and succulents. **Known for:** creative breakfast fare; fried eggs with chicharrón regio (made with pork jowl); leisurely afternoon meals in a charming neighborhood. [$] *Average main: MP410* ✉ *Calle General Antonio León 72, San Miguel Chapultepec* ☎ *55/8931–8136* 🌐 *www.madereros.mx* 🕒 *No dinner Sun.* [M] *Juanacatlán.*

★ **Mari Gold**

$$ | **MEXICAN FUSION** | In this narrow minimalist space with one long communal table, you can feast on a lighter and slightly more casual version of the Indian-Mexican-fusion fare popularized by noted Masala y Maiz chefs Norma Listman and Saqib Keval. **Known for:** chilaquiles with tatemada (charred-tomato) salsa, cream, and cheese in the morning; gajar ka halwa (North Indian dessert made with grated carrots and coconut milk) with maracuya sorbet; well-chosen wine list. [$] *Average main: MP200* ✉ *Calle Gobernador Protasio Tagle 66A,*

San Miguel Chapultepec ☎ *55/3726–2228* 🌐 *www.instagram.com/mari.gold.mx* 🕓 *Closed Mon. and Tues. No dinner* [M] *Juanacatlán.*

Coffee and Quick Bites

Deli Lou

$ | **CAFÉ** | A cheerful bakery-café near San Miguel Chapultepec's art galleries, Deli Lou serves crusty-baguette sandwiches with distinctive toppings (turkey with olives, goat cheese, Camembert, jamón serrano, and the like), plus freshly baked cakes, brownies, and cookies. There's also a small selection of jams, wines, artisanal juices and teas, and other gourmet goodies, plus a variety of espresso drinks. **Known for:** satisfying salads with the same ingredient options as the outstanding baguettes; dark-chocolate brownies; picnic supplies for visiting nearby Bosque de Chapultepec. [$] *Average main: MP110* ✉ *Calle Gobernador Gregorio V. Gelati 78, San Miguel Chapultepec* ☎ *55/4444–6334* 🌐 *www.delilou.com.mx* 🕓 *Closed Sun. No dinner Sat.* [M] *Constituyentes.*

Hotels

Green Park Hotel

$$ | **HOTEL** | This inviting, reasonably priced hotel on the edge of increasingly trendy San Miguel Chapultepec and adjacent to Bosque de Chapultepec conveys an old-world sensibility with its floor-to-ceiling curtains, British antiques, and large marble-accented bathrooms, some with steam showers and Jacuzzi tubs. **Pros:** a short walk from several art galleries and museums; rooftop terrace with lovely park views; spacious, elegantly furnished suites. **Cons:** slightly old-fashioned design and atmosphere may not suit every taste; beside a busy highway; a bit of a walk from the heart of Condesa. [$] *Rooms from: MP2980* ✉ *Av. Constituyentes 99, San Miguel Chapultepec* ☎ *55/5276–6565* 🌐 *www.thegreenparkhotel.com.mx* 🛏 *33 rooms* 🍴 *Free Breakfast* [M] *Constituyentes.*

HS Hotsson Hotel CDMX–Condesa Sur

$$ | **HOTEL** | **FAMILY** | Part of a growing Mexican chain of mid-range hotels, this eight-story property is technically in Tacubaya, just south of Condesa, but it's an easy walk from the neighborhood's wealth of trendy restaurants and shops, making it a great affordable base. **Pros:** close to San Miguel Chapultepec's galleries and restaurants; spacious rooms outfitted with kitchens; excellent value for the neighborhood. **Cons:** noise from neighboring busy streets can be obtrusive; room decor is a bit cookie-cutter; on the south edge of the neighborhood. [$] *Rooms from: MP2600* ✉ *Av. Revolución 67, Tacubaya, La Condesa* ☎ *55/8844–0101* 🌐 *www.hotsson.com* 🛏 *103 rooms* 🍴 *No Meals* [M] *Tacubaya.*

Shopping

★ **Xocolate DF**

CHOCOLATE | You could easily miss this tiny artisanal chocolate shop if you walked by too quickly, but there's a pretty good chance the brightly colored handmade bonbons in the display cases might catch your eye. These beautiful little gems with speckles and swirls that look like abstract paintings have distinctive fillings like passionfruit, pistachio, chipotle, and tamarind—more than 50 varieties in all. The boxes of assorted flavors make lovely gifts. You can also order hot chocolate, lattes, and teas to enjoy on one of the handful of sidewalk seats. ✉ *Calle Ignacio Esteva, La Condesa* ✥ *Corner of Calle General Francisco Molinos del Campo* ☎ *55/3425–3376* 🌐 *www.facebook.com/xocolatedf* [M] *Constituyentes.*

Chapter 10

BENITO JUÁREZ

Updated by
Megan Frye

⊙ Sights   🍴 Restaurants   🛏 Hotels   🛍 Shopping   🍸 Nightlife

★★☆☆☆   ★★★☆☆   ★★☆☆☆   ★☆☆☆☆   ★★★☆☆

NEIGHBORHOOD SNAPSHOT

TOP EXPERIENCES

■ **Diverse architecture.** Rent an Eco-Bici and ride through the side streets of Colonia del Valle Centro and Colonia Narvartes, admiring the varied architectural styles.

■ **San Pedro de los Pinos.** This charming residential neighborhood is ideal for exploring by foot, especially during a weekday afternoon. Stop for an authentic lunch at any of the many comida corrida spots, and take a stroll through the main Mercado San Pedro de los Pinos.

■ **City parks.** Being a predominantly residential borough, Benito Juárez is brimming with leafy parks. Parque de los Venados is a popular one for families, with its permanent carnival rides and even a planetarium while Parque Hundido is beloved by joggers and dog walkers, and its sunken design makes it a great place to cool off when the sun gets too intense.

■ **City skyline views.** The World Trade Center's rotating restaurant, Bellini, offers fine dining and literal panoramic views of the city.

■ **Zona Arqueológica de Mixcoac.** This small but significant archaeological site reminds us that Mexico City was not long ago a great capital of Meso-American indigenous peoples. Mixcoac means "serpent in the clouds" in Náhuatl, the language of the Mexica people.

GETTING HERE

Sitting about 4 km (2½ miles) south of Centro Histórico, the borough of Benito Juárez spans more than 26 square km (10 square miles), with the northeastern edge bordering Roma Sur. Uber fares from the airport or the city center run about MP120–MP180. Due to the size of the delegation, there are four subway lines that cross through it (2, 3, 7, and 12) and two lines of the Metrobus (1 and 2).

PAUSE HERE

■ **Metro Zapata.** This busy metro station linking lines 3 and 12 is also one of the city's most interesting public transit hubs. It hosts frequent large-scale art exhibitions that most people are moving too fast to fully enjoy. Most of the work is by local and emerging artists, with occasional special collections. It's a good place to come to take a moment to appreciate the heartbeat of the city's underground—just perhaps not at rush hour. ⊠ *Intersection of Av. Félix Cuevas and Av. Universidad.*

PLANNING YOUR TIME

■ Benito Juárez is largely safe to explore on foot, and there's usually a subway or Metrobus line close to major points of interest. To cross the entire delegation, you could walk the length of División del Norte, one of its main north–south arteries, in 1½ hours (it's just over 5 km [3 miles]). Street parking is common and most establishments have parking available for their customers.

Named in honor of Mexico's first indigenous president, Benito Juárez is one of Mexico City's 16 *alcaldías*, or boroughs (which cover a larger space than its *colonias*, or neighborhoods). Covering more than 41 square km (16 square miles) of the central city, Benito Juárez is primarily residential with the exception of the bustling business district that lines Insurgentes Avenue, an area that includes the World Trade Center and a number of international financial and engineering institutions.

Blessed with ample green parks, wide sidewalks, and charming mom-and-pop *tiendas de abarrotes* (corner stores) and restaurants, its 43 colonias are about as relaxed as you can get this close to the action in Mexico City. Every corner of the borough is well connected to the city's public transport system, including the subway, the metrobus, the trolleybus, and a deluge of other buses in varying degrees of decrepitation—the smaller ones are known as combis, or *peseros*. Each neighborhood has its age-old cantina (some classier than others) and its favorite coffee shops, many of which have been there for decades.

Certain neighborhoods, such as the Narvartes and Del Valles, are seeing a plethora of new restaurants and bars geared to the young and hip. Meanwhile, big-block movie theaters, malls filled with international brands, multifloor apartment buildings, microbreweries, organic coffee shops, and foreign cuisine restaurants are springing up next to the little cafés and houses that have been passed down through the generations. In general, walking or biking through Benito Juárez is the best way to get to know its neighborhood-on-the-verge charm.

◉ Sights

Alberca Olímpica Francisco Márquez

POOL | If you've ever wanted to swim in an Olympic-size pool, this one from the 1968 Olympic games (and the largest pool in all of Mexico) might be your best option. Created just for the 1968 games, today it serves as a neighborhood pool that offers open swim for all levels. Water polo and scuba diving are also options in the pool area, while the neighboring Gimnasio Olímpico Juan de la Barrera hosts

Benito Juárez

volleyball and basketball pick-up and league games; tae kwon do classes, and other sports. ⊠ *División del Norte 2333, Benito Juárez* ✢ *Colonia General Anaya* ☎ *55/5604–8344* 🖾 *MP361 (unlimited visits for a month)* Ⓜ *Eje Central.*

Parque de los Venados

CITY PARK | FAMILY | This 25-acre park represents one of the best of Mexico City's outdoor spaces. With more than 10,000 trees, a fountain, kids' carnival rides and games, a dog park, and food trucks, it can make for a whole day of fun and people-watching. Weekdays see the park filled with dog-walkers, people exercising, and kids on carnival rides after school. Weekends turn into a full-on spectacle, packed with people lining its Talavera-tiled benches and snacking at the many different food stands. Though popular, it maintains its neighborhood friendly vibe and provides a lot of shade and oxygen to an otherwise not heavily treed zone. ⊠ *Miguel Laurent between Av. Division del Norte and Dr. José María Vertiz, Santa Cruz Atoyac, Benito Juárez* Ⓜ *Parque de los Venados.*

★ Parque Hundido

CITY PARK | FAMILY | Known as the "sunken park" in Spanish, this 22-acre green space is exceedingly quiet, especially considering that it lies on busy Insurgentes Avenue. With jogging and walking paths that curve through the lush greenery, fountains, and statues, the park is a good place to escape the city and its stresses. When you descend into the park via the ramp or steps, the temperature always seems to drop about 10 degrees: an excellent antidote for a hot day. ⊠ *Av. Insurgentes between Av. Porfirio Díaz and Calle Millet, Extremadura Insurgentes, Benito Juárez* Ⓜ *Insurgentes Sur.*

Poliforum Siqueiros

ARTS CENTER | The history of Poliforum Siqueiros has been and remains turbulent, but it still remains one of the city's most beloved cultural treasures.

The cultural space was first opened in 1971 and features the largest mural of the world, "The March of Humanity" painted by Mexican muralist and political dissenter David Siqueiros. The interior mural covers more than 93,646 square feet and depicts the struggle of humanity across four sections, narrated by the late artist himself as a rotating platform carries visitors on a journey through the mural. The space also features galleries and a theater. The facade, a dodeca-hedron by design, brings Siqueiros' art to the outside world. Over the years, numerous groups have worked to restore the building, now officially declared as part of the city's cultural heritage. While it is officially closed to visitors, you can still see the mural itself just from the outside. ⊠ *Insurgentes Sur 701, Benito Juárez* ☎ *55/5536–4520* ⊕ *www.facebook.com/ www.polyforumsiqueiros.com.mx.*

World Trade Center Mexico City

NOTABLE BUILDING | Originally built to be a hotel, Mexico City's World Trade Center now stands as the third tallest building in the city and hosts a number of office spaces, functioning as a grand-scale meeting place and convention center. Construction began in 1966, and while it never lived its life as a hotel due to financial and bureaucratic troubles, it opened officially as a world commerce building in 1995. Atop the 52-story glass and aluminum building sits what Guinness World Records calls the largest rotating restaurant in the world, the pricey Bellini, which specializes in views of the city and Italian food. Also within the WTC are a number of cafés, a cinema, a concert venue, and several restaurants. ⊠ *Montecito 38, Benito Juárez* ☎ *55/9000–6000* ⊕ *www.wtcmexico.mx* Ⓜ *San Pedro de los Pinos.*

Zona Arqueológica de Mixcoac

RUINS | Located relatively close to the city center in the San Pedro de los Pinos colonia, near San Ángel and Del Valle, this important archaeological site is on

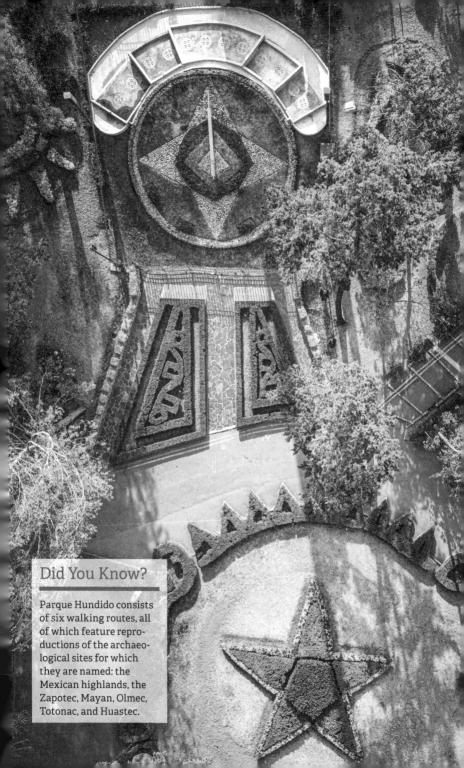

Did You Know?

Parque Hundido consists of six walking routes, all of which feature reproductions of the archaeological sites for which they are named: the Mexican highlands, the Zapotec, Mayan, Olmec, Totonac, and Huastec.

what centuries ago was the southwestern shore of Lake Texcoco, an area fed by streams from the western mountains. Its name, which in the Nahuatl language of the Mexica who resided here means "viper of the cloud," is believed to refer to the swirl of stars above that we call the Milky Way. The physical structure preserved at this site is relatively young, having been inhabited from around AD 900 to 1521. One of Mexico's smallest archaeological sites (it's just under 2 acres), Mixcoac only opened to the public for visits in summer 2019, under the aegis of Instituto Nacional de Antropología e Historia (INAH). Visitors can tour the remaining structures, which include a central courtyard surrounded by east and west platforms, with a ceremonial plaza, residential rooms, and other spaces. ✉ *Calle Pirámide 7, Benito Juárez* ☎ 🌐 *www.inah.gob.mx* 🎫 *Free* [M] *San Antonio.*

🍴 Restaurants

Bellini

$$$$ | **ECLECTIC** | Revolving slowly on the 45th floor of the World Trade Center, Bellini maintains a formal, reserved character. While it's definitely known less for its food than the views (romantically twinkling city lights at night and a pair of volcanoes on a clear day), it's still worth the dining experience, especially for its beloved osso buco and French onion soup. **Known for:** pricey international cuisine; panoramic views of the city; excellent lobster. [$] *Average main: MP1000* ✉ *Torre WTC (World Trade Center), Montecito 38, 45th fl., Benito Juárez* ☎ *55/9000–8305* 🌐 *www.bellini.com.mx* [M] *Metro San pedro de los Pinos.*

Branca Parilla

$$$ | **SOUTH AMERICAN** | Sitting on a quiet corner on a residential street, Branca Parilla is stunning both inside and out. It's snazzy enough to dress up a bit, but casual enough not to worry about it if you're not. **Known for:** pasta and steaks; nice variety of wine by the glass or bottle; romantic outdoor seating. [$] *Average main: MP400* ✉ *Av. Universidad 626, Benito Juárez* ✣ *Narvarte Oriente* ☎ *55/6550–0644* 🌐 *www.brancaparrilla.com.mx* [M] *División del Norte.*

★ Cantina La Valenciana

$$ | **MEXICAN** | While one side of the cantina speaks more to drinking, party-heavy crowds and the other to family outings focused on watching soccer, they merge as one on evenings and weekends with live cumbia and salsa. The building has been on this popular stretch of Narvarte for more than 100 years, with more than 50 years under the same ownership, making it a true neighborhood cantina. **Known for:** thick, juicy steaks; dancing on the weekends; hefty cocktail and liquor list. [$] *Average main: MP250* ✉ *Av. Universidad 48, Benito Juárez* ✣ *Narvarte Oriente* ☎ *55/3330–7505* 🌐 *www.facebook.com/CantinaLaVale* 💳 *No credit cards* [M] *Xola.*

★ Charcutería Hinojosa y Baguetería

$$ | **SANDWICHES** | This charming, European-style charcuterie is one of few in the city. With a couple of outdoor seats and a bar where you can watch all the action, sandwiches are served on fluffy or crunchy baguettes and feature smoked cheeses and sausages. **Known for:** neighborhood charcuterie catering to locals; excellent price-to-quality ratio; lovely sidewalk seating. [$] *Average main: MP250* ✉ *Dr. José María Vertiz 1251, Benito Juárez* ✣ *Vertiz Narvarte* ☎ *55/5601–1181* 🌐 *www.facebook.com/CharcuteriaHinojosayBaguetteria* 💳 *No credit cards* [M] *Parque de los Venados.*

★ Corazón de Libano

$$ | **LEBANESE** | Lebanese cuisine has a long history in Mexico thanks to an immigration wave in the early 20th century, and this spot is one of the city's best. The small, casual sidewalk restaurant in the lovely, leafy neighborhood of Narvarte Poniente has just a few items on the menu, but they're done very well. **Known**

Changing Demographics

Benito Juárez has long been considered one of Mexico City's most residential delegations. Since the era of Porfirio Diaz's dictatorship era in the late 19th and early 20th century and its park-building extravaganza aimed at making the city more European, it has attracted people from both high society and from the working class. When the financial and international business sectors took up shop on Insurgentes in the late 20th century, it became an even more desirable place to live.

As rents have risen over the past decade in areas like Roma and Condesa, much of the artistic community that called those colonias home has shifted south of the Viaducto Alemán in search of more ample, affordable, and quiet living. This movement started to incorporate more young expats following the devastating September 19, 2017, earthquake that rocked Roma and Condesa particularly hard and left many buildings there uninhabitable. As a result, new restaurants, cafés, and bars have popped up in Benito Juárez in order to cater to these migrations of mostly young and single professionals.

While Benito Juárez largely remains a place to call home more than a place to work, sightsee, or party, the changing vibe of its neighborhoods is noticeable and only expected to evolve as the years pass.

for: inviting space that feels like you're in someone's living room; just a handful of tables so be prepared to wait; excellent lamb kebabs. 💲 *Average main: MP250* ✉ *Heriberto Frias 573, Benito Juárez* ☎ *55/2213–7342* ⊕ *www.facebook.com/corazondelibanocdmx* Ⓜ *Eugenia.*

★ Fonda Margarita
$ | MEXICAN | Everyone from postclubbing revelers to early morning workers to ardent foodies (the late Anthony Bourdain was a big fan) wait in line for a chance to feast on the hearty guisados served in this legendary breakfast joint. Come with a big appetite, and try a few specialties, such as *refritos huevos* (eggs whipped with refried beans), chilaquiles with salsa verde, and eggs stewed with longaniza sausage. **Known for:** stick-to-your-ribs breakfast fare; no-frills dining room with communal seating; early closure at noon so get here early. 💲 *Average main: MP150* ✉ *Adolfo Prieto 1364B, Benito Juárez* ☎ *55/5559–6358* ☉ *Closed Mon. No lunch or dinner* Ⓜ *20 de Noviembre.*

La Secina
$$ | MEXICAN | On the northwest edge of La Narvarte, this ample-size restaurant is great for big parties and sitting out on the terrace in the evening. The menu is specific: *cecina* (cured beef) in all of its mighty forms, including an appetizing ceviche. **Known for:** upscale Mexican fare focusing on cured beef; craft beer and cocktails; outdoor dining in the evenings. 💲 *Average main: MP250* ✉ *Calzada Obrero Mundial 305, Benito Juárez* ✛ *Narvarte Poniente* ☎ *55/6730–2462* ⊕ *www.lasecina.com* Ⓜ *Centro Médico.*

★ Las Tlayudas
$$ | MEXICAN | Quick and reliably good, Las Tlayudas is a small sidewalk eatery specializing in Oaxacan cuisine. Come here for the *tlayudas*, of course—massive tortillas covered with beans, cheese, and meat. **Known for:** chill vibe; Oaxacan delicacies; small-batch mezcal menu. 💲 *Average main: MP200* ✉ *Luz Saviñon 1211–A, Benito Juárez* ☎ *55/6379–2496* ⊕ *www.facebook.com/LasTlayudas* Ⓜ *Eugenia.*

★ Los Chamorros de Tlacoquemécatl

$$ | MEXICAN | A bustling restaurant with no frills, but plenty of flavor, Los Chamorros is dark, hot, and popular. In business since 1974, the restaurant offers an array of Mexican specialties that take diners on a gastronomic voyage into Mexico's countryside. **Known for:** chamorro (juicy, butter-soft pork knuckle); huazontles (native herbs) battered and stuffed with cheese and doused in pasilla chile sauce; hearty soups like sopa de haba (lima bean soup). $ *Average main: MP200* ⊠ *Calle Tlacoquemécatl 177, Del Valle Centro, Benito Juárez* ☎ *55/5575–1235* ⊕ *www.facebook.com/loschamorrosdetlacoquemecatl* ⊘ *No dinner* Ⓜ *Insurgentes Sur, Hospital 20 de Noviembre.*

Mazurka

$$$$ | POLISH | The glowing reputation of this long-standing Polish restaurant shone even brighter after people got word that the establishment had served Pope John Paul II on several of his visits to Mexico City; the generous *Degustación del Papa* (Pope's Menu) includes small portions of various entrées served to the pope. Its best days might be behind it, but it's an interesting slice of the city's diverse culinary history, and still a source for terrific duck dishes. **Known for:** the best kielbasa for miles; impressive international wine collection; pierogi with piano accompaniment. $ *Average main: MP600* ⊠ *Nueva York 150, between Calles Texas and Oklahoma, Benito Juárez* ☎ *55/5543–4509* ⊕ *www.mazurka.com.mx* ⊘ *Closed Mon.* Ⓜ *San Pedro de los Pinos.*

★ Mictlán Antojitos Veganos

$$ | MEXICAN | One of the best vegan eateries in the city, Mictlán prepares traditional Mexican meals without meat or cheese, and without depending too heavily on non-Mexican food products such as tofu or seitan. Everything sold here is Mexican in origin, with a special focus on ancestral cuisine and sauces. **Known for:** excellent vegan Mexican dishes; agua de cacao; LGBTQ+-friendly vibes. $ *Average main: MP150* ⊠ *Luz Saviñon 1354, Benito Juárez* ☎ *55/4036–2821* ⊕ *mictlanantojitosveganos.com* ⊘ *Closed Tues.* Ⓜ *Eugenia.*

★ Piloncillo y Cascabel

$ | MEXICAN | On a verdant corner in Narvarte, this neatly decorated space has plenty of room and a quickly rotating lunch crowd. Known for its lines down the block, diners come for an updated take on traditional Mexican cuisine and reasonable prices. **Known for:** casual gourmet Mexican dishes; lunch specials; charming outdoor space. $ *Average main: MP100* ⊠ *Torres Adalid 1263, Narvarte Poniente, Benito Juárez* ☎ *55/3330–2121* ⊕ *www.facebook.com/piloncilloycascabel* ⊘ *Closed Sun.* Ⓜ *Eugenia.*

Pinche Gringo BBQ

$$$ | BARBECUE | While you wouldn't want to push gringo cuisine on anyone visiting Mexico, Pinche Gringo BBQ has created a little barbecue sanctuary for itself, with live music and football on the television screens. Serving Texas-style brisket at Texas prices, it has a small but loyal following of patrons who enjoy food it's hard to find elsewhere in CDMX. **Known for:** excellent brisket and mac-and-cheese; laid-back ambience; fun outdoor patio. $ *Average main: MP350* ⊠ *Cumbres de Maltrata 360, Benito Juárez* ☎ *55/6389–1129* ⊕ *www.pgbbq.mx* Ⓜ *Etiopía-Plaza de la Transparencia.*

★ Pizza Local

$$ | PIZZA | Most visitors to Mexico City don't come here in search of New York–style pizza, but that's not to say a fine pie isn't appreciated in the city. Mexican pizza is typically light on the sauce, but Pizza Local is the rare exception with thin-crust options such as roasted tomato and garlic or classic, charcuterie-style pepperoni (also a rarity in the city). **Known for:** pizza that even a New Yorker could love; thin-crust pies; pretty patio for outdoor dining. $ *Average main: MP300* ⊠ *Uxmal 88, Benito Juárez* ☎ *55/4632–1669* ⊕ *www.*

You'll find archeological sites that blend into the cityscape all over CDMX, like the Zona Arqueológica de Mixcoac.

pizzalocal.mx ⊟ *No credit cards* ⊘ *Closed Mon.* Ⓜ *Etiopía/Plaza de la Transparencia.*

☕ Coffee and Quick Bites

Almanegra Café

$ | CAFÉ | As its name would suggest (it translates to "black soul"), you'll find lots of brooding music and black attire here. With two locations in Benito Juárez, the Narvarte Poniente spot was the first and is still the coziest, with just a small coffee counter and a few benches outside to sit along Avenida Universidad. **Known for:** a rotating menu of Mexican coffee from different states; fast service; good people-watching. ⓢ *Average main: MP50* ⊠ *Av. Universidad 420–A, Benito Juárez* ⊹ *Narvarte Poniente* ☎ *55/4162–5899* ⊕ *www.almanegracafe.mx* Ⓜ *Eugenia.*

★ Bajo Sombra Café

$ | CAFÉ | While it specializes in espresso, pour-overs, and other hipster coffee-lover delights, this café has more of a neighborhood vibe than many of its counterparts. Mexican coffee is its specialty,

though it occasionally features standout imports as well. **Known for:** house-made tea infusions; herbal soda waters; mezcal and coffee-based Mexican craft beer. ⓢ *Average main: MP100* ⊠ *Diagonal San Antonio 1507, Benito Juárez* ⊹ *Narvarte Oriente* ☎ *55/5530–8216* ⊕ *www.face-book.com/bajosombracafe* ⊘ *Closed Sun.* Ⓜ *Etiopía/Plaza de la Transparencia.*

Costra

$ | CAFÉ | Fresh-baked bread, doughnuts, muffins, and croissants are eye-catching from the display just inside the window at Costra. With only a few seats inside, it is a cozy spot to catch up on some work or with a friend. **Known for:** house-made baked goods; varieties of tea; friendly service. ⓢ *Average main: MP100* ⊠ *Av. Universidad 482, Benito Juárez* ⊹ *Narvarte Poniente* ☎ *55/7457–2240* ⊕ *www.instagram.com/costramx* Ⓜ *Eugenia.*

El Vilsito

$ | MEXICAN | With its quirky setting inside a large industrial building that also houses an auto repair shop, this Colonia Narvarte Poniente hot spot was featured on Netflix's *Tacos Chronicles* and is a serious contender in the city's crowded battle for al pastor primacy. Overflowing with happy eaters into the wee hours of the night, as late as 5 am on Friday and Saturday, Vilsito serves pastor tacos with or without cheese along with a good variety of the usual suspects (tacos choriqueso, tortas Cubanas). **Known for:** tacos al pastor; refreshing horchata; crowded but festive scene. $ *Average main: MP100* ⊠ *Petén 248, Benito Juárez* ☎ *55/5536–3636* ⊕ *www.facebook.com/VilsitoDiamante.*

La Divina Culpa

$ | **MEXICAN** | **FAMILY** | This perpetually packed sidewalk diner offers the quintessential quick bite experience in Mexico City. Serving breakfast and lunch, it's popular for the daily *comida corrida* (three-course meal); tables turn over fast. **Known for:** mole enchiladas stuffed with chicken; lunch deals including a three-course option; exceedingly delicious pozole (a Mexican soup made with hominy and pork). $ *Average main: MP80* ⊠ *Eje Central Lázaro Cárdenas 514, Benito Juárez* ✛ *Portales Sur* ☎ *55/5605–3019* ⊕ *www.facebook.com/DivinaCulpaRestaurante* ▤ *No credit cards* ☾ *Closed Sun.* Ⓜ *Xola.*

★ Mimo Café Bueno

$ | **CAFÉ** | Serving up caffeinated beverages in a variety of forms from all over the country, this attractive space maintains a chill vibe and attracts passersby looking for a beverage on the go. Sit at one of the three tables inside or two by the sidewalk, where you can expect to be serenaded by wandering buskers. **Known for:** varieties of Mexican coffee, served several different ways; shots of carajillo (espresso with Licor 43); relaxed atmosphere. $ *Average main: MP60* ⊠ *Amores 1403, Benito Juárez* ✛ *Del Valle Centro* ☎ *55/7826–6900* ⊕ *www.facebook.com/MimoCAFEBUENO* Ⓜ *Hospital 20 de Noviembre.*

Back in the Day

The pyramids of Teotihuacán and Templo Mayor get most of the attention in terms of the city's archaeological zones, but they are far from being the only vestiges of an ancient past here. Located in the charming colonia San Pedro de los Pinos, literally right on the east side of the highway that encircles much of the city, you'll find the ruins of a postclassic Mexica temple dedicated to Mixcoatl, a serpentlike god of the sky and the hunt. La Zona Arqueológica de Mixcoac is open daily and is accompanied by a small museum.

Pan de Nube

$ | **BAKERY** | There is always something in the oven at Pan de Nube, a quiet nook near the lovely Parque Mariscal Sucre. Daily breakfast and brunch specials range from house-made granola and yogurt to quiches and Spanish tortillas. **Known for:** pastries and sweets prepared fresh daily; cozy atmosphere; clientele with a refreshing lack of laptops. $ *Average main: MP70* ⊠ *Diagonal San Antonio 922, Benito Juárez* ✛ *Narvarte Poniente* ☎ *55/5687–3949* ⊕ *www.instagram.com/pandenubemex* ▤ *No credit cards* Ⓜ *Etiopía/Plaza de la Transparencia.*

★ Té Cuento

$ | **CAFÉ** | Looking out on vibrant Parque Tlacoquemécatl, this cozy, bright teahouse and eatery is run by an Argentine journalist and specializes in dozens of teas and infusions. It also doubles as a cultural space in the evenings, offering workshops on topics such as film and literature. **Known for:** mouthwatering baked goods; house-made organic foods; excellent tea menu. $ *Average main: MP100* ⊠ *C. Tlacoquemecatl Exterior 171, Benito Juárez* ✛ *Corner of Adolfo*

Mexico City's World Trade Center is the third tallest building in the city.

Prieto and Tlacoquemécatl ☎ *55/7589–9210* 🌐 *www.facebook.com/TeCuentoC-asadeTe* [M] *Hospital 20 de Noviembre.*

Village Café

$ | **INTERNATIONAL** | Facing Parque Hundido with a view of nothing but trees (okay, and some parked cars and an EcoBici stand), Village Café is a great place to unwind and take in a bit of tranquillity in one of the busier parts of the city. Massive windows open to the sidewalk, where diners take their time on sandwiches, coffees, and pastries. **Known for:** lovely views of the park; tasty bagel sandwiches; peaceful atmosphere. [$] *Average main: MP120* ✉ *Av. Porfirio Díaz 69–A, Benito Juárez* ✣ *Noche Buena* ☎ *55/1107–6072* 🌐 *www.villagecafe.com.mx.*

Hotels

Alia Inn Boutique

$$ | **HOTEL** | Just a few blocks from the World Trade Center and busy Insurgentes Avenue, this small boutique hotel is a charmer, with a hint of luxury. **Pros:** great location in a quiet neighborhood; impeccably clean; nice rooftop with pool. **Cons:** add-ons are pricey; some loud party nights; generic rooms. [$] *Rooms from: MP2100* ✉ *C. Nueva York 178, Benito Juárez* ☎ *55/9055–8520* 🌐 *aliainnboutique.com* 🛏 *32 rooms* 🍴 *No Meals* [M] *San Pedro de los Pinos.*

Aura For Living

$$ | **HOTEL** | The suites here are perfect for any length of stay in the city, and the location is well situated whether you're visiting for business or pleasure. **Pros:** kitchenettes in every room; equipped for extended stays; great service. **Cons:** gets busy; international franchise so not much local flavor; style is a bit impersonal. [$] *Rooms from: MP2100* ✉ *Montecito 19, Benito Juárez* ☎ *55/5523–1047* 🌐 *www.auraforliving.com* 🛏 *24 rooms* 🍴 *Free Breakfast* [M] *San Pedro de los Pinos.*

Hotel Beverly

$ | **HOTEL** | Meant to be a business luxury experience, Hotel Beverly has more local flair than most of the hotels in the area.

Bullfighting in Mexico City

Fair warning: the topic of the legality and morality of bullfighting in Mexico City might bring out stronger opinions than talking about Mexican politics. That said, Mexico is one of only eight countries in the world where bullfighting is legal, and Mexico City is home to the biggest bullfighting ring in the world. The Plaza de Toros opened in 1946 with stands that are designed to fit over 40,000 spectators.

While bullfighting in the city was banned for a little over a year during 2022 and 2023, the Mexico Supreme Court has once again deemed it legal and you'll see it still draws quite a crowd of those who come to imbibe, listen to live mariachi, and watch what those in favor of bullfighting call tradition, and what others would call pure brutality.

Bills to ban bullfighting (in which, spoiler, the bull always dies), especially in Mexico City, have been routinely introduced and then rejected by a majority of city officials. As it currently stands, animal rights activists are still tirelessly trying to stop the events, while those who are neutral turn a blind eye and those who are passionate spectators line up to buy tickets, especially for the novice matador show in November and the largest of the city's bullfighting events, La Temporada Grande, in February.

Pros: good price-to-quality ratio; luxurious suites; good location. **Cons:** occasional Wi-Fi issues in rooms; some rooms/bathrooms are small; updating needed in some areas. Ⓢ *Rooms from: MP1250* ✉ *C. Nueva York 301, Benito Juárez* ☏ *55/5523–6065* ⊕ *hotelbeverly.com.mx* 🛏 *79 rooms* ⑩ *No Meals* Ⓜ *San Antonio.*

Nightlife

Kaito Bar Izakaya
BARS | This small bar serves up some of the best sushi in Del Valle as well as inventive cocktails featuring Mexican and international liquors. Dark and intimate, the space relies heavily on a Japanese industrial aesthetic, with concrete, stainless steel, and wood all put to good use. There are DJs on the weekends, and it gets pretty rollicking at night. ✉ *Calle J. Enrique Pestalozzi 1238, Colonia del Valle Centro, Benito Juárez* ☏ *55/5605–6317* ⊕ *www.facebook.com/kaitodelvalle* Ⓜ *División del Norte.*

La Maraka
DANCE CLUB | Many locals consider the merengue and salsa music played at this dance hall, southeast of Colonia Roma, to be some of the city's best. It also offers dance classes and live music. ✉ *Mitla 410, at Eje 5, Benito Juárez* ☏ *55/5682–0636* ⊕ *www.lamaraka.com.mx* Ⓜ *Eugenia.*

★ La Paloma Azul
BARS | Specializing in one thing and one thing only (pulque, the fermented nectar of the agave plant), his bar is decorated with wall paintings of Mexico's pre-Columbian past. The pulque (about 4.5% ABV) comes in a variety of flavors to sample, and be sure to enjoy the ever-revolving cast of characters here, including students, neighborhood fixtures, and older folks. ✉ *Av. Popocatépetl 154D, Benito Juárez* ✛ *Portales Sur* ☏ *55/5688–5662* ⊕ *www.facebook.com/Palomaazuloficial* Ⓜ *Eje Central.*

★ Manada Bar

BARS | Craft cocktails are served in this tiny but fashionable bar ideal for a date or catching up with a close friend. Owned by tour guide Anais Martinez, the space has a hip and charming allure, with a location in the welcoming and laid-back neighborhood of Narvarte Oriente. Small snacks are available to accompany the fine cocktails and wine. ⊠ *Diag. San Antonio 1923, Benito Juárez* ⊕ *www. instagram.com/manadabar* Ⓜ *Viaducto.*

Taberna Calacas

BARS | Serving Mexican and imported artisanal beer, including three brands brewed on-site (you'll be engulfed by the scent of malt while you imbibe), seating at this small bar is mostly communal and against dark walls with tattoo-style art. Snacks (including charcuterie plates and guacamole with grasshoppers and pork rinds) are served each afternoon, with a special brunch menu on Sunday. ⊠ *Eje. Central Lazaro Cardenas 409, Portales Sur, Benito Juárez* ☎ *55/1381–4359* ⊕ *www.facebook.com/TabernaCalacas* Ⓜ *Portales.*

🔟 Performing Arts

★ Cineteca Nacional

FILM | Since 1984, the Cineteca Nacional (or National Film Archive) has been one of the highlights of Mexico City's contemporary offerings, hosting local and foreign films as well as film classes. The massive 41,172 square-foot complex houses coffee shops, restaurants, bars, bookstores, 10 viewing rooms (including three auditoriums), and more than 15,000 film titles. An outdoor viewing amphitheater invites filmgoers to take in movies on the grass at the entrance, a popular date activity. Affordable prices and edgy titles make it popular among youths, while the overall variety keeps it interesting for all ages. ⊠ *Av. México Coyoacán 389, Xoco, Benito Juárez* ☎ *55/4155–1200* ⊕ *www.cinetecanacional.net* Ⓜ *Coyoacán, Eje Central.*

Pepsi Center WTC

CONCERTS | Since its opening in 2012, the Pepsi Center WTC has quickly risen to fame as one of the most modern concert venues in Mexico. With a capacity of 7,500 people, it's much smaller (and therefore slightly more intimate) than the other local arenas of Foro Sol, Estadio Azteca, and Palacio de los Deportes. It regularly receives international touring acts and sells out quickly. ⊠ *Dakota S/N, Colonia Nápoles, Benito Juárez* ☎ *55/9000–6000* ⊕ *www.pepsicenterwtc.com/conoce* Ⓜ *San Pedro de los Pinos.*

Teatro Insurgentes

THEATER | With a Diego Rivera mural covering 5,920 square feet of space above its entrance, this 1,000-seat theater intrigues from its stately location along Insurgentes Avenue. Opened in 1953, it regularly hosts theatrical works, concerts, and even the occasional sporting event. Even if you don't get a chance to see a performance in this historic theater, even just glimpsing it from the street invites its own fair share of drama as the Rivera mural represents the theatrics of Mexico, from Mexica rituals to scenes of the Mexican Revolution and 20th-century film stars. Check the website for upcoming shows. ⊠ *Av. de los Insurgentes Sur 1587, San José Insurgentes, Benito Juárez* ☎ *55/5611–4253* ⊕ *www.carteleradeteatro.mx/teatro/sur/ teatro-de-los-insurgentes* Ⓜ *Barranca Del Muerto.*

Shopping

Torre Manacar

MALL | What Benito Juárez might lack in boutique shops, it certainly makes up for with international fashion brands within this 29-story skyscraper. Expect the normal stores you'd find in the United States, but with a few upscale additions like Mango, Uterqüe, Massimo Dutti, and Julio (a Mexican clothing brand). There's also a cinema and a number of restaurants, all of which are international or Mexican chains. ⊠ *1457 Av. de los Insurgentes Sur, Benito Juárez* ⊕ *www.manacarmx.com* Ⓜ *Hospital 20 de Noviembre.*

Chapter 11

COYOACÁN

Updated by
Andrew Collins

⊙ Sights	🍴 Restaurants	🛏 Hotels	🛍 Shopping	🍸 Nightlife
★★★★☆	★★★☆☆	★★★★☆	★★★☆☆	★★★☆☆

NEIGHBORHOOD SNAPSHOT

TOP EXPERIENCES

■ **Museo Frida Kahlo.** The rambling "Casa Azul" provides a fascinating look into the tumultuous life of an iconic artist.

■ **Mercado de Coyoacán.** If you visit only one of the city's rambling and historic markets, make it this bustling space famed for its stalls serving ceviche tostadas, squash-blossom quesadillas, fresh-squeezed juices, and other delights.

■ **Jardín Centenario y Plaza Hidalgo.** Anchoring Coyoacán's vibrant historic center, these adjacent plazas take on a festive air with their street performers, food and craft vendors, statuary and fountains, restaurant terraces, and cheerful crowds of all ages.

■ **Avenida Francisco Sosa.** To get a sense of Coyoacán's bohemian spirit and Spanish Colonial aesthetic, amble along this narrow, cobblestone street that also provides a pleasing route to San Ángel.

■ **Café culture.** Although less of a culinary destination than many other CDMX neighborhoods, Coyoacán nevertheless abounds with lively, open-air cafés serving delicious breakfast fare, artisan espresso drinks, and decadent pastries.

GETTING HERE

Along with its neighbor San Ángel, Coyoacán is one of the city's southern neighborhoods—the center of the neighborhood is about 9 km (6 miles) south of Roma and Condesa and 12 km (7 miles) south of Centro Histórico. Uber fares from the airport or the city center run about MP120–MP200. By Metro, you can take the 3 line to the Coyoacán, Viveros, or Miguel Ángel de Quevedo stops or the 2 line to General Anaya, but none of these stations are in the center of the neighborhood, so expect a 15- to 25-minute walk to most points of interest (Coyoacán is very safe for walking). From San Ángel, it's a quick Uber ride (around MP60) or picturesque 45- to 60-minute walk via Avendia Francisco Sosa. The neighborhood also has a fair amount of free street parking as well as several inexpensive and secure lots.

VIEWFINDER

■ The name Coyoacán roughly translates to "place of coyotes" in the Nahuatl language of the Mexica, who populated the area when Hernan Cortés named it Spain's new capital in 1521. Appropriately, a favorite spot for a selfie today is in front of Jardín Centenario's famed 1967 fountain, in which two regal coyotes cavort beneath streams of water.

PLANNING YOUR TIME

■ Even allowing time to visit Museo Frida Kahlo and a couple other key attractions, Coyoacán can easily be explored in a day. You could combine your visit with nearby San Ángel, but that only allows you to see a couple of top sites in each place. Extremely safe and pleasant to walk through, you can visit Coyoacán at any time of day. Mornings provide the chance to dine at one of several excellent breakfast spots, while staying until after dark is fun—especially on weekends—for people-watching in the main plazas, which hum with activity until late.

Founded by Toltecs in the 10th century and later settled by Mexica (commonly known as Aztecs), then Spanish conquistador Cortés, and then—over the past century or so—by a steady stream of artists, writers, intellectuals, and creative spirits, Coyoacán is as much a mood as a physical place.

About 12 km (7 miles) south of Centro Histórico, this colonial neighborhood of quiet tree-lined streets feels like its own little village, and indeed, until it was officially incorporated as a part of Mexico City in 1857, it functioned as a distinct—and quite rural—municipality. When Cortés arrived, the settlement sat on the southwestern shore of Lake Texcoco. Today it's a wonderful place for strolling and people-watching, especially around its festive central squares (or zócalo), Plaza Hidalgo and adjacent Jardín Centenario; it's also home to one of the country's most popular attractions, Casa Azul, where painter Frida Kahlo resided.

Coyoacán has actually been the home of many illustrious creatives and intellectuals, including artists David Alfaro Siqueiros and Diego Rivera; directors Luis Buñuel and Emilio "El Indio" Fernández; actors Dolores del Río, Mario Moreno, Daniel Giménez Cacho, and Diego Luna; singer Lila Downs; and writers Octavio Paz, Laura Esquivel, Jorge Ibargüengoitia, Juan Villoro, and Salvador Novo. It's also the neighborhood where the exiled Leon Trotsky met his violent death. The neighborhood's bohemian spirit is still palpable, and during the day, its artsy cafés, shaded parks and plazas, and bounty of cultural centers and excellent, often underrated museums (Museo Frida Kahlo is by no means the only game in town) overflow with both locals and tourists.

Bear in mind that Coyoacán is both one of Mexico City's 16 official delegaciónes (comparable to boroughs) and the name commonly used to refer to the much smaller historic neighborhood that's covered here. When most Chilangos (residents of Mexico City) refer to Coyoacán, they mean this small historic core (also known as Colonia Del Carmen) that's home to Museo Frida Kahlo, Avenida Francisco Sosa, Plaza Hidalgo, and Jardín Centenario. The delegación of Coyoacán spans well beyond this historic center and is home to some 650,000 residents; the major attractions in the delegación outside the historic core—such as Museo Anahuacalli, Universidad Nacional Autónoma de México (UNAM), and Estadio Azteca—are farther afield and thus covered in the Greater Mexico City section.

Historic Coyoacán is largely without the hipster cachet and expat popularity of Roma and Condesa, and its relatively out-of-the-way location insulates it—to a degree—from the faster pace and urban sprawl that characterizes much of the rest of the city. As popular as it is for breakfast, coffee, and daytime exploring, it quiets down a bit in the evening, except for the handful of locals-oriented cantinas and bars around the zócalo. This historic core of the neighborhood buzzes with merriment day and night, but especially on weekends. Mostly locals of all ages and a smaller number of tourists mill about Plaza Hidalgo, Jardín Centenario, and the surrounding blocks, which are lined with souvenir shops, inexpensive restaurants, and vendors selling classic Mexican treats like elote, tamales, candies, chile-dusted snacks, tacos, and more. The cheerful, family-friendly vibe is similar to that of a street fair.

The neighborhood's one unwelcome recent development was the 2021 construction of lipstick-shape Torre Mítikah, a menacingly banal emblem of hubristic postmodernism that lies on the border between Del Valle and Coyoacán and is now the tallest building in Mexico City. Like an awkwardly tall, uninvited party guest, Torre Mítikah now routinely photo bombs everyone's otherwise enchanting pictures of Coyoacán, whose skyline had previously barely changed since the days of Cortés.

Although lacking big hotels, the neighborhood is rife with charming Airbnbs and a handful of inviting, beautifully appointed inns. It's a perfect hub if you're seeking a relatively tranquil base for exploring the city, and you don't mind having to Uber or take the Metro to more central neighborhoods. Many who stay here combine their visit with a few days closer to the city center, which is a nice strategy for experiencing two very distinct sides of Mexico City. The most ardent devotees of Coyoacán's bohemian spirit and manageable pace can't imagine staying, or living, anywhere else in the city.

 # Sights

★ Avenida Francisco Sosa

STREET | One of the prettiest and most historic streets in the city, this narrow tree-lined thoroughfare paved with stone is a delightful destination for a short stroll or (if you're feeling a bit more ambitious) as the most scenic way to walk between the historic centers of Coyoacán and San Ángel. From Jardín Centenario, it runs west for just under 2 km (a little over a mile), ending at Avendia Universidad beside the tiny and historic San Antonio de Padua Chapel. Along the route you'll pass grand 19th-century mansions hidden behind, or towering over, colorfully painted walls. The surrounding neighborhood has been home to various celebrities over the years, from Dolores del Río, Luis Buñuel, and Octavio Paz to, more recently, actor Diego Luna, singer Lila Downs, and *Like Water for Chocolate* novelist Laura Esquivel. The sidewalks become narrower the farther west you walk, and ancient tree roots have in places pushed up and broken the pavement to an almost comical degree (it can feel more like bouldering than walking in a couple of spots).

The plaza surrounding 16th-century Santa Catarina Chapel is especially picturesque, hung with strings of colorful papel picado and dotted with stone benches and pretty trees. Across the street, the shaded, peaceful grounds of Casa de Cultura Jesús Reyes Heroles are also lovely to walk around, and you may witness a dance or crafts class taking place in one of the cultural center's workshops. Up and down Sosa, and especially closer to Jardín Centenario, you'll pass by inviting cafés and boutiques. There are a few attractions of note on or near this street, such as Fonoteca Nacional and Museo Nacional de la Acuarela Alfredo Guati Rojo. The narrow lanes that intersect with Francisco Sosa are also quite pretty, especially the allegedly haunted and oft-photographed Callejon Aguacate, an alley lined with ivy and flowering shrubs that's reached via a quick turn south onto Calle Tata Vasco. To reach San Ángel, cross Universidad where Francisco Sosa ends and continue west on Calle Arenal and Avenida de la Paz (past Parque de la Bombilla); without stops, it's about a one-hour stroll from Jardín Centenario to San Ángel's Plaza del Carmen. ⊠ *Av. Francisco Sosa, Coyoacán* ✛ *Between Jardin Centenario and Av. Universidad* Ⓜ *Viveros.*

Casa Municipal (*Casa de Cortés*)
GOVERNMENT BUILDING | The place where the Mexica emperor Cuauhtémoc was held prisoner by Cortés is often alleged to have been rebuilt in the 18th century from the stones of the conquistador's original house, although historians agree that Cortés himself lived not here but several blocks away by La Conchita Church. Topped by two coyote figures, this long, single-story building on the north side of Plaza Hidalgo houses Coyoacán's municipal government offices and a small tourism visitor center (as well as the local library in the adjacent building). You can wander through the wide arches to see the handsomely tiled courtyard. ⊠ *Plaza Hidalgo 1, Coyoacán* ⧆ *Free* Ⓜ *Viveros.*

★ Fonoteca Nacional de México
LIBRARY | On the western end of picturesque Avenida Francisco Sosa, this grand mansion with a dramatic facade was built in the Moorish and Andulusian style in the 18th century and eventually became the home of Mexican Nobel poet Octavio Paz, who lived here in the late 1990s until his death in 1998. In 2008, the building—known as Casa Alvarado—became the home of Mexico's national sound archive. Today, visitors can explore the archives and, in the listening rooms, hear digitized recordings from the archive's immense collection, which includes Frida Kahlo, Álvaro Obregón, and dozens of other historical figures. There's also an extensive library of books related to music and

sound, and you can saunter through the gracious gardens and grounds, which are a perfect spot to relax with a book or rest your feet for a bit. Fonoteca also hosts a rich array of lectures, concerts, and other events—check the online calendar for details. ⊠ *Av. Francisco Sosa 383, Coyoacán* ☎ *55/4155–0950* ⊕ *www.fonotecanacional.gob.mx* ⧆ *Free* ☾ *Closed Sun.* Ⓜ *Viveros.*

★ Jardín Centenario and Plaza Hidalgo
PLAZA/SQUARE | These infectiously festive plazas function as Coyoacán's zócalo and are barely separated from each other by a narrow street with slow-moving traffic. The Jardín, with its shady trees, an oft-photographed fountain with two snarling coyotes, and a fringe of lively patio bars and restaurants (of varying quality), is the more commercial of the two but also arguably prettier. Note the the often-overlooked concrete obelisk with a tile fountain and four coyote gargoyles. A wander through here is even more enjoyable while savoring a dish of traditional Mexican ice cream (mamey, *leche quemada* [burnt milk], and elote are among the unique flavors) from Tepoznieves, which is located on the Francisco Sosa side of Jardín Centenario.

The larger Plaza Hidalgo hosts children's fairs, music and dance performances, clowns, bubble-blowers, and cotton candy and balloon sellers, especially on weekends and holidays. It's anchored by an ornate old bandstand and the impressive Parroquia de San Juan Bautista, one of the first churches to be built in New Spain. Each afternoon of September 15, before the crowds become suffocating at nightfall, these delightful plazas are perhaps the best place in the capital to enjoy Independence Day celebrations. More recently, they've become a must-visit for Día de Muertos in early November, with throngs of people of all ages cavorting about in costume and face paint. Both plazas are filled with landscaped courtyards, sculptures, and

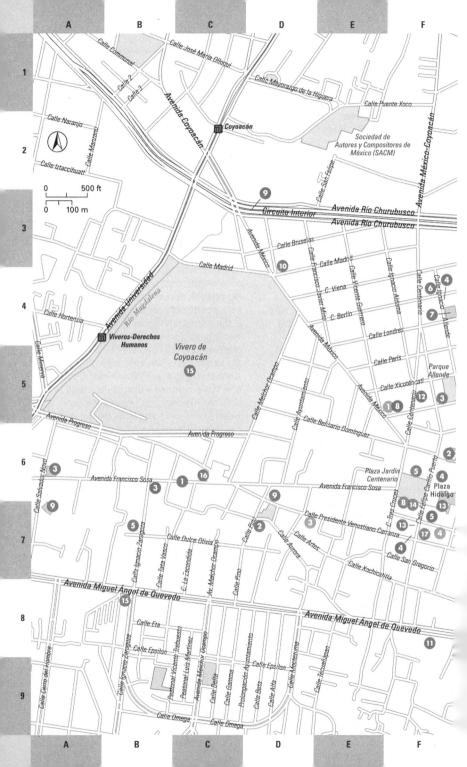

Coyoacán

Sights ▼

1 Avenida Francisco Sosa C6
2 Casa Municipal F6
3 Fonoteca Nacional de México A6
4 Jardín Centenario and Plaza Hidalgo............. F6
5 Monumental Casa de Emilio el "Indio" Fernández B7
6 Museo Casa de León Trotsky............. H3
7 Museo Frida Kahlo F4
8 Museo Nacional de Culturas Populares G6
9 Museo Nacional de la Acuarela Alfredo Guati Rojo............... A7
10 Museo Nacional de las Intervenciones............ I3
11 Parque Frida Kahlo H8
12 Parque Xicoténcatl....... I3
13 Parroquia San Juan Bautista.................. F7
14 Plaza de la Conchita.... H7
15 Viveros de Coyoacán.... C5

Restaurants ▼

1 Alverre Café Bistró H5
2 Café Ruta de la Seda... D7
3 Cancino Coyoacán F5
4 Cochinita Country Coyoacán................ F4
5 Corazón de Maguey..... F6
6 Croasán................... F4
7 El Beneficio de la Duda..................... H5
8 El Entrevero F6
9 El Olvidado.............. D6
10 El Sheik D4
11 El Tajín.................... F8
12 La Barraca Valenciana F5
13 Los Amantes Café & Bistro............. F7
14 Los Danzantes F7
15 Mercado Roma Coyoacán................ B8
16 Merendero Las Lupitas C6
17 Mi Compa Chava F7

Quick Bites ▼

1 Café Avellaneda G7
2 Café El Jarocho......... G6
3 Happy Banh Mi B6
4 Il Vicolo Panadería F7
5 Kahwen Café............. F7
6 Mercado de Antojitos Mexicanos.............. G6
7 Pastefam Caramel........ I4
8 Picnic Helados........... F5
9 Super Tacos Chupacabras............ D3

Hotels ▼

1 Agata Hotel Boutique ... E5
2 Casa Moctezuma....... G6
3 Casa Tamayo............ D7
4 Casa Tuna F7
5 H21 Hospedaje Boutique G7

KEY

1 Sights
1 Restaurants
1 Quick Bites
1 Hotels

Stroll down Avenida Francisco Sosa to admire the colorful architecture.

dozens of park benches, and they're a memorable destination for people-watching. You'll see passersby of all ages and backgrounds, from multigenerational families and young couples of all sexual orientations cuddling, kissing, and holding hands to tourists from all over the world, and locals walking their dogs (who are often gussied up in sweaters and bows). Of the streets emanating from the plazas, Felipe Carrillo Puerto—which runs due south—has the best selection of high-quality shops and restaurants, including branches of popular Mexico City businesses like Churrería El Moro, Boicot coffeehouse, and Gandhi bookstore. ■ TIP→ **There are public bathrooms (for a small fee) in the lovely, landscaped courtyard beside the Parroquia.** ⊠ *Coyoacán* ✛ *Bounded by Calle Centenario and Calle Ignacio Allende at Av. Francisco Sosa and Av. Miguel Hidalgo* Ⓜ *Viveros.*

Monumental Casa de Emilio el "Indio" Fernández

HISTORIC HOME | FAMILY | Although open only on weekends, this palatial former home of Emilio "El Indio Fernández"—one of the greatest directors in Mexican cinematic history—is well worth a visit any time of year, but is especially a must-see during the weeks around Día de Muertos, when its rooms and gardens abound with remarkably extensive and colorful *ofrendas* (altars). The fortresslike home, built in the 1940s of volcanic rock with a design influenced by prehistoric temples, is filled with movie memorabilia, and vendors sell crafts, food, and other goods in the house's tree-shaded front courtyard. There are also theatrical presentations and other events throughout the year, some with additional admission charges. ⊠ *Ignacio Zaragoza 51, Coyoacán* ☎ *55/6475–2670* ⊕ *www. facebook.com/casafuerteindiofernandez* 🎫 *MP150* 🕙 *Closed weekdays* Ⓜ *Viveros.*

★ Museo Casa de León Trotsky

HISTORIC HOME | From the house's original entrance on Calle Morelos (around the corner from the current museum entrance) with its forbidding high walls and turrets for armed guards, you get a sense of just how precarious life was for its final resident, León Trotsky, one of the most important figures of the Russian Revolution. Living in exile, Trotsky moved his family here in 1939 at the behest of his friends Diego Rivera and Frida Kahlo (who resided in Casa Azul, just a few blocks away). Less than a year later, he would be assassinated. The house and adjoining exhibit galleries make for an eerily fascinating glimpse of Trotsky's later life and death. As you walk through the house, which looks largely as it did the day of his death, you'll see bullet holes still in the walls from the first assassination attempt, in which the muralist David Alfaro Siqueiros was implicated. The rooms include his bedroom, his wife's study, the dining room and kitchen, and the study where assassin Ramón Mercader (a man of many aliases) drove a pickax into Trotsky's head. On his desk, cluttered with writing paraphernalia and an article he was revising in Russian, the calendar is open to that fateful day: August 20, 1940. ✉ *Av. Río Churubusco 410, Coyoacán* ☎ *55/5554–4083* ⊕ *www.museotrotsky.org.mx* ✆ *MP40* ☾ *Closed Mon.* Ⓜ *Coyoacán.*

★ Museo Frida Kahlo

ART MUSEUM | Casa Azul (Blue House), where the iconic artist was born in 1907 (not 1910, as she wanted people to believe) and died 47 years later, is both museum and shrine. Kahlo's astounding vitality and originality are reflected in the house itself, from the giant papier-mâché skeletons outside and the *retablos* (small religious paintings on tin) on the staircase to the gloriously decorated kitchen and the bric-a-brac in her bedroom. The house displays relatively few of Kahlo's original paintings, but you can admire her early sketches, diary entries, tiny

outfits, and wheelchair at her easel, plus her four-poster bed fitted with a mirror above, and in a separate exhibit space across the garden, a collection of her dresses presented in the context of her physical disabilities. The relaxing garden also has a small but excellent gift shop and café.

The museum has become astoundingly popular in recent years and carefully limits ticket sales to avoid the house becoming too crowded at any given time. Tickets can only be purchased online. You can buy them from the museum website, but these tend to sell out quickly. If this happens, you can try buying tickets from a third-party tour site, such as ⊕ *Tiqets.com,* ⊕ *GetYourGuide.com,* or ⊕ *Viator.com.* You'll pay a surcharge, but these sites sometimes have tickets available on shorter notice, and they also sell tickets many weeks in advance, which the museum's official site does not. For all the hassle of buying tickets, it's worth the effort to visit this very special place, and once you're inside, you can explore at a leisurely pace (and be glad the museum is never allowed to become too crowded). ✉ *Londres 247, Coyoacán* ☎ *55/5554–5999* ⊕ *www.museofridakahlo.org.mx* ✆ *MP250 weekdays, MP270 weekends (includes admission to Museo Diego Rivera–Anahuacalli)* ☾ *Closed Mon.* Ⓜ *Coyoacán.*

Museo Nacional de Culturas Populares

SPECIALTY MUSEUM | FAMILY | A huge *arbol de la vida* (tree of life) sculpture stands in the courtyard of this museum devoted to popular culture and regional arts and crafts and located just a few steps from Plaza Hidalgo. Its exhibits rotate (there's no permanent collection), and the variety of events include children's workshops, traditional music concerts, and dance performances. On certain weekends the courtyard becomes a small crafts-and-sweets market with some worthwhile exhibitors from throughout the country displaying their wares. The museum

Within Plaza Hidalgo, you'll find a popular fountain featuring two snarling coyotes.

shop stocks an exceptional selection of books on everything from Mexican art to anthropology as well as high-quality crafts. ⊠ *Av. Hidalgo 289, Coyoacán* 🖷 *55/4155–0920* ⊕ *mncp.cultura.gob.mx* ◲ *MP18; free Sun.* Ⓜ *Viveros.*

Museo Nacional de la Acuarela Alfredo Guati Rojo

ART MUSEUM | Founded in 1964 by the late artist Alfredo Guati Rojo, this museum devoted entirely to watercolor painting makes for an enjoyable detour if you're strolling along nearby Avenida Francisco Sosa. Admission is free, and the two-story white house that contains the galleries is surrounded by pretty flower gardens and hedges, which you can admire from the terrace of the small museum café. The art includes dozens of works by Rojo and his wife, plus galleries devoted to watercolor paintings by Mexican, international, and contemporary artists; a separate building across the garden stages temporary exhibits. ⊠ *Calle Salvador Novo 88, Coyoacán* 🖷 *55/5554–1801* ⊕ *www.acuarela. org.mx* ◲ *Free* Ⓜ *Viveros.*

★ Museo Nacional de las Intervenciones

HISTORY MUSEUM | Surrounded by a park with mature trees and greenery, cannons, and a towering statue of General Anaya, this fascinating museum in San Diego Churubusco—a pleasant 15-minute walk east of Coyoacán's historic center—may just be the city's best museum you've never heard of. It's devoted to relating the surprisingly lengthy and storied history of Mexico's wars, dating from the 1810–21 War of Independence to the Mexican Revolution a century later. The exceptionally well-executed exhibits within the building's many galleries provide an impressive explanation of how exactly Mexico became, well, Mexico. But you don't need to be a history buff to appreciate the building, which occupies the former Nuestra Señora de los Angeles de Churubusco monastery, a glorious structure built in the late 1600s and converted into an ad-hoc military fort in 1847 during the Mexican-American War. In the exhibits, history is told through displays of uniforms, guns, flags, paintings, and other artifacts, including a diorama of the Battle of Churubusco and photos of Pershing's 1914 punitive expedition in search of the elusive Pancho Villa. The museum also contains a remarkable collection of original frescoes, religious paintings, and ex-votos from the building's period as a monastery. In addition, there's a tranquil community garden as well as galleries that host rotating shows. Part of the fun of touring the museum is observing the building's well-preserved sloping floors, beamed ceilings, fine tile work, and ancient arches. ⊠ *20 de Agosto s/n, at Calle Xicoténcatl, Coyoacán* ☎ *55/5604–0699* ⊕ *www.intervenciones. inah.gob.mx* ⊠ *MP90* ⊗ *Closed Mon.* Ⓜ *General Anaya.*

Parque Frida Kahlo

CITY PARK | Offering a small oasis of calm only a few blocks from Coyoacán's joyfully frenetic main plazas, this green space of topiaries, life-size bronze statues of Frida and Diego, and a central fountain with three vertical streams of water has a relaxing ambience. Open only during the day, the narrow, fenced-in park prohibits pets, skates, bikes, and sporting equipment. For this reason, it's a lovely place to read, catch your breath, and listen to songbirds chirping in the trees overhead. It's diagonally across the street from Plaza de La Conchita, with its historic chapel. ⊠ *Calle Fernández Leal, at Av. Pacífico, Coyoacán* ⊠ *Free* Ⓜ *Viveros.*

Parque Xicoténcatl

CITY PARK | This less-visited but beautiful little park is in the San Diego Churubusco neighborhood, just steps from the excellent Museo Nacional de las Intervenciones. The 1.5-acre patch of lush gardens is fenced in (and open only during the day). There's a central kiosk and fountain, a huge statue of Cortés, stone and brick paths, a couple of children's playgrounds, and plenty of benches to relax on. The tranquil oasis is a perfect spot to sip coffee and munch on pastries (Pastelería Caramel is right on the way if

you're making the 15-minute walk here from the center of Coyoacán). ⊠ *Calle Xicoténcatl s/n, east of Av. División del Norte, Coyoacán* Ⓜ *General Anaya.*

Parroquia de San Juan Bautista

CHURCH | One of the earliest churches built in New Spain, this huge and striking church dates to 1527, although construction wasn't completed until 1550, and it's been rebuilt and extensively remodeled at various times (its spire had to be repaired after it was badly damaged in the city's 2017 earthquake). The interior is quite spectacular, with priceless artwork and a gorgeous vaulted ceiling. Next door, the cloister of the former convent is a peaceful spot to relax and reflect. ⊠ *Centenario 8, Coyoacán* ☎ *55/5554–6310* ⊕ *www.facebook. com/parroquiasanjuanbautistacoyoacan* ⊠ *Free* Ⓜ *Viveros.*

Plaza de La Conchita

PLAZA/SQUARE | Connected to the neighborhood's other central plazas by café-lined Calle Higuera, this tree-shaded plaza with red-painted cement benches and pretty gardens is anchored by a little chapel known officially as La Chapel of the Immaculate Conception Church—although everyone calls it by its nickname, "La Conchita." The twin-spired, relatively modest structure has an impressive pedigree: it stands on the site of a pre-Hispanic ceremony ground, and it was built by none other than Spanish conquistador Hernán Cortés in 1525 (although, like so many of the city's ancient structures, it was extensively rebuilt later—in this case sometime around the late 1600s). Cortés, incidentally, is said to have had a home overlooking the church. The interior is closed indefinitely for renovations, but you can admire the striking facade of the *tezontle* (volcanic stone) that's so common in this part of the city. ⊠ *Calle Fernández Leal 74, Coyoacán* Ⓜ *Viveros.*

Frida and Diego's Mexico City

The two most recognized figures in Mexican art, Frida Kahlo and Diego Rivera enjoy an almost fanatical following among visitors to the capital, which is where they lived (in both San Ángel and Coyoacán) and where much of their work can be viewed today. The two larger-than-life personalities were married from 1929 through Kahlo's death, at age 47, in 1954—except for a one-year gap in 1929–30, when the pair divorced. Their tumultuous relationship endured numerous affairs by both parties, but they also remained a joint artistic and political force—both were committed to leftist causes—until the end.

Rivera enjoyed greater fame as a painter, especially for his murals, during their lifetimes, but Kahlo's deeply personal paintings began to earn wider acclaim during the final decade of her life. And by the 1990s—as she became a symbol of feminist, LGBTQ+, Indigenous, and Mexican-American rights—Kahlo surpassed Rivera as the better recognized of the two. Ironically, the rejection of more commercial artistic styles that cost Kahlo financial success during her life is in part what fuels her vaunted reputation today. In 2021, Kahlo's 1949 oil painting *Diego y yo* fetched $34.9 million at auction, shattering the previous record for the sale of work by a Latin American artist, set in 2018 by a Diego Rivera painting that sold for $9.76 million.

Although you'll find works by Kahlo and Rivera throughout the city center (especially Palacio Nacional and Palacio de Bellas Artes for his murals and Museo de Arte Moderno for her paintings), their art is best explored in the south of the city, which is home to four key attractions: **Museo Frida Kahlo**, **Museo Casa Estudio Diego Rivera y Frida Kahlo**, **Museo Anahuacalli**, and **Museo Dolores Olmedo**.

★ Viveros de Coyoacán

CITY PARK | Officially this 96-acre swath of greenery is a nursery that was developed in 1913 to grow tree seedlings to be transplanted to the forests in and around Mexico City, but today Viveros functions for visitors as a glorious park (it has, in fact, been an official national park since 1938). A 2.2-km (1.4-mile) gravel walking and jogging trail laces the perimeter of the property, and a series of narrow trails crisscross the park, each one lined with specimen trees that are planted around the city: acacia, sweet gum, jacaranda, cedar, and so on. There are five entrances around the park: the southwest one is closest to Viveros metro, but the northeast one is better if you're walking over from elsewhere in Coyoacán or from the Coyoacán metro stop. Each entrance is staffed by security, and although admission is free, the gates shut to the public promptly at 6 pm and don't reopen until the next morning at 6 am. This is one of the most enjoyable (and popular) spots in the city for jogging, but throughout Viveros you'll also find benches, rows of ornamental plants, hundreds of colorful and friendly black and gray squirrels, swatches of grass to set up picnic blankets, and a central plaza that's often the site of small groups informally practicing fencing, yoga, dancing, and the like. Unless you glimpse the unfortunately bland Torre Mítikah, which was completed in 2021 on the neighborhood's northern border, you can easily imagine that you're miles from urban civilization while relaxing in this enchanting urban sanctuary. Near the northeast entrance, an actual nursery sells plants, flowers, and garden statuary and gifts of every imaginable kind. ⊠ *Av. México and Calle Madrid, Coyoacán* ⌷ *Free* Ⓜ *Viveros.*

🍴 Restaurants

Alverre Café Bistró

$$ | **ECLECTIC** | A cute, unpretentious local favorite, Alverre has the sort of extensive international menu that's perfect when you and your friends aren't exactly sure what you're hungry for. Excellent bets here include the bountiful jamón serrano salad with arugula and goat cheese, the oven-baked lasagna with Bolognese sauce, and enchiladas suizas with chicken, but you'll also find crepes, omelets, quiches, empanadas, pizzas, and sandwiches. **Known for:** hearty breakfasts; remarkably extensive and varied menu; good selection of artisanal Mexican beers and kombuchas. Ⓢ *Average main: MP175* ⊠ *Calle Gómez Farias 42, Coyoacán* ☎ *55/5658–9027* ⊕ *www.facebook.com/alverrecafe* Ⓜ *Viveros.*

★ Café Ruta de la Seda

$ | **CAFÉ** | Named for the Silk Road, this inviting café with an enchanting outdoor patio overlooking tranquil Parque Santa Catarina does indeed draw its culinary inspiration from both East and West, serving delectable kimchi omelets, Cuban sandwiches, soba noodle and toasted sesame salads, and anise–avocado leaf cakes. Most of the fair-trade ingredients, from the coffee beans and teas to the whole grains and flours used in the artisan breads and pastries, are sourced organically. **Known for:** matcha cakes and lattes; extensive list of organic Asian teas; location overlooking a beautiful park near Avenida Francisco Sosa. Ⓢ *Average main: MP120* ⊠ *Calle Aurora 1, Coyoacán* ☎ *55/3869–4888* ⊕ *www.caferutadelaseda.com* Ⓜ *Viveros.*

★ Cancino Coyoacán

$$ | **PIZZA** | Quite possibly the most beautifully designed location of this hugely popular gourmet pizza chainlet, Cancino Coyoacán is in a stunning bi-level space with brick walls, soft lighting, high ceilings, and soaring windows that offer views of tree-shaded Jardín Allende. There are wood-fired pizzas with toppings like pureed huitlacoche, Oaxaca cheese, elote, jalapeños, and Bolognese sauce with red wine and tomatoes, and there's a tempting assortment of appetizers, from blistered shishito peppers to truffled Parmesan potatoes. **Known for:** lovely park views from the upper level; house-made gnocchi and other pastas; warm chocolate brownie with vanilla ice cream. Ⓢ *Average main: MP180* ⊠ *Malintzin 151, Coyoacán* ☎ *55/9026–1545* ⊕ *www.archipielagomx.com/cancino* Ⓜ *Coyoacán.*

Cochinita Country Coyoacán

$$ | **MEXICAN** | In a creaky old house that practically backs up to Museo Frida Kahlo, this unpretentious restaurant with friendly servers and reasonable prices serves well-crafted, authentic Yucatecan cuisine, including classics like rich and flavorful *papadzules* (tortillas stuffed with hard-boiled eggs and smothered in a pumpkin seed-tomato sauce) and tender cochinita pibil. Be sure to start with a cup of *sopa de lima* (a soup of shredded chicken, tortillas, and lime), and perhaps an order of *panuchos* (fried tortillas stuffed with beans and topped with different meats and sauces). **Known for:** charming outdoor seating along the sidewalk; eggs with longaniza sausage from Valladolid for breakfast; several delicious vegetarian options. Ⓢ *Average main: MP230* ⊠ *Ignacio Allende 161, Coyoacán* ☎ *55/5661–2840* ⊕ *www.cochinitacountrycoyoacan.com* ⊗ *Closed Mon.* Ⓜ *Coyoacán.*

11

Coyoacán

Corazón de Maguey

$$$ | **MODERN MEXICAN** | A stylish bi-level bistro and mezcal bar with a prime views across Jardín Centenario, Corazón de Maguey is a pleasing setting for artfully presented regional Mexican fare and creative cocktails. You could easily put together a meal of several starters—the guacamole with chapulines and a sampler of five moles with tortillas among them—or opt for one of the substantial main dishes, such as Acapulco-style seared octopus with fried plantains, jicama, and pineapple, or tender Oaxacan tlayudas with *arrachera* (a grilled, thin steak) marinated in a guajillo chile sauce. **Known for:** superb cocktails using the acclaimed Alipús house brand mezcal; great views of Jardín Centenario from the landscaped patio; lime merengue with house-made lime ice cream. [$] *Average main: MP380* ✉ *Parque Centenario 9A, Coyoacán* ☎ *55/7406–8199* 🌐 *www.corazondemaguey.com* [M] *Viveros.*

★ **Croasán**

$$ | **CAFÉ** | Drop by this smart café just steps from Museo Frida Kahlo for generous portions of creatively prepared Mexican and European breakfast and lunch fare, along with a vast selection of pastries and espresso drinks. The Yucatecan-style chilaquiles, topped with cochinita pibil and pickled onions, are a highlight in the morning, while standouts later in the day include avocado-smoked salmon toast and a Croque monsieur on a freshly baked brioche. **Known for:** extensive selection of fresh-squeezed juices; Nutella-stuffed pancakes with a mixed berry jam; lovely outdoor seating along a quiet street. [$] *Average main: MP180* ✉ *Ignacio Allende 168, Coyoacán* ☎ *55/4027–4639* 🌐 *www.croasanmx.com* 🕒 *Closed Mon. No dinner* [M] *Coyoacán.*

El Beneficio de la Duda

$$ | **CAFÉ** | This dapper all-day café with white-brick walls, colorful peltre dishware, and fresh flowers on every table is in a semi-residential section of Coyoacán, well-removed from the crowds and an easy stroll from Museo Frida Kahlo. The owner uses organic coffees and, as much as possible, locally sourced ingredients in the European-influenced Mexican fare, which includes superb chilaquiles (order them with both the green and red sauces), panfried potatoes with paprika and chipotle aioli, and ham-gruyere croissant sandwiches. **Known for:** wide assortment of fresh-baked pastries and desserts; fresh fruit plates (with honey and granola); bright and cheerful space. [$] *Average main: MP225* ✉ *Calle Xicoténcatl 275, Coyoacán* ☎ *55/1741–8979* 🌐 *www.facebook.com/elbeneficiodeladuda* [M] *Coyoacán.*

El Entrevero

$$$ | **ARGENTINE** | Although a Uruguayan owns this fashionable eatery on Coyoacán's lively Jardín Centenario, the menu will be familiar to fans of Argentine cuisine: the superb *provoleta* (grilled provolone cheese with oregano), for example, and the stellar steaks. Uruguay's Italian heritage appears on the menu as well, with good pizzas and gnocchi with a creamy gorgonzola sauce. **Known for:** aged steaks; clericot (a classic Argentine drink of red wine, sugar, lemon juice, and soda water); dulce de leche imported from Uruguay. [$] *Average main: MP360* ✉ *Jardín Centenario 14, Coyoacán* ☎ *55/5659–0066* 🌐 *www.grupoentrevero.com* [M] *Viveros.*

★ **El Olvidado**

$$ | **CAFÉ** | Detour just a short block off Francisco Sosa to find this inviting, light-filled café that offers up gorgeous breakfast and lunch fare as well as exquisite cakes and pastries based on recipes from the owner's British grandmother, including scones with jam and *nata* (clotted cream), trifle, and cardamom cakes. Other menu options include lentil salad; eggs Benedict; smoked salmon, ricotta, and egg croissants; and roast beef, gouda, Dijon mustard, and caramelized onion sandwiches on rustic bread. **Known for:**

Mueso Frida Kahlo, also known as Casa Azul, was where the painter was born and where she died.

fine black teas and organic coffee drinks; modern takes on classic British baked goods and breakfasts; attractive sidewalk seating. $ *Average main: MP170* ⊠ *Calle Presidente Carranza 267, Coyoacán* ☎ *55/7095–6125* ⊕ *www.elolvidado.com* Ⓜ *Viveros.*

El Sheik

$$ | **MIDDLE EASTERN** | The flavorful Lebanese cuisine—including baked eggs, raw kibbeh, falafel, grilled kofta, dolmas, and cucumber salad—at this charming restaurant with amiable servers is perfect for filling up before or after a stroll or run in nearby Viveros park. If you're not sure what to order, the best approach is the extensive sampler platter, or dine here on the weekend, when there's a huge buffet offering. **Known for:** boldly flavored mint tea, Turkish coffee, and lassi drinks; generous weekend buffet offering a huge sampling of dishes; scrumptious Arabic cookies and other desserts. $ *Average main: MP180* ⊠ *Calle Madrid 129, Coyoacán* ☎ *55/5659–3311* ⊕ *www.elsheik. com.mx* Ⓜ *Coyoacán.*

El Tajín

$$ | **MEXICAN** | Named after El Tajín pyramid in Veracruz state and a longtime proponent of the "slow food" movement, this elegant lunch spot inside Jardin Cultural Del Centro Veracruzano sizzles with pre-Hispanic influences. Innovative appetizers include *chilpachole,* a delicate crab-soup with epazote and macha chile paste, while main dishes might include rabbit in a guajillo mole sauce and octopus cooked in its own ink with red wine, olives, and almonds. **Known for:** lovely setting overlooking a garden courtyard; impressive wine list; artfully prepared pre-Hispanic Mexican cuisine. $ *Average main: MP260* ⊠ *Jardin Cultural Del Centro Veracruzano, Av. Miguel Ángel de Quevedo 687, Coyoacán* ☎ *55/5659–5759* ⊕ *www.facebook.com/eltajinrestaurante* ☉ *No dinner* Ⓜ *Viveros.*

★ La Barraca Valenciana

$$ | **SPANISH** | This casual Spanish restaurant is known both for traditional tapas like *tartar de atún con ajillo, croquetas de jamón serrano,* and *patatas bravas,* and

for its Iberian take on tortas, the classic Mexican sandwich. The tortas are among the best in the city, some with Mexican touches—like the *secretaria* (pork leg, chorizo, and cheese)—but the specialties are the *calamar* (chopped baby squid in chimichurri sauce) and *vegetariana* (a hearty stack of roasted eggplant and melted cheese). **Known for:** anything with squid or octopus (including tortas and tapas); house-brewed artisanal beers (available by the bottle); a pretty good wine list. $ *Average main: MP160* ⊠ *Av. Centenario 91, Coyoacán* ☎ *55/5658–1880* ⊕ *www.facebook.com/barracavalencianacoyoacan* Ⓜ *Viveros.*

★ Los Amantes Café & Bistro

$$ | CAFÉ | Stroll just a block south of Jardín Centenario's inevitable crowds to find this little gem with simple red-and-white-checked tablecloths and a front window lined with tantalizing displays of fresh-made cakes and pies. Indeed, sweets—as well as finely curated teas and well-crafted espresso drinks—are the specialty here, but you'll also find excellent breakfast, lunch, and dinner options, ranging from vegetable frittatas and mollettes with beans and ham in the morning to spinach-and-artichoke casserole and salmon burgers later in the day. **Known for:** enticing cakes, cookies, and brownies; plenty of sidewalk seating and a quiet courtyard; generous portions. $ *Average main: MP160* ⊠ *Calle Felipe Carrillo Puerto 19, Coyoacán* ☎ *55/7576–0946* ⊕ *www.cafelosamantes.mx* Ⓜ *Viveros.*

Los Danzantes

$$$ | MODERN MEXICAN | On the fancy side for the neighborhood, this outpost of a famed Mexican fusion restaurant in Oaxaca occupies a handsome two-story space overlooking Jardín Centenario. Artfully plated dishes like *guajolote* (organic wild turkey) smothered in mole poblano and negro sauces, and achiote-marinated *huachinango* (Gulf red snapper) with plantains, avocado, and cotija cheese reflect the kitchen's creative approach, although service can be a tad stiff, especially for laid-back Coyoacán **Known for:** regional Mexican cuisine with an emphasis on Oaxaca; romantic patio with retractable awning overlooking Jardín Centenario; impressive wine and mezcal lists. $ *Average main: MP410* ⊠ *Parque Centenario 12, Coyoacán* ☎ *55/4356–7185* ⊕ *www.losdanzantescoyoacan.com* Ⓜ *Viveros.*

Mercado Roma Coyoacán

$$ | ECLECTIC | The hip Mercado Roma has replicated its success on a slightly smaller scale with this attractive, three-story food hall a couple of blocks from both Avendia Francisco Sosa and the swanky Oasis Coyoacán shopping mall and cinema. You'll find a good variety of options, including mini-outposts of some popular restaurants around town (including El Auténtico Pato Manila and Butcher & Sons, which occupies the entire top floor), serving everything from pizza and burgers to kebabs and Thai curry bowls. **Known for:** fun, lively space; nice variety of cuisine types; craft beer and mojito stalls. $ *Average main: MP150* ⊠ *Av. Miguel Ángel de Quevedo 353, Coyoacán* ☎ *55/2155–9435* ⊕ *mrc.mercadoroma.com* Ⓜ *Miguel Ángel de Quevedo.*

Merendero Las Lupitas

$$ | MEXICAN | Eclectic paintings of Mexican scenes, colorful tilework and papel picado banners, and ladderback rush-seated chairs capture the traditional vibe of this cozy restaurant that opened here in 1959 on a lovely corner of Avenida Francisco Sosa. The charming setting is the top reason to dine here, but home-style machaca with eggs, chorizo gorditos, carne asada, and other Norteño-style dishes are affordable and tasty. **Known for:** Northern Mexico–style ("Norteño") comfort food; historic setting overlooking a famous church; atole (a traditional Mesoamerican corn-masa beverage served warm). $ *Average main: MP150* ⊠ *Calle Jardín Santa Catarina 4, Coyoacán*

☎ *55/5554–3353* 🌐 *www.facebook.com/merenderolaslupitas* [M] *Viveros.*

★ Mi Compa Chava

$$ | **SEAFOOD** | Prepare to wait for a table at this hugely popular seafood restaurant a couple of blocks from Jardín Centenario—it's known for serving big, gorgeously plated portions of sublime ceviche and aguachile. There's also a great variety of raw bar options, including oysters on the half shell, as well as fish tacos, smoked-fish pâté, seared bluefin tuna, and more. **Known for:** Pacific-style grilled, fried, and raw seafood; fried fish of the day with a seasoned-mayo dipping sauce; cajeta cheesecake. [$] *Average main: MP300* ✉ *Calle Presidente Carranza 109, Coyoacán* ☎ *55/9219–0294* 🌐 *www.instagram.com/micompachava* ⏲ *Closed Mon. No dinner* [M] *Viveros.*

Coffee and Quick Bites

★ Café Avellaneda

$ | **CAFÉ** | One of the few spots in Coyoacán with the hip factor of Roma or Condesa, this tiny artisan roaster turns out some of the best, and most interesting, coffee drinks in city as well as selling connoisseur-worthy beans to go. The classics, including single-origin pour-overs and lattes, are superb, but you'll also find tasty iced drinks, like the refreshing Greench (green tea, kefir, and soda water) and the soothing Trago Tranquila with coffee, coconut cream, pineapple, and tonic water. **Known for:** carefully sourced and roasted coffee beans; creative iced coffee and tea elixirs; meticulous brewing techniques. [$] *Average main: MP80* ✉ *Calle Higuera 40–A, Coyoacán* ☎ *55/6553–3441* 🌐 *www.facebook.com/avellanedakf* [M] *Viveros.*

Café El Jarocho

$ | **CAFÉ** | **FAMILY** | A block from Plaza Hidalgo, this old-time café whose name translates to "native of Veracruz" has a nearly fanatical following. It has stood at this prime street corner in 1953—many evenings the line for coffee, hot chocolate, mochas, and doughnuts extends down the block well past midnight. **Known for:** hot chocolate and mochas; colorful people-watching; crafts vendors selling their wares out front. [$] *Average main: MP60* ✉ *Cuauhtémoc 134, Coyoacán* ☎ *55/5554–5418* 🌐 *www.facebook.com/cafeljarocho* 💳 *No credit cards* [M] *Viveros.*

★ Happy Banh Mi

$$ | **VIETNAMESE** | This tiny counter-service Vietnamese sandwich shop with a few tables overlooking lovely Avenida Francisco Sosa serves just a few items, all of them utterly delicious. The four banh mi options (lemongrass chicken, beef, pork, or tofu) are all made with traditional fixings (jalapeños, pickled carrots, daikon, cilantro) and perfectly crunchy baguettes, and the summer roll makes for a refreshing starter. **Known for:** best banh mi sandwiches in the city; coconut panna cotta with lemongrass for dessert; attractive sidewalk seating. [$] *Average main: MP150* ✉ *Av. Francisco Sosa 266, Coyoacán* ☎ *55/5659–4494* 🌐 *www.happybanhmi.mx* ⏲ *Closed Mon. No dinner* [M] *Viveros.*

Il Vicolo Panaderia

$ | **BAKERY** | A friendly family with Italian and Mexican roots operates this tiny artisan bakery that's tucked inside a shop near Jardín Centenario and open only Thursday through Saturday, from mid-morning until they sell out (usually by 2 pm or so). You'll find crisp-but-chewy sundried-tomato-Parmesan and cranberry-walnut-fennel baguettes, flaky scones, soft and chewy amaretto and orange pastries, and lusciously gooey chocolate-banana cakes. **Known for:** savory and sweet breads made with simple, natural ingredients; baguettes in several flavors; delicious sweets. [$] *Average main: MP50* ✉ *Calle Presidente Carranza 115, Coyoacán* ☎ *55/4137–4756* 🌐 *www.facebook.com/ilvicolopanaderia* ⏲ *Closed Sun.–Wed.* [M] *Viveros.*

Kahwen Café

$ | CAFÉ | This cozy café is perfect for a pick-me-up from the well-curated list of artisan coffees and wines, all of them from highly respected producers found throughout Mexico. Just a couple of blocks from Jardín Centenario and Plaza Hidalgo, Kahwen is a happily chill space far from the crowds. **Known for:** pet-friendly seating; first-rate coffee beans available for purchase; friendly, knowledgeable staff. $ *Average main: MP80* ⊠ *Francisco Ortega 17, Coyoacán* ⊕ *www.kahwen.cafe* Ⓜ *Viveros.*

★ Mercado de Antojitos Mexicanos

$ | MEXICAN | Just a few steps down Calle Higuera from Plaza Hidalgo, this covered, open-air market with about a dozen stalls is home to some of the best street food in the neighborhood: barbacoa tacos, squash-blossom quesadillas, fresh-squeezed juices and smoothies, and plenty more, all of it affordably priced. There's nothing trendy about this bustling space where you may have to jostle a bit for a seat, but young buskers often entertain the crowds with great music. **Known for:** inexpensive, old-school street food; great people-watching; open until 11 nightly. $ *Average main: MP60* ⊠ *Calle Higuera 10, Coyoacán* Ⓜ *Viveros.*

Pastefam Caramel

$ | BAKERY | Skip the more touristy bakeries near Coyoacán's main plazas and head to this cute traditional shop on tree-lined Calle Londres, a short walk from Museo Frida Kahlo. The chocolatines, cinnamon rolls, and almond pastries are fresh, delicious, and generously portioned, and you'll also find savory poblano and other breads. **Known for:** affordable, generously sized pastries and cakes; locals snacking on the white iron benches out front; coffee or juices available from the bakery's adjacent beverage counter. $ *Average main: MP60* ⊠ *Corina 117, Coyoacán* ☎ *55/5601–3472* ⊕ *pastefam.com.mx* Ⓜ *Coyoacán.*

★ Picnic Helados

$ | ICE CREAM | This simple take-out window on a quiet side street serves the best hand-crafted ice cream and sorbet in the neighborhood, always featuring just a handful of flavors that change regularly but might include coffee-cardamom, plum–goat cheese, guava-cinnamon, or matcha tea. Picnic also sells a few kinds of delicious cookies and brownies, too. **Known for:** interesting flavors, often with seasonal fruits; cute take-out window (but no seating); chocolate brownies. $ *Average main: MP50* ⊠ *Calle Malintzin 205–2, Coyoacán* ☎ *55/5510–9209* ⊕ *picnic-helados.negocio.site* ⊗ *Closed Mon. and Tues.* Ⓜ *Coyoacán.*

Super Tacos Chupacabras

$ | MEXICAN | Open all night and drawing a particularly spirited crowd during the wee hours, this no-frills taco stand named for the vampire-ish "goat sucker" of Latin American folklore serves joyfully messy, overstuffed pastor, chorizo, beef, cecina, and other meaty tacos for around just MP25 apiece. The casual seating area, set below a highway overpass, has several metal picnic tables. **Known for:** generous array of free fixings (potatoes, grilled onions, jicama, salsas, and more); late-night dining; steps from Torre Mítikah and Coyoacán metro. $ *Average main: MP75* ⊠ *Av. Río Churubusco 187, Coyoacán* Ⓜ *Coyoacán.*

 Hotels

★ Agata Boutique Hotel

$$ | B&B/INN | With its helpful staff that loves to pamper guests, an extensive spa menu, and gorgeously appointed rooms and bathrooms, this intimate wellness-focused guesthouse an easy walk from both Museo Frida Kahlo and Coyoacán's main plazas appeals to guests seeking a mindful getaway. A creative multicourse breakfast, which you order from an extensive menu, is included in the rates, and several excellent bars and restaurants are within a block or two. **Pros:** soothing

facials, massages, and other spa treatments are available; thoughtful staff that can arrange cooking classes and other experiences; lovely rooftop terrace. **Cons:** not suitable for families or travelers with pets; often books up well in advance; on a busy street with some traffic noise. $ *Rooms from: MP2900* ✉ *Av. México 21, Coyoacán* ☎ *55/1741–8670* ⊕ *www. agatahotelboutiquespa.com* ⇆ *4 rooms* ❑ *Free Breakfast* Ⓜ *Coyoacán.*

Casa Moctezuma

$$ | B&B/INN | FAMILY | On a quiet side street a few blocks east of Coyoacán's historic plazas, this elegant red hacienda captures the neighborhood's Spanish Colonial charm while offering modern in-room amenities like kitchens and fast Wi-Fi. **Pros:** great for longer stays; free use of bikes; each room has its own terrace or outdoor space. **Cons:** no on-site parking; eclectic, somewhat quirky decor isn't for everyone; far from the city center. $ *Rooms from: MP2200* ✉ *Moctezuma 79, Coyoacán* ☎ *55/6070– 4670* ⊕ *www.casamoctezuma.com* ⇆ *12 rooms* ❑ *No Meals* Ⓜ *Viveros.*

Casa Tamayo

$ | B&B/INN | This unassuming and exceptionally affordable guesthouse on pretty Calle Presidente Carranza, which parallels Avenida Francisco Sosa and is just a short hop from Jardín Centenario, offers pleasantly furnished rooms and public areas decorated with a carefully curated collection of contemporary Mexican art. **Pros:** peaceful setting just steps from Avenida Francisco Sosa; beautiful yard with flowering plants; very reasonable rates. **Cons:** far from city center; some rooms are a bit cozy; no on-site parking. $ *Rooms from: MP1200* ✉ *Calle Presidente Carranza 220, Coyoacán* ☎ *55/5554–0655* ⊕ *www.casatamayo. com* ⇆ *4 rooms* ❑ *No Meals* Ⓜ *Viveros.*

Casa Tuna

$$ | B&B/INN | This peaceful oasis that's just a couple of blocks from Jardín Centenario is set around an art-filled,

early 20th-century mansion abundant with inviting common spaces, including a shared kitchen, entertainment lounge, and patios shaded by orange and magnolia trees. Some rooms have kitchenettes and terraces. **Pros:** in the heart of Coyoacán; stunning rooftop terrace; within two blocks of several excellent restaurants. **Cons:** breakfast, though excellent, costs extra; you can hear some noise from the nearby plazas (especially on weekends); far from city center. $ *Rooms from: MP2600* ✉ *Francisco Ortega 8, Coyoacán* ☎ *55/6070–4670* ⊕ *www.tunacoyoacan.com* ⇆ *12 rooms* ❑ *No Meals* Ⓜ *Viveros.*

★ H21 Hospedaje Boutique

$$ | B&B/INN | From the unassuming exterior on lively Calle Higuera, you'd never guess such a plush retreat lies within, complete with lushly landscaped gardens and seven individually furnished guest rooms with air-conditioning and heating (uncommon in Mexico City guest houses) and smart TVs with fast streaming—some also have kitchenettes. **Pros:** lots of bar and café options nearby; chic design; personal, thoughtful service. **Cons:** far from city center; on a narrow bar-lined street with a lot of foot traffic; no breakfast available. $ *Rooms from: MP3500* ✉ *Calle Higuera 21, Coyoacán* ☎ *55/6414–2782* ⊕ *www.h21.mx* ⇆ *7 rooms* ❑ *No Meals* Ⓜ *Viveros.*

 Nightlife

Centenario 107

BARS | Midway between Coyoacán's plazas and the Cineteca Nacional film center, this spacious, conversation-filled bar and grill stands out for its extensive selection of both Mexican and international craft beers on tap and by the bottle. But there's also a big all-day-and-night food menu featuring pretty tasty pizzas, burgers, pastas, sandwiches, and the like. ✉ *Centenario 107, Coyoacán* ☎ *55/4752–6369* ⊕ *www.facebook.com/ centenario107* Ⓜ *Coyoacán.*

El Convento

BARS | Although this dramatic space in a former 16th-century convent is better known as a restaurant, having drinks on the cloistered central patio is the best way to enjoy a visit here. The food is fine, but it's more about the setting, which is especially lovely around dusk, making it a great option for predinner cocktails. There's live music some evenings, too. ⊠ *Fernández Leal 96, Coyoacán* ☎ *55/7426–5545* ⊕ *www.conventocoyoacan.com* Ⓜ *Viveros.*

El Hijo del Cuervo

BARS | Students and intellectuals of all ages pack "the Raven's Son," thanks to an interesting mix of rock, jazz, and other live music performances as well as intriguing art shows on the walls. Set on the northwest corner of Jardín Centenario, it's also a nice spot to enjoy a beer or a light bite to eat on the patio. It stages occasional theater shows, too. ⊠ *Jardín Centenario 17, Coyoacán* ☎ *55/5658–7824* ⊕ *www.elhijodelcuervo.com.mx* Ⓜ *Viveros.*

★ Júpiter Cervecería

BEER GARDENS | This bustling, stylish craft beer bar stands out for its attractive setting inside a high-ceilinged space with vertical-garden walls and an exceptionally varied selection of bottled and draft beers, most of them Mexican. There's also a great menu of elevated tacos, tortas, and other bar food, plus ping-pong and live music many evenings. ⊠ *Malintzin 199, Coyoacán* ☎ *55/5280–6987* ⊕ *www.facebook.com/jupitercerveceria* Ⓜ *Viveros.*

La Bipo

BARS | A trendy, youthful crowd congregates in this always-busy bar co-owned by actor Diego Luna and decorated with pop-art murals. You can sometimes catch alternative and rock bands performing, and there's better-than-average bar food

(burgers, Jamaica quesadillas, seafood tacos, etc.) along with an extensive selection of mezcal and other top-shelf booze. ⊠ *Calle Malintzin 155, Coyoacán* ☎ *55/5484–8230* Ⓜ *Viveros.*

★ La Calaca

BARS | Talented mariachis, a long drinks list, and very tasty (though slightly expensive for the neighborhood) contemporary Mexican food are among the draws of this trendy modern cantina across the street from Jardín Centenario. But the biggest boast is the gracious setting: the main dining and drinking area is in a scenic courtyard with giant trees and a glass roof. There's a cozier bar upstairs, and next to the entrance, La Calaca has a cute little shop that sells fun gifts, crafts, and artwork. ⊠ *Av. Centenario 2, Coyoacán* ☎ *55/5554–7652* ⊕ *www.facebook.com/lacalacacoyoacan* Ⓜ *Viveros.*

La Coyoacana

BARS | A few steps from Plaza Hidalgo, this venerable cantina has been a neighborhood fixture for years. It's nothing fancy, but the food and drink are inexpensive, and mariachis perform on the cheerful covered patio out back. ⊠ *Calle Higuera 14, Coyoacán* ☎ *55/5658–5337* ⊕ *www.facebook.com/la.coyoacanaoficial* Ⓜ *Viveros.*

Mezcalero

BARS | As the name suggests, the considerable selection of mezcal is the big draw at this very popular cocktail bar behind San Juan Batista Church. If you're not sure what you'd like, try a flight of three or five one-ounce pours. DJs spin good music later in the evening, and there's pretty tasty bar food to pair with your sips. ⊠ *Calle Caballocalco 14, Coyoacán* ☎ *55/5554–7027* ⊕ *www.facebook.com/mezcalerocoyoacan* Ⓜ *Viveros.*

🎭 Performing Arts

La Titería

PUPPET SHOWS | FAMILY | Also known as Casa de las Marionetas, or House of Puppets, this small kids-oriented cultural center and theater uses (you guessed it) puppets in its theater and music performances but also shows films and offers other kinds of family-friendly programming. ⊠ *Calle Vicente Guerrero 7, Coyoacán* ☎ *55/5662–6023* ⊕ *www.latiteria.mx* Ⓜ *Coyoacán.*

★ Teatro Bar El Vicio

THEATER | Since 2005, this fabulous little cabaret theater and bar has been delighting crowds with irreverent, original shows, often with a decidedly queer and provocatively political bent. ⊠ *Calle Madrid 13, Coyoacán* ☎ *55/3753–3529* ⊕ *www.elvicio.com.mx* Ⓜ *Coyoacán.*

★ Teatro La Capilla

THEATER | FAMILY | Founded in 1953 by the gay playwright and poet Salvador Novo, who's sometimes referred to as Mexico's Oscar Wilde, this intimate theater hosts a wide range of mostly contemporary indie plays. Productions rotate often, and there's something going on virtually every night of the week. It's one of the best small theaters in the city, and many performances are geared to kids and teens. There's also a bar and restaurant attached. ⊠ *Calle Madrid 13, Coyoacán* ☎ *55/5658–6285* ⊕ *www.teatrolacapilla.com* Ⓜ *Coyoacán.*

Teatro Santa Catarina UNAM

THEATER | Situated just off Avendia Francisco Sosa across the courtyard from beautiful Santa Catarina Chapel, this fairly intimate black box theater operates through the acclaimed drama program at UNAM (Universidad Nacional Autónoma de México). It's the site of often experimental and contemporary works. Although small, its productions are top-notch. ⊠ *Jardín Santa Catarina 10, Coyoacán* ✣ *Corner of Av. Francisco Sosa and Av. Progreso* ☎ *55/5658–0560* ⊕ *www.teatrounam.com.mx/teatro* Ⓜ *Viveros.*

🛍 Shopping

★ Centro Cultural Elena Garro

BOOKS | FAMILY | Named for the late novelist and screenwriter Elena Garro, this huge bookstore occupies an early-20th-century mansion that's been enclosed within a stunning contemporary glass-walled, two-story addition. You'll find a terrific selection of literary and artistic titles as well as concerts, lectures, children's events (from puppet shows to storytelling), and other cultural programming. There's also a café with an enchanting garden seating area. ⊠ *Calle Fernández Leal 43, Coyoacán* ☎ *55/5554–6198* ⊕ *www.educal.com.mx/elenagarro* Ⓜ *Viveros.*

Ecosentli

FOOD | This cute family-run shop specializes in artisanal or handmade foods and some other products (soaps, jewelry, crafts) primarily from the state of Puebla. There's a selection of coffee beans and mezcals from small producers, plus mezquite honey, salsas, sweets, and other organic products. The shop also has a small coffee bar and a tortillería serving up handmade corn quesadillas filled with chicken and mole, nopales, mushrooms, and other tasty ingredients. ⊠ *Calle Presidente Carranza 138, Coyoacán* ☎ *222/521–7802* ⊕ *www.ecosentli.com* Ⓜ *Viveros.*

Fuerza Mítica Bazar

MARKET | Located in a narrow courtyard along lovely Avenida Francisco Sosa, this lively market is devoted to locally made crafts, gifts, clothing, body-care products, and artisanal foods. Edible treats include homemade fudge, hand pies, chocolates, and mezcals. ⊠ *Av. Francisco Sosa 171, Coyoacán* ☎ *55/5184–5778* Ⓜ *Viveros.*

HomoHabilis

LEATHER GOODS | At this friendly boutique, artisans hand-craft gorgeous, stylish leather products, including backpacks, computer bags, wallets, purses, journals, and aprons. The level of quality is superb, and the goods have a timeless look. ⊠ *Higuera 56, Coyoacán* ☎ *55/7156–7112* ⊕ *www.homohabilis.mx* Ⓜ *Viveros.*

★ Mercado de Coyoacán

MARKET | Although it's not as big as some of the city's other markets, this lively mercado just a couple of blocks from Frida Kahlo's house is one of the most popular with visitors, in large part because of the famous food stalls at its center doling out plates of delicious ceviche, octopus, shrimp, chicken tinga, picadillo, and other fillings for about MP40 to MP50 per portion. But you'll also find aisles of the usual fresh juices, produce, spices, candies, and other goodies typical of Mexican markets as well as a number of souvenir and homeware vendors (mostly near the northwest entrance) and many other food vendors. Arguably even better than the tostadas are the quesadillas sold from a tiny little stand at the west entrance, directly across from pretty Jardín Allende, a small landscaped park with benches and pathways; on weekends, artists sell their wares in the park and a DJ spins traditional Latin music, which locals of all ages dance to—it's great fun to watch. For a sweet treat, stop by Chocolate Mexicano Dulce Olivia, which serves sipping chocolates and carries a vast array of artisan chocolate bars produced by small, often family-run makers from throughout the country. ⊠ *Calle Ignacio Allende at Calle Xicoténcatl, Coyoacán* ☎ *55/4072–1596* ⊕ *www. facebook.com/mercadodecoyoacanno.89* Ⓜ *Coyoacán.*

Mineralia

SPECIALTY STORE | Pick up an actual piece of Mexico at this colorful gem shop that specializes in both rough and polished minerals and stones from all around the country, including obsidian, jasper, lapis lazuli, rose quartz, amethyst, and more. Fossils and sculptures are also sold here, and prices are quite reasonable. ⊠ *Francisco Ortega 32, Coyoacán* ☎ *55/5554–5922* ⊕ *www.mineralia.com. mx* Ⓜ *Viveros.*

★ Taller Experimental de Cerámica

CERAMICS | At this tree-shaded compound founded in 1964 and situated midway between Museo Frida Kahlo and Jardín Centenario, exquisite Japanese-inspired bowls, plates, vases, tea sets, and other ceramics are produced and sold at quite reasonable prices. Ceramics workshops are offered as well, and as you're browsing the wares, you can say hello to the owners' friendly cadre of xoloitzcuintlis (the distinctive hairless dogs that have been a part of Mexican culture for more than 3,500 years). ⊠ *Centenario 63, Coyoacán* ☎ *55/5554–6960* ⊕ *www. facebook.com/ceramicadiazdecossio* Ⓜ *Coyoacán.*

Chapter 12

SAN ÁNGEL

Updated by
Andrew Collins

⊙ Sights	🍴 Restaurants	🛏 Hotels	🛍 Shopping	🍸 Nightlife
★★★☆☆	★★★☆☆	★★☆☆☆	★★★★★	★★☆☆☆

NEIGHBORHOOD SNAPSHOT

TOP EXPERIENCES

■ **Museo Casa Estudio Diego Rivera y Frida Kahlo.**
This compound of angular, modernist buildings filled
with artwork and some of Rivera's personal effects is
a must for fans of these two creative icons.

■ **Museo del Carmen.** View ancient mummies,
saunter through a leafy garden sanctuary, and admire
an eclectic collection of art and history exhibits in this
beautifully preserved early-17th-century religious
building.

■ **Parroquia de San Jacinto.** It's a short stroll from
the neighborhood's main shopping area to the peaceful courtyard of this centuries-old church constructed
of volcanic rock and known for its ornate interior.

■ **El Cardenal.** Kick off your afternoon of hunting for
handicrafts and gifts with a leisurely late breakfast at
this gracious bi-level restaurant serving well-prepared
Mexican classics.

■ **Shopping around Plaza San Jacinto.** Dozens of
street vendors, numerous boutiques, and the neighborhood's most famous retail draw, El Bazaar Sábado,
make this one of the best shopping districts in
Mexico.

GETTING HERE

Along with neighboring Coyoacán, San Ángel is in
the city's southern section; it's about 9 km (6 miles)
south of Roma and Condesa and 12 km (7 miles)
south of Centro Histórico. Uber fares from the
airport or the city center run about MP100–MP180.
By Metro, you can take the 3 line to Coyoacán,
Viveros, or Miguel Ángel de Quevedo or the 7 line to
the final stop Barranca del Muerto, but none of these
stations is in the center of the neighborhood, so
expect a 15- to 25-minute walk to most points of
interest (but the area is very safe for walking). From
Coyoacán, it's a quick Uber ride (around MP60) or
picturesque 45- to 60-minute walk via Avendia de la
Paz, Calle Arenal, and Avendia Francisco Sosa. The
neighborhood also has a fair amount of free street
parking as well as several inexpensive but secure
lots.

OFF-THE-BEATEN PATH

■ **Plaza Loreto.** A 15-min-
ute walk south of the
neighborhood's heart,
this shopping center built
around converted ware-
houses contains a handful
of stylish retailers, the
refined La Taberna del León
restaurant, and an under-
rated branch of free Museo
Soumaya. ⊠ *Altamirano
46* ☏ *M. A. de Quevedo.*

PLANNING YOUR TIME

■ Allow at least four hours
and ideally a full day to
visit this neighborhood
known for its boutiques
and street vendors selling
authentic Mexican crafts
and artwork. The most
impressive of these retail
spaces, Bazaar Sábado, is
open only on Saturday,
making that the most desirable but also most crowded
day to go; you'll contend
with fewer people but still
find plenty of great shopping if you come another
day. Avoid Monday, though,
as the handful of excellent
museums are closed then.
Consider combining your
visit to San Ángel with
nearby Coyoacán.

A small colonial enclave of cobblestone streets, stone walls, stately pastel houses, lush foliage, blooming jacaranda trees, and gardens drenched in bougainvillea, San Ángel is one of the city's most inviting outlying neighborhoods. Its historic core abounds with boutiques, design shops, arts and crafts galleries, and both casual and fashionable restaurants. It's an especially popular destination on Saturday, when its famed Bazaar Sábado draws legions of shoppers.

Many who come to San Ángel combine their adventure with adjacent Coyoacán, which can be an effective strategy if you're short on time. But there are a few excellent museums and some good restaurants in San Ángel, so if you can, set aside a full day to shop, dine, and take your time exploring its three most noteworthy attractions: Museo del Carmen, Museo Casa Estudio Diego Rivera y Frida Kahlo, and Museo de Arte Carrillo Gil.

Like Coyoacán, this community functioned as its own distinct, agrarian municipality from the precolonial Mexica (Aztec) era and its settlement in the late 1500s by the Spaniards—who constructed the San Jacinto and El Carmen monasteries that came to define the area—to the early 20th century, when San Ángel became fully part of Mexico City. The construction in the 1950s of sprawling Ciudad Universitaria to the south as well as two wide and modern (if not especially pleasant) north–south boulevards, Avenida de los Insurgentes (the longest street in the city) and Avenida Revolución, spurred the area's rapid urbanization. Today you'll find a number of high-rise office buildings, residential towers, and shopping malls on the busy streets just beyond San Ángel's charming and historic core.

Enamored of the area's pleasant climate, rural character, and striking setting atop fields of volcanic rock, Mexico City's wealthy elite built lavish haciendas and mansions in San Ángel during the late 18th and 19th centuries to use as country homes. The neighborhood has maintained a reputation for affluence ever since. Some of the grandest of these homes have been converted into high-end restaurants or shopping arcades. On either sides of Avenidas Revolución and Insurgentes, however, you'll also discover blocks of narrow cobblestone lanes flanked by gorgeous old houses. When you need a break from the hubbub of retail activity around the main plazas, take a stroll through these tranquil, picturesque residential districts, which lie immediately west and north of Plaza San Jacinto and south and east of Parque de la Bombilla.

Sights

Centro Cultural Isidro Fabela and Museo Casa del Risco

HISTORIC HOME | This 1681 mansion, which contains both a cultural center and Museo Casa del Risco, is one of the prettiest houses facing the Plaza San Jacinto. The huge 18th-century Risco Fountain—exploding with colorful porcelain tiles, shells, and mosaics—dominates the eastern wall of the enclosed courtyard. Inside, the upper galleries contain a splendid if slightly somber collection of 17th- and 18th-century European baroque and colonial Mexican paintings and furnishings, all donated by the house's last owner, statesman and politician Isidro Fabela, who died in 1964. Fabela also donated books and magazines to a small library behind the museum (by way of a lovely patio) that's open to the public. Events and rotating art exhibits are staged throughout the year. ⊠ *Plaza San Jacinto 15, San Angel* ☎ *55/5616–2711* ⊕ *www.isidrofabela.org.mx* ✉ *Free* ⊙ *Closed Mon.* Ⓜ *M. A. de Quevedo.*

★ Museo Casa Estudio Diego Rivera y Frida Kahlo

ART MUSEUM | This small museum compound is where Diego and Frida lived, painted, loved, and fought (they divorced briefly in 1939) from 1934 to 1940; its three angular red and blue buildings with large multipane windows and a cacti-filled courtyard is stylistically the antithesis of the traditional Spanish Colonial Museo Frida Kahlo just a few miles away in Coyoacán. In the red main house, some of Rivera's final paintings rest on easels, and you can see his denim jacket and shoes on a wicker chair with his modest little bed and side table made up as though the artist might return at any moment. In the building's studio you can view giant papier-mâché sculptures (some of the pre-Hispanic pottery that Rivera collected) and other curious figurines and colorful folk art. The buildings' unusual, and at the time highly avant garde, designs are a big part of what makes a visit here so interesting. Architect Juan O'Gorman, who devised these buildings in 1931, was a close friend of Rivera's and lived on the property in a third structure that today, like the blue house that Frida resided in, contains rotating exhibits.

Interesting architectural features include several curving concrete exterior and interior staircases, and a bridge that connects the rooftops of Diego's and Frida's homes—a convenient passageway that allowed the two simultaneous access to and space from one another. ⊠ *Calle Diego Rivera, at Av. Altavista, San Angel* ☎ *55/8647–5470* ⊕ *www.inba.gob.mx/ recinto/51* ✉ *MP45; free Sun.* ⊙ *Closed Mon.* Ⓜ *Barranco Del Muerto.*

Museo de Arte Carrillo Gil

ART MUSEUM | This cube-shape art museum built in 1972 by businessman and collector Dr. Alvar Carrillo Gil is one of the top venues in the city for viewing vanguard art. Rotating exhibits showcase contemporary art in a wide range of media, often by young, emerging artists. At times you can also view portions of the immense permanent collection, which consists of more than 2,000 works, about 1,400 of which Gil collected himself. These include more than 150 murals and paintings by José Clemente Orozco, 45 works by David Alfaro Siqueiros, and important pieces by Rivera, Klee, and Picasso. ⊠ *Av. Revolución 1608, San Angel* ☎ *55/8647–5450* ⊕ *www.*

museodeartecarrillogil.com ✉ MP65;
free Sun. ⏱ Closed Mon. Ⓜ M. A. de
Quevedo.

★ Museo del Carmen

CHURCH | Erected by Carmelite friars
with the help of an Indigenous chieftain
between 1615 and 1628, this church—
with its domes, frescoes, vaulted
archways, fountains, and gardens—was
never actually a convent, despite its
name. Though some locals might tell you
otherwise, nuns never actually lived here.
The church still operates (you can enter
it for free from a separate entrance next
door), but part of the church complex
has been converted into Museo del
Carmen, with a fine collection of 16th-
to 18th-century religious paintings and
icons. Much of the religious art (along
with a captivating collection of photos
that depict San Ángel and the southern
portions of the city during the early 20th
century) is on the second floor of the
adjoining Casa de Acueducto, which
overlooks another courtyard fringed by
an interesting ancient aqueduct. It's also
worth visiting the dozen-or-so mummified corpses tucked away in the crypt—a
creepy but fascinating sight, for sure. For
a perhaps much-needed breath of fresh
air, saunter out to the gracious rear garden, with its shady trees and benches.
There's usually an excellent temporary
exhibit as well, typically touching on
some element of Mexico City history and
culture. ✉ Av. Revolución 4, San Angel
☎ 55/5616–1504 ⊕ lugares.inah.gob.mx/
es/museos-inah/museo/404-museo-de-el-
carmen ✉ MP60 ⏱ Closed Mon. Ⓜ M.
de Quevedo.

Museo Soumaya Plaza Loreto

ART MUSEUM | The Plaza Loreto branch
of the famed art museum in Polanco
contains several huge exhibition rooms
set inside the upper level of a colonial-era
warehouse building that now houses
shops and restaurants. It's a bit south of
the heart of San Ángel, and not necessarily worth a trip all on its own, but

admission is free and the exhibits are
quite interesting and include an extensive
look at the life and work of renowned
Mexican architect Pedro Ramírez Vázquez
(of Estadio Azteca and Museo Nacional
de Antropologia fame). There are also
wonderful collections of Venetian paintings, Flemish tapestries, and early Mexican photography. ✉ Rio de la Magdalena
at Av. Revolución, San Angel ☎ 55/1103–
9866 ⊕ www.museosoumaya.org ✉ Free
Ⓜ M. A. de Quevedo.

Parque de la Bombilla

CITY PARK | At the eastern edge of the
neighborhood, not far from the border
with Coyoacán, this handsome park is
anchored by a striking art deco obelisk
monument to Álvaro Obregón, the
much-lauded general of the Mexican
Revolution and 39th president of Mexico.
In 1928, shortly after his reelection to the
presidency, Obregón was assassinated
while dining in La Bombilla restaurant,
which stood exactly where the monument and park are today—they opened
seven years after his death, in 1935.
A long, shallow reflecting pool frames
the monument, which is illuminated
dramatically at night, and is surrounded
by beautifully tended gardens and rows
of trees. Rife with benches, the park is
a perfect place to enjoy a picnic or relax
with a book; it also makes a nice break if
you're strolling to or from Coyoacán via
Avendia Francisco Sosa. Along Avendia
de la Paz, which forms the park's northern border, you'll find a series of well-
stocked, bargain-filled used-book stalls.
The streets immediately south of the
park, a neighborhood known as Chimal-
istac, are lined with lovely old homes and
gardens. ✉ Av. de los Insurgentes Sur at
Av. de la Paz, San Angel ✉ Free Ⓜ M. A.
de Quevedo.

Parroquia de San Jacinto

CHURCH | With its ancient dome and roof
line rising above the shops that flank
the west edge of Plaza San Jacinto, this
church built by Dominican friars during

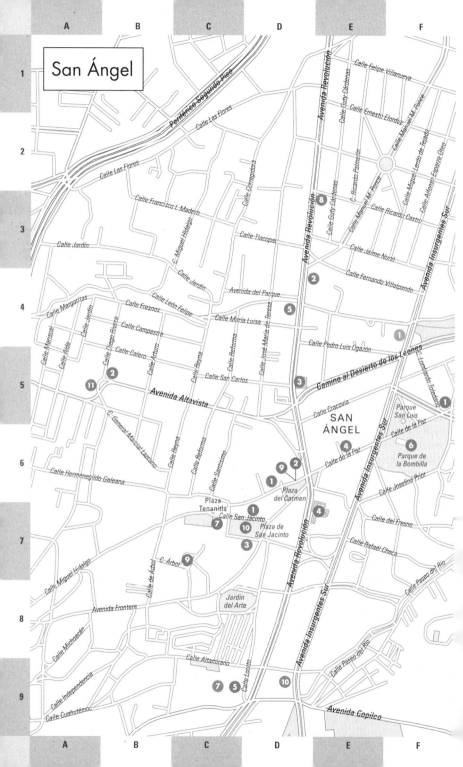

San Ángel

Sights ▼

1 Centro Cultural
Isidro Fabela and Museo
Casa del Risco **D7**

2 Museo Casa Estudio
Diego Rivera y Frida Kahlo........ **B5**

3 Museo de Arte Carrillo Gil........ **D5**

4 Museo del Carmen **E7**

5 Museo Soumaya Plaza Loreto **C9**

6 Parque de la Bombilla.............. **F6**

7 Parroquia de San Jacinto **C7**

8 Parroquia de
San Sebastián Mártir **G6**

9 Plaza de los Arcángeles **C7**

10 Plaza San Jacinto **D7**

Restaurants ▼

1 Bistro 83 .... **D6**

2 Cafebrería El Péndulo **D4**

3 Cataly **D7**

4 El Cardenal **E6**

5 Eloise................................ **D4**

6 Gruta Ehden **I1**

7 La Taberna del León................ **C9**

8 Loretta Chic Bistrot................ **E3**

9 Mercado del Carmen.............. **D6**

10 Mojama Oyster Bar **D9**

11 Restaurante San Angel Inn....... **A5**

12 Taro................................ **H7**

Quick Bites ▼

1 Bakers **F5**

2 Díaz de Cafe **D6**

3 Tierra Garat........................ **G1**

Hotels ▼

1 Krystal Grand Suites **F4**

12

San Ángel

KEY

1 Sights

1 Restaurants

1 Quick Bites

1 Hotels

The Museo del Carmen features religious art, a crypt with mummified bodies, and a charming garden.

the 16th and 17th centuries is best viewed from its gracious courtyard. From the beautiful gardens, you can take in the view of the church's distinctive facade of volcanic stone and chipped and faded salmon-pink stucco. It's a peaceful spot to relax and catch your breath after shopping around San Ángel, and the interior—with its ornate Spanish Rococo–style retablo behind the altar—is stunning. ⊠ Plaza San Jacinto 18 Bis, San Angel ☎ 55/5616–2059 ⊕ www.facebook.com/sanjacintoarqmx ⊠ Free.

Parroquia San Sebastián Mártir

CHURCH | Built in the mid-1500s and containing a remarkably ornate, 18th-century altarpiece, this small oft-photographed church with high, timber-beam ceilings anchors a small plaza in a quiet section of the charmingly historic Chimalistac neighborhood. More intimate than many of the city's noteworthy places of worship, the church is unusual for having a sanctuary that's much wider than it is deep. ⊠ Plaza Federico Gamboa 11, Chimalistac, San Angel ☎ 55/5661–6041 ⊠ Free ⊙ Closed Sun. Ⓜ M. A. de Quevedo.

Plaza de Los Arcángeles

CITY PARK | From Plaza San Jacinto, it's a leisurely 10-minute stroll through an elegant neighborhood of cobblestone streets to reach this tiny, tranquil park that few people, except for the residents of its surrounding homes, ever see. The verdant sliver of dense shrubbery, specimen trees, bougainvillas, and flower beds is laced with flagstone pathways and contains several statues as well as three ornate stone benches named for the three arcángeles for whom the little park is dedicated: San Miguel, San Gabriel, and San Rafael. Virtually free of car traffic, it's an idyllic place to sneak away from the crowds of weekend shoppers and briefly imagine life as a resident of this historic neighborhood. ⊠ 2a Frontera 37, San Angel ⊠ Free Ⓜ M. A. de Quevedo.

★ Plaza San Jacinto

PLAZA/SQUARE | This picturesque plaza lined with palatial 18th- and 19th-century homes as well as a number of galleries, boutiques, and restaurants constitutes the heart of San Ángel. On the north side of the plaza, the superb arts-and-crafts market Bazaar Sábado is held all day Saturday, and just west up Calle Benito Juarez there's an additional covered market on weekends where you can find less expensive knickknacks and goods. Continue a block down the hill along shop-lined Calle Madero to reach Plaza del Carmen, a smaller park with pathways and benches where still more artists sell their works on Saturday. A memorial plaque on Plaza San Jacinto's west side lists the names of about 50 Irish soldiers from St. Patrick's Battalion who helped Mexico during the "unjust North American invasion" of 1847. These men had been enticed to desert the ranks of U.S. General Zachary Taylor by appeals to the historic and religious ties between Spain and Ireland, siding with the Mexicans in the Mexican-American War. Following their capture by U.S. forces, all were hanged (16 of them on Plaza San Jacinto). ■ TIP→ **If the crowds around the Plaza become a little overwhelming (as often happens on Saturday), walk down quiet, cobblestone Calle de la Amargura, behind Bazaar Sábado, toward Avenida Revolución. It's a lovely lane that's absent of vendors and leads past several beautiful homes.** ⊠ *Plaza San Jacinto, San Angel* Ⓜ *M. A. de Quevedo.*

🍴 Restaurants

Bistro 83

$$$ | **MODERN MEXICAN** | Set in the back of a small but posh contemporary shopping arcade overlooking a tranquil formal garden just off Plaza del Carmen, chic Bistro 83 is a go-to for lavish contemporary Euro-Mexican fare, such as escargot sautéed in garlic butter, grilled red snapper

Art in the Wild

On Saturday, San Ángel's two historic central squares—Plaza San Jacinto and Plaza del Carmen—morph into vibrant, colorful art markets. Take your time as you venture through these two spaces, which are connected by a short, narrow lane. Even if you're not looking to buy something, it's a wonderful opportunity to view local art and chat with those who create it.

with a lemon-caper sauce, and tuna tartare tostadas with a soy-ginger marinade. During the day, enjoy a drawn-out feast on the classy patio. **Known for:** views of lush green gardens; perfectly grilled steaks and burgers; weekend brunch. Ⓢ *Average main: MP420* ⊠ *Calle de la Amargura 17, San Angel* ☎ *55/5616–4911* ⊕ *www.bistro83.com.mx* ⊗ *No dinner Sun.* Ⓜ *M. A. de Quevedo.*

★ Cafebrería El Péndulo

$$ | **ECLECTIC** | Located beside Centro Cultural Helénico, this latest branch of the chainlet of stylish bookstore-restaurants contains three levels designed with massive glass windows, loft mezzanines, and wide bridges and staircases—it's basically a modern tree house for hungry book lovers. The encyclopedic menu of creatively conceived food and drink includes Mexican, American, and European staples, from burgers to breakfast sandwiches to macadamia-nut cheesecake, but what makes this place special is the artful aesthetic. **Known for:** well-prepared gastropub fare; seating placed throughout a well-stocked bookstore; late-night dining. Ⓢ *Average main: MP200* ⊠ *Av. Revolución 1500, San Angel* ☎ *55/3640–4540* ⊕ *www.pendulo. com* Ⓜ *Barranca del Muerto.*

Meal Times in Mexico City

Traditionally, in Mexico the most substantial meal of the day is *la comida*, and it happens roughly between 1:30 and 4:30 pm. Breakfast is usually served in restaurants starting around 8 am, while Mexicans tend to prefer eating light at night, often enjoying a simple dinner (*la cena*) between 8:30 or 9:30.

These customs sometimes confound visitors used to lunching around noon and saving their largest meal for dinnertime. But in diverse and cosmopolitan Mexico City, you'll find plenty of restaurants that serve meals at times that suit both visitors and locals, not too mention countless cafés, taquerías, and street vendors doling out tacos and other quick bites throughout the day. Just keep in mind that some establishments—especially more traditional ones—may not open for lunch until 1 pm, and if you show up for dinner before 8, you may encounter a fairly empty dining room. Also note that on Sunday, even many

trendy international restaurants close by 6 pm.

Although not many restaurants in Mexico City offer specific "brunch" menus, plenty do offer late-morning and early afternoon dining that's very typical of what might be called brunch in other parts of the world. Think expansive menus featuring a mix of breakfast and lunch dishes, along with free-flowing cocktails and a charming setting—there may even be live music. Especially in affluent neighborhoods like Polanco and San Ángel, wonderfully inviting brunchlike experiences abound on weekends and even at some restaurants during the week.

Finally, if you're a fan of the morning meal, take comfort in knowing that breakfast (*el desayuno*) is highly popular in Mexico City, and typically a great value. Many restaurants offer package deals (*paquetes*) that include your main dish, coffee, fresh fruit or fresh-squeezed juice, and—best of all—a decadently delicious pastry of your choosing.

Cataly

$$ | **ITALIAN** | Just off Plaza San Jacinto, this smart and contemporary café offers a relatively calm respite from the bustle of weekend shoppers and is particularly popular for brunch. The menu focuses on creative thin-crust pizzas, bountiful salads, avocado toast, and panini sandwiches, and the mimosas are always flowing. **Known for:** adjacent boutique, de Corazón, selling beautiful decorative arts; charming, dog-friendly terrace; gelato in interesting (cardamom, amaretto-mascarpone) flavors. [$] *Average main: MP210* ⊠ *Calle del Dr. Gálvez 20, San Angel* ☎ *55/5106–0299* ⊕ *www.cataly.com.mx* Ⓜ *M. A. de Quevedo.*

★ El Cardenal

$$ | **MEXICAN** | Although not as historic as the original in El Centro (there are four locations in all), this beloved outpost of one of the city's most highly regarded traditional Mexican restaurants occupies a courtly redbrick mansion with high ceilings and expansive terraces, a setting that's ideal for a leisurely weekend brunch before shopping around nearby Plaza San Jacinto. The menu is extensive and includes consistently well-executed renditions of such regional specialties as chilaquiles rojo with cecina, Oaxacan-style chicken mole, pan de elote with clotted cream, and chiles en nogada (in September). **Known for:** exceptionally

Within Parque de la Bombilla, you'll find a monument to Álvaro Obregón, one of the heroes of the Mexican Revolution.

thoughtful and knowledgeable servers; grand, elegant setting; weekend brunch or dinner. $ *Average main: MP290* ✉ *Av. de la Paz 32, San Angel* ☎ *55/5550–0293* ⊕ *www.restauranteelcardenal.com* ⊘ *No dinner* Ⓜ *M. A. de Quevedo.*

Eloise
$$$ | MODERN FRENCH | A swanky spot for celebrating a special meal or simply savoring artful plates of opulent modern French fare—including crème brûlée de foie gras, truffled asparagus with Parmesan, and flank steak–frites Béarnaise—Eloise could be faulted only for its slightly ho-hum decor. The food is consistently excellent, right down to the indulgent desserts and globally representative wine list. **Known for:** dressy, special-occasion ambience; eight-hour-braised short ribs bourguignonne; outstanding wine list. $ *Average main: MP430* ✉ *Av. Revolución 1521, San Angel* ☎ *56/3017–7603* ⊕ *www.facebook.com/restauranteeloise* ⊘ *No dinner Sun.* Ⓜ *Barranca del Muerto.*

Gruta Ehden
$$ | LEBANESE | Established in 1976 by owners whose grandparents emigrated from Lebanon to Mexico in 1930, this casual spot with red tiles and hammered-tin light fixtures serves some of the most authentic and flavorful Middle Eastern food in the city. A rewarding way to approach a feast here is to share a variety of smaller and larger plates—kibbeh, jocoque, baba ghanoush, fattoush, shawarma, and alambre-style grilled shrimp among them. **Known for:** flavorful hummus and other Middle Eastern dips; welcoming service; wide range of grilled and raw meat dishes. $ *Average main: MP240* ✉ *Calle Pino 69, San Angel* ☎ *55/5661–1994* ⊕ *www.grutaehden. com.mx* Ⓜ *Coyoacán.*

La Taberna del León
$$$$ | MODERN EUROPEAN | Set in a pretty 1920s chalet-style house, this dignified destination for sophisticated modern European–Mexican cuisine is surrounded by the historic redbrick buildings of the Plaza Loreto shopping center. Once

you're seated on the shaded side patio or old-world dining rooms—supping on beef tartare with caviar, roasted duck with a mango sauce and wild rice, or ribeye steak with a Roquefort sauce and Lyonnaise potatoes—it's easy to feel like you've been transported to a wealthy friend's hideaway in the French Alps. **Known for:** solicitous, slightly formal service; refined old-world ambience; beautifully presented cuisine. [$] *Average main: MP670* ✉ *Antonio Plaza, Altamirano 46, San Angel* ☎ *55/5616–2110* 🌐 *www.tabernadelleon.rest* 🕓 *No dinner Sun.* [M] *M. A. de Quevedo.*

★ Loretta Chic Bistrot

$$$$ | MEDITERRANEAN | With a chic terrace upstairs and a modern white-on-white interior space on the ground floor, Loretta is one of the few restaurants in the southern half of the city that consistently makes it onto critics' top dining lists. Celebrated chef Abel Hernández presents contemporary takes on classic Provençal, Tuscan, Greek, and Middle Eastern dishes, like pork belly confit–and–heirloom tomato crostini, followed by creative pastas, steaks, moussakas, seafood grills, and a generous selection of vegetable sides. **Known for:** knowledgeable, efficient service; superb pan-Mediterranean wine list; creatively prepared vegetable sides that could be combined into a full meal. [$] *Average main: MP540* ✉ *Av. Revolución 1426, San Angel* ☎ *55/2747–9305* 🌐 *www.facebook.com/lorettarest* 🕓 *No dinner Sun.* [M] *Barranca del Muerto.*

★ Mercado del Carmen

$$ | ECLECTIC | One of the most beautifully designed and eclectic of the city's many contemporary food hall–style mercados, this bustling complex occupies a stylishly converted colonial home off Plaza del Carmen. The front contains hip boutiques selling sophisticated gourmet goodies, designer sunglasses, and mod housewares, and the open-air rear section is anchored by a bi-level seating area with a retractable roof that's fringed with trendy food stalls dispensing elevated pork buns, American barbecue, sushi, burgers, tortas, pizzas, tacos, and a range of wine, craft beer, and cocktail options. **Known for:** wide variety of cuisine and drink options; beautiful open-air dining area; trendy shops to browse while you wait for your food. [$] *Average main: MP160* ✉ *Calle de la Amargura 5, San Angel* ☎ *56/1900–1419* 🌐 *www.mercadodelcarmen.net* [M] *M. A. de Quevedo.*

Mojama Oyster Bar

$$$$ | SEAFOOD | Tantalizing displays of oysters on the half shell, Alaskan crab legs, jumbo prawns, fish roe, and sashimi anchor the fashionable, high-ceilinged dining room of this bustling seafood restaurant in a modern office tower by Plaza Loreto shopping center. Here at one of the top seafood restaurants on the city's south side, treat yourself to selections from the extensive raw bar as well as grilled octopus, Maine lobster, and soft-shell crab sandwiches. **Known for:** sushi nigiri and rolls; oysters Rockefeller with escamoles (ant larvae); fine selection of sparkling and still wines. [$] *Average main: MP480* ✉ *Aleph San Ángel, Av. Insurgentes Sur 2475, San Angel* ☎ *55/8913–8038* 🌐 *www.facebook.com/mojamaoysterbar* 🕓 *No dinner Sun.* [M] *M. A. de Quevedo.*

Restaurante San Angel Inn

$$$$ | MEXICAN | Dark mahogany furniture, crisp white table linens, exquisite blue-and-white Talavera place settings, and refined service strike a note of restrained opulence at this 18th-century estate whose dining rooms surround a central courtyard with fragrant gardens and a circular fountain. Although you'll find European-influenced classic fare like chateaubriand for two and crispy calves' brains in brown butter, the Mexican delicacies are the stars—consider the crepes of huitlacoche, or a jewel-like dish of escamoles panfried in butter and herbs. **Known for:** gorgeous indoor and outdoor dining areas; weekend brunch; elaborate dessert cart. Ⓢ *Average main: MP580* ✉ *Calle Diego Rivera 50, San Angel* ☎ *55/5550–5807* ⊕ *www.sanangelinn. com* Ⓜ *Barranca del Muerto.*

Taro

$$$ | JAPANESE | A bit south of San Ángel on the main street leading to UNAM, this clean and simple restaurant has been serving some of the finest Japanese food in the city since it opened in 1980. Sushi and sashimi prepared exactly as it is in Japan is a highlight, but you'll also find an extensive menu of izakaya-style dishes: gyozas, chicken karaage, seafood teppanyaki, tempura vegetables, beef katsu curry, and a variety of udon and soba noodle dishes. **Known for:** authentic sushi and sashimi; beef and seafood teppanyaki; outstanding sake selection. Ⓢ *Average main: MP430* ✉ *Av. Universidad 1861, San Angel* ☎ *55/5661–4083* ⊕ *www.facebook.com/resttaro* ⊗ *Closed Mon.* Ⓜ *M. A. de Quevedo.*

🅒 Coffee and Quick Bites

★ Bakers

$ | BAKERY | This sunny, easygoing bakery/café—part of a popular Mexico City chainlet—lies conveniently across the street from handsome Parque de La Bombilla, which is the perfect spot to savor some of the exquisite, freshly baked tarts, cookies, and pastries sold here, along with a coffee or tea. For a heartier meal, choose one of the more substantial options, such as the Jamón serrano-Manchego sandwich or vegetable quiche. **Known for:** cheerful park-side setting; chewy alfajores (dulce de leche cookies); lemon balm rooibos tea. Ⓢ *Average main: MP110* ✉ *Av. Miguel Ángel de Quevedo 50, Chimalistac, San Angel* ☎ *55/9155–1515* ⊕ *www.mesalibre.com. mx/bakers* Ⓜ *M. A. de Quevedo.*

Díaz de Cafe

$ | CAFÉ | You'll find this cozy but warmly lit coffeehouse immediately on your left as you enter trendy Mercado del Carmen—it's separate from the main food hall and thus a bit more intimate and peaceful. The menu features an extensive list of espresso and tea drinks, breakfast and lunch fare (from chilaquiles to sandwiches), and pies, cakes, and other sweets. **Known for:** grilled cheese sandwiches; date pie; carajillos and other boozy coffee cocktails. Ⓢ *Average main: MP105* ✉ *Calle de la Amargura 5, San Angel* ☎ *55/3723–4135* ⊕ *www.diazdecafe.com* Ⓜ *M. A. de Quevedo.*

Tierra Garat

$ | CAFÉ | With an airy design, comfortable seating, good Wi-Fi, and large windows that let in plenty of light, this branch of the popular local coffee franchise is ideal for meeting up with friends, getting some work done on your laptop, or grabbing a quick snack or meal. Tierra Garat offers an extensive range of espresso drinks but particularly excels with its sweet chai teas, flavored hot chocolates, and frozen drinks—it's a favorite for anyone with a sweet tooth. **Known for:** inviting atmosphere for reading or working; hot chocolates, chais, and other dessert drinks; late hours. Ⓢ *Average main: MP80* ✉ *Av. de los Insurgentes Sur 1722, San Angel* ☎ *55/6588–1950* ⊕ *www.tierragarat.mx* Ⓜ *Barranca Del Muerto.*

🅗 Hotels

★ Krystal Grand Suites

$$ | HOTEL | Hotels are rare in this neighborhood, but this stylish all-suites property steps from San Ángel's main shopping area and major sights is also a great base for visiting Coyoacán, Tlalpan, and UNAM. **Pros:** well-designed for extended stays; great restaurant with landscaped terrace; closest hotel to historic center

of San Ángel. **Cons:** on a busy street; traffic noise can be a problem with some rooms; gym equipment is a bit dated. [$] *Rooms from: MP2400* ✉ *Av. Insurgentes Sur 1991, San Angel* ☎ *55/5322–1580* 🌐 *www.krystal-grand-suites.com* 🛏 *150 rooms* 🍴 *No Meals* [M] *M. A. de Quevedo.*

Nightlife

El Depósito

BEER GARDENS | A bustling branch of Mexico City's self-proclaimed world beer store, this dark and otherwise nondescript bar and bottle shop stands out for its vast selection of both Mexican and international craft beers. There are about 15 other branches around the city, and light pub fare is available as well. ✉ *Av. Insurgentes Sur 2098, Chimalistac, San Angel* ☎ *55/5647–8015* 🌐 *www.eldeposito.com.mx* [M] *M. A. de Quevedo.*

La Barra del Patrón

BARS | The largest bar inside the inviting and seemingly always busy Mercado del Carmen, La Barra sits right at the entrance to the food hall and is a great spot for creative cocktails and artisanal mezcal. You can drink at the bar or enjoy your libations with food at one of the hall's communal tables. ✉ *Mercado del Carmen, Calle de la Amargura 5, San Angel* ☎ *55/4515–3842* 🌐 *www.facebook.com/labarradelpatron* [M] *M. A. de Quevedo.*

Performing Arts

★ Centro Cultural Helénico

THEATER | One of the most stately performance spaces in Mexico City, the Hellenic Cultural Center was constructed in 1954 using portions of a Spanish cloister and chapel from the 12th and 14th centuries as well as a baroque Guanajuato facade from the 17th century. The stately building became a cultural center in 1973 and showcases a wide range of popular plays, musicals, and festivals. It adjoins the handsome bookstore and café, Cafebrería El Péndulo. ✉ *Av. Revolución 1500, San Angel* ☎ *55/4155–0900* 🌐 *www.helenico.gob.mx* [M] *Barranca del Muerto.*

Centro Cultural San Ángel

PERFORMANCE VENUES | A variety of plays, musicals, concerts, and other events are presented in this elegant cultural center's Teatro López Tarso. The building opened in 1887 as a municipal palace and was later used as the government offices of President Álvaro Obregón. ✉ *Av. Revolución s/n, San Angel* ☎ *55/5616–1254 culture center, 55/5207–1498 box office* 🌐 *www.cultura.cdmx.gob.mx* [M] *M. A. de Quevedo.*

Cinemanía Loreto

FILM | In the same converted historic building that houses Museo Soumayo in Plaza Loreta, this inviting indie cineplex shows a steady roster of indie films and retrospectives. ✉ *Altamirano 46, San Ángel, San Angel* ☎ *55/5616-4836* 🌐 *www.cinemanias.mx* [M] *M. A. de Quevedo.*

Shopping

Casa del Obispo

CRAFTS | Beautiful handicrafts and folk art—including alebrijes animal figurines, carved masks, bracelets, ceramics, and Día de Muertos decor—are sold in the rooms of this alluring shop set inside a rambling 18th-century mansion with a gorgeous courtyard and exterior gardens. It's a few steps from Plaza San Jacinto, offering a bit of calm from the bustle of vendors found there. ✉ *Calle Benito Juárez 1, San Angel* ☎ *55/5616–9079* [M] *M. A. de Quevedo.*

Citlali

JEWELRY & WATCHES | Established in 1968, this highly respected, family-run artisan jewelry shop carries artful, silver-plated earrings, pendants, rings, necklaces, and other pieces, often in shapes and forms of objects associated with Mexico: nopales, hummingbirds, rabbits, and

San Angel's El Bazaar Sábado is one of the city's most popular shopping experiences.

the like. There are additional locations in Centro Histórico as well as in Guadalajara. ⊠ *C. Benito Juárez 2–2A, San Angel* ☎ *55/5616–2263* ⊕ *www.joyascitlali.com* Ⓜ *M. A. de Quevedo.*

⭐ El Bazaar Sábado

MARKET | It's worth visiting San Ángel on a Saturday just to visit this upscale artisan market that's been going strong since 1960. Before you even make it into the grandiose colonial mansion, you'll encounter dozens of vendors selling crafts, wood carvings, embroidered clothing, leather goods, wooden masks, beads, *amates* (bark paintings), and trinkets at stalls just outside and around Plaza San Jacinto and adjacent Calle Benito Juárez. (Just be warned that more than a few businesses around Plaza San Jacinto, perhaps misleadingly, include the word "Bazaar" in their name.) Inside, on two levels that encircle a beautiful courtyard, are the generally top-quality—although higher priced—goods, including *alebrijes* (painted wooden animals from

Oaxaca), miniature ofrendas, glassware, pottery, jewelry, fashion, furniture, kitchenware, and a smattering of gourmet goods and beauty products. There's also a decent traditional Mexican restaurant in the courtyard, which has a massive tree looming over it. The bazaar is open only on Saturday, but many shops sell their wares online and will ship abroad. ⊠ *Plaza San Jacinto 11, San Angel* ☎ *55/5616–0082* ⊕ *www.elbazaarsabado. mx* Ⓜ *M. A. de Quevedo.*

Librería Octavio Paz

BOOKS | This huge contemporary bookstore that's part of the nonprofit Fondo de Cultura Económica is named for the Mexican poet and diplomat who lived the final years of his life in nearby Coyoacán. Inside you'll find a huge inventory of titles as well as a small café. ⊠ *Av. Miguel Ángel de Quevedo 115, San Angel* ☎ *55/5480–1801* ⊕ *www.fondodecultur-aeconomica.com* Ⓜ *M. A. de Quevedo.*

★ Local México

CRAFTS | Offering top-quality, fair-trade goods (much of it made in Chiapas), this small compound between Plaza and Parroquia San Jacinto contains six different enterprises, one of which is entirely devoted to Día de Muertos figures and artwork. Other highlights include the artists' co-op Jolom Mayaetik for beautifully designed apparel, Fou Fou Chat for jewelry and gifts, Maestras Artesanas for home textiles, and Maka México for leather jewelry boxes and handbags. ✉ *Calle Benito Juárez 2, San Angel* ☎ *55/1702–2850* Ⓜ *M. A. de Quevedo.*

Villa San Jacinto

SHOPPING CENTER | Set around a modern, attractive courtyard landscaped with cacti and succulents, this fashionable cluster of boutiques contains some shops worth seeking out, especially the contemporary Mexican fashion label Pineda Covalin, known for its colorful-print handbags, shoes, scarves, and neckties, and Casa Mendiola, with its selection of stylish housewares crafted by artisans from throughout the country. A jewelry shop and a couple of other clothiers round out mix, and there's also a café and rooftop bar, both of which have lovely settings if fairly ordinary food and drinks. ✉ *Plaza San Jacinto 16, San Angel* ☎ *55/5550–2548* ⊕ *villasanjacinto.com* Ⓜ *M. A. de Quevedo.*

GREATER MEXICO CITY

Updated by
Andrew Collins

◉ Sights	🍴 Restaurants	🛏 Hotels	⬤ Shopping	🍸 Nightlife
★★★★☆	★★★★☆	★★☆☆☆	★★★☆☆	★★☆☆☆

NEIGHBORHOOD SNAPSHOT

TOP EXPERIENCES

■ **La Villa de Guadalupe.** Everyone from devoted pilgrims to history buffs come here to visit both the 17th-century Antigua Basílica and the modern (if aesthetically less pleasing) 1976 Nueva Basílica.

■ **Estadio Azteca.** Join up to around 84,000 other fans to watch a Club América or Cruz Azul soccer game at this stadium that will also be a host during the 2026 FIFA World Cup.

■ **Parque Nacional Desierto de los Leones.** On the mountainous western edge of the city limits, you can stroll tranquil wooded trails and explore an early 19th-century convent at Mexico's oldest national park.

■ **Universidad Nacional Autónoma de México (UNAM).** The attractive campus of Mexico's most prestigious university is dotted with architectural wonders and is home to an impressive collection of cultural attractions and gardens, including the stellar MUAC (Museo Universitario Arte Contemporáneo).

■ **Xochimilco Canals.** Make the journey to the far southeast edge of the city to ride a gondola-like *trajinera* through a dense network of canals and *chinampas* at this colorful and fascinating UNESCO World Heritage Site.

GETTING HERE

The attractions and businesses in this chapter are spread throughout greater Mexico City, some of them relatively close to the city center and reachable via Metro, Metrobus, or a short Uber ride. Others are well outside the range of public transportation and are best visited by Uber or a hired driver, or by renting a car and driving yourself, which is not as daunting as it sounds if you're fairly used to driving in big cities. Renting a car for just a day or two to hit the farther afield sites is fairly cost-effective and more comfortable compared to car-shares. You'll find specific directions and transportation tips throughout this chapter.

PLANNING YOUR TIME

■ For the closer attractions, restaurants, and shops, you may only need to set aside a couple of hours for a visit. But for experiences located more on the city's outskirts, such as the national parks and more far-flung neighborhoods like Xochimilco, Tlalpan, Santa Fe, and the UNAM campus, think of your visit as more of a half- or even full-day trip. Traffic can be heavy at any time, although usually a bit less so on Sunday. It's best to check the latest driving times and conditions before you set out, but always build in a cushion to account for potential delays.

Those who venture beyond the city's immediate central neighborhoods, and even beyond popular Coyoacán and San Ángel to the south, will be rewarded with the opportunity to visit some fascinating attractions, including several charming historic neighborhoods (such as Tlalpan Centro and Xochimilco, with its extensive canal network and gondolalike boats), some outstanding museums (especially on the beautiful campus of UNAM), and a selection of both inexpensive and high-end restaurants and shops.

In the north, there's the iconic Basílica de Guadalupe, a gigantic church dedicated to Mexico's patron saint, as well as the underrated Parque Bicentenario. CDMX's western mountains are also home to Mexico's first national park, the alpine-aired Desierto de los Leones as well as the futuristic edge city of Santa Fe, with its forest of contemporary skyscrapers.

Many of the top sites worth visiting are located in the south of the city, a large district of lava-covered foothills and slopes that include not just Tlalpan Centro and Xochimilco, but also a number of interesting parks, restaurants, and museums. UNAM's picturesque and culturally rich main campus was constructed in the 1950s on a particularly scenic patch of lava—now known as Ciudad Universiteria (University City)—and contains some truly superb cultural attractions and performing arts venues; the campus is one

of four UNESCO World Heritage Sites in the metro region. You'll also find a couple of key Frida Kahlo and Diego Rivera sites in this part of the city: Museo Anahuacalli and Museo Dolores Olmedo.

How to best balance your time while exploring Greater Mexico City depends a lot on your particular interests and your tolerance for potentially dense traffic, which can be tiring whether you're the driver or a passenger in this sprawling metropolis. Most of the sites on the city's immediate periphery can be reached without too much effort by public transportation or a short Uber ride. To fully appreciate Xochimilco, give yourself at least a half-day, and perhaps consider combining that trip with nearby Tlalpan. Exploring Desierto de los Leones pairs nicely with lunch, dinner, or a movie in Santa Fe, and if you're visiting the outstanding Museo Universitario

Arte Contemporáneo (MUAC) at UNAM, consider seeing a performance in one of the adjacent performance halls. If you're in Mexico City for at least four full days, it's well worth setting aside at least a day to embark on some of these side trips. Many travelers who do make the effort to venture farther afield discover some of their favorite attractions or meals of the trip.

Greater Mexico City North

Sights

Estadio Alfredo Harp Helú

SPORTS VENUE | Thanks to batter-friendly thin air, baseball fans here are often treated to slugfests at Diablos Rojos games in this dramatic stadium near the airport. The season for the Mexican League pro team (they play at roughly the caliber of U.S. MLB Triple A minor league teams) runs from April to August, with playoffs lasting into September. ⊠ *Av. Viaducto Río de la Piedad Ciudad de los Deportes Magdalena Mixihuca, Granjas México, Greater Mexico City* ☎ *55/9128–7223* ⊕ *www.diablos.com.mx* Ⓜ *Puebla.*

La Villa de Guadalupe

CHURCH | La Villa—the local moniker of the site of the two basilicas of the Virgin of Guadalupe, about 7 km (4 miles) north of the Zócalo—is Mexico's holiest shrine. Its importance derives from the miracle that the devout believe occurred here on December 12, 1531: a Mexica named Juan Diego received from the Virgin a cloak permanently imprinted with her image so he could prove to the priests that he had experienced a holy vision. Although the story of the miracle and the cloak itself have been challenged for centuries, they are hotly defended by clergy and laity alike. Every December 12,

millions of pilgrims arrive, many crawling on their knees for the last few hundred yards, praying for divine favors.

Outside the **Antigua Basílica** (Old Basilica) stands a statue of Juan Diego, who became the first indigenous saint in the Americas when he was canonized in 2002. The canonization of Juan Diego was wildly popular among Mexican Catholics, although a vocal minority of critics (both in and out of the Church) argued that, despite the Church's extensive investigation, the validity of Juan Diego's existence is suspect. Many critics see the canonization of this polarizing figure as a strategic move by the Church to retain its position among Mexico's indigenous population. The old basilica dates from 1536; various additions have been made since then. The altar was executed by sculptor Manuel Tolsá. The basilica now houses an excellent museum of ex-votos (hand-painted depictions of miracles, dedicated to Mary or a saint in gratitude) and popular religious, decorative, and applied arts from the 15th through 18th centuries.

Because the structure of the Antigua Basílica had weakened over the years and the building was no longer large enough or safe enough to accommodate all the worshippers, Pedro Ramírez Vázquez, the architect responsible for Mexico City's splendid Museo Nacional de Antropología, was commissioned to design a shrine, which was consecrated in 1976. In this case, alas, the architect's inspiration failed him: the **Nueva Basílica** (New Basilica) is a gigantic, circular mass of wood, steel, and polyethylene that feels like a stadium rather than a church. The famous image of the Virgin is encased high up in its altar at the back and can be viewed from a moving sidewalk that passes below. The holiday itself is a great time to visit if you don't mind crowds; it's celebrated with various kinds of music and dancers.

It's possible to take the metro here—La Villa-Basílica station is just a couple of blocks south. But it's not the safest or most scenic part of town, and it's quicker and more secure to go by Uber. ✉ *Calz de Guadalupe, Greater Mexico City* ☎ *55/5118–0500* 🌐 *www.virgendeguadalupe.org.mx* 🎟 *Nueva Basílica free; Antigua Basílica MP15.*

★ **Museo del Juguete Antiguo México**
SPECIALTY MUSEUM | A riotously colorful and curious collection of some 45,000 toys, some dating back to the 19th century, fill this playful museum and ode to pop culture in the Doctores neighborhood. There's little rhyme or reason to the manner in which everything is arranged, other than, perhaps, the whimsical eye and sly sense of humor of the museum's founder, architect Roberto Shimizu Kinoshita. You'll find cases of Barbie dolls, model cars and planes, stuffed animals, dioramas, and tons of Lucha Libre and other elements of Mexican culture. The shop on the ground floor sells some very cool antique toys. The district is just a 15-minute walk east of Roma and although it is becoming safer and even an increasingly popular as a place to live, Doctores can be a bit dicey, especially at night or if you're walking alone. Consider taking an Uber. ✉ *Calle Dr. Olvera 15, Doctores* ☎ *55/5588–2100* 🌐 *www.facebook.com/museodeljuguete* 🎟 *MP50* [M] *Obrera.*

Parque Bicentenario
CITY PARK | **FAMILY** | It's perhaps unsurprising that in a city where disused hydroelectric and garbage heaps have been reimagined as parks and new neighborhoods, a badly polluting former oil refinery has been converted into a stunning, family-friendly green space with seven sections to replicate different climate-vegetation zones. The 136-acre preserve in the north of the city opened in 2010 on the bicentennial of the country's independence from Spain (hence the park's name). Key features include a lake that's lovely to walk around, picnic areas, playgrounds, jogging tracks, sporting fields and courts, an orchid greenhouse, and a gorgeous botanical garden that's definitely the highlight of any visit. Food stalls are located throughout the park, and there's even a little bar and grill with outdoor seating next to the lake. Concerts, festivals, and other noteworthy events take place here throughout the year—check the online calendar for what's coming up next. The park is a 15- to 20-minute drive north of Polanco (the vehicle entrance is at Av. F.F.C.C. Nacionales 221, on the east side of the park) and easily accessed from the Estación Refinería metro stop, which is at the park's northeast corner. ✉ *Puerta 1, Av. 5 de Mayo 290, Ángel Zimbrón, Greater Mexico City* ☎ *55/9154–2244* 🌐 *www.parquebicentenario.com.mx* 🎟 *Free, parking from MP40* 🕒 *Closed Mon.*

🍴 Restaurants

★ **Carmela y Sal**
$$$ | **INTERNATIONAL** | Named the country's top chef by the Mexican Gastronomical Council in 2019, young chef Gabriela Ruíz helms this handsome space with a high "living" green ceiling in fashionable Lomas de Chapultepec. Offering inventive interpretations on recipes she grew up with in her native Tabasco, Ruíz wows diners with complexly flavored dishes like goose pâté with a guava compote or beef tongue in a traditional *puchero* (stew) with plantains and malanga root. **Known for:** molcajete-ground salsas and moles; first-rate cocktail mixology program; flourless chocolate cake with a Tabasco-chiles crumble. [$] *Average main: MP430* ✉ *Torre Virreyes, Calle Pedregal N.24, Lomas de Chapultepec, Greater Mexico City* ☎ *55/7600–1280* 🌐 *www.carmelaysal.mx* 🕒 *No dinner Sun.*

★ **Hotaru Lomas**
$$$ | **SUSHI** | Venture just up the hill from Polanco into similarly upscale Lomas de Chapultepec to sample some of the

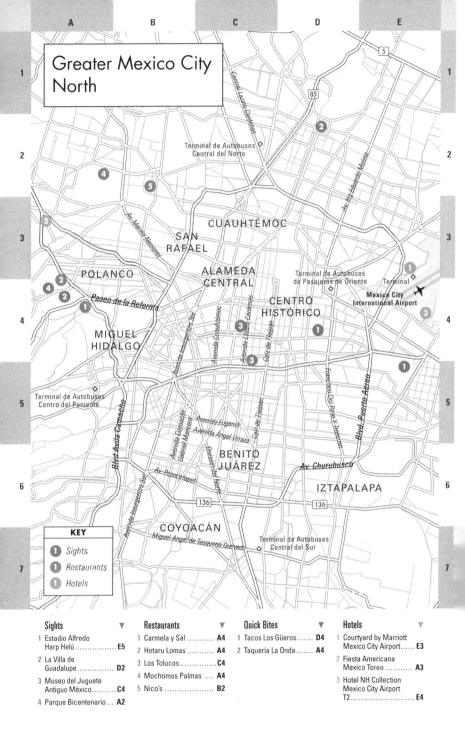

Greater Mexico City North

KEY

- ① Sights
- ① Restaurants
- ① Hotels

Sights ▼	Restaurants ▼	Quick Bites ▼	Hotels ▼
1 Estadio Alfredo Harp Helú................. **E5**	1 Carmela y Sal **A4**	1 Tacos Los Güeros........ **D4**	1 Courtyard by Marriott Mexico City Airport...... **E3**
2 La Villa de Guadalupe............... **D2**	2 Hotaru Lomas **A4**	2 Taquería La Onda........ **A4**	2 Fiesta Americana Mexico Toreo **A3**
3 Museo del Juguete Antiguo México.......... **C4**	3 Los Tolucos............... **C4**		3 Hotel NH Collection Mexico City Airport T2........................ **E4**
4 Parque Bicentenario... **A2**	4 Mochomos Palmas **A4**		
	5 Nico's **B2**		

most exquisitely presented and sublime sushi in the city, including king crab hand rolls with truffle mayo and butter soy, and hamachi marinated in ponzu-yuzu with sliced serrano chiles. The varnished wood sushi bar is a fun place to sit and watch the chefs in action. **Known for:** omakase tasting menus; wagyu, enoki mushroom, and pork belly skewers; macadamia cheesecake for dessert. [$] *Average main: $360* ✉ *Calle San Isidro 44, Reforma Social, Greater Mexico City* ☎ *55/8022–2325* 🌐 *www.costeno.com/hotaru* [M] *Polanco.*

★ Los Tolucos

$ | MEXICAN | Hungry diners come from all over the city to savor bowls of green pozole—a Guerrero specialty—at this casual, old-fashioned Mexican restaurant situated in working-class Algarin (by the Lázaro Cárdenas metro, a short way east of Roma Sur). Piled high with shredded chicken, chicharrón, avocado, and other savory ingredients, this is some of the best pozole around, and there's also a good selection of tacos. **Known for:** pozole Guerrerense-style; big, affordable portions; agua de horchata and Jamaica. [$] *Average main: MP85* ✉ *Calle Juan E. Hernández y Davalos 40, Greater Mexico City* ☎ *55/5440–3318* 🌐 *www.facebook.com/resturantelostolucos* [M] *Lázaro Cárdenas.*

Mochomos Palmas

$$$$ | MODERN MEXICAN | The original Mexico City location of this empire of swanky restaurants founded by celebrity chef and proponent of modern Sonoran cuisine Alfonso Lira Valenzuela (there are additional outposts in the Mitikah tower mall near Coyoacán and in Santa Fe) occupies a spacious, high-ceiling space with verdant living walls in Lomas de Chapultepec. A fleet of solicitous servers works the room, carrying out plates piled high with slow-cooked pork belly, mixed octopus-shrimp-scallop grills, and rib-eye steaks—everything presented with great artistic flourish. **Known for:** impressively extensive wine list; swanky ambience perfect for celebrating a special occaision; over-the-top desserts. [$] *Average main: MP560* ✉ *Av. Paseo de las Palmas 781, Lomas de Chapultepec, Greater Mexico City* ☎ *55/5919–4211* 🌐 *www.mochomos.mx* [M] *Auditorio.*

★ Nico's

$$$ | MEXICAN | A must-visit for fans of traditional Mexican cuisine who think they've tasted it all, this barely adorned, simply elegant restaurant in a pleasant workaday neighborhood—a 20-minute Uber ride from Polanco—is the domain of chef Gerardo Vázquez Lugo (whose parents opened Nicos in 1957), a stickler for ingredients sourced from small producers and dishes that can seem *nuevo* but are all rooted in history. The *sopa seca de natas*—several crepes layered with cream, tomato, and poblano chiles—is a 19th-century recipe from a convent in Guadalajara, and the octopus stewed in its ink with pecans, almonds, and pine nuts is a generations-old recipe from Veracruz. **Known for:** beef fillet with caramelized oranges and a Jamaica sauce; extensive artisanal mezcal selection; chiles en nogada (available only in September). [$] *Average main: MP380* ✉ *Av. Cuitlahuac 3102, Greater Mexico City* ☎ *55/5396–7090* 🌐 *www.nicosmexico.mx* ⏲ *No dinner Sun.–Wed.* [M] *Cuitláhuac.*

☕ Coffee and Quick Bites

★ Tacos Los Güeros

$ | MEXICAN | If you watched the addictively tantalizing Netflix food show *Taco Chronicles*, you may have witnessed the scenes of al pastor deliciousness filmed in this humble but beloved taqueria on Calle Lorenzo Boturini, which is actually lined with great eats, including a few others featured on the program (such as Taquería la Autentica and El Buen Taco). In this no-frills spot that's open until at least 1 am nightly (it doesn't open, however, until around 4 pm), you'll of course want to sample the al pastor tacos, but you'll find dozens of other kinds, plus fantastic birria. **Known for:** flavorful tacos and tortas; hearty birria stew; Jamaica and horchata beverages. $ *Average main: MP50 ⊠ Calle Lorenzo Boturini 4354, Aeronáutica Militar ☎ No phone Ⓜ Fray Servando.*

Taquería La Onda

$ | **MEXICAN** | This unpretentious taco shop on a modest street in otherwise posh Lomas de Chapultepec draws a mix of workers, foodies, and even the occasional celebrity for its flavorful tacos. La Onda opened in 1970 and was one of the first places on this side of town to specialize in tacos al pastor, which remain its signature dish. **Known for:** late night snacking; affordable dining in a pricey neighborhood; large outdoor seating area. $ *Average main: MP140 ⊠ Barrilaco 420, Lomas de Chapultepec, Greater Mexico City ☎ 55/5520–9146 ⊕ www.laonda.com.mx Ⓜ Auditorio.*

 # Hotels

★ Courtyard by Marriott Mexico City Airport

$$ | **HOTEL** | Several hotels are found along the main road across from Aeropuerto Internacional Benito Juárez Terminal 1, and this airy and smartly designed mid-price member of the popular Courtyard Marriott brand is easily the most appealing, with its spacious and contemporary rooms, unusually efficient and friendly service, and attractive common spaces. **Pros:** good location for seeing concerts at Foro Sol and Palacio de los Deportes; convenient for flights out of Terminal 1; rooms set around cheerful glass-roofed atrium. **Cons:** dull neighborhood; need to take (free) shuttle bus to get to Terminal 2; no pool. $ *Rooms from: MP2850 ⊠ Sinaloa 31, Peñón de los Baños, Greater Mexico City ☎ 55/4631–4000 ⊕ www.marriott.com ⇗ 288 rooms ⑩ No Meals Ⓜ Terminal Aérea.*

Fiesta Americana Mexico Toreo

$$$ | **HOTEL** | This contemporary tower with plush rooms and myriad amenities—a member of Mexico's largest hotel brand—rises 12 floors above the fashionable Toreo shopping center in Lomas de Sotelo, a short drive northwest of Polanco and Lomas de Chapultepec. **Pros:** nice city and mountain views from high floors (and a rooftop pool); short walk from Cuatro Caminos Metro station; direct access to upscale shopping mall. **Cons:** rates can climb steeply during busy periods; sometimes books up with meetings or weddings; not in a walkable neighborhood (beyond the mall). $ *Rooms from: MP4300 ⊠ Perif. Blvd. Manuel Ávila Camacho 5, Lomas de Sotelo, Greater Mexico City ☎ 55/2794–0300 ⊕ www.fiestamericana.com ⇗ 252 rooms ⑩ No Meals Ⓜ Cuatro Caminos.*

Hotel NH Collection Mexico City Airport T2

$$ | **HOTEL** | This sleek, circular three-story hotel is set directly above Aeropuerto Internacional Benito Juárez Terminal 2 and is the most convenient lodging if you're flying on Aeroméxico or Delta (which are both based in this terminal), offering well-appointed accommodations with wood floors, premium bedding, and nicely updated bathrooms. **Pros:** very nice gym and outdoor pool; thick windows keep out any noise from planes; literally steps from Terminal 2. **Cons:** need to take (free) airport shuttle to Terminal 1 or the Metro; uninteresting location for sightseeing; rooms have a rather drab courtyard view. $ *Rooms from: MP2900 ⊠ Aeropuerto Internacional Benito Juárez, Terminal 2, Capitán Carlos León Gonzales s/n, Venustiano Carranza, Greater Mexico City ☎ 55/9596–8237 ⊕ www.nh-hotels.com ⇗ 287 rooms ⑩ No Meals Ⓜ Terminal Aérea.*

Estadio Azteca is the second largest soccer stadium in Latin America.

Nightlife

★ Barba Azul

CABARET | Since 1951 (minus a two-year closure during the pandemic), this unabashedly campy cabaret in the eastern reaches of Doctores has been luring even shy patrons onto the central dance stage for salsa, merengue, and cumbia music. The live orchestra is almost as much fun to watch as the completely diverse crowd that includes everyone from white-haired couples to gay teens. Upstairs by the restrooms, be sure to check out the kitschy, obscene artwork. Although not terribly far from Roma or El Centro, the area can get a bit dodgy at night—it's best to Uber here. ⊠ *Simon Bolivar 291, Doctores, Doctores* ☎ *55/5588–6070* ⊕ *www.facebook.com/barba.azul.cabaret* Ⓜ *Obrera.*

Performing Arts

Palacio de los Deportes

CONCERTS | Constructed in 1968 for basketball and volleyball games during the Mexico City Olympics, this massive arena relatively near the airport still hosts occasional sporting events but is best known as a venue for major music concerts. In recent years, Ariana Grande, Imagine Dragons, The Killers, Billie Eilish, Beyoncé, and Madonna have performed here. ⊠ *Granjas México, Iztacalco, Greater Mexico City* ☎ *55/4743–1100* ⊕ *www.palaciodelosdeportes.mx* Ⓜ *Velódromo.*

🛍 Shopping

Mercado Jamaica

MARKET | As sensory experiences go, the city's most impressive floral market, located about a mile east of Roma and south of Centro Histórico, is quite impressive. The nearly 1,200 stalls proffering boldly colored, radiant arrangements and cut flowers along with a huge variety of potted plants fill the air with fragrant aromas. You'll find more than 300 vendors selling other goods, including snacks, fruits, and fresh juices, plus a good variety of ornate piñatas. ✉ *Guillermo Prieto 45, Jamaica, Greater Mexico City* ☎ *55/5741–0002* Ⓜ *Jamaica.*

Greater Mexico City South

◉ Sights

Espacio Escultórico UNAM

ART MUSEUM | At the northern edge of UNAM's cultural center and an easy stroll from MUAC (Museo Universitario Arte Contemporáneo) and the concert halls, this mesmerizing and tranquil complex of contemporary sculpture is more of a wilderness than a garden. Opened in 1979, it contains strikingly dramatic and in some cases massive sculpture installations by six renowned artists: the frequent Barragán collaborator Mathias Goeritz as well as Helen Escobedo, Manuel Felguérez, Sebastian, Hersúa, and Federico Silva, who came up with the idea of creating a natural space to display large-scale, abstract shapes. The property adjoins a massive nature preserve; if you have time, take a stroll through the rugged, arid landscape of rusty-hued volcanic rock and the flora that thrives here. It's a peaceful spot, although with little protection from the sun. Note that it closes at 4 in the afternoon. ✉ *UNAM, Centro Cultural Universitario, Ciudad Universiteria, Greater Mexico City* ⊕ *www.cultura. unam.mx* ✉ *Free* ☉ *Closed weekends* Ⓜ *Universidad.*

★ Estadio Azteca

SPORTS VENUE | Fútbol is the sport that Mexicans are most passionate about, which is evident in the size of their soccer stadium, Estadio Azteca, which holds 83,264 spectators and is the second largest in all of Latin America. Located in the south of the city, about 8 km (5 miles) beyond historic Coyoacán, it's the home turf of Club América, one of Mexico's top fútbol teams, as well as the Primera División's Cruz Azul, repeat winners of the CONCACAF Champions League. Additionally, Mexico's national team plays here often, and there's an American NFL football game held here once a year. The stadium will also be one of three in Mexico (and the only one in Mexico City) to host games during the FIFA World Cup in 2026. In preparation for this, the stadium will be undergoing significant renovations and improvements throughout 2024 and early 2025, although most games are still expected to take place throughout this period, with the exception of the annual NFL football game, which may not resume until after the World Cup. You can buy tickets at the stadium ticket windows on the same day of any minor game. For more important games, try to buy tickets a week in advance—it's easiest to do so via Ticketmaster.

You can't get to Azteca by Metro, but there is a light rail stop (Estadio Azteca) outside the stadium and it's a short walk to catch the light rail from the Tasqueña metro stop. Hour-long tours are also offered daily for MP150. ✉ *Calz. de Tlalpan 3465, Sta. Úrsula Coapa, Greater Mexico City* ☎ *55/5487–3215 tours* ⊕ *www.estadioazteca.com.mx.*

Estadio Olímpico Universitario

SPORTS VENUE | This hulking 72,000-seat stadium is near the south end of San Ángel, but is part of Ciudad Universitaria, the main campus for UNAM (National Autonomous University of Mexico). The striking elliptical building was an icon of modern architecture when it opened in 1952 and it played host to the main events of the 1968 Olympics and 1986 FIFA World Cup. Today it hosts soccer games of UNAM's Pumas as well as a number of other events. Be sure to view

The Estadio Olímpico Universitario hosted the main events of the 1968 Olympics as well as the 1986 World Cup.

the sprawling relief mural by Diego Rivera that hangs above the main entrance of the stadium, on the east side of the building. ✉ *Av. de los Insurgentes Sur s/n, Greater Mexico City* ☎ *55/5622–0580* ⊕ *www.pumas.mx/estadio-olimpico-universitario* Ⓜ *Copilco.*

Jardín Botánico del IB-UNAM

GARDEN | On the west side of UNAM's campus, this sprawling 32-acre swatch of greenery is Mexico's oldest botanical garden. Created in 1959 to preserve and encourage the study of the nation's diverse flora that spans the tropical, high-desert, and forested mountain regions, a walk through this remarkable landscape and its many greenhouses truly showcase Mexico's incredible biodiversity. The garden consists of 15 different collections, and contains more than 1,600 specimens, with a particularly diverse and remarkable array of cacti. A critical aspect of the garden's mission is protecting endangered flora as well as developing methods for sustaining them. ✉ *Cto. Zona Deportiva, Greater Mexico City* ⊹ *Entrance next to Instituto de Biología, on the west side of UNAM campus, south of the sports fields* ☎ *55/5622–9047* ⊕ *www.ib.unam.mx/ib/jb* ▱ *Free* ⊘ *Closed Sun.* Ⓜ *Copilco.*

Museo del Axolotl

SCIENCE MUSEUM | **FAMILY** | In this small, slightly quirky museum and aquarium inside Parque Ecológico Presa Tarango, in a hilly west-side neighborhood between Santa Fe and San Ángel, you can learn about one of Mexico's strangest and seemingly unlikely creatures, the axolotl. This small (averaging about 10 inches in length) and entirely aquatic relative of a tiger salamander once proliferated in the lakes beneath Mexico City, but rampant urbanization has almost entirely destroyed their natural habitats and axolotls have become nearly extinct in the wild. Lake Xochimilco and Lake Chalco, on the southeast side of the city, are the only places in the world where these underwater animals are still found. In the three geodesic-dome buildings and surrounding gardens that make up

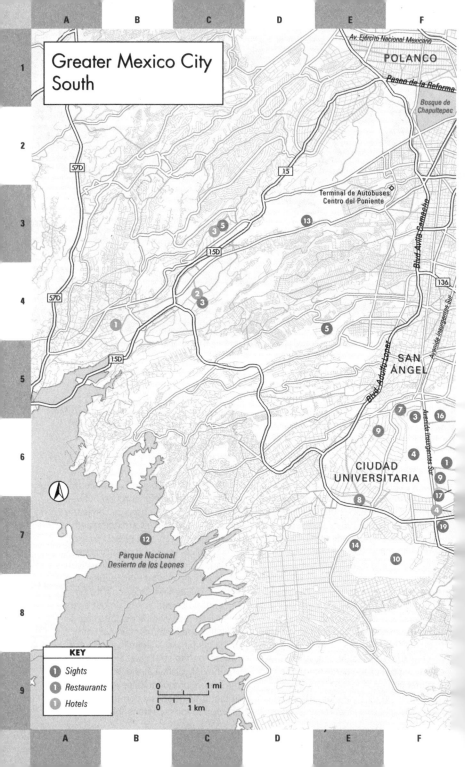

Greater Mexico City South

KEY
- Sights
- Restaurants
- Hotels

POLANCO

Av. Ejército Nacional Mexicano

Paseo de la Reforma

Bosque de Chapultepec

Blvd Ávila Camacho

57D

15

15D

57D

15D

Terminal de Autobuses
Centro del Poniente

Blvd Adolfo López

Avenida Insurgentes Sur

SAN ÁNGEL

CIUDAD UNIVERSITARIA

Parque Nacional
Desierto de los Leones

136

13

5

3 5

2
3

1

5

7 3 16

9

4

8

12

14

10

1

9

17

4

19

0   1 mi
0   1 km

Sights ▼

1 Espacio Escultórico UNAM **F6**
2 Estadio Azteca **H7**
3 Estadio Olímpico Universitario.... **F5**
4 Jardín Botánico del IB-UNAM.... **F6**
5 Museo del Axolotl **E4**
6 Museo del Tiempo Tlalpan **G7**
7 Museo Diego Rivera–
   Anahuacalli......................... **H6**
8 Museo Dolores Olmedo........... **I8**
9 Museo Universitario Arte
   Contemporáneo (MUAC) **F6**
10 Parque Nacional
   Bosque del Pedregal.............. **F7**
11 Parque Nacional
   Cumbres del Ajusco **H9**
12 Parque Nacional
   Desierto de los Leones........... **B7**
13 Santa Fe **D3**
14 Six Flags México.................. **E7**
15 Tlalpan Centro **G7**
16 Universidad Nacional
   Autónoma de México (UNAM).... **F5**
17 Universum **F6**
18 Xochimilco Canals................. **J9**
19 Zona Arqueológica Cuicuilco **F7**

Restaurants ▼

1 Antigua Hacienda de Tlalpan **G7**
2 Arroyo............................. **G7**
3 K-ntina **C4**
4 Michoacanissimo.................. **G6**
5 Nobu **C3**
6 Porco Rosso........................ **H5**
7 Restaurante Casa
   Club de Académico................ **F5**
8 Sud 777............................. **E7**
9 Tetetlán **E6**

Hotels ▼

1 Hyatt House Mexico City/
   Santa Fe **B4**
2 JW Marriott Hotel
   Mexico City Santa Fe............. **C4**
3 Live Aqua Urban Resort
   Mexico............................. **C3**
4 Suites Perisur **F7**

The Museo Diego Rivera–Anahuacalli was built by Diego Rivera himself to house his own personal art collection.

this museum, you can view exhibits about these unique amphibians and their conservation, and view them up-close in aquariums. The easiest way to get here is by Uber—it's a 15- to 20-minute ride from Santa Fe and San Ángel (or its nearest Metro stop, Barranca del Muerto). ⊠ *Parque Ecológico Presa Tarango, Prol. 5 de Mayo 521, Álvaro Obregón, Greater Mexico City* ☎ *55/7898–7876* ⊕ *www. museodelaxolote.org.mx* ✉ *MP50* ⊗ *Closed Mon.* Ⓜ *Barranca del Muerto.*

Museo del Tiempo Tlalpan

SPECIALTY MUSEUM | This offbeat gem of a museum located in a handsome 19th-century former home on the west side of historic Tlalpan's Plaza de la Constitución contains an unexpectedly fascinating collection of antique clocks as well as old gramophones, movie cameras, phones, typewriters, jukeboxes, and even relatively modern gadgets from the 2000s, like old flip phones and adding machines. The owner is quite happy to show visitors around, but he does keep fairly irregular hours, so always call ahead. ⊠ *Plaza de la*

Constitución 7 ☎ *55/4219–4082* ⊕ *www. museodeltiempo.com.mx* ✉ *MP150* ☞ *By appointment only.*

★ Museo Diego Rivera–Anahuacalli

ART MUSEUM | FAMILY | A devoted collector of pre-Hispanic art, Diego Rivera built his own museum to house the more than 45,000 artifacts he collected over his lifetime—which, sadly, came to an end several years before this impressive volcanic-rock building with a design inspired by ancient Mexican pyramids was completed in 1964. The third-floor studio, with its massive wall of windows, displays sketches for some of Rivera's most celebrated murals. Be sure to make your way to the rooftop, which affords sweeping city and mountain views, especially if it's a clear day; look out for the museum's small adjacent nature reserve, which you can also walk through. During the weeks surrounding Día de Muertos, you can view a remarkable altar in honor of Rivera himself. Although located in the larger delegación of Coyoacán, the museum is in the neighborhood of San Pablo

Tepetlapa, about a 15-minute Uber ride south of Coyoacán's historic center; it's also a short walk from the Nezahualpilli light rail station. ⊠ *Calle del Museo 150* ☎ *55/5619–7652* ⊕ *www.museoanahua-calli.org.mx* 🚇 *MP100* 🕐 *Closed Mon.*

★ Museo Dolores Olmedo

ART MUSEUM | In Xochimilco, on the out-skirts of the city, you'll find this superb collection of paintings by Frida Kahlo and the largest private collection of works by Diego Rivera. The museum was established by Dolores Olmedo, Rivera's lifelong model, patron, and onetime mistress. The lavish display of nearly 150 pieces from his cubist, postcubist, and mural periods hangs in a magnificent 17th-century hacienda with lovely gar-dens. Kahlo's paintings are in a separate, adjacent hall; the museum sometimes lends these for traveling exhibitions, so check ahead to ensure they're here if this is the main reason you're visiting. Concerts and entertainment for children are presented on many weekends, while gaggles of geese and strutting peacocks amble about the grounds, adding to the clamor. There is a lovely small café in a glassed-in gazebo, and a variety of compelling rotating exhibits are held in other buildings around the proper-ty. During the month of October, the museum presents one of the better Día de Muertos displays in the city. You can reach the museum by taking the metro to Tasqueña station, and then catching the light-rail to La Noria (*not* Xochimilco), which is a five- to seven-minute walk away. By car, it's about a 40- to 50-minute drive from El Centro, but many visitors combine a stop here with boating on the canals in Xochimilco or strolling around historic Tlalpan. Just note, however, that currently the museum has been closed since the pandemic; it's expected to reopen sometime in 2024, and visitors are advised to check the museum's Face-book page for updates. ⊠ *Av. México 5843, Xochimilco, Greater Mexico City* ☎ *55/5555–1221* ⊕ *www.facebook. com/elolmedomx* 🚇 *MP100; free Tues.* 🕐 *Closed Mon.*

★ Museo Universitario Arte Contemporáneo (MUAC)

ART MUSEUM | Although this gleaming, expansive contemporary art museum on the campus of UNAM—in the same clus-ter of buildings that make up the univer-sity's cultural center—has no permanent installation, the several gallery spaces, some intimate and some enormous, are staged with exceptional changing shows throughout the year. Additionally, parts of the university's extensive collection are shown at different times. MUAC is on par with any of the city's contemporary art museums, partly thanks to the gorgeous, angular design of noted architect Teodoro González de Leon, who also designed Reforma 222, Torre Manacar, and—in col-laboration—Museo Rufino Tamayo (which bears a resemblance to MUAC). The glass facade rises at a sharp angle over a long reflecting pool, facing a broad court-yard that leads to the cultural center's performance venues. A long curving window in the back of the building looks out over the volcanic landscape on which the museum and the university are built, and a grand, freestanding staircase leads to a lower-level museum restaurant (the food is fine, if not spectacular, but the space is beautiful) and some additional galleries as well as a lecture hall. There are usually five or six shows taking place at any given time, and these rotate two or three times per year. Past shows have been devoted to works by Ai Weiwei, Zaha Hadid, Anish Kapoor, Lawrence Abu Hamdan, and Pola Weiss. The museum shop is also superb and carries a number of reasonably priced household items. ⊠ *Cto. Centro Cultural, Ciudad Univer-siteria* ☎ *55/5622–6972* ⊕ *muac.unam. mx* 🚇 *MP40* 🕐 *Closed Mon. and Tues.* Ⓜ *Universidad.*

Parque Nacional Bosque del Pedregal

NATIONAL PARK | Although part of the country's national park system, this hilly, arid 623-acre expanse of oak scrubland south of the city—just 3 km (2 miles) west of Tlalpan Centro—feels a bit more like a city park, given that its completely surrounded by residential neighborhoods. It's also a highly popular destination for running and walking, with its paved central pathways easily accessible from the bustling neighborhood at the park's main entrance, where you'll also find the stately Casa de la Cultura Tlalpan cultural center as well as a good-size parking area and a playground. Once you venture deeper into the park, along the gravel and dirt paths, it starts to feel a bit more like you're actually in a wilderness (signs with park maps are placed strategically throughout the park, making it easy to navigate). Jagged lava outcroppings are evidence of the eruption some 2,000 years ago of nearby Xitle volcano, and the park contains more than 200 kinds of flora, from wild orchids to towering palms, and around 135 types of birds, snakes, and mammals. If you make a complete circuit around the park and venture out to its northwestern border, you'll also spy some strange, curving towers in the mid-distance, at which point the gleeful screams of passengers will clue you in that you're viewing the back side of Six Flags México amusement park. ✉ *Camino de Sta. Teresa 703, Tlalpan* ☏ *55/5171–4558* ✆ *Free.*

Parque Nacional Cumbres del Ajusco

NATIONAL PARK | Mexico City is flanked by huge mountains, including the cloud-scraping peaks of 5,230-meter (17,160-foot) Iztaccíhuatl and its neighbor Popocatépetl, an extremely active volcano that's also the country's second-highest peak, at 5,426 meters (17,802 feet). Visible on clear days from the city center, Popocatépetl is more than 3,300 feet taller than the highest peak in the Lower 48, California's Mount Whitney. But Izzi and Popo, as these twins are affectionately

known, aren't actually within city limits (they're about 56 to 72 km [35 to 45 miles] south of El Centro). The highest peak within city limits is Mount Ajusco, which is the centerpiece of Parque Nacional Cumbres del Ajusco, the third oldest national park in Mexico. Located in the southwestern corner of CDMX, it's a highly popular destination for hikers. Summiting its 3,930-meter (12,894-foot) peak is no easy feat, however. You'll want to allow at least seven hours to make it up and back, and as trails aren't always well-marked and crime isn't unheard of in this minimally patrolled wilderness, it's best to attempt a hike here with a guide or locals who've done the climb before. At the very least, go with a friend and research online for good trail maps and directions—under no circumstances should you go it alone. The elevation gain from any of the hike's starting points is around 2,500 to 3,000 feet, and it is a steep 10-km (6-mile) round-trip or loop hike (depending on the route), beginning in lush coniferous meadows and rising well above the tree line. You should also be in good shape to make it all the way. But it's a wonderfully rewarding adventure, and the views from the summit of neighboring mountains as well as the entirety of Mexico City to the north are spectacular. An excellent starting point is the trail that leads up from beside the casual Mexican restaurant, Cabaña Mireles La Polea, which is on the north side of the mountain, on the road that encircles it. Uber drivers shouldn't have trouble finding it, and if you drive yourself, you can park at the restaurant (or others near it) if you dine here before or after (the food is quite tasty)—just ask permission first. ⊕ *Best trailhead: beside Cabaña Mireles La Polea restaurant, Carretera Picacho-Ajusco, Km 21.5* ☏ *55/5449–7000* ✆ *Free.*

★ Parque Nacional Desierto de los Leones

NATIONAL PARK | The air is rare in this stunning alpine preserve, which in 1917 was declared Mexico's first national

Parque Nacional Desierto de los Leones was declared Mexico's first national park in 1917.

park. The 4,600-acre oasis of mostly conifer forest (with significant stands of oak trees as well) ranges in elevation between 2,600 meters (8,530 feet) and 3,700 meters (12,140 feet), and when you're scampering along the trails and beside the babbling brooks that lace this verdant wonderland, it's hard to believe that you're still completely within Mexico City limits (albeit close to the border with Estado de México). If the name had you picturing a vast arid plain of savage wild cats, note that "Desierto" is a reference to the distance from civilization, and while "leones" reportedly does relate to the one-time prevalence of wild critters living in the area, there were never any true lions out here, of course. The area was settled in 1606 by the Spaniards, who constructed a Carmelite convent nestled amid the pines. Now the focal point of the park and a must for any visitor, the current **Ex-Convento del Desierto de los Leones**—with its curving domes, high walls, and cloistered courtyards—was constructed in 1814, long after its predecessor had deteriorated through gradual

weathering and wear. After exploring the ex-convent and the huge forest sanctuary behind it, stroll around the immediate grounds, where you'll find a number of crafts and food vendors as well as a colorful little restaurant with table service, El Leon Dorado. The park lies 20 km (12 miles) southwest of the city center, and just 10 km (6 miles) beyond the modern commercial district of Santa Fe, at the junction of the 134 and 57 federal highways. ⊠ *Calz. Desierto de los Leones, Greater Mexico City* ✛ *Off Carretera Toluca-México (Federal 15)* ☎ *55/5814–1171* 🖼 *MP40* ⊗ *Closed Mon.*

Santa Fe

NEIGHBORHOOD | It rises like a postmodern Oz or perhaps (depending on your ideas about urbanization) a Bladerunner-esque dystopia, but regardless, the district of Santa Fe looks and feels entirely distinct from the rest of Mexico City. And if you're headed to this thicket of futuristic high-rises situated about 18 km (11 miles) from the city center, there's a high probability you're going for work-related reasons. Developed in the early 2000s atop a massive garbage landfill, Santa Fe was designed emphatically with cars in mind as more of an edge city than a proper neighborhood. It's home to some interesting examples of contemporary architecture, one of the most impressive shopping malls in Latin America (Centro Santa Fe), a massive convention center (Expo Santa Fe), a slew of major corporate offices, mostly upscale chain hotels (Westin, JW Marriott, Hilton, Hyatt House, and Camino Real among them), and high-end restaurants. Many of the latter are also major chains or outposts of other restaurants located elsewhere around the city. If business brings you here or you're simply curious to check out this thoroughly posh if rather antiseptic district, do make a point of visiting Parque La Mexicana, a beautifully designed 74-acre urban green space offering a playground, skate park, dog park, running and bicycling trails, and an outdoor terrace café. Santa Fe is also relatively close to Desierto de los Leones National Park, and it's a good stepping off point for venturing farther west to the city of Toluca. To get here, driving or taking an Uber is practically a requirement, as there's no metro service and getting here by bus is time-consuming and a bit complicated for tourists. In late 2023, the new Mexico City–Toluca commuter rail finally opened its first phase (four stations in the state of Mexico), but the three Mexico City stations are expected to open by mid- to late 2024. The line will provide easier and faster access, with a stop right in the center of Santa Fe. ✉ *Vasco de Quiroga* ✛ *Off México 134D/ México 15D freeways.*

Six Flags México

AMUSEMENT PARK/CARNIVAL | FAMILY | Amusement park giant Six Flags operates this enormous, well-designed park in the south of Mexico City, near Tlalpan and about 18 km (11 miles) from the city center. You'll find acres of both extreme and fairly mild rides (nine rollercoasters in all), plus live entertainment and other diversions, including multiple restaurants and souvenir stands. Areas have colorful themes, such as DC Super Heroes, Bugs Bunny Boom Town, and Polynesian Village. It's possible to get here cheaply via the Insurgentes Sur Metrobus, but Uber is more efficient. The company also operates Six Flags Hurricane Harbor Oaxtepec, a similarly popular water park near Cuernavaca, about a 90-minute drive southeast of Mexico City. ✉ *Carretera Picacho-Ajusco Km 1.5, Jardines del Ajusco, Greater Mexico City* ☎ *55/5339– 3600* ⊕ *www.sixflags.com.mx* ✉ *From MP1039* ⊙ *Closed many weekdays (check website for exact details).*

★ **Tlalpan Centro**

NEIGHBORHOOD | Extremely popular with Mexican families, especially as a place to stroll and people-watch on weekends, this historic and enchanting historic center laid out in the 1600s is sometimes described as what Coyoacán felt and looked like 30 years ago, before it became more of a must-see destination. Slowly but surely, Tlalpan's narrow lanes of colorful, historic houses and its charming tree-shaded hub, Plaza de la Constitución, are drawing more sizable crowds, but a visit here still feels manageable and relaxed, like you've stumbled upon a small colonial village far from the big city.

Do visit the Capilla de las Capuchinas, a few blocks away, to admire the strikingly modernist interior, which Luis Barragán completely redesigned in the late 1950s. You can also walk through the courtyard and view the interior of the imposing Parroquia de San Agustín de las Cuevas, on the east side of the plaza. Next door are a couple of good quick stops for a refreshment: historic La Jalisciense cantina for Spanish food and tortas, and an atmospheric branch of the local ice-cream chain, La Nueva Michoacana (which has been going strong since the early 1950s). If you can visit on a Sunday, you can enjoy watching locals, many of them seniors, dancing around the grand kiosco in the Plaza. Vendors sell crafts, souvenirs, and food while just a few steps south, Mercado de la Paz is a traditional market that also has plenty of food vendors. And although Tlalpan isn't flashy as a dining destination, there are a number of mostly traditional restaurants, cantinas, and food vendors on the blocks around the plaza, especially along pedestrianized Calle Guadalupe Victoria (which extends south from the plaza western's edge). Along here you'll also find the quirky but excellent Museo del Tiempo Tlalpan and the Museo de Historia de Tlalpan that, while not a must, offers free admission and gives a good overview of the neighborhood's history.

Finally, on the north side of the Plaza, the performance venue Multiforo Tlalpan often has concerts and other interesting shows—it's worth checking to see what's on. Tlalpan is in the south, easily visited in conjunction with Xochimilco, and most conveniently via Uber. But you could also save some pesos by taking the Metro to Universidad or the light rail to Huipulco, and taking much shorter Uber rides from either. Or you can take the Insurgentes Metrobus line south to the Fuentes Brotantes stop in Tlalpan Centro. ⊠ *Plaza de la Constitución 1.*

★ **Universidad Nacional Autónoma de México (UNAM)**

COLLEGE | Some of the country's most celebrated modern architects—including Mario Pani, Enrique del Moral, and Teodoro González de Leon—designed buildings on the massive campus of UNAM, which sprawls across its own city within a city, the 2,500-acre (10-square-km) Ciudad Universitaria. Located in the southern reaches of the city, a little south of Coyoacán and San Ángel, the current campus was constructed in the 1950s on a then completely desolate field of petrified lava produced by the roughly AD 300 eruption of Xitle Volcano (a now

dormant 1,000-foot-tall ash cone volcano about 8 km [5 miles] to the south). The university itself was established in 1910 and is one of the largest and most prestigious educational institutions in the world, with about 213,000 undergraduate and 30,000 graduate students enrolled across its numerous campuses around the country (as well as in extension schools in the United States and Canada). UNAM accepts only about 8% of applicants, and the campus here at Ciudad Universiteria is by far the largest and includes a number of outstanding architectural works and cultural attractions. Murals by Diego Rivera, David Alfaro Siqueiros, and Juan O'Gorman appear on some buildings, most notably the 1956 functionalist Central Library, which O'Gorman designed in collaboration with Gustavo Saavedra and Juan Martinez de Velasco (and on which his massive murals appear). In addition to its outstanding museums and performance spaces, another highlight on campus is Jardín Botánico. UNAM also operates some other important institutions around the city, including Palacio de Mineria and Colegio de San Ildefonso (with its famous murals) in Centro Histórico, Casa del Lago in Parque Chapultepec, and Museo Universitario del Chopo in Santa Maria la Ribera. ⊠ *Cto. Interior, Ciudad Universiteria* ✛ *Off Av. Insurgentes Sur at Cto. Escolar* ⊕ *www.cultura.unam.mx* Ⓜ *Universidad.*

Universum

SCIENCE MUSEUM | FAMILY | The Museo de las Ciencias de la UNAM (or UNAM Science Museum) lies at the southeastern edge of the university's cultural center and is packed with touch-friendly, interactive exhibits as well as a planetarium and a particularly good oceanography area. Especially popular with families, highlights include an actual, touchable piece of the moon, a butterfly exhibit, dinosaurs, and more. ⊠ *UNAM, Cto. Centro Cultural, Ciudad Universiteria, Greater Mexico City* ☎ *55/5622–7260* ⊕ *www.*

The Universidad Nacional Autónoma de México campus contains some of the city's most stunning buildings.

universum.unam.mx ✉ *MP90* ⊘ *Closed Mon. and Tues.* Ⓜ *Universidad.*

★ Xochimilco Canals

BODY OF WATER | A former pre-Hispanic city 21 km (13 miles) south of current-day CDMX city center, the Xochimilco neighborhood is well worth a visit to explore its vast, ancient network of canals and *chinampas* (man-made islands), which have been declared a UNESCO World Heritage Site. When the first indigenous settlers arrived in the Valley of Mexico, they found an enormous lake. As the years passed and their population grew, the land could no longer satisfy their agricultural needs. They solved the problem by devising a system of chinampas, rectangular structures akin to barges, which they filled with reeds, branches, and mud. They planted the barges with willows, whose roots anchored the floating gardens to the lake bed, creating a labyrinth of small islands and canals on which vendors carried flowers and produce grown on the chinampas to market.

Today Xochimilco is the only place in Mexico where the gardens still exist. Go on a Saturday, when the *tianguis* (market stalls) are most active, or, though it's crowded, on a Sunday. On weekdays the distinctive community is usually much less crowded, so it loses some of its vibrancy but also its chaos. It's considered almost a mandatory custom to hire a *trajinera* (a flower-painted boat that's roughly akin to a large gondola); a colorfully painted arch over each boat spells out its name. You can hire the trajineras at several different points in town—the launch point along Calle de Mercado (just north of Camino a Nativitas) tends to be a little less crowded, as it's farther from the light-rail station, and a pretty pedestrian bridge crosses the canal, allowing for some great photos of these colorful boats. Expect to pay MP600 per hour for a boat that can accommodate up to around 18 passengers. Optional extras include beer, micheladas, and soft drinks along with mariachi and marimba bands, Bluetooth speakers, tour guides, and decorative arches for your boat made of actual flowers. As you

The Island of the Dolls

Situated among the ancient canals of Xochimilco, one of the city's most intriguing—and creepiest—photo ops is Isla de las Muñecas (Island of the Dolls), which you'll get a good view of if you book a ride in one of the famous, floral-painted *trajineras* that ply these waters. The island's late caretaker, Don Julián Santana Barrera, allegedly found a drowned little girl near the island and soon after located a doll floating in the canal. Believing the doll to be hers, he hung it on a tree on this island, as a tribute or memorial of sorts, and over time, he hung more and more dolls in an effort to appease her apparently restless spirit. Barrera's death was also the result of drowning, and as the story goes, his body was found exactly where he discovered the little girl.

sail through the canals, you'll pass mariachis and women selling tacos from other trajineras, and you'll pass by the bizarre Isla de las Munecas (the Island of Dolls), which you'll know when you see it. While a Xochimilco boat tour has become one of Mexico City's top experiences, note that it's not an activity for everyone—these are basically party boats that ply some pretty murky, badly polluted waters, and while the tours can be a lot of fun for groups of friends (less so for just a couple of passengers), Xochimilco is a long way to go for a touristy tour on a crowded canal. To get here, it's about a 45-minute to 1-hour drive, or you can take the metro to Tasqueña station, and then catch the light-rail commuter train to Xochimilco (a journey of about two hours each way). ✉ *Embarcadero Nuevo Nativitas, Calle del Mercado at Camino a Nativitas, Xochimilco, Greater Mexico City.*

Zona Arqueológica Cuicuilco

RUINS | The occupants of cars and buses speeding along the city's Anillo Periférico (southern beltway) are sometimes surprised to see an ancient, conical pyramid rising just off the side of the highway, standing out rather strangely among the modern buildings that dominate the surrounding landscape of the city's Pedregal area. From around 1400 to 200 BC, a Mexica settlement with as many as 20,000 residents thrived here along the southern shoreline of Lake Texcoco, the now drained body of water on which Mexico City now stands. They built this impressive pyramid likely around 800 BC, several centuries before the construction of the massive pyramids of Teotihuacán (a settlement that some believe was created by descendants of Cuicuilco inhabitants). It's thus considered the oldest of the major archaeological sites in metro CDMX. Today you can visit the site, which has been remarkably well preserved in part because it was covered in lava by the eruption of nearby Xitle around 100 BC. A small museum designed by noted Mexican architect Luis Macgregor Krieger houses excellent exhibits tracing the settlement's history as well as countless pots, figurines, tools, and other artifacts unearthed on the site. You can also walk the grassy, verdant grounds and stand atop the pyramid. Cuicuilco is a five-minute drive from Tlalpan Centro and about a 15-minute drive from UNAM and Ciudad Universitaria. You can Uber here, or take the Insurgentes Sur Metrobus to the Villa Olímpica stop, from which it's an easy five-minute walk. ✉ *Espacio Ecológico Cuicuilco, Insurgentes Sur at Anillo Anillo Periférico* ☎ *55/5606–9758* ⊕ *www.inah. gob.mx/zonas/zona-arqueologica-cuicuilco* 🎫 *Free* 🕐 *Closed Mon.*

Spend a day with friends drinking and enjoying mariachi music on the Xochimilco Canals.

🍽 Restaurants

Antigua Hacienda de Tlalpan

$$$ | **MEXICAN** | One of the most beautiful restaurant settings in the city, this gracious 1837 hacienda in Tlalpan Centro oozes history and personality, from the peacocks strutting about the sweeping lawns and gardens to the plates of sophisticated, haute Mexican and European cuisine served on hand-painted plates. Although open late most evenings, it's especially nice to relax here over midday comida, soaking up the garden views while supping on chile relleno stuffed with duck and topped with tamarind sauce, or filet mignon topped with a rich mushroom sauce. **Known for:** elegant, historic setting; outdoor seating overlooking the beautiful grounds; rich traditional Mexican and European cuisine. $ *Average main: MP420* ✉ *Calz. de Tlalpan 4619* ☎ *55/5655–7888* ⊕ *www. aht.mx* ⊗ *No dinner Sun.*

Arroyo

$$$ | **MEXICAN** | Whether it's truly the largest restaurant in Mexico, as it boasts, this cavernous spectacle on the edge of Tlalpan Centro is undoubtedly enormous and renowned for big family-style platters of pit-cooked lamb barbacoa and other traditional Mexican fare (carnitas, cecina, chicken leg, etc). Opened in 1940, Arroyo is decorated with tiled walls, brick archways, murals, and overhead rows of colorful papales picados. **Known for:** huge portions of barbacoa; live entertainment on weekends; a kids' playground. $ *Average main: MP420* ✉ *Av. Insurgentes Sur 4003* ☎ *55/5573–4344* ⊕ *www.arroyorestaurante.mx.*

★ K-ntina

$$$$ | **MODERN MEXICAN** | The swanky Santa Fe business district has plenty of good restaurants, but this buzzy spot serving inventive takes on regional Mexican cuisine is one of the few truly worth making the trip. Decorated with Mexican pottery and eye-catching artwork, the contemporary space is perfect

for feasting on short rib tacos with spicy glazed grapes and an arugula-peanut salsa, grilled salmon with garlic-chile sauce and Oaxacan-style polenta-huitlacoche tamal, and other boldly flavored, creative fare. **Known for:** ceviche and other raw-bar dishes; wood-grilled steaks and seafood; inventive cocktails. $ *Average main: MP620* ✉ *Park Plaza, Av. Javier Barros Sierra 540, Santa Fe, Greater Mexico City* ☎ *55/5292–4688* ⊕ *www.facebook.com/ kntinamx* ⊙ *No dinner Sun.*

Michoacanissimo

$$ | **MEXICAN** | Renowned for birria, this unfussy restaurant popular with families and locals serves a few kinds of the spicy stew popular in western Mexico states like Michoacán, including *surtida* (goat and a mix of other meaty bits like ribs, tongue, skin, and such) and the less adventurous but still robustly flavorful *maciza* (with pork). Expect a crowd— and maybe a wait—on weekends, when there's also sometimes mariachi music. **Known for:** Michoacán-style birria; micheladas; refreshing paleta (ice-cream bars). $ *Average main: MP180* ✉ *Calle San Valentín 866, Pedregal de Sta Úrsula, Greater Mexico City* ☎ *55/5421–5576* ⊕ *www.michoacanisimo.com* ⊙ *No dinner* Ⓜ *Universidad.*

Nobu

$$$$ | **JAPANESE FUSION** | One of two (the other is in Polanco) Mexico City locations of the famous, see-and-be-seen Nobu Japanese restaurant empire, this stylish space with soaring ceilings, a long sushi bar, and plush booths is in the affluent Arcos Bosques complex, between Santa Fe and Lomas Altas. Signature dishes from the extensive menu include salmon tataki with cilantro sauce, a Peruvian-style tiradito of Japanese scallops, grilled black cod with miso, and gyozas filled with wagyu and foie gras. **Known for:** stunningly plated food; seven-course omikase meals; long and interesting dessert menu. $ *Average main: MP630* ✉ *Paseo de los Tamarindos 90, PB21A,*

Bosques de las Lomas, Greater Mexico City ☎ *66/9135–0062* ⊕ *www.noburestaurants.com/mexicocity* ⊙ *No dinner Sun.*

Porco Rosso

$$ | **BARBECUE** | Located in the Coyoacán delegación but about 2 miles (3 km) south of the historic area, this lively outpost of the popular Mexico City chainlet specializing in tasty and reasonably authentic U.S.-style barbecue is a fun lunch or dinner stop when visiting nearby Museo Anahuacalli or on your way back from Xochimilco or Tlalpan. Grab a seat at one of the communal picnic tables and tuck into platters of tender, slow-cooked baby-back ribs, brisket, and pulled pork, along with burgers, queso fries, and even pretty decent ramen. **Known for:** large covered outdoor seating area; sides of mac-and-cheese and grilled Cajun-spiced corn; deep-fried oreos. $ *Average main: MP240* ✉ *Av. División del Norte 3103, El Rosedal, Greater Mexico City* ☎ *55/5336–3522* ⊕ *www.porcorossobbq.mx.*

Restaurante Casa Club de Académico

$$ | **INTERNATIONAL** | **FAMILY** | It's worth making your way south to Cuidad Universitaria to dine at this distinctive and generally untouristy venue inside the UNAM faculty club, with a terrace that overlooks beautiful gardens and volcanic rocks. Open to the public and especially enjoyable for a late afternoon lunch, the restaurant serves a diverse, affordable menu of globally inspired dishes, such as penne pasta with a puttanesca sauce, panela cheese enchiladas with mole verde, and roasted rosemary chicken with a Chardonnay reduction. **Known for:** live music, cultural programs, and kids' activities on weekend afternoons; lovely, peaceful setting; creative cocktails and mocktails. $ *Average main: MP200* ✉ *Av. Cd Universitaria 301, Greater Mexico City* ☎ *55/6381–2691* ⊕ *www. facebook.com/casaclubdelacademico* ⊙ *No dinner* Ⓜ *Copilco.*

★ Sud 777

$$$ | MODERN MEXICAN | Celebrated chef Edgar Nunez has developed a thoroughly ambitious approach to contemporary cuisine that uses both Mexican and international ingredients—consider seared tuna with jocoque, fennel, smoked grapefruit, and citrus butter, or sea scallops with coconut, purple onions, and rice vinegar. The gently modern space (a 10-minute drive south of San Ángel) merges indoors with outdoors and is one of the sexiest spots in town. **Known for:** stellar wine list; elaborate tasting menus, including a vegan option; a separate sushi bar within the restaurant, Hokusai. $ Average main: MP425 ⊠ Blvd. de la Luz 777, Greater Mexico City ☎ 55/5568–4777 ⊕ www.sud777.com.mx ⊗ No dinner Sun.

★ Tetetlán

$$$ | MODERN MEXICAN | Adjacent to a gorgeous 1947 Luis Barragán–designed house (Casa Pedegral), this dramatic space with plexiglass floors that reveal a volcanic-rock landscape beneath is a favorite destination of both foodies and architecture aficionados. The kitchen turns out fancy, organic fare from early morning until late at night, like gently scrambled eggs with *escamoles* (ant larvae) and salsa verde for breakfast, and artisan pizza or roasted octopus with squid ink, caramelized onions, and a pineapple puree at dinner. **Known for:** stunning Luis Barragán–designed space; exceptional ceviche and aguachile; first-rate clothing boutique on-site. $ Average main: MP410 ⊠ Av. de Las Fuentes 180-B ☎ 55/5668–5335 ⊕ www.facebook.com/tetetlan Ⓜ Copilco.

 Hotels

Hyatt House Mexico City/Santa Fe

$ | HOTEL | With lower rates than most properties in the corporate-centered Santa Fe district, this eight-story hotel is a great deal considering the roomy accommodations, attractive pool and fitness center, and safe and relatively quiet location. **Pros:** pretty mountain views from upper floors; suites with full kitchens are perfect for longer stays; on the calmer western edge of Santa Fe. **Cons:** 20- to 30-minute walk or short Uber ride from most key Santa Fe attractions; 30- to 45-minute drive from main city neighborhoods; limited restaurant options nearby. $ Rooms from: MP2000 ⊠ Vasco de Quiroga 4001, Santa Fe, Greater Mexico City ☎ 55/5282–1234 ⊕ www.hyatt.com ⤢ 119 rooms ❑ Free Breakfast.

★ JW Marriott Hotel Mexico City Santa Fe

$$ | HOTEL | Among the most luxurious and centrally located of the cluster of hotels in business-oriented Santa Fe, this stylish contemporary urban retreat caters primarily to corporate travelers, but leisure visitors willing to contend with the out-of-the-way location will appreciate the extremely reasonable rates and proximity to several excellent restaurants and the enormous Centro Santa Fe shopping mall. **Pros:** within walking distance of many excellent restaurants and shops; upscale stay at low prices, especially on weekends; beautifully designed full-service spa and health club. **Cons:** 30- to 45-minutes from central Mexico City; corporate, futuristic Santa Fe lacks charm; pets not allowed. $ Rooms from: MP2550 ⊠ Av. Santa Fe 160, Santa Fe, Greater Mexico City ☎ 55/5292–7272 ⊕ www.marriott.com ⤢ 221 rooms ❑ No Meals.

Live Aqua Urban Resort Mexico

$$$ | RESORT | Situated in the stylish Arcos Bosques mixed-use district on the eastern edge of Santa Fe about 6 miles (10 km) from Parque Chapultepec, the only CDMX location of this growing Mexico brand of posh resorts offers plenty of creature comforts, including huge rooms with 65-inch smart TVs (and smaller TVs in the bathrooms), a gorgeous full spa, and an acclaimed restaurant serving rarefied Spanish cuisine. **Pros:** adjacent to upscale shopping and dining complex;

ultraluxurious amenities and design; highly personal service. **Cons:** slightly formal ambience can feel fussy; 10-minute drive from Santa Fe's core attractions; 20- to 40-minute drive from central Mexico City. $ *Rooms from: MP4700 ⊠ Paseo de los Tamarindos 98, Bosques de Lomas, Greater Mexico City* ☎ *55/9177–8400* ⊕ *www.liveaqua.com* ⤴ *135 rooms* ⫟ *No Meals.*

Suites Perisur

$ | **HOTEL** | **FAMILY** | For families, those spending a lot of time at UNAM or in the south of the city, or visitors with a rental car who don't mind a bit of driving, this well-maintained and attractively furnished extended-stay property offers an outstanding value and a relatively quiet location at the axis of two major roads, just across the highway from the fascinating Zona Arqueológica Cuicuilco. **Pros:** rooftop terrace with mountain views; spacious furnished suites with kitchens are perfect for long-term stays; good base for UNAM, Tlalpan, and anything south of the city. **Cons:** 45- to 60-minute drive to city center; no restaurant on-site (except for breakfast) and few nearby; breakfast is at extra cost. $ *Rooms from: MP1467 ⊠ Alba 15, Insurgentes Cuicuilco, Greater Mexico City* ☎ *55/8873–8758* ⊕ *www.suiteperisur.com.mx* ⤴ *69 suites* ⫟ *No Meals.*

Nightlife

Barra Alipus

COCKTAIL BARS | One of the most revered artisanal mezcal makers in the country, Oaxaca-based Alipus—which also runs the restaurants/bars Los Danzantes and Corazón de Maguey in Coyoacán—operates this stylish little spot in historic Tlalpan Centro. Stop by to sample the mezcal either straight up or in the extensive list of interesting cocktails, and note the well-prepared traditional Mexican food, including a number of Oaxacan specialties. ⊠ *Guadalupe Victoria 15, Tlalpan Centro, Greater Mexico City*

☎ *55/6363–4375* ⊕ *www.facebook.com/barraalipus15.*

Krox International Beer

BEER GARDENS | This small, lively craft beer bar and garden abuts the eastern edge of the CENART campus and is a great spot for drinks and a light bite before or after seeing a performance or perhaps a movie at the neighboring Cineteca Nacional Churubusco. You'll find one of the city's largest selections of domestic and international beers here, and most everything is available to go. ⊠ *Av. Río Churubusco 85, El Prado, Greater Mexico City* ☎ *55/3875–4520* Ⓜ *General Anaya.*

★ **La Jalisciense**

BARS | Since 1870, this convivial cantina has been a favorite spot for socializing, drinking, and dining on hearty Spanish fare in historic Tlalpan. The long, narrow space with an ornate wooden bar, vintage artwork, and brick archways is lively day or night. You can order delicious tortas and other items to go from a small take-out window up front and enjoy eating them on a picnic bench in nearby Plaza de la Constitución. ⊠ *Plaza de la Constitución 6* ☎ *55/3498–4174.*

🎭 Performing Arts

★ **Centro Cultural Universitario de la UNAM**

PERFORMANCE VENUES | A sprawling campus of exceptional museums, art spaces, and performance halls in the heart of Ciudad Universitaria, UNAM's cultural center is an excellent place to see concerts by the superb Orquesta Filarmónica de la UNAM (OFUNAM), which take place in the acoustically renowned Sala Nezahualcóyotl. Neighboring venues include the Centro Universitario de Teatro (CUT), Foro Sor Juana Ines de la Cruz, Teatro Juan Ruiz de Alarcón, Sala Carlos Chavez, and Filmoteca UNAM–Sala Miguel Covarrubias. Among these beautifully designed modern buildings, there's virtually always some sort of interesting performance (or several) taking place (except during occasional school breaks), including ballet, modern dance, choral, film, lecture, and theater. Tickets to performances are very reasonably priced. ✉ *Cto. Centro Cultural, Ciudad Universiteria* ⊕ *www.cultura.unam.mx* Ⓜ *Universidad.*

Centro Nacional de las Artes (CENART)

PERFORMANCE VENUES | Situated a little east of Coyoacán and adjacent to Estudios Churubusco, CENART is the largest and most important film studio in Latin America. It was built in 1994 by a group of acclaimed Mexican architects led by Ricardo Legorreta, who clearly had Luis Barragán in mind with the design, which relies heavily on bright colors and geometric shapes. Created by the country's National Council for Culture and the Arts, the huge campus consists of performing arts schools and several venues, and there's virtually always something interesting going on, from dance and theater to music of all kinds. Check out the terrific bookshop and hip little café on-site, and during the day, take a stroll through the surrounding gardens and walking paths. There's also now a satellite branch of the famed indie film center, Cineteca, on the east edge of the campus. ✉ *Av. Río Churubusco 79, Country Club Churubusco, Greater Mexico City* ☎ *55/4155–0000* ⊕ *www.cenart.gob.mx* Ⓜ *General Anaya.*

Shopping

Centro Santa Fe

SHOPPING CENTER | Remarkable for its sheer enormity, the country's largest shopping mall is in the heart of the appropriately upscale (although a bit soulless) modern Santa Fe commercial district. Centro Santa Fe contains more than 500 shops and restaurants, a huge central ice-skating rink, a luxury multiplex cinema, and a kids theme park; it's also in immediate proximity to a giant convention center and several hotels. Anchor stores include some noted Mexican brands, including Casa Palacio, Liverpool, and El Palacio de Hierro, and you'll find a number of luxury boutiques, most of which have branches in Polanco or other more central neighborhoods. For ardent shopping enthusiasts, it's worth the 18-km (11-mile) trip from downtown. Until the Toluca–Mexico City commuter rail opens by the end of 2024, a car is the best way to get here. ✉ *Av. Vasco de Quiroga 3800, Greater Mexico City* ☎ *55/3003–4300* ⊕ *www.centrosantafe.com.mx.*

Paseo Arcos Bosques

SHOPPING CENTER | In the affluent Bosques de las Lomas neighborhood near Santa Fe, in the rolling hills west of the city center, this exclusive shopping mall stands out as much for its chic boutiques as for its location inside the iconic Arcos Bosques towers. They were designed by Teodoro González de León in 1996 and comprise two angular 35-story towers joined at the top by a four-story lintel. The shopping center isn't huge, but it contains an upscale food court and restaurants along with such retailers as Brooks Brothers, Kiehl's, and Lululemon. ✉ *Paseo de Los Tamarindos 90, Bosques de las Lomas* ☎ *55/2167–9607* ⊕ *www.paseoarcosbosques.mx.*

Chapter 14

SIDE TRIPS FROM MEXICO CITY

Updated by
Andrew Collins

◉ Sights   🍴 Restaurants   🛏 Hotels   🛍 Shopping   🍸 Nightlife

★★★★★   ★★★★☆   ★★★★☆   ★★★★☆   ★★☆☆☆

WELCOME TO
SIDE TRIPS FROM MEXICO CITY

TOP REASONS TO GO

★ **Ancient ruins.** In addition to visiting the iconic pyramids of Teotihuacán, you can explore fascinating pre-Hispanic settlements in Cholula, Malinalco, and near Cuernavaca.

★ **Delicious regional food and wine.** Puebla is one of the country's most celebrated centers of gastronomy, and Querétaro is increasingly famous for its respected wine, but you'll find exceptional dining in even many small towns.

★ **Incredible natural vistas.** Part of the fun of traveling round the formidable mountain ranges and towering volcanoes that surround Mexico City is taking in the splendid natural scenery, which extends for miles in every direction.

★ **World-class art and history museums.** Enrich your cultural understanding of central Mexico by visiting Puebla's Museo Amparo and Cuernavaca's Museo Robert Brady, and exploring the hundreds of meticulously preserved churches, haciendas, and civic buildings throughout this area.

1 **Teotihuacán.** A breathtakingly immense 2,000-year-old archaeological site that includes the world's third largest pyramid.

2 **Tepotzotlán.** The closest of Mexico's enchanting Pueblos Mágicos to Mexico City.

3 **Querétaro.** One of Mexico's fastest-growing cities, with a burgeoning wine country.

4 **Puebla.** Mexico's fifth most populous city, famed for regional cuisine (mole and chiles en nogada are specialties).

5 **Cholula.** A lively city home to both a dramatic 2,400-year-old pyramid and a hip and youthful café, bar, and restaurant scene.

6 **Tepoztlán.** A favorite destination among CDMX residents seeking nature and relaxation.

7 **Cuernavaca.** An attractive midsize city offering a sunny and warm year-round climate.

8 **Malinalco.** A small, lush town with an eco- and spirituality-focused resort scene.

9 **Taxco.** A striking colonial-era silver-mining town rife with high-quality jewelry and crafts shops.

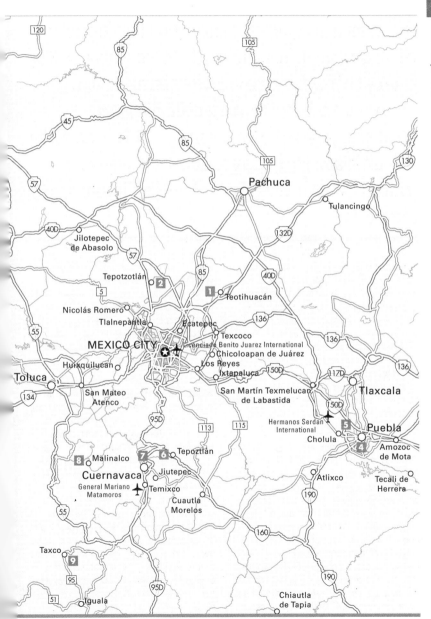

In every direction, via every major highway leading outside Mexico City, locals and increasing numbers of tourists fill cars and buses headed to the dozens of intriguing towns and cities known for everything from awe-inspiring natural scenery to bewitching colonial-era centers. If you're traveling to Mexico City for at least four days, even on your first visit, it's well worth making at least one side trip.

The most popular and closest destination is Teotihuacán, which is just an hour away and whose legendary Mesoamerica archaeological sites can be explored in a half-day or so. If you're feeling ambitious, you could even combine this adventure with a detour to Tepotzotlán, which is also on the north side of the metro area, about an hour west of Teotihuacán. Both of these places can be efficiently visited by bus or even Uber, which is particularly economical if you're sharing your ride with two or more passengers.

The other six destinations covered in depth in this chapter are all far enough away—between 1½ and 3 hours by bus or car—that it's best to plan at least an overnight stay or ideally a couple of nights to enjoy them. Puebla and Cholula are part of a quite sizable metro area about two hours east of CDMX and actually offer enough to see and do to keep you busy for several days or more. But you can cover their key sites and get a sense of each city in two or three days. Another sizable city that's also a base for

several outlying attractions is Querétaro, which lies about three hours northwest of Mexico City and is again best explored over two or three days. You could also combine a trip here with a longer tour of popular San Miguel de Allende and Guanajuato, which are only an hour or two further northwest.

The chapter's other four destinations—Tepoztlán, Cuernavaca, Taxco, and Malinalco—all lie within a relatively compact but extremely mountainous area that extends south and southwest of Mexico City. Tepoztlán and Cuernavaca are close to one another and roughly 90 minutes from CDMX—you could even visit one or the other (but both would be too much) on a long day trip. But ideally give yourself two to three days to visit the pair, and the same amount of time for a trip to Taxco or Malinalco, which are a bit farther away. You could also visit all four of these towns, especially if you rent a car, by driving one big scenic loop—give yourself five to seven days, however, to visit them all together.

Given the distances and logistics, it helps to think about your objectives and how much time you'll be in Mexico City before planning side trips beyond Teotihuacán and Tepotzotlán. If you're spending a week to 10 days in CDMX, consider spending two or three of those nights on a side trip—Puebla and Cholula if you love cities and worldly restaurants, and either Tepoztlán (which can be easily combined with Cuernavaca), Taxco, or Malinalco if you're seeking a relaxing small-town getaway with gorgeous natural scenery. Because it's farther away and also a large city with a lot to see and do, Querétaro is perhaps better saved if you're visiting Mexico City for an extended period, you've already been a couple of times, or you're planning a longer trip up north that will also include San Miguel de Allende.

MAJOR REGIONS
North of CDMX. The state of Mexico (Estado de México, or Edomex for short) wraps around Mexico City, or Ciudad de México (CDMX) to the east, north, and west and makes up a good chunk of the metro population, encompassing a bit of the vast, high-elevation Valley of Mexico. Just beyond the city's border in Edomex, you can visit the legendary pyramids of Teotihuacán and the charming historic center of the small city of Tepotzotlán.

The state of Querétaro, which is one of the smallest in Mexico, lies due north of Estado de México. Its capital city, Querétaro (officially Santiago de Querétaro) is a hub of culture and tourism. It's also a popular stop with travelers headed farther northwest to nearby San Miguel de Allende and Guanajuato.

Puebla. The state of Puebla lies east of Mexico City, just beyond the mammoth peaks of the Popocatépetl and Iztaccíhuatl volcanoes. Its government seat and largest city, Puebla, is just a two-hour drive east of CDMX and offers plenty to see and do along with the smaller neighboring city of Cholula.

South of CDMX. Due south of Mexico City, the curving toll Highway 95D winds down a couple of thousand feet in elevation into another of the country's smallest states, Morelos, which is home to Tepoztlán, an inviting hub of spa getaways and outdoor recreation. A short distance southwest lies the state's largest city, Cuernavaca, which is also its seat of government. And barely 30 km (18 miles) west of the Morelos border at the north-central tip of the very large state of Guerrero—which is also home to the coastal resort cities of Acapulco and Zihuatanejo—you'll find the picturesque and extremely hilly town of Taxco. Finally, technically in the southwest corner of the state of Mexico, on the border with Morelos, Malinalco's splendid natural scenery awaits.

Planning

Getting Here and Around

AIR
It's not possible to fly to most of the destinations in this chapter and not worth the expense and effort to fly to Querétaro, the one city with direct flights from CDMX. However, both Querétaro and Puebla are served by efficient, relatively modern airports that have some direct flights to the United States. Given that both airports are generally more pleasant to fly in and out of than Mexico City's massive Benito Juárez International Airport, you might consider booking both or one of your flights to these smaller facilities if you're already planning a trip to either place.

For example, you could plan an excursion to Querétaro or Puebla (with Cholula) at the start or end of your CDMX trip. Another advantage to this strategy is that if you're planning to rent a car, doing so when you arrive at either of these airports is less intimidating than doing so in Mexico City. Some car rental companies don't charge high fees for one-way rentals, so you could potentially rent your car at the airport in Querétaro or Puebla and return it in CDMX or elsewhere.

Both airports fly to a number of other major cities in Mexico, including Cancún, Guadalajara, Monterrey, and Tijuana. Currently, United Airlines flies from Puebla International Airport (PBC) and Querétaro Intercontinental Airport (QRO) to Houston. And also from Querétaro, American Airlines flies to Dallas/Fort Worth, Aeroméxico (which partners with Delta) flies to Detroit, Viva Aerobus flies to Houston and San Antonio, and Volaris flies to Chicago.

CONTACTS Puebla International Airport.
✉ *Carretera Federal México-Puebla Km 91.5, Puebla* ✛ *35 km (21 miles) northwest of city center* ☎ *227/102–5080.*
Querétaro Intercontinental Airport. ✉ *State Hwy. 200, Querétaro* ✛ *35 km (22 miles) east of city center* ☎ *442/192–5500* ⊕ *www.aiq.com.mx.*

BUS

Although inter-city train travel is nearly nonexistent in greater CDMX, dozens of private bus lines provide a safe, affordable, and generally quite comfortable way to explore the region—and for that matter, just about every nook and cranny of the country. The main bus lines that serve the regions covered in this chapter are ADO, Estrella Blanca, ETN, Flecha Roja, Grupo Pullman de Morelos, and Primera Plus, along with their many subsidiary brands. Most towns in Mexico are served by at least two lines. You'll find details along with basic (second-class) fares in the individual Getting Here and Around sections for each town in this chapter, along with additional information about a few destination-specific bus lines.

Here are a few general thoughts to keep in mind if you're planning to travel by bus. Mexico City is served by four major bus stations, which are located in the

northern, eastern, southern, and western sides of the city. Buses depart from the station that corresponds with the direction of the destination in relation to CDMX. For example, buses to Puebla—which is east of Mexico City—depart from Terminal de Autobuses de Pasajeros Oriente (aka TAPO), which is on the east side of the city.

If choosing between first-class (which may be called *ejecutivo* or *primera*) and second-class bus service, it's well-worth the expense to book the former. The fares usually aren't significantly higher, and first-class buses are extremely comfortable, with reclining seats that offer plenty of legroom, in-cabin bathrooms, and TVs that show movies (albeit often pretty random ones). Second-class buses are sometimes you're only option if traveling to smaller towns; these can be slower because they often stop to pick up and drop off passengers. But they'll still typically clean and efficient.

You can usually find bus schedules and fares by searching online. The websites ⊕ *Busbud.com* and ⊕ *Rome2Rio.com* are both pretty reliable. With Busbud, you can also book tickets online for many routes. Many of the bus lines also let you book directly on their websites; however, many of these do not accept payments from foreign credit cards. Some do accept PayPal. You can also buy tickets with most bus lines at the ubiquitous convenience store OXXO, which has hundreds of branches throughout Mexico City and in most major towns.

That all being said, generally, when traveling from Mexico City to other towns and cities in the region, it's not necessary to book your tickets in advance. You can just show up at the bus station and buy your ticket at the window. Arrive at the station at least an hour in advance if you haven't booked your ticket yet, and a half-hour in advance if you have, just so that you're not rushing to find your boarding gate. If you're traveling at a busy time

(Friday and Sunday afternoons or holidays), you might want to play it safe and book in advance.

CONTACTS ADO. ⊕ *www.ado.com.mx.* **Estrella Blanca.** ☎ *55/8854–7158* ⊕ *www. estrellablanca.com.mx.* **ETN.** ☎ *800/800– 0386* ⊕ *viajes.etn.com.mx.* **Flecha Roja.** ☎ *55/1555–9519* ⊕ *www.flecharoja. com.mx.* **Grupo Pullman de Morelos.** ☎ *800/624–0360* ⊕ *www.pullman.mx.* **Primera Plus.** ☎ *477/710–0610* ⊕ *www. primeraplus.com.mx.*

CAR

The calculus that goes into whether to rent a car or let others (buses or maybe even Uber and taxi drivers) do the driving is a bit complicated in Mexico, and especially in Mexico City. If you find driving in big cities or foreign countries stressful, the answer is very simple: don't rent a car. Mexico City is a giant, sprawling place with notorious traffic and often confusing signage. Narrow, winding roads as well as even narrower bumpy streets (along with Mexico's notorious unmarked and unpainted speed bumps) are commonplace throughout not just Mexico City but the surrounding region.

If the idea of driving in Mexico still doesn't make you anxious, renting a car does have some advantages. It's true that you generally don't need a car to explore the centers of the region's towns and cities—these tend to be very pedestrian-friendly and often quite compact, and a car can actually be a liability in historic, densely settled neighborhoods. But driving does allow you some freedom and flexibility. Once you get outside of Mexico City, central Mexico's network of safe and direct toll highways make for relatively smooth navigating, and a car allows you to detour to interesting spots along the way. Additionally, there are a number of attractions outside of city centers—especially in the vicinity of Cuernavaca and Querétaro—that are hard to get to via public transportation. And if you're planning more than one side trip

or a multicity adventure, and especially if Malinalco is on your itinerary (as it isn't served by buses or Uber), a car can be especially useful.

Just remember that renting a car—once you add in insurance, the relatively high cost of gas in Mexico (about MP24 per liter, which works out to about US$5.50 per gallon), and the cost of highway tolls—can be far more costly than taking buses and potentially even more expensive than hiring an Uber for a long-distance journey. If you do drive, be sure to bring at least MP1,000 in cash with you, as tolls add up quickly in this part of the world. Driving toll roads to Puebla or Taxco will set you back around MP300 in tolls; the drive to Querétaro is closer to MP350.

UBER AND TAXI

All of the destinations in this chapter are served by taxis. They're easy to hail or find around the town plazas in smaller communities like Malinalco and Tepoztlán, and Taxco is rather famous for its hundreds of vintage Volkswagen Beetles—these intrepid little cars seem to handle the town's steep, narrow, cobblestone lanes without the slightest difficulty. Taxis are generally quite safe in these areas, but always agree on a fare before you set out, and if in doubt, ask someone at your hotel or the restaurant you're eating in to call a taxi for you.

When it's available, Uber service is preferable to taxis—it's usually cheaper, and it's also generally quite safe and reliable. Of the towns in this chapter, Uber serves all of them except for Malinalco, Taxco, and Tepoztlán.

It may sound extravagant to call an Uber for a long-distance trip, but rates in Mexico are fairly reasonable. For example, you can Uber from Mexico City to Teotihuacán or Tepotzlán for around MP500 to MP800, depending on traffic and the time of day. For longer trips, you might want to factor in whether you'll really enjoy sitting in a stranger's potentially very small car for a couple of hours, but again, the fares aren't bad when compared with what you'd pay for a rental car and gas. A trip to Tepoztlán or Cuernavaca should cost around MP1,500 to MP1,800. To Puebla, an Uber will run between MP2,000 and MP2,400, and a three-hour trip to Taxco or Querétaro should cost between MP2,800 and MP3,200. You can also book a larger car with Uber XL for about twice the regular fare, and an even more luxurious Uber Black car for about 2½ times the regular fare.

There is one catch to keep in mind: although you can book an Uber from Mexico City to a town that the company doesn't serve, you won't be able to book a return trip with Uber. In that scenario, your best bet would be to ask your hotel or Airbnb if they can recommend a local taxi to take you.

Tours

Booking a guided tour is a great way to explore the many interesting towns outside of Mexico City without having to worry about the logistics of ground transportation while also ensuring that knowledgeable locals are showing you the area's best sites. You'll generally pay a bit more for a guided excursion than if you arrange transportation yourself, but the convenience can be well worth it—many tour companies can pick guests up and return them to their Mexico City hotel or Airbnb.

Amigo Tours
GUIDED TOURS | This well-respected international tour company is a great source for planning side trips from Mexico City. Group offerings include exploring the pyramids of Teotihuacán, a trip to Freixenet Wine Cellar and a hike up Pena de Bernal in Querétaro, a full-day excursion to Puebla and Cholula, and a trip to explore Taxco, Cuernavaca, and a pre-Hispanic

mine. You can also arrange private tours to a number of places in the region, and Amigo has lots of tours in other popular destinations around Mexico as well. ☎ 55/5512–5207 ⊕ www.amigotours. com/mexico-city-tours ✉ From MP750.

Travis Adventures
GUIDED TOURS | Based in Mexico City, this reputable tour operator specializes in history- and gastronomy-oriented trips to different parts of the metro area, including Puebla and Cholula, Taxco and the Cacahuamilpa Caves, and Querétaro's Peña de Bernal and Tequisquiapan wine country. Travis Adventures also has several Teotihuacán trips, plus adventures farther afield to Valle de Bravo and Tlalpujahua. ☎ 55/5409–4250 ⊕ www.travisadventures.com.mx ✉ From MP1500.

Teotihuacán

50 km (31 miles) northeast of Mexico City.

Teotihuacán is one of the most significant and haunting archaeological sites in the world. Imagine yourself walking down a pathway called Calzada de los Muertos (Avenue of the Dead). You are surrounded by some of Earth's most mysterious ancient structures, among them the Palace of the Jaguars, the Pyramid of the Moon, and the Temple of the Plumed Serpent. From the top of the awe-inspiring Pyramid of the Sun—at about 210 feet, the third-tallest pyramid in the world—you begin to appreciate your 248-stair climb as you survey a city that long ago was the seat of a powerful empire. This is Teotihuacán, meaning "place where men become gods." You can easily spend several hours here seeing all of the key sites.

Nearly everyone visits Teotihuacán as a day trip from Mexico City, as there's not a whole lot to see and do in the immediate vicinity. But there are a couple of inviting places to stay in the area if you'd like to avoid spending two hours or more (round-trip) getting to and from the site on the same day.

GETTING HERE AND AROUND

There are several ways to approach a visit to Teotihuacán. A number of companies give guided tours that include transportation. As good English-language guidebooks are sold at the site, it's actually quite easy to explore and learn about Teotihuacán on your own—don't feel a guided tour is a necessity, although a knowledgeable guide can greatly enhance your understanding of the site's fascinating and complex history, and leaving the transportation to a guide service does greatly reduce the hassle of getting here.

Another relatively efficient option is taking an Uber here and back. The cost generally runs between MP900 to MP1,200 each way. If you're comfortable driving in and around Mexico City, another option is renting a car for the day and making the one-hour drive yourself (there's ample, reasonably priced parking on-site). There's also frequent and very affordable bus service from the city on Autobuses Teotihuacan.

CONTACTS Autobuses Teotihuacan. ⊕ www.autobusesteotihuacan.com. mx. **BlueBus.** ☎ 55/8154–5006 ⊕ www. bluebus.com.mx.

TOURS

Dozens of outfitters offer guided tours of Teotihuacán that include transportation from Mexico City—many of them can pick you up and drop you off right at your hotel. You'll find a number of official tour guides inside the five main entrances to Teotihuacán; they generally charge anywhere from MP800 to MP1,600, depending on the length of the tour.

★ Teotihuacán Express Private Tours

CULTURAL TOURS | Offered through the popular outfitter Local Vibes Mexico City, these half-day tours include private transportation from the city. The company also offers an option that includes a 45-minute

shared hot-air balloon ride over the pyramids; this also includes a light breakfast. ☎ 55/1854–3354 ⊕ www.localvibesmexico.com ☒ From MP2000.

Tekpan Tours

GUIDED TOURS | With extremely knowledgeable and friendly guides, this highly reputable operator offers full-day excursions that provide an in-depth history of the ruins. Tours leave very early in the morning and last about eight hours door-to-door, including private round-trip transportation from Mexico City. ☎ 55/1479–3082 ⊕ www.facebook.com/tekpantours ☒ From MP2200.

 Sights

★ Teotihuacán

RUINS | At its zenith, around AD 600, Teotihuacán (*teh*-oh-tee-wa- *can*) was one of the world's largest cities and the center of an empire that inhabited much of central Mexico. Archaeologists believe that Teotihuacán was once home to some 100,000 people. The questions of just who built this city, at whose hands it fell, and even its original name, remain a mystery, eluding archaeologists and fueling imaginations the world over.

Excavations here first began as part of the dictator Porfirio Díaz's efforts to prepare for the centennial celebration of Mexican independence. Between 1905 and 1910, he sent his official archaeologist, Leopoldo Batres, to work principally on the Pyramid of the Sun. Later studies of these excavations have shown that several elements of this pyramid were destroyed in the excavation and others were falsely presented as being part of the original pyramid.

In 2010, archaeologists took part in another commemorative excavation, this time to celebrate 100 years of archaeological work at Teotihuacán. They discovered a tunnel, about 40 feet down, that passes below the Templo de Quetzalcóatl and is thought to have

As one of the world's most impressive archeological sites, Teotihuacán is a popular day trip from Mexico City.

been intentionally closed off between AD 200 and AD 250. The tunnel leads to chambers into which thousands of objects were thrown, perhaps as a kind of offering. Archaeologists hoped that after a couple of months of digging they might find the remains of some of the city's earliest rulers. Although rulers were often deified at other sites, no tombs or even depictions of rulers have ever been found at Teotihuacán.

The **Ciudadela** is a massive citadel ringed by more than a dozen temples, with the **Templo de Quetzalcóatl** (Temple of the Plumed Serpent) as the centerpiece. Here you'll find incredibly detailed carvings of the benevolent deity Quetzalcóatl, a serpent with its head ringed by feathers, jutting out of the facade.

One of the most impressive sights in Teotihuacán is the 4-km-long (2½-mile-long) **Calzada de los Muertos** (Avenue of the Dead), which once held great ceremonial importance. The Mexica gave it this name because they mistook the temples lining

either side for tombs. It leads all the way to the 126-foot-high **Pirámide de la Luna** (Pyramid of the Moon), which dominates the northern end of the city. Atop this structure, you can scan the entire ancient city. Some of the most exciting recent discoveries, including a royal tomb, have been unearthed here. In late 2002 a discovery of jade objects gave important evidence of a link between the Teotihuacán rulers and the Maya.

On the west side of the spacious plaza facing the Pyramid of the Moon is the **Palacio del Quetzalpápalotl** (Palace of the Plumed Butterfly); its expertly reconstructed terrace has columns etched with images of various winged creatures. Nearby is the **Palacio de los Jaguares** (Palace of the Jaguars), a residence for priests. Spectacular bird and jaguar murals wind through its underground chambers.

The awe-inspiring **Pirámide del Sol** (Pyramid of the Sun), the first monumental structure constructed here, stands in the center of the city. With a base nearly as broad as that of the pyramid of Cheops in Egypt, it is one of the largest pyramids ever built. Its size takes your breath away, often quite literally, during the climb up 248 steps on its west face. Deep within the pyramid, archaeologists have discovered a natural clover-shape cave that they speculate may have been the basis for the city's religion and perhaps the reason the city was built in the first place.

The best artifacts uncovered at Teotihuacán are on display at the exceptional Museo Nacional de Antropología in Mexico City. Still, the **Museo de la Sitio,** adjacent to the Pirámide del Sol, contains a number of noteworthy pieces, such as the stone sculpture of the saucer-eyed Tlaloc, some black-and-green obsidian arrowheads, and the skeletons of human sacrifices arranged as they were when first discovered.

More than 4,000 one-story adobe and stone dwellings surround the Calzada de los Muertos; these were occupied by artisans, warriors, and tradesmen. The best example, a short walk east of the Pirámide del Sol, is called **Tepantitla.** Here you'll see murals depicting a watery realm ruled by the rain god Tláloc. Restored in 2002, its reds, greens, and yellows are nearly as vivid as when they were painted more than 1,500 years ago.

There are five entrances to Teotihuacán, each close to one of the major attractions. Around these entrances there are food and craft vendors as well as several restaurants. Among these, the most famous and interesting is La Gruta, which is near Pirámide del Sol and just a short walk east of Museo de Sitio Teotihuacán. ✉ *Carretera Federal 132 (follow signs), San Juan Teotihuacán* ☎ *59/4958–2081* 🌐 *www.inah.gob.mx/zonas/23-zona-arqueologica-de-teotihuacan* 🎟 *MP90.*

🍴 Restaurants

★ Conejo en la Luna Teotihuacán

$$ | MEXICAN | Although best known for the artisanal mezcals produced by its widely known and well-regarded Conejo en La Luna label, this bustling restaurant with a long, covered patio is a great option for grabbing a meal before or after your time visiting the adjacent pyramids. It's one of the area's better breakfast options, with a nice range of classic Mexican egg and chilaquiles dishes, and later in the day you can enjoy hearty fare like lamb barbecue (on weekends only), *escamoles* (ant larvae) sauteed in herb butter, and tacos filled with *cecina* (locally produced cured beef). **Known for:** creative mezcal-based cocktails; great location beside Teotihuacán's pyramids; lovely patio seating. [$] *Average main: MP255* ✉ *Circuito Arqueológico S/N, Purificacion* ☎ *55/7226–9853* 🌐 *www.instagram.com/conejoenlalunateotihuacan.*

La Gruta

$$$ | MEXICAN | FAMILY | Easily the most famous—though also touristy—dining option in the area, this hulking restaurant dates to 1906 and is set within an immense cave with dramatic rock ceilings. The traditional Mexican fare served here is consistently good, including handmade corn quesadillas filled with seasonal ingredients, tortilla soup, *albóndigas* (meatballs) in a tomato-chipotle stew, and traditional barbecue. **Known for:** lots tour groups and big crowds; truly unique and Instagram-worthy setting; short walk from Pirámide del Sol. [$] *Average main: MP340* ✉ *Circuito Arqueologico, Av. del Puente S/N, San Francisco Mazapa* ☎ *55/5191–9799* 🌐 *www.lagruta.mx.*

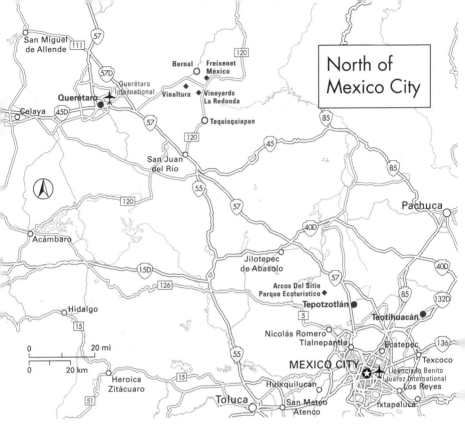

Hotels

Kali Teepee

$ | **B&B/INN** | For an unusual overnight adventure just a 10-minute drive from Teotihuacán's ruins, spend a night glamping under the stars at this small compound of stylishly appointed canvas and geodesic-dome teepees. **Pros:** attentive and friendly hosts; hot-air balloon and dinner packages are available; you can watch movies on a giant projection screen from your tent or teepee. **Cons:** it's possible to hear some street traffic; not within walking distance of any restaurants; in a residential area lacking the natural scenery typically associated with camping. $ *Rooms from: MP1800* ⊠ *Calle Laureles at Av. Tuxpan, San Martín de las Pirámides* ☎ *55/2860–2263* ⊕ *www.facebook.com/kaliteepees* ⤵ *3 units* ❀ *Free Breakfast.*

Posada Colibrí

$$ | **B&B/INN** | Located in the small city of San Juan Teotihuacán, just a few minutes' drive (or half-hour walk) from the nearest entrance gate to the pyramids, this charming inn is set in a walled 18th-century hacienda with a pool, a small candlelit spa, a restaurant, and beautifully landscaped grounds. **Pros:** close to pyramids; spa services and temazcal rituals available; peaceful and lushly landscaped common spaces. **Cons:** rooms are a little dark; in a nondescript neighborhood; not a lot to do in town beyond the pyramids. $ *Rooms from: MP2000* ⊠ *Av. Miguel Hidalgo 37, Teotihuacán de Arista* ☎ *594/933–2025* ⊕ *www.posadacolibri.com* ⤵ *5 rooms* ❀ *Free Breakfast.*

Tepotzotlán

40 km (25 miles) north of Mexico City.

Not to be confused with the similar-sounding town of Tepoztlán, which is just a little farther from Mexico City in the opposite direction (to the south), Tepotzotlán on the northside of the metro area makes for a pleasing half-day getaway. One of country's designated Pueblos Mágicos (and the closest one to CDMX), Tepotzotlán traces its human history back to around 2500 BC and became a center of religious training and education when Spanish Jesuits established a foothold here in the mid-16th century. The most prestigious of the city's institutions, the College of San Francisco Javier, is now the splendid Museo Nacional del Virreinato, and a must for visitors. It adjoins the city's striking cathedral, Templo de San Francisco Javier, and is situated in the picturesque and pedestrian-friendly Centro Histórico, officially known as the San Martín neighborhood. From here, you can stroll around the plaza, admire views of the surrounding mountains, and visit the smattering of galleries, shops, and eateries nearby. There's no shortage of lively—mostly traditional—cafés and restaurants, and if you'd prefer to make a night of it, Puerta Al Virreinato Hotel Boutique offers comfortable, upscale accommodations.

GETTING HERE AND AROUND

Depending on traffic, it's about a 45-minute to 1-hour drive to Tepotzotlán via the toll Highway 57D (going toward Querétaro) from Mexico City. An Uber ride costs around MP500 to MP800 each way. Primera Plus buses depart to the center of Tepotzotlán regularly from Terminal Central de Autobuses del Poniente/Observatorio, on the west side of CDMX, not far from Condesa. The fare is around MP110 each way.

Tepotzotlán itself is easy to explore on foot, and you can catch an Uber to any points slightly farther afield.

TOURS

★ Paseos Turisticos Tepotzotlan

GUIDED TOURS | The tour operator Paseos Turísticos Tepotzotlán, based in the center of town, offers a variety of guided tours, including one-hour history walks, a five-hour tour out to Arcos Del Sitio Parque Ecoturistico, and a full-day tour that takes in the city's historic sites and natural history. Tours are typically given in Spanish, but it's possible to arrange English-speaking tours as well as transportation from Mexico City in advance. Note that sister company Escapadas Estado de México also offers a number of tours throughout the region and is especially known for its excursions to Michoacán's Reserva de la Biósfera Santuario Mariposa Monarca (Monarch Butterfly Sanctuary). ☎ 55/5494–3965 ⊕ www.turismotepotzotlan.com.mx ⛵ From MP120.

VISITOR INFORMATION

CONTACTS Tepotzotlán Tourism Office. ✉ Ayuntamiento De Tepotzotlán (City Hall), Pl. Virreinal No. 1, San Martin, Tepotzotlán ☎ 55/5876–0808 ⊕ www.tepotzotlan.gob.mx/turismo.

Sights

Arcos Del Sitio Parque Ecoturistico

RUINS | FAMILY | This privately run, 130-acre park about 30 km (19 miles) west of Tepozotlán is centered on the massive Aqueduct of Xalpa. Construction of this huge aqueduct was begun in the mid-18th-century by Tepozotlán's Jesuits as a project to supply the town and its monastery with water from a nearby river. The Jesuits were kicked out of Mexico before they could finish the job, but the site's later owner completed the project, and in the 1990s, the 200-foot-tall structure was restored as part of the development of the land into a park. It's a dramatic site, and a beautiful place to

A highlight of visiting Tepotzotlán is getting a glimpse of the Aqueduct of Xalpa within the Arcos Del Sitio Parque Ecoturistico.

stroll around. A number of recreational activities are offered here for an additional price, including horseback rides, ziplining over the river, boating on a small lake, and swimming in a pool. There's also a playground, a casual restaurant, and picnic areas. ⊠ *Off San José Piedra Gorda, Tepotzotlán* ✛ *Follow the signs from Hwy. 2, west of Tepotzotlan; it's about a 45-minute drive from the center of town* ☎ *55/8894–5523* ⊕ *www.arcosdelsitio.com* ✉ *MP35.*

Museo Nacional del Virreinato

HISTORY MUSEUM | No visit to the lovely Spanish colonial city of Tepotzotlán is complete without checking out the National Museum of Viceroyalty of New Spain, which contains an exceptional collection of art, furniture, and other items from primarily the 1500s through the mid-1800s. The museum is set inside the former College of San Francisco Javier, which was built by Jesuit priests in 1580. The ornate baroque architecture—in particular the gilded interiors—of the museum and its surrounding complex of

colonial buildings is reason alone to visit. But the decorative arts inside, including stunning carved cedar retablos covered in 23-karat gold-leaf, as well as fascinating exhibits that detail the 300 years of Mexico's New Spain period, are also tremendously impressive. The museum sits right on Centro Tepotzotlán's main Plaza de la Cruz, which can sometimes be packed with crowds. For some quiet and a breath of fresh air, head out to explore the tree-shaded lawns and gardens in the back, which you can access from the lower floor in the rear of the museum. ⊠ *Plaza Hidalgo 99* ☎ *55/5876–0332* ⊕ *virreinato.inah.gob.mx* ✉ *Free* ☉ *Closed Mon.*

🍽 Restaurants

Los Virreyes

$$ | MEXICAN | The best seats at this sprawling, multilevel restaurant in the heart of Tepotzotlán's historic center are on the upstairs terrace and take in sweeping views of Templo de San Francisco Javier and the surrounding mountains—it's especially dramatic and romantic at sunset. The kitchen turns out reliably good, quite traditional Mexican and European fare from rib-eye steaks to mole poblano, but the big draw here is the view. **Known for:** terrace views of Tepoztlán's historic center; hearty steaks and seafood grills; escamoles (ant larvae) and gusanos de maguey (mezcal worms). $ Average main: MP260 ⊠ Plaza Virreinal 32 ☎ 55/5876–0235 ⊕ www. restaurantelosvirreyes.com.

★ Pulpo Negro

$$$ | **ITALIAN** | Walk a couple blocks south of Tepoztlán's main plaza, which is lined with mostly unmemorable restaurants, to reach this beautifully designed modern Italian spot set in a handsome old building with towering windows and brick walls. The extensive menu features creative pastas, pizzas, and sandwiches served on house-baked artisan breads—try the linguine with shrimp and octopus sauteed in garlic or the Argentinean-style choripán sandwich, with chorizo, a mix of cheeses, and chimichurri sauce. **Known for:** delicious breakfasts; inventive craft cocktails; house-made sodas with unusual flavors, like basil-jasmine-cardamom. $ Average main: MP320 ⊠ Ignacio Manuel Altamirano 8, Tepotztlán ☎ 55/1100–8846 ⊕ www.pulponegro.mx ♡ Closed Mon.

 Hotels

Puerta al Virreinato Hotel Boutique

$$ | **B&B/INN** | Tepotztlán has few noteworthy lodging options, but this elegantly furnished property just around the block from Museo Nacional del Virreinato is a lovely place to spend a night or two. **Pros:** steps from key attractions; splendid views from rooftop restaurant and bar; sophisticated old-world ambience. **Cons:** neighborhood often teems with visitors; no pool or gym; uneven service and quality in the restaurant. $ Rooms from: MP2400 ⊠ Av. Lic. Benito Juárez 1A, Tepotztlán ☎ 55/5876–7213

⊕ puerta-al-virreinato.hotelesentepoztlan. com ⟿ 8 rooms ⓄⅠ Free Breakfast.

Querétaro

205 km (127 miles) northwest of Mexico City.

Querétaro is a modern city with one of the fastest-growing populations in Mexico—there are currently more than 1.1 million inhabitants in the city proper, about a 30% increase over the past decade. The city's high quality of life, low crime rate, pleasant climate, and proximity to a number of worthwhile attractions makes it not only a wonderful place for a short visit but also a desirable place to live, and many people from throughout Mexico as well as the United States, Canada, and Europe are relocating here. This growth in popularity has led to an influx of sophisticated restaurants, bars, and theaters. And within an hour's drive of the city, you can also explore the state of Querétaro's increasingly well-known and impressive wine country.

Querétaro's historical center, which has been designated a UNESCO World Heritage Site, also holds its own against the region's other colonial cities, with wide, tree-lined boulevards and wonderfully manicured parks adorned with fountains and statues of its heroes. Even the large factories and offices rising around the city's perimeter manage to look nice.

Historically, Querétaro is notable as the former residence of Josefa Ortíz de Domínguez, popularly known as La Corregidora, who warned the conspirators gathered in San Miguel and its environs that their independence plot had been discovered. It is here that the ill-fated Emperor Maximilian made his last stand and was executed by firing squad on the Cerro de Las Campanas (Hill of Bells), and where the Mexican Constitution was eventually signed in 1917.

318

The city's relatively small historic center is easily explored by walking along its streets and *andadores* (pedestrian walkways). To the east, the streets climb gradually into the lively and fashionable La Cruz district, which has a number of welcoming cafés and bars. Here you can also stop and catch your breath at the Mirador de los Arcos, a small park on a bluff named for its expansive view of Acueducto de Querétaro, a dramatic 4,200-foot-long aqueduct that extends east into the hills and was built in the 18th century to supply the city with water. Back in the city center, at Plaza de Armas, you can pick up information about the city and surrounding state at the small tourist kiosk.

GETTING HERE AND AROUND
By car, it's a fairly straight shot northwest through picturesque mountainous terrain on toll Highway 57D from Mexico City to Querétaro; the drive takes about three hours. The city makes a convenient and enjoyable overnight stop if you're headed farther north to San Miguel de Allende (an hour northwest) or the city of Guanajuato (another 45 minutes west of San Miguel del Allende). It also has a modern, relatively small, and highly efficient airport with direct flights to several U.S. cities. So if you're planning a trip to Mexico City as well as San Miguel de Allende and Guanajuato, you might consider flying in and out of Querétaro, which has frequent and affordable bus connections to all three cities and is a less chaotic place to rent a car and get acclimated to driving in Mexico than CDMX.

Three bus lines—Futura, Chihuahuenses, and Elite Select, all of which are brands within Estrella Blanca group—offer direct service from Mexico City's Terminal del Norte bus station (which is on the CDMX's metro line 5). The fares are around MP470 each way.

Once you arrive in Querétaro, it's quite easy to get around on foot within the historic city center, which also has several secure parking garages. A relatively modern network of roads and highways makes getting around the metro area and visiting nearby attractions and wineries pretty easy either by car or using Uber.

VISITOR INFORMATION
CONTACTS Querétaro State Tourism Office.
✉ *Calle Pasteur Norte 4, Querétaro* ☎ *442/238–5067* ⊕ *queretaro.travel.*

Sights

Bernal
TOWN | Just a short hop from Tequisquiapan and the state's growing wine country, and about an hour's drive northeast of Querétaro, this officially designated Pueblo Mágico is famous for its scenic peña, one of the largest rock monoliths in the world, which rises 1,150 feet above the town and can be seen for miles away. Though some people come to climb it, many more come for an invigorating walk up its lower half, or just to bask in its supposedly mystical aura. The village itself, with about 4,000 people, makes for a sweet stopover, with its lively restaurants, cafés, and shops selling very nice woolen blankets and clothing in addition to minerals, jewelry, and tchotchkes. ✉ *Hwy. 100, Bernal, Querétaro.*

★ Freixenet México
WINERY | If you have time to visit just one vineyard in the region's increasingly acclaimed wine country, consider heading to this respected operation in the Ezequiel Montes countryside, which offers a variety of tours and tasting experiences, including one that lets you horseback around the property's 125 acres of fields and plantings. Freixenet is especially known for its champagne-style sparkling wines, but the winery also produces some excellent

still wines, including a dry white blend of Macabeo, Chardonnay, and Muscat, and an inky Malbec that pairs well with steak and pastas. ⊠ *Carretera San Juan del Río–Cadereyta, Km 40.5, Querétaro* ☎ *441/277–0147* ⊕ *www.freixenetmex-ico.com.mx* ✉ *MP240 for tour and tasting.*

Fuente de Neptuno

FOUNTAIN | Renowned Mexican architect and Bajío native Eduardo Tresguerras built this fountain in an orchard of the San Antonio monastery in 1797. According to one story, the monks sold some of their land and the fountain along with it when they were facing serious economic problems. It now stands next to the Templo de Santa Clara. ⊠ *Calle Ignacio Allende Norte 32, Querétaro.*

Jardín de la Corregidora

PLAZA/SQUARE | This plaza is prominently marked by a statue of its namesake and War of Independence heroine, Josefa Ortiz de Domínguez. Behind the monument stands the Arbol de la Amistad (Tree of Friendship). Planted in 1977 in a mixture of soils from around the world, the tree symbolizes Querétaro's hospitality to all travelers. This is the town's calmest square, with plenty of choices for patio dining. ⊠ *Corregidora at Av. 16 de Septiembre, Querétaro.*

★ MUCAL (Museo del Calendario)

SPECIALTY MUSEUM | Querétaro has a number of smaller museums with idiosyncratic themes, and this one with an impressively extensive collection set among the many rooms, courtyards, and gardens of a historic house in the city center is one of the best. Exhibits touch on the history of calendars and calendar-making in different cultures around the world. You'll also find a vast array of framed calendars from the past century or so, including quite a few kitschy ones depicting pets, families, and suggestively posed women that were often distributed as advertising material. There's a nice view of the city skyline from the rooftop

terrace, and a small café in the peaceful back garden serves coffee and light food. ⊠ *Calle Francisco I. Madero 91, Querétaro* ☎ *442/212–2187* ⊕ *www.facebook. com/museodelcalendario* ✉ *MP60* ⊙ *Closed Mon.*

Museo de Arte Contemporáneo Querétaro (MACQ)

ART MUSEUM | Although less visited than some of the city's better-known attractions, this excellent (and free) art museum shows thoughtful and well-curated rotating exhibits of contemporary art. It's on a hilltop in the attractive La Cruz neighborhood, in a beautiful historic building beside the imposing Santuario de la Santa Cruz de Los Milagros. There are two floors of galleries, and the art is by a mix of regional and international artists. ⊠ *Av. Reforma Oriente 158, Querétaro* ☎ *442/119–8251* ⊕ *www. macq.mx* ✉ *Free* ⊙ *Closed Mon.*

Museo de Arte de Querétaro

ART MUSEUM | Focusing mostly on European and Mexican artwork, this baroque 18th-century Augustinian monastery-turned-museum exhibits paintings from the 17th through 19th centuries, as well as multiple rotating exhibits of contemporary art. Ask about the symbolism of the columns and the figures in conch shells atop each arch on the fascinating baroque patio. ⊠ *Calle Ignacio Allende Sur 14, Querétaro* ☎ *442/212–2357* ⊕ *www.museodeartedequeretaro.com. mx* ✉ *Free* ⊙ *Closed Mon.*

★ Museo Regional de Querétaro

HISTORY MUSEUM | This elegant 17th-century Franciscan monastery displays pre-Hispanic and indigenous artifacts from cultures of the region plus rooms dedicated to the colonial history of Querétaro and the general history of Mexico. There are early copies of the Mexican Constitution and the table on which the Treaty of Guadalupe Hidalgo was signed. ⊠ *Corregidora Sur 3, Querétaro* ☎ *442/220–2031* ⊕ *lugares. inah.gob.mx* ✉ *MP95* ⊙ *Closed Mon.*

Palacio del Gobierno del Estado

GOVERNMENT BUILDING | Dubbed La Casa de la Corregidora, this building now houses the city's municipal government offices, but in 1810 it was home to Querétaro's mayor-magistrate (El Corregidor) and his wife, Josefa Ortíz de Domínguez (La Corregidora). La Corregidora's literary salon was actually a cover for conspirators—including Ignacio Allende and Father Miguel Hidalgo—to plot a course for independence. When he discovered the salon's true nature, El Corregidor imprisoned his wife in her room, but not before she alerted Allende and Hidalgo. Soon after, on September 15, Father Hidalgo tolled the bell of his church to signal the onset of the fight for freedom. A replica of that bell caps this building, and two contemporary murals in the central courtyard depict key players in Querétaro's history. ☒ *Plaza de la Independencia, Calle 5 de Mayo, Querétaro* ☎ *442/211-7070* ⊕ *www.queretaro.gob.mx* ☒ *Free* ⊙ *Closed weekends.*

★ **Plaza de Armas**

PLAZA/SQUARE | Also known as Plaza de la Independencia, this immaculate square is bordered by carefully restored colonial mansions and is especially lovely at night, when the central fountain is lit-up. Built in 1842, the fountain is dedicated to the Marqués de la Villa del Villar, who constructed Querétaro's elegant aqueduct. The old stone aqueduct, with its 74 towering arches, stands at the town's east end. Patio tables under the portico in front of Hotel Mesón de Santa Rosa are the perfect place for a respite from shopping and museum hopping. ☒ *And. 5 de Mayo at Av. Luis Pasteur Sur, Querétaro.*

Templo de Santa Rosa de Viterbo

RELIGIOUS BUILDING | This former convent, constructed from 1727 to 1752 and attributed to the Queretano Don Ignacio Mariano de las Casas, is noteworthy for its whimsical arches and the Arab influence of its facade. Inside, the church is one of the joys of the Mexican baroque, famous for its five fantastically carved, gold-leaf altarpieces as well as its rich paintings and statues. ☒ *José María Arteaga 89, Querétaro* ☎ *442/214-1691* ⊕ *www.facebook.com/templosantarosa* ☒ *Free.*

Tequisquiapan

TOWN | Drenched in sun, bougainvillea, and flowering trees, Tequis (as the locals call it) is a pleasant stop for a day or overnight trip—it lies about an hour's drive east of Querétaro, and is also close to the region's wine country. Join the many families who come to stroll through the main square with its neoclassical Templo de Santa María de la Asunción, whose facade has been said to resemble swirls of cotton more than stone. Stop for lunch in one of the outdoor cafés under the arcades that front the plaza and visit the surrounding streets and the Mercado de Artesanías to shop for handicrafts. Tequis has a well-deserved reputation for high-quality craftwork, including wicker baskets, opal jewelry, woven goods, wood, and ceramics. The town is also known for its mineral swimming pools (many of the hotels have them) and spas. ☒ *Hwy. 120 at Hwy. 200, Querétaro.*

Vinaltura

WINERY | This elegant boutique winery in a contemporary building on a mesa with stunning views toward Peña de Bernal is known both for its excellent wines and its outstanding restaurant, Envero, which is open for lunch and dinner. You can book a classic tour and tasting of two wines, which lasts about 90 minutes, or opt for the sensory experience in which you'll try three different wines blindfolded, along with small tapas to better understand the relationship foods have on wine tasting. Vinaltura makes a wide range of wines, from crisp and minerally Chenin Blanc and Gewürztraminer with floral notes to a bold Bordeaux blend called Terruño Ladera. ☒ *Ignacio Zaragoza, Sta Rosa de Lima S/N, Querétaro*

☎ 442/824–7701 ⊕ www.vinaltura.mx
🍴 Tours and tastings from MP450.

Vineyards La Redonda
WINERY | **FAMILY** | Fairly close to Freixenet México and therefore popular to visit when heading there or to the nearby town of Bernal, La Redonda is one of the most prestigious and popular wineries in central Mexico. The sprawling property is laced with pathways and beautiful landscaping, and it's very accommodating of families and even visitors with dogs. You can come and sample the many varieties of wine produced here by booking a full meal in the restaurant or opting for a more casual experience in the wine garden and wine bar. La Redonda also offers overnight winery glamping experiences, and festivals and events open to the public take place throughout the year. ⊠ Carr. San Juan del Río a Ezequiel Montes Km 33.5, Querétaro ☎ 442/230–1636 ⊕ www.laredonda.com.mx 🍴 Grounds free; wine and food available for purchase.

🍴 Restaurants

★ Di Vino
$$ | **ITALIAN** | Clean, bright, and charming, this Italian restaurant has an inviting location on pedestrian-only Andador Cinco de Mayo, just steps away from Plaza de Armas. Customers return again and again for the creative thin-crust pizzas, pastas, and cheese and charcuterie plates served in a historic old home converted to a three-story restaurant. **Known for:** friendly, knowledgeable staff; outstanding wine list; exquisite desserts. $ Average main: MP240 ⊠ Andador 5 de Mayo 12, Querétaro ☎ 442/214–1273 ⊕ www.divino.com.mx.

El Mesón de Chucho el Roto
$$ | **MEXICAN** | This tremendously popular restaurant, named after Querétaro's version of Robin Hood, is on the handsome Plaza de Armas. It's strong on regional dishes like goat-filled tacos and shrimp with nopal (cactus) and corundas (a kind of tamale from the neighboring state of Michoacán). **Known for:** romantic covered patio overlooking Plaza de Armas; leisurely breakfasts; hearty steaks and seafood grills. $ Average main: MP245 ⊠ Av. Luis Pasteur Sur 16, Querétaro ☎ 442/182–0855 ⊕ www.chuchoelroto.com.mx.

★ Hacienda La Laborcilla
$$$$ | **MODERN EUROPEAN** | A favorite destination for romantic date nights and special occasions, this elegant restaurant is set within the grand high-ceiling salons and elaborately landscaped terraces of a 17th-century hacienda a short drive north of the city center. The upscale cuisine borrows heavily from France and Italy—consider foie gras with fig compote on a baguette and roasted beets with labneh and pistachios to start, followed by fish of the day with a puttanesca sauce or beef filet with a rich tarragon-butter sauce. **Known for:** refined setting in a 17th-century hacienda; artfully plated modern cuisine; drinks and live music in the restaurant's Carter and Horus bars. $ Average main: MP470 ⊠ Prol. Corregidora Norte 911 bis, Querétaro ☎ 442/245–1695 ⊕ www.haciendalalaborcilla.com.

Hacienda Los Laureles Restaurante
$$$ | **MEXICAN** | The flower-filled grand patio in this perfectly restored hacienda a 15-minute drive north of the city offers inviting outdoor dining shaded by umbrellas. The house specialty is carnitas, chunks of pork stewed overnight and served with oodles of guacamole, beans, and homemade tortillas. **Known for:** impressive wine and cocktail list; relaxing garden setting; live music. $ Average main: MP370 ⊠ 5 Carretera México-San Luis Potosí, Km. 8 5, Querétaro ☎ 237/119–3592 ⊕ www.restauranteloslaureles.com.mx.

Hank's Oyster Bar
$$ | **CREOLE** | You'll find surprisingly authentic Creole and Cajun fare at this festive New Orleans–style restaurant in the

historic city center that's decorated with photos and paintings of jazz musicians and indeed features live bands in the evening from Wednesday through Saturday. Oysters fried, roasted, or on the half shell are a must for fans of bivalves, but also consider such classic recipes such as seafood gumbo, barbecue ribs, and blackened redfish along with po'boys and burgers. **Known for:** festive, chatter-filled dining room; oysters prepared in a wide variety of ways; pecan pie à la mode. [$] *Average main: MP290* ✉ *Calle Benito Juárez Sur 7, Querétaro* ☎ *442/214–2620* 🌐 *www.hanksmexico.com.*

La Biznaga Arte y Café

$ | **ECLECTIC** | This colorful restaurant set in a historic building in the trendy La Cruz district is filled with hanging plants, climbing vines, and eccentric paintings and folk art. Although popular for every meal of the day, the restaurant is especially known during the day for crepes, omelets, salads, sandwiches, pizzas, and traditional Mexican dishes. **Known for:** cash-only policy; festive breakfast and brunches; long dessert menu of milk shakes, pies, and cakes. [$] *Average main: MP140* ✉ *Manuel Gutiérrez Nájera 17, Querétaro* ☎ *442/807–0111* 🌐 *www.instagram.com/labiznagaarteycafe* 💳 *No credit cards* 🕒 *Closed Sun.*

Restaurante Josecho

$$$$ | **INTERNATIONAL** | Situated a 10-minute drive southwest of the city center, this elegant spot specializing in sophisticated contemporary Mexican and international cuisine is a lovely destination for an unhurried dinner. The house specialties change regularly, but typical fare includes steak Rossini with foie gras and a red wine glaze or rare-seared tuna with risotto and a balsamic–black olive reduction. **Known for:** live classical music many evenings; one of the best selections of Mexican and international wine in the city; rich and creative house-made desserts. [$] *Average main: MP520* ✉ *Dalia 1, Querétaro* ☎ *442/216–0201* 🌐 *www.josecho.com.mx* 🕒 *No dinner Sun.*

Coffee and Quick Bites

Cafe Racine

$ | **CAFÉ** | Perfect for a quick caffeine pick-me-up or a more leisurely session of catching up with friends, this plant-filled café serves a full range of coffee and tea drinks along with a selection of tasty baked goods. It's right in the heart of the city center, steps from local museums. **Known for:** decadent cookies; extensive menu of espresso drinks; chai and matcha teas. [$] *Average main: MP70* ✉ *Calle José María Pino Suárez 25, Querétaro* ☎ *442/245–7258* 🌐 *www.instagram.com/caferacine.qro* 🕒 *Closed Sun.*

★ **Kremsha Cafe & Bakery**

$ | **BAKERY** | Set in a quiet residential area several blocks south of the city center, this cozy and inviting spot with a small pet-friendly terrace is a terrific option for delicious breakfasts and lunches, or even just a rich latte or a slice of cake. Highlights from the menu include avocado toast, ham-and-Manchego baguette sandwiches, and chilaquiles verde. **Known for:** luscious desserts; quiet location away from the bustle of the city center; sandwiches and toasts on house-baked artisan breads. [$] *Average main: MP130* ✉ *Calle Motolinia 12B, Querétaro* ☎ *442/323–2437* 🌐 *www.kremsha.com* 🕒 *No dinner.*

Hotels

Fiesta Americana Hacienda Galindo Resort & Spa

$$ | **RESORT** | **FAMILY** | Offering a great variety of activities for guests of all ages—from a sophisticated spa and elegant pool area to a game room, bike rentals, horseback riding, and a billiards room—this stylish resort built around a grand early 1600s hacienda makes a wonderful base for exploring the region. **Pros:** beautifully landscaped grounds; lovely pool

and full-service spa; en route from CDMX and close to the wine country. **Cons:** need a car to get around; 40-minute drive from the city; often fills up with weddings and events. [$] *Rooms from: MP3500* ✉ *Carretera Amealco–Hacienda Galindo Km 5.5, San Juan del Río, Querétaro* ☎ *443/310–8137* 🌐 *www.fiestamericana.com* 🛏 *168 rooms* 🍴 *No Meals.*

★ **Hacienda Jurica**

$$ | RESORT | FAMILY | Families from Mexico City escape to this sprawling 16th-century ex-hacienda, part of the upscale Brisas chain, which is replete with topiary gardens, a horse stable, access to a nearby golf course, and acres of grassy sports fields. **Pros:** spectacular grounds; no shortage of activities; romantic restaurant. **Cons:** need a car or Uber to get around; lots of weddings and corporate events; a bit far from CDMX. [$] *Rooms from: MP2400* ✉ *Paseo Jurica 700, Querétaro* ☎ *442/218–0022* 🌐 *www.lasbrisashotels.com.mx/queretaro* 🛏 *182 rooms* 🍴 *No Meals.*

Hotel Criol

$ | HOTEL | With a sleek modern design and a terrific location within walking distance of Plaza de Armas and the restaurants and nightlife of the La Cruz district, the reasonably priced Hotel Criol has a peaceful courtyard and pool, a library, a small restaurant for guests to relax in, and compact but smartly furnished rooms. **Pros:** convenient, central location; alluring contemporary architecture; very reasonable rates. **Cons:** some rooms are a little dark; breakfast, though quite good, costs extra; no parking. [$] *Rooms from: MP1650* ✉ *Hotel Criol de Hoteles Calle 1, Querétaro* ☎ *442/213–5357* 🌐 *www.facebook.com/hotelcriol* 🛏 *24 rooms* 🍴 *No Meals.*

Hotel de Piedra

$$ | HOTEL | Short of camping along the trail, you can't get a whole lot closer to the famed Peña de Bernal monolith than staying in this imaginatively designed boutique inn constructed of local stone and offering a very nice restaurant and wine cellar bar, plus a terrace, pool, and hot tub with great views of the countryside. **Pros:** steps from the trail to Peña de Bernal; beautiful architecture with smartly designed guest rooms; excellent base for exploring the wine country. **Cons:** 20-minute walk from center of Bernal; an hour's drive from Querétaro's city center; some rooms hear noise from the restaurant. [$] *Rooms from: MP3200* ✉ *Calle de la Corregidora 67, Bernal, Querétaro* ☎ *441/296–4680* 🌐 *www.hoteldepiedra.com* 🛏 *13 rooms* 🍴 *Free Breakfast.*

★ **Hotel Doña Urraca**

$$$ | RESORT | Located a few blocks east of the city center in the lively La Cruz neighborhood, this enchanting and rather posh urban resort set within the thick walls of a stunningly updated 18th-century hacienda contains 24 spacious, minimalist-chic suites along with a romantic restaurant, a central pool and courtyard, and a spa offering a wide range of services and treatments. There's a second Doña Urraca resort in San Miguel de Allende. **Pros:** in a lively central neighborhood; opulent rooms and common spaces; serene setting. **Cons:** not a good fit for families; expensive; noise from corridors and public spaces can be an issue. [$] *Rooms from: MP5000* ✉ *Calle 5 de Mayo 117, Querétaro* ☎ *442/238–5400* 🌐 *www.donaurraca.com* 🛏 *24 rooms* 🍴 *Free Breakfast.*

★ **La Casa de la Marquesa**

$$$ | HOTEL | A stately 1756 mansion has been converted into a handsome hotel in Querétaro's center, with each of the spacious guest rooms decorated with fine antiques, tasteful art, parquet floors, and area rugs. **Pros:** distinctly decorated rooms and interesting Moorish architecture; steps from museums and restaurants; solicitous service. **Cons:** may be a bit too old-fashioned for some tastes; in a busy, loud neighborhood; not suitable for children. [$] *Rooms from: MP4700* ✉ *Calle Francisco I. Madero 41, Querétaro*

☎ 442/227–0500 ⊕ lacasadelamarquesa.
mx ⇜ 13 rooms ⏐⊙⏐ No Meals.

Nightlife

★ College Bar Querétaro
BARS | The name of this lively lounge
in the city center's bustling La Cruz
district may give you pause if you last
attended college in the previous century,
but College Bar actually appeals to a
wide range of ages thanks to its pretty
rooftop lounge with great views and an
extensive menu of legitimately tasty pub
fare, including pizzas, Cobb salads, and
gigantic burgers. Musicians entertain the
crowds, and TV monitors air soccer as
well as NFL football games. ⊠ Av. Circunvalación 46, Querétaro ☎ 442/537–7452
⊕ www.instagram.com/collegebarqro.

La Internacional Querétaro
BARS | The Querétaro outpost of a
Mexican chainlet of popular bottle
shop-bars known for the vast selections
of craft beer is a fun place to mingle
with locals and dine on light pub fare.
⊠ Av. Circunvalación 30, Querétaro
☎ 442/213–0082 ⊕ www.instagram.com/
lainternacionalqro.

Wicklow Irish Pub
PUB | A few blocks up the hill from Plaza
de Armas in the La Cruz neighborhood,
this classic Irish pub lives up to its theme
with a great selection of imported whiskies and beers, plus live rock bands many
evenings. It has pretty tasty burgers,
wings, and the like as well. ⊠ Calle de
Mayo 86, Querétaro ☎ 442/141–2714
⊕ www.wicklowirishpub.mx.

Shopping

★ Casa Queretana de las Artesianias
CRAFTS | Located just a few steps down
a pedestrian alley from Plaza de Armas,
this beautiful boutique run by the state's
department of culture promotes Querétaro's rich heritage of arts and crafts.
The traditional weavings, woodwork,

ceramics, and other fine pieces here
have been created by fairly compensated
artisans young and old. It's one of the
best places in the city to pick up a keep-
sake. ⊠ Andador Libertad 52, Querétaro
☎ 442/214–1235 ⊕ www.casaquereta-
naartesanias.gob.mx.

Puebla

130 km (81 miles) east of Mexico City.

The country's fifth largest city, Puebla has
long been popular with visitors interested
in exploring its well preserved Centro
Histórico and sampling its famously
delicious traditional Mexican cuisine.
But this city of around 1.7 million people
has also been saddled with a somewhat
stodgy and staid reputation that befits the
business-minded and religiously devoted
mind-set of many of its residents, who are
known as Poblanos. But the city's vibe is
steadily changing, especially as younger
residents move here for the abundance of
high-paying jobs, especially in the automotive industry—both Audi and Volkswagen
have huge factories here.

A mix of sleek spa-boutique hotels and
restaurants offering contemporary dining
have opened in recent years, many in artfully transformed historic buildings. Puebla
is a beautiful city to walk around, fairly
bursting with baroque flourishes and the
bright colors of its famed Talavera tiles.
The downtown area in particular overflows
with religious structures; it might just
have more ex-convents and monasteries,
chapels, and churches per square mile
than anywhere else in the country. The
city was established by the Spanish in
1531 as a strategic stopover between
Mexico City and the port city of Veracruz,
and its ornate architecture is a key reason
the Centro Histórico was named a UNES-
CO World Heritage Site in 1987.

It's possible to see the city's top
attractions and even sneak in a detour
to neighboring Cholula in a couple of

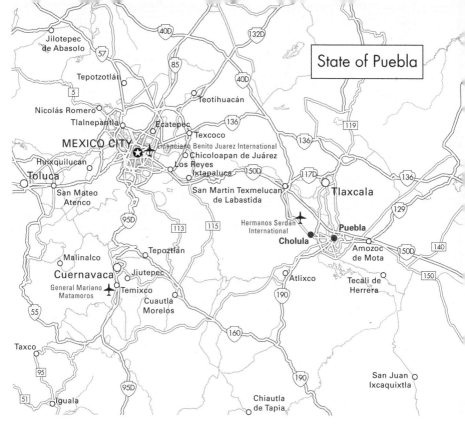

State of Puebla

days, but you could easily spend a few additional days just savoring the exquisite cuisine. Two of Mexico's most popular dishes are said to have originated here: mole, the wonderfully rich and complex sauce with as many as 30 ingredients, which is also claimed by the neighboring state of Oaxaca; and *chiles en nogada,* a dish of poblano chiles filled with meats, fruits, and nuts then covered with a sauce of chopped walnuts and cream and topped with pomegranate seeds; the colors represent the Mexican flag, and this hearty plate is served predominantly in September in honor of Mexican Independence Day. Other recipes for which the city is known are *pelonas,* fried rolls filled with lettuce, beef, cream, and sauce; and *cemitas,* a type of torta made with a sweeter bread and filled with avocado, meat, and cheese.

The city center generally follows a tidy grid pattern, made up of *avenidas* and *calles,* and most are numbered.

GETTING HERE AND AROUND

Allow about two hours, maybe a bit less if traffic is on your side, for the drive via toll Highway 150D from Mexico City. This very direct route runs over a high mountain pass to the north—offering great views on clear days—of the Iztaccíhuatl and Popocatépetl volcanoes. For an even more scenic but much longer (about four hours) drive that runs along the lower western slopes of the volcanoes, take Highway 115D southeast to Highway 160 east, and then Highway 438D east through the charming small city of Atlixco to Highway 190, which leads north to Puebla. Cholula is an easy 20-minute drive west of Puebla's historic center by way of Via Volkswagen.

Bus travel is a convenient option as well, especially since you don't really need a car to explore Puebla, which has a densely populated city center that's best explored on foot. Buses bound for Puebla's main station (CAPU, or Central de Autobuses de Puebla) depart several times an hour from TAPO terminal, which is a few kilometers east of Mexico City's Centro Histórico. On ADO, the most reliable company, the two-hour ride costs about MP230 to MP400.

If you do arrive by car, park at your hotel or in a municipal garage rather than trying to contend with the slow traffic of the city center. Uber is reliable for longer trips or to get back and forth between Puebla and Cholula.

The double-decker Turibus (⊕ *www. turibus.com.mx*) is a good option for exploring the city and the neighboring town of Cholula. Every day from morning through evening, these open-top buses follow a circuit around the city and on to neighboring Cholula; you can board the buses at stops marked with Turibus signs. The fare is MP150.

VISITOR INFORMATION

CONTACTS Puebla State Tourism Office.
⊠ *Módulo de Información Turística, Av. 5 Oriente 3, Centro Histórico, Puebla* ☎ *22/2246–2490* ⊕ *www.visitpuebla.mx.*

 Sights

Barrio del Artista
NEIGHBORHOOD | Watch painters and sculptors at work in the galleries in this small district set amid bronze monuments to Poblano authors and poets. Farther down Calle 8 Norte, you can buy Talavera pottery and other local crafts from the dozens of small stores and street vendors. There are occasional weekend concerts and open-air theater performances. ⊠ *Calle 8 at Av. 6 Oriente, Puebla.*

Calle de los Dulces
STREET | Puebla is famous for all kinds of homemade goodies. Calle de Santa Clara, also known as Sweets Street, is lined with shops selling a wide variety of sugary treats in the shape of sacred hearts, guitars, and sombreros. Don't miss the cookies—they're even more delicious than they look. ⊠ *Av. 6 Oriente, between Av. 5 de Mayo and Calle 4 Norte, Puebla.*

★ Callejón de los Sapos
STREET | This narrow and charming pedestrian lane, whose name means "Alley of the Toads," cuts diagonally behind the cathedral. The adjacent square has a bustling weekend antiques market with all sorts of Mexican art and crafts, from elaborately carved doors to small paintings on pieces of tin offering thanks to a saint for favors. There are also hip cafés filled with people listening to live music on weekends. ⊠ *Calle 6 Sur from Av. 5 to 7 Oriente, Puebla.*

Capilla del Rosario
RELIGIOUS BUILDING | The magnificent church of St. Dominic is famous for its overwhelming Capilla del Rosario (Chapel of the Rosary), where almost every inch of the walls and ceilings is covered with gilded carvings. Dominican friars arrived here in 1534, barely a dozen years after the Spanish conquered this region. The Capilla de la Tercera Orden (Chapel of the Third Order) was originally called the "Chapel of the Dark-Skinned Ones," named for the mixed-race population born a short time later. ⊠ *Av. 5 de Mayo at Av. 4 Poniente, Puebla* ☎ *222/242–3643* ⊕ *www.capilladelrosariopuebla. com.mx* 🎫 *Free* ☺ *Closed Mon.*

Catedral de Puebla
RELIGIOUS BUILDING | Construction on Puebla's immense and impressive cathedral began between 1536 and 1539. Work was completed by the city's most famous son, Bishop Juan de Palafox y Mendoza, who donated his personal fortune to build its famous tower, the

Once a convent, the Museo de Arte Religioso de Santa Mónica features several religious exhibits.

second largest in the country. The altar was constructed between 1797 and 1818. Manuel Tolsá, Mexico's most illustrious colonial architect, adorned it with onyx, marble, and gold. The meticulously preserved interior is among the most impressive of Mexico's churches. ✉ *Calle 16 de Septiembre at Calle 3, Puebla* ☎ *222/232–2316* ⊕ *www.arquidiocesis-depuebla.mx* ✉ *Free.*

Mercado de Artesanías El Parián

MARKET | More than 100 craft vendors sell their wares in this bustling open-air market decorated with Talavera tiles that's been a fixture of the city center since 1961. It's a fun place to shop for tourist souvenirs, such as toy guitars and colorful sombreros, but you'll also find a good selection of higher-quality jewelry, tapestries, metalwork, and ceramics. ✉ *Av. 2 Oriente and Calle 6 Norte, Puebla* ☎ *222/232–5484.*

★ Museo Amparo

HISTORY MUSEUM | This impressive art and history museum is housed in a pair of adjoining Spanish Colonial hospital buildings from the 1800s with a gorgeous contemporary atrium, several galleries, and a dramatic rooftop terrace with a bar, glass walls, and grand views of the Zócalo. Home to the private collection of pre-Columbian and colonial-era art of Mexican banker and philanthropist Manuel Espinoza Yglesias, Museo Amparo exhibits unforgettable pieces from all over Mexico, including nearly 5,000 pre-Hispanic artifacts. The collection includes colonial-era painting, sculpture, and decorative objects as well as a small modern art section notable for works by Diego Rivera, Frida Kahlo, Miguel Felguérez, and Vicente Rojo. ✉ *Calle 2 Sur 708, Puebla* ☎ *222/229–3850* ⊕ *www.museoamparo. com* ✉ *MP85* ☾ *Closed Tues.*

Museo de Arte Religioso de Santa Mónica

HISTORY MUSEUM | This former convent (sometimes called Ex-Convento de Santa Mónica) opened in 1688 as a spiritual refuge for women whose husbands were away on business. Despite the Reform Laws of the 1850s, it continued to function until 1934. It is said that the women here invented the famous dish called chiles en nogada, a complex recipe that incorporates the red, white, and green colors of the Mexican flag. In the museum's 23 permanent exhibit galleries, curiosities include the gruesome display of the preserved heart of the convent's founder and paintings in the Sala de los Terciopelos (Velvet Room), in which the feet and faces seem to change position as you view them from different angles. ⊠ *Av. 18 Poniente 103, Puebla* ☎ *222/232–0178* ⊕ *www.facebook.com/ ExConventodeSantaMonica* 🖼 *MP70* 🕙 *Closed Mon.*

Museo del Fuerte de Loreto

MILITARY SIGHT | A five-minute drive north of the Zócalo in an otherwise nondescript industrial area, you'll find this excellent museum inside the Zona Histórica de los Fuertes, an expansive park that commemorates the city's colorful military history, including the famous Battle of Puebla between France and the nascent Mexican Republic, in which the latter prevailed against what was considered to be far more formidable force. Unless you're a big history buff, you may not be familiar with this battle, but you probably recognize the date: May 5, 1862, or Cinco de Mayo, which though a popular holiday outside Mexico is a far less important date than that of Mexican Independence Day, on September 16. Nevertheless, the museum here inside this well-preserved fort is one of the more interesting, and underrated, ones in the city; it's filled with exhibits and artifacts that tell the story of this battle. Across the park, Museo del Fuerte de Guadalupe is interesting as well but not quite as comprehensive. It's worth a look, though, if you have time. ⊠ *De los, Calz. de los Fuertes s/n, Puebla* ☎ *222/234–8513* ⊕ *www.facebook.com/LosFuertesPuebla* 🖼 *MP70* 🕙 *Closed Mon.*

★ **Museo Internacional del Barroco**

ART MUSEUM | Located in a modern business district in Puebla's southwestern outskirts, a 15-minute drive from the city center, this striking white contemporary building with curving white-concrete walls facing a courtyard with a reflecting pool is arguably as famous for its architecture as for the collection within. Renowned Japanese architect Toyo Itō designed the museum, paying homage to Puebla's rich history of Baroque art and design, which traces back to the city's settlement by the Spanish in the 1530s. One exhibit that interprets this relationship with a particular flourish is an interactive scale-model of Puebla's Centro Histórico that lets you see just how many buildings have been influenced by this important movement that spanned the early 17th through the mid-18th centuries. Other galleries are devoted to Baroque paintings, classical music, literature, theater, and other disciplines. On the second level, a stylish restaurant continues the building's beautiful design and serves quite tasty contemporary Mexican cuisine. ⊠ *Atlixcáyotl 2501, Puebla* ☎ *222/326–7130* ⊕ *www. museospuebla.puebla.gob.mx* 🖼 *MP95* 🕙 *Closed Mon.*

Museo Nacional de los Ferrocarriles

SPECIALTY MUSEUM | FAMILY | Occupying a train station inaugurated by President Juárez in 1869, the National Railway Museum extends a nostalgic treat. Period engines sit on the now-unused platforms, and several vintage cars—including a caboose—can be explored. ⊠ *Calle 11 Norte 1005, Puebla* ☎ *222/774–0100* ⊕ *www.museoferrocarrilesmexicanos. gob.mx* 🖼 *MP19* 🕙 *Closed Mon.*

Twin Peaks

[👁]

Driving from Mexico City to Puebla on toll Highway 150D (known as the Carretera a Puebla, or the Puebla Highway), you'll see Mexico's second- and third-highest peaks, Popocatépetl and Iztaccíhuatl, to your right (looking south)—if the clouds and climate allow. "Popo," at 17,887 feet high, is the pointed volcano farther away, sometimes graced with a plume of smoke; Izta is slightly shorter but has a larger girth. Both are often covered with snow. Popo has seen a renewed period of activity since the mid-1990s; light volcanic activity has been consistent and you might see steam and gas emissions (the mountain is still in "yellow" alert level).

As legend has it, Aztec warrior Popocatépetl was sent by the emperor—father of his beloved Iztaccíhuatl—to bring back the head of a feared enemy in order to win her hand. He returned triumphantly only to find that Iztaccíhuatl had killed herself, believing him dead. Grief-stricken, Popo laid out her body on a small knoll and lighted an eternal torch that he watches over. Each of Iztaccíhuatl's four peaks is named for a different part of her body, and its silhouette conjures up its nickname, "Sleeping Woman" (although the correct Nahuatl translation is "the white woman").

Popo is strictly off-limits for climbing, but several of Izta's rugged peaks can be explored, although anyone other than extremely experienced high-peak mountaineers should go only with an established guide company. Those who make the climb are rewarded with sublime views of Popo and other volcanoes, with the Pico de Orizaba (or Citlaltépetl, which at 18,491 feet is the country's highest peak) to the east and the Nevado de Toluca to the west.

★ Uriarte Talavera

FACTORY | Founded in 1824, this is one of the few authentic Talavera workshops left today. To be the real deal, pieces must be hand-painted in intricate designs with natural dyes derived from minerals. That's why only five colors are used: blue, black, yellow, green, and a reddish pink. English- and Spanish-language tours take place daily except for Sunday, but visitors are also welcome to visit the shop and terrace for free. ✉ *Av. 4 Poniente 911, Puebla* ☎ *222/232–1598* 🌐 *www.uriartetalavera.com.mx* 🎟 *Free; tours from MP80* 🕑 *No tours Sun.*

🍴 Restaurants

★ Augurio

$$ | **MODERN MEXICAN** | High ceilings, dangling wood beams, and distinctive light features hint at the marriage of traditional and contemporary approaches to Mexican cuisine at this stylish restaurant across from Museo Amparo. Creative takes on mole are a specialty, including sweetbreads with (ant larvae) and a white mole sauce, and 36-hour-braised short rib with an ancho chile adobo sauce, but you'll also find dried-beef tartare with jalapeño oil and blue-corn masa filled with black beans, pork shank, and cotija cheese. **Known for:** attractive outdoor seating; deals on food and craft beer on Taco Tuesdays; chilaquiles with a chicken and mole poblano for breakfast. [$] *Average main: MP265* ✉ *Privada*

9 Oriente 16, Puebla 222/290–2378 www.augurio.mx No dinner Sun.

La Casa del Mendrugo

$$ | **MEXICAN FUSION** | Many are drawn to this restaurant for its dramatic setting in an early 19th-century former Jesuit college that now contains a museum filled with pre-Hispanic artifacts and exhibits, but the superbly crafted traditional Pueblan food is excellent, too. Start with a breakfast of eggs in a stew of poblano chiles, corn, and epazote, or later in the day, try the pork chalupas or guacamole with *chapulines* (grasshopper) followed by chicken in a green pumpkin-seed mole sauce. **Known for:** memorable historic setting; hearty traditional breakfasts; attentive service. *Average main: MP270* *Calle 4 Sur 304, Puebla* 222/326–8060 www.casadelmendrugo.com No dinner Sun.

★ **Moyuelo**

$$ | **MEXICAN** | This eatery does a welcome, contemporary take on the cemita, Puebla's version of the classic Mexican torta sandwich. The smoked brisket comes with a plantain puree and flavorful pepper sauce while the chilaquiles are garnished with watercress in avocado oil. **Known for:** hip, stylish vibe; inventive appetizers like beef tongue carpaccio with coriander seeds; creative cocktails. *Average main: MP260* *Av. 7 Poniente 312, Puebla* 222/232–4270 www.moyuelo.com.mx Closed Mon. No dinner Sun.

★ **Mural de los Poblanos**

$$$ | **MEXICAN** | Among the city's countless restaurants specializing in Pueblo-style mole sauces, this relaxing spot set in a gracious galleried building with wood-beam ceilings, soaring arches, and tile floors is one of the finest. The sampler plate with chicken or cheese enchiladas smothered under three different kinds of mole sauce are a delicious way to learn about the differences in preparation of these complex sauces. **Known for:** refined setting; excellent wine

list; pan de elote (corn cake) with eggnog ice cream. *Average main: MP355* *Calle 16 de Septiembre 506, Puebla* 222/242–0503 www.elmuraldelospoblanos.com.

Coffee and Quick Bites

Cafe Cultura

$ | **CAFÉ** | Break up your explorations of Pueblo's Centro Histórico with perfectly crafted single-origin coffee or cold brew featuring locally roasted beans from acclaimed Subversivo Roasters at this hip little café around the corner from the colorful Sapos Alley. There are a few tasty food items, too, including flatbread with cheese and ham. **Known for:** fine teas; flat whites and lattes; croissants, cheesecake, and other sweets. *Average main: MP45* *Calle 4 Sur 506, Puebla* 221/528–2451 www.instagram.com/cafecultura_p Closed Sun.

Mary Barragan Helados

$ | **ICE CREAM** | A few blocks south of the Zócalo, there's often a line outside at this beloved ice-cream parlor known for rich and creamy frozen treats. Favorite flavors include avocado, cajeta, and hibiscus. **Known for:** banana splits; luscious tiramisu or Baileys Irish Cream milk shakes; nieves (sorbets) in fresh fruit flavors like guayaba and passionfruit. *Average main: MP50* *Calle 16 de Septiembre 1501, Puebla* 222/240–2098.

Hotels

★ **Banyan Tree Puebla**

$$ | **HOTEL** | Set in an imaginatively updated 19th-century building with stone walls, high ceilings, and floor-to-ceiling windows, this posh and peaceful urban oasis on the edge of Centro Histório abounds with pleasing amenities, including three excellent restaurants, two bars, and a sublime spa offering Thai-style massages and body treatments. **Pros:** outstanding, highly personalized service; gorgeous rooftop terrace with bar and

pool; multiple excellent dining options. **Cons:** 15-minute walk to the Zócalo; pool is quite small; rates can rise considerably during busy periods. $ *Rooms from: MP3300* ✉ *Calle 10 Norte 1402, Puebla* ☎ *222/122–2300* ⊕ *www.banyantree. com* ⇝ *78 rooms* ❄❄❄ *No Meals.*

★ Cartesiano Boutique & Wellness Hotel
$$ | **HOTEL** | Occupying a magnificently transformed pair of 17th-century buildings, one of which formerly held a ceramic-tile factory, this plush urban oasis with a rooftop pool and a soothing spa is part of Puebla's new wave of chic—and surprisingly affordable—boutique hotels. **Pros:** great downtown location; stunning rooftop with bar and pool; stunning, distinctive design. **Cons:** very crowded neighborhood; often books up well in advance on weekends; wellness treatments and meals can greatly add to your tab. $ *Rooms from: MP2700* ✉ *Calle 3 Oriente 610, Puebla* ☎ *222/478–6900* ⊕ *www.cartesiano360.com* ⇝ *78 rooms* ❄❄❄ *Free Breakfast.*

★ Casona de la China Poblana
$$ | **B&B/INN** | This marvelously renovated colonial building may no longer be a private home, but it still has the same cozy environment, with an enchanting mix of original accents, antique and modern furnishings, and luxe linens. **Pros:** romantic restaurant; spacious rooms with lots of personality; easy walk to downtown sights. **Cons:** largest rooms are quite pricey; not suitable for kids; noise from the restaurant and the street can be an issue. $ *Rooms from: MP3600* ✉ *Calle 4 Norte 2, Puebla* ☎ *222/242–0361* ⊕ *www.casonadelachinapoblana.mx* ⇝ *10 rooms* ❄❄❄ *Free Breakfast.*

La Purificadora
$$ | **HOTEL** | Part of the trendy Grupo Habita brand, this striking hotel set in a former 19th-century water-purification plant helped put Puebla on the map with

fans of design and architecture when it opened in 2008, and although it's been somewhat overshadowed by even newer and swankier properties in recent years, it's still a memorable place to spend the night without spending a fortune. **Pros:** distinctive design that blends old and new; rooftop terrace with great views; full-service spa. **Cons:** noise from street and restaurant can be a problem; a bit of a walk from central attractions; service, especially in the bar and restaurant, can be uneven. $ *Rooms from: MP2300* ✉ *Callejon de la 10 Norte 802, Puebla* ☎ *222/309–1920* ⊕ *www.lapurificadora. com* ⇝ *26 rooms* ❄❄❄ *No Meals.*

Mesón Sacristía de la Compañía
$ | **B&B/INN** | If any of the antiques that decorate your room in this beautifully converted colonial mansion strike your fancy, you might consider taking home a souvenir; they're all for sale. **Pros:** terrific restaurant that offers cooking classes; reasonable rates; convenient, central location. **Cons:** some rooms hear noise from the street; decor may feel a bit old-fashioned to some; on a charming but very busy street. $ *Rooms from: MP1600* ✉ *Calle 6 Sur 304, at Callejón de los Sapos, Puebla* ☎ *322/221–2277* ⊕ *www.hotelesboutique.com* ⇝ *8 rooms* ❄❄❄ *Free Breakfast.*

Nightlife

Bilderberg Taproom Centro
BREWPUBS | Set in a cozy and convivial historic space with stone walls and a ornate tile floor, you can sample the superb European-style craft beers of this acclaimed local brewer, including a light and refreshing Hefeweizen and heady Dunkles Bock. The bar also serves well-made cocktails and fine mezcals. There's an additional location in Cholula. ✉ *Av. 5 Oriente 402* ☎ *246/262–4200* ⊕ *www. bilderberg.mx.*

Cholula

14 km (9 miles) west of Puebla, 125 km (78 miles) southeast of Mexico City.

A smaller (population 120,000) neighbor of Puebla, lively Cholula has a more youthful and avant garde art, food, and nightlife scene thanks largely to it being home to the prestigious Universidad de la Américas (UDLA). For centuries prior to the Spanish conquest, this settlement inhabited since 500 BCE had hundreds of temples and rivaled Teotihuacán as a cultural and ceremonial center. On his arrival, Cortés ordered every temple destroyed and replaced by a church.

The claim that Cholula has 365 church cupolas, one for every day in the year, should be taken with a grain of salt, but there are a lot of religious structures here, the most famous of which—the bright yellow Nuestra Señora de los Remedios—sits directly atop the Great Pyramid of Cholula, which was built some 2,500 years ago. Together, these structures are the top reasons to visit Cholula, but the increasingly hip and trendy dining scene may tempt you to stay longer. Another notable feature is the often awesome view of Popocatépetl, which dominates the horizon just 30 km (19 miles) east of the city.

There are a few notable hotels in the city core, which is divided between the historic San Pedro Cholula district and the younger San Andrés Cholula district (where you'll find the campus of UDLA). But it's also quite easy to use Puebla, which has many more hotels, as a base for exploring Cholula. An Uber between the two cities costs around MP130–MP150.

Weekends are the liveliest time to visit Cholula, when you can catch the Sunday market and some live music with dinner. The town's even busier during one of its many festivals, especially the Feria de San Pedro, during the first two weeks of September.

GETTING HERE AND AROUND

Just a 20- to 30-minute drive or Uber ride from Puebla's city center, depending on traffic, Cholula is most easily reached from Mexico City by heading first to Puebla. If you're driving, follow the same route you would to drive to Puebla, but head west rather than east from Highway 190 once you get here. By bus, take ADO to Puebla's main CAPU terminal, and then catch an Uber (MP160–MP220) from there to the center of Cholula.

VISITOR INFORMATION

CONTACTS San Pedro Cholula Tourist Office. ⊠ *Kiosko, Plaza de la Concordia, Av. 4 Oriente at Calle 2 Norte, Cholula* ☎ *222/261–2393* ⊕ *www.vivecholula. com.*

Sights

Ex-Convento de San Gabriel

RELIGIOUS BUILDING | This impressive, huge, former convent includes a trio of churches. The most unusual is the Moorish-style Capilla Real, with 49 domes. Construction began in the 1540s, and the building was originally open on one side to facilitate the conversion of huge masses of people. A handful of Franciscan monks still live in one part of the premises, so be respectful of their privacy. La Biblioteca Franciscana is a fascinating on-premises library of over 24,000 volumes from the 16th through 19th centuries, with occasional exhibitions. ⊠ *Calle 2 Norte 4, Cholula* ☎ *2222/247–0028* ⊕ *www.facebook.com/conventodesanga-brielcholula* ⊠ *Free.*

Iglesia de Santa María Tonantzintla

CHURCH | The exterior of this 16th-century church might be simple, but inside waits an explosion of color and swirling shapes. To facilitate the conversion of the indigenous population, Franciscan monks incorporated elements recalling the local cult of the goddess Tonantzin in the ornamentation of the chapel. The result is a jewel of the style known as

The yellow-hued Ex-Convento de San Gabriel is a highlight of Cholula.

churrigueresque. The polychrome wood-and-stucco carvings—inset columns, altarpieces, and the main archway—were completed in the late 17th century. The carvings, set off by ornate gold-leaf figures of plant forms, angels, and saints, were made by local craftspeople. ⊠ *Av. M. Hidalgo at Av. Reforma, Cholula* 📞 *222/666–6214* 🎫 *Free.*

★ Museo Regional de Cholula

HISTORY MUSEUM | Resting in the shadows of the Zona Arqueológica de Cholula, this engrossing museum inside a beautifully transformed 1910 psychiatric hospital has corridors connecting with the tunnels beneath the Great Pyramid. There are eight exhibit areas, each one touching on a different aspect of the region's art and history, including the nearby and quite active Popocatépetl and Iztaccíhuatl volcanoes, Pueblan pottery and meticulously painted alebrijes folk art, and, of course, the fascinating history of the pyramids. It's a pleasure walking through this extensive property's tree-shaded pathways and landscaped grounds. The outstanding gift shop, which is filled with interesting books and artwork, is set inside a contemporary structure with a curving roof and glass walls. ⊠ *Calle 14 Poniente 307, Cholula* 📞 *222/247–7243* 🌐 *www.museospuebla.puebla.gob.mx* 🎫 *MP45* ⏱ *Closed Mon.*

Templo de San Francisco Acatepec

RELIGIOUS BUILDING | Manuel Toussaint, an expert in colonial art, likened this church to "a temple of porcelain, worthy of being kept beneath a crystal dome." Construction began in 1590, with the elaborate Spanish baroque decorations added between 1650 and 1750. Multicolor Talavera tiles cover the exceptionally ornate facade. The interior blazes with polychrome plasterwork and gilding; a sun radiates overhead. Unlike that of the nearby Santa María Tonantzintla, the ornamentation hews to the standard representations of the Incarnation, the Evangelists, and the Holy Trinity. Look for St. Francis, to whom the church is dedicated, between the altarpiece's spiraling columns. ⊠ *Puebla 6, La Purísima,*

Cholula ☎ *222/643–4252* 🌐 *www.facebook.com/snfcoacatepec* 🎫 *Free.*

★ Zona Arqueológica de Cholula
(The Great Pyramid)

RUINS | The remarkable center of this archaeological site in the center of Cholula is the Gran Pirámide, once the hub of Olmec, Toltec, and Aztec religious centers and, by volume, the largest pyramid in the world. It consists of seven superimposed structures connected by tunnels and stairways. Ignacio Márquina, the architect in charge of the initial explorations in 1931, decided to excavate two tunnels partly to prove that *el cerrito* (the little hill), as many still call it, was an archaeological trove. When seeing the Zona Arqueológica, you'll walk through these tunnels to a vast 43-acre temple complex that was dedicated to the god Quetzalcóatl.

On top of the pyramid stands the Spanish chapel Nuestra Señora de los Remedios (Our Lady of the Remedies). Almost destroyed by an earthquake in 1999, it has been impressively restored. From the top of the pyramid you'll have a clear view of other nearby churches, color-coded by period: oxidized red was used in the 16th century, yellow in the 17th and 18th centuries, and pastel colors in the 19th century. You can obtain an English-language guide for a small fee. The vistas of Popocatépetl volcano are extremely impressive as well. ✉ *C. 14 Pte. s/n, Cholula* ☎ *222/235–1478* 🌐 *lugares.inah.gob.mx* 🎫 *MP90* 🕒 *Closed Sun. and Mon.*

🍴 Restaurants

★ Antojería Nacional

$ | **MEXICAN** | Decorated with brightly colored papeles picados and tables with Talavera tile tops, friendly and traditional Antojería Nacional is a bit of a contrast with the many hip and modern spots in this neighborhood of Cholula close to the campus of Universidad de las Americas. The specialty of this hugely popular spot is traditional street food—tortas milanesas, chicken pelonas, chorizo gorditas, and more. **Known for:** refreshing, and spicy on request, michelada cocktails; artfully prepared, boldly flavored renditions of classic Mexican snacks and street foods; lively multigenerational mix of locals, students, and tourists. [$] *Average main: MP130* ✉ *Calle 10 Oriente 210, Cholula* ☎ *222/934–4492* 🌐 *www.facebook.com/LaAntojeriaNacional* 🕒 *Closed Mon.*

★ Ciudad Sagrada

$$ | **MODERN MEXICAN** | Set in a beautiful, open-air space with enchanting terraces, gardens, and views of Cholula's famous pyramid and church, which is just a block away, this is one of the town's most romantic destinations for any meal of the day—it's open from early in the morning until late (except for Sunday, when it closes at 6). The menu focuses mostly on modern interpretations of Mexican favorites like chiles en nogada (which can be prepared vegetarian on request) and chicken enchiladas bathed in a rich mole poblano, but some pastas and international dishes are served, too. **Known for:** enchanting outdoor dining; artfully plated cuisine; late-night dining. [$] *Average main: MP280* ✉ *Av. 2 Oriente 615, Cholula* ☎ *222/247–9425* 🌐 *www.ciudadsagrada.mx* 🕒 *No dinner Sun.*

Dang! Noodle Bar

$$ | **ASIAN** | Cholula is one of the few places in central Mexico outside of CDMX with some pretty good Asian restaurants, and this cozy, colorfully painted spot in the heart of city center is one of the best. It's known for robustly flavored bowls and soups, including spicy ramen with Mexican longaniza sausage and eggplant sofrito, and Thai ramen with shrimp and a fragrant green curry base. **Known for:** creatively prepared ramens using a mix of authentic and nontraditional ingredients; hip, youthful staff; pork dumplings. [$] *Average main: MP160* ✉ *Calle 6 Norte 408, Cholula*

📠 *222/419–2200* ⊕ *www.instagram.com/ dang.noodlebar* ⊘ *Closed Mon.*

★ Harina y Sal
$$ | ECLECTIC | One of several noteworthy artisan bakeries in Cholula, this stylish two-story café with an industrial-chic vibe turns out generous portions of creative brunch fare in the morning—think avocado toast on organic sourdough bread or rich Croque monsieur sandwiches. Later in the day, the specialty shifts to burgers, baguette sandwiches, and exceptionally delicious pizzas; try the white pie with locally made truffled goat cheese, ricotta, Parmesan, and garlic and herbs. **Known for:** decadent house-made pastries and doughnuts; extensive selection of artisan espresso drinks and natural wines; inviting upstairs terrace with pyramid views. $ *Average main: MP225* ✉ *Av. 5 de Mayo 205, Cholula* 📠 *221/330–3606* ⊕ *www.instagram.com/harinaysal.mx.*

Spezzia Pasta Bar
$$ | ITALIAN | Italian food may just be Mexico's favorite international cuisine, but it's still rare to find house-made pasta that's as delicious and reasonably priced as the noodles served at this stylishly contemporary trattoria that draws foodies from far and near. Favorites include agnolotti stuffed with shrimp, mascarpone, and spring peas in a light olive oil-herb sauce, and tagliatelle with a rich short rib-and-red wine ragout. **Known for:** freshly made burrata with rustic bread and either a savory or fruity sauce; creative pizzas; excellent Italian-focused wine list. $ *Average main: MP220* ✉ *Calle 14 Poniente 104, Cholula* 📠 *222/985–7573* ⊕ *www. spezziapastabar.com* ⊘ *Closed Mon.*

Coffee and Quick Bites

Barbarista
$ | CAFÉ | Duck into this minimalist-chic third-wave coffeehouse for a hot or cold sip to take with you on your walk to the Zona Arqueológica de Cholula. Baguette sandwiches, salads, and other light fare

is served alongside a menu of coffee and espresso featuring locally roasted beans. **Known for:** friendly, unpretentious vibe; well-crafted lattes and other espresso drinks; three-layer carrot cake and other decadent sweets. $ *Average main: MP60* ✉ *Calle 8 Poniente 103, Cholula* ⊕ *www.instagram.com/barbarista.mx.*

★ San Pedro Tortas and Cemitas
$ | MEXICAN | Across the street from the dramatic spires of Parroquia de San Andrés Cholula, this simple sandwich shop serves delicious versions of classic tortas as well as Puebla's beloved version of these hearty sandwiches, the cemita. Try it with chicken milanesa (with thinly pounded and breaded chicken) or local sausage with all the fixings, including cheese, avocado, jalapeños, and chipotles in adobado sauce. **Known for:** simple, unfussy digs; egg or cheese-and-ham breakfast tortas; large portions. $ *Average main: MP50* ✉ *Av. Reforma 10, Cholula* 📠 *222/247–8406* ⊕ *www. facebook.com/sanpedrotortasycemitas* ⊘ *No dinner Sun.*

Hotels

Casa Eva Hotel Boutique & Spa
$$ | HOTEL | Sustainably designed and located on a central street just a few blocks south of the pyramid, this hotel set in an updated Spanish colonial house offers plenty of pleasing amenities for a small property, including an all-day restaurant and a small spa offering a good variety of treatments. **Pros:** close to San Pedro Cholula attractions and restaurants; gym, day spa, and small heated lap pool; restaurant serves very good food throughout the day. **Cons:** restaurant service can be a little slow; some rooms are dark and lack ventilation; 15-minute walk from San Andrés Cholula dining and nightlife. $ *Rooms from: MP2300* ✉ *Av. Miguel Alemán 705, Cholula* 📠 *222/375–4567* ⊕ *www.casaeva.travel* 🛏 *11 rooms* 🍽 *Free Breakfast.*

Estrella De Belem

$ | **B&B/INN** | This stately 19th-century home contains one of Cholula's most welcoming accommodations, and it's just a stone's throw from the Great Pyramid and a short walk from numerous restaurants and bars. **Pros:** terrific breakfasts; rooftop terrace with pool; beautifully restored historic building. **Cons:** some rooms are a little dark; street noise from nearby bars can be a problem; often books up well in advance. $ *Rooms from: MP1850* ⊠ *Av. 2 Oriente 410, Cholula* ☎ *222/261–1925* ⊕ *estrelladebelem.com.mx* ↝ *7 rooms* ⦿| *Free Breakfast.*

★ Hotel Boutique Xoxula

$ | **B&B/INN** | Although the sometimes intense bustle of pedestrians is right outside, along with a slew of fun bars and restaurants, you'll find quiet rooms and an enchantingly tranquil garden at this welcoming, bright-blue-stucco B&B just a block from Cholula's famous archeological site. **Pros:** steps from pyramid/chapel and many restaurants; budget-friendly rates; friendly and helpful staff. **Cons:** no on-site parking; on a busy and sometimes noisy street; rooms are on the small side. $ *Rooms from: MP1800* ⊠ *Av. 2 Oriente 403, Cholula* ☎ *222/889–0316* ⊕ *www.hotelxoxula.com* ↝ *6 rooms* ⦿| *Free Breakfast.*

★ Hotel Quinta Luna

$$ | **B&B/INN** | A five-minute walk from the Zócalo, this elegant boutique hotel set inside a grand 17th-century mansion with a central patio and fountain was restored (and is now operated) using environmentally conscious practices and with as many of the original materials as possible; the well-stocked library was built entirely from repurposed *vigas,* or beams. **Pros:** alluring gardens; spacious rooms; acclaimed restaurant. **Cons:** a bit of a walk from San Andrés Cholula dining and nightlife; some rooms pick up noise from the street; romantic adult vibe may not be ideal for families. $ *Rooms from: MP2800* ⊠ *Calle 3 Sur 702, Cholula*

☎ *222/247–8915* ⊕ *www.laquintaluna.com* ↝ *7 rooms* ⦿| *Free Breakfast.*

Nightlife

★ Cervecería Cholula

BEER GARDENS | This open-air beer garden is extremely popular with students and ale aficionados and is located a 10-minute walk west of Cholula's pyramid. In addition to the extensive selection of artisanal beers, you'll find plenty of tasty snacks, including empanadas, tacos, and salads. ⊠ *Av. 13 Oriente 412, Cholula* ☎ *222/947–7190* ⊕ *www.cerveceriacholula.com.*

Container City

BARS | You'll find a wide range of bars, food stalls, and other diversions at this trendy and festive complex made up entirely of repurposed shipping containers, featuring plenty of outdoor seating. You'll also find galleries and shops that are great for people-watching. It's a favorite stop after visiting the nearby pyramid and Museo Regional de Cholula. ⊠ *Casi Esquina 2 Norte, Cholula* ☎ *222/888–6172* ⊕ *www.facebook.com/containercity.*

★ Jazzatlan

LIVE MUSIC | Right in the heart of town, some of Mexico's most talented jazz musicians perform at this well-respected and lively music club that also turns out excellent gastropub fare, such as burgers, cheese fondue, and pizzas. There's a second branch in Roma Norte in Mexico City. ⊠ *Av. 2 Oriente 406, Cholula* ☎ *222/838–7569* ⊕ *www.jazzatlan.club/cholula.*

Licorería San Pedrito

BARS | Drop by this cozy lounge with a pleasant terrace to sample some of the best craft cocktails in town, along with an extensive list of fine mezcals. There's a good selection of food as well. ⊠ *De San Miguel Tianguisnahuitl, Av. Morelos 405B, Cholula* ☎ *221/194–3795* ⊕ *www.instagram.com/licoreriasanpedritocholula.*

Tepoztlán

90 km (56 miles) south of Mexico City, 27 km (17 miles) northeast of Cuernavaca.

When Chilangos seek a relaxing, sunny break from the big city that's easy to get to and blessed with beautiful natural scenery, many of them head to this wellness-oriented town just over the mountains that form CDMX's southern border. Surrounded by sandstone monoliths that throw off a russet glow at sunset, Tepoztlán is a magical place. It's a popular with fans of meditation and yoga, as well as outdoorsy types looking for light hikes—there are several easy trails in neighboring Parque Nacional El Tepozteco that locals and hotel staff can point out, including Ruta Miradores and Cerro Tepozteco, which leads from town up to the famous 900-year-old Aztec pyramid devoted to the Sun God.

You'll still find vendors selling homegrown produce and street food in the lively weekend market surrounding the Zócalo, and the main street through town (Del Tepozteco) as well as the blocks just off of it are lined with boutiques selling everything from artisanal chocolate to fine art and furniture. It's a perfect destination for leisurely pursuits, and it's close enough to Cuernavaca if you're seeking a slightly more urbane excursion. Although there are several appealing boutique resorts in town, Tepoztlán also has a wealth of beautiful Airbnb listings. The region's temperatures fluctuate, from intensely warm around midday to sometimes quite chilly at night. Pack layers and a jacket, especially if visiting late fall through late winter.

GETTING HERE AND AROUND

Driving from Mexico City, it takes around 75 to 90 minutes to get here via the toll Highway 95D, which climbs rather dramatically over the foothills in the south of the city before plummeting a few thousand feet in elevation to where you pick up toll Highway 115D for the final few kilometers to Tepoztlán. It's a beautiful drive, and as road trips in this part of the country go, it's a fairly easy journey that tends to see less traffic than the drives west, north, and east of CDMX. If you were tempted to try renting a car for a Mexico City side trip, this—potentially combining your journey with nearby Cuernavaca—would be a good one.

That said, it's also very easy and affordable to get to Tepoztlán by bus from Mexico City's Terminal del Sur/Taxqueña, using either of two reliable bus companies: Ómnibus Cristóbal Colón (OCC), which is a subsidiary of ADO, or Grupo Pullman de Morelos. The fare is around MP180 to MP200. If you're continuing to Cuernavaca, just 40 minutes southwest, you can catch a regional bus (these run frequently throughout the day) for about MP40 or take a taxi for about MP400 to MP500. Note that you can book an Uber from Cuernavaca to Tepoztlán, but not the other way around. Tepoztlán is served only by taxis, and they are generally a quick and inexpensive way to get around this town, which is also quite walkable (though hilly).

Sights

Museo Ex-Convento de Tepoztlán (*Museo de la Natividad*)

RELIGIOUS BUILDING | Rising high above Tepoztlán's low skyline is this buttressed former convent. It dates from the mid-16th century and has a facade adorned with icons dating from before the introduction of Christianity. Many of the walls, especially on the ground floor, have fragments of old paintings in earthen tones on the walls and decorating the arches. It is worth a visit just to see the building, which also houses temporary exhibits and a bookstore with a good selection of literature and music. ⊠ *Envila and No Reelección s/n, Tepoztlán* ☎ *739/395–0255* ⊕ *lugares.inah.gob.mx* 🎫 *Free.*

★ Zona Arqueológica Tepozteco

RUINS | Perched on a mountaintop, this small temple is dedicated to—depending on who you believe—either the Aztec deity Tepoztécatl, the god of the alcoholic drink pulque, or the Ahuizotl, the eighth Aztec emperor. The pyramid was part of a city that has not been uncovered, but was of such importance that pilgrims flocked here from as far away as Guatemala. Today it attracts hikers and sightseers willing to undertake the somewhat arduous climb up a well-maintained but rather steep trail of about a mile each way. At the top you can walk around the base and the top of the pyramid—the view over the valley is absolutely dazzling. Note that the last access to the trailhead is 3 pm. You'll find several snack bars and casual eateries lining the street to the trailhead. ✉ *North end of Av. del Tepozteco, Tepoztlán* 🎟 *MP90* 🕑 *Closed Mon. and Tues.*

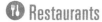

🍴 Restaurants

Axitla

$$ | **MEXICAN** | This smart establishment near the town's mountains is surrounded by ponds and bridges. Among the delicious concoctions are pork chops with a mango-pineapple salsa and grilled octopus in a rich garlic sauce. **Known for:** live music many afternoons and evenings; lushly landscaped outdoor seating; beef, chicken, and seafood with rich traditional sauces. [$] *Average main: MP190* ✉ *Av. del Tepozteco, near start of pathway to pyramid, Tepoztlán* ☎ *739/395–0519* 🌐 *www.facebook.com/restauranteaxitla* 🕑 *Closed Tues.*

El Ciruelo

$$$ | **MEXICAN** | Tables at this casually stylish restaurant are centered on a partially open patio with grand views of the mountains. The varied menu includes contemporary takes on regional Mexican fare, including a fragrant soup of corn, zucchini, squash blossoms, and huitlacoche; spaghetti with duck ragu; and salmon cooked over a charcoal fire and served with cauliflower puree and grilled asparagus. **Known for:** stunning views of the pyramid; children's play area; a very nice wine list. [$] *Average main: MP320* ✉ *Av. Ignacio Zaragoza 17, Tepoztlán* ☎ *55/8565–9029* 🌐 *www.facebook.com/elciruelotepoztlan.*

La Sombra del Sabino

$$ | **CAFÉ** | Head to this friendly and festive open-air café and shop that hosts a range of musical and literary events for a delicious breakfast. The eclectic options include traditional English bangers and mash with sautéed tomatoes and mushrooms, chilaquiles verdes, and baguette French toast. **Known for:** boutique selling books, gourmet goods, natural soups, and interesting gifts; live music, book readings, and cultural events; brunch with mimosas. [$] *Average main: MP240* ✉ *Prolongación Zaragoza 450, Tepoztlán* ☎ *739/596–0998* 🌐 *www.lasombradelsabino.com.mx* 🕑 *Closed Mon. and Tues. No dinner.*

Los Colorines

$$ | **MEXICAN** | **FAMILY** | Hung with colorful *papeles picados* (paper cutouts), this family-friendly restaurant with bright pink walls and regional folk art serves great soups (try the creamy fava bean or earthy lentil varieties), sopes topped with grilled chicken or cecina, and mole enchiladas made in an open kitchen. A specialty is the *huauzontles* (a broccoli-like vegetable you scrape from the stalk with your teeth). **Known for:** welcoming, unpretentious vibe; machaca (seasoned, shredded dried beef) with eggs at breakfast; margaritas and mezcal cocktails. [$] *Average main: MP160* ✉ *Tepozteco 13, Tepoztlán* ☎ *739/395–0198* 💳 *No credit cards.*

★ Parcela Restaurante

$$ | **MODERN MEXICAN** | This unusual restaurant and organic farm in the lush Atongo Valley to the east of town produces artfully plated salads, such as fresh-made burrata with roasted beets, as well as heartier dishes like an earthy huitlacoche

risotto with Parmesan, all made using ingredients grown on-site. Dining is in an open-air garden structure with an arched ceiling as well as at tables amid the flowers and plants, and the views of the surrounding mountains are breathtaking. **Known for:** lush setting amid organic gardens; creative herb-infused cocktails and desserts; friendly and thoughtful service. [$] *Average main: MP220 ✉ Av. Ignacio Zaragoza 408, Tepoztlán ☎ 739/395–4348 🌐 www.parcela.com.mx/restaurante ⏲ Closed Mon.*

Coffee and Quick Bites

★ Tepoznieves Matriz
$ | **ICE CREAM** | **FAMILY** | The colorful flagship branch of the popular ice cream and sorbet parlor stands out for its beautiful displays of Day of the Dead figures and other sculptures and crafts. You'll find an encyclopedic menu of flavors, including local fruits and vegetables (date, mango, mamey, beets, corn) and other distinctive options like coconut with chiles, pine nut, rose petal, and tres leches. **Known for:** a number of flavor-combo options; colorful artwork and Day of the Dead figures; several other locations around town. [$] *Average main: MP60 ✉ 5 de Mayo 21, Tepoztlán ☎ 739/395–4839 🌐 www.tepoznieves.mx.*

Hotels

★ Amomoxtli
$$$$ | **RESORT** | For the ultimate luxury spa getaway, treat yourself to a couple of days at the supremely cushy Amomoxtli, a hideaway that offers an extensive array of wellness services, including temazcal sessions, yoga classes, cleansing ceremonies, reflexology, and deep-tissue massage. **Pros:** relaxing setting away from the bustle of town; stunning pool set amid lushly landscaped grounds; excellent farm-to-table restaurant. **Cons:** expensive; not suitable for families; too far to walk to town. [$] *Rooms from: MP7800 ✉ Calle Netzahualcóyotl 115, Tepoztlán ☎ 739/395–0012 🌐 www.amomoxtli.com 🔑 37 rooms 🍴 Free Breakfast.*

Hostal de la Luz Spa Holistic Resort
$$ | **RESORT** | From the traditional adobe structure to the use of feng shui, this tranquil, holistic-oriented eco-resort at the foot of the Quetzalcóatl mountains in the village of Amatlán has an expansive spa and has been designed to blend with the environment. **Pros:** secluded surroundings with awesome views; excellent spa facilities and treatments; personal, friendly service. **Cons:** there's Wi-Fi on the property but it doesn't reach most rooms; remote location; not a good fit for families. [$] *Rooms from: MP3500 ✉ Carretera Federal Tepoztlán–Amatlán, Km 4, Amatlán de Quetzalcóatl, Tepoztlán ☎ 739/393–3076 🌐 www.hostaldelaluzresort.com 🔑 41 rooms 🍴 Free Breakfast.*

★ Hotel Boutique Casa Fernanda
$$ | **HOTEL** | Among Tepoztlán's several holistic-minded spa resorts, this centrally located boutique hotel known for its polished service and peaceful setting is one of the best, thanks to its soothing spa and first-rate restaurant, La Veladora, which is worth seeking out even if you aren't an overnight guest. **Pros:** lovely spa with extensive treatment menu; tranquil setting with splendid mountain views; one of the best restaurants in the area. **Cons:** not a good fit for kids; sometimes books up with weddings; steep walk up to downtown's main street. [$] *Rooms from: MP3500 ✉ Del Niño Artillero 20, Tepoztlán ☎ 739/395–0522 🌐 www.casafernanda.com 🔑 12 rooms 🍴 Free Breakfast.*

Posada del Tepozteco
$$ | **HOTEL** | Enjoy splendid views of both the village and the pyramid as you stroll through the terraced gardens of this grand and historic hotel that has hosted numerous celebrities over the years—including Diego Rivera, Dolores Del Rio, and Gael García Bernal—and enjoys an

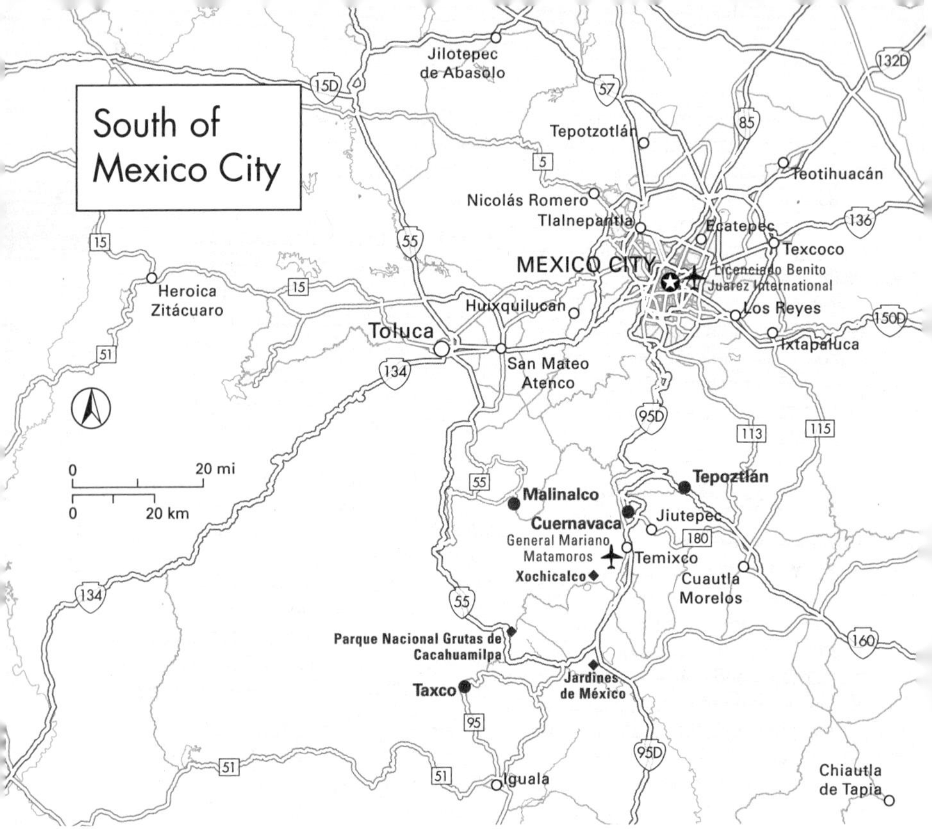

ideal hilltop setting steps from downtown restaurants, shops, and attractions. **Pros:** unbeatable views; excellent service; temazcal rituals and in-room spa services can be arranged. **Cons:** restaurant has gorgeous views but so-so food; short but steep uphill walk from downtown; some rooms pick up noise from the restaurant. *[$] Rooms from: MP3700 ✉ Calle del Paraíso 3, Tepoztlán ☎ 739/395–0010 🌐 www.posadadeltepozteco.com.mx 🛏 25 rooms 🍴 Free Breakfast.*

Cuernavaca

88 km (55 miles) south of Mexico City.

The drive from Mexico City to Cuernavaca will likely heighten your anticipation—you'll catch your first glimpse of the city's lush surroundings from high up on a mountain highway, through lacy pine branches. This mid-size metropolis with around 370,000 residents has nearly perfect weather—it's typically several degrees warmer than Mexico City, which is nearly 2,500 feet higher in elevation, and thus it's popular as a place for wealthy Chilangos to own second homes.

That ideal climate has earned Cuernavaca the nickname City of the Eternal Spring, and it's the reason you'll find so many stunning gardens here, many of them abundant with flowering bougainvilleas. Open to the public, Jardín Borda—where José de la Borda (who made his fortune in Taxco silver) lived and died in the 18th century—is perhaps the most famous. It's been a private garden for centuries, and it's where Emperor Maximilian and his empress came to rest. Undoubtedly, many of the best gardens lie behind high walls, although some grace the grounds of inviting hotels and Airbnbs.

Beyond lazing by the hotel pool, the city has much to offer. There are enough museums and historic sites in the historic city center to keep you busy for an afternoon, and a few other notable attractions farther afield. Downtown also abounds with mostly casual restaurants and bars, many of the latter lining pedestrian-only alley Fray Bartolomé de Las Casas, which is just south of the Plaza de Armas. It's also easy to combine a visit to Cuernavaca with Taxco, which is less than an hour and a half to the southeast.

GETTING HERE AND AROUND

The drive from Mexico City to Cuernavaca is, for the first 82 km (50 miles) or so, identical to the drive to Tepoztlán, except that you follow toll Highway 95D the entire way—a total of 95 km (59 miles)—instead of cutting east on toll Highway 115D. It's a quite scenic drive that initially ascends up and over the mountains on the south side of CDMX and then switchbacks down a few thousand feet in elevation to the warm and sunny city of Cuernavaca. The entire drive takes about 90 minutes if you don't run into any traffic.

Buses from Mexico City's Terminal del Sur/Taxqueña make the roughly 75-minute journey to Cuernavaca numerous times per hour throughout the day. Several bus companies—including Futura (a subsidiary of Estrella Blanca), Grupo Pullman de Morelos, and ETN (as well as its subsidiary Turistar)—make this generally quite pleasant trip, and fares typically run about MP180 to MP200.

Once in Cuernavaca, the historic city center is easy to navigate on foot, and both street and garage parking are pretty easy to find as well. You'll either need a car or you can call an Uber to get to the handful of resorts and restaurants located beyond the city center, as well

as attractions and businesses elsewhere in Morelos. Note that while Uber serves Cuernavaca itself, it does not serve the surrounding region, so if you're returning to Cuernavaca from, say, Tepoztlán or the ruins at Xochicalco, you'll need to call a taxi that's local to those areas.

VISITOR INFORMATION
CONTACTS Cuernavaca Tourist Office. ✉ *Motolinía 2, Centro Cuernavaca, Cuernavaca* ☎ *777/329–5500* ⊕ *www. cuernavaca.gob.mx.* **Morelos State Tourism Office.** ✉ *Calle Hidalgo 239, Cuernavaca* ☎ *777/318–6200* ⊕ *www.turismoycultura. morelos.gob.mx.*

 Sights

Catedral de Cuernavaca
CHURCH | Cortés ordered the construction of this cathedral, also known as Catedral de Nuestra Señora de la Asunción, with work beginning in 1525. Like his palace, the cathedral doubled as a fortress. Cannons mounted above the flying buttresses helped bolster the city's defenses. The facade may give you a sense of foreboding, especially when you catch sight of the skull and crossbones over the door. The interior is much less ominous, though, thanks to the stained-glass windows and the murals uncovered during renovations. ✉ *Hidalgo and Av. Morelos, Cuernavaca* ☎ *777/312–1290* ⊕ *www. facebook.com/catedralcuer* ⊠ *Free.*

Jardín Borda
GARDEN | Among the most popular sights in the state of Morelos, the Borda Gardens were designed in the late 18th century for Don Manuel de la Borda, son of Don José de la Borda, a wealthy miner who established the beautiful church of Santa Prisca in Taxco. The gardens were once so famous they attracted royalty. Maximilian and Carlotta visited frequently. Here the emperor reportedly dallied with the gardener's wife, called La India Bonita, who was immortalized in a famous portrait. Novelist Malcolm

Lowry turned the formal gardens into a sinister symbol in his 1947 novel *Under the Volcano.* A pleasant café and a well-stocked bookstore sit just inside the gates, and there's a cultural center that shows rotating art exhibits as well. ⊠ *Av. Morelos 271, Cuernavaca* ☎ *777/318–1050* ⊕ *www.facebook.com/jardinborda* 🖭 *MP40* ⊘ *Closed Mon.*

Jardines de México

GARDEN | FAMILY | About a 40-minute drive south of Cuernavaca, just off toll Highway 95D, this sprawling 125-acre mashup between a theme park and a botanic garden is one of the region's leading attractions. The park claims to be the largest floral gardens in the world, and indeed, it takes two to three hours to walk the entire property, which is divided into a number of sections, each with its own theme and design: Italian, Japanese, cactus, tropical, labyrinth of senses, children's garden, and several more. A big focus of the owners are weddings and events, and there's also a large restaurant and gift shop—in other words, this experience is more commercial than a lot of traditional botanic gardens. That said, the whimsical animal-shape topiaries, thoughtfully designed paths, and sweeping views of the surrounding mountains make for a fun visit. Keep in mind that there isn't a lot of shade, so bring a hat and wear sunscreen. ⊠ *Autopista México–Acapulco, Km 129, Tequesquitengo, Cuernavaca* ☎ *777/333–0140* ⊕ *www.jardinesdemexico.com* 🖭 *MP275* ⊘ *Closed Mon.*

★ Museo Regional de los Pueblos de Morelos

HISTORY MUSEUM | On the southeast side of Plaza de Armas, you'll find this fascinating museum that reopened following a massive renovation that was needed after the building was badly damaged in the major earthquake that struck the region in 2017. Prior to that, the building was named Museo Regional Cuauhnáhuac, but it's also known as the Palacio

de Cortés. The fortresslike building was constructed as a stronghold for Hernán Cortés in 1522, as the region had not been completely conquered at that time. His palace sits atop the ruins of Aztec buildings, some of which have been partially excavated. There are plenty of stone carvings from the area on display among the 19 exhibit galleries, with a highlight being the murals Diego Rivera painted between 1927 and 1930 on the second floor, depicting the history of Morelos. ⊠ *Francisco Leyva 100, Cuernavaca* ☎ *777/312–8171* ⊕ *lugares.inah.gob.mx* 🖭 *MP90* ⊘ *Closed Mon.*

Plaza de Armas

PLAZA/SQUARE | The city's tree-shaded main square, which is partially lined with restaurants and shops, is marked by a hefty, volcanic-stone statue of revolutionary hero José María Morelos and a couple of little fountains. On weekdays the square fills with vendors from throughout the region. On weekends it is crowded with balloon sellers, amateur painters, and stalls for crafts, jewelry, and knickknacks. Opposite the northwest corner of the square is leafy Jardín Juárez, which hosts concerts in its bandstand, and on the southeast side of the square you can explore the excellent Museo Regional de los Pueblos de Morelos. ⊠ *Calle Gutemberg and Miguel Hidalgo, Cuernavaca.*

★ Robert Brady Museum

ART MUSEUM | This remarkable museum on a quiet street south of the Plaza de Armas showcases the collection of the decidedly eccentric artist, antiquarian, and decorator from Fort Dodge, Iowa, who traveled the world amassing an incredible array of works before settling in Cuernavaca in 1962. Ceramics, antique furniture, sculptures, paintings, and tapestries fill the restored 16th-century monastery, which is directly behind the Catedral de Cuernavaca. A number of Brady's works depict his illustrious friends, who included Josephine Baker,

Peggy Guggenheim, and actor Geoffrey Holder. They're all magnificently arranged in rooms decorated with brightly painted tiles. Upon his death in 1986, Brady left the house and collection to the city government to be turned into a museum. ⊠ *Calle Nezahualcóyotl 4, Cuernavaca* ☎ *777/318–8554* ⊕ *www.museorobert-brady.com* ✉ *MP70* ⊗ *Closed Mon.*

★Xochicalco

RUINS | A trip to these ruins, which are a roughly 45-minute drive southwest of Cuernavaca, is one of the best reasons to visit the state of Morelos. Built by the Olmeca-Xicalanca people, the mighty hilltop city reached its peak between AD 700 and 900. It was abandoned a century later after being destroyed, perhaps by its own inhabitants. With its several layers of fortifications, the city appears unassailable. The most eye-catching edifice is the Pyrámide de Quetzalcóatl (Temple of the Plumed Serpent). Carvings of vicious-looking snakes—all in the style typical of the Maya to the south—wrap around the lower level, while figures in elaborate headdresses sit above. Be sure to seek out the Observatorio in a man-made cave reached through a tunnel on the northern side of the city. Through a narrow shaft in the ceiling, the Xochical-co astronomers could observe the heavens. Twice a year—May 14 and 15 and July 28 and 29—the sun passes directly over the opening, filling the room with light. From the ruins, you're also treated to an impressive view of the surrounding mountains.

Be sure to set aside at least a half-hour to explore the excellent solar-powered museum, where a wonderfully mount-ed exhibit of a wide variety of artifacts from Xochicalco are on display, includ-ing gorgeous sculptures of Xochicalco deities found nearby. There are dozens of other structures here, including three impressive ball courts. ⊠ *Carretera Federal Xochicalco, Tetlama, Cuernavaca* ☎ *737/374–3090* ✉ *MP90.*

🍴 Restaurants

Casa Hidalgo

$$$ | **MEXICAN** | The marvelous view of the Palacio de Cortés is a major draw of this rambling restaurant with sprawl-ing patios, leafy plants, and traditional artwork. The menu mixes Mexican and international foods; you might try the breaded veal stuffed with Serrano ham and manchego cheese, the trout stuffed with shrimp and roasted red peppers, or the tacos filled with grilled cactus. **Known for:** great views of Plaza de Armas and Palacio de Cortés; live jazz on weekends; excellent breakfasts. $ *Average main: MP315* ⊠ *Calle Hidalgo 6, Cuernavaca* ☎ *777/312–2749* ⊕ *www.casahidalgo. com.*

★ Casa Manzano Restaurante

$$ | **MEXICAN** | This sprawling, open-air restaurant in an affluent neighborhood northeast of downtown has a lush garden setting that makes it a perfect choice for a relaxing meal on a balmy day, of which there are many in Cuernavaca. The farm-to-table-inspired menu features a mix of classic and contemporary dishes, such as shrimp tacos with a mildly spicy sambal salsa, aguachile with tangy passionfruit sauce, or pasta with classic fettuccine carbonara. **Known for:** friendly, attentive service; nice selection of craft beer and Mexican wines; ginger-carrot cake. $ *Average main: MP255* ⊠ *Av. Teopan-zolco 400, Cuernavaca* ☎ *777/317–3711* ⊕ *www.casamanzano.mx.*

El Madrigal

$$$$ | **MODERN MEXICAN** | It should come as no surprise that one of the most cele-brated and refined restaurants in the City of the Eternal Spring overlooks a lushly landscaped garden—the beautiful dining room is decorated with candlelit tables, arched ceilings, and well-curated artwork. The elegantly plated modern Mexican cuisine relies heavily on seasonal, locally sourced ingredients and might include a cream of avocado soup with cilantro

Traditional Medicine in Modern Mexico

Herbal medicine remains an integral part of Mexican life, and still predominates in remote areas where modern medicines are hard to come by or are too expensive for rural laborers. Even in the capital, most markets will have distinctive stalls piled with curative herbs and plants.

The Aztecs were excellent botanists, and their extensive knowledge impressed the Spanish, who borrowed from Mexico's indigenous herbarium and cataloged the intriguing plants. Consequently, medicine remains one of the few examples of cultural practices and indigenous wisdom that have not been lost to history. Visitors to Mexico City can find a display of medicinal plants used by the Aztecs in the Museum of Medicine, in the former Palace of the Inquisition, at the northwest corner of Plaza Santo Domingo.

A rich variety of herbs is harvested in the 300 rural communities of the fertile state of Morelos, where *curanderos* (natural healers) flock to the markets on weekends to give advice and sell their concoctions. Stores in the state capital, Cuernavaca, sell natural antidotes for every ailment imaginable and potions for sexual prowess, lightening the skin, colic in babies, and IQ enhancement.

Chamanes (shamans) and healers abound at the weekend market in the main square of the delightful mountain village of Tepoztlán. Long known for its *brujas* (witches), Tepoztlán continues to experience a boom in

spiritual retreats and shops. Visitors can benefit from the healing overload without getting hoodwinked by booking a session in one of the many good temazcales (Aztec sweat lodges) in town.

The temazcal is a "bath of cleansing" for body, mind, and spirit; a session consists of a ritual that lasts at least an hour, ideally (for first-timers) with a guide. Temazcales are igloo-shape clay buildings, round so as not to impede the flow of energy. They usually seat 6 to 12 people, who can participate either naked or in a swim suit. Each guide develops his own style, under the tutelage of a shaman, so practices vary. In general your aura (or energy field) is cleaned with a bunch of plants before you enter the temazcal, so that you start off as pure as possible. You will have a fistful of the same plants—usually rosemary, sweet basil, or eucalyptus—to slap or rub against your skin. You walk in a clockwise direction and take your place, and water is poured over red-hot stones in the middle to create the steam. Usually silence is maintained, although the guide may chant or pray, often in Nahuatl. The procedure ends with a warm shower followed by a cold one to close the pores.

The experience helps eliminate toxins, cure inflammations, ease pains in the joints, and relieve stress. They've become extremely popular in recent years and are offered at a number of spa hotels in the region.

and serrano chiles, filet mignon with a rich chipotle sauce and new potatoes, and grilled shrimp stuffed with crabmeat and served in a lemon-butter sauce. **Known for:** leisurely breakfasts; creative cocktails; extensive dessert list. [$] *Average main: MP530* ✉ *Av. Sonora 115, Cuernavaca* ☎ *777/100–7700* 🌐 *www.facebook.com/elmadrigal.mx* ⏲ *Closed Mon.*

★ House Restaurant

$$$ | FUSION | Downtown Cuernavaca is a bit lacking in trendy dining, but this casually fashionable open-air restaurant in stylish Las Casas B&B Hotel serves some of the most beautifully plated and delicious food in the city. It's a mix of contemporary Mexican and Mediterranean dishes, from sea bass risotto with roasted artichokes and kalamata olives to grilled chicken in a rich mole negro with caramelized bananas and hand-made blue-corn tortillas. **Known for:** outstanding wine list; romantic terrace overlooking gardens and a pool; molten chocolate cake with vanilla-bean ice cream, berries, and rosemary. [$] *Average main: MP435* ✉ *Las Casas B+B Hotel, Fray Bartolomé de Las Casas 110, Cuernavaca* ☎ *777/318–7777* 🌐 *www.lascasasbb.com* ⏲ *No dinner Sun.*

Hotels

★ Anticavilla

$$$$ | HOTEL | Set in an affluent, outlying neighborhood, this fashionable adults-only resort is set in a cloistered 1600s Spanish colonial hacienda but has been made over with a minimalist, contemporary Italian flair that extends to its chic bar and restaurant. **Pros:** lush and idyllic gardens and common spaces; one of the region's best spas; superb restaurant. **Cons:** expensive; 10-minute drive from city center; kids aren't permitted. [$] *Rooms from: MP7700* ✉ *Río Amacuzac 10, Vista Hermosa, Cuernavaca* ☎ *777/313–3131* 🌐 *www.anticavilla.com* 🔑 *12 rooms* 🍴 *No Meals.*

★ Hacienda San Gabriel de las Palmas

$$$ | RESORT | A colorful history distinguishes this grand hacienda, built in 1529 under the orders of Cortés, now a magnificent oasis of quiet and lush gardens disturbed only by birdcalls, the splashing of a waterfall, and the ringing of a chapel bell. **Pros:** less than an hour's drive from Cuernavaca and Taxco; lots of intriguing gardens, nooks, and salons to explore and relax in; relaxing, magical setting. **Cons:** need a car (or an expensive taxi/Uber ride) to get here; sometimes books up with weddings or groups; although the restaurant is very good, it's the only good place to eat for miles. [$] *Rooms from: MP4400* ✉ *Carretera Federal Cuernavaca–Chilpancingo, Km 41.8, Amacuzac, Cuernavaca* ☎ *751/348–0636* 🌐 *www.haciendasangabriel.com* 🔑 *20 rooms* 🍴 *No Meals.*

Hotel & Spa Hacienda de Cortés

$$ | HOTEL | Wandering around the gardens and discovering cascades, fountains, abandoned pillars, and sculptures in this 16th-century former sugar mill that once belonged to the famed conquistador makes for an enchanting experience, especially at dusk. **Pros:** the entire property exudes history; romantic rooms, restaurant, and spa; plenty of quiet, inviting common spaces. **Cons:** a 15-minute drive from town; a bit old-fashioned for some tastes; noisy events often take over the hotel. [$] *Rooms from: MP2800* ✉ *Plaza Kennedy 90, Col. Atlacomulco, Jiutepec, Cuernavaca* ☎ *777/315–8844* 🌐 *www.hotelhaciendadecortes.com.mx* 🔑 *23 rooms* 🍴 *Free Breakfast.*

Huayacan Cuernavaca Curamoria Collection

$$ | RESORT | FAMILY | Set amid the gardens and weekend homes just south of Cuernavaca in exclusive Lomas de Jiutepec, this sustainably designed member of Fiesta Americana's luxury boutique Curamoria brand offers an array of eco-minded amenities to ensure a relaxing stay, including bike rentals, a good restaurant and bar, a conventional pool as well as a unique "biopiscina" natural swimming pond, an aviary, and a butterfly enclosure. **Pros:** extensive, well-maintained facilities; reasonably priced among the area's luxury resorts; very family-friendly. **Cons:** hosts lots of weddings and events; no spa; a 20-minute drive south of the city center. $ *Rooms from: MP3400* ⊠ *Tezontepec 200, Lomas de Jiutepec, Cuernavaca* ☎ *777/516–1010* ⊕ *www.curamoria. com* ⇆ *40 rooms* ⦿ *Free Breakfast.*

★ Las Casas B&B Hotel

$$$ | B&B/INN | Although just a stone's throw from central Cuernavaca's museums, restaurants, and bars, this tastefully understated but quite cushy compound feels completely relaxing, with a fabulous spa, intimate pool, lush gardens, and a destination-worthy restaurant. **Pros:** steps from many museums and restaurants; rates include a delicious full breakfast; welcoming, personal service. **Cons:** some rooms are a bit small; on the pricey side; neighborhood can get very noisy, especially at night. $ *Rooms from: MP4200* ⊠ *Fray Bartolomé de Las Casas 110, Cuernavaca* ☎ *777/318–7777* ⊕ *www. lascasasbb.com* ⇆ *11 rooms* ⦿ *Free Breakfast.*

Las Mañanitas

$$$$ | RESORT | An American expat opened this hacienda-style hotel in the 1950s, and it remains one of the most exclusive lodgings in Cuernavaca, even though its somewhat stodgy personality doesn't appeal to every taste, especially younger travelers. **Pros:** stunning grounds and landscaping; stylish sizable rooms; terrific modern Mexican art collection. **Cons:** overly formal and old-fashioned for some tastes; very expensive; 15-minute walk or short drive from city center. $ *Rooms from: MP7000* ⊠ *Ricardo Linares 107, Cuernavaca* ☎ *777/362–0000* ⊕ *las-mananitas.com.mx* ⇆ *23 suites* ⦿ *Free Breakfast.*

Malinalco

100 km (62 miles) southwest of Mexico City

Nestled in a spectacular, verdant valley flanked by sheer cliffs, the town and surrounding municipality of Malinalco is an idyllic place to relax and decompress for a couple of days—bearing in mind that you may be awakened by roosters each morning. Many of the accommodations in town have pools, spas or in-room massage and body treatments, and restaurants, making it tempting for guests to never leave the property. Harder to get to than Tepoztllán but similarly appealing to nature lovers and spirituality seekers, this unhurried town with around 7,500 residents lies amid the lofty mountain peaks southwest of Mexico City, about midway between the smaller cities of Toluca and Cuernavaca. Also like Tepoztlán, the town is home to a famously dramatic Aztec ruin and a large, carefully preserved ex-convent. Most easily reached by private car, Malinalco draws mostly Mexican tourists seeking peaceful weekend getaways—it's pretty quiet during the week—but is steadily becoming discovered by more and more foreigners.

On the small central plaza of this walkable village, vendors sell crafts, tamales, and homemade ice cream, and a handful of restaurants and bars serve locally raised trout and other regional dishes, some with pre-Hispanic influences, on terraces with grand views of the countryside. The surrounding area abounds with natural wonders, which are helping turn the town into a hub of eco-tourism and outdoor adventure—a couple of well-respected tour companies in town offer hiking, rappelling, canyoneering, and other adrenaline-inducing pursuits. If you're thinking of going to Taxco, Malinalco is a great potential stopover en route.

GETTING HERE AND AROUND

Getting to Malinalco using public transportation is a bit cumbersome, as there's no direct bus service to here from Mexico City. The closest option is taking a Flecha Roja bus from Mexico City's Terminal Central de Autobuses del Poniente/Observatorio, which is southwest of Condesa, to the town of Chalma; the ride takes about two hours and costs around MP130. From there, it's a 15- to 20-minute taxi ride to Malinalco (expect to pay around MP80 to MP100 pesos), which is 10 km (6 miles) away; Uber doesn't serve Malinalco or Chalma.

If you're willing to rent a car, driving to Malinalco—which is a quite picturesque experience once you get beyond CDMX—offers the most flexibility. The drive takes around two hours by way of toll Highway 15D, which you take toward Toluca, before turning south in Lerma on toll Highway 6D and then taking the windy local roads over the mountains through the villages of Santa María Jajalpa, San Francisco Tepexoxuca, and El Guarda de Guerrero.

An alternate route, which takes only about 15 to 30 minutes longer, is to exit toll Highway 15D at the town of La Marquesa and follow the winding Highways 6 and 4 through Santiago Tilapa, Santa Martha, and Chalma. The latter town is famous for its ornate late-17th-century church, Santuario El Señor de Chalma, which is considered the second-most prominent Christian pilgrimage site in the country (after Mexico City's Basilica of Santa María de Guadalupe).

Once you arrive, parking is plentiful in tiny and safe Malinalco, although it's also quite easy to get around the heart of the village on foot.

TOURS

Maliemociones Tours

ADVENTURE TOURS | The friendly guides with this company based in the village of Malinalco can get you acquainted with the region's natural scenery and thrilling adventures, including hikes through lush canyons, rappelling down waterfalls, and camping. Other tours touch on the town's rich culinary heritage and artisanal mezcal production, or lead visitors to the Zona Arqueológica de Malinalco. ✉ *Malinalco* ☎ *722/108–1461* ⊕ *www.maliemociones.com.mx* ✉ *From MP350.*

Promotora Turística AMD

ADVENTURE TOURS | Most of the tours and adventures offered by this popular agency in the center of Malinalco focus on the outdoors, including waterfall hikes and rappelling, ziplining through canyons, horseback riding, and tandem paragliding. You can also book an ATV excursion, tour local honey- and mezcal producers, and take a guided walk through Zona Arqueológica de Malinalco and the town's museums. ✉ *Malinalco* ☎ *712/157–1865* ⊕ *www.algomasde.com* ✉ *From MP200.*

VISITOR INFORMATION

CONTACTS Malinalco Tourism Office. ✉ *Av. Del Progreso 3, Malinalco* ☎ *714/147–0111* ⊕ *www.malinalco.gob.mx.*

Sights

Ex-Convento Agustino

RELIGIOUS BUILDING | The largest and most dramatic of a few different historic churches in town, this imposing, ornately designed church and former Augustine monastery sits in the very center of town, overlooking Malinalco's small but bustling main plaza. Exceptionally detailed murals created by indigenous artists when the building was constructed in the mid-16th century line the walls and arched ceilings of the central atrium, and there's a remarkable crucifix carved of stone on the expansive tree-shaded grounds out front. The building is also known as the Parroquia del Divino Salvador, or Parish of the Divine Savoir. ⊠ *Plaza Principal Manzana, at the corner of Av. Hidalgo, Malinalco* ☎ *712/313–9697* 🖃 *Free.*

Museo de Malinalco

HISTORY MUSEUM | Officially called the Museo Universitario Dr. Luis Mario Schneider and located near the entrance to Zona Arqueológica de Malinalco, this small but informative museum installed within a gracious orange mansion with galleries surrounding a plant-filled courtyard makes an excellent companion piece to the archaeological site. Exhibits are filled with both original and reproduced artifacts and artwork dating back to the Aztec period as well as photos and dioramas that interpret the region's history right up until the present day. ⊠ *Corner of Amajac and Agustín Melgar, Malinalco* ☎ *714/147–1288* ⊕ *www.facebook.com/mudrluismarioschneider* 🖃 *MP15* 🕙 *Closed Mon.*

★ Museo Vivo, Los Bichos de Malinalco

SCIENCE MUSEUM | FAMILY | Kids and adults alike enjoy wandering through the galleries, gardens, and animal enclosures of this offbeat natural history museum that's devoted to the region's remarkable biodiversity and incredible vast array of *bichos*, or critters. Insects, spiders, butterflies, scorpions, snakes, turtles, and lizards native to the area take center stage here, where you'll have the chance to actually touch and maybe even hold many creatures (at least the ones that don't pose any threat). There's also a well-tended botanical garden, a very cool shop that sells all sorts of dried animal specimens as well as cacti and other plants, and a terrace café serving light snacks (some of them made with insects) and refreshments. Be sure to try a "bichelada," the museum's version

of a michelada—the rim of the glass is coated with *sal de chapulines* (grasshopper salt). ⊠ *Pensamientos S/N, Malinalco* ☎ *714/147–2242* ⊕ *www.museovivo.org* 🖃 *MP125* 🕙 *Closed Tues. and Wed.*

★ Zona Arqueológica de Malinalco

RUINS | If you have time for just one attraction, do not miss this impressive site—known officially as Cuauhtinchan—located high on a hill on the west side of town and comprising six ceremonial sites constructed by the Aztecs between the late 1400s and early 1500s (although archaeologists have determined that Indigenous people have worshipped on this site for centuries longer). You reach the site by walking west from Malinalco's colorful main plaza along Calle Vicente Guerrero, which is lined with crafts shops (some of them quite good) and cute bars and cafés. Turn left at the end and then continue a short way on Calle Amajac to the entrance gate, where you'll pay admission and be warned about the arduous—but well-maintained and quite beautiful—trail with 426 steps leading to the site itself. The trail has several resting spots with interpretative signs in English, Spanish, and Nahuatl, and you'll also likely encounter a guide or two whom you can hire, if you wish, to provide an informative tour of the site. At the top, you can climb atop several of the ruins, which have been constructed with local stone. The most interesting of these, the palapa-roof Cuauhcalli (or House of the Eagles), has been carved with great effort and engineering sophistication directly into the steep mountainside. ⊠ *Amajac s/n, Malinalco* ☎ *722/215–8569* ⊕ *www.inah.gob.mx/zonas/135-zona-arqueologica-malinalco* 🖃 *MP75* 🕙 *Closed Mon.*

Restaurants

La Casa de Valentina

$$ | ECLECTIC | Located across the street from Malinalco's striking Agustino de la Transfiguración convent, this convivial taverna filled with whimsical artwork and lush hanging plants serves creative, eclectic fare with both Mexican and Mediterranean influences. You might start with beef carpaccio seasoned with lemon and olive oil or marinated-tuna tostadas with chipotle dressing, before graduating to grilled pistachio-crusted sea bass with roasted vegetables or linguine with a sauce of goat cheese, basil, and white wine. **Known for:** burgers and sausage sandwiches with creative toppings; weekend brunch; extensive menu of house-baked desserts. [$] *Average main: MP270* ✉ *Av. Hidalgo 213, Malinalco* ☎ *55/4075–5459* 🌐 *www.lacasadevalentina.com* 🕐 *Closed Tues.*

★ Restaurante Casa Colibrí

$$ | ECLECTIC | Although there's a charming downstairs seating area, the rooftop terrace of this delightful bistro serving creative Mexican dishes as well as pizzas and gastropub fare is hard to beat, with its views overlooking the town's central plaza and the steep cliffs that frame Malinalco. Highlights from the diverse menu include a tiradito of raw cecina with serrano chiles, marinated wild-boar tacos, and trout topped with pineapples, ham, and cheese in a lightly spicy sauce. **Known for:** roof terrace with stunning views; several dishes with locally sourced trout and wild boar; delicious breakfasts. [$] *Average main: MP260* ✉ *Plaza Principal 106, Malinalco* ☎ *712/157–1689* 🌐 *www.restaurante-casacolibri.com* 🕐 *Closed Tues.*

Hotels

★ Canto de Aves Hotel Malinalco

$$ | B&B/INN | Fragrant gardens, mature shade trees, and a small pond dot the tranquil grounds of this small, sustainably designed eco-resort with six contemporary suites and a quiet location a few kilometers south of Malinalco's village center. **Pros:** very good breakfast; beautifully landscaped grounds with a pool; peaceful setting. **Cons:** a long walk or 10-minute taxi ride from town; spotty Wi-Fi; not suitable for kids. [$] *Rooms from: MP2900* ✉ *Paraje el Trapichito s/n, Malinalco* ☎ *722/561–9176* 🌐 *www.cantodeaves.com* 🛏 *6 rooms* 🍴 *Free Breakfast.*

Paradise Hotel

$$ | HOTEL | Although located on the south side of town along the main road connecting Malinalco to Chalma and beyond, this friendly and informal spa retreat is quiet and surrounded by lush gardens, lawns, and terraces with grand vistas of the countryside. **Pros:** friendly, helpful staff; dry sauna and pools with massage and hydrotherapy treatments offered; splendid setting with sweeping mountain views. **Cons:** not suitable for kids under 10; rooms are a bit dark and rustic; a 20-minute walk or short taxi ride from town. [$] *Rooms from: MP2650* ✉ *Pedregal 409, Carretera Toluca-Chalma, Malinalco* ☎ *714/147–0421* 🌐 *www.hotelparadisemalinalco.com* 🛏 *9 rooms* 🍴 *Free Breakfast.*

Quinta Cielo

$$ | B&B/INN | This sophisticated country inn, which has both a pool and an inviting restaurant, is just a few blocks from Malinalco's main plaza and is filled with contemporary artwork and interesting decorative pieces collected by the well-traveled owner. **Pros:** excellent breakfast included; beautiful architecture and grounds; short walk to local restaurants and attractions. **Cons:** least expensive rooms are quite small; rooms in the outbuildings have thin walls; spotty Wi-Fi. $ Rooms from: MP2600 ⊠ Calle San Juan 16, Malinalco ☎ 55/6066–1341 ⊕ www.casaquintacielo.com ⤻ 7 rooms ❏❏ Free Breakfast.

Taxco

185 km (115 miles) southwest of Mexico City.

In Mexico's renowned "Silver City"—an officially designated Pueblos Mágico—marvelously preserved white-stucco, red-tile-roof colonial buildings hug cobblestone streets that wind up and down the foothills of the Sierra Madre. Taxco (pronounced *tahss*-ko) is a living work of art, For centuries, its silver mines drew foreign mining companies, and in 1928 the government made it a national monument. Today its charm, abundant sunshine, flowers, and silversmiths make it a tremendously popular getaway.

The town's name was derived from the Nahuatl word *tlacho* meaning "the place where ball is played." Spanish explorers discovered a wealth of minerals in the area in 1524, just three years after Hernán Cortés entered the Aztec city of Tenochtitlán in present-day Mexico City. Soon Sovácon del Rey, the first mine in the New World, was established on the present-day town square. The first mines were soon depleted of riches, however, and the town went into stagnation for the next 150 years. In 1708 two Frenchmen, Francisco and José de la Borda, resumed the mining. Francisco soon died, but José discovered the silver vein that would soon make him the region's wealthiest man. The main square in the town center is named Plaza Borda in his honor.

After the Borda era, however, Taxco's importance again faded, until the 1930s and the arrival of William G. Spratling,

a writer-architect from New Orleans. Enchanted by the city and convinced of its potential as a center for silver jewelry, Spratling set up an apprentice shop. His talent and fascination with pre-Columbian design combined to produce silver jewelry and other artifacts that once again earned Taxco its worldwide reputation as the Silver City. Spratling's inspiration lives on in his students and their descendants, many of whom are now famous silversmiths.

It takes about three hours to get from Mexico City to this magical village that clings precipitously to a mountainside in the very northern tip of the state of Guerrero, but Taxco is nevertheless one of the most popular weekend destinations among residents of CDMX.

This enchanting town is also quite compact and easy to explore in a day or two, but as it's perched on the side of a mountain 5,800 feet above sea level, you'll swear some of its narrow, winding streets run nearly vertical. Bring some good walking shoes and be prepared to get some lung-gasping exercise.

GETTING HERE AND AROUND

Allow about 2½ to 3 hours for the drive from Mexico City to Taxco via the safe and efficient toll Highway 95D. You'll pass through Cuernavaca along the way. Alternatively, a longer but highly scenic option is driving to Taxco by heading west toward Toluca and then south through Ixtapan de la Sal and the famous Parque Nacional Grutas de Cacahuamilpa. This drive takes the better part of a day (about four hours without stops), but the scenery is dazzling and you could potentially break things up with an overnight in Malinalco along the way. If you have five to seven days, you could easily make a scenic road-trip adventure from CDMX by looping through Malinalco to Taxco and then returning by way of Cuernavaca and Tepoztlán, spending a night or two in each place.

Comfy Estrella de Oro and Costa Line buses travel the route between Mexico City's Terminal del Sur/Taxqueña and Taxco's city center numerous times throughout the day. One-way fares run between MP190 and MP320, depending on the level of service.

Once you arrive, it's fairly easy to navigate Taxco's narrow, winding, and hilly streets on foot, but the steep inclines—especially if you're not used to the town's 6,000-foot elevation—can be challenging. The town's famously colorful (and intrepid) Volkswagen Beetle taxis are another option—Taxco is not served by Uber. Although driving to Taxco can be fun, driving within this vertiginous and densely settled town is another story; most lodgings don't have parking, but there are quite a few safe off-site lots around town. It's best to park your car there when you arrive, and leave it for the duration of your stay.

VISITOR INFORMATION
CONTACTS Taxco Tourist Office. ⊠ *Calle Benito Juárez 06, Taxco* ☎ *72/622–1379* ⊕ *www.taxco.gob.mx.*

 Sights

Mercado Tetitlán
MARKET | Locals from surrounding towns come to sell and buy produce, crafts, and everything from peanuts to cell phone covers at this bustling market. It's directly down the hill from Santa Prisca, accessed through a series of pedestrian alleyways and staircases. Look for the market's chapel to the Virgin of Guadalupe. ⊠ *Off Calle Luis Montes de Oca, Taxco* ☎ *762/105–5897* ⊕ *www.facebook.com/MercadoMunicipalTetitlan.*

Museo de Arte Virreinal de Taxco, Casa Humboldt
ART MUSEUM | This Moorish-style 18th-century house with archways, an ornate fireplace, soaring beam ceilings, and a finely detailed facade contains a wonderful little art museum that includes a mix of colonial works, historic photographs, and rotating contemporary exhibits. The space also occasionally hosts music and cultural events. It's also commonly known as Casa Humboldt, in honor of the German naturalist Alexander von Humboldt, who stayed here in 1803. ⊠ *Calle Juan Ruíz de Alarcón 12, Taxco* ☎ *762/627–4258* ⊕ *www.facebook.com/museooficial* ⊠ *MP20* ⊙ *Closed Mon.*

Museo Guillermo Spratling
ART MUSEUM | The former home of renowned mid-20th-century silversmith William G. Spratling houses some 140 of the artist's original designs plus a vast collection of both original and reproduction pre-Columbian artifacts. Exhibits also explain the working of colonial mines. ⊠ *Calle Porfirio Delgado 1, Taxco* ☎ *762/622–1660* ⊕ *www.taxcodealarcon.org/museo-guillermo-spratling* ⊠ *MP70* ⊙ *Closed Mon.*

★ Parque Nacional Grutas de Cacahuamilpa
CAVE | Mexico's largest caverns are located within this 4,000-acre national park about 30 km (19 miles) northeast of Taxco. Guides (it's usually possible to arrange for one who speaks English) lead visitors along a 2 km (1 mile) illuminated walkway with fascinating limestone geological formations that ranks among the world's largest networks of caverns. A tour takes around two hours, after which you're free to spend more time on your own exploring. The road from Taxco is steep and winding but well-maintained and quite beautiful—it's also possible to visit the caverns as a side trip from Cuernavaca or Malinalco. If you don't have a car, it's easy to find taxis willing to make the trip here from any of these cities, and several tour operators also offer trips to Taxco that include an excursion to the caves. ⊠ *Hwys. 55 and 166, Taxco* ☎ *721/104–0156* ⊕ *www.facebook.com/lasgrutasdecacahuamilpaoficial* ⊠ *MP150.*

★ Parroquia de Santa Prisca y San Sebastián

RELIGIOUS BUILDING | This church has dominated the town's Plaza Borda since the 18th century, and throughout the Spanish colonial era, it was Mexico's tallest structure. Usually just called Santa Prisca, it was built by French silver magnate José de la Borda after he literally stumbled upon a rich silver vein, although the expense nearly bankrupted him. According to legend, first-century Christian martyr St. Prisca appeared to workers during a storm and prevented a wall of the church from tumbling. Soon after, the church was named in her honor. The style of the church—a sort of Spanish baroque known as *churrigueresque*—and its pale pink exterior have made it Taxco's most important landmark. Its facade, naves, and *bovedas* (vaulted ceilings), as well as important paintings by Mexican Juan Cabrera, are slowly being restored. A soft light illuminates the church each night until midnight. Around Plaza Borda are several *neverías* where you can treat yourself to ice cream in such unique flavors as tequila, corn, avocado, and burnt-milk. Currently the church is undergoing renovations, and its twin spires and much of the exterior are cloaked in scaffolding; it'll likely be the end of 2024 or sometime in 2025 when you'll again be able to take clear photos of the spectacular facade. ✉ *Southeast side of Plaza Borda, Taxco* ☎ *762/622–0183* 🌐 *www.facebook.com/StaPriscaSnSebastian* 🎟 *Free.*

🍴 Restaurants

Casa Spratling–Scaffecito

$ | ECLECTIC | Although the food is consistently good—omelets, chilaquiles, tamales with mole sauce at breakfast, and salads, pastas, and pizzas in the afternoon—the best reason to dine in this home that once belonged to famed silversmith William Spratling is the elegant setting. The high-ceilinged dining room and terraces of the gracious colonial building exude old-world charm, and tables have wonderful views of the town's red-roofed homes. **Known for:** gracious, historic building; ravioli with seasonal fillings; early closing at 6 pm. [$] *Average main: MP130* ✉ *Delicias 23, Taxco* ☎ *762/627–6177* 🌐 *www.facebook.com/casaspratling* 🕓 *Closed Thurs. No dinner.*

Restaurante El Adobe

$$ | MEXICAN | This intimate spot has excellent food and hanging lamps and masks. You'll find a fairly typical selection of meat, poultry, and seafood dishes, including salmon with grilled onions and spicy chile de árbol sauce and steak with a savory mustard sauce, but the favorites are garlic-and-shrimp soup and the *queso al cilantro,* fried cheese on a bed of potato skins, covered with salsa verde. **Known for:** charming covered terrace; mole dishes; dessert crepes with nutella and berries. [$] *Average main: MP235* ✉ *Plazuela de San Juan 13, Taxco* ☎ *762/622–1416* 🌐 *www.eladoberestaurante.info.*

★ Rosa Amaranto

$$ | MODERN MEXICAN | This stylish restaurant set on the rooftop terrace of the enchanting Hotel Boutique Pueblo Lindo offers not only some of the best views in town, but also delicious, beautifully presented modern Mexican dishes. Start the day with huevos rancheros, fresh seasonal fruit, and one of the decadent house-baked pastries; later in the day, try the grilled fish of the day with pureed potatoes and a mango salsa, or enchiladas with chicken and hibiscus flowers. **Known for:** brunch with splendid views; friendly and welcoming staff; freshly baked pastries. [$] *Average main: MP230* ✉ *Hotel Boutique Pueblo Lindo, Calle Don Miguel Hidalgo 30, Taxco* ☎ *762/622–2872* 🌐 *www.facebook.com/RosaAmarantoTaxco.*

★ **Tía Calla**

$ | **MEXICAN** | Be prepared to wait for a table, especially on weekend evenings, at this hugely popular no-nonsense restaurant just off Plaza Borda that's famous for pozole. There are three options—green (available only on Thursday and Saturday), red (served only on Thursday), and white, the classic version that's on the menu daily. **Known for:** hearty, flavorful pozole; queso fundido; simple, unpretentious dining room. [$] *Average main: MP75* ✉ *Plaza Borda 1, Taxco* ☎ *762/622–5602* 🌐 *www.facebook.com/PozoleriaTiaCalla* ⏲ *Closed Tues.*

Hotels

★ **De Cantera y Plata Hotel Boutique**

$$$ | **B&B/INN** | This chic, contemporary inn located on the lower slopes of Montetaxco contains nine airy, beautifully appointed rooms with large windows, contemporary artwork, and luxurious bathrooms, all with access to a small pool and lawn with chaise lounges overlooking all of Taxco. **Pros:** romantic restaurant; spectacular views; beautiful, quiet setting. **Cons:** not within walking distance of town; expensive; some rooms lack views of town. [$] *Rooms from: MP4600* ✉ *Camino a La Posada 39, Taxco* ☎ *762/622–8682* 🌐 *www.hotelboutiquedecanterayplata.com* 🛏 *9 rooms* 🍴 *Free Breakfast.*

Hotel Boutique Pueblo Lindo

$ | **HOTEL** | This small, moderately priced hotel just down the hill from Santa Prisca has spacious, pleasant rooms with tile floors, colorful fabrics and curtains, and in some cases kitchenettes, but the best reasons to stay here are the superb restaurant and the outstanding views from the pool and terraces. **Pros:** pool and sundeck; wonderful vistas of town; outstanding restaurant. **Cons:** pool is quite small; some rooms lack balconies and views; on a very busy street. [$] *Rooms from: MP1900* ✉ *De Miguel Hidalgo 30, Taxco* ☎ *762/622–3481* 🌐 *www.pueblolindo.com.mx* 🛏 *11 rooms* 🍴 *Free Breakfast.*

★ **Hotel Los Arcos**

$ | **HOTEL** | This 1620 converted monastery just a short uphill stroll from Plaza Borda offers simple but pleasantly decorated rooms with traditional furnishings, but the stars of the show here are the inviting restaurant in the tree-shaded courtyard and the expansive rooftop terrace that's absolutely perfect for stargazing or taking in views of Santa Prisca's spires. **Pros:** very good restaurant; beautifully landscaped courtyard and rooftop terrace; central location. **Cons:** rooms pick up lots of noise from the street and restaurant; some rooms and bathrooms are very small; no pool. [$] *Rooms from: MP1400* ✉ *Juan Ruiz de Alarcón 4, Taxco* ☎ *762/622–1836* 🌐 *www.hotellosarcosdetaxco.com* 🛏 *21 rooms* 🍴 *Free Breakfast.*

Hotel Montetaxco

$ | **RESORT** | **FAMILY** | With a knockout view of town, multiple dining and nightlife options, a pool, Saturday night fireworks, a golf course, a spa, and kids' activities, this modern, upscale resort named for the mountain on which it's perched has the most extensive amenities of any property in town. **Pros:** reasonable rates; stupendous views of town; lots of activities and amenities. **Cons:** need to take a taxi or the funicular (MP120 round-trip) to get to town; restaurant has mixed reviews; some rooms lack views. [$] *Rooms from: MP1800* ✉ *Calle Alfredo Checa Curi s/n, Taxco* ☎ *762/622–1300* 🌐 *www.montetaxcohotel.mx* 🛏 *200 rooms* 🍴 *No Meals.*

★ **Hotel William de Diseno**

$$ | **HOTEL** | The chic, contemporary rooms in this imaginatively transformed mansion in the center of Taxco—just down the hill from Plaza Borda—are decorated with green-tile floors, high beds with plush linens, and soft lighting, and amenities include an excellent shop specializing in locally crafted silver jewelry and a fashionable restaurant and bar. **Pros:** appealing decor; lovely staff;

great value. **Cons:** among the highest rates in town; smallish rooms; rooms near street can be noisy. [$] *Rooms from: MP3600* ✉ *Juan Ruíz de Alarcón 7, Taxco* ☎ *727/627–3920* 🌐 *www.hotelwilliam.mx* 🛏 *15 rooms* 🍴 *Free Breakfast.*

🍸 Nightlife

★ Bar Berta

BARS | At what's said to be Taxco's oldest bar (it opened in the 1930s), a tequila, lime, and club soda concoction called a Berta is the specialty. Watch out for Taxco's high curbs and ankle-turning cobblestones after you down a few of those. You can also sample local mezcal here. ✉ *Plaza Borda 9, Taxco* ☎ *762/622–0172* 🌐 *www.instagram.com/barberta_taxco.*

YOLOTL Cerveza Artesanal

BREWPUBS | Drop by this cozy, festive brewpub to sample the well-crafted blonde, amber, and brown ales or to sip traditional mezcal and pulque. There's a lovely tree-shaded terrace illuminated by hanging lanterns and offering nice views of town. ✉ *Estacadas 24, Taxco* ☎ *762/627–2280* 🌐 *www.instagram.com/yolotl_cerveza.*

🛍 Shopping

Most shoppers come to Taxco with silver in mind. Three types are available: sterling, which is always stamped 0.925 (925 parts in 1,000) and is the most expensive; plated silver; and the inexpensive, so-called *alpaca,* a nickel/copper/zinc alloy that looks like silver, but doesn't actually contain any (it's also sometimes referred to as "nickel silver"). Sterling pieces are usually priced by weight according to world silver prices. Fine workmanship will add to the cost. The smallest of bangles start at around MP120 but larger and more elaborate bracelets and necklaces can run for MP5,000 or more. Designs range from traditional bulky necklaces (often inlaid with turquoise and other semiprecious stones) to streamlined bangles and chunky earrings. Many of the dozens of silver shops carry identical merchandise—it's best to compare prices and designs at a two or three shops in the center of town before making a purchase.

Hecho A Mano Idearte

JEWELRY & WATCHES | This well-respected shop just off Plaza Borda carries an extensive selection of top-quality silver and other jewelry. Prices tend to be a little higher here, but you can trust what you're buying, and even if you're not looking to purchase anything, it's a beautiful shop to browse through. ✉ *Plaza Borda 1, Taxco* ☎ *762/622–7771.*

Index

Photo Credits

Front Cover: Claudia Uripos/eStock Photo[Descr:Mexico, Mexico City, Angel de la Independencia]. **Back cover, from left to right:** Brett Welcher/Shutterstock. Janinejerez/Shutterstock.Marcos Castillo/Shutterstock. **Spine:** Luis Boucault/Shutterstock. **Interior, from left to right:**Bill Perry/Shutterstock (1). Fatima Reyes 13/Shutterstock (2). **Chapter 1: Experience Mexico:** Rubi Rodriguez Martinez/ Shutterstock (6-7). Luis Boucault/Shutterstock (8-9). Santiago Castillo Chomel/Shutterstock (9). Marketa1982/Shutterstock (9). Javarman/ Shutterstock (10). Anton_Ivanov/Shutterstock (10). Dpa Picture Alliance/Alamy Stock Photo (10). Kit Leong/Shutterstock (10). Janinejerez/ Shutterstock (11). Aleksandar Todorovic/Shutterstock (11). Angel Malo/Shutterstock (12). Aleksandar Todorovic/Shutterstock (12). Kmiragaya/ Dreamstime (12). Sun_Shine/Shutterstock (13). Alexandra Lande/Shutterstock (13). Nekomura/Shutterstock (14). Victor SG/Shutterstock (14). Another Believer/Wikimedia Commons (14). Aleksandr Medvedkov/Shutterstock (14). Leonid Andronov/Shutterstock (15). Pshaw_Photo/ Shutterstock (15). Marcos Castillo/Shutterstock (20). Fabian Montano/iStockphoto (20). Dominique Caron/iStockphoto (20). Marcos Castillo/ Shutterstock (20). Natspel/Dreamstime (21). Antwonm/Dreamstime (21). Carlosrojas20/iStockphoto (21). Elihuconh/Dreamstime (21). Brett Welcher/Shutterstock (22). Tout Chocolat (22). Curiosopl/Dreamstime (22). Araujogarcia/Dreamstime (23). Lizzy Komen/Shutterstock (23). Richie Chan/Shutterstock (24). Sun_Shine/Shutterstock (24). Victor SG/Shutterstock (24). 123455543/Shutterstock (25). Kamira/Shutterstock (25). Aberu.Go/Shutterstock (26). Dacerv01/Dreamstime (26). Ibrester/Dreamstime (26). Anton_Ivanov/Shutterstock (27). JorgePM/Shutterstock (27). **Chapter 3: Centro Histórico:** Aleksandar Todorovic/Shutterstock (61). E Rojas/Shutterstock (69). Eddygaleotti/iStockphoto (71). WitR/Shutterstock (72). Elijah-Lovkoff/iStockphoto (75). Brett Welcher/Shutterstock (78). **Chapter 4: Alameda Central:** KaryBntz/ Shutterstock (87). Eskystudio/Shutterstock (90). Nelson Antoine/Shutterstock (95). Elijah-Lovkoff/iStockphoto (96). **Chapter 5: Juárez and Anzures with La Zona Rosa:** AgCuesta/Shutterstock (105). Eskystudio/Shutterstock (113). Sergio Mendoza Hochmann/Shutterstock (114). Fchm/Shutterstock (117). **Chapter 6: San Rafael and Santa María la Ribera:** Brester Irina/Shutterstock (123). Aberu.Go/Shutterstock (126-127). Aberu.Go/Shutterstock (137). **Chapter 7: Polanco and Bosque de Chapultepec:** Sedgraphic/Shutterstock (139). Indivcidual/ Shutterstock (146). Jeffrey Isaac Greenberg 7+/Alamy Stock Photo (148). ItzaVU/Shutterstock (154). Jeffrey Isaac Greenberg 7+/Alamy Stock Photo (161). **Chapter 8: Roma:** Jennifer DePrima (163). Ibrester/Dreamstime (170). Just Another Photographer/Shutterstock (174). Kamira/Shutterstock (180). Cathyrose Melloan/Alamy Stock Photo (182). Omar Bárcena/Flickr (184). **Chapter 9: Condesa:** Mehdi33300/ Shutterstock (197). Wirestock Creators/Shutterstock (208). ForgimindArchimedia/WikimediaCommons (219). **Chapter 10: Benito Juárez:** Cathyrose Melloan/Alamy Stock Photo (223). Santiago Castillo Chomel/Shutterstock (229). Sailingstone Travel/Shutterstock (233). Abel Gonzalez/iStockphoto (235). **Chapter 11: Coyoacán:** Lucas Vallecillos/Alamy Stock Photo (239). Lucas Vallecillos/Alamy Stock Photo (246). Elovkoff/Dreamstime (248). R.M. Nunes/Shutterstock (253). **Chapter 12: San Ángel:** Inspired By Maps/Shutterstock (261). Brester Irina/Shutterstock (268). Gill_figueroa/Shutterstock (271). Kamira/Shutterstock (275). **Chapter 13: Greater Mexico City:** Santiago reyna córona/Shutterstock (277). Jkraft5/Dreamstime (285). Dani3alex21/Dreamstime (287). Coralimages2020/Dreamstime (290). Frank Nowikowski/Alamy Stock Photo (293). Kmiragaya/Dreamstime (296). Ulita/Dreamstime (298). **Chapter 14: Side Trips from Mexico City:** Photo Spirit/Shutterstock (303). Witr/Dreamstime (312). Specialmarck/Dreamstime (316). Bosiljka Zutich/Alamy Stock Photo (327). Leonid Andronov/Shutterstock (333). **About Our Writers:** All photos are courtesy of the writers except for the following. Andrew Collins Courtesy of Fernando Nocedal.

Every effort has been made to trace the copyright holders, and we apologize in advance for any accidental errors. We would be happy to apply the corrections in the following edition of this publication.

Notes

Notes

Fodor's MEXICO CITY

Publisher: Stephen Horowitz, *General Manager*

Editorial: Douglas Stallings, *Editorial Director;* Jill Fergus, Amanda Sadlowski, *Senior Editors;* Brian Eschrich, Alexis Kelly, *Editors;* Angelique Kennedy-Chavannes, Yoojin Shin, *Associate Editors*

Design: Tina Malaney, *Director of Design and Production;* Jessica Gonzalez, *Senior Designer;* Jaimee Shaye, *Graphic Design Associate*

Production: Jennifer DePrima, *Editorial Production Manager;* Elyse Rozelle, *Senior Production Editor;* Monica White, *Production Editor*

Maps: Rebecca Baer, *Map Director;* David Lindroth, Mark Stroud (Moon Street Cartography), *Cartographers*

Photography: Viviane Teles, *Director of Photography;* Namrata Aggarwal, Neha Gupta, Payal Gupta, Ashok Kumar, *Photo Editors;* Jade Rodgers, Shanelle Jacobs, *Photo Production Intern*

Business and Operations: Chuck Hoover, *Chief Marketing Officer;* Robert Ames, *Group General Manager*

Public Relations and Marketing: Joe Ewaskiw, *Senior Director of Communications and Public Relations*

Fodors.com: Jeremy Tarr, *Editorial Director;* Rachael Levitt, *Managing Editor*

Technology: Jon Atkinson, *Executive Director of Technology;* Rudresh Teotia, *Associate Director of Technology;* Alison Lieu, *Project Manager*

Writers: Andrew Collins, Roshida Dowe, Megan Frye

Editor: Amanda Sadlowski

Production Editor: Jennifer DePrima

1st Edition

ISBN 978-1-64097-699-3

ISSN 2996-9085

All details in this book are based on information supplied to us at press time. Always confirm information when it matters, especially if you're making a detour to visit a specific place. Fodor's expressly disclaims any liability, loss, or risk, personal or otherwise, that is incurred as a consequence of the use of any of the contents of this book.

SPECIAL SALES
This book is available at special discounts for bulk purchases for sales promotions or premiums. For more information, e-mail SpecialMarkets@fodors.com.

PRINTED IN CANADA

10 9 8 7 6 5 4 3 2

About Our Writers

 Former Fodor's staff editor **Andrew Collins** lives in Coyoacán with his partner and two friendly cats. A lifelong nomad, he spends about half his time on the road, much of it in New England and the Pacific Northwest. A contributor to more than 200 Fodor's guidebooks, including National Parks, Utah, Santa Fe, Pacific Northwest, Oregon, and New England, he's also a regular travel contributor to The Points Guy. He's written for dozens of mainstream and LGBTQ publications—*Travel + Leisure*, *New Mexico Magazine*, *Yankee Magazine*, and *The Advocate* among them. Additionally, Collins teaches travel writing and food writing for New York City's Gotham Writers Workshop. You can find more of his work at ⊕ *AndrewsTraveling.com* and follow him on Instagram at TravelAndrew. For this book, he updated and wrote the Experience, Travel Smart, Roma, Condesa, Coyoacán, San Ángel, Greater Mexico City, and Side Trips From Mexico City chapters.

 After falling in love with Mexico City on a vacation, **Roshida Dowe** moved to the city of her dreams in 2019 and has never looked back. A lover of big cities, cultural experiences, and great food, Mexico City provides everything she could ask for. Creating content about Mexico City feeds her curiosity and allows her to wander its streets with no other goal than to find something new to see or eat. She updated the Centro Histórico, Alameda Central, and Polanco and Bosque de Chapultepec chapters this edition.

Megan Frye is an independent journalist, photographer, and translator specializing in stories about regenerative travel and conservation. Following a history of newsroom journalism and nonprofit management in Detroit, Michigan, along with escapades across the American West, she settled in Mexico City in 2015, where today she appreciates the charms and tranquility of her chosen neighborhood of Coyoacán. She updated the Juárez and Anzures, San Rafael and Santa María la Ribera, and Benito Juárez chapters for this book.

Mexico City Metro

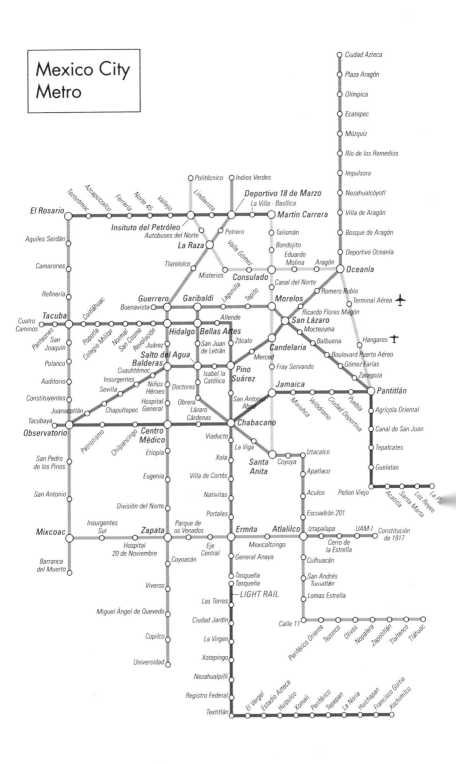